THE TANK McNAMARA CHRONICLES

Books in the Sheed Andrews and McMeel Treasury Series

The Family Circus Treasury by Bil Keane

The Ziggy Treasury by Tom Wilson

The Momma Treasury by Mell Lazarus

The Marmaduke Treasury by Brad Anderson

The Tank McNamara Chronicles by Jeff Millar and Bill Hinds

The Cathy Chronicles by Cathy Guisewite

THE TANK McNAMARA CHRONICLES

by Jeff Millar and Bill Hinds

Foreword by Roger Staubach

Sheed Andrews and McMeel, Inc.
Subsidiary of Universal Press Syndicate
Kansas City

The Tank McNamara Chronicles copyright © 1978 by Universal Press Syndicate All rights reserved. Printed in the United States of America. No part of this book may be used or reproduced in any manner whatsoever without written permission except in the case of reprints in the context of reviews. For information write Sheed Andrews and McMeel, Inc., Subsidiary of Universal Press Syndicate, 6700 Squibb Road, Mission, Kansas 66202.

ISBN: 0-8362-1118-9 cloth
       0-8362-1119-7 paper
Library of Congress Catalog Card Number: 78-67227

Foreword

As with most challenges in life, sports, whether amateur or professional, can make insistent demands. They require not only the obvious hard work, but more importantly, the special qualities of a desire and dedication to win. And like so many other things in our lives, despair, too, can be present: Sports can take you down as quickly as they can bring you up.

The too-few moments of sitting back and reflecting — smiling at it all — sometimes bring the ups and downs of this profession into a better focus. This is why *Tank McNamara* is so unique: it offers that opportunity for those of us actively involved in sports to smile at ourselves, and for the fan a chance to realize that we are not often the mythical figures we are sometimes made out to be. When Tank, himself a caricature of the football-player-turned-sports-announcer, bumbles his way through a newscast or (usually accidentally) comes up with a "scoop" that frequently pokes a little fun at a topical sports issue or star, it brings a quick smile to my face and helps remind me that this hectic world of sports is something I relish, and not just a paycheck. I think one of our greatest God-given gifts is the ability to laugh, not so much at others, but at ourselves. It's part of the "game" (if you will) I hope I never lose.

I first spotted *Tank McNamara* several years back, and since then I've seen it in many of the cities I've played in. I've found it frequently to be right on target and as current as the headlines in the day's sports pages. Tank is a delightful eye through which to see what *is* going on in sports, and his cast of supporting characters touches many of the fringes of the world of sports, both stars and fans.

Last year, Jeff Millar, the writer of the strip, and Bill Hinds, the artist behind *Tank*, flew with the Cowboys to one of our games. Hinds was drawing frantically — caricatures of all of us — while Millar, we suspected, was committing to memory everything we said. After following the strip, I wouldn't have been surprised to see our whole game plan in a Sunday color comic section (though I'm sure the team playing us might have been).

At the least, I'm sure the duo behind *Tank McNamara* learned a bit more about the thinking of professional football players, and we learned a lot more about the thinking and what goes into making a successful, popular comic strip. The session helped add to my respect for their combined talents and appreciation of the effort it actually takes to get a comic strip out every day of the week, every week of the year.

But I'm sure I've said enough about Tank, and Jeff, and Bill. So just enjoy the best of *Tank McNamara*. It shows that all of us, professional players and fans alike, should take our games a bit less seriously.

Roger Staubach
Dallas

The sweetest music to my ears is when somebody tells me that he knows for sure the *real* person upon whom Tank McNamara is based.

"It's [name deleted], right? He's the guy who does the sports in my hometown. He's the whole bit: Ex-jock, big and he screws everything up the same way Tank does. *Gotta* be that guy, right?"

Tank is *all* these guys. There's one — or more — in every major television market: The guy who got his job as a sportscaster not because he has any talent at reading scores but because he's got a semimarketable name which the station management thinks might have some novelty value. When I came up with the idea that became *Tank McNamara,* there was no one jockcaster who functioned as a role model. But I can tell you the specific incident which started me off. I was watching a Tank-type struggling through the sports on a local newscast (not necessarily in Houston, where I live). He fumblemouthed through the baseball scores with marginal intelligibility; but when the poor guy came to the results of an important European car race, you could tell he was about ready to buy the farm. "Jacky Ickx" nearly sent him into a labial arrhythmia; but the name of the race, which occurred last in the sentence, was the heart punch. Guess how he pronounced "Grand Prix." Yep.

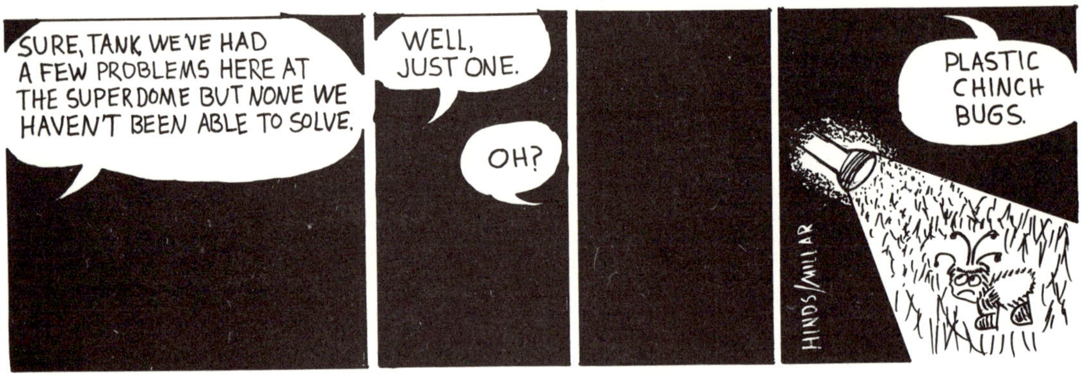
SURE, TANK WE'VE HAD A FEW PROBLEMS HERE AT THE SUPERDOME BUT NONE WE HAVEN'T BEEN ABLE TO SOLVE.
WELL, JUST ONE.
OH?
PLASTIC CHINCH BUGS.
HINDS/MILLAR

This strip was drawn by Jeff Millar and written by Bill Hinds (ME) to demonstrate why Jeff does the writing and I do the drawing. As a critique of his artwork I would say the first three panels were overworked and the last panel suggests he missed his true calling - entomology.

That was in 1973. I was working — still do — for the *Houston Chronicle* as the paper's film critic and twice-a-week humor columnist (well, at least I *tell* my editor the column is funny). In doing the humor column, I came to believe that I had acquired an unusual perspective on sports. For just about the same reasons that everyone else gives it a shot — ego and money — I thought about seeking a national audience for it. I briefly considered a wry sports column; but the market is overburdened with syndicated columns and my chances of persuading a syndicate to take me on seemed slim. And then I thought about a comic strip. I had long read comic strips — from habit and enjoyment as a child, with admiration and interest as an adult. Ah-ha, I thought. There's nothing quite like the strip which I propose on the market. A niche presents itself. Seize the time.

There was only one thing that kept me from becoming quickly rich and famous as a cartoonist: I cannot draw. Not even stick figures. Were I lost in the desert and dying of thirst, I could not draw a recognizable glass of water to communicate to a passing Arab that I thirst.

A couple of inquiries put me onto Bill Hinds. He was then 23 years old, freshly graduated from Stephen F. Austin University in Nacogdoches, Texas, and was in the process of genteelly starving to death as a freelance cartoonist.

I called up Bill, went out to see him, gave him some strip ideas and asked him to pencil them. It was immediately clear that he was very, very good. We worked up six weeks of daily strips and three of the big Sunday drawings and showed them, on the advice of Jack Loftis, my editor at the *Chronicle* who buys the paper's strips, first to Universal Press Syndicate (yaaay!) because they would most likely be receptive to iconoclasm, satire and other impolite attitudes.

Bingo.

They liked it, basically. Oh, they didn't like the name we had for the strip, *Jocks* (there was some thought that, referring as it does to the item of lingerie, there would be some sales resistance in small newspapers). Or the principal character. Or the second name we came up with for the strip *(Sweatsox)*. Or the new principal character. But other than that . . .

Tank was there all the time, as a supporting player. When we suggested that we make him the title character, bingo. Break out the contracts.

We started syndication August 5, 1974, learning as we earned.

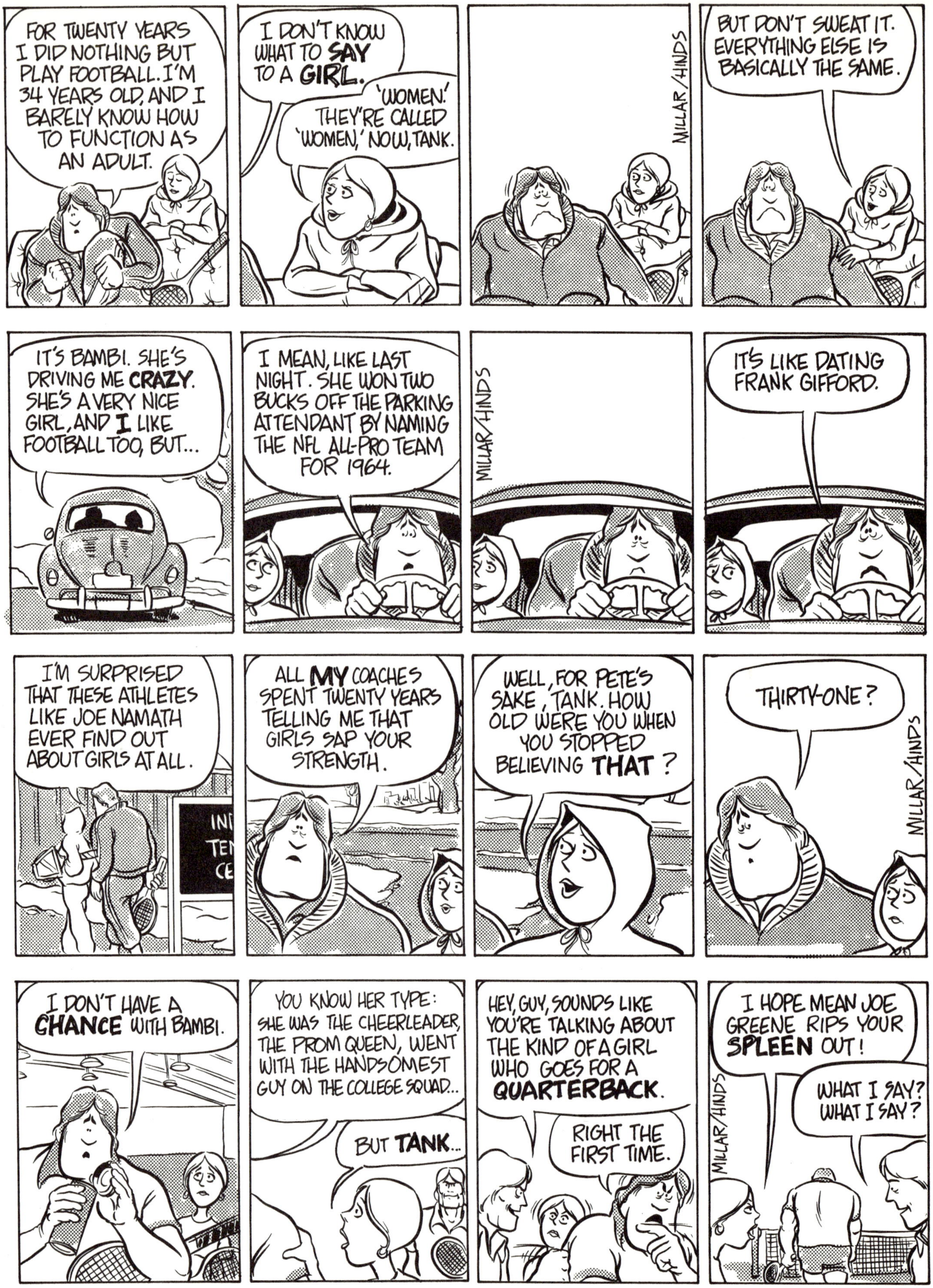
FOR TWENTY YEARS I DID NOTHING BUT PLAY FOOTBALL. I'M 34 YEARS OLD, AND I BARELY KNOW HOW TO FUNCTION AS AN ADULT.
I DON'T KNOW WHAT TO SAY TO A GIRL.
'WOMEN.' THEY'RE CALLED 'WOMEN,' NOW, TANK.
MILLAR/HINDS
BUT DON'T SWEAT IT. EVERYTHING ELSE IS BASICALLY THE SAME.
IT'S BAMBI. SHE'S DRIVING ME CRAZY. SHE'S A VERY NICE GIRL, AND I LIKE FOOTBALL TOO, BUT...
I MEAN, LIKE LAST NIGHT. SHE WON TWO BUCKS OFF THE PARKING ATTENDANT BY NAMING THE NFL ALL-PRO TEAM FOR 1964.
MILLAR/HINDS
IT'S LIKE DATING FRANK GIFFORD.
I'M SURPRISED THAT THESE ATHLETES LIKE JOE NAMATH EVER FIND OUT ABOUT GIRLS AT ALL.
ALL MY COACHES SPENT TWENTY YEARS TELLING ME THAT GIRLS SAP YOUR STRENGTH.
WELL, FOR PETE'S SAKE, TANK. HOW OLD WERE YOU WHEN YOU STOPPED BELIEVING THAT?
THIRTY-ONE?
MILLAR/HINDS
I DON'T HAVE A CHANCE WITH BAMBI.
YOU KNOW HER TYPE: SHE WAS THE CHEERLEADER, THE PROM QUEEN, WENT WITH THE HANDSOMEST GUY ON THE COLLEGE SQUAD...
BUT TANK...
HEY, GUY, SOUNDS LIKE YOU'RE TALKING ABOUT THE KIND OF A GIRL WHO GOES FOR A QUARTERBACK.
RIGHT THE FIRST TIME.
MILLAR/HINDS
I HOPE MEAN JOE GREENE RIPS YOUR SPLEEN OUT!
WHAT I SAY? WHAT I SAY?

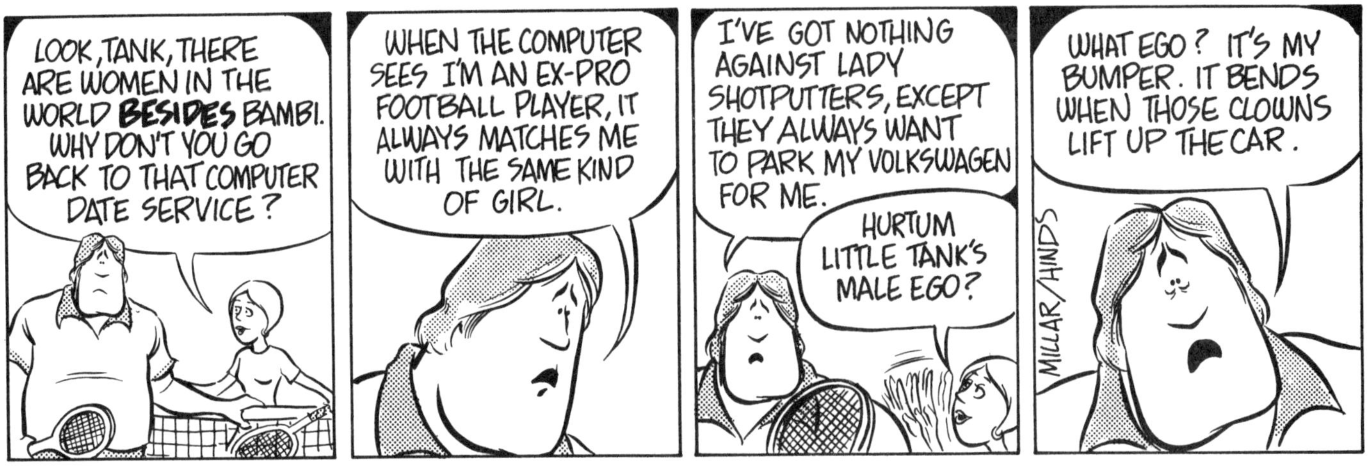
LOOK, TANK, THERE ARE WOMEN IN THE WORLD **BESIDES** BAMBI. WHY DON'T YOU GO BACK TO THAT COMPUTER DATE SERVICE?
WHEN THE COMPUTER SEES I'M AN EX-PRO FOOTBALL PLAYER, IT ALWAYS MATCHES ME WITH THE SAME KIND OF GIRL.
I'VE GOT NOTHING AGAINST LADY SHOTPUTTERS, EXCEPT THEY ALWAYS WANT TO PARK MY VOLKSWAGEN FOR ME.
HURTUM LITTLE TANK'S MALE EGO?
MILLAR/HINDS
WHAT EGO? IT'S MY BUMPER. IT BENDS WHEN THOSE CLOWNS LIFT UP THE CAR.

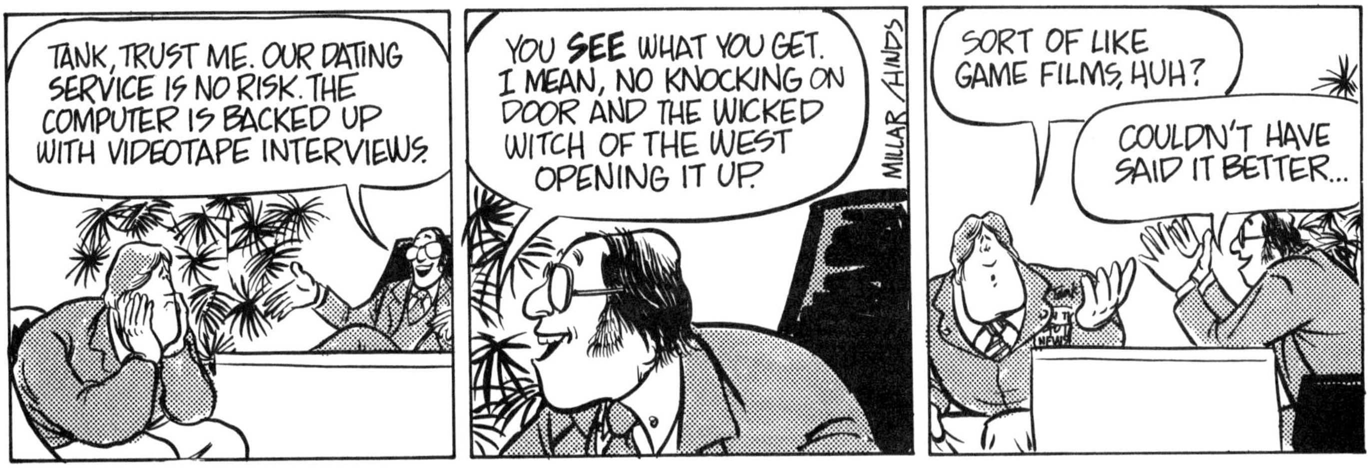
TANK, TRUST ME. OUR DATING SERVICE IS NO RISK. THE COMPUTER IS BACKED UP WITH VIDEOTAPE INTERVIEWS.
YOU **SEE** WHAT YOU GET. I MEAN, NO KNOCKING ON DOOR AND THE WICKED WITCH OF THE WEST OPENING IT UP.
MILLAR/HINDS
SORT OF LIKE GAME FILMS, HUH?
COULDN'T HAVE SAID IT BETTER...

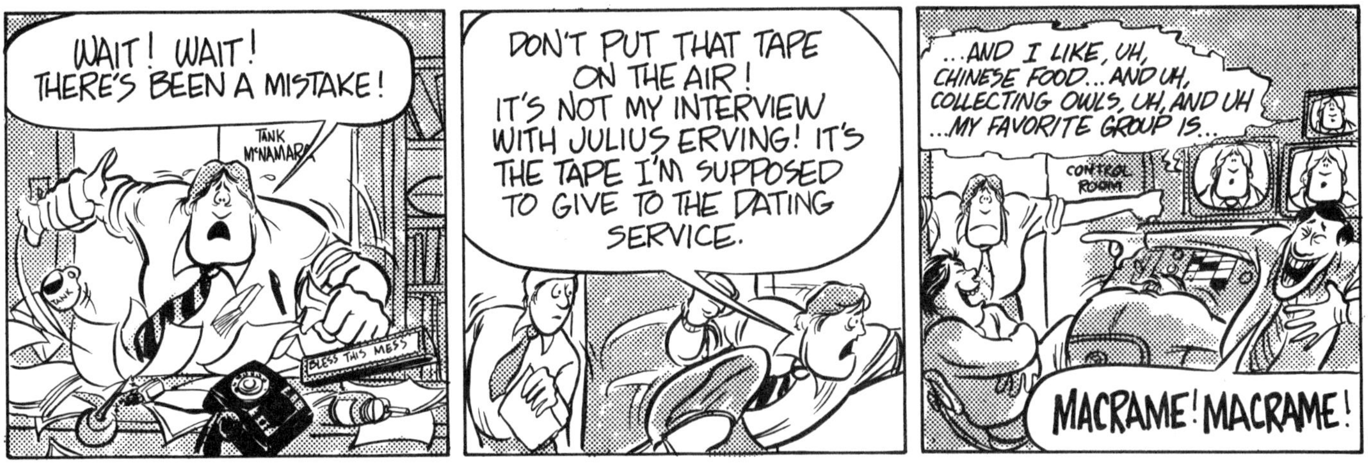
WAIT! WAIT! THERE'S BEEN A MISTAKE!
TANK McNAMARA
BLESS THIS MESS
DON'T PUT THAT TAPE ON THE AIR! IT'S NOT MY INTERVIEW WITH JULIUS ERVING! IT'S THE TAPE I'M SUPPOSED TO GIVE TO THE DATING SERVICE.
...AND I LIKE, UH, CHINESE FOOD... AND UH, COLLECTING OWLS, UH, AND UH ...MY FAVORITE GROUP IS...
CONTROL ROOM
MACRAME! MACRAME!

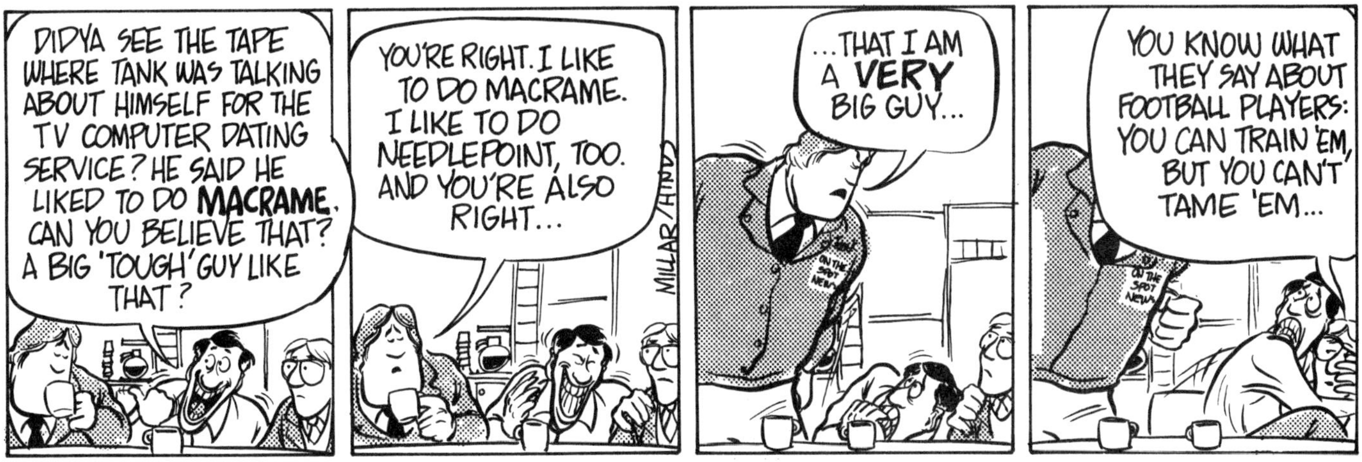
DIDYA SEE THE TAPE WHERE TANK WAS TALKING ABOUT HIMSELF FOR THE TV COMPUTER DATING SERVICE? HE SAID HE LIKED TO DO **MACRAME**. CAN YOU BELIEVE THAT? A BIG 'TOUGH' GUY LIKE THAT?
YOU'RE RIGHT. I LIKE TO DO MACRAME. I LIKE TO DO NEEDLEPOINT, TOO. AND YOU'RE ALSO RIGHT...
MILLAR/HINDS
...THAT I AM A **VERY** BIG GUY...
YOU KNOW WHAT THEY SAY ABOUT FOOTBALL PLAYERS: YOU CAN TRAIN 'EM, BUT YOU CAN'T TAME 'EM...

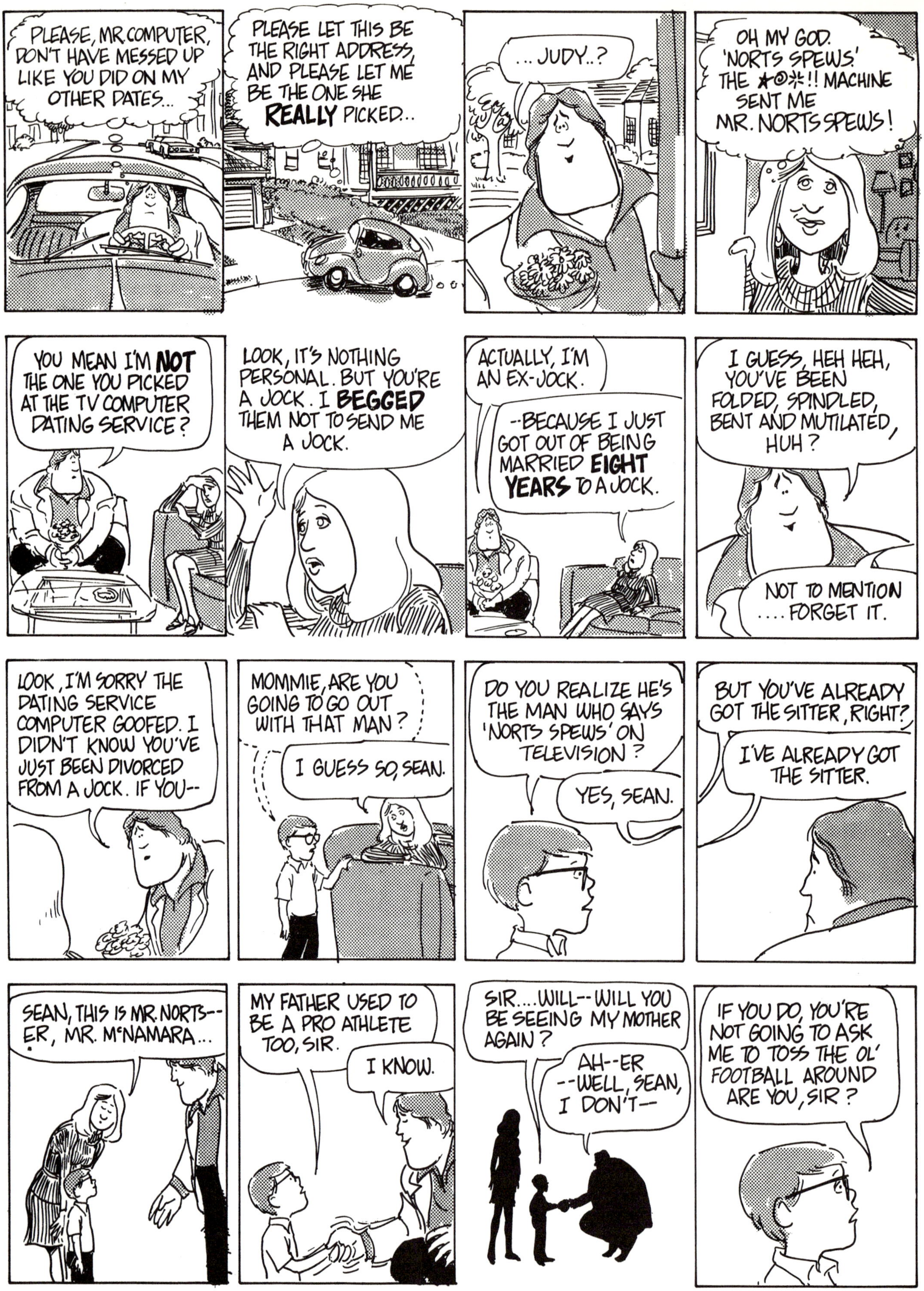
PLEASE, MR. COMPUTER, DON'T HAVE MESSED UP LIKE YOU DID ON MY OTHER DATES...
PLEASE LET THIS BE THE RIGHT ADDRESS, AND PLEASE LET ME BE THE ONE SHE REALLY PICKED...
...JUDY..?
OH MY GOD. 'NORTS SPEWS.' THE ★@*!! MACHINE SENT ME MR. NORTS SPEWS!
YOU MEAN I'M NOT THE ONE YOU PICKED AT THE TV COMPUTER DATING SERVICE?
LOOK, IT'S NOTHING PERSONAL. BUT YOU'RE A JOCK. I BEGGED THEM NOT TO SEND ME A JOCK.
ACTUALLY, I'M AN EX-JOCK.
--BECAUSE I JUST GOT OUT OF BEING MARRIED EIGHT YEARS TO A JOCK.
I GUESS, HEH HEH, YOU'VE BEEN FOLDED, SPINDLED, BENT AND MUTILATED, HUH?
NOT TO MENTION .... FORGET IT.
LOOK, I'M SORRY THE DATING SERVICE COMPUTER GOOFED. I DIDN'T KNOW YOU'VE JUST BEEN DIVORCED FROM A JOCK. IF YOU--
MOMMIE, ARE YOU GOING TO GO OUT WITH THAT MAN?
I GUESS SO, SEAN.
DO YOU REALIZE HE'S THE MAN WHO SAYS 'NORTS SPEWS' ON TELEVISION?
YES, SEAN.
BUT YOU'VE ALREADY GOT THE SITTER, RIGHT?
I'VE ALREADY GOT THE SITTER.
SEAN, THIS IS MR. NORTS-- ER, MR. McNAMARA...
MY FATHER USED TO BE A PRO ATHLETE TOO, SIR.
I KNOW.
SIR.... WILL-- WILL YOU BE SEEING MY MOTHER AGAIN?
AH--ER --WELL, SEAN, I DON'T--
IF YOU DO, YOU'RE NOT GOING TO ASK ME TO TOSS THE OL' FOOTBALL AROUND ARE YOU, SIR?

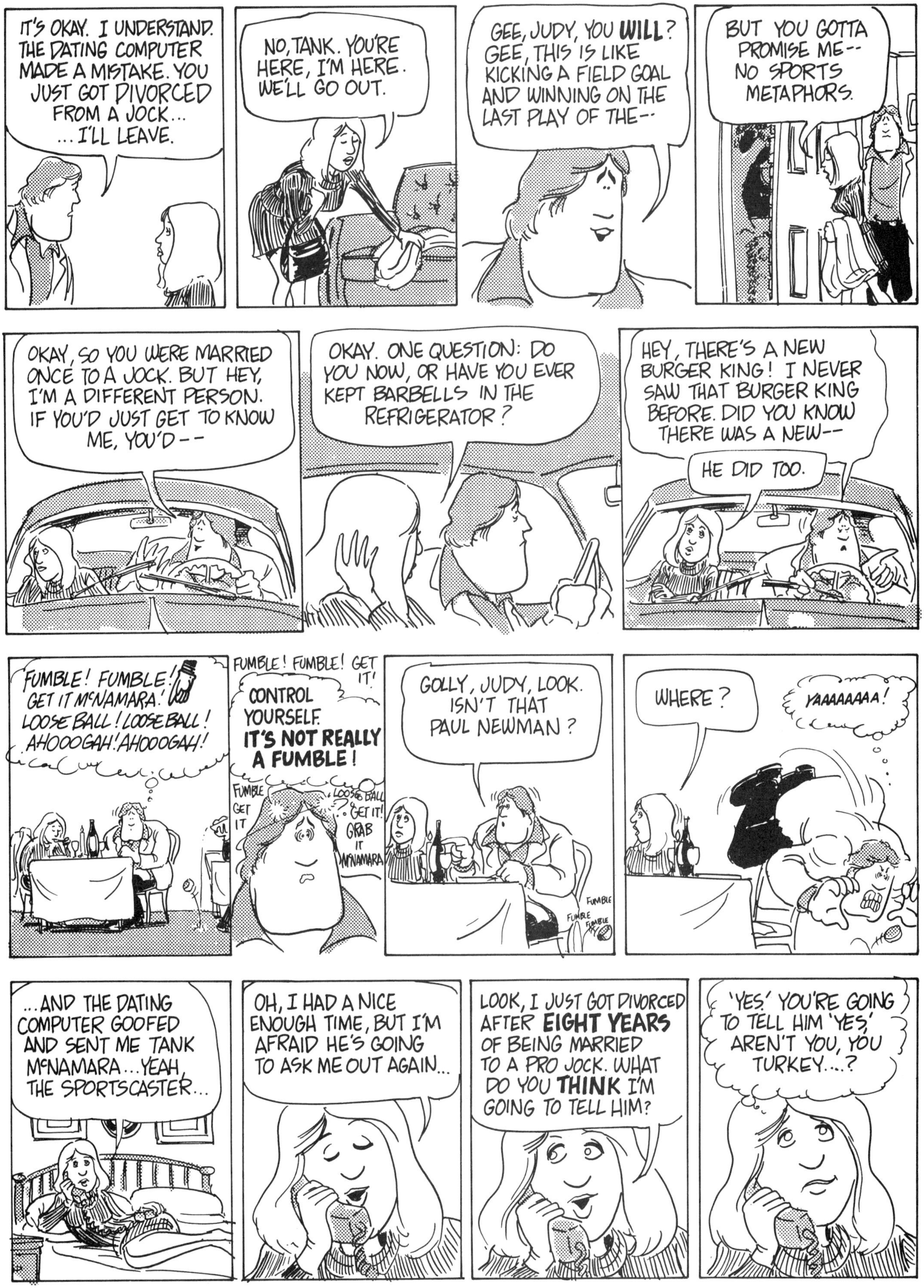
IT'S OKAY. I UNDERSTAND. THE DATING COMPUTER MADE A MISTAKE. YOU JUST GOT DIVORCED FROM A JOCK... ...I'LL LEAVE.
NO, TANK. YOU'RE HERE, I'M HERE. WE'LL GO OUT.
GEE, JUDY, YOU **WILL**? GEE, THIS IS LIKE KICKING A FIELD GOAL AND WINNING ON THE LAST PLAY OF THE--
BUT YOU GOTTA PROMISE ME-- NO SPORTS METAPHORS.
OKAY, SO YOU WERE MARRIED ONCE TO A JOCK. BUT HEY, I'M A DIFFERENT PERSON. IF YOU'D JUST GET TO KNOW ME, YOU'D --
OKAY. ONE QUESTION: DO YOU NOW, OR HAVE YOU EVER KEPT BARBELLS IN THE REFRIGERATOR?
HEY, THERE'S A NEW BURGER KING! I NEVER SAW THAT BURGER KING BEFORE. DID YOU KNOW THERE WAS A NEW--
HE DID TOO.
FUMBLE! FUMBLE! GET IT McNAMARA! LOOSE BALL! LOOSE BALL! AHOOOGAH! AHOOOGAH!
FUMBLE! FUMBLE! GET IT!
CONTROL YOURSELF. **IT'S NOT REALLY A FUMBLE!**
FUMBLE GET IT
LOOSE BALL GET IT! GRAB IT McNAMARA
GOLLY, JUDY, LOOK. ISN'T THAT PAUL NEWMAN?
FUMBLE
FUMBLE
FUMBLE
WHERE?
YAAAAAAAA!
...AND THE DATING COMPUTER GOOFED AND SENT ME TANK McNAMARA...YEAH, THE SPORTSCASTER...
OH, I HAD A NICE ENOUGH TIME, BUT I'M AFRAID HE'S GOING TO ASK ME OUT AGAIN...
LOOK, I JUST GOT DIVORCED AFTER **EIGHT YEARS** OF BEING MARRIED TO A PRO JOCK. WHAT DO YOU **THINK** I'M GOING TO TELL HIM?
'YES.' YOU'RE GOING TO TELL HIM 'YES,' AREN'T YOU, YOU TURKEY...?

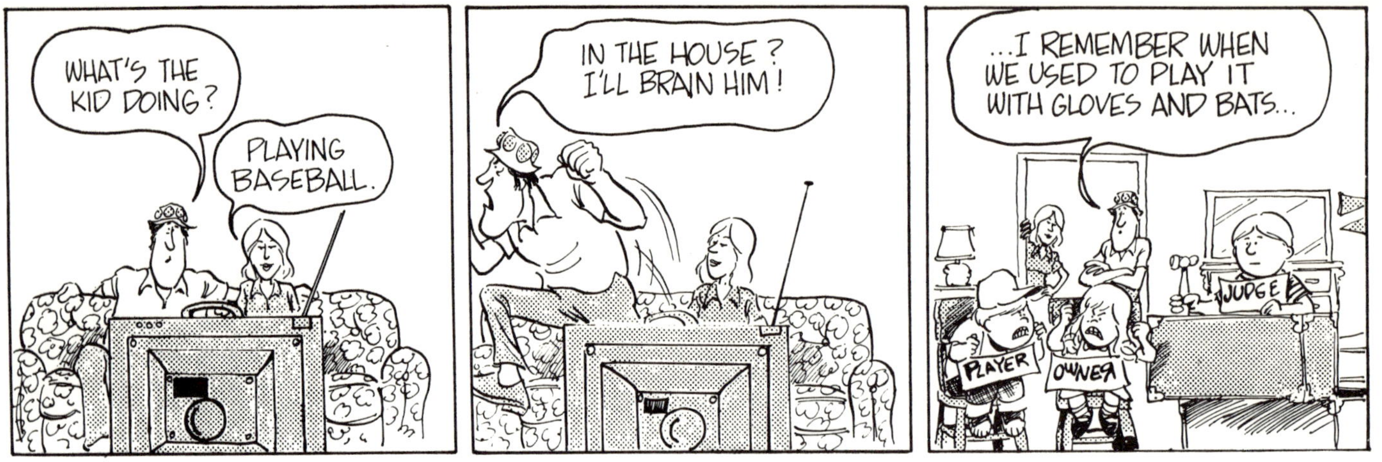
WHAT'S THE KID DOING?
PLAYING BASEBALL.
IN THE HOUSE? I'LL BRAIN HIM!
...I REMEMBER WHEN WE USED TO PLAY IT WITH GLOVES AND BATS...
PLAYER
OWNER
JUDGE

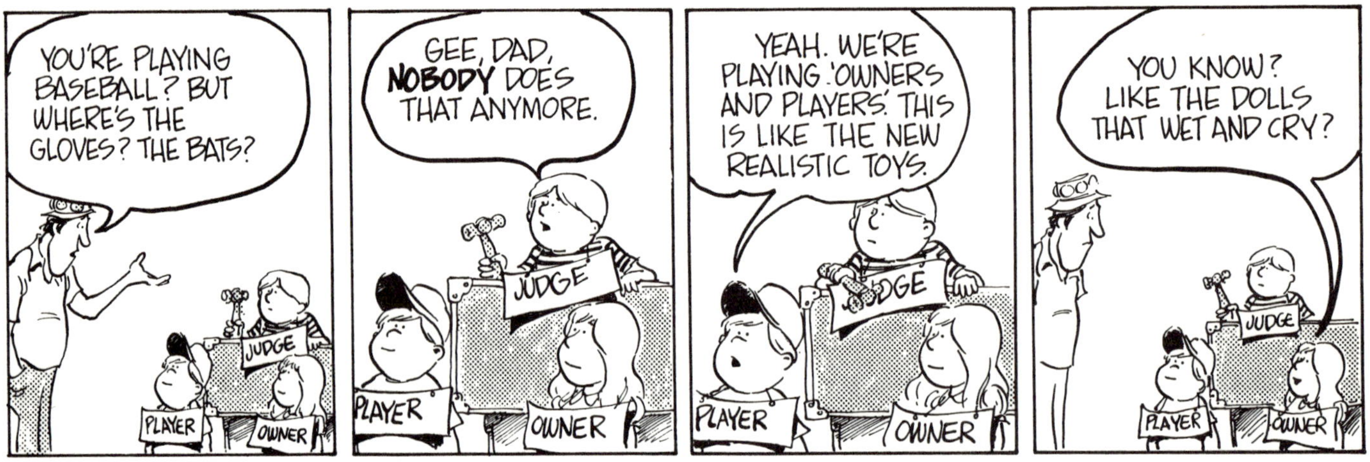
YOU'RE PLAYING BASEBALL? BUT WHERE'S THE GLOVES? THE BATS?
JUDGE
PLAYER
OWNER
GEE, DAD, **NOBODY** DOES THAT ANYMORE.
YEAH. WE'RE PLAYING 'OWNERS AND PLAYERS.' THIS IS LIKE THE NEW REALISTIC TOYS.
YOU KNOW? LIKE THE DOLLS THAT WET AND CRY?

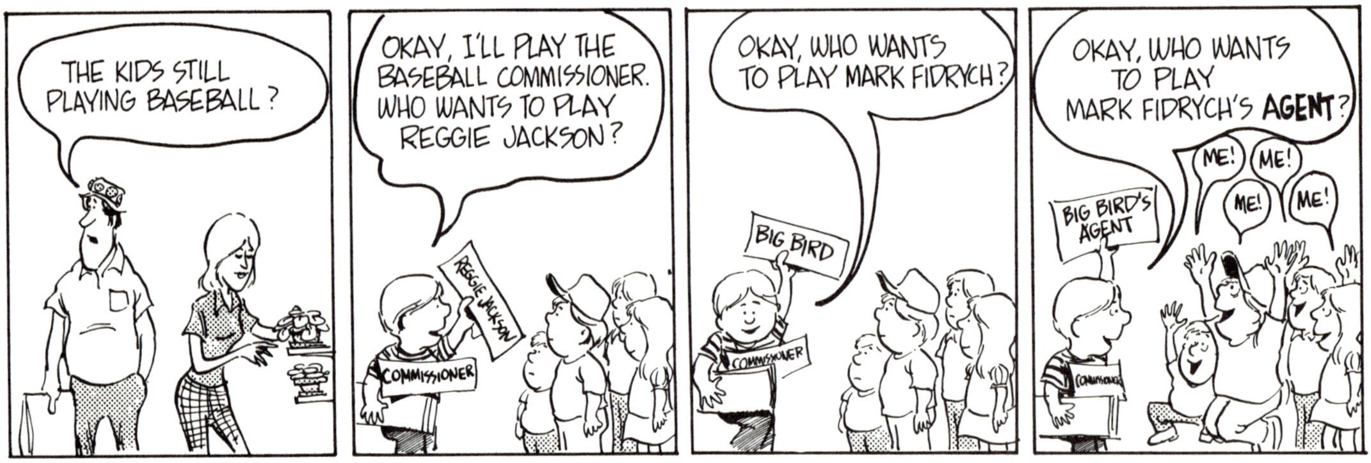
THE KIDS STILL PLAYING BASEBALL?
OKAY, I'LL PLAY THE BASEBALL COMMISSIONER. WHO WANTS TO PLAY REGGIE JACKSON?
REGGIE JACKSON
COMMISSIONER
OKAY, WHO WANTS TO PLAY MARK FIDRYCH?
BIG BIRD
OKAY, WHO WANTS TO PLAY MARK FIDRYCH'S **AGENT**?
BIG BIRD'S AGENT
ME!
ME!
ME!
ME!

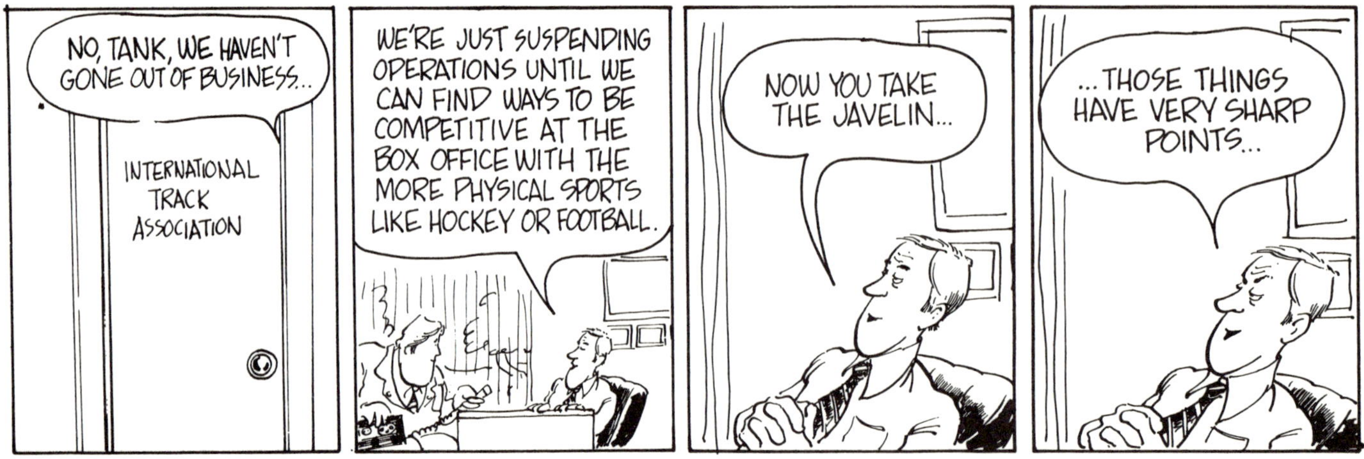
NO, TANK, WE HAVEN'T GONE OUT OF BUSINESS...
INTERNATIONAL TRACK ASSOCIATION
WE'RE JUST SUSPENDING OPERATIONS UNTIL WE CAN FIND WAYS TO BE COMPETITIVE AT THE BOX OFFICE WITH THE MORE PHYSICAL SPORTS LIKE HOCKEY OR FOOTBALL.
NOW YOU TAKE THE JAVELIN...
...THOSE THINGS HAVE VERY SHARP POINTS...

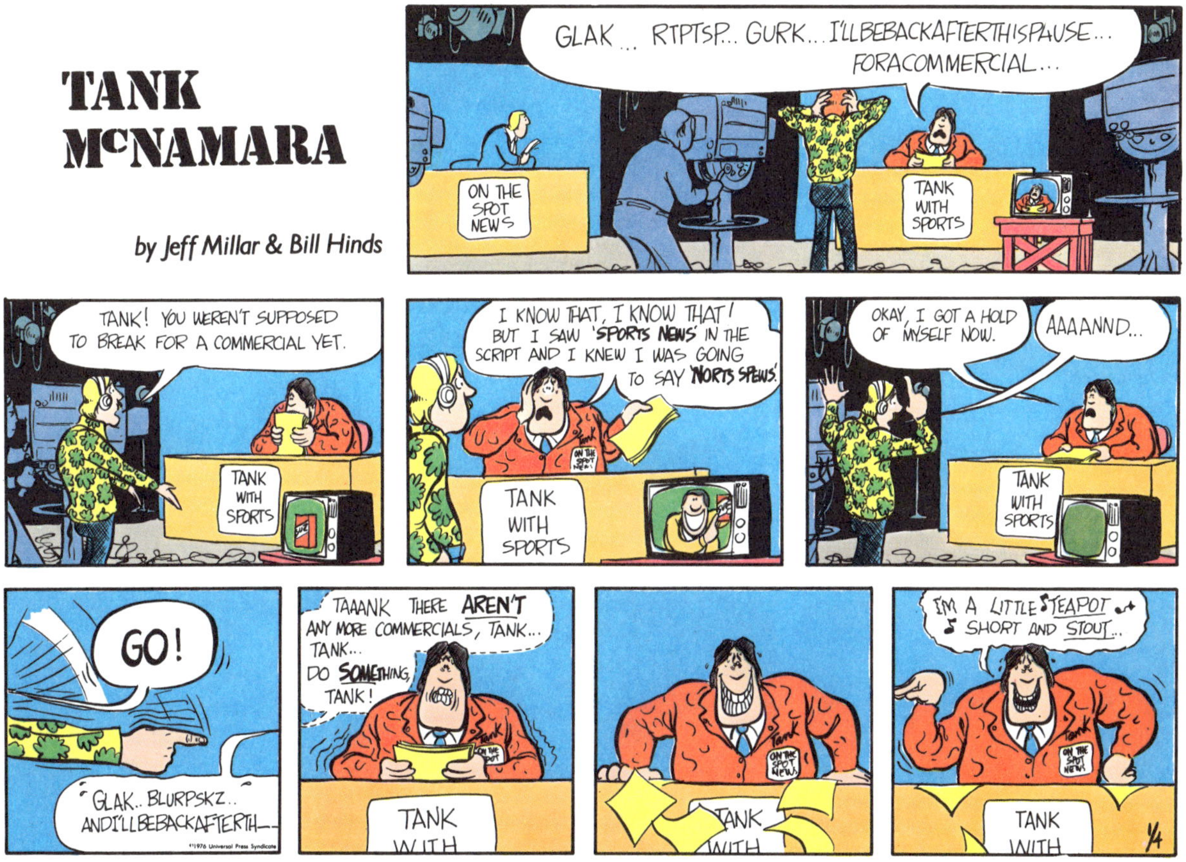
TANK McNAMARA
by Jeff Millar & Bill Hinds
GLAK ... RTPTSP... GURK... I'LLBEBACKAFTERTHISPAUSE... FORACOMMERCIAL...
ON THE SPOT NEWS
TANK WITH SPORTS
TANK! YOU WEREN'T SUPPOSED TO BREAK FOR A COMMERCIAL YET.
TANK WITH SPORTS
I KNOW THAT, I KNOW THAT! BUT I SAW 'SPORTS NEWS' IN THE SCRIPT AND I KNEW I WAS GOING TO SAY 'NORTS SPEWS'.
TANK WITH SPORTS
OKAY, I GOT A HOLD OF MYSELF NOW.
AAAANND...
TANK WITH SPORTS
GO!
GLAK.. BLURPSKZ.. ANDI'LLBEBACKAFTERTH—
©1976 Universal Press Syndicate
TAAANK THERE AREN'T ANY MORE COMMERCIALS, TANK... TANK... DO SOMETHING, TANK!
TANK
I'M A LITTLE TEAPOT SHORT AND STOUT...
TANK
1/4

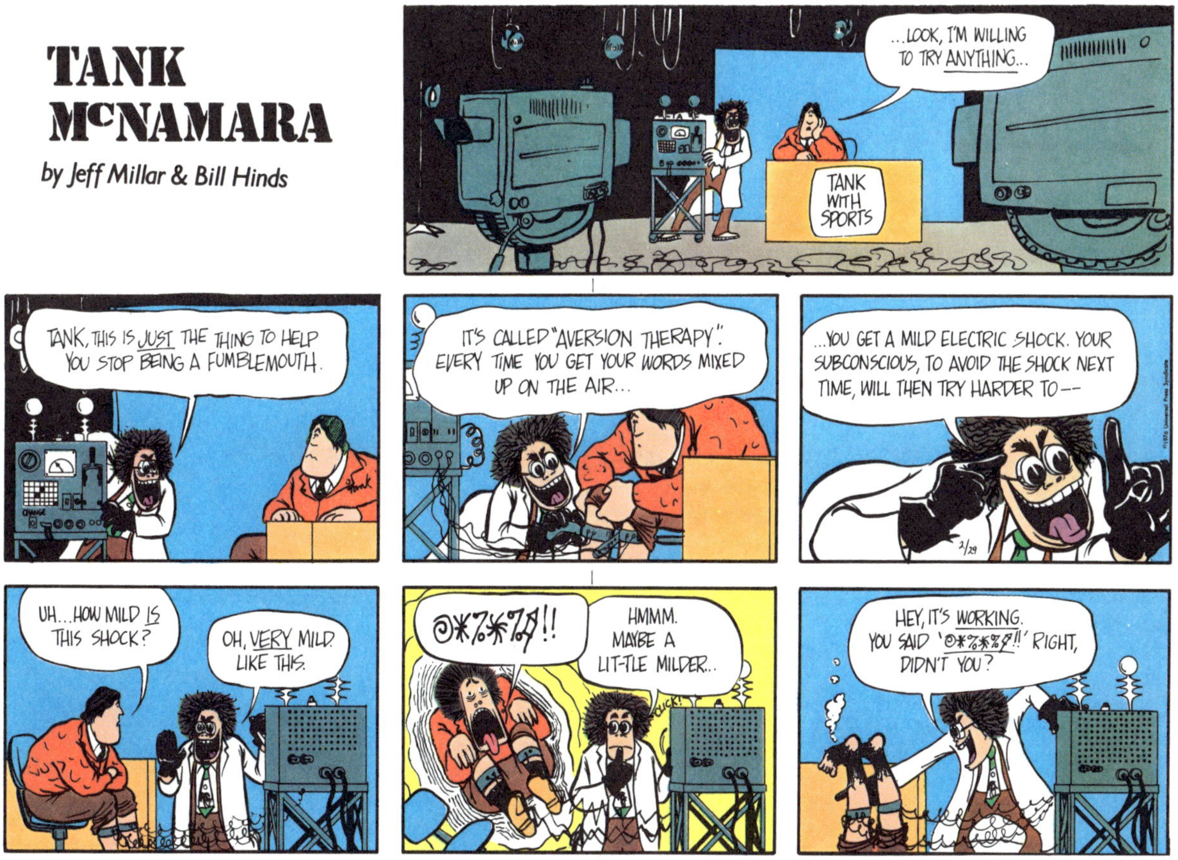
TANK McNAMARA
by Jeff Millar & Bill Hinds
...LOOK, I'M WILLING TO TRY ANYTHING...
TANK WITH SPORTS
TANK, THIS IS JUST THE THING TO HELP YOU STOP BEING A FUMBLEMOUTH.
IT'S CALLED "AVERSION THERAPY". EVERY TIME YOU GET YOUR WORDS MIXED UP ON THE AIR...
...YOU GET A MILD ELECTRIC SHOCK. YOUR SUBCONSCIOUS, TO AVOID THE SHOCK NEXT TIME, WILL THEN TRY HARDER TO—
3/29
UH...HOW MILD IS THIS SHOCK?
OH, VERY MILD. LIKE THIS.
@*%*%!!
HMMM. MAYBE A LIT-TLE MILDER..
HEY, IT'S WORKING. YOU SAID '@*%*%!!' RIGHT, DIDN'T YOU?

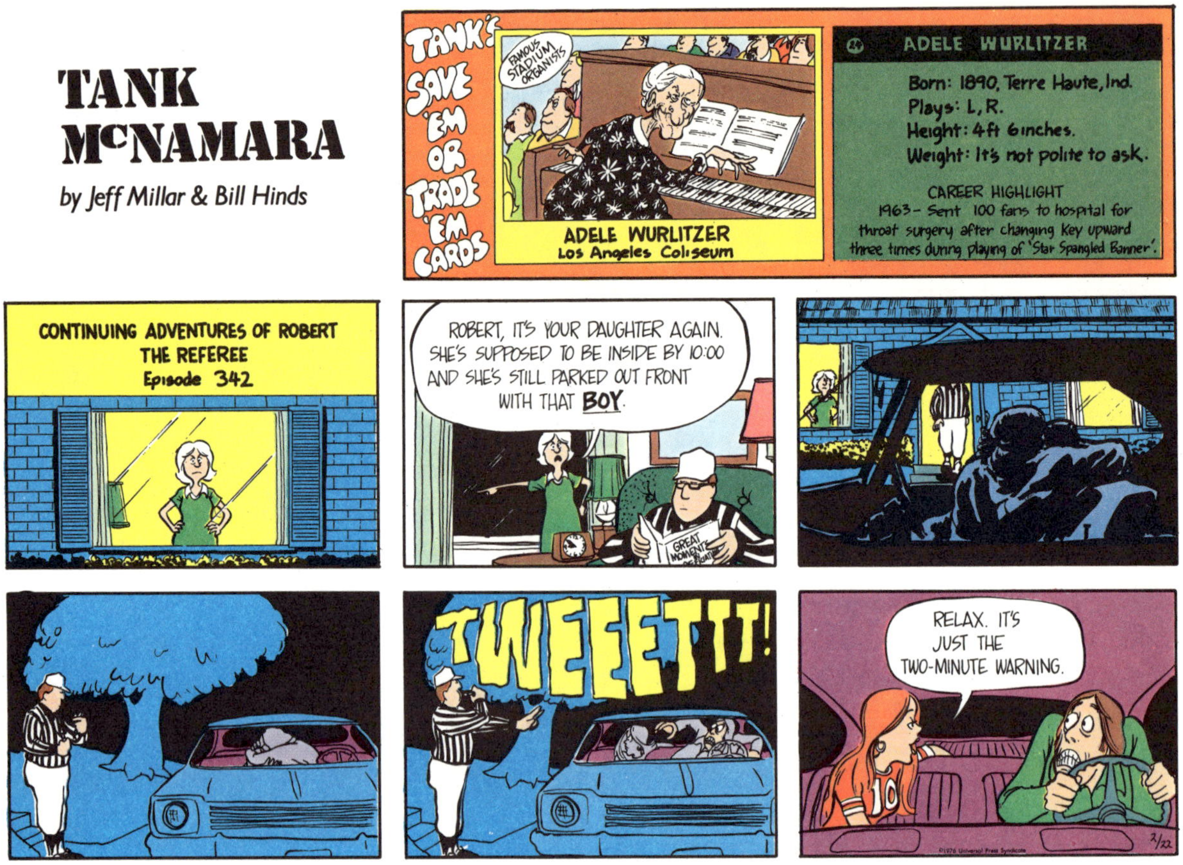

TANK McNAMARA
by Jeff Millar & Bill Hinds
TANK'S SAVE 'EM OR TRADE 'EM CARDS
FAMOUS STADIUM ORGANISTS
ADELE WURLITZER
Los Angeles Coliseum
24 ADELE WURLITZER
Born: 1890, Terre Haute, Ind.
Plays: L, R.
Height: 4 ft 6 inches.
Weight: It's not polite to ask.
CAREER HIGHLIGHT
1963 – Sent 100 fans to hospital for throat surgery after changing key upward three times during playing of "Star Spangled Banner".
CONTINUING ADVENTURES OF ROBERT THE REFEREE
Episode 342
ROBERT, IT'S YOUR DAUGHTER AGAIN. SHE'S SUPPOSED TO BE INSIDE BY 10:00 AND SHE'S STILL PARKED OUT FRONT WITH THAT BOY.
GREAT MOMENTS
TWEEETTT!
RELAX. IT'S JUST THE TWO-MINUTE WARNING.
10
2/22

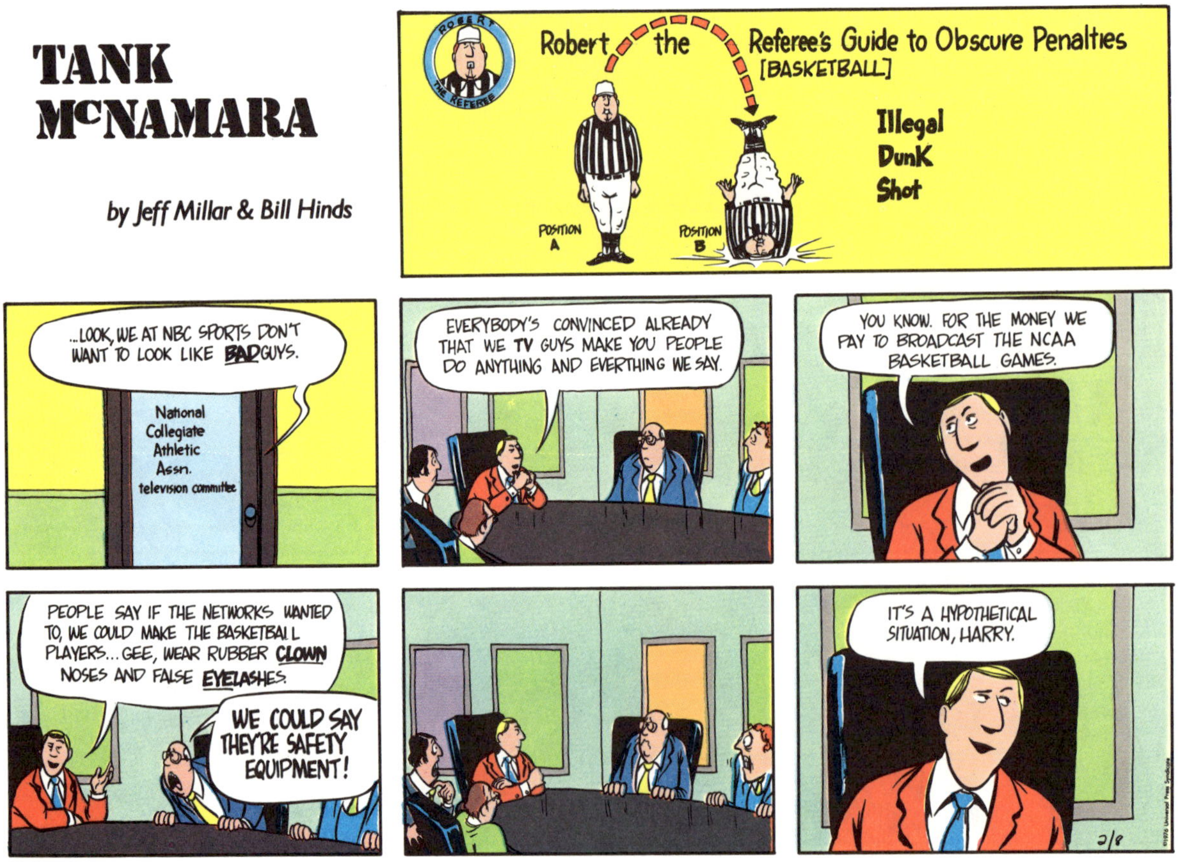

TANK McNAMARA
by Jeff Millar & Bill Hinds
ROBERT THE REFEREE
Robert the Referee's Guide to Obscure Penalties
[BASKETBALL]
Illegal Dunk Shot
POSITION A
POSITION B
...LOOK, WE AT NBC SPORTS DON'T WANT TO LOOK LIKE BAD GUYS.
National Collegiate Athletic Assn. television committee
EVERYBODY'S CONVINCED ALREADY THAT WE TV GUYS MAKE YOU PEOPLE DO ANYTHING AND EVERTHING WE SAY.
YOU KNOW. FOR THE MONEY WE PAY TO BROADCAST THE NCAA BASKETBALL GAMES.
PEOPLE SAY IF THE NETWORKS WANTED TO, WE COULD MAKE THE BASKETBALL PLAYERS... GEE, WEAR RUBBER CLOWN NOSES AND FALSE EYELASHES.
WE COULD SAY THEY'RE SAFETY EQUIPMENT!
IT'S A HYPOTHETICAL SITUATION, HARRY.
2/8

TANK McNAMARA

by Jeff Millar & Bill Hinds

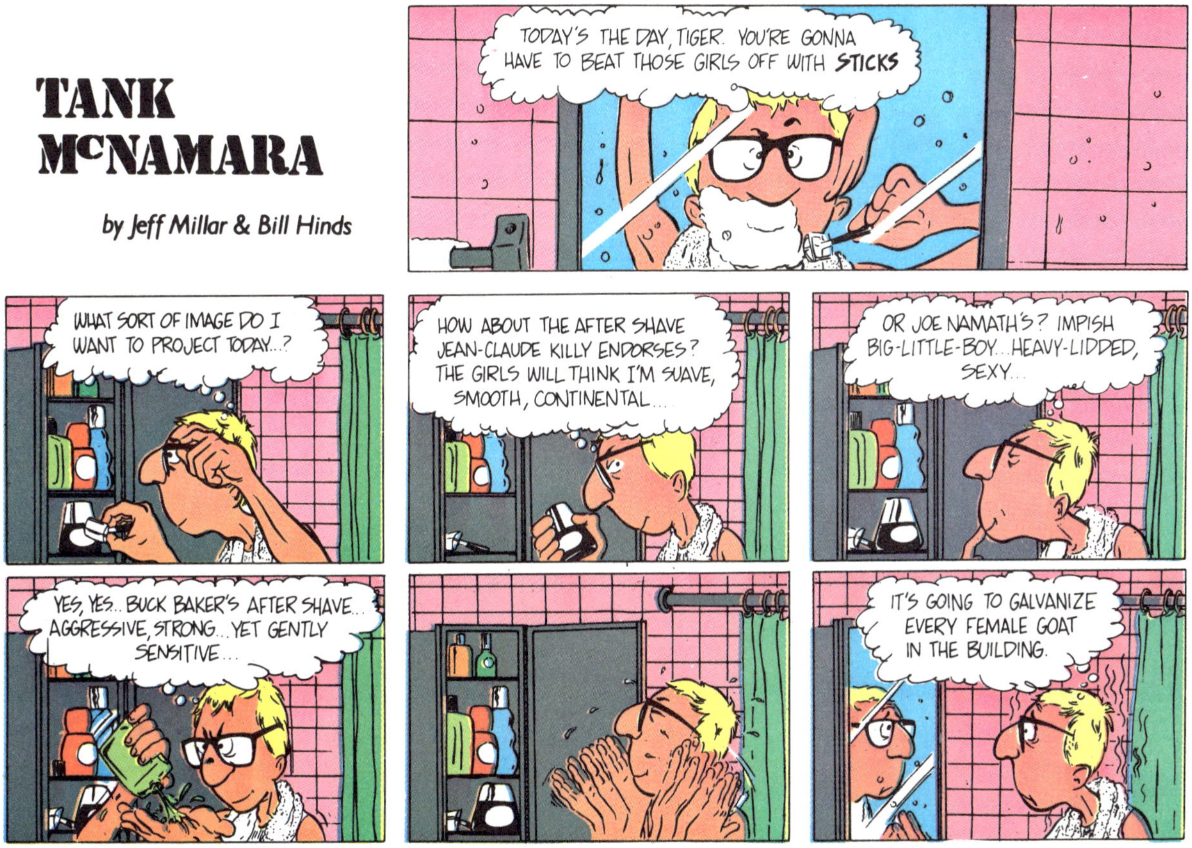
TODAY'S THE DAY, TIGER. YOU'RE GONNA HAVE TO BEAT THOSE GIRLS OFF WITH STICKS
WHAT SORT OF IMAGE DO I WANT TO PROJECT TODAY...?
HOW ABOUT THE AFTER SHAVE JEAN-CLAUDE KILLY ENDORSES? THE GIRLS WILL THINK I'M SUAVE, SMOOTH, CONTINENTAL...
OR JOE NAMATH'S? IMPISH BIG-LITTLE-BOY...HEAVY-LIDDED, SEXY...
YES, YES...BUCK BAKER'S AFTER SHAVE... AGGRESSIVE, STRONG...YET GENTLY SENSITIVE...
IT'S GOING TO GALVANIZE EVERY FEMALE GOAT IN THE BUILDING.

TANK McNAMARA

by Jeff Millar & Bill Hinds

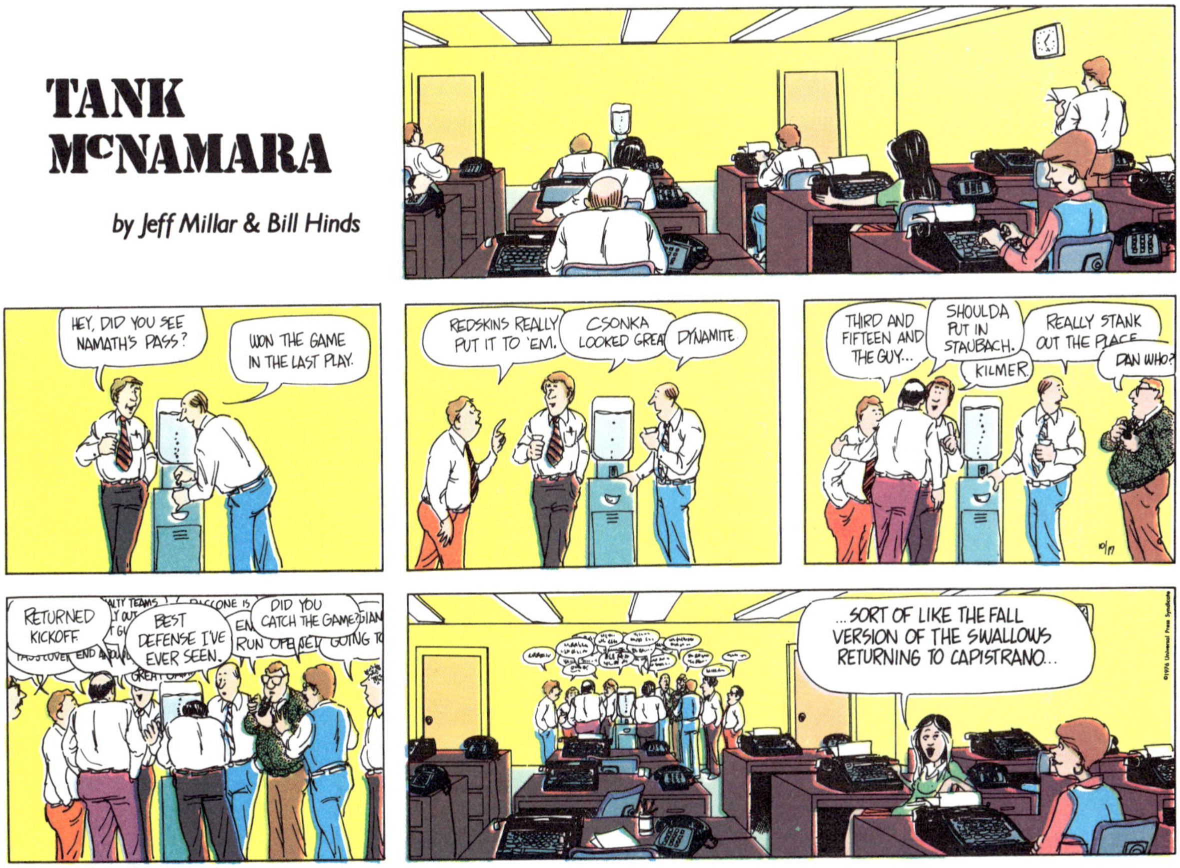
HEY, DID YOU SEE NAMATH'S PASS?
WON THE GAME IN THE LAST PLAY.
REDSKINS REALLY PUT IT TO 'EM.
CSONKA LOOKED GREA
DYNAMITE
THIRD AND FIFTEEN AND THE GUY...
SHOULDA PUT IN STAUBACH.
KILMER
REALLY STANK OUT THE PLACE
DAN WHO?
RETURNED KICKOFF
BEST DEFENSE I'VE EVER SEEN.
DID YOU CATCH THE GAME?
...SORT OF LIKE THE FALL VERSION OF THE SWALLOWS RETURNING TO CAPISTRANO...

TANK McNAMARA

by Jeff Millar & Bill Hinds

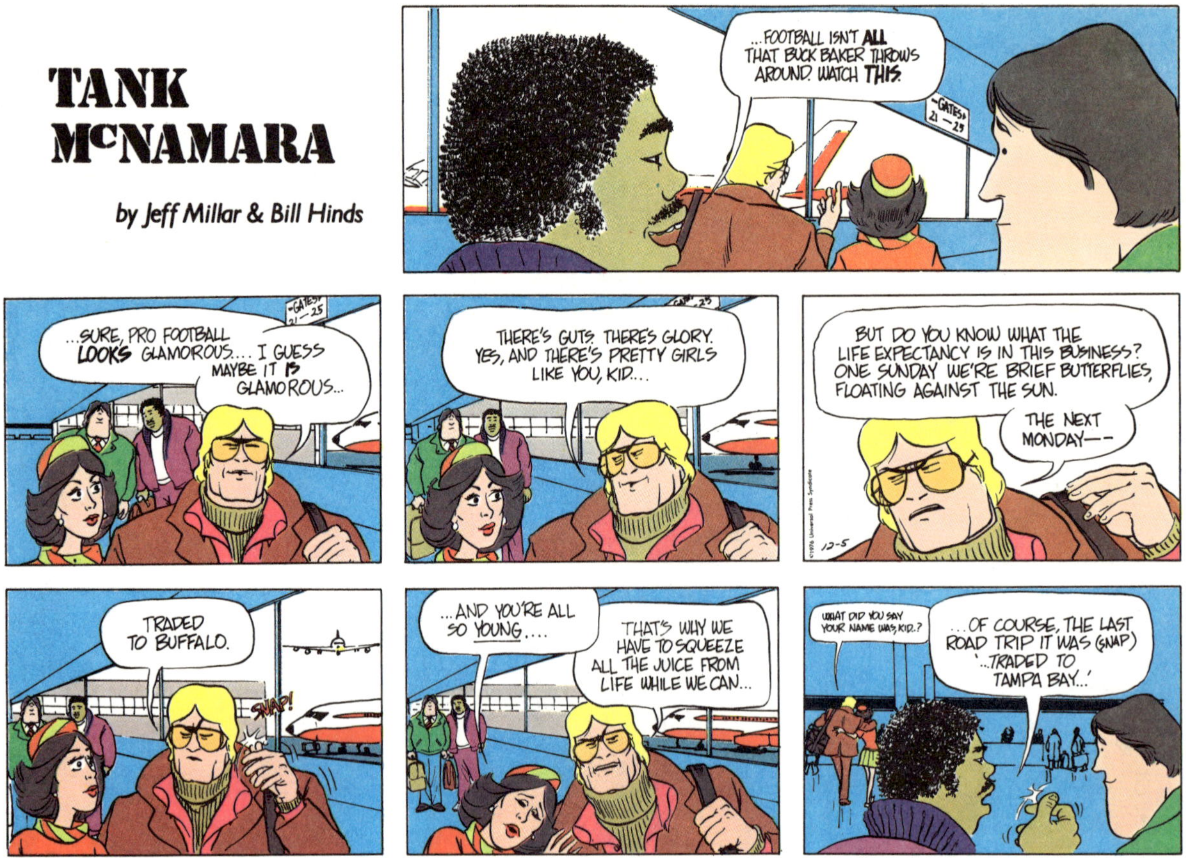

...FOOTBALL ISN'T ALL THAT BUCK BAKER THROWS AROUND. WATCH THIS.
GATES 21—25
...SURE, PRO FOOTBALL LOOKS GLAMOROUS.... I GUESS
MAYBE IT IS GLAMOROUS...
THERE'S GUTS. THERE'S GLORY. YES, AND THERE'S PRETTY GIRLS LIKE YOU, KID...
BUT DO YOU KNOW WHAT THE LIFE EXPECTANCY IS IN THIS BUSINESS? ONE SUNDAY WE'RE BRIEF BUTTERFLIES, FLOATING AGAINST THE SUN.
THE NEXT MONDAY——
TRADED TO BUFFALO.
SNAP!
...AND YOU'RE ALL SO YOUNG....
THAT'S WHY WE HAVE TO SQUEEZE ALL THE JUICE FROM LIFE WHILE WE CAN...
WHAT DID YOU SAY YOUR NAME WAS, KID..?
...OF COURSE, THE LAST ROAD TRIP IT WAS (SNAP) '...TRADED TO TAMPA BAY...'

TANK McNAMARA

by Jeff Millar & Bill Hinds

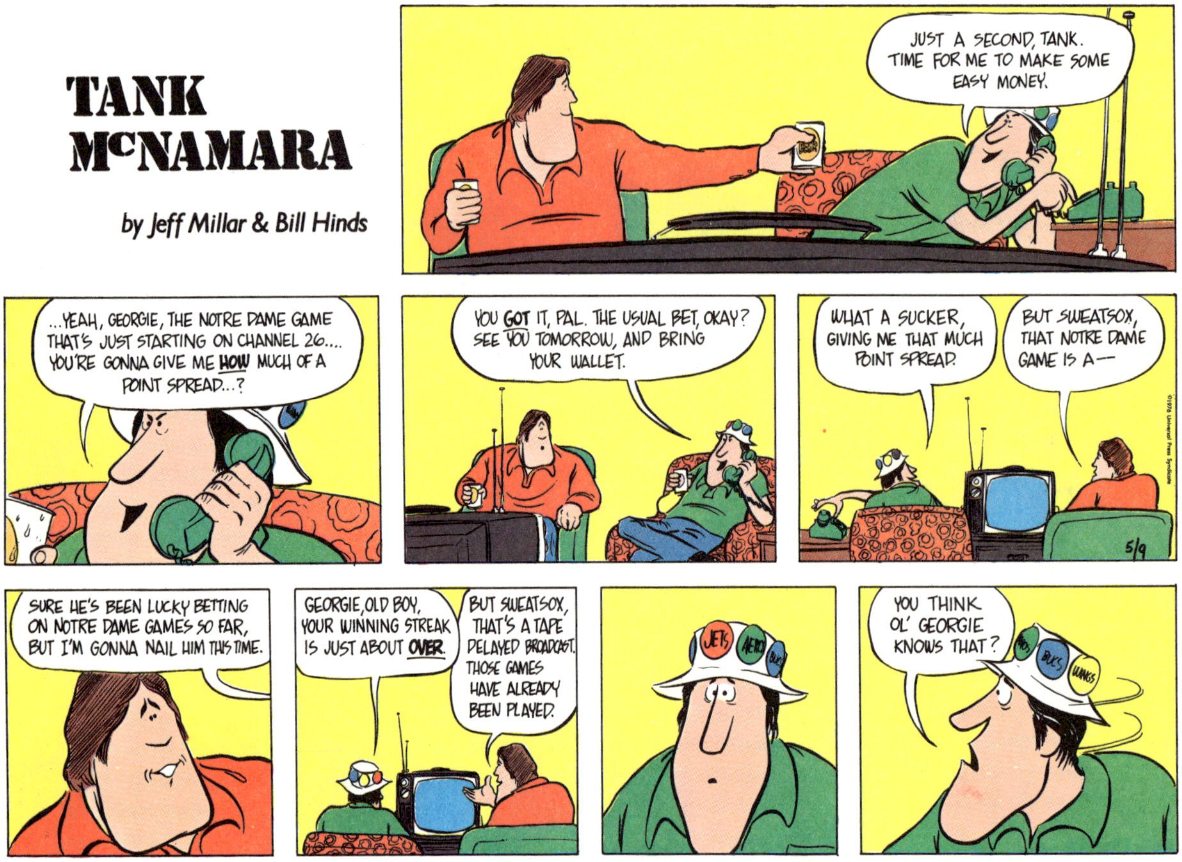

JUST A SECOND, TANK. TIME FOR ME TO MAKE SOME EASY MONEY.
...YEAH, GEORGIE, THE NOTRE DAME GAME THAT'S JUST STARTING ON CHANNEL 26.... YOU'RE GONNA GIVE ME HOW MUCH OF A POINT SPREAD...?
YOU GOT IT, PAL. THE USUAL BET, OKAY? SEE YOU TOMORROW, AND BRING YOUR WALLET.
WHAT A SUCKER, GIVING ME THAT MUCH POINT SPREAD.
BUT SWEATSOX, THAT NOTRE DAME GAME IS A—
SURE HE'S BEEN LUCKY BETTING ON NOTRE DAME GAMES SO FAR, BUT I'M GONNA NAIL HIM THIS TIME.
GEORGIE, OLD BOY, YOUR WINNING STREAK IS JUST ABOUT OVER.
BUT SWEATSOX, THAT'S A TAPE DELAYED BROADCAST. THOSE GAMES HAVE ALREADY BEEN PLAYED.
JETS
YOU THINK OL' GEORGIE KNOWS THAT?

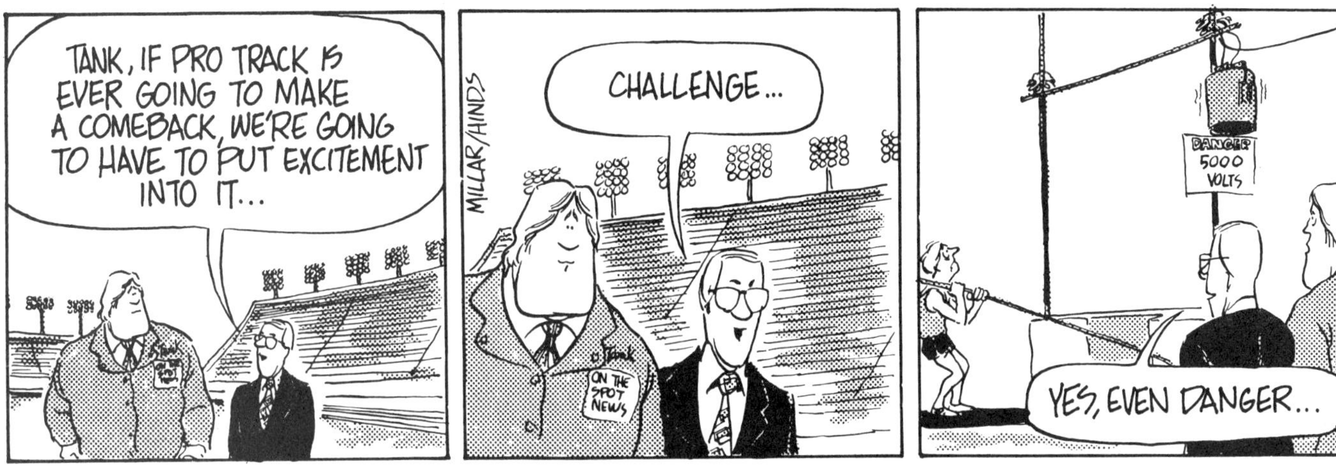
TANK, IF PRO TRACK IS EVER GOING TO MAKE A COMEBACK, WE'RE GOING TO HAVE TO PUT EXCITEMENT INTO IT...
MILLAR/HINDS
CHALLENGE...
ON THE SPOT NEWS
DANGER 5000 VOLTS
YES, EVEN DANGER...

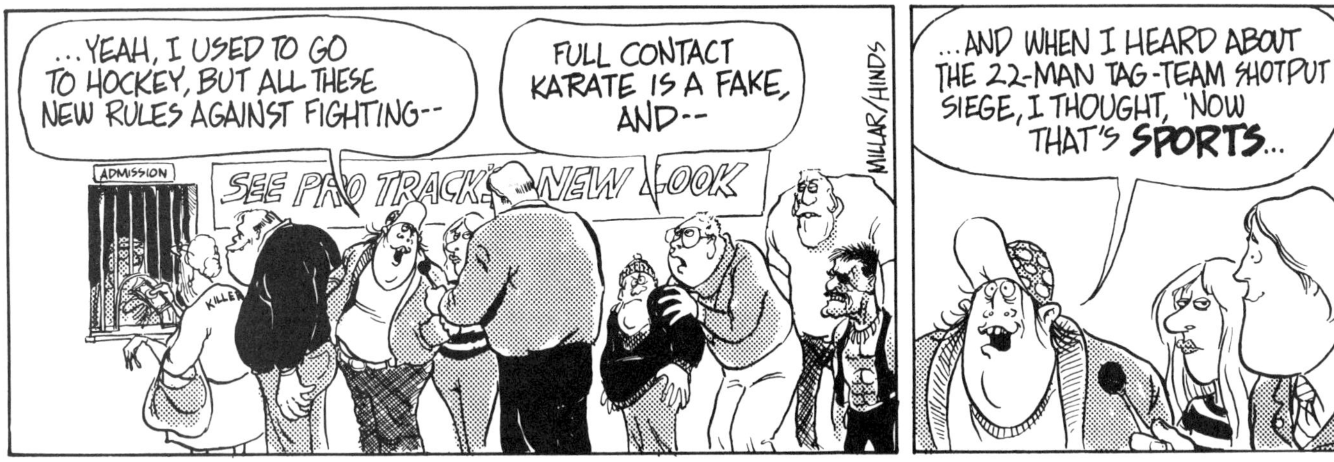
...YEAH, I USED TO GO TO HOCKEY, BUT ALL THESE NEW RULES AGAINST FIGHTING--
FULL CONTACT KARATE IS A FAKE, AND--
ADMISSION
MILLAR/HINDS
...AND WHEN I HEARD ABOUT THE 22-MAN TAG-TEAM SHOTPUT SIEGE, I THOUGHT, 'NOW THAT'S **SPORTS**...

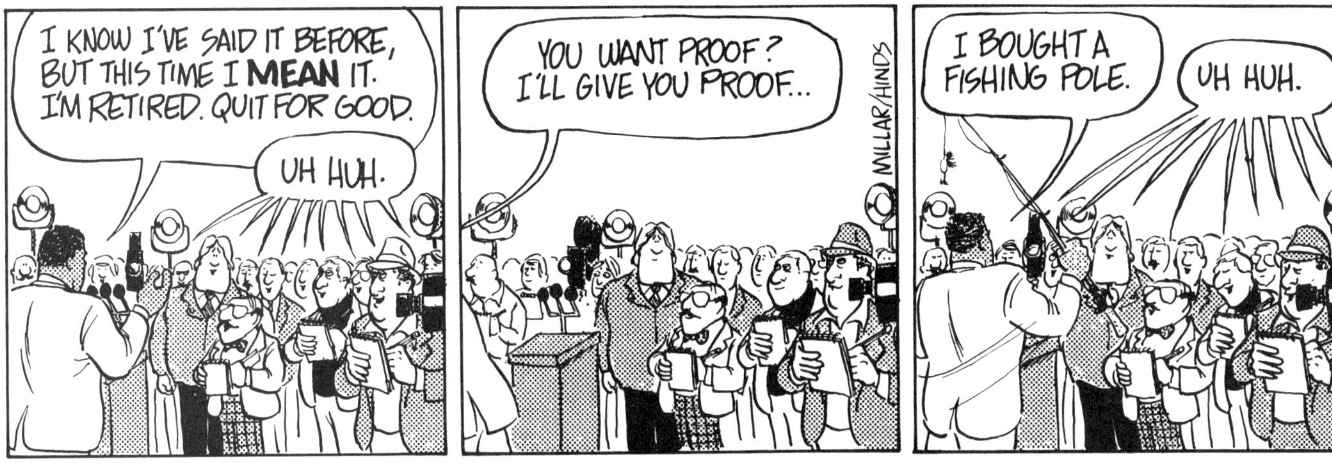
I KNOW I'VE SAID IT BEFORE, BUT THIS TIME I **MEAN** IT. I'M RETIRED. QUIT FOR GOOD.
UH HUH.
YOU WANT PROOF? I'LL GIVE YOU PROOF...
MILLAR/HINDS
I BOUGHT A FISHING POLE.
UH HUH.

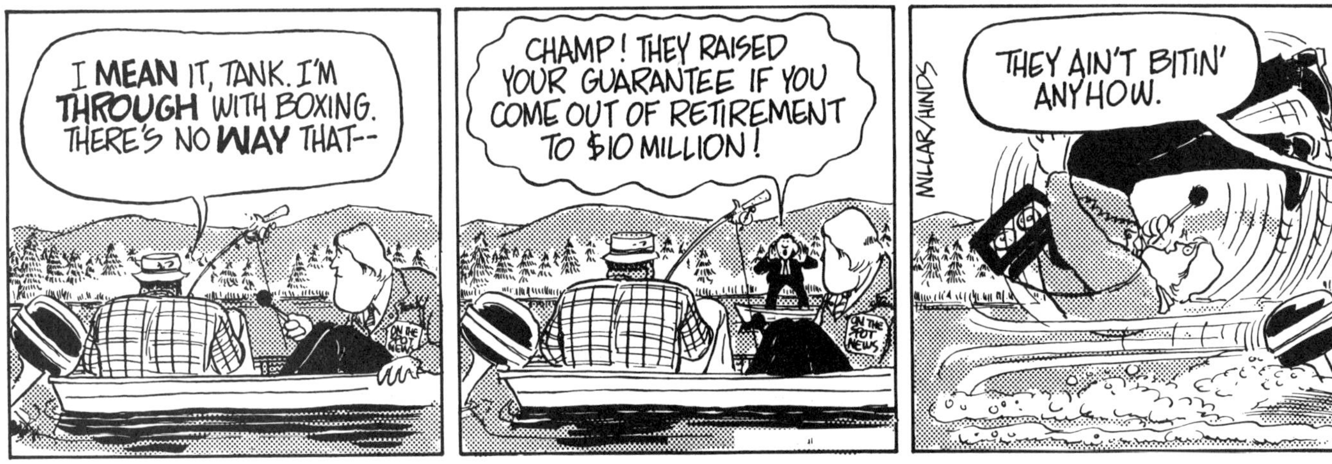
I **MEAN** IT, TANK. I'M **THROUGH** WITH BOXING. THERE'S NO **WAY** THAT--
CHAMP! THEY RAISED YOUR GUARANTEE IF YOU COME OUT OF RETIREMENT TO $10 MILLION!
ON THE SPOT NEWS
MILLAR/HINDS
THEY AIN'T BITIN' ANYHOW.

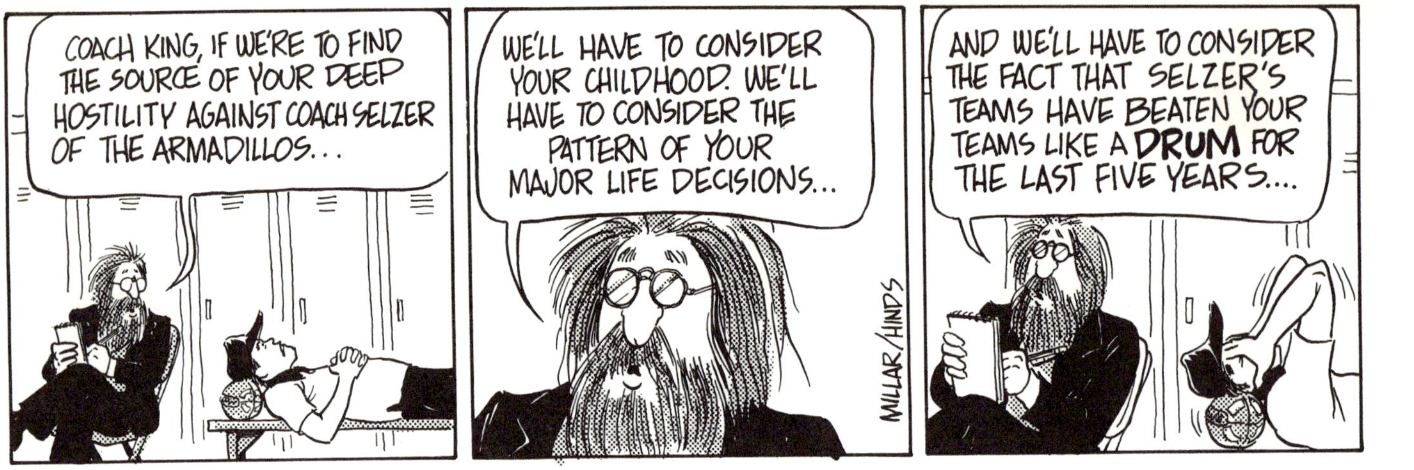
COACH KING, IF WE'RE TO FIND THE SOURCE OF YOUR DEEP HOSTILITY AGAINST COACH SELZER OF THE ARMADILLOS...
WE'LL HAVE TO CONSIDER YOUR CHILDHOOD. WE'LL HAVE TO CONSIDER THE PATTERN OF YOUR MAJOR LIFE DECISIONS...
MILLAR/HINDS
AND WE'LL HAVE TO CONSIDER THE FACT THAT SELZER'S TEAMS HAVE BEATEN YOUR TEAMS LIKE A **DRUM** FOR THE LAST FIVE YEARS....

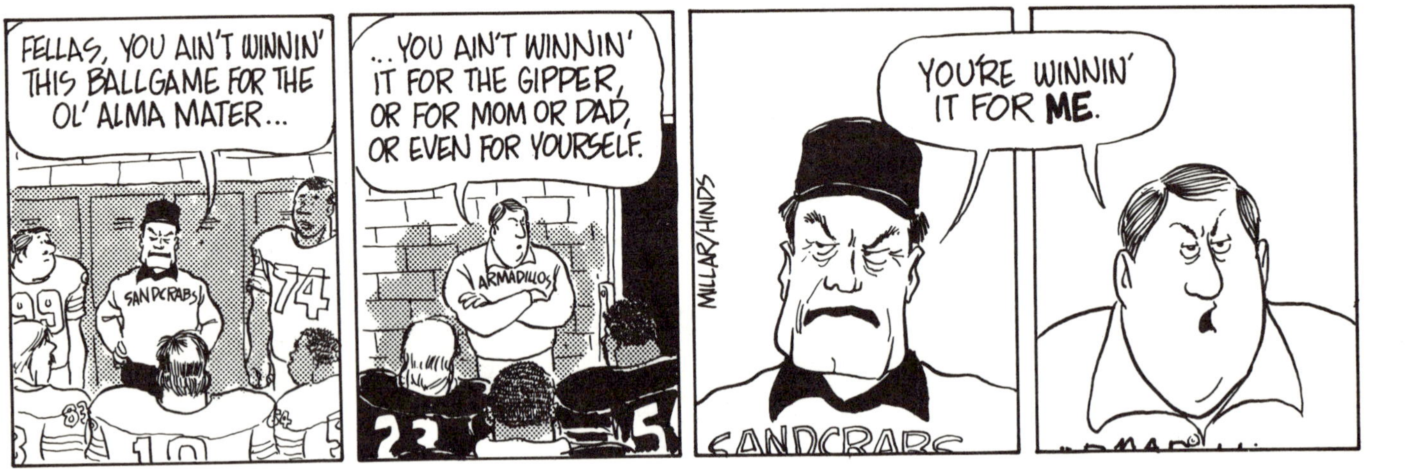
FELLAS, YOU AIN'T WINNIN' THIS BALLGAME FOR THE OL' ALMA MATER...
SANDCRABS
...YOU AIN'T WINNIN' IT FOR THE GIPPER, OR FOR MOM OR DAD, OR EVEN FOR YOURSELF.
ARMADILLOS
MILLAR/HINDS
YOU'RE WINNIN' IT FOR **ME**.

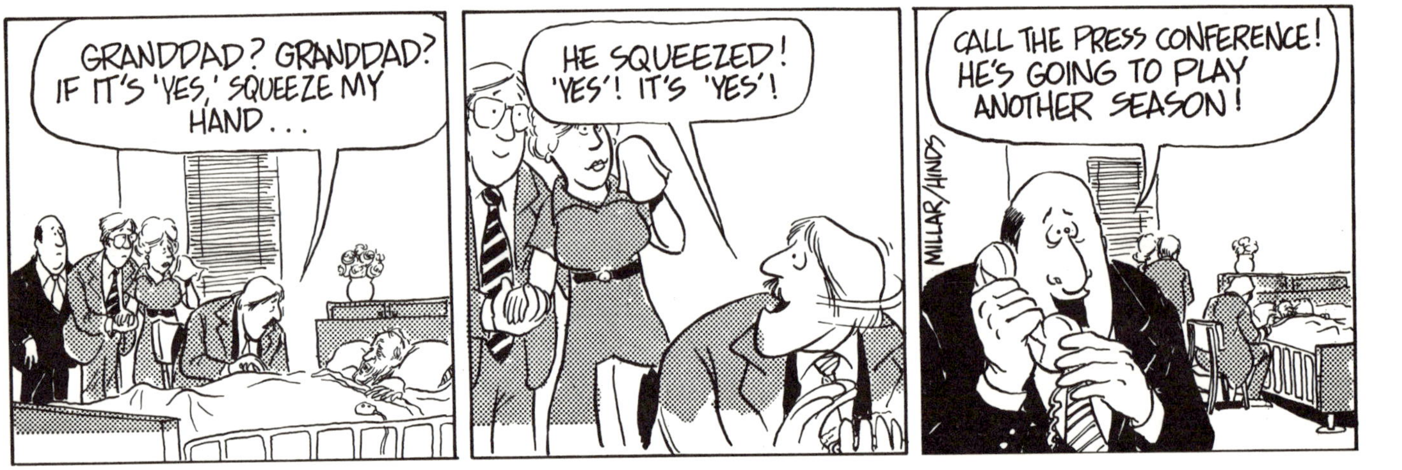
GRANDDAD? GRANDDAD? IF IT'S 'YES,' SQUEEZE MY HAND...
HE SQUEEZED! 'YES'! IT'S 'YES'!
MILLAR/HINDS
CALL THE PRESS CONFERENCE! HE'S GOING TO PLAY ANOTHER SEASON!

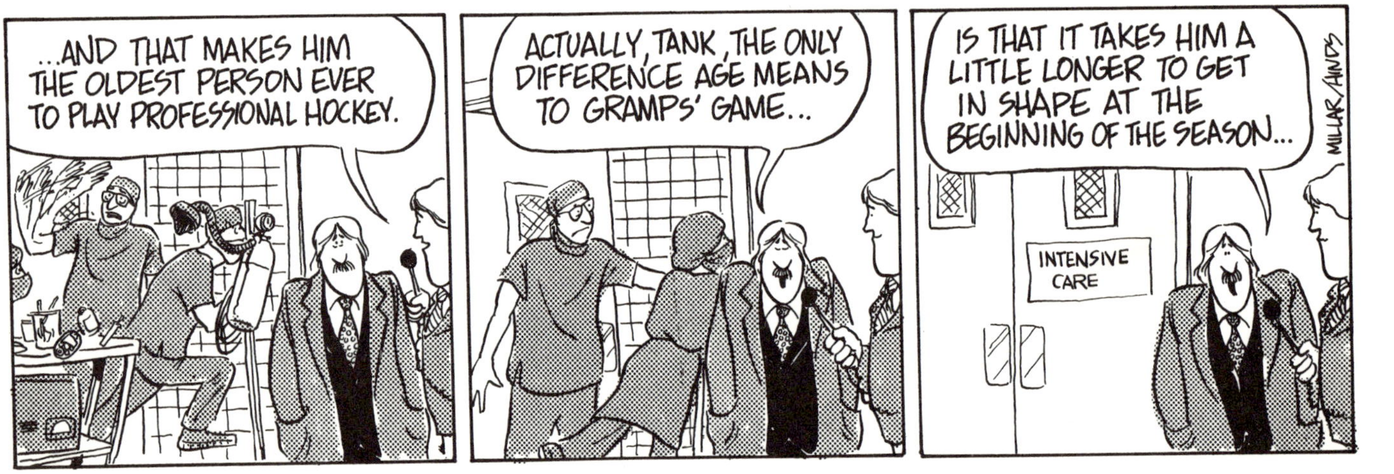
...AND THAT MAKES HIM THE OLDEST PERSON EVER TO PLAY PROFESSIONAL HOCKEY.
ACTUALLY, TANK, THE ONLY DIFFERENCE AGE MEANS TO GRAMPS' GAME...
IS THAT IT TAKES HIM A LITTLE LONGER TO GET IN SHAPE AT THE BEGINNING OF THE SEASON...
MILLAR/HINDS
INTENSIVE CARE

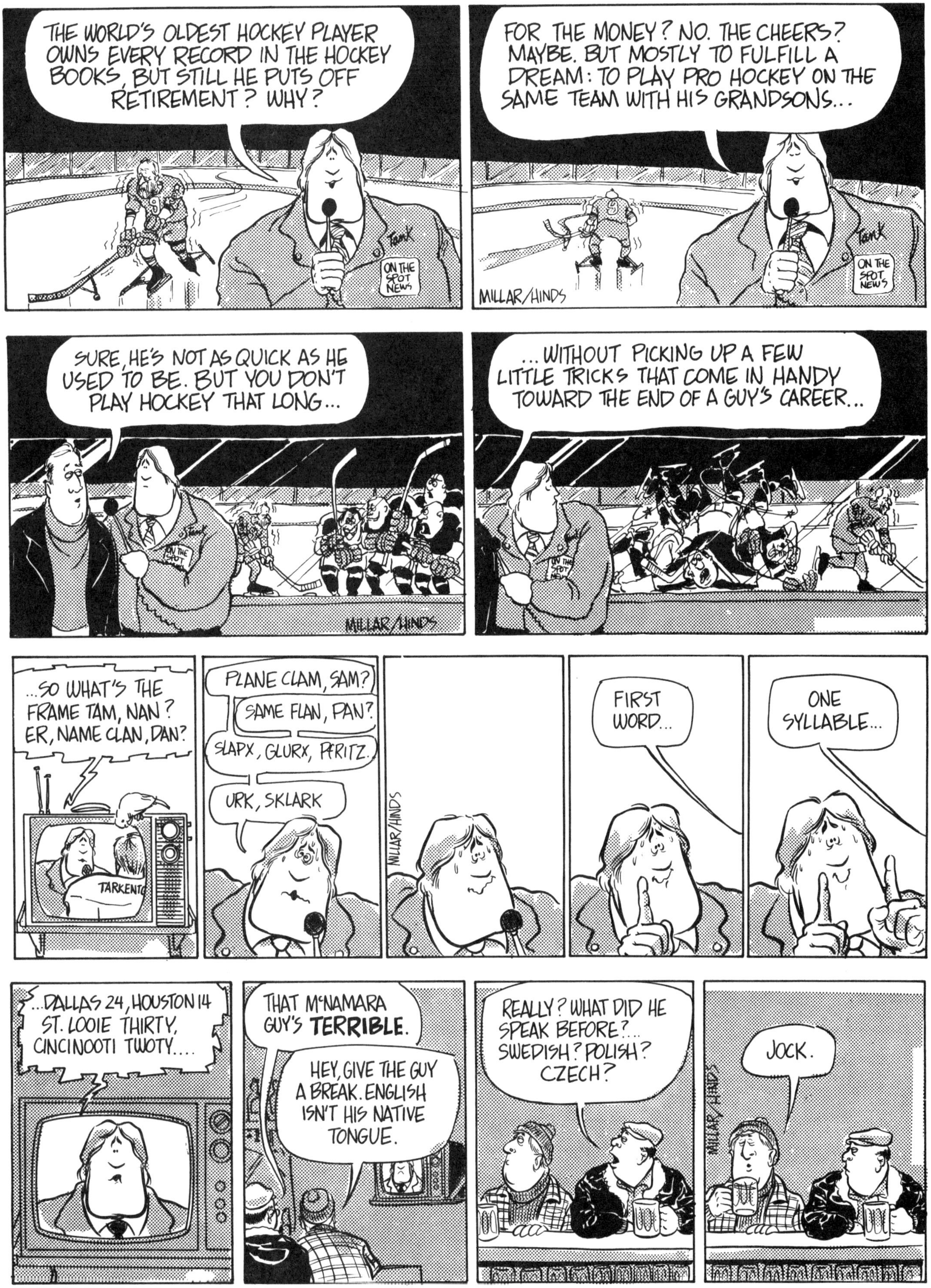
THE WORLD'S OLDEST HOCKEY PLAYER OWNS EVERY RECORD IN THE HOCKEY BOOKS, BUT STILL HE PUTS OFF RETIREMENT? WHY?
ON THE SPOT NEWS
FOR THE MONEY? NO. THE CHEERS? MAYBE. BUT MOSTLY TO FULFILL A DREAM: TO PLAY PRO HOCKEY ON THE SAME TEAM WITH HIS GRANDSONS...
ON THE SPOT NEWS
MILLAR/HINDS
SURE, HE'S NOT AS QUICK AS HE USED TO BE. BUT YOU DON'T PLAY HOCKEY THAT LONG...
MILLAR/HINDS
...WITHOUT PICKING UP A FEW LITTLE TRICKS THAT COME IN HANDY TOWARD THE END OF A GUY'S CAREER...
...SO WHAT'S THE FRAME TAM, NAN? ER, NAME CLAN, DAN?
TARKENTO
PLANE CLAM, SAM?
SAME FLAN, PAN?
SLAPX, GLURX, PFRITZ.
URK, SKLARK
MILLAR/HINDS
FIRST WORD...
ONE SYLLABLE...
...DALLAS 24, HOUSTON 14 ST. LOOIE THIRTY, CINCINOOTI TWOTY....
THAT McNAMARA GUY'S **TERRIBLE**.
HEY, GIVE THE GUY A BREAK. ENGLISH ISN'T HIS NATIVE TONGUE.
REALLY? WHAT DID HE SPEAK BEFORE?... SWEDISH? POLISH? CZECH?
MILLAR/HINDS
JOCK.

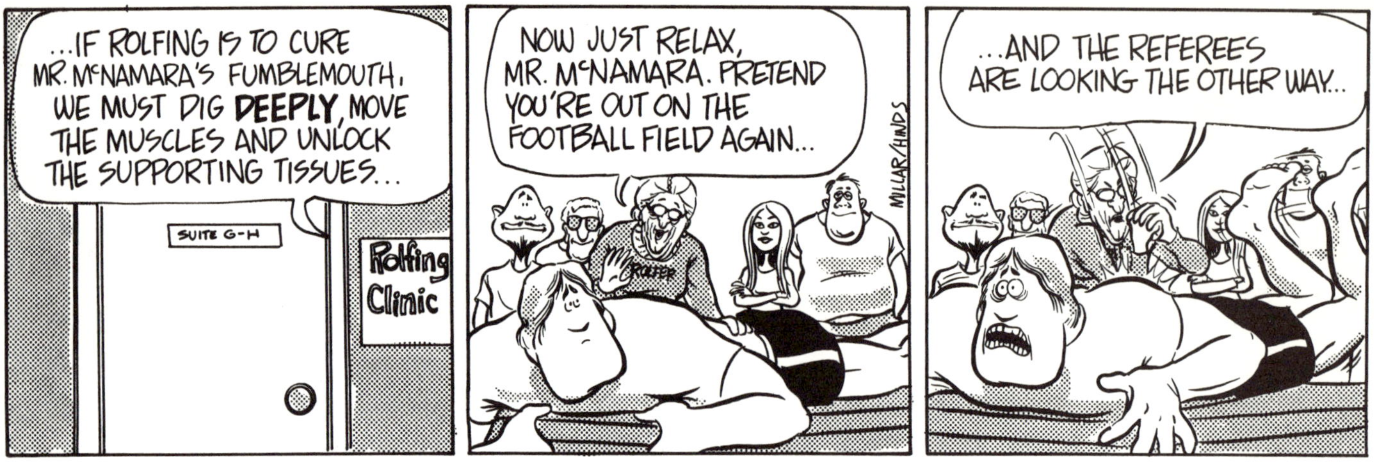
...IF ROLFING IS TO CURE MR. McNAMARA'S FUMBLEMOUTH, WE MUST DIG DEEPLY, MOVE THE MUSCLES AND UNLOCK THE SUPPORTING TISSUES...
SUITE G-H
Rolfing Clinic
NOW JUST RELAX, MR. McNAMARA. PRETEND YOU'RE OUT ON THE FOOTBALL FIELD AGAIN...
ROLFER
MILLAR/HINDS
...AND THE REFEREES ARE LOOKING THE OTHER WAY...

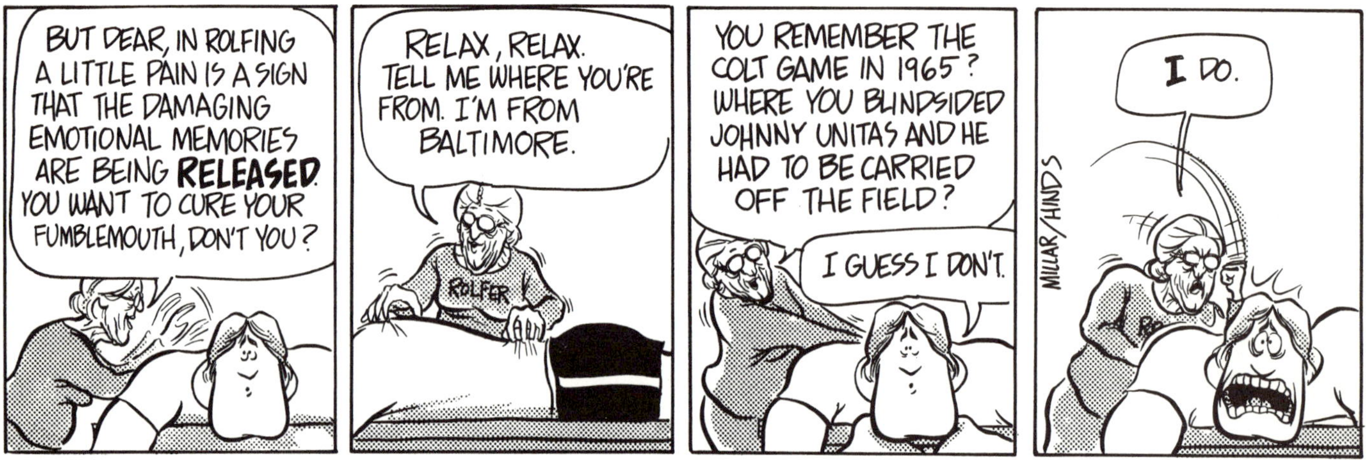
BUT DEAR, IN ROLFING A LITTLE PAIN IS A SIGN THAT THE DAMAGING EMOTIONAL MEMORIES ARE BEING RELEASED. YOU WANT TO CURE YOUR FUMBLEMOUTH, DON'T YOU?
RELAX, RELAX. TELL ME WHERE YOU'RE FROM. I'M FROM BALTIMORE.
ROLFER
YOU REMEMBER THE COLT GAME IN 1965? WHERE YOU BLINDSIDED JOHNNY UNITAS AND HE HAD TO BE CARRIED OFF THE FIELD?
I GUESS I DON'T.
MILLAR/HINDS
I DO.

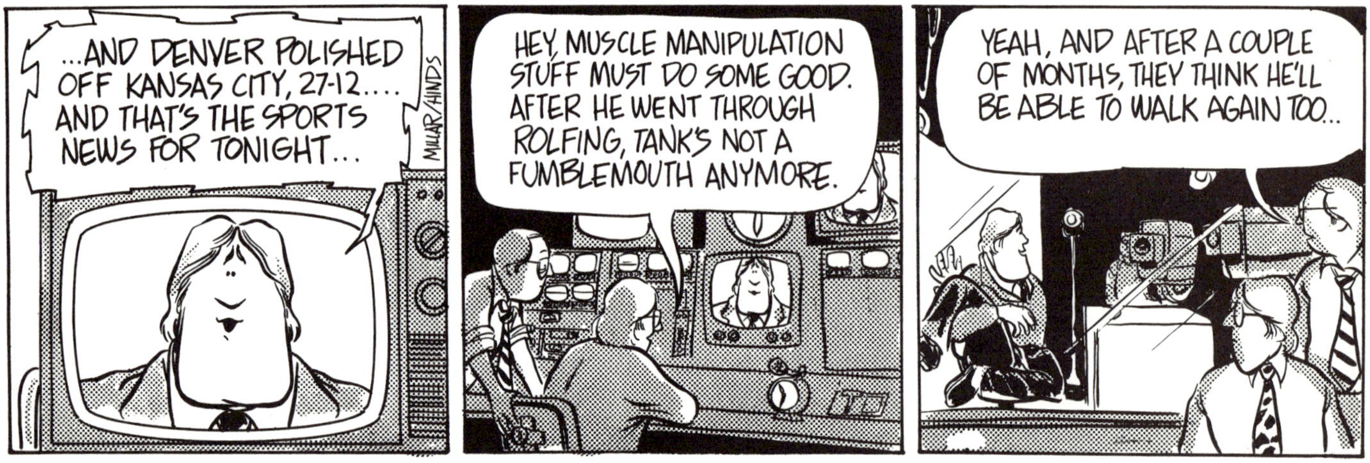
...AND DENVER POLISHED OFF KANSAS CITY, 27-12.... AND THAT'S THE SPORTS NEWS FOR TONIGHT...
MILLAR/HINDS
HEY, MUSCLE MANIPULATION STUFF MUST DO SOME GOOD. AFTER HE WENT THROUGH ROLFING, TANK'S NOT A FUMBLEMOUTH ANYMORE.
YEAH, AND AFTER A COUPLE OF MONTHS, THEY THINK HE'LL BE ABLE TO WALK AGAIN TOO...

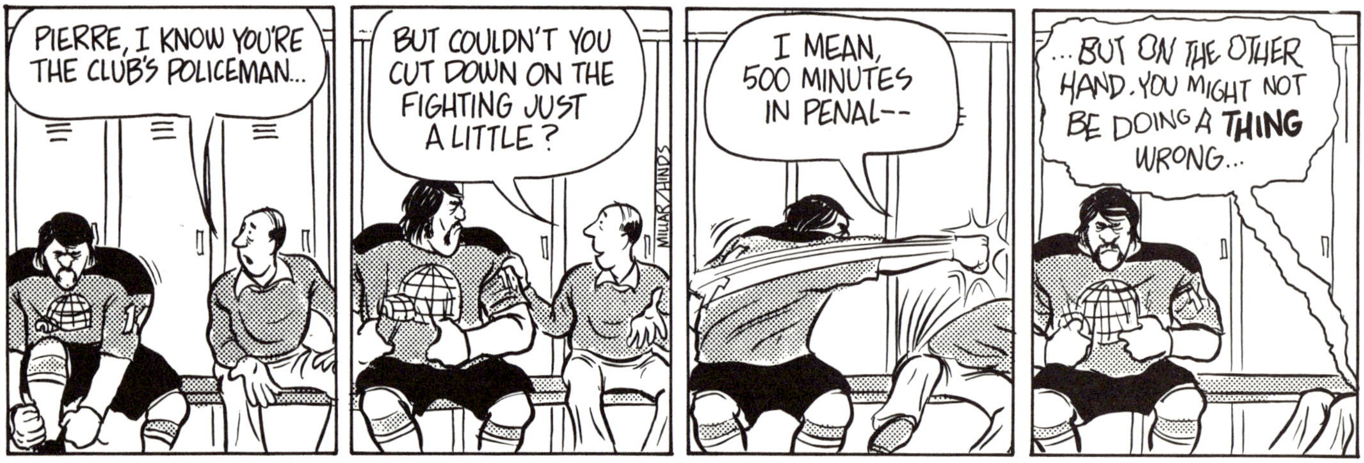
PIERRE, I KNOW YOU'RE THE CLUB'S POLICEMAN...
BUT COULDN'T YOU CUT DOWN ON THE FIGHTING JUST A LITTLE?
MILLAR/HINDS
I MEAN, 500 MINUTES IN PENAL--
...BUT ON THE OTHER HAND, YOU MIGHT NOT BE DOING A THING WRONG...

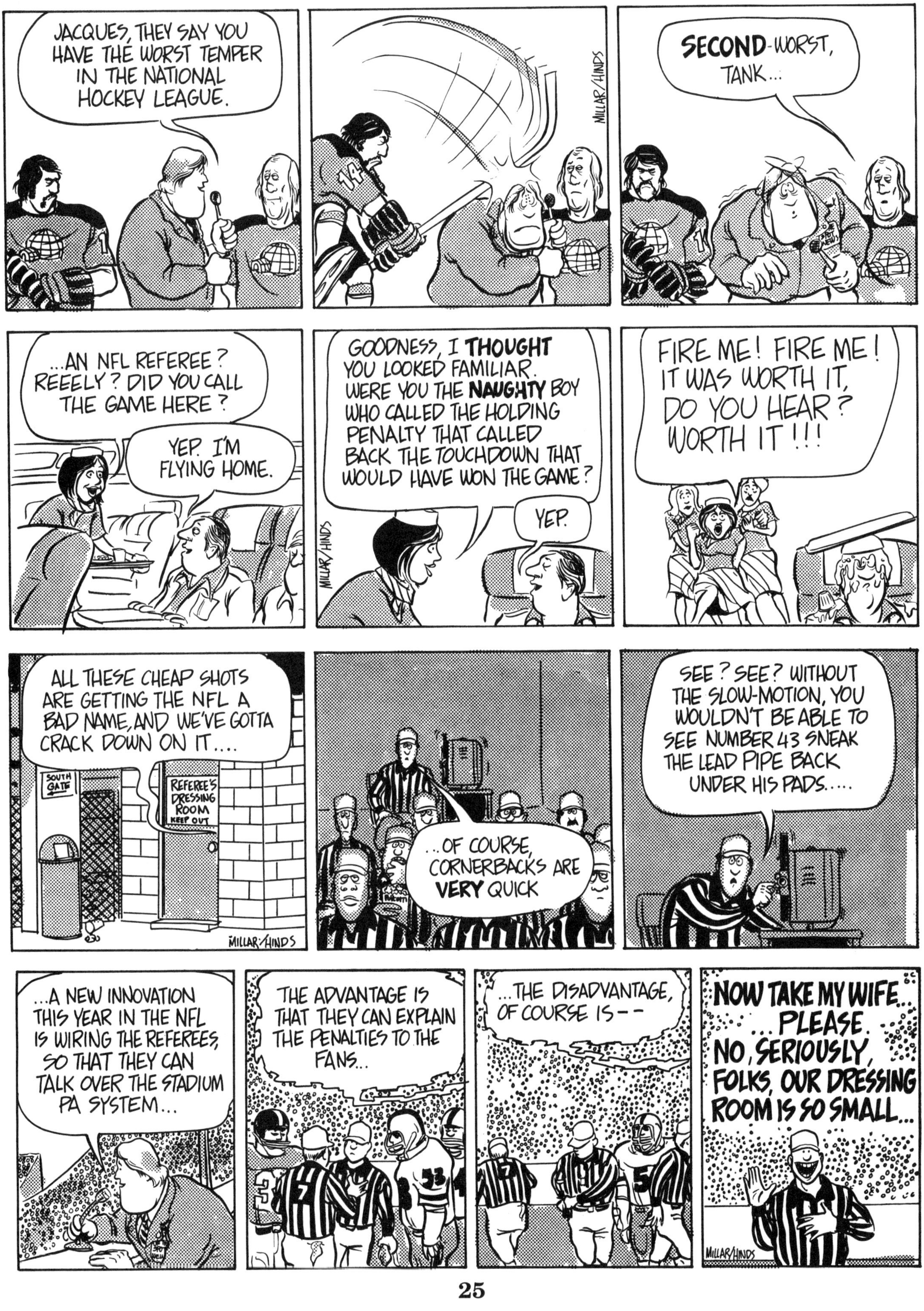
JACQUES, THEY SAY YOU HAVE THE WORST TEMPER IN THE NATIONAL HOCKEY LEAGUE.
MILLAR/HINDS
SECOND-WORST, TANK...
...AN NFL REFEREE? REEELY? DID YOU CALL THE GAME HERE?
YEP. I'M FLYING HOME.
GOODNESS, I THOUGHT YOU LOOKED FAMILIAR. WERE YOU THE NAUGHTY BOY WHO CALLED THE HOLDING PENALTY THAT CALLED BACK THE TOUCHDOWN THAT WOULD HAVE WON THE GAME?
YEP.
MILLAR/HINDS
FIRE ME! FIRE ME! IT WAS WORTH IT, DO YOU HEAR? WORTH IT!!!
ALL THESE CHEAP SHOTS ARE GETTING THE NFL A BAD NAME, AND WE'VE GOTTA CRACK DOWN ON IT....
SOUTH GATE
REFEREE'S DRESSING ROOM KEEP OUT
MILLAR/HINDS
...OF COURSE, CORNERBACKS ARE VERY QUICK
SEE? SEE? WITHOUT THE SLOW-MOTION, YOU WOULDN'T BE ABLE TO SEE NUMBER 43 SNEAK THE LEAD PIPE BACK UNDER HIS PADS.....
...A NEW INNOVATION THIS YEAR IN THE NFL IS WIRING THE REFEREES, SO THAT THEY CAN TALK OVER THE STADIUM PA SYSTEM...
THE ADVANTAGE IS THAT THEY CAN EXPLAIN THE PENALTIES TO THE FANS...
...THE DISADVANTAGE, OF COURSE IS--
NOW TAKE MY WIFE... PLEASE. NO, SERIOUSLY, FOLKS, OUR DRESSING ROOM IS SO SMALL...
MILLAR/HINDS

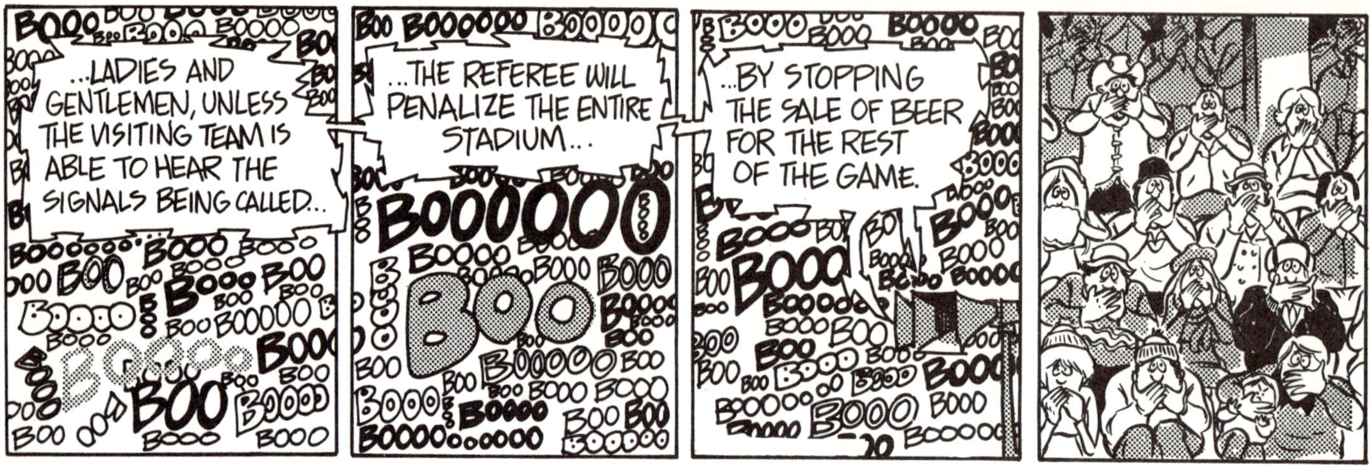
...LADIES AND GENTLEMEN, UNLESS THE VISITING TEAM IS ABLE TO HEAR THE SIGNALS BEING CALLED...
...THE REFEREE WILL PENALIZE THE ENTIRE STADIUM...
...BY STOPPING THE SALE OF BEER FOR THE REST OF THE GAME.

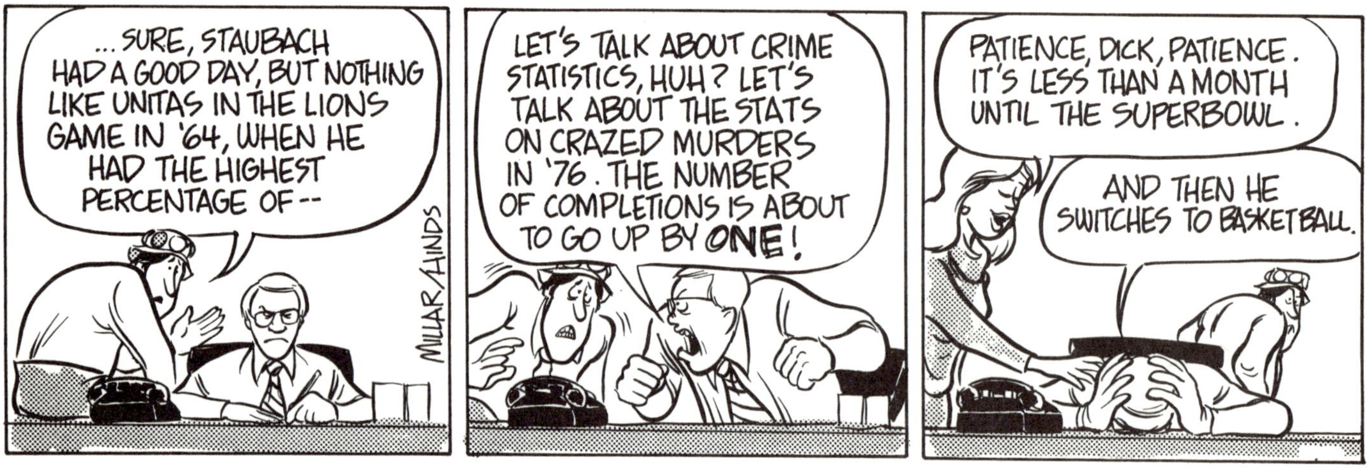
...SURE, STAUBACH HAD A GOOD DAY, BUT NOTHING LIKE UNITAS IN THE LIONS GAME IN '64, WHEN HE HAD THE HIGHEST PERCENTAGE OF--
MILLAR/HINDS
LET'S TALK ABOUT CRIME STATISTICS, HUH? LET'S TALK ABOUT THE STATS ON CRAZED MURDERS IN '76. THE NUMBER OF COMPLETIONS IS ABOUT TO GO UP BY ONE!
PATIENCE, DICK, PATIENCE. IT'S LESS THAN A MONTH UNTIL THE SUPERBOWL.
AND THEN HE SWITCHES TO BASKETBALL.

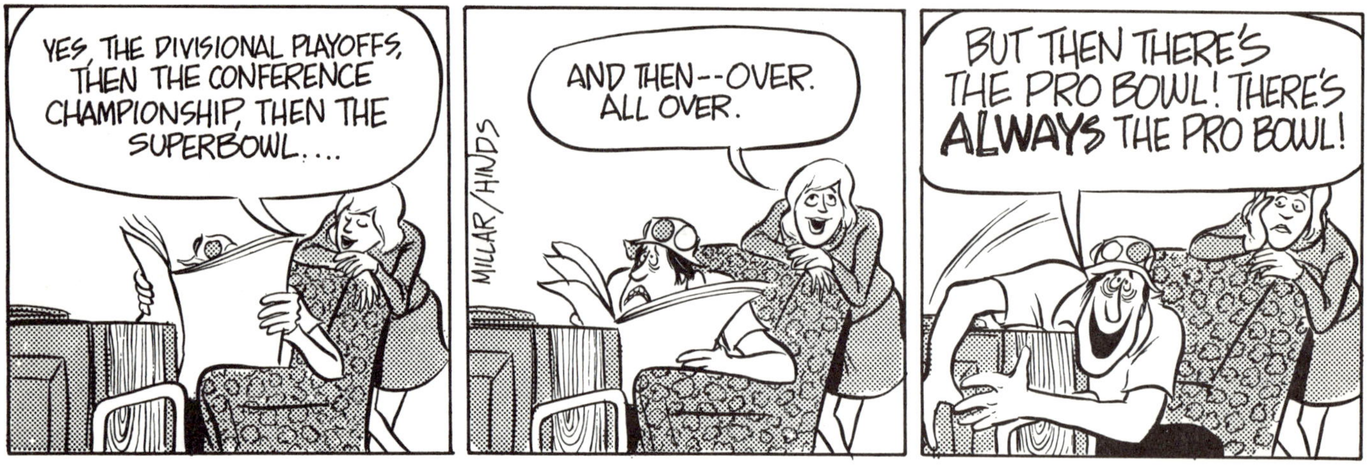
YES, THE DIVISIONAL PLAYOFFS, THEN THE CONFERENCE CHAMPIONSHIP, THEN THE SUPERBOWL....
MILLAR/HINDS
AND THEN--OVER. ALL OVER.
BUT THEN THERE'S THE PRO BOWL! THERE'S ALWAYS THE PRO BOWL!

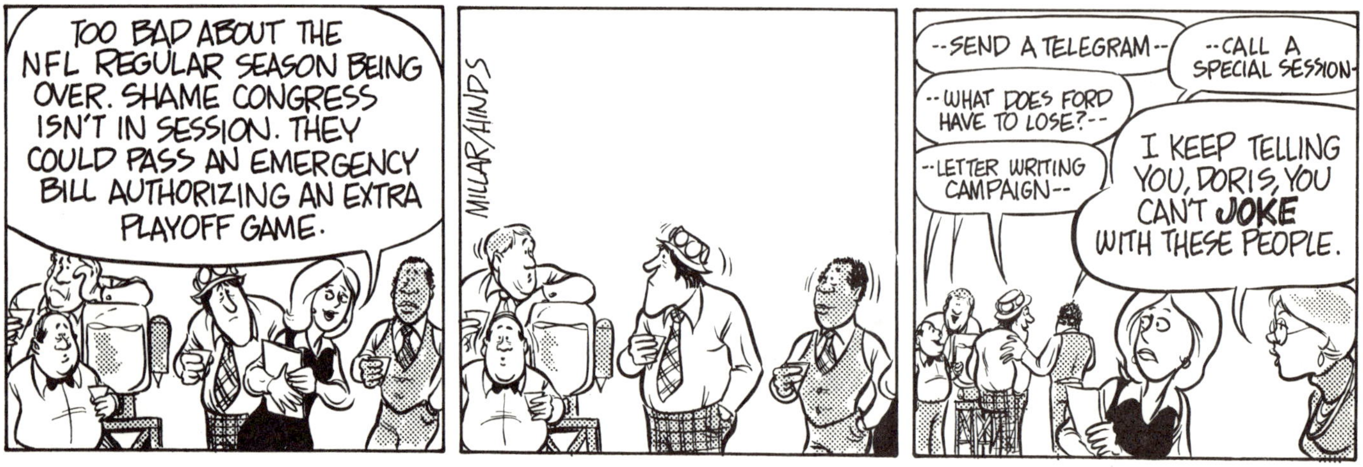
TOO BAD ABOUT THE NFL REGULAR SEASON BEING OVER. SHAME CONGRESS ISN'T IN SESSION. THEY COULD PASS AN EMERGENCY BILL AUTHORIZING AN EXTRA PLAYOFF GAME.
MILLAR/HINDS
--SEND A TELEGRAM--
--CALL A SPECIAL SESSION--
--WHAT DOES FORD HAVE TO LOSE?--
--LETTER WRITING CAMPAIGN--
I KEEP TELLING YOU, DORIS, YOU CAN'T JOKE WITH THESE PEOPLE.

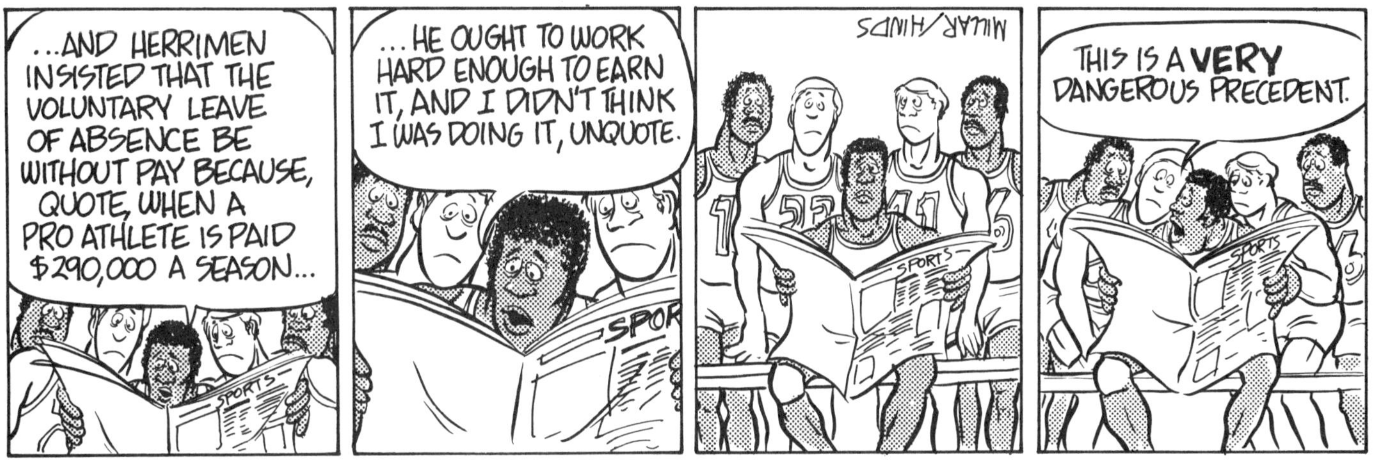
...AND HERRIMEN INSISTED THAT THE VOLUNTARY LEAVE OF ABSENCE BE WITHOUT PAY BECAUSE, QUOTE, WHEN A PRO ATHLETE IS PAID $290,000 A SEASON...
...HE OUGHT TO WORK HARD ENOUGH TO EARN IT, AND I DIDN'T THINK I WAS DOING IT, UNQUOTE.
MILLAR/HINDS
THIS IS A **VERY** DANGEROUS PRECEDENT.

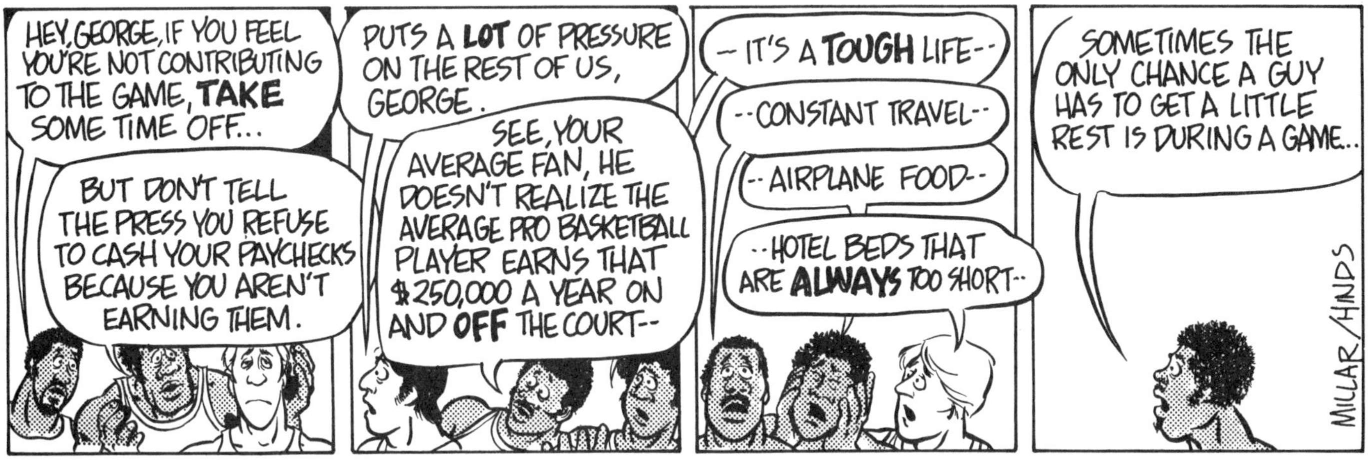
HEY, GEORGE, IF YOU FEEL YOU'RE NOT CONTRIBUTING TO THE GAME, **TAKE** SOME TIME OFF...
BUT DON'T TELL THE PRESS YOU REFUSE TO CASH YOUR PAYCHECKS BECAUSE YOU AREN'T EARNING THEM.
PUTS A **LOT** OF PRESSURE ON THE REST OF US, GEORGE.
SEE, YOUR AVERAGE FAN, HE DOESN'T REALIZE THE AVERAGE PRO BASKETBALL PLAYER EARNS THAT $250,000 A YEAR ON AND **OFF** THE COURT--
--IT'S A **TOUGH** LIFE--
--CONSTANT TRAVEL--
--AIRPLANE FOOD--
--HOTEL BEDS THAT ARE **ALWAYS** TOO SHORT--
SOMETIMES THE ONLY CHANCE A GUY HAS TO GET A LITTLE REST IS DURING A GAME...
MILLAR/HINDS

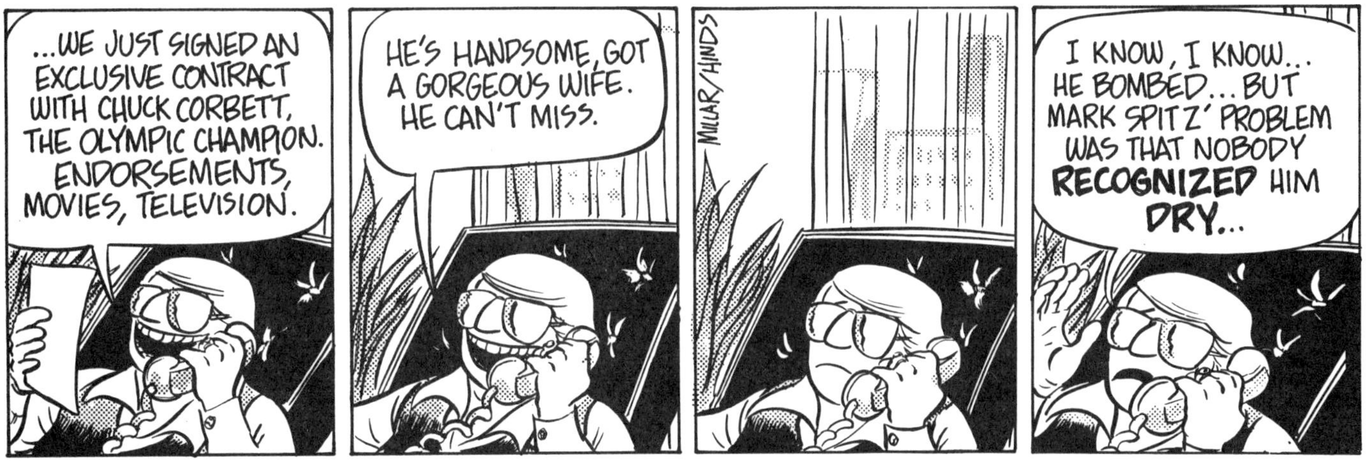
...WE JUST SIGNED AN EXCLUSIVE CONTRACT WITH CHUCK CORBETT, THE OLYMPIC CHAMPION. ENDORSEMENTS, MOVIES, TELEVISION.
HE'S HANDSOME, GOT A GORGEOUS WIFE. HE CAN'T MISS.
MILLAR/HINDS
I KNOW, I KNOW... HE BOMBED... BUT MARK SPITZ' PROBLEM WAS THAT NOBODY **RECOGNIZED** HIM **DRY**...

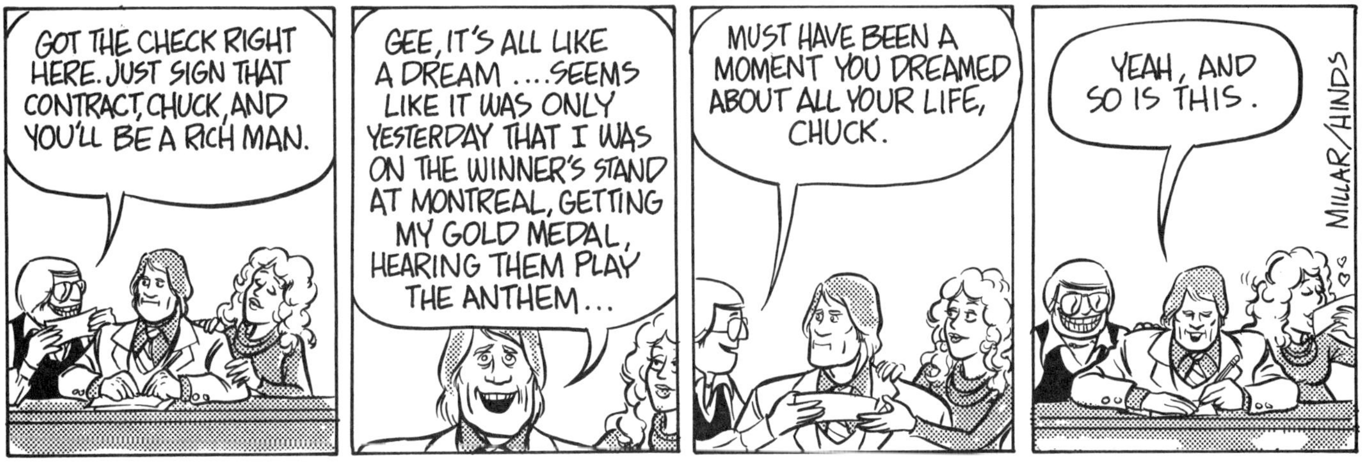
GOT THE CHECK RIGHT HERE. JUST SIGN THAT CONTRACT, CHUCK, AND YOU'LL BE A RICH MAN.
GEE, IT'S ALL LIKE A DREAM ....SEEMS LIKE IT WAS ONLY YESTERDAY THAT I WAS ON THE WINNER'S STAND AT MONTREAL, GETTING MY GOLD MEDAL, HEARING THEM PLAY THE ANTHEM...
MUST HAVE BEEN A MOMENT YOU DREAMED ABOUT ALL YOUR LIFE, CHUCK.
YEAH, AND SO IS THIS.
MILLAR/HINDS

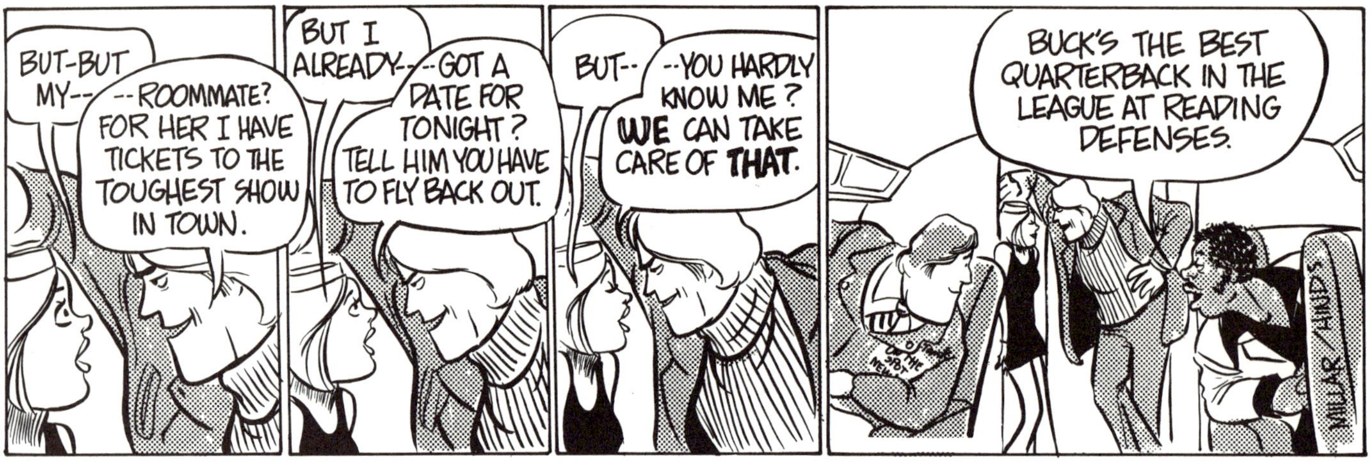
BUT-BUT MY--
--ROOMMATE? FOR HER I HAVE TICKETS TO THE TOUGHEST SHOW IN TOWN.
BUT I ALREADY--
--GOT A DATE FOR TONIGHT? TELL HIM YOU HAVE TO FLY BACK OUT.
BUT--
--YOU HARDLY KNOW ME? **WE** CAN TAKE CARE OF **THAT**.
BUCK'S THE BEST QUARTERBACK IN THE LEAGUE AT READING DEFENSES.
MILLAR/HINDS

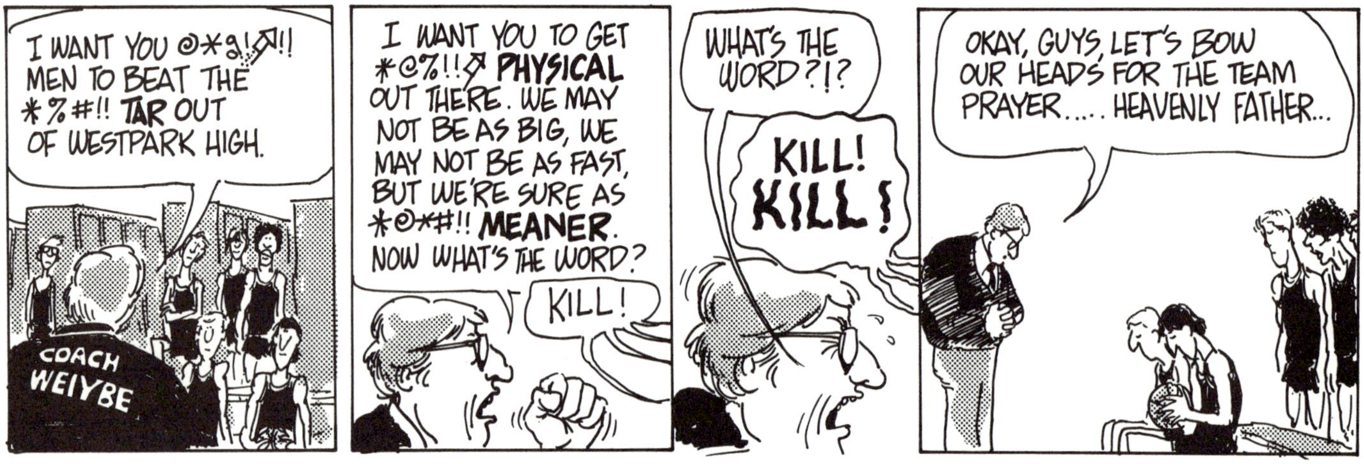
I WANT YOU @*&!↗!! MEN TO BEAT THE *%#!! **TAR** OUT OF WESTPARK HIGH.
COACH WEIYBE
I WANT YOU TO GET *@%!!↗ **PHYSICAL** OUT THERE. WE MAY NOT BE AS BIG, WE MAY NOT BE AS FAST, BUT WE'RE SURE AS *@*#!! **MEANER**. NOW WHAT'S THE WORD?
KILL!
WHAT'S THE WORD?!?
KILL! KILL!
OKAY, GUYS, LET'S BOW OUR HEADS FOR THE TEAM PRAYER..... HEAVENLY FATHER...

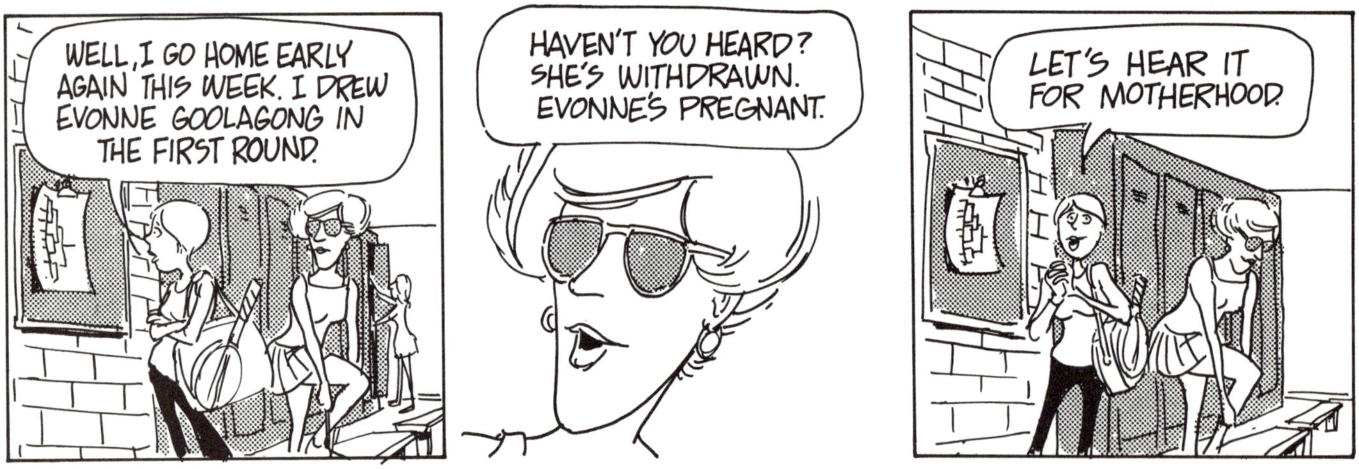
WELL, I GO HOME EARLY AGAIN THIS WEEK. I DREW EVONNE GOOLAGONG IN THE FIRST ROUND.
HAVEN'T YOU HEARD? SHE'S WITHDRAWN. EVONNE'S PREGNANT.
LET'S HEAR IT FOR MOTHERHOOD.

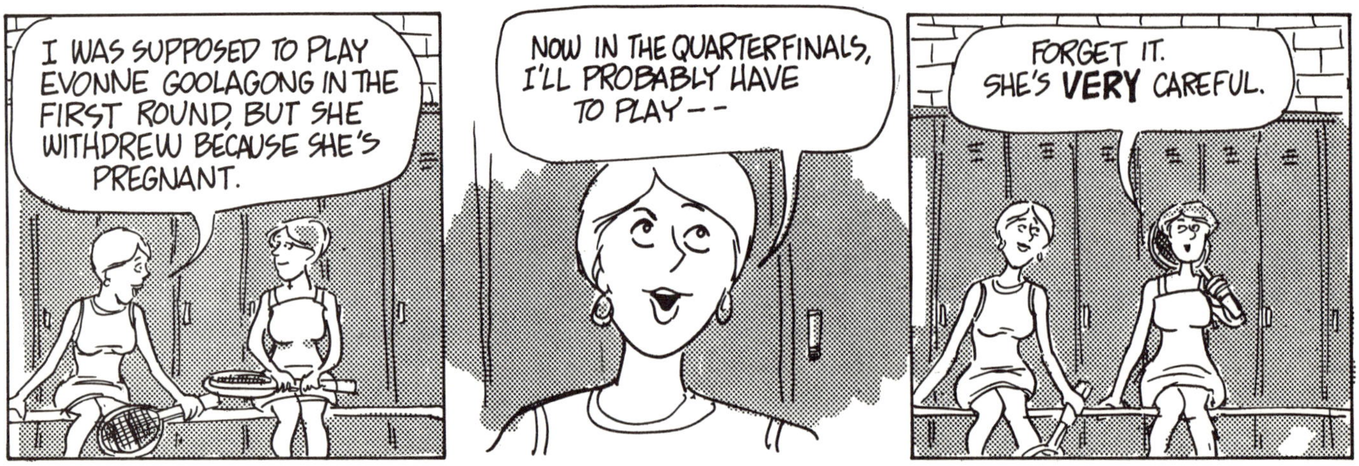
I WAS SUPPOSED TO PLAY EVONNE GOOLAGONG IN THE FIRST ROUND, BUT SHE WITHDREW BECAUSE SHE'S PREGNANT.
NOW IN THE QUARTERFINALS, I'LL PROBABLY HAVE TO PLAY--
FORGET IT. SHE'S **VERY** CAREFUL.

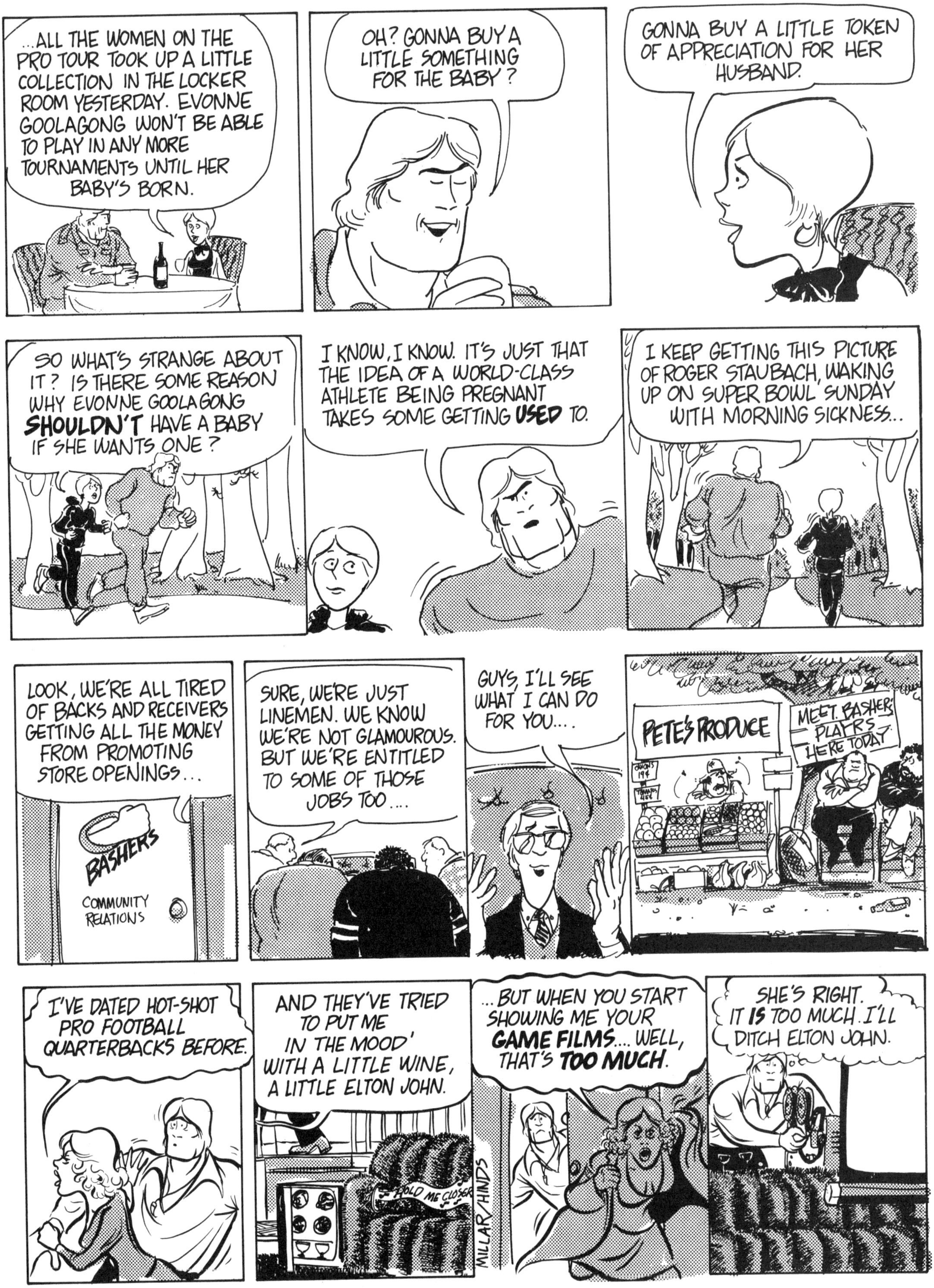

...ALL THE WOMEN ON THE PRO TOUR TOOK UP A LITTLE COLLECTION IN THE LOCKER ROOM YESTERDAY. EVONNE GOOLAGONG WON'T BE ABLE TO PLAY IN ANY MORE TOURNAMENTS UNTIL HER BABY'S BORN.
OH? GONNA BUY A LITTLE SOMETHING FOR THE BABY?
GONNA BUY A LITTLE TOKEN OF APPRECIATION FOR HER HUSBAND.
SO WHAT'S STRANGE ABOUT IT? IS THERE SOME REASON WHY EVONNE GOOLAGONG **SHOULDN'T** HAVE A BABY IF SHE WANTS ONE?
I KNOW, I KNOW. IT'S JUST THAT THE IDEA OF A WORLD-CLASS ATHLETE BEING PREGNANT TAKES SOME GETTING **USED** TO.
I KEEP GETTING THIS PICTURE OF ROGER STAUBACH, WAKING UP ON SUPER BOWL SUNDAY WITH MORNING SICKNESS...
LOOK, WE'RE ALL TIRED OF BACKS AND RECEIVERS GETTING ALL THE MONEY FROM PROMOTING STORE OPENINGS...
BASHERS
COMMUNITY RELATIONS
SURE, WE'RE JUST LINEMEN. WE KNOW WE'RE NOT GLAMOUROUS. BUT WE'RE ENTITLED TO SOME OF THOSE JOBS TOO....
GUYS, I'LL SEE WHAT I CAN DO FOR YOU....
PETE'S PRODUCE
MEET BASHERS PLAYERS HERE TODAY
I'VE DATED HOT-SHOT PRO FOOTBALL QUARTERBACKS BEFORE.
AND THEY'VE TRIED TO PUT ME 'IN THE MOOD' WITH A LITTLE WINE, A LITTLE ELTON JOHN.
HOLD ME CLOSER
MILLAR/HINDS
...BUT WHEN YOU START SHOWING ME YOUR **GAME FILMS**.... WELL, THAT'S **TOO MUCH**.
SHE'S RIGHT. IT **IS** TOO MUCH. I'LL DITCH ELTON JOHN.

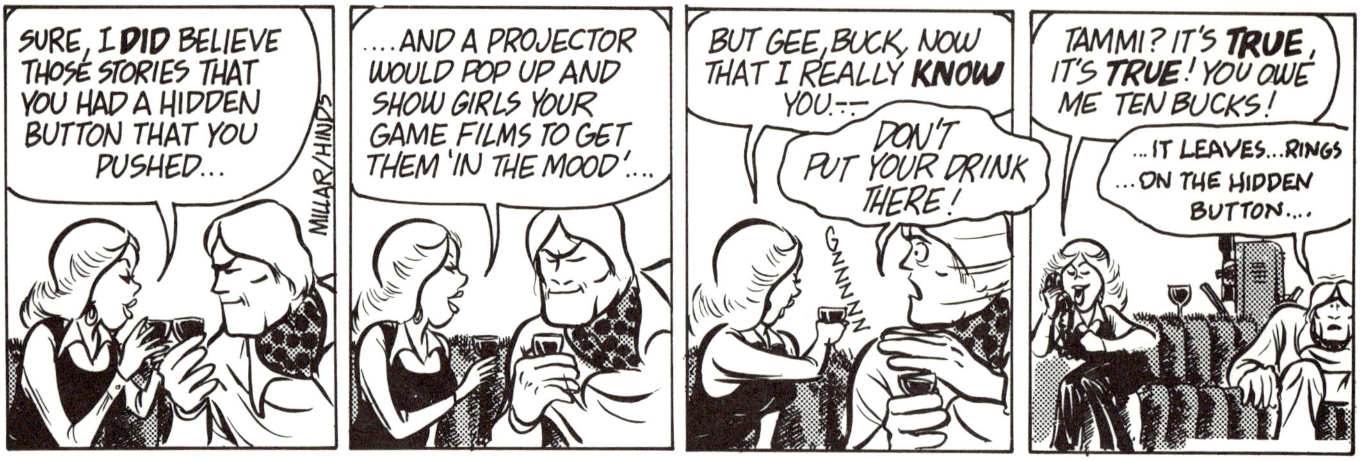
SURE, I DID BELIEVE THOSE STORIES THAT YOU HAD A HIDDEN BUTTON THAT YOU PUSHED...
MILLAR/HINDS
....AND A PROJECTOR WOULD POP UP AND SHOW GIRLS YOUR GAME FILMS TO GET THEM 'IN THE MOOD'....
BUT GEE, BUCK, NOW THAT I REALLY KNOW YOU.--
DON'T PUT YOUR DRINK THERE!
GNNNNN
TAMMI? IT'S TRUE, IT'S TRUE! YOU OWE ME TEN BUCKS!
...IT LEAVES...RINGS ...ON THE HIDDEN BUTTON....

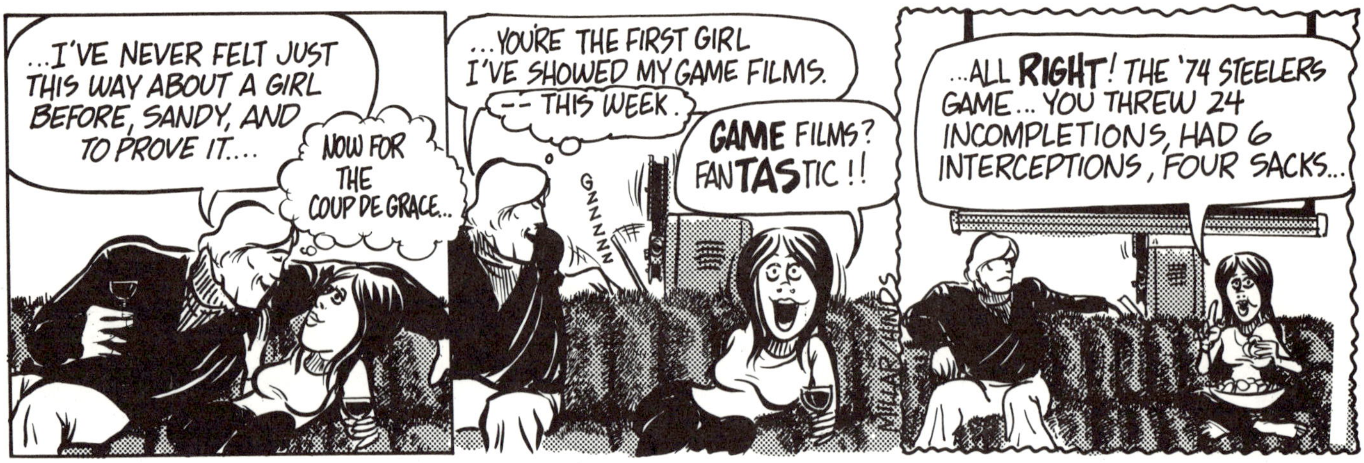
...I'VE NEVER FELT JUST THIS WAY ABOUT A GIRL BEFORE, SANDY, AND TO PROVE IT....
NOW FOR THE COUP DE GRACE...
...YOU'RE THE FIRST GIRL I'VE SHOWED MY GAME FILMS.
-- THIS WEEK.
GAME FILMS? FANTASTIC!!
GNNNNN
MILLAR/HINDS
...ALL RIGHT! THE '74 STEELERS GAME... YOU THREW 24 INCOMPLETIONS, HAD 6 INTERCEPTIONS, FOUR SACKS...

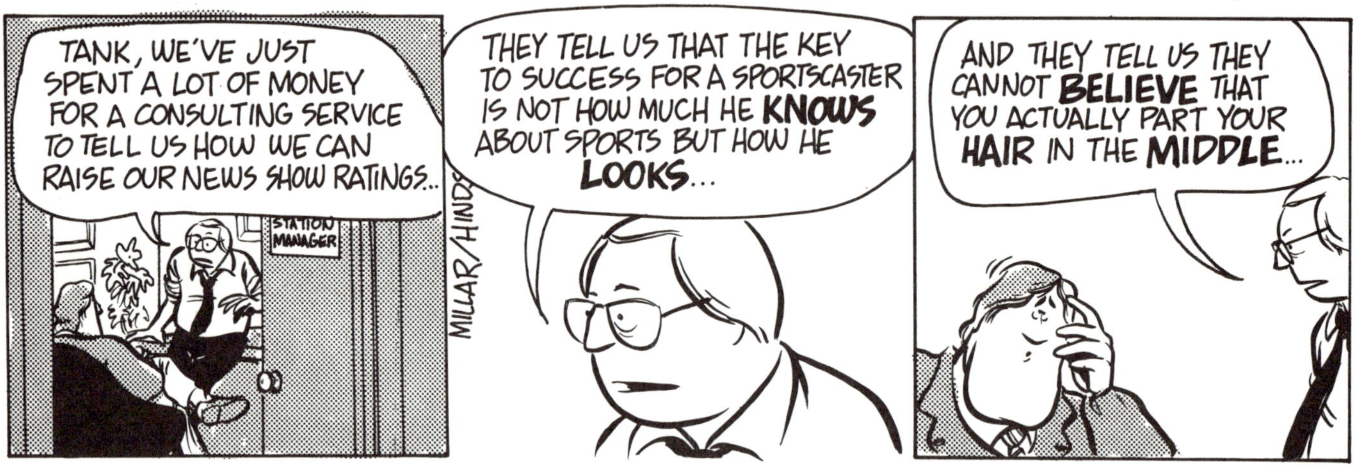
TANK, WE'VE JUST SPENT A LOT OF MONEY FOR A CONSULTING SERVICE TO TELL US HOW WE CAN RAISE OUR NEWS SHOW RATINGS...
STATION MANAGER
MILLAR/HINDS
THEY TELL US THAT THE KEY TO SUCCESS FOR A SPORTSCASTER IS NOT HOW MUCH HE KNOWS ABOUT SPORTS BUT HOW HE LOOKS...
AND THEY TELL US THEY CANNOT BELIEVE THAT YOU ACTUALLY PART YOUR HAIR IN THE MIDDLE...

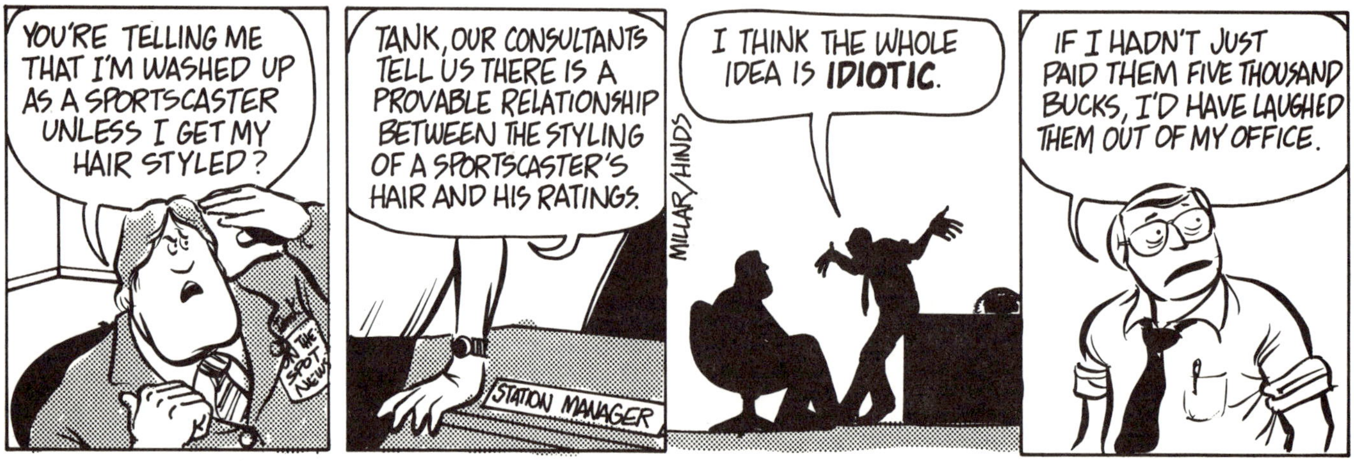
YOU'RE TELLING ME THAT I'M WASHED UP AS A SPORTSCASTER UNLESS I GET MY HAIR STYLED?
ON THE SPOT NEWS
TANK, OUR CONSULTANTS TELL US THERE IS A PROVABLE RELATIONSHIP BETWEEN THE STYLING OF A SPORTSCASTER'S HAIR AND HIS RATINGS.
STATION MANAGER
MILLAR/HINDS
I THINK THE WHOLE IDEA IS IDIOTIC.
IF I HADN'T JUST PAID THEM FIVE THOUSAND BUCKS, I'D HAVE LAUGHED THEM OUT OF MY OFFICE.

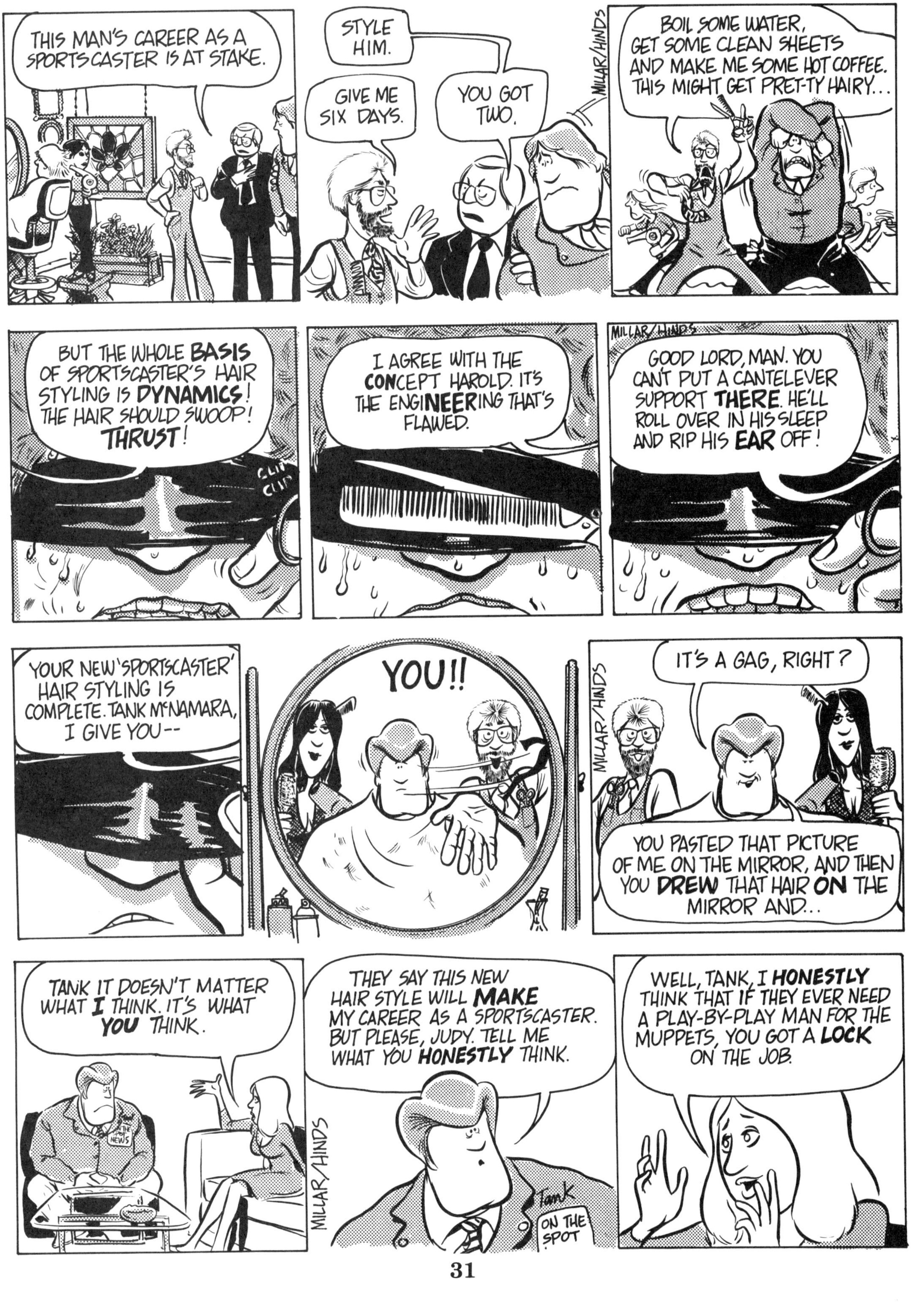
THIS MAN'S CAREER AS A SPORTSCASTER IS AT STAKE.
STYLE HIM.
GIVE ME SIX DAYS.
YOU GOT TWO.
MILLAR/HINDS
BOIL SOME WATER, GET SOME CLEAN SHEETS AND MAKE ME SOME HOT COFFEE. THIS MIGHT GET PRET-TY HAIRY...
BUT THE WHOLE BASIS OF SPORTSCASTER'S HAIR STYLING IS DYNAMICS! THE HAIR SHOULD SWOOP! THRUST!
I AGREE WITH THE CONCEPT HAROLD. IT'S THE ENGINEERING THAT'S FLAWED.
MILLAR/HINDS
GOOD LORD, MAN. YOU CAN'T PUT A CANTELEVER SUPPORT THERE. HE'LL ROLL OVER IN HIS SLEEP AND RIP HIS EAR OFF!
YOUR NEW 'SPORTSCASTER' HAIR STYLING IS COMPLETE. TANK McNAMARA, I GIVE YOU--
YOU!!
MILLAR/HINDS
IT'S A GAG, RIGHT?
YOU PASTED THAT PICTURE OF ME ON THE MIRROR, AND THEN YOU DREW THAT HAIR ON THE MIRROR AND...
TANK IT DOESN'T MATTER WHAT I THINK. IT'S WHAT YOU THINK.
MILLAR/HINDS
THEY SAY THIS NEW HAIR STYLE WILL MAKE MY CAREER AS A SPORTSCASTER. BUT PLEASE, JUDY. TELL ME WHAT YOU HONESTLY THINK.
ON THE SPOT
WELL, TANK, I HONESTLY THINK THAT IF THEY EVER NEED A PLAY-BY-PLAY MAN FOR THE MUPPETS, YOU GOT A LOCK ON THE JOB.

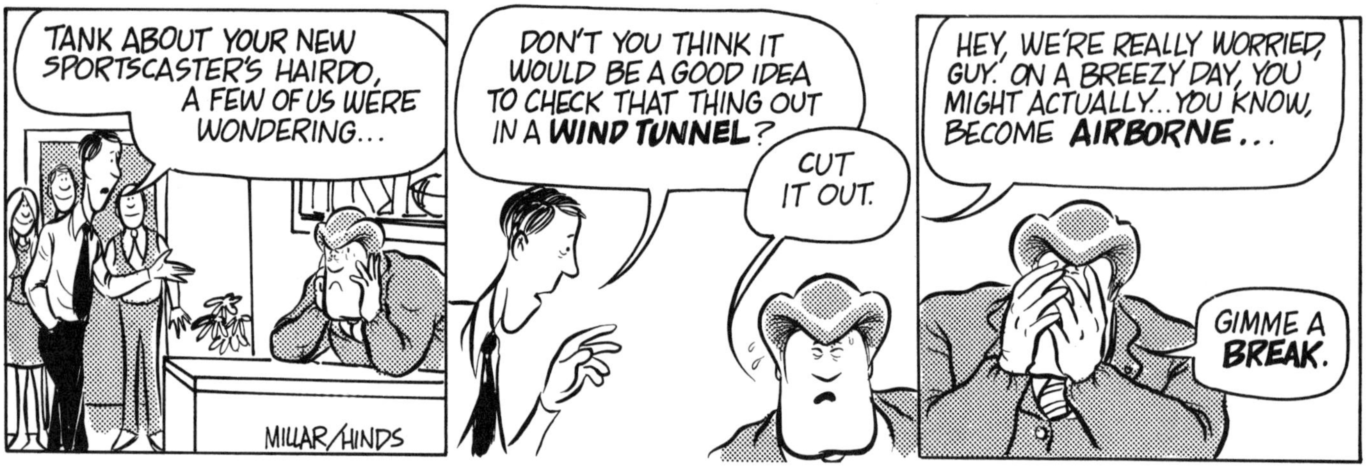
TANK ABOUT YOUR NEW SPORTSCASTER'S HAIRDO, A FEW OF US WERE WONDERING...
MILLAR/HINDS
DON'T YOU THINK IT WOULD BE A GOOD IDEA TO CHECK THAT THING OUT IN A WIND TUNNEL?
CUT IT OUT.
HEY, WE'RE REALLY WORRIED, GUY. ON A BREEZY DAY, YOU MIGHT ACTUALLY... YOU KNOW, BECOME AIRBORNE...
GIMME A BREAK.

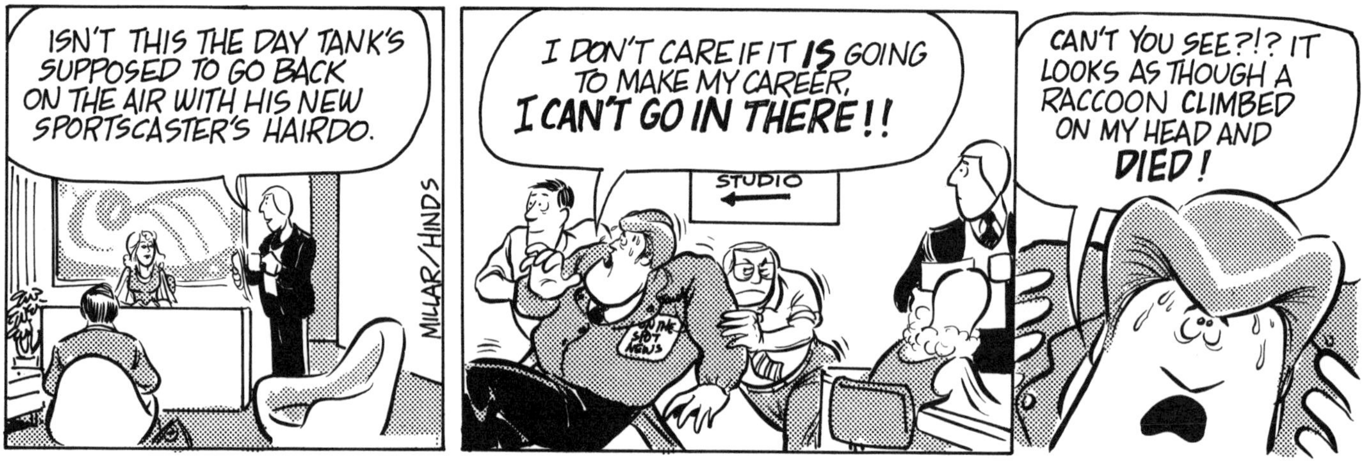
ISN'T THIS THE DAY TANK'S SUPPOSED TO GO BACK ON THE AIR WITH HIS NEW SPORTSCASTER'S HAIRDO.
MILLAR/HINDS
I DON'T CARE IF IT IS GOING TO MAKE MY CAREER, I CAN'T GO IN THERE!!
STUDIO
CAN'T YOU SEE?!? IT LOOKS AS THOUGH A RACCOON CLIMBED ON MY HEAD AND DIED!

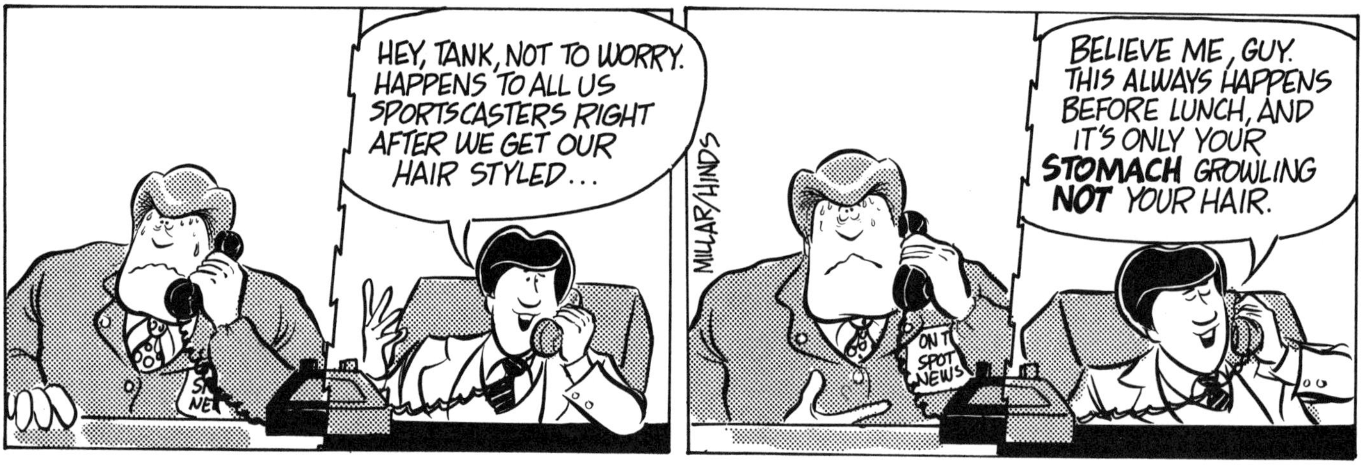
HEY, TANK, NOT TO WORRY. HAPPENS TO ALL US SPORTSCASTERS RIGHT AFTER WE GET OUR HAIR STYLED...
MILLAR/HINDS
BELIEVE ME, GUY. THIS ALWAYS HAPPENS BEFORE LUNCH, AND IT'S ONLY YOUR STOMACH GROWLING NOT YOUR HAIR.

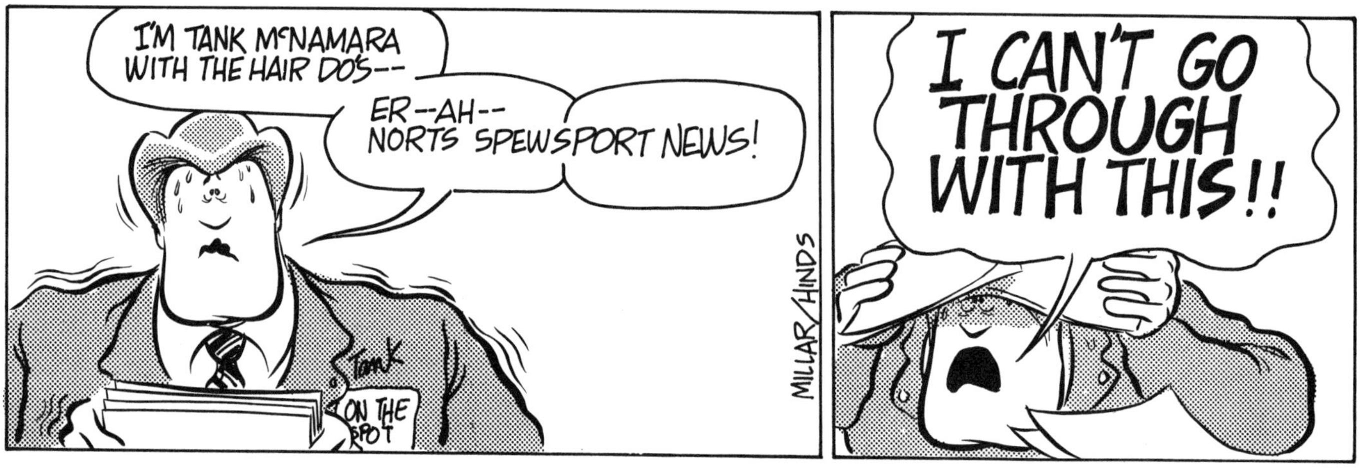
I'M TANK McNAMARA WITH THE HAIR DO'S--
ER--AH-- NORTS SPEWSPORT NEWS!
ON THE SPOT
MILLAR/HINDS
I CAN'T GO THROUGH WITH THIS!!

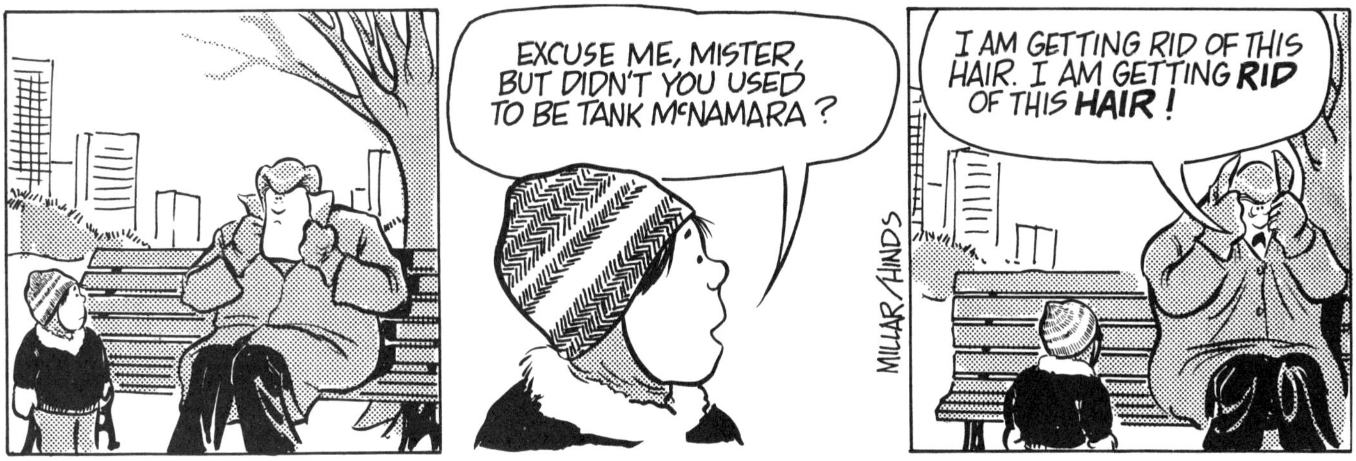
EXCUSE ME, MISTER, BUT DIDN'T YOU USED TO BE TANK McNAMARA?
I AM GETTING RID OF THIS HAIR. I AM GETTING **RID** OF THIS **HAIR**!
MILLAR/HINDS

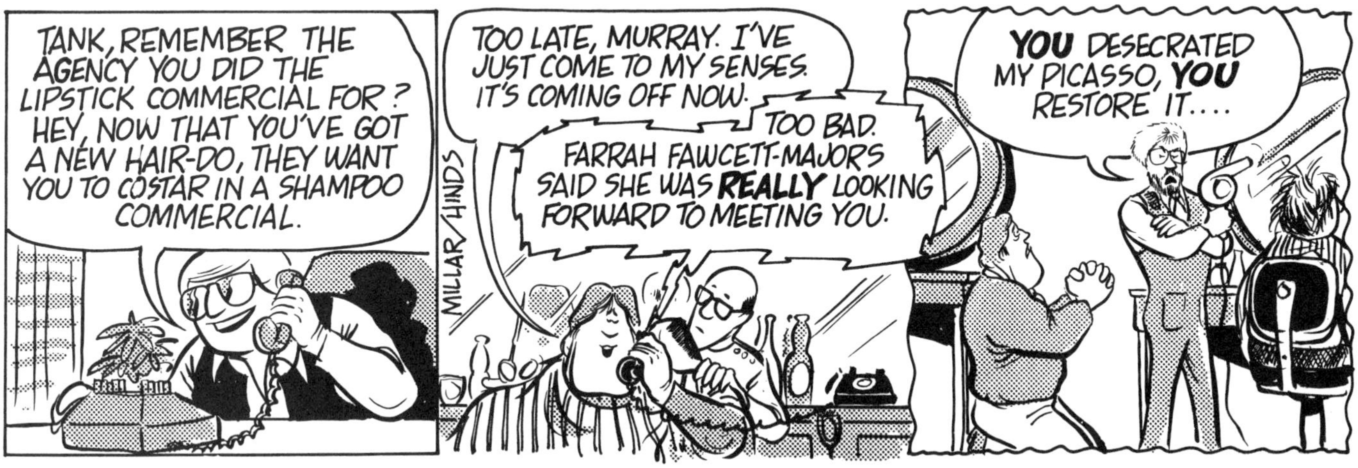
TANK, REMEMBER THE AGENCY YOU DID THE LIPSTICK COMMERCIAL FOR? HEY, NOW THAT YOU'VE GOT A NEW HAIR-DO, THEY WANT YOU TO COSTAR IN A SHAMPOO COMMERCIAL.
MILLAR/HINDS
TOO LATE, MURRAY. I'VE JUST COME TO MY SENSES. IT'S COMING OFF NOW.
TOO BAD. FARRAH FAWCETT-MAJORS SAID SHE WAS **REALLY** LOOKING FORWARD TO MEETING YOU.
YOU DESECRATED MY PICASSO, **YOU** RESTORE IT....

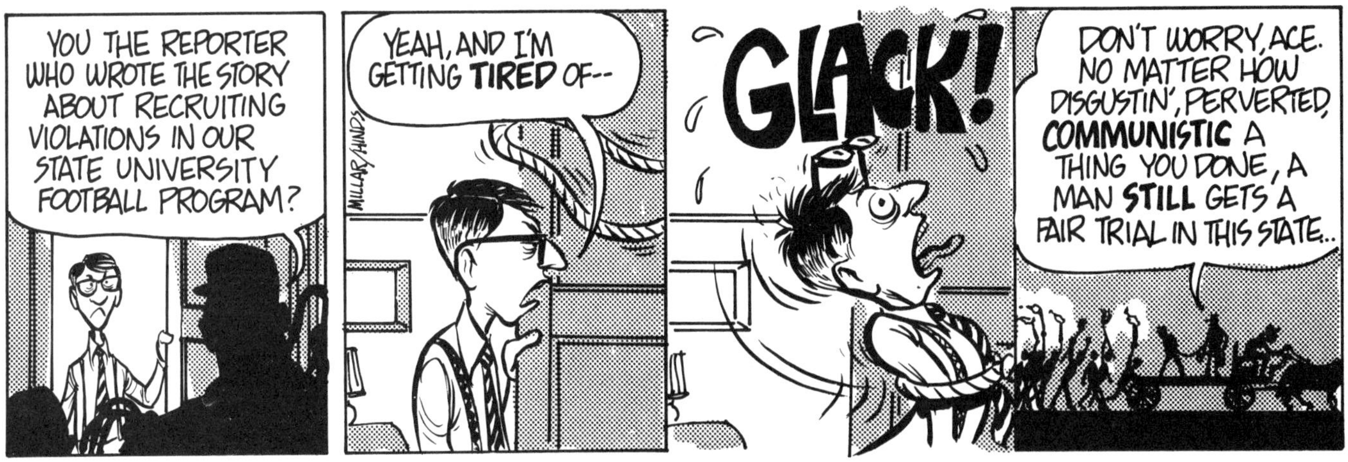
YOU THE REPORTER WHO WROTE THE STORY ABOUT RECRUITING VIOLATIONS IN OUR STATE UNIVERSITY FOOTBALL PROGRAM?
YEAH, AND I'M GETTING **TIRED** OF--
MILLAR/HINDS
GLACK!
DON'T WORRY, ACE. NO MATTER HOW DISGUSTIN', PERVERTED, **COMMUNISTIC** A THING YOU DONE, A MAN **STILL** GETS A FAIR TRIAL IN THIS STATE...

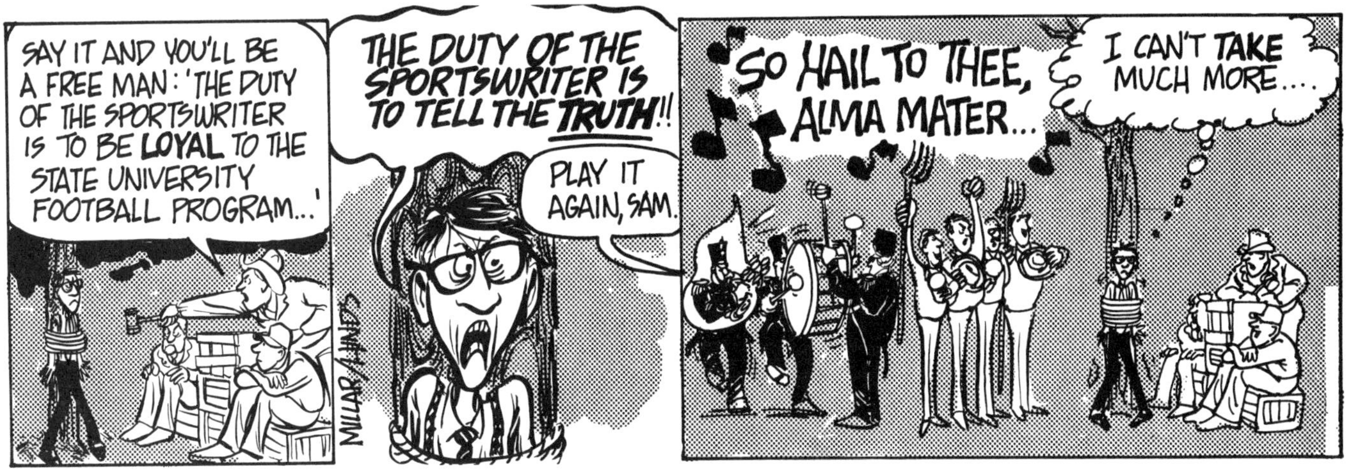
SAY IT AND YOU'LL BE A FREE MAN: 'THE DUTY OF THE SPORTSWRITER IS TO BE **LOYAL** TO THE STATE UNIVERSITY FOOTBALL PROGRAM...'
THE DUTY OF THE SPORTSWRITER IS TO TELL THE TRUTH!!
PLAY IT AGAIN, SAM.
MILLAR/HINDS
SO HAIL TO THEE, ALMA MATER...
I CAN'T **TAKE** MUCH MORE....

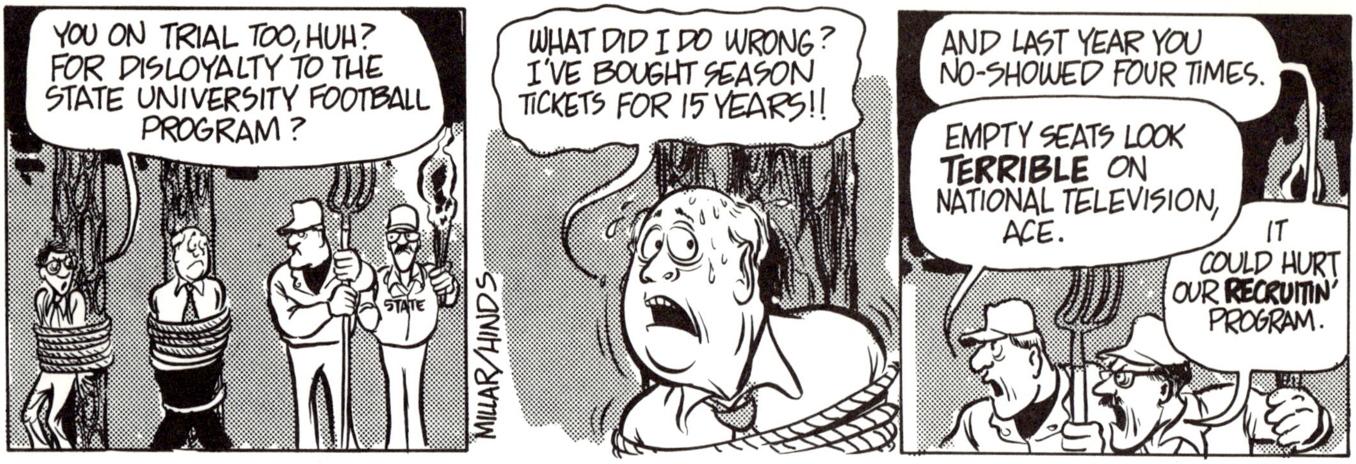
YOU ON TRIAL TOO, HUH? FOR DISLOYALTY TO THE STATE UNIVERSITY FOOTBALL PROGRAM?
STATE
MILLAR/HINDS
WHAT DID I DO WRONG? I'VE BOUGHT SEASON TICKETS FOR 15 YEARS!!
AND LAST YEAR YOU NO-SHOWED FOUR TIMES.
EMPTY SEATS LOOK **TERRIBLE** ON NATIONAL TELEVISION, ACE.
IT COULD HURT OUR **RECRUITIN'** PROGRAM.

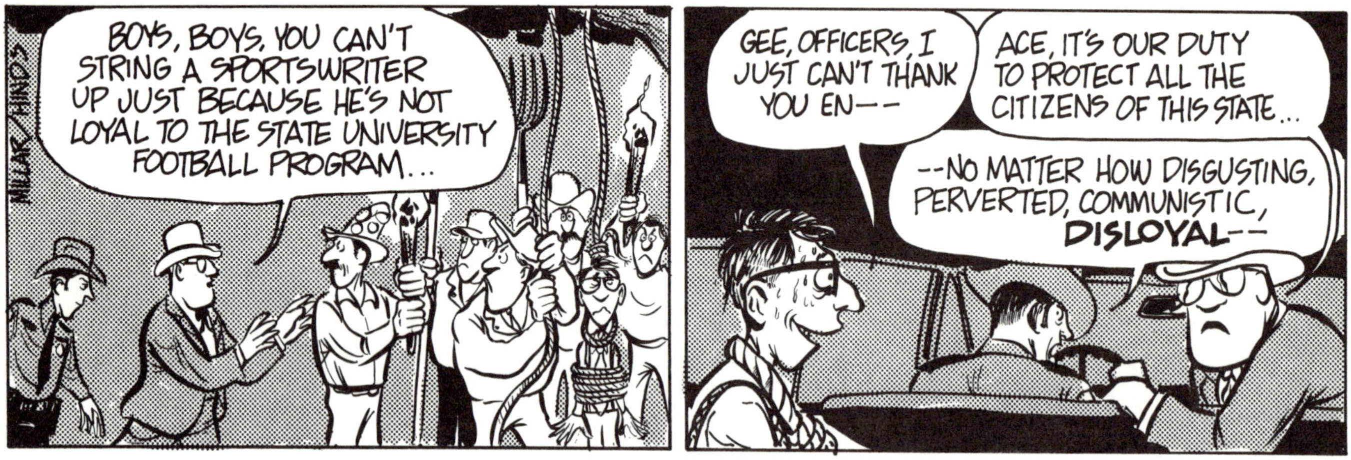
MILLAR/HINDS
BOYS, BOYS, YOU CAN'T STRING A SPORTSWRITER UP JUST BECAUSE HE'S NOT LOYAL TO THE STATE UNIVERSITY FOOTBALL PROGRAM...
GEE, OFFICERS, I JUST CAN'T THANK YOU EN--
ACE, IT'S OUR DUTY TO PROTECT ALL THE CITIZENS OF THIS STATE...
--NO MATTER HOW DISGUSTING, PERVERTED, COMMUNISTIC, **DISLOYAL**--

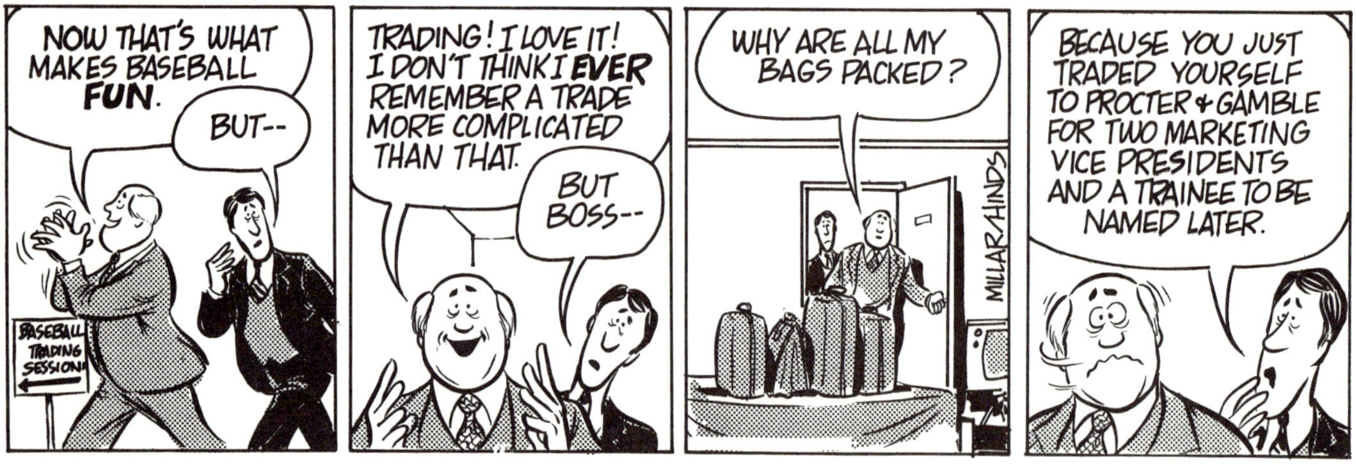
NOW THAT'S WHAT MAKES BASEBALL **FUN**.
BUT--
BASEBALL TRADING SESSION
TRADING! I LOVE IT! I DON'T THINK I **EVER** REMEMBER A TRADE MORE COMPLICATED THAN THAT.
BUT BOSS--
WHY ARE ALL MY BAGS PACKED?
MILLAR/HINDS
BECAUSE YOU JUST TRADED YOURSELF TO PROCTER & GAMBLE FOR TWO MARKETING VICE PRESIDENTS AND A TRAINEE TO BE NAMED LATER.

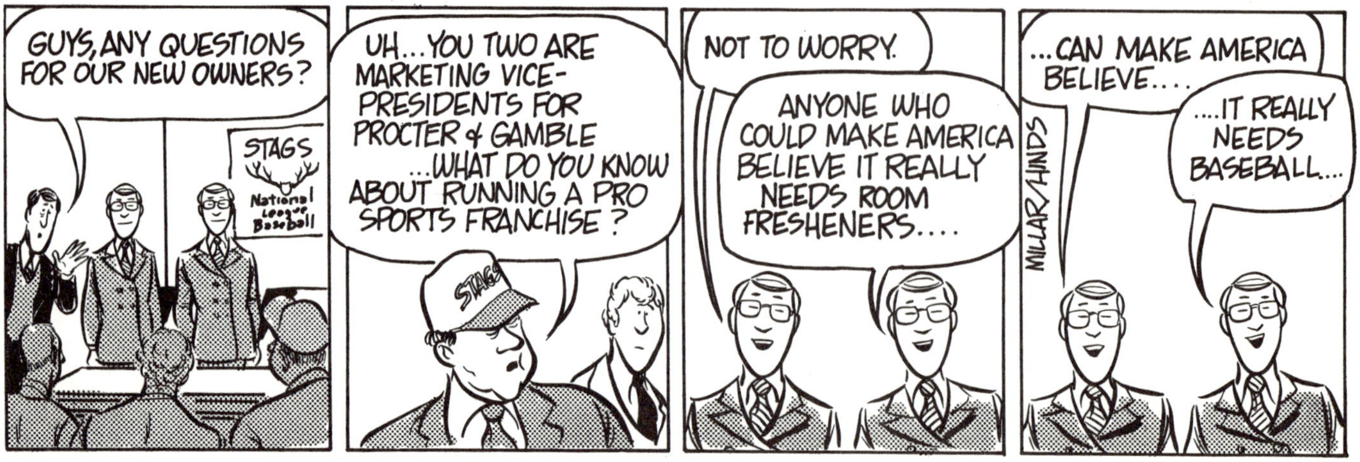
GUYS, ANY QUESTIONS FOR OUR NEW OWNERS?
STAGS National League Baseball
UH...YOU TWO ARE MARKETING VICE-PRESIDENTS FOR PROCTER & GAMBLE ...WHAT DO YOU KNOW ABOUT RUNNING A PRO SPORTS FRANCHISE?
STAGS
NOT TO WORRY.
ANYONE WHO COULD MAKE AMERICA BELIEVE IT REALLY NEEDS ROOM FRESHENERS....
MILLAR/HINDS
...CAN MAKE AMERICA BELIEVE....
....IT REALLY NEEDS BASEBALL....

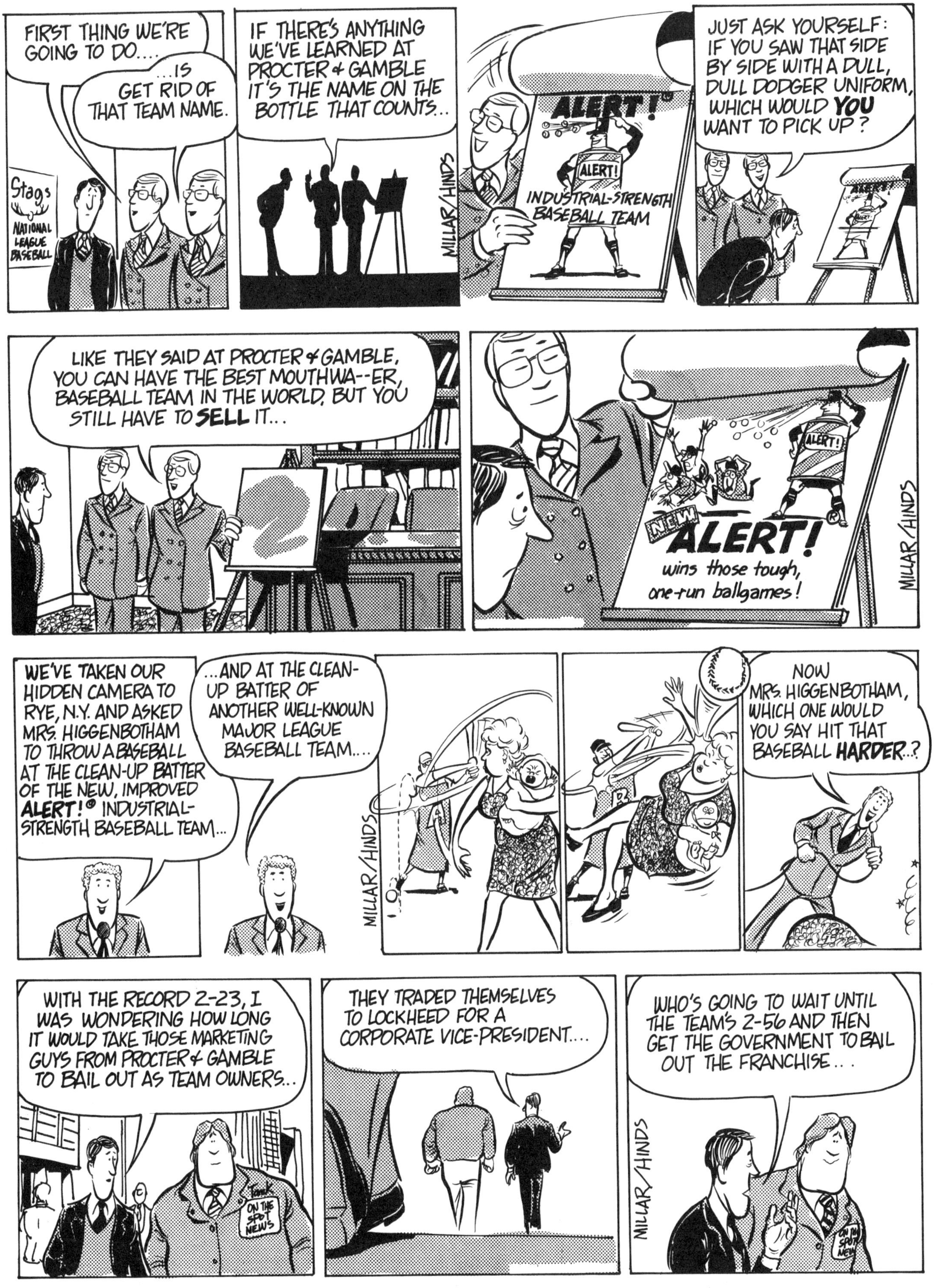
FIRST THING WE'RE GOING TO DO....
...IS GET RID OF THAT TEAM NAME.
Stags NATIONAL LEAGUE BASEBALL
IF THERE'S ANYTHING WE'VE LEARNED AT PROCTER & GAMBLE IT'S THE NAME ON THE BOTTLE THAT COUNTS...
MILLAR/HINDS
ALERT!
ALERT!
INDUSTRIAL-STRENGTH BASEBALL TEAM
JUST ASK YOURSELF: IF YOU SAW THAT SIDE BY SIDE WITH A DULL, DULL DODGER UNIFORM, WHICH WOULD **YOU** WANT TO PICK UP?
LIKE THEY SAID AT PROCTER & GAMBLE, YOU CAN HAVE THE BEST MOUTHWA--ER, BASEBALL TEAM IN THE WORLD, BUT YOU STILL HAVE TO **SELL** IT...
ALERT!
NEW ALERT!
wins those tough, one-run ballgames!
MILLAR/HINDS
WE'VE TAKEN OUR HIDDEN CAMERA TO RYE, N.Y. AND ASKED MRS. HIGGENBOTHAM TO THROW A BASEBALL AT THE CLEAN-UP BATTER OF THE NEW, IMPROVED **ALERT!®** INDUSTRIAL-STRENGTH BASEBALL TEAM...
...AND AT THE CLEAN-UP BATTER OF ANOTHER WELL-KNOWN MAJOR LEAGUE BASEBALL TEAM....
MILLAR/HINDS
NOW MRS. HIGGENBOTHAM, WHICH ONE WOULD YOU SAY HIT THAT BASEBALL **HARDER**..?
WITH THE RECORD 2-23, I WAS WONDERING HOW LONG IT WOULD TAKE THOSE MARKETING GUYS FROM PROCTER & GAMBLE TO BAIL OUT AS TEAM OWNERS...
Tank
ON THE SPOT NEWS
THEY TRADED THEMSELVES TO LOCKHEED FOR A CORPORATE VICE-PRESIDENT....
WHO'S GOING TO WAIT UNTIL THE TEAM'S 2-56 AND THEN GET THE GOVERNMENT TO BAIL OUT THE FRANCHISE...
MILLAR/HINDS

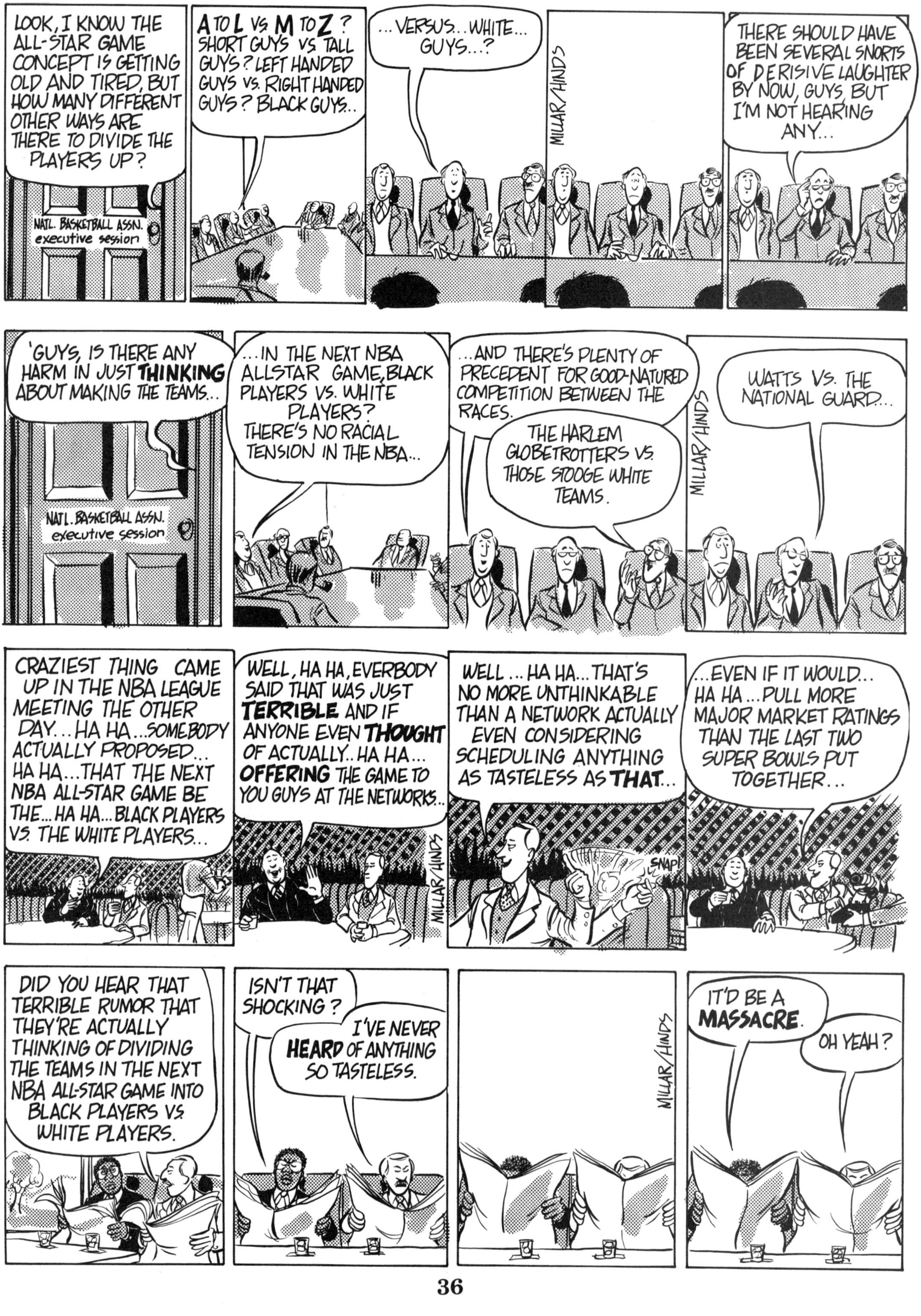
LOOK, I KNOW THE ALL-STAR GAME CONCEPT IS GETTING OLD AND TIRED, BUT HOW MANY DIFFERENT OTHER WAYS ARE THERE TO DIVIDE THE PLAYERS UP?
NATL. BASKETBALL ASSN. executive session
A TO L VS. M TO Z? SHORT GUYS VS. TALL GUYS? LEFT HANDED GUYS VS. RIGHT HANDED GUYS? BLACK GUYS...
...VERSUS...WHITE...GUYS...?
MILLAR/HINDS
THERE SHOULD HAVE BEEN SEVERAL SNORTS OF DERISIVE LAUGHTER BY NOW, GUYS, BUT I'M NOT HEARING ANY...
'GUYS, IS THERE ANY HARM IN JUST THINKING ABOUT MAKING THE TEAMS...
NATL. BASKETBALL ASSN. executive session
...IN THE NEXT NBA ALLSTAR GAME, BLACK PLAYERS VS. WHITE PLAYERS? THERE'S NO RACIAL TENSION IN THE NBA...
...AND THERE'S PLENTY OF PRECEDENT FOR GOOD-NATURED COMPETITION BETWEEN THE RACES.
THE HARLEM GLOBETROTTERS VS. THOSE STOOGE WHITE TEAMS.
MILLAR/HINDS
WATTS VS. THE NATIONAL GUARD...
CRAZIEST THING CAME UP IN THE NBA LEAGUE MEETING THE OTHER DAY...HA HA...SOMEBODY ACTUALLY PROPOSED... HA HA...THAT THE NEXT NBA ALL-STAR GAME BE THE...HA HA...BLACK PLAYERS VS. THE WHITE PLAYERS...
WELL, HA HA, EVERBODY SAID THAT WAS JUST TERRIBLE AND IF ANYONE EVEN THOUGHT OF ACTUALLY..HA HA... OFFERING THE GAME TO YOU GUYS AT THE NETWORKS...
MILLAR/HINDS
WELL ... HA HA... THAT'S NO MORE UNTHINKABLE THAN A NETWORK ACTUALLY EVEN CONSIDERING SCHEDULING ANYTHING AS TASTELESS AS THAT...
SNAP!
...EVEN IF IT WOULD... HA HA ...PULL MORE MAJOR MARKET RATINGS THAN THE LAST TWO SUPER BOWLS PUT TOGETHER...
DID YOU HEAR THAT TERRIBLE RUMOR THAT THEY'RE ACTUALLY THINKING OF DIVIDING THE TEAMS IN THE NEXT NBA ALL-STAR GAME INTO BLACK PLAYERS VS. WHITE PLAYERS.
ISN'T THAT SHOCKING?
I'VE NEVER HEARD OF ANYTHING SO TASTELESS.
MILLAR/HINDS
IT'D BE A MASSACRE.
OH YEAH?

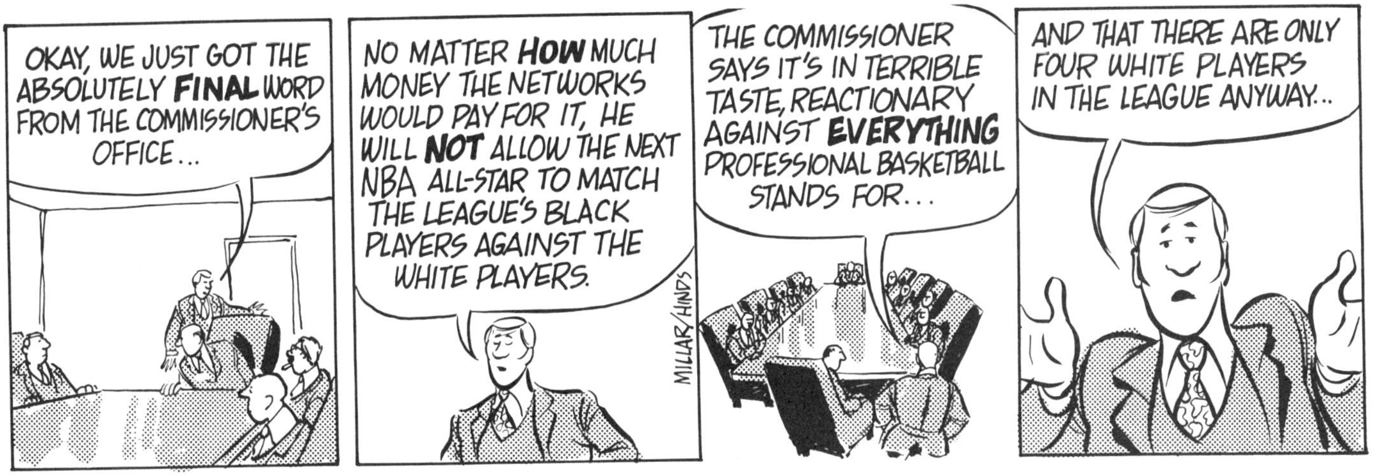
OKAY, WE JUST GOT THE ABSOLUTELY FINAL WORD FROM THE COMMISSIONER'S OFFICE...
NO MATTER HOW MUCH MONEY THE NETWORKS WOULD PAY FOR IT, HE WILL NOT ALLOW THE NEXT NBA ALL-STAR TO MATCH THE LEAGUE'S BLACK PLAYERS AGAINST THE WHITE PLAYERS.
MILLAR/HINDS
THE COMMISSIONER SAYS IT'S IN TERRIBLE TASTE, REACTIONARY AGAINST EVERYTHING PROFESSIONAL BASKETBALL STANDS FOR...
AND THAT THERE ARE ONLY FOUR WHITE PLAYERS IN THE LEAGUE ANYWAY...

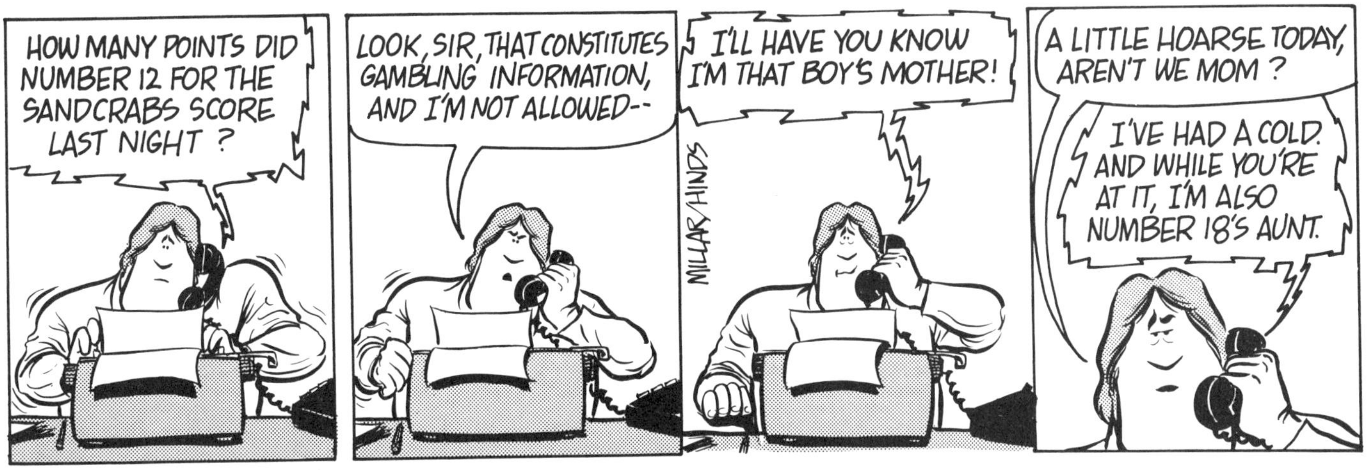
HOW MANY POINTS DID NUMBER 12 FOR THE SANDCRABS SCORE LAST NIGHT ?
LOOK, SIR, THAT CONSTITUTES GAMBLING INFORMATION, AND I'M NOT ALLOWED--
MILLAR/HINDS
I'LL HAVE YOU KNOW I'M THAT BOY'S MOTHER!
A LITTLE HOARSE TODAY, AREN'T WE MOM ?
I'VE HAD A COLD. AND WHILE YOU'RE AT IT, I'M ALSO NUMBER 18'S AUNT.

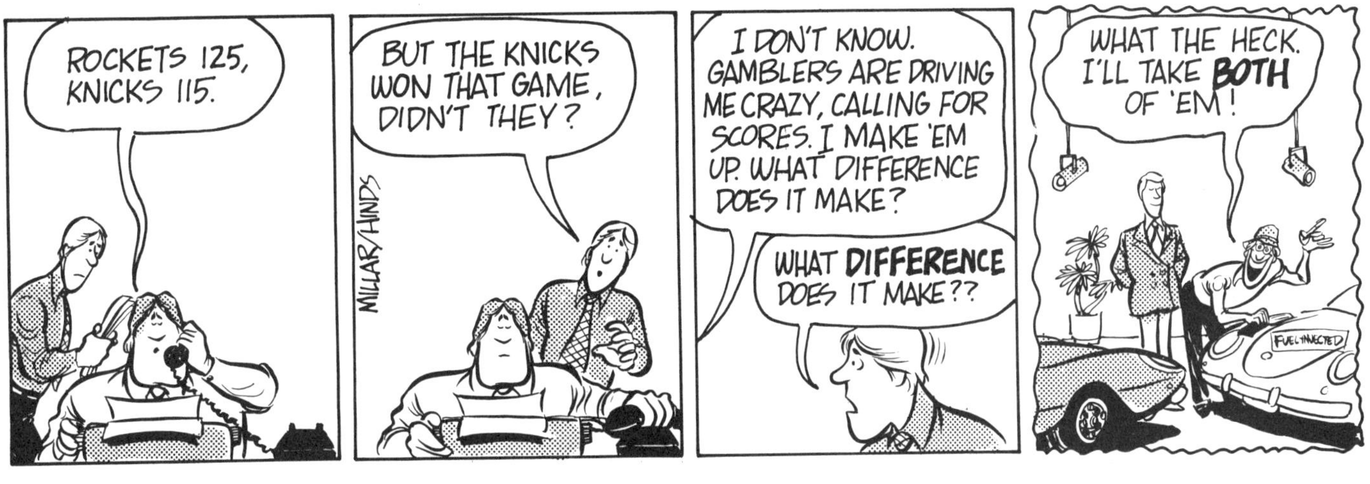
ROCKETS 125, KNICKS 115.
MILLAR/HINDS
BUT THE KNICKS WON THAT GAME, DIDN'T THEY?
I DON'T KNOW. GAMBLERS ARE DRIVING ME CRAZY, CALLING FOR SCORES. I MAKE 'EM UP. WHAT DIFFERENCE DOES IT MAKE?
WHAT DIFFERENCE DOES IT MAKE??
WHAT THE HECK. I'LL TAKE BOTH OF 'EM!
FUEL INJECTED

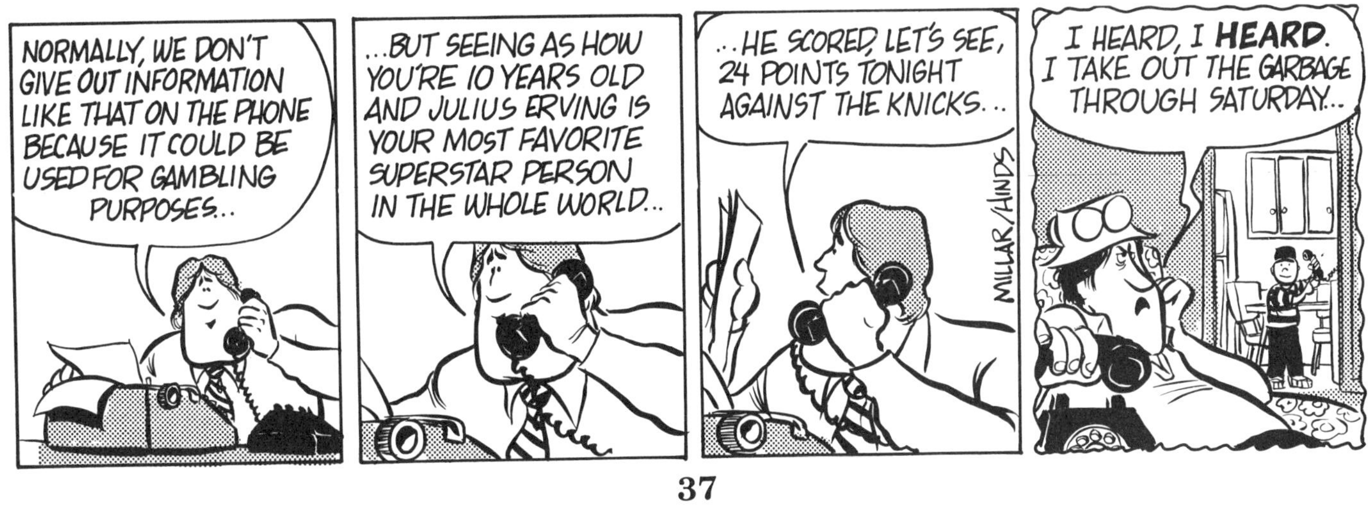
NORMALLY, WE DON'T GIVE OUT INFORMATION LIKE THAT ON THE PHONE BECAUSE IT COULD BE USED FOR GAMBLING PURPOSES...
...BUT SEEING AS HOW YOU'RE 10 YEARS OLD AND JULIUS ERVING IS YOUR MOST FAVORITE SUPERSTAR PERSON IN THE WHOLE WORLD...
...HE SCORED, LET'S SEE, 24 POINTS TONIGHT AGAINST THE KNICKS...
MILLAR/HINDS
I HEARD, I HEARD. I TAKE OUT THE GARBAGE THROUGH SATURDAY...

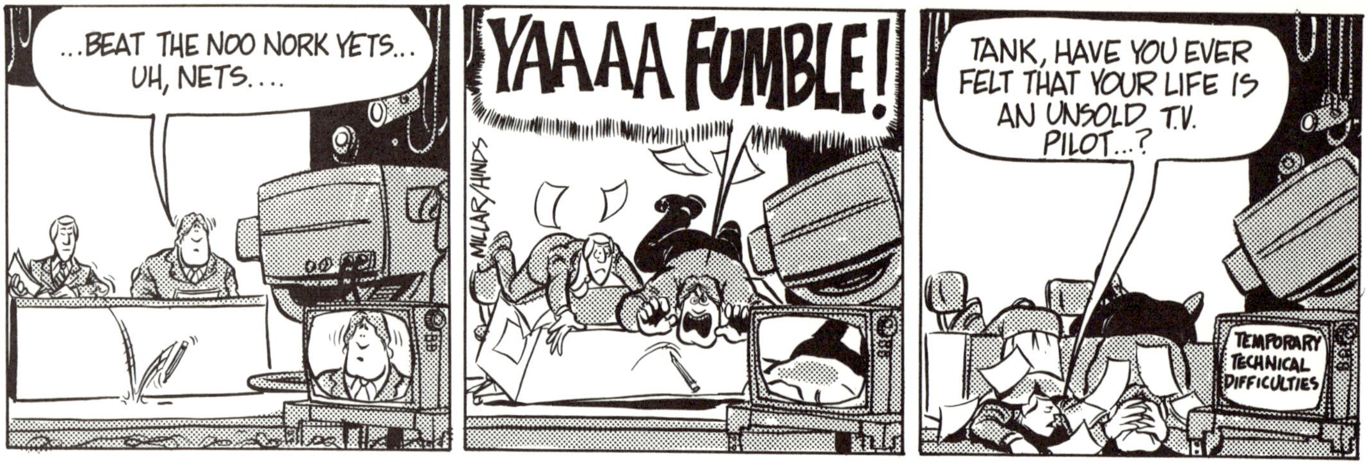
...BEAT THE NOO NORK YETS... UH, NETS....
YAAAA FUMBLE!
MILLAR/HINDS
TANK, HAVE YOU EVER FELT THAT YOUR LIFE IS AN UNSOLD T.V. PILOT...?
TEMPORARY TECHNICAL DIFFICULTIES

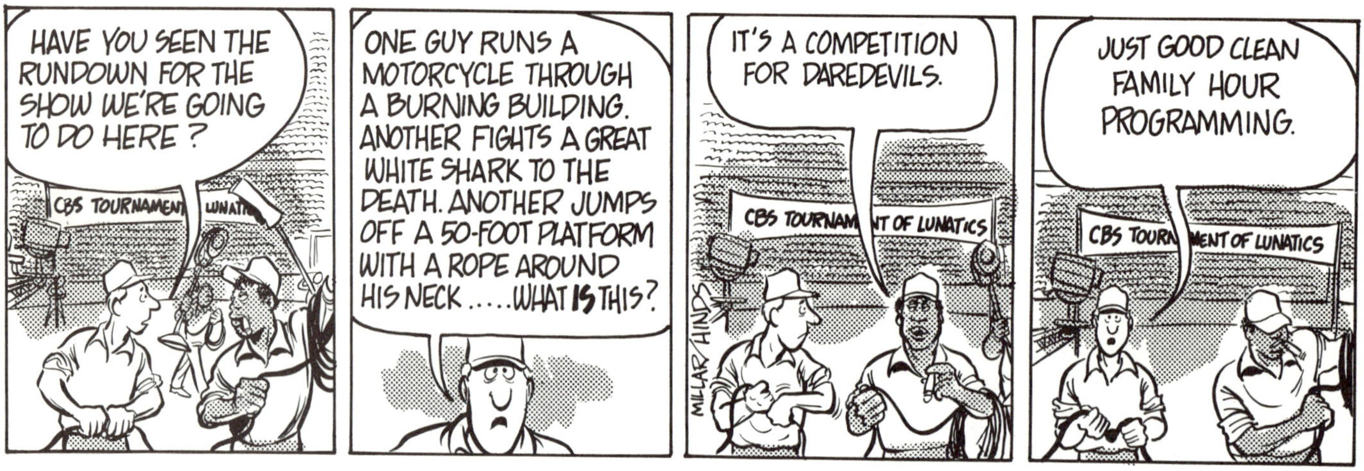
HAVE YOU SEEN THE RUNDOWN FOR THE SHOW WE'RE GOING TO DO HERE?
ONE GUY RUNS A MOTORCYCLE THROUGH A BURNING BUILDING. ANOTHER FIGHTS A GREAT WHITE SHARK TO THE DEATH. ANOTHER JUMPS OFF A 50-FOOT PLATFORM WITH A ROPE AROUND HIS NECK.....WHAT IS THIS?
IT'S A COMPETITION FOR DAREDEVILS.
CBS TOURNAMENT OF LUNATICS
MILLAR/HINDS
JUST GOOD CLEAN FAMILY HOUR PROGRAMMING.
CBS TOURNAMENT OF LUNATICS

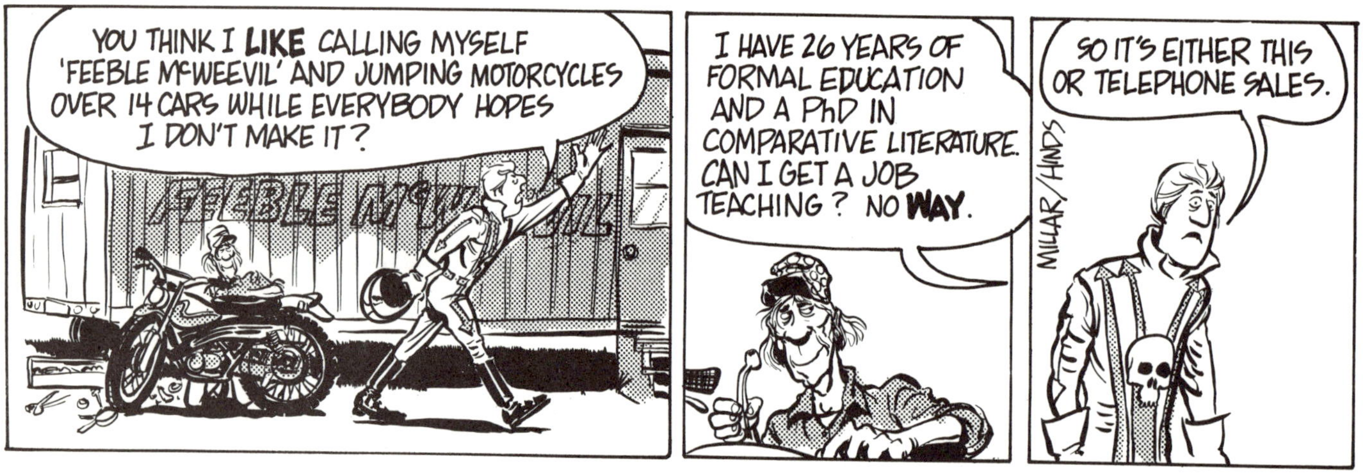
YOU THINK I LIKE CALLING MYSELF 'FEEBLE McWEEVIL' AND JUMPING MOTORCYCLES OVER 14 CARS WHILE EVERYBODY HOPES I DON'T MAKE IT?
I HAVE 26 YEARS OF FORMAL EDUCATION AND A PhD IN COMPARATIVE LITERATURE. CAN I GET A JOB TEACHING? NO WAY.
MILLAR/HINDS
SO IT'S EITHER THIS OR TELEPHONE SALES.

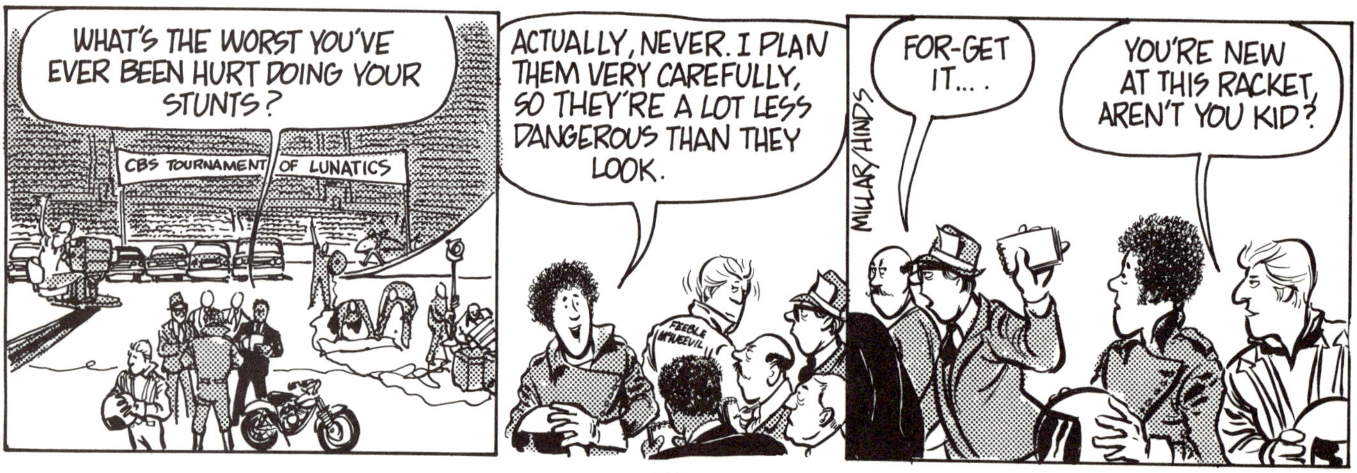
WHAT'S THE WORST YOU'VE EVER BEEN HURT DOING YOUR STUNTS?
CBS TOURNAMENT OF LUNATICS
ACTUALLY, NEVER. I PLAN THEM VERY CAREFULLY, SO THEY'RE A LOT LESS DANGEROUS THAN THEY LOOK.
FEEBLE McWEEVIL
MILLAR/HINDS
FOR-GET IT....
YOU'RE NEW AT THIS RACKET, AREN'T YOU KID?

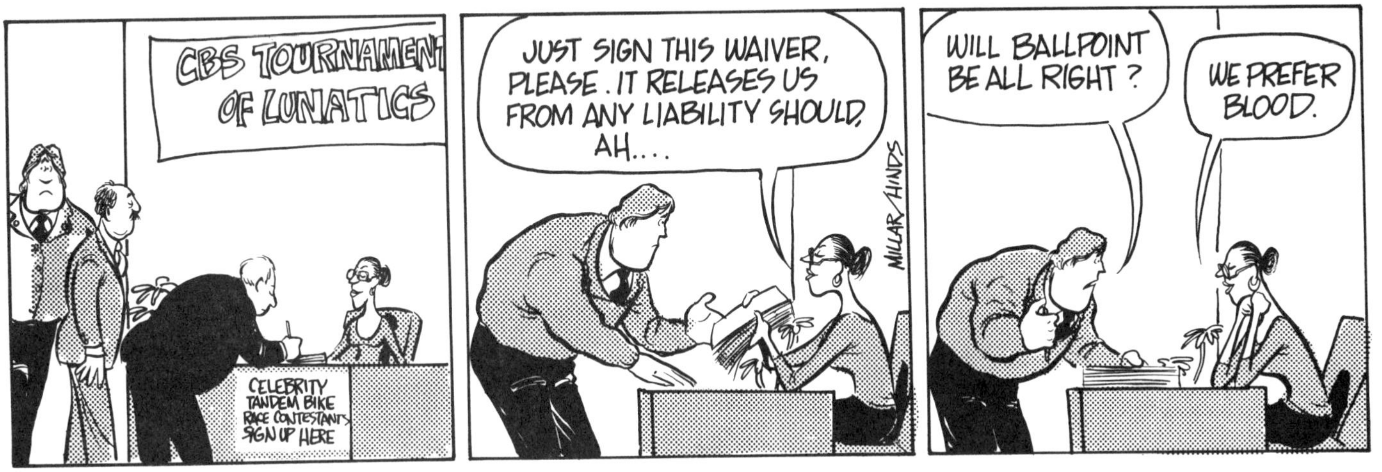
CBS TOURNAMENT OF LUNATICS
CELEBRITY TANDEM BIKE RACE CONTESTANTS SIGN UP HERE
JUST SIGN THIS WAIVER, PLEASE. IT RELEASES US FROM ANY LIABILITY SHOULD, AH....
MILLAR/HINDS
WILL BALLPOINT BE ALL RIGHT?
WE PREFER BLOOD.

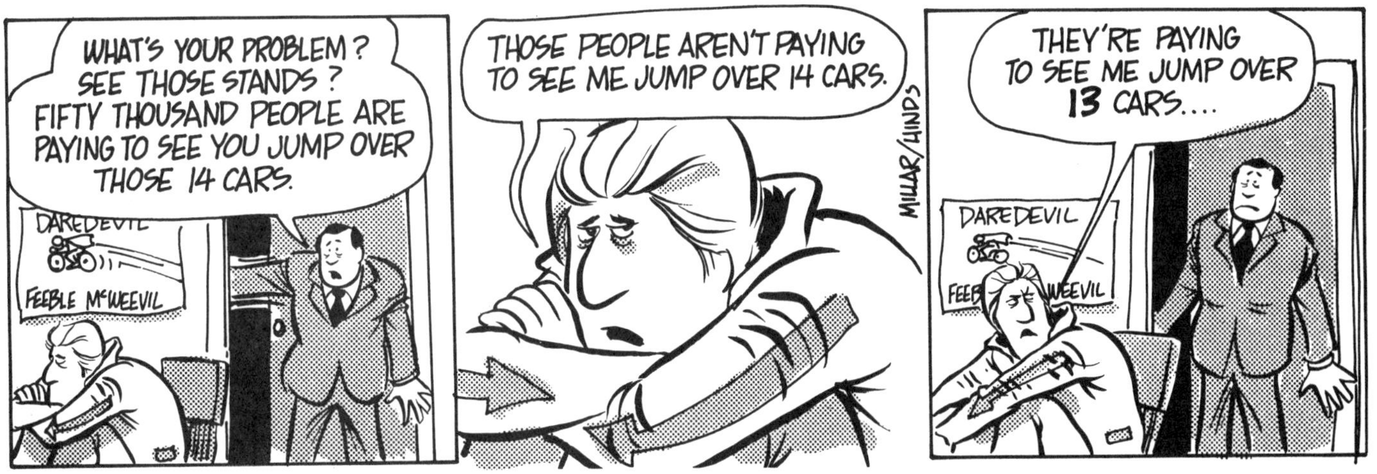
WHAT'S YOUR PROBLEM? SEE THOSE STANDS? FIFTY THOUSAND PEOPLE ARE PAYING TO SEE YOU JUMP OVER THOSE 14 CARS.
DAREDEVIL
FEEBLE McWEEVIL
THOSE PEOPLE AREN'T PAYING TO SEE ME JUMP OVER 14 CARS.
MILLAR/HINDS
THEY'RE PAYING TO SEE ME JUMP OVER **13** CARS....
DAREDEVIL

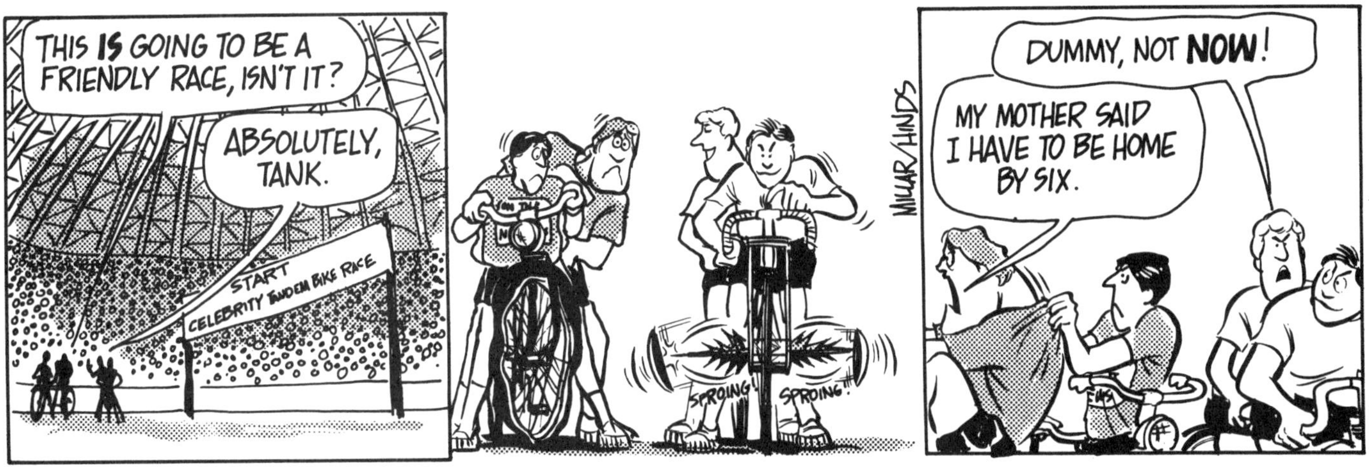
THIS **IS** GOING TO BE A FRIENDLY RACE, ISN'T IT?
ABSOLUTELY, TANK.
START
CELEBRITY TANDEM BIKE RACE
SPROING! SPROING!
MILLAR/HINDS
DUMMY, NOT **NOW**!
MY MOTHER SAID I HAVE TO BE HOME BY SIX.

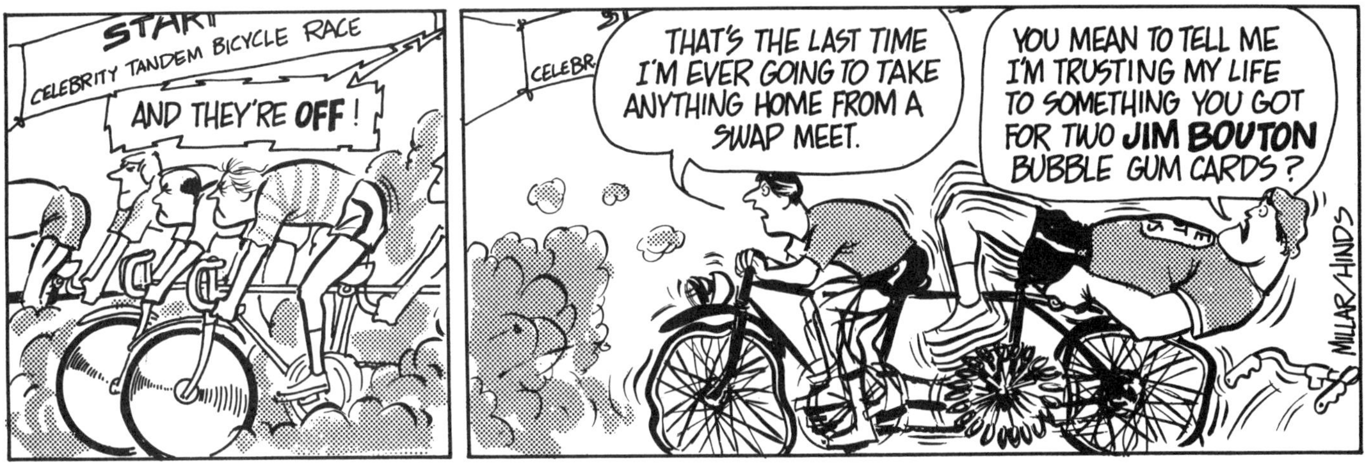
START
CELEBRITY TANDEM BICYCLE RACE
AND THEY'RE **OFF**!
THAT'S THE LAST TIME I'M EVER GOING TO TAKE ANYTHING HOME FROM A SWAP MEET.
YOU MEAN TO TELL ME I'M TRUSTING MY LIFE TO SOMETHING YOU GOT FOR TWO **JIM BOUTON** BUBBLE GUM CARDS?
MILLAR/HINDS

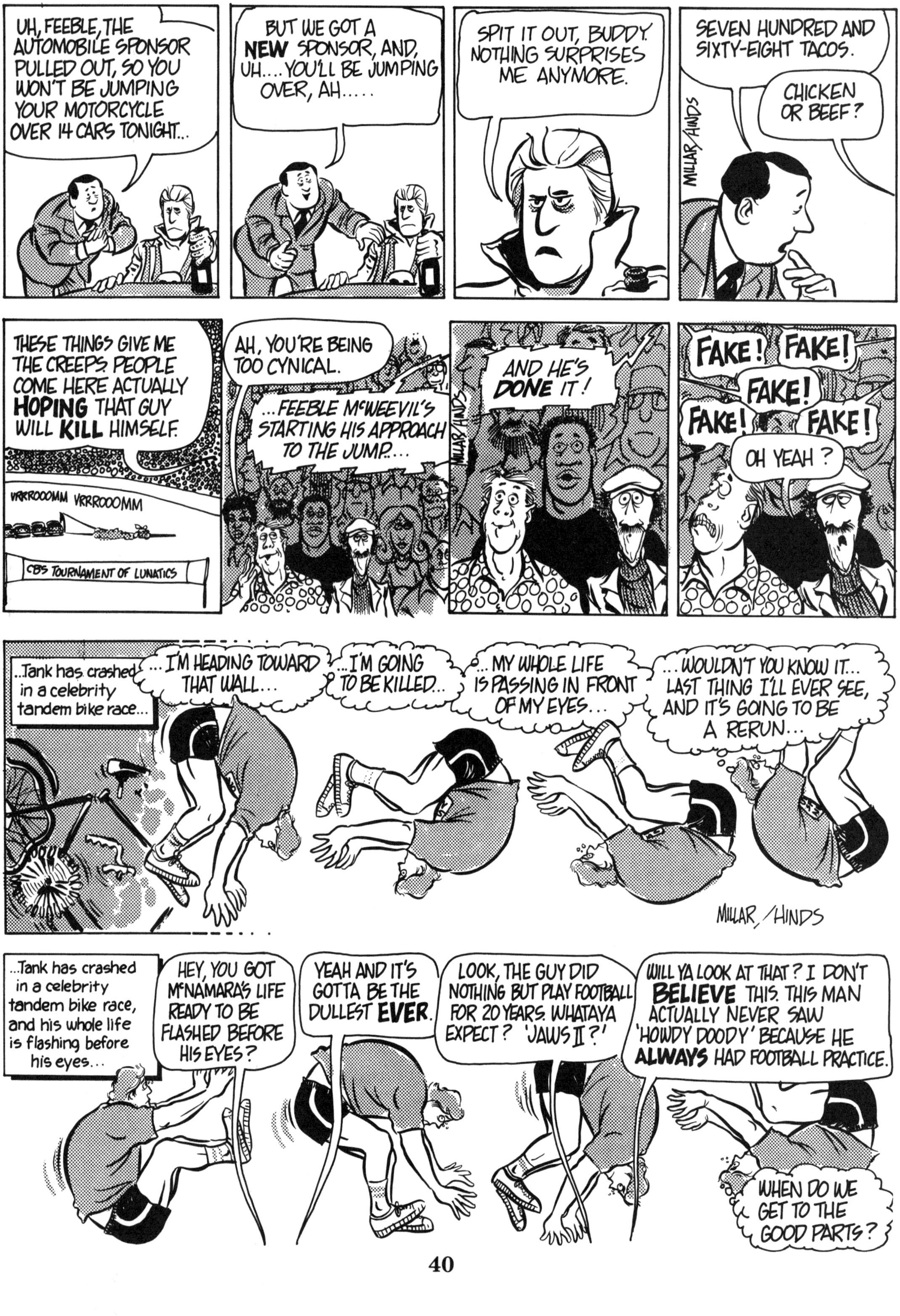
UH, FEEBLE, THE AUTOMOBILE SPONSOR PULLED OUT, SO YOU WON'T BE JUMPING YOUR MOTORCYCLE OVER 14 CARS TONIGHT...
BUT WE GOT A NEW SPONSOR, AND, UH.... YOU'LL BE JUMPING OVER, AH.....
SPIT IT OUT, BUDDY. NOTHING SURPRISES ME ANYMORE.
SEVEN HUNDRED AND SIXTY-EIGHT TACOS.
CHICKEN OR BEEF?
MILLAR/HINDS
THESE THINGS GIVE ME THE CREEPS. PEOPLE COME HERE ACTUALLY HOPING THAT GUY WILL KILL HIMSELF.
VRRROOOMM VRRROOOMM
CBS TOURNAMENT OF LUNATICS
AH, YOU'RE BEING TOO CYNICAL.
...FEEBLE McWEEVIL'S STARTING HIS APPROACH TO THE JUMP....
MILLAR/HINDS
AND HE'S DONE IT!
FAKE! FAKE! FAKE! FAKE! FAKE!
OH YEAH?
...Tank has crashed in a celebrity tandem bike race...
... I'M HEADING TOWARD THAT WALL...
...I'M GOING TO BE KILLED...
... MY WHOLE LIFE IS PASSING IN FRONT OF MY EYES...
... WOULDN'T YOU KNOW IT... LAST THING I'LL EVER SEE, AND IT'S GOING TO BE A RERUN...
MILLAR/HINDS
...Tank has crashed in a celebrity tandem bike race, and his whole life is flashing before his eyes...
HEY, YOU GOT McNAMARA'S LIFE READY TO BE FLASHED BEFORE HIS EYES?
YEAH AND IT'S GOTTA BE THE DULLEST EVER.
LOOK, THE GUY DID NOTHING BUT PLAY FOOTBALL FOR 20 YEARS. WHATAYA EXPECT? 'JAWS II?'
WILL YA LOOK AT THAT? I DON'T BELIEVE THIS. THIS MAN ACTUALLY NEVER SAW 'HOWDY DOODY' BECAUSE HE ALWAYS HAD FOOTBALL PRACTICE.
WHEN DO WE GET TO THE GOOD PARTS?

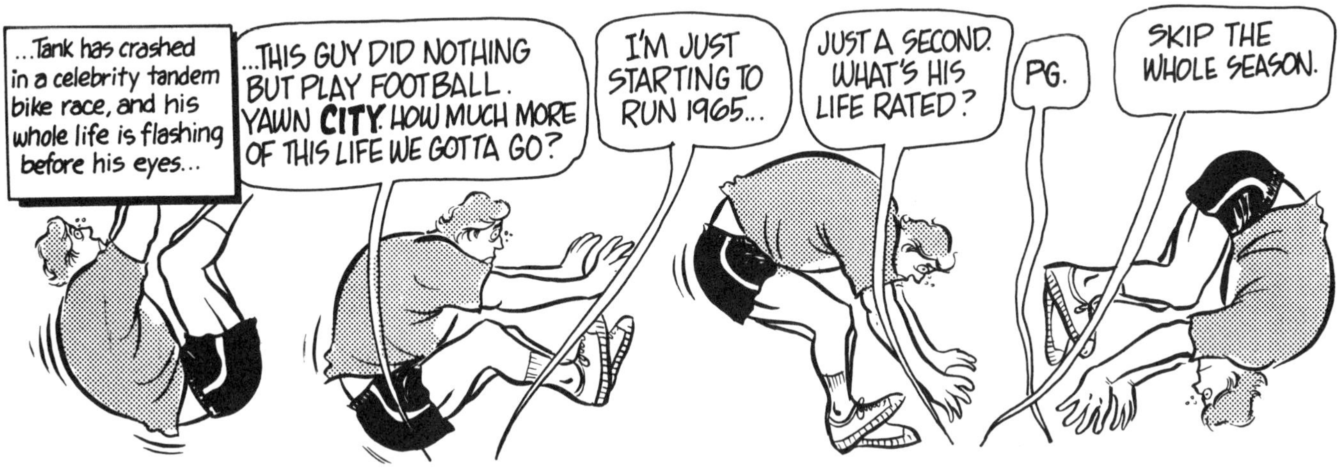
...Tank has crashed in a celebrity tandem bike race, and his whole life is flashing before his eyes...
...THIS GUY DID NOTHING BUT PLAY FOOTBALL. YAWN CITY. HOW MUCH MORE OF THIS LIFE WE GOTTA GO?
I'M JUST STARTING TO RUN 1965...
JUST A SECOND. WHAT'S HIS LIFE RATED?
PG.
SKIP THE WHOLE SEASON.

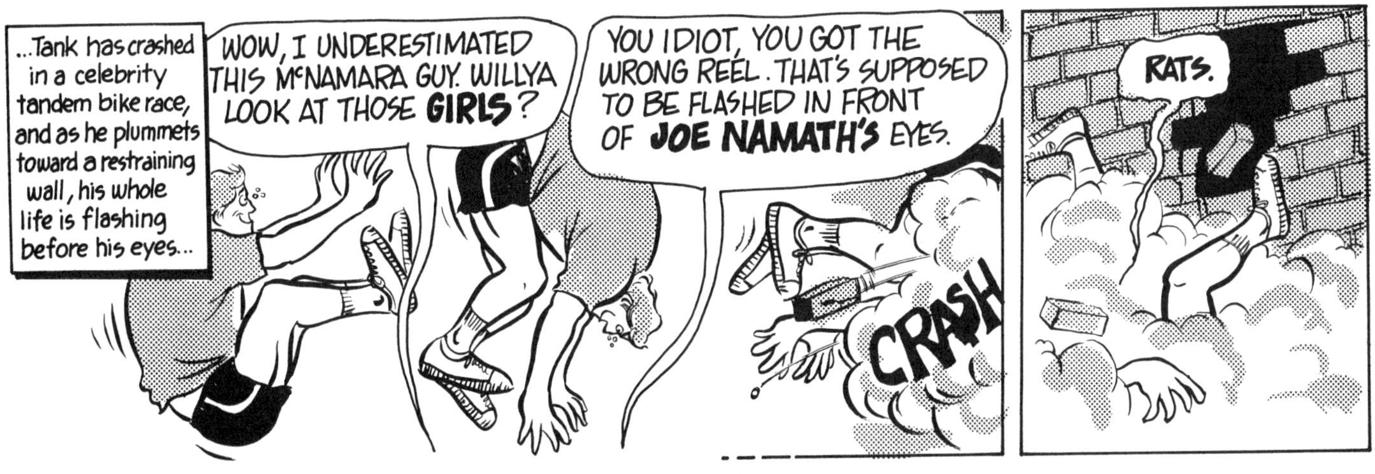
...Tank has crashed in a celebrity tandem bike race, and as he plummets toward a restraining wall, his whole life is flashing before his eyes...
WOW, I UNDERESTIMATED THIS McNAMARA GUY. WILLYA LOOK AT THOSE GIRLS?
YOU IDIOT, YOU GOT THE WRONG REEL. THAT'S SUPPOSED TO BE FLASHED IN FRONT OF JOE NAMATH'S EYES.
CRASH
RATS.

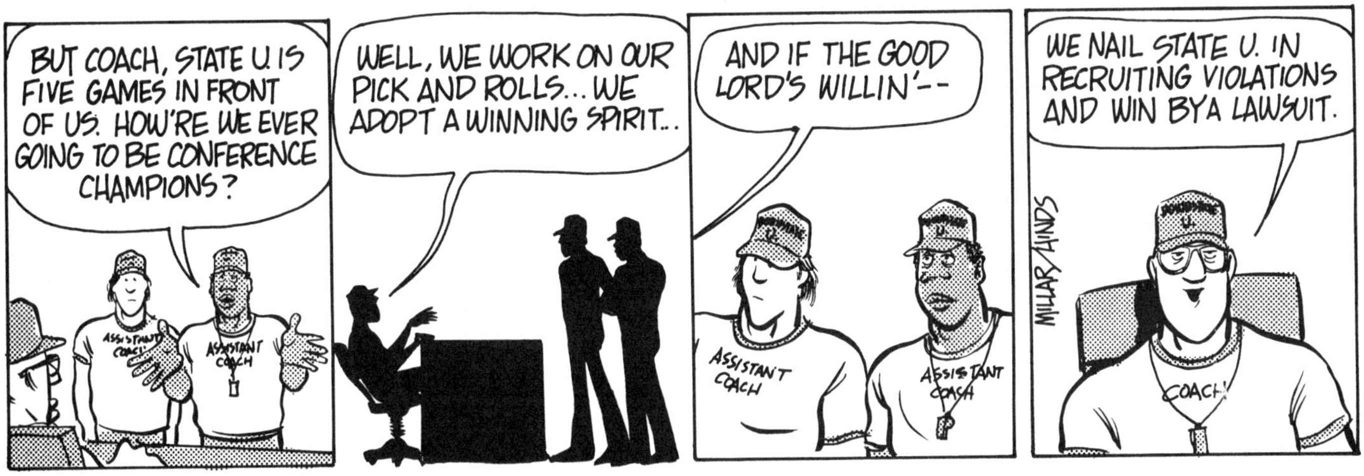
BUT COACH, STATE U. IS FIVE GAMES IN FRONT OF US. HOW'RE WE EVER GOING TO BE CONFERENCE CHAMPIONS?
ASSISTANT COACH
ASSISTANT COACH
WELL, WE WORK ON OUR PICK AND ROLLS... WE ADOPT A WINNING SPIRIT...
AND IF THE GOOD LORD'S WILLIN'--
ASSISTANT COACH
ASSISTANT COACH
MILLAR/HINDS
WE NAIL STATE U. IN RECRUITING VIOLATIONS AND WIN BY A LAWSUIT.
COACH

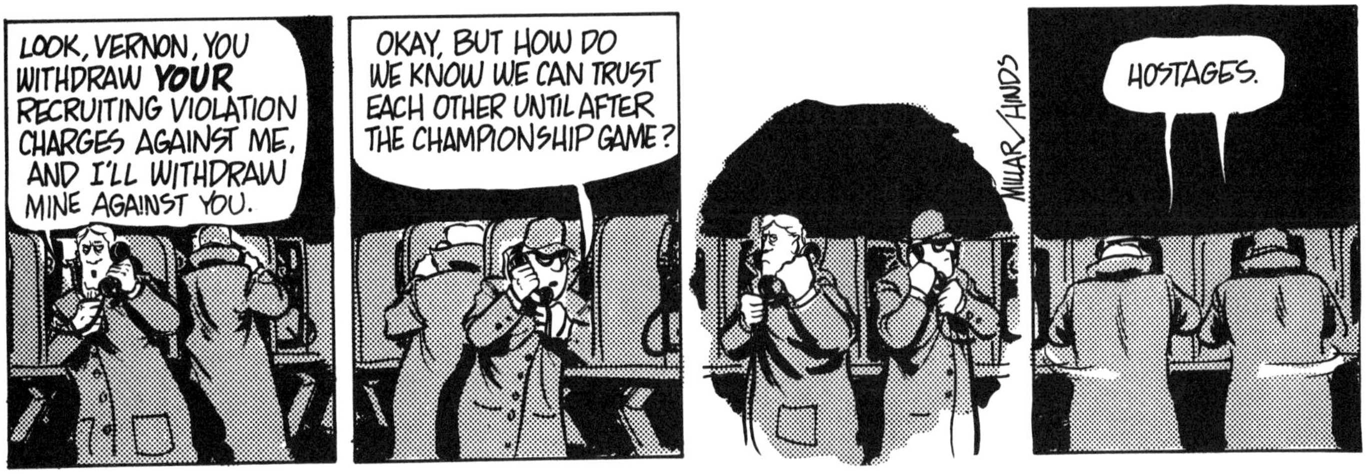
LOOK, VERNON, YOU WITHDRAW YOUR RECRUITING VIOLATION CHARGES AGAINST ME, AND I'LL WITHDRAW MINE AGAINST YOU.
OKAY, BUT HOW DO WE KNOW WE CAN TRUST EACH OTHER UNTIL AFTER THE CHAMPIONSHIP GAME?
MILLAR/HINDS
HOSTAGES.

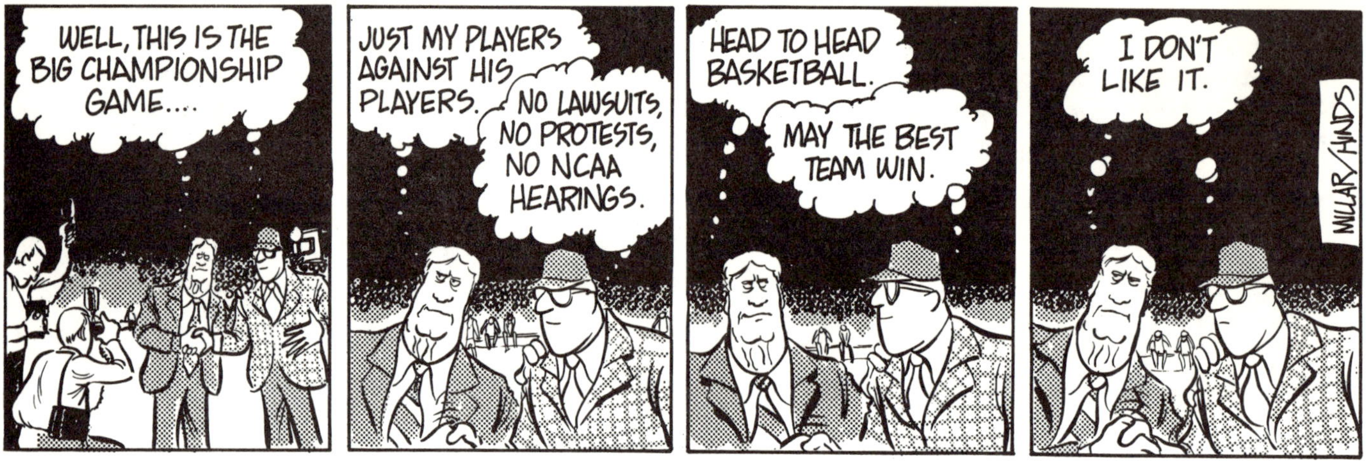
WELL, THIS IS THE BIG CHAMPIONSHIP GAME....
JUST MY PLAYERS AGAINST HIS PLAYERS.
NO LAWSUITS, NO PROTESTS, NO NCAA HEARINGS.
HEAD TO HEAD BASKETBALL.
MAY THE BEST TEAM WIN.
I DON'T LIKE IT.
MILLAR/HINDS

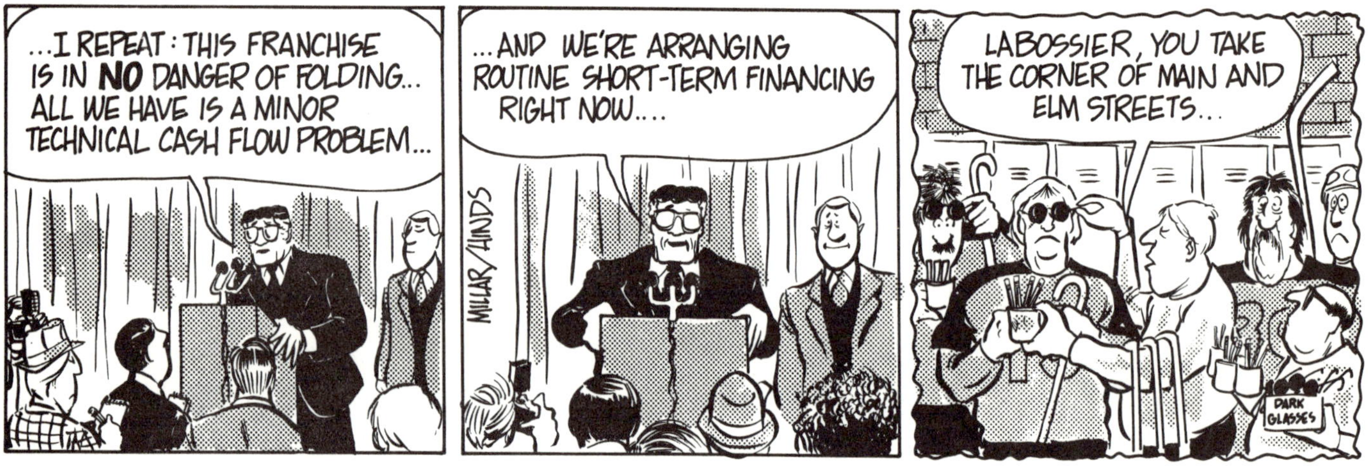
...I REPEAT: THIS FRANCHISE IS IN NO DANGER OF FOLDING... ALL WE HAVE IS A MINOR TECHNICAL CASH FLOW PROBLEM...
...AND WE'RE ARRANGING ROUTINE SHORT-TERM FINANCING RIGHT NOW....
MILLAR/HINDS
LABOSSIER, YOU TAKE THE CORNER OF MAIN AND ELM STREETS...
DARK GLASSES

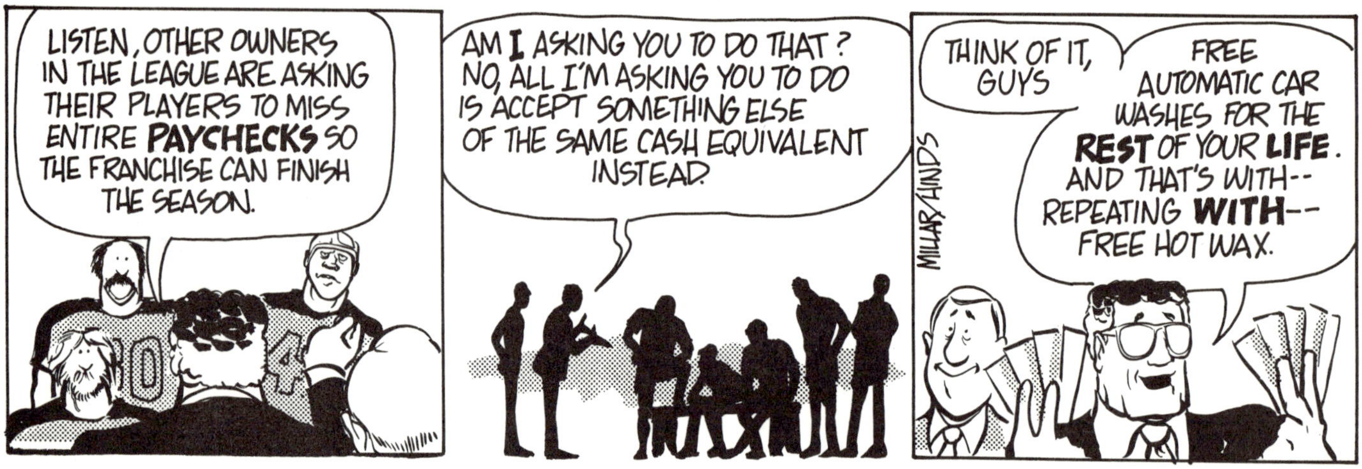
LISTEN, OTHER OWNERS IN THE LEAGUE ARE ASKING THEIR PLAYERS TO MISS ENTIRE PAYCHECKS SO THE FRANCHISE CAN FINISH THE SEASON.
AM I ASKING YOU TO DO THAT? NO, ALL I'M ASKING YOU TO DO IS ACCEPT SOMETHING ELSE OF THE SAME CASH EQUIVALENT INSTEAD.
MILLAR/HINDS
THINK OF IT, GUYS
FREE AUTOMATIC CAR WASHES FOR THE REST OF YOUR LIFE. AND THAT'S WITH-- REPEATING WITH-- FREE HOT WAX.

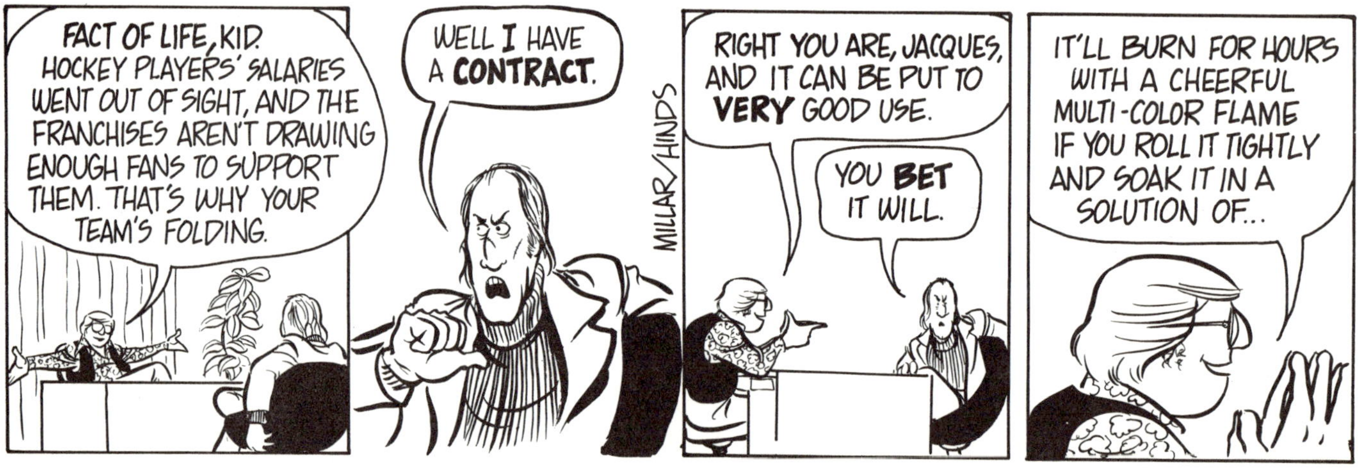
FACT OF LIFE, KID. HOCKEY PLAYERS' SALARIES WENT OUT OF SIGHT, AND THE FRANCHISES AREN'T DRAWING ENOUGH FANS TO SUPPORT THEM. THAT'S WHY YOUR TEAM'S FOLDING.
WELL I HAVE A CONTRACT.
MILLAR/HINDS
RIGHT YOU ARE, JACQUES, AND IT CAN BE PUT TO VERY GOOD USE.
YOU BET IT WILL.
IT'LL BURN FOR HOURS WITH A CHEERFUL MULTI-COLOR FLAME IF YOU ROLL IT TIGHTLY AND SOAK IT IN A SOLUTION OF...

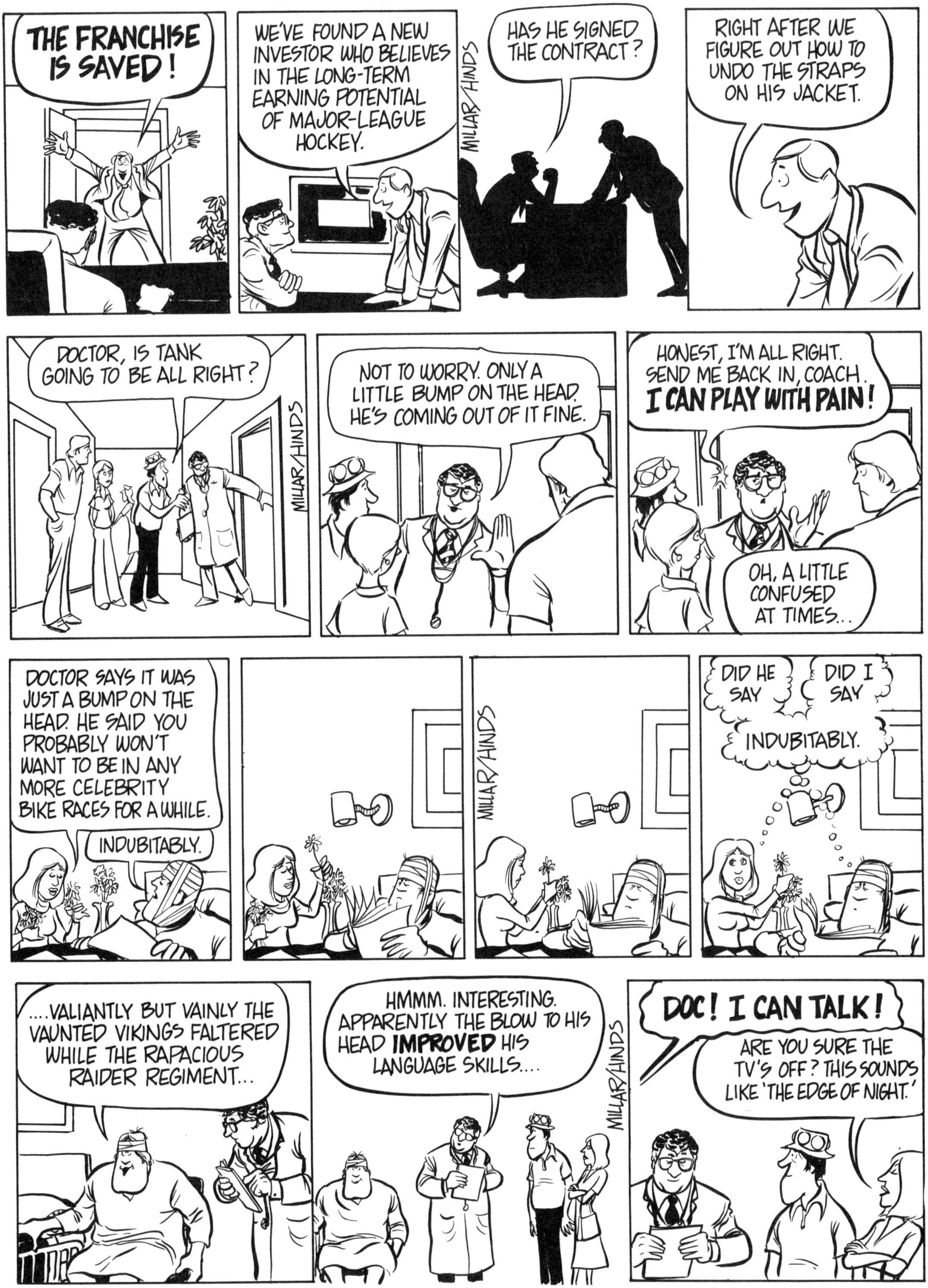
THE FRANCHISE IS SAVED!
WE'VE FOUND A NEW INVESTOR WHO BELIEVES IN THE LONG-TERM EARNING POTENTIAL OF MAJOR-LEAGUE HOCKEY.
MILLAR/HINDS
HAS HE SIGNED THE CONTRACT?
RIGHT AFTER WE FIGURE OUT HOW TO UNDO THE STRAPS ON HIS JACKET.
DOCTOR, IS TANK GOING TO BE ALL RIGHT?
MILLAR/HINDS
NOT TO WORRY. ONLY A LITTLE BUMP ON THE HEAD. HE'S COMING OUT OF IT FINE.
HONEST, I'M ALL RIGHT. SEND ME BACK IN, COACH. I CAN PLAY WITH PAIN!
OH, A LITTLE CONFUSED AT TIMES...
DOCTOR SAYS IT WAS JUST A BUMP ON THE HEAD. HE SAID YOU PROBABLY WON'T WANT TO BE IN ANY MORE CELEBRITY BIKE RACES FOR A WHILE.
INDUBITABLY.
MILLAR/HINDS
DID HE SAY
DID I SAY
INDUBITABLY.
....VALIANTLY BUT VAINLY THE VAUNTED VIKINGS FALTERED WHILE THE RAPACIOUS RAIDER REGIMENT...
HMMM. INTERESTING. APPARENTLY THE BLOW TO HIS HEAD IMPROVED HIS LANGUAGE SKILLS....
MILLAR/HINDS
DOC! I CAN TALK!
ARE YOU SURE THE TV'S OFF? THIS SOUNDS LIKE 'THE EDGE OF NIGHT.'

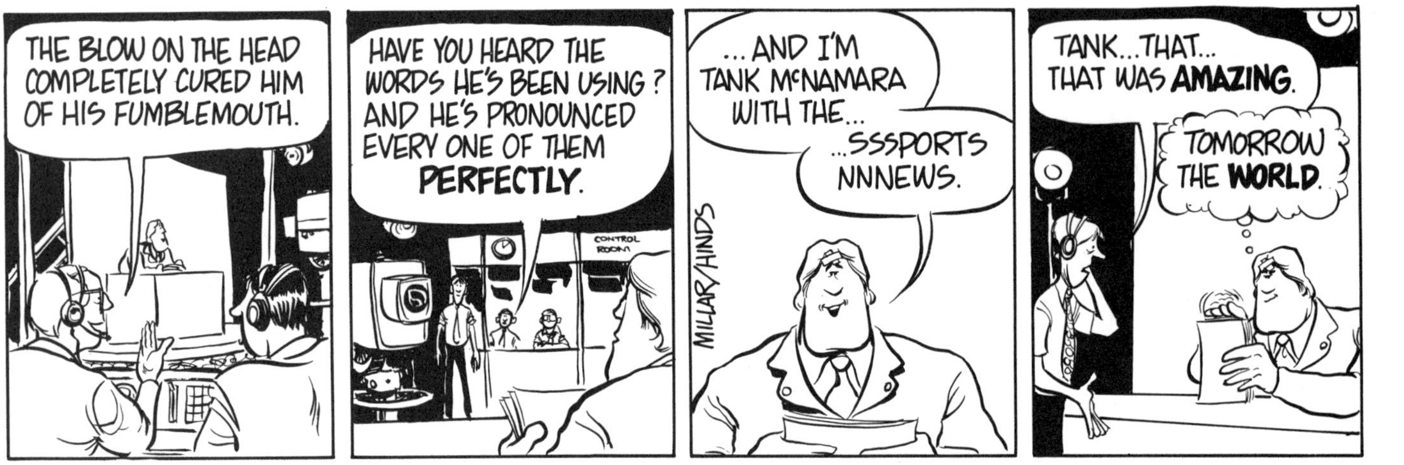
THE BLOW ON THE HEAD COMPLETELY CURED HIM OF HIS FUMBLEMOUTH.
HAVE YOU HEARD THE WORDS HE'S BEEN USING ? AND HE'S PRONOUNCED EVERY ONE OF THEM PERFECTLY.
CONTROL ROOM
... AND I'M TANK McNAMARA WITH THE...
...SSSPORTS NNNEWS.
MILLAR/HINDS
TANK...THAT... THAT WAS AMAZING.
TOMORROW THE WORLD.

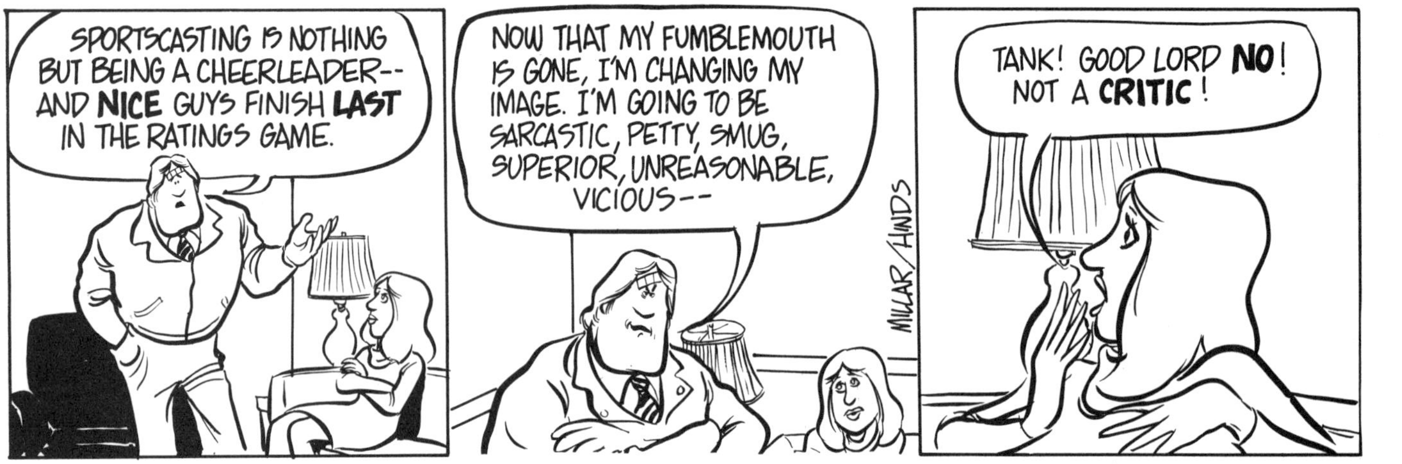
SPORTSCASTING IS NOTHING BUT BEING A CHEERLEADER-- AND NICE GUYS FINISH LAST IN THE RATINGS GAME.
NOW THAT MY FUMBLEMOUTH IS GONE, I'M CHANGING MY IMAGE. I'M GOING TO BE SARCASTIC, PETTY, SMUG, SUPERIOR, UNREASONABLE, VICIOUS--
MILLAR/HINDS
TANK! GOOD LORD NO! NOT A CRITIC!

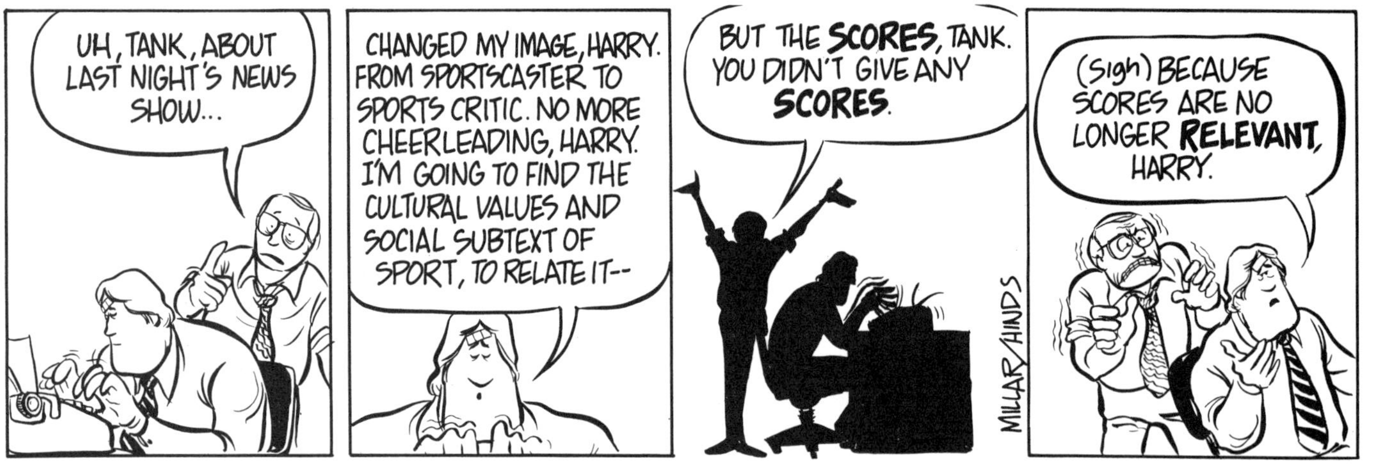
UH, TANK, ABOUT LAST NIGHT'S NEWS SHOW...
CHANGED MY IMAGE, HARRY. FROM SPORTSCASTER TO SPORTS CRITIC. NO MORE CHEERLEADING, HARRY. I'M GOING TO FIND THE CULTURAL VALUES AND SOCIAL SUBTEXT OF SPORT, TO RELATE IT--
BUT THE SCORES, TANK. YOU DIDN'T GIVE ANY SCORES.
MILLAR/HINDS
(Sigh) BECAUSE SCORES ARE NO LONGER RELEVANT, HARRY.

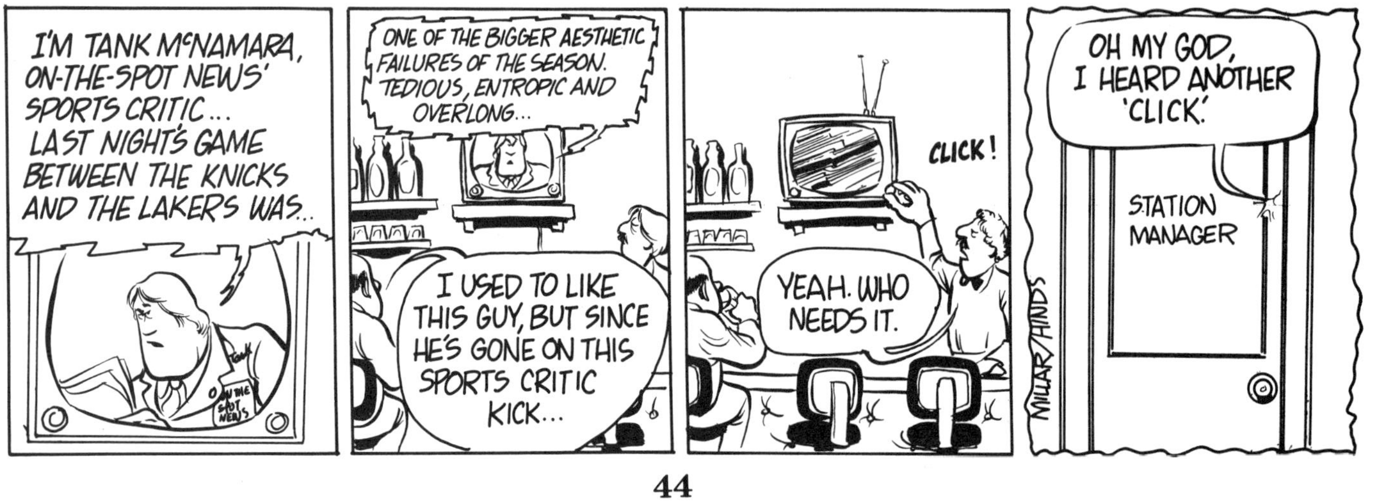
I'M TANK McNAMARA, ON-THE-SPOT NEWS' SPORTS CRITIC... LAST NIGHT'S GAME BETWEEN THE KNICKS AND THE LAKERS WAS...
ON THE SPOT NEWS
ONE OF THE BIGGER AESTHETIC FAILURES OF THE SEASON. TEDIOUS, ENTROPIC AND OVERLONG...
I USED TO LIKE THIS GUY, BUT SINCE HE'S GONE ON THIS SPORTS CRITIC KICK...
CLICK!
YEAH. WHO NEEDS IT.
MILLAR/HINDS
OH MY GOD, I HEARD ANOTHER 'CLICK.'
STATION MANAGER

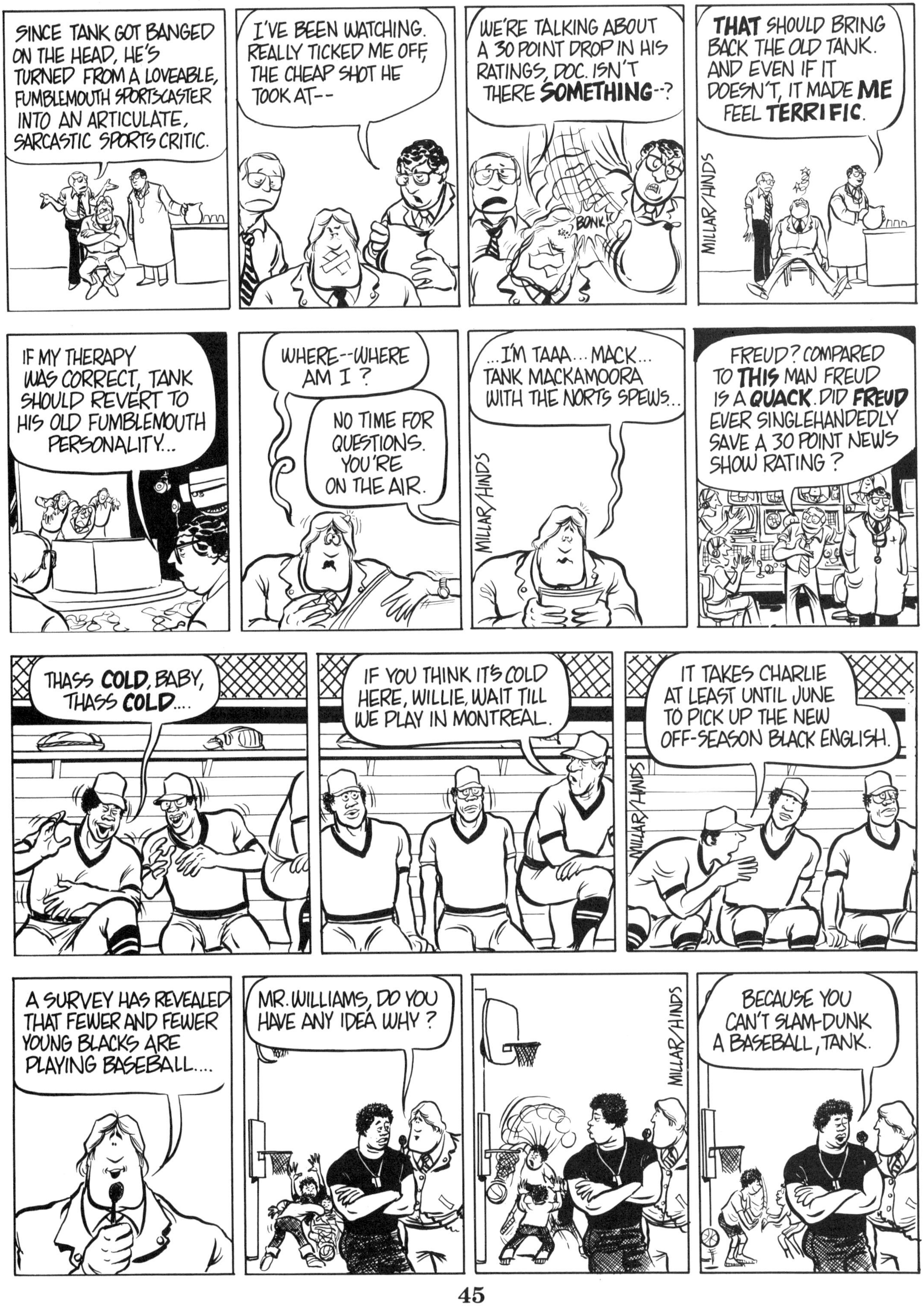
SINCE TANK GOT BANGED ON THE HEAD, HE'S TURNED FROM A LOVEABLE, FUMBLEMOUTH SPORTSCASTER INTO AN ARTICULATE, SARCASTIC SPORTS CRITIC.
I'VE BEEN WATCHING. REALLY TICKED ME OFF, THE CHEAP SHOT HE TOOK AT--
WE'RE TALKING ABOUT A 30 POINT DROP IN HIS RATINGS, DOC. ISN'T THERE **SOMETHING**--?
BONK!
THAT SHOULD BRING BACK THE OLD TANK. AND EVEN IF IT DOESN'T, IT MADE **ME** FEEL **TERRIFIC**.
MILLAR/HINDS
IF MY THERAPY WAS CORRECT, TANK SHOULD REVERT TO HIS OLD FUMBLEMOUTH PERSONALITY...
WHERE--WHERE AM I ?
NO TIME FOR QUESTIONS. YOU'RE ON THE AIR.
...I'M TAAA... MACK... TANK MACKAMOORA WITH THE NORTS SPEWS...
MILLAR/HINDS
FREUD? COMPARED TO **THIS** MAN FREUD IS A **QUACK**. DID **FREUD** EVER SINGLEHANDEDLY SAVE A 30 POINT NEWS SHOW RATING ?
THASS **COLD**, BABY, THASS **COLD**....
IF YOU THINK IT'S COLD HERE, WILLIE, WAIT TILL WE PLAY IN MONTREAL.
MILLAR/HINDS
IT TAKES CHARLIE AT LEAST UNTIL JUNE TO PICK UP THE NEW OFF-SEASON BLACK ENGLISH.
A SURVEY HAS REVEALED THAT FEWER AND FEWER YOUNG BLACKS ARE PLAYING BASEBALL....
MR. WILLIAMS, DO YOU HAVE ANY IDEA WHY ?
MILLAR/HINDS
BECAUSE YOU CAN'T SLAM-DUNK A BASEBALL, TANK.

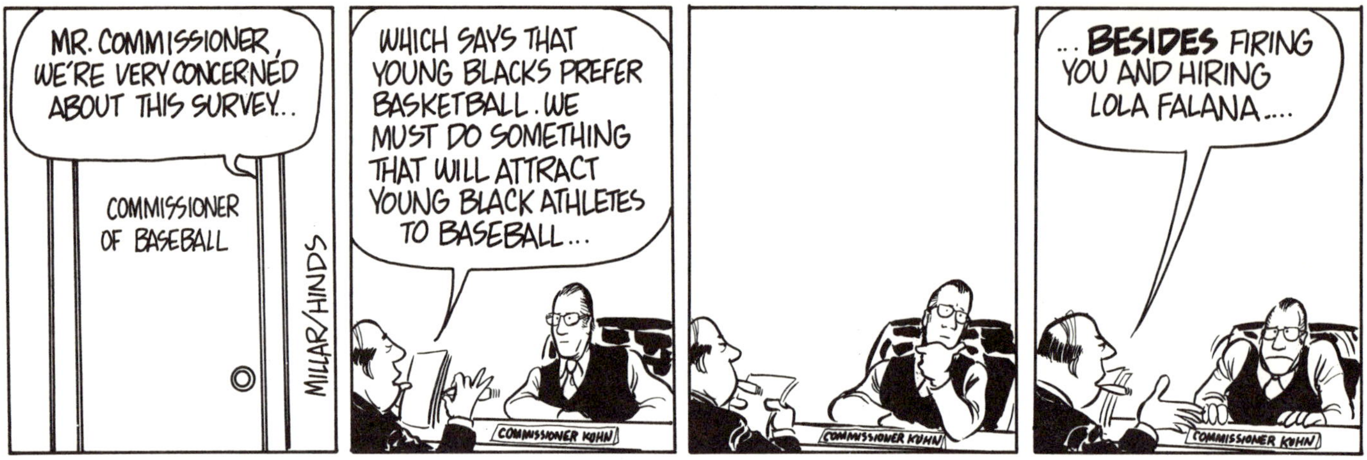
MR. COMMISSIONER, WE'RE VERY CONCERNED ABOUT THIS SURVEY...
COMMISSIONER OF BASEBALL
MILLAR/HINDS
WHICH SAYS THAT YOUNG BLACKS PREFER BASKETBALL. WE MUST DO SOMETHING THAT WILL ATTRACT YOUNG BLACK ATHLETES TO BASEBALL...
COMMISSIONER KUHN
COMMISSIONER KUHN
... **BESIDES** FIRING YOU AND HIRING LOLA FALANA....
COMMISSIONER KUHN

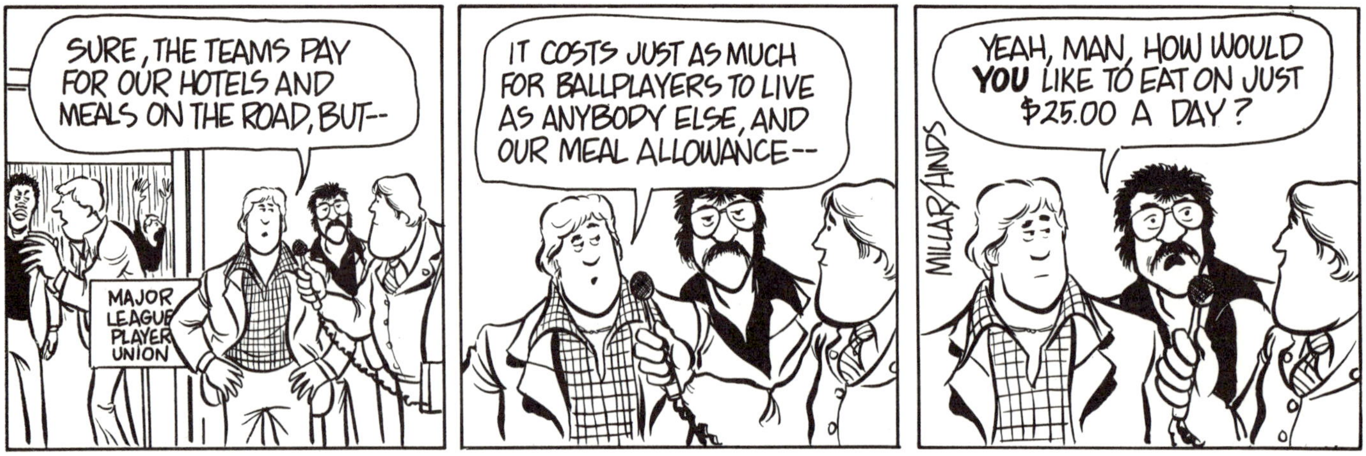
SURE, THE TEAMS PAY FOR OUR HOTELS AND MEALS ON THE ROAD, BUT--
MAJOR LEAGUE PLAYER UNION
IT COSTS JUST AS MUCH FOR BALLPLAYERS TO LIVE AS ANYBODY ELSE, AND OUR MEAL ALLOWANCE--
MILLAR/HINDS
YEAH, MAN, HOW WOULD **YOU** LIKE TO EAT ON JUST $25.00 A DAY?

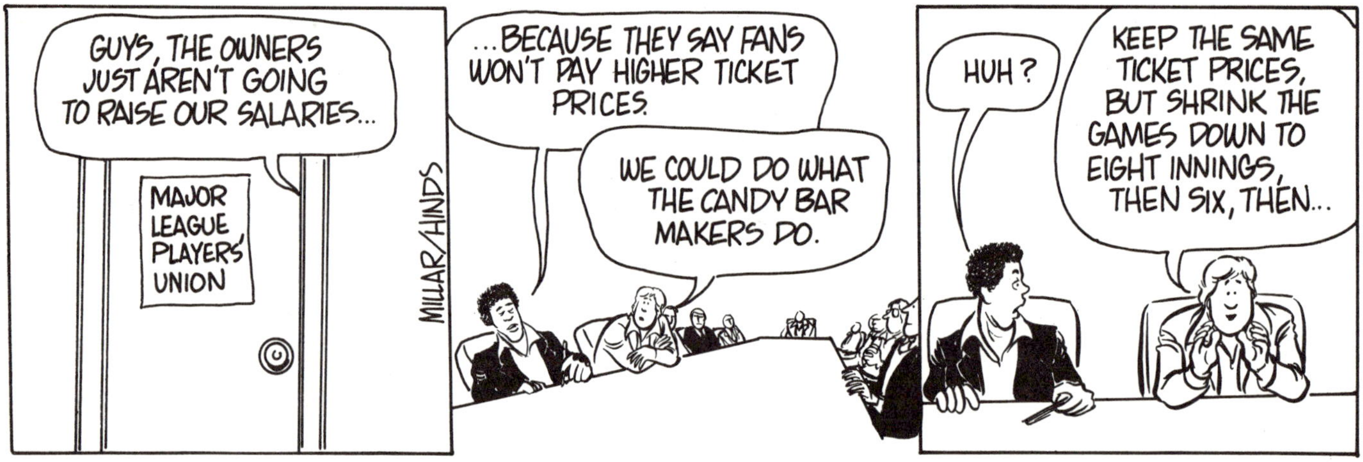
GUYS, THE OWNERS JUST AREN'T GOING TO RAISE OUR SALARIES...
MAJOR LEAGUE PLAYERS' UNION
MILLAR/HINDS
...BECAUSE THEY SAY FANS WON'T PAY HIGHER TICKET PRICES.
WE COULD DO WHAT THE CANDY BAR MAKERS DO.
HUH?
KEEP THE SAME TICKET PRICES, BUT SHRINK THE GAMES DOWN TO EIGHT INNINGS, THEN SIX, THEN...

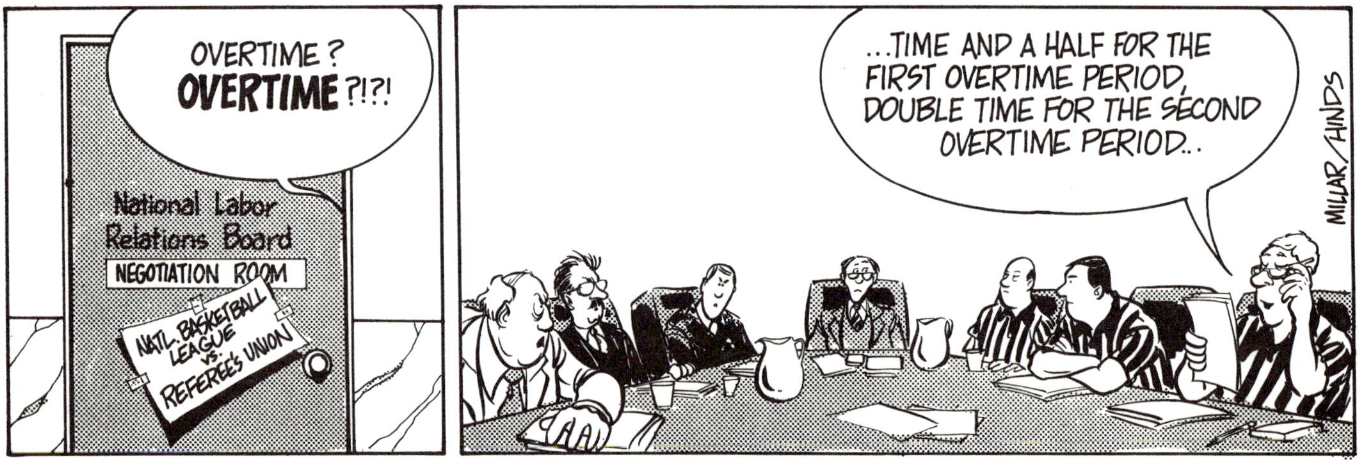
OVERTIME? **OVERTIME**?!?!
National Labor Relations Board
NEGOTIATION ROOM
NAT'L BASKETBALL LEAGUE VS. REFEREE'S UNION
...TIME AND A HALF FOR THE FIRST OVERTIME PERIOD, DOUBLE TIME FOR THE SECOND OVERTIME PERIOD...
MILLAR/HINDS

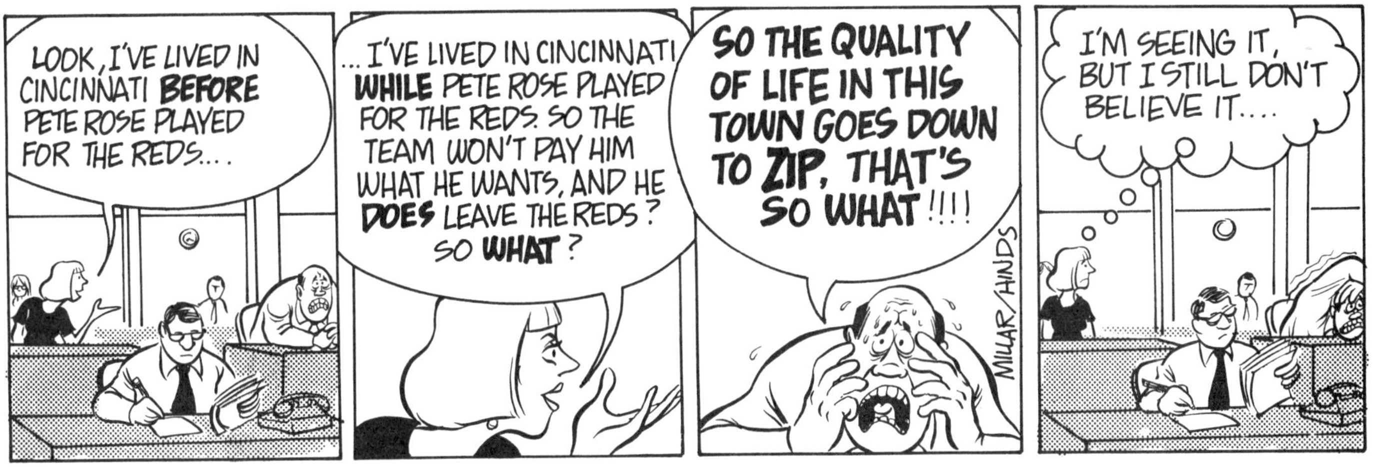
LOOK, I'VE LIVED IN CINCINNATI **BEFORE** PETE ROSE PLAYED FOR THE REDS...
...I'VE LIVED IN CINCINNATI **WHILE** PETE ROSE PLAYED FOR THE REDS. SO THE TEAM WON'T PAY HIM WHAT HE WANTS, AND HE **DOES** LEAVE THE REDS? SO **WHAT**?
SO THE QUALITY OF LIFE IN THIS TOWN GOES DOWN TO ZIP, THAT'S SO WHAT!!!!
MILLAR/HINDS
I'M SEEING IT, BUT I STILL DON'T BELIEVE IT....

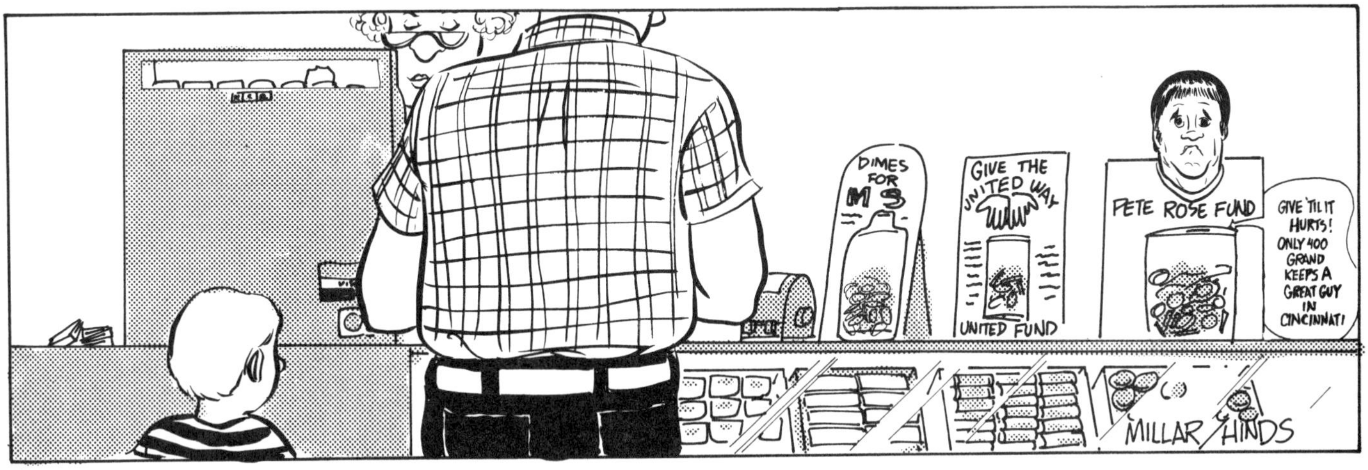
DIMES FOR MS
GIVE THE UNITED WAY
UNITED FUND
PETE ROSE FUND
GIVE 'TIL IT HURTS! ONLY 400 GRAND KEEPS A GREAT GUY IN CINCINNATI
MILLAR/HINDS

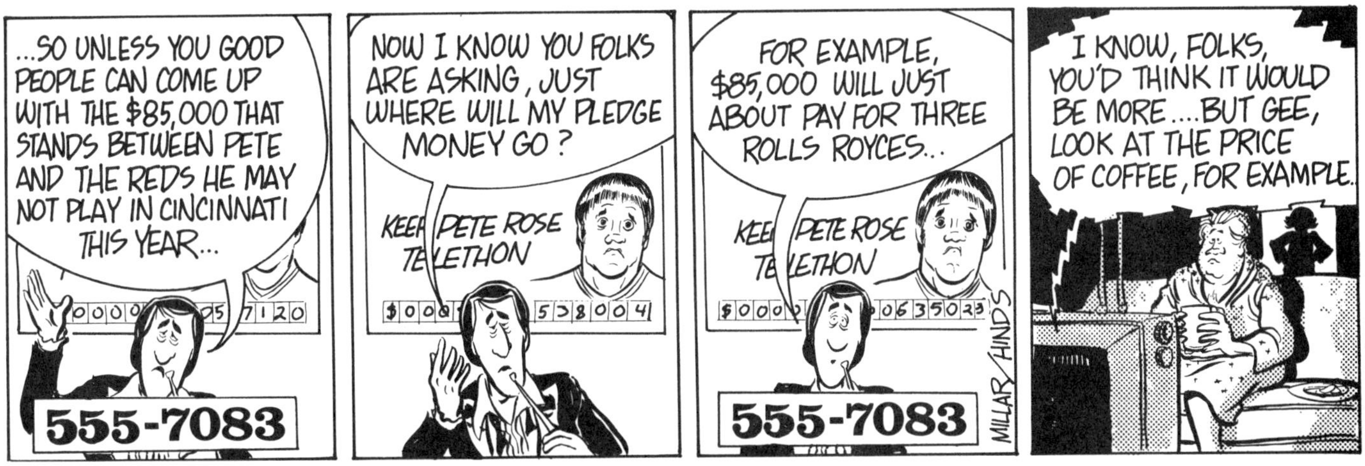
...SO UNLESS YOU GOOD PEOPLE CAN COME UP WITH THE $85,000 THAT STANDS BETWEEN PETE AND THE REDS HE MAY NOT PLAY IN CINCINNATI THIS YEAR...
555-7083
NOW I KNOW YOU FOLKS ARE ASKING, JUST WHERE WILL MY PLEDGE MONEY GO?
KEEP PETE ROSE TELETHON
FOR EXAMPLE, $85,000 WILL JUST ABOUT PAY FOR THREE ROLLS ROYCES...
TELETHON
555-7083
MILLAR/HINDS
I KNOW, FOLKS, YOU'D THINK IT WOULD BE MORE....BUT GEE, LOOK AT THE PRICE OF COFFEE, FOR EXAMPLE.

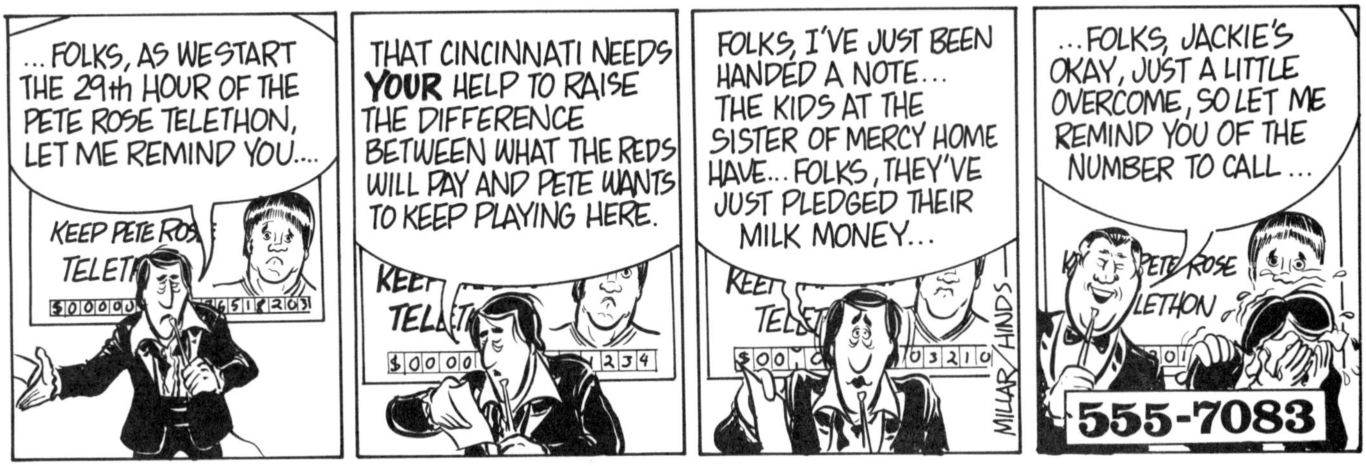
...FOLKS, AS WE START THE 29th HOUR OF THE PETE ROSE TELETHON, LET ME REMIND YOU....
KEEP PETE ROS
THAT CINCINNATI NEEDS **YOUR** HELP TO RAISE THE DIFFERENCE BETWEEN WHAT THE REDS WILL PAY AND PETE WANTS TO KEEP PLAYING HERE.
FOLKS, I'VE JUST BEEN HANDED A NOTE... THE KIDS AT THE SISTER OF MERCY HOME HAVE... FOLKS, THEY'VE JUST PLEDGED THEIR MILK MONEY...
MILLAR/HINDS
...FOLKS, JACKIE'S OKAY, JUST A LITTLE OVERCOME, SO LET ME REMIND YOU OF THE NUMBER TO CALL...
555-7083

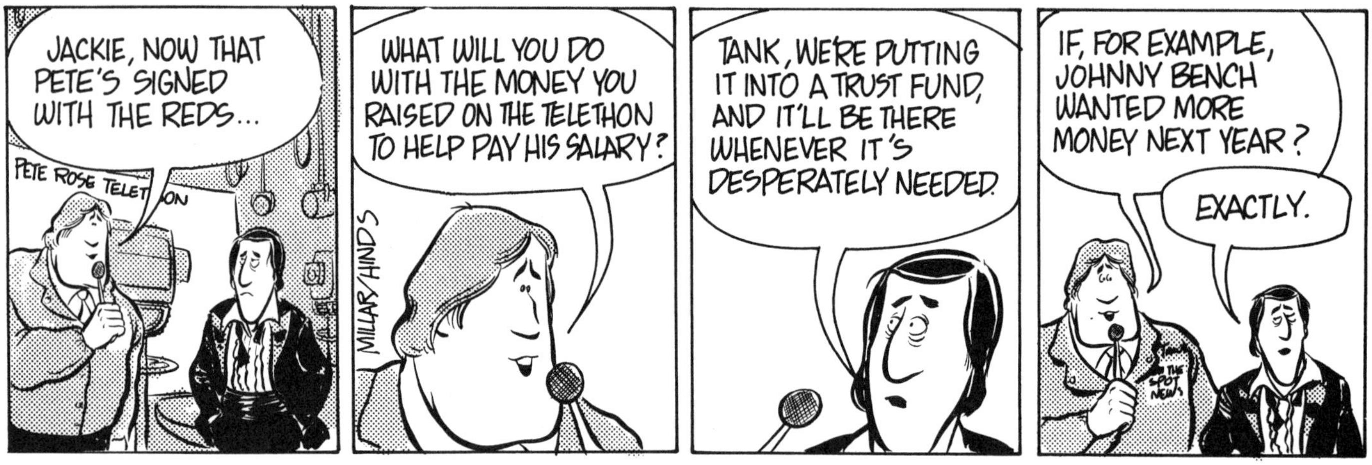
JACKIE, NOW THAT PETE'S SIGNED WITH THE REDS...
WHAT WILL YOU DO WITH THE MONEY YOU RAISED ON THE TELETHON TO HELP PAY HIS SALARY?
MILLAR/HINDS
TANK, WE'RE PUTTING IT INTO A TRUST FUND, AND IT'LL BE THERE WHENEVER IT'S DESPERATELY NEEDED.
IF, FOR EXAMPLE, JOHNNY BENCH WANTED MORE MONEY NEXT YEAR?
EXACTLY.

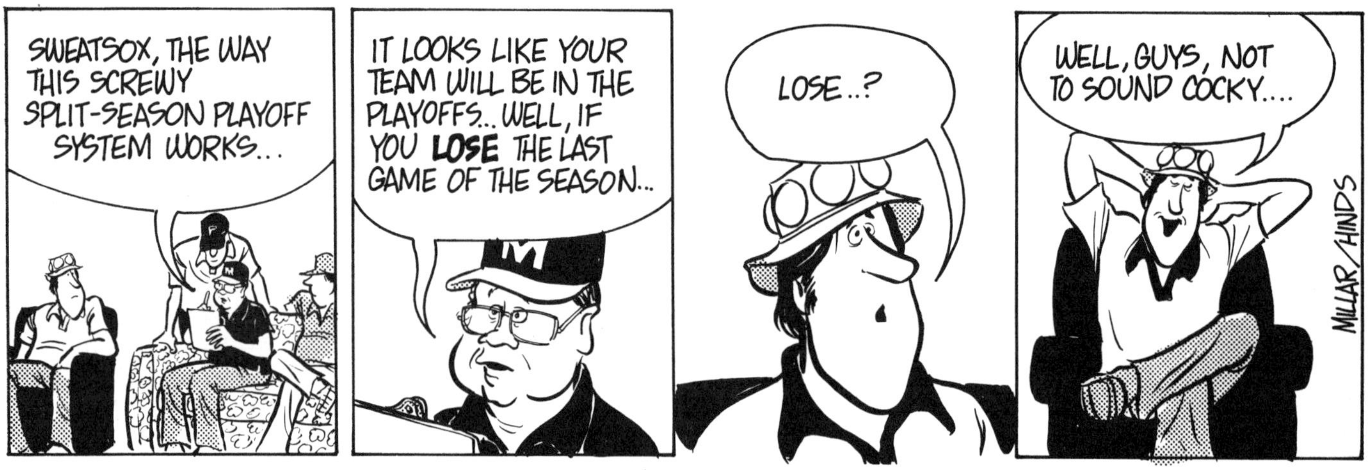
SWEATSOX, THE WAY THIS SCREWY SPLIT-SEASON PLAYOFF SYSTEM WORKS...
IT LOOKS LIKE YOUR TEAM WILL BE IN THE PLAYOFFS... WELL, IF YOU **LOSE** THE LAST GAME OF THE SEASON...
LOSE...?
WELL, GUYS, NOT TO SOUND COCKY....
MILLAR/HINDS

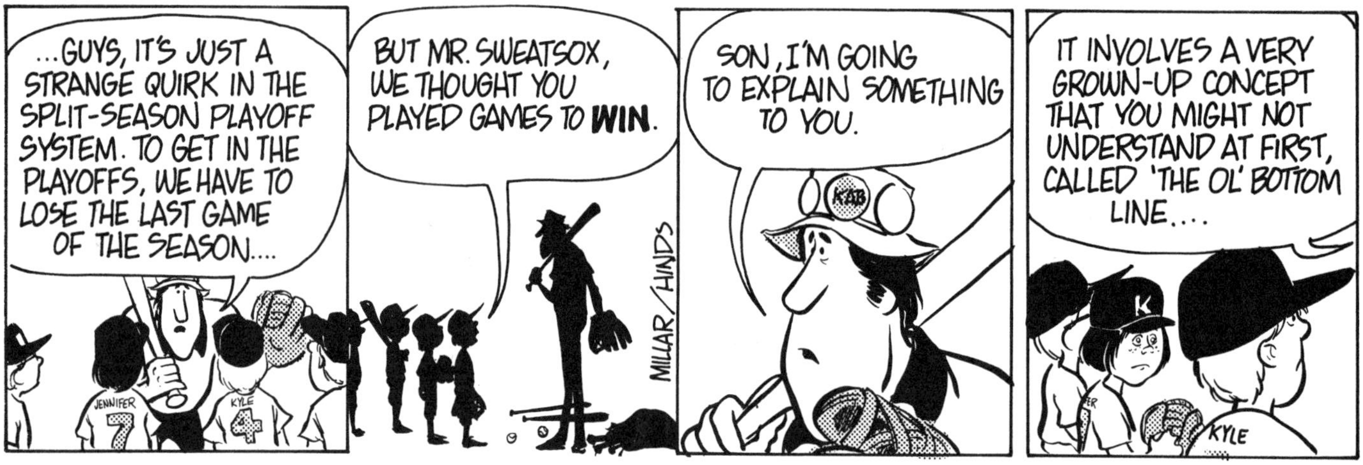
...GUYS, IT'S JUST A STRANGE QUIRK IN THE SPLIT-SEASON PLAYOFF SYSTEM. TO GET IN THE PLAYOFFS, WE HAVE TO LOSE THE LAST GAME OF THE SEASON....
JENNIFER 7
KYLE 4
BUT MR. SWEATSOX, WE THOUGHT YOU PLAYED GAMES TO **WIN**.
MILLAR/HINDS
SON, I'M GOING TO EXPLAIN SOMETHING TO YOU.
KAB
IT INVOLVES A VERY GROWN-UP CONCEPT THAT YOU MIGHT NOT UNDERSTAND AT FIRST, CALLED 'THE OL' BOTTOM LINE....
K
KYLE

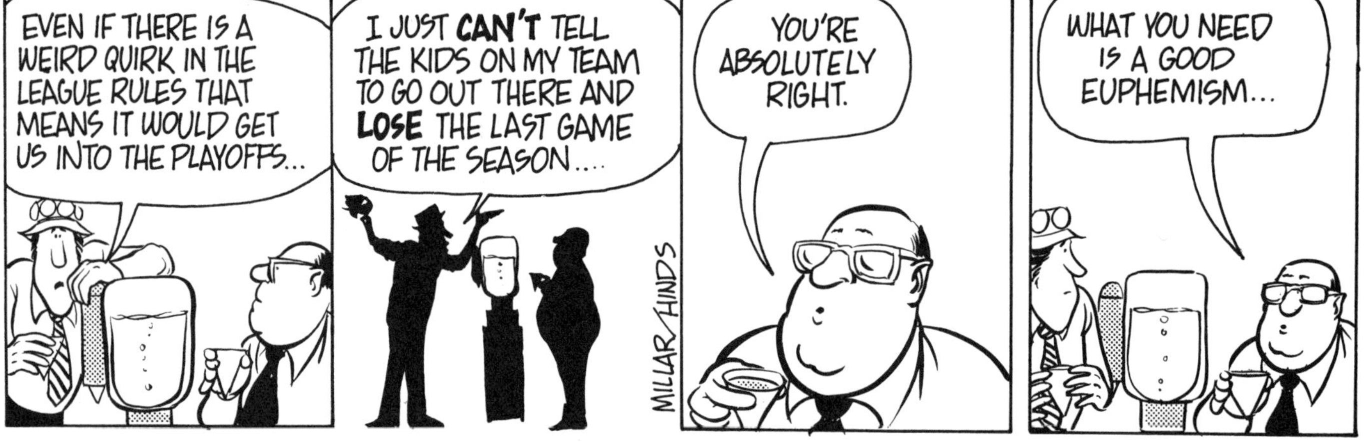
EVEN IF THERE IS A WEIRD QUIRK IN THE LEAGUE RULES THAT MEANS IT WOULD GET US INTO THE PLAYOFFS...
I JUST **CAN'T** TELL THE KIDS ON MY TEAM TO GO OUT THERE AND **LOSE** THE LAST GAME OF THE SEASON....
MILLAR/HINDS
YOU'RE ABSOLUTELY RIGHT.
WHAT YOU NEED IS A GOOD EUPHEMISM...

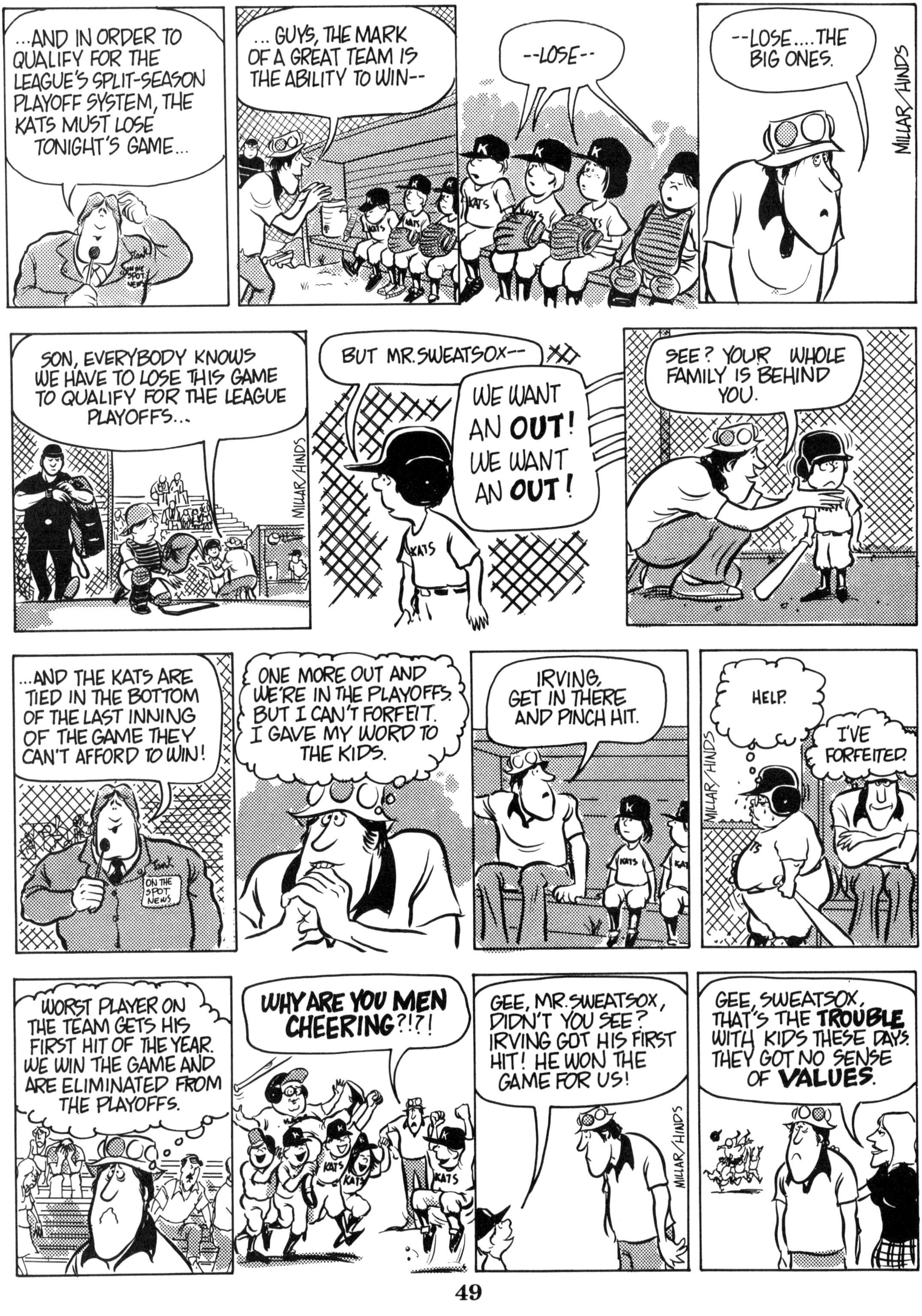
...AND IN ORDER TO QUALIFY FOR THE LEAGUE'S SPLIT-SEASON PLAYOFF SYSTEM, THE KATS MUST LOSE TONIGHT'S GAME...
... GUYS, THE MARK OF A GREAT TEAM IS THE ABILITY TO WIN--
--LOSE--
--LOSE.... THE BIG ONES.
MILLAR/HINDS
SON, EVERYBODY KNOWS WE HAVE TO LOSE THIS GAME TO QUALIFY FOR THE LEAGUE PLAYOFFS...
MILLAR/HINDS
BUT MR. SWEATSOX--
WE WANT AN OUT! WE WANT AN OUT!
SEE? YOUR WHOLE FAMILY IS BEHIND YOU.
...AND THE KATS ARE TIED IN THE BOTTOM OF THE LAST INNING OF THE GAME THEY CAN'T AFFORD TO WIN!
ON THE SPOT NEWS
ONE MORE OUT AND WE'RE IN THE PLAYOFFS. BUT I CAN'T FORFEIT. I GAVE MY WORD TO THE KIDS.
IRVING, GET IN THERE AND PINCH HIT.
MILLAR/HINDS
HELP.
I'VE FORFEITED.
WORST PLAYER ON THE TEAM GETS HIS FIRST HIT OF THE YEAR. WE WIN THE GAME AND ARE ELIMINATED FROM THE PLAYOFFS.
WHY ARE YOU MEN CHEERING?!?!
GEE, MR. SWEATSOX, DIDN'T YOU SEE? IRVING GOT HIS FIRST HIT! HE WON THE GAME FOR US!
MILLAR/HINDS
GEE, SWEATSOX, THAT'S THE TROUBLE WITH KIDS THESE DAYS. THEY GOT NO SENSE OF VALUES.

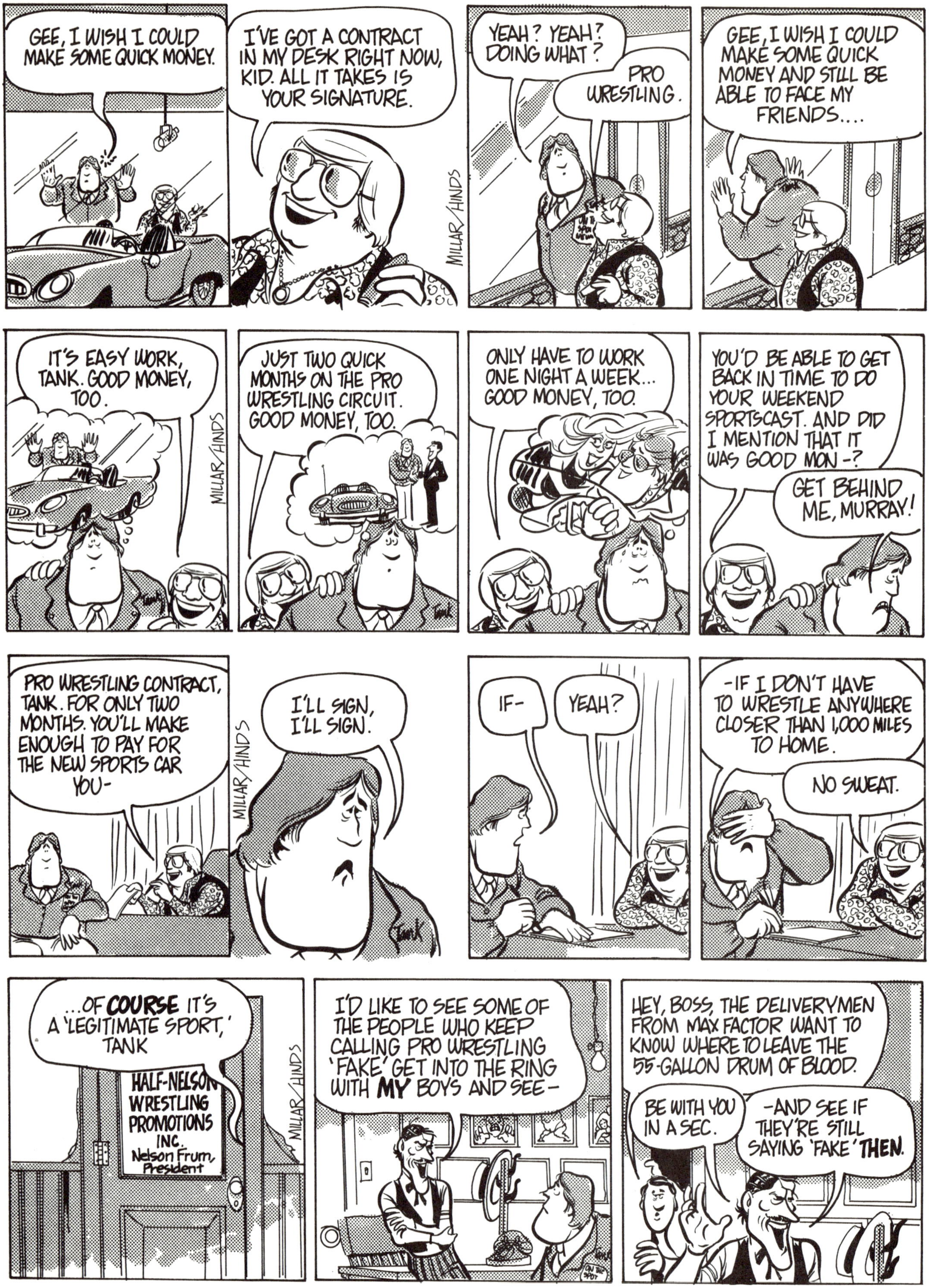

GEE, I WISH I COULD MAKE SOME QUICK MONEY.
I'VE GOT A CONTRACT IN MY DESK RIGHT NOW, KID. ALL IT TAKES IS YOUR SIGNATURE.
MILLAR/HINDS
YEAH? YEAH? DOING WHAT?
PRO WRESTLING.
GEE, I WISH I COULD MAKE SOME QUICK MONEY AND STILL BE ABLE TO FACE MY FRIENDS....
IT'S EASY WORK, TANK. GOOD MONEY, TOO.
MILLAR/HINDS
JUST TWO QUICK MONTHS ON THE PRO WRESTLING CIRCUIT. GOOD MONEY, TOO.
ONLY HAVE TO WORK ONE NIGHT A WEEK... GOOD MONEY, TOO.
YOU'D BE ABLE TO GET BACK IN TIME TO DO YOUR WEEKEND SPORTSCAST. AND DID I MENTION THAT IT WAS GOOD MON-?
GET BEHIND ME, MURRAY!
PRO WRESTLING CONTRACT, TANK. FOR ONLY TWO MONTHS. YOU'LL MAKE ENOUGH TO PAY FOR THE NEW SPORTS CAR YOU-
MILLAR/HINDS
I'LL SIGN, I'LL SIGN.
IF-
YEAH?
-IF I DON'T HAVE TO WRESTLE ANYWHERE CLOSER THAN 1,000 MILES TO HOME.
NO SWEAT.
...OF COURSE IT'S A 'LEGITIMATE SPORT,' TANK
HALF-NELSON WRESTLING PROMOTIONS INC. Nelson Frum, President
MILLAR/HINDS
I'D LIKE TO SEE SOME OF THE PEOPLE WHO KEEP CALLING PRO WRESTLING 'FAKE' GET INTO THE RING WITH MY BOYS AND SEE-
HEY, BOSS, THE DELIVERYMEN FROM MAX FACTOR WANT TO KNOW WHERE TO LEAVE THE 55-GALLON DRUM OF BLOOD.
BE WITH YOU IN A SEC.
-AND SEE IF THEY'RE STILL SAYING 'FAKE' THEN.

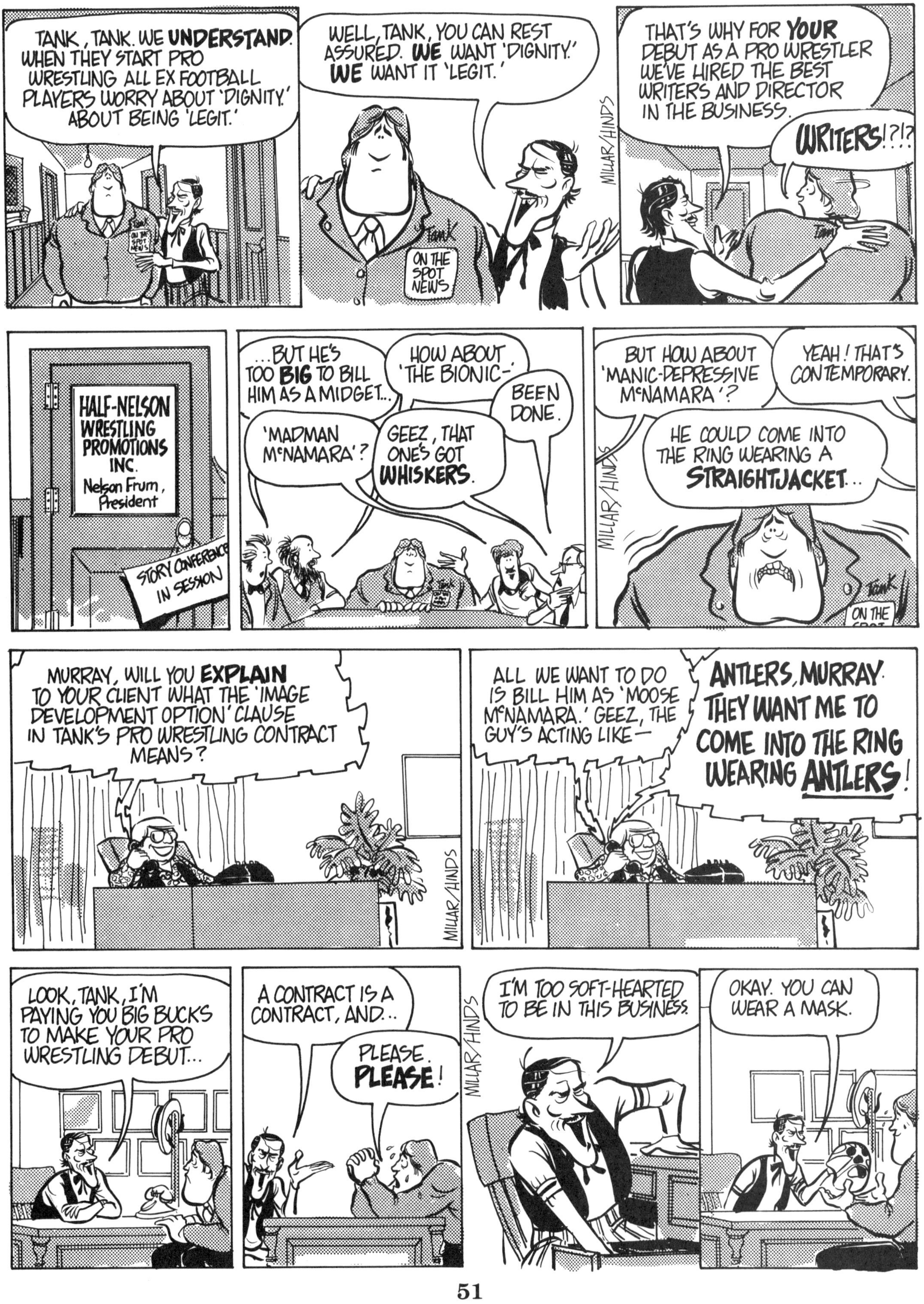
TANK, TANK. WE UNDERSTAND. WHEN THEY START PRO WRESTLING ALL EX FOOTBALL PLAYERS WORRY ABOUT 'DIGNITY.' ABOUT BEING 'LEGIT.'
WELL, TANK, YOU CAN REST ASSURED. WE WANT 'DIGNITY.' WE WANT IT 'LEGIT.'
TANK
ON THE SPOT NEWS
MILLAR/HINDS
THAT'S WHY FOR YOUR DEBUT AS A PRO WRESTLER WE'VE HIRED THE BEST WRITERS AND DIRECTOR IN THE BUSINESS.
WRITERS!?!?
HALF-NELSON WRESTLING PROMOTIONS INC.
Nelson Frum, President
STORY CONFERENCE IN SESSION
...BUT HE'S TOO BIG TO BILL HIM AS A MIDGET...
HOW ABOUT 'THE BIONIC-'
BEEN DONE.
'MADMAN McNAMARA'?
GEEZ, THAT ONE'S GOT WHISKERS.
MILLAR/HINDS
BUT HOW ABOUT 'MANIC-DEPRESSIVE McNAMARA'?
YEAH! THAT'S CONTEMPORARY.
HE COULD COME INTO THE RING WEARING A STRAIGHTJACKET...
MURRAY, WILL YOU EXPLAIN TO YOUR CLIENT WHAT THE 'IMAGE DEVELOPMENT OPTION' CLAUSE IN TANK'S PRO WRESTLING CONTRACT MEANS?
MILLAR/HINDS
ALL WE WANT TO DO IS BILL HIM AS 'MOOSE McNAMARA.' GEEZ, THE GUY'S ACTING LIKE—
ANTLERS, MURRAY. THEY WANT ME TO COME INTO THE RING WEARING ANTLERS!
LOOK, TANK, I'M PAYING YOU BIG BUCKS TO MAKE YOUR PRO WRESTLING DEBUT...
A CONTRACT IS A CONTRACT, AND...
PLEASE. PLEASE!
MILLAR/HINDS
I'M TOO SOFT-HEARTED TO BE IN THIS BUSINESS.
OKAY. YOU CAN WEAR A MASK.

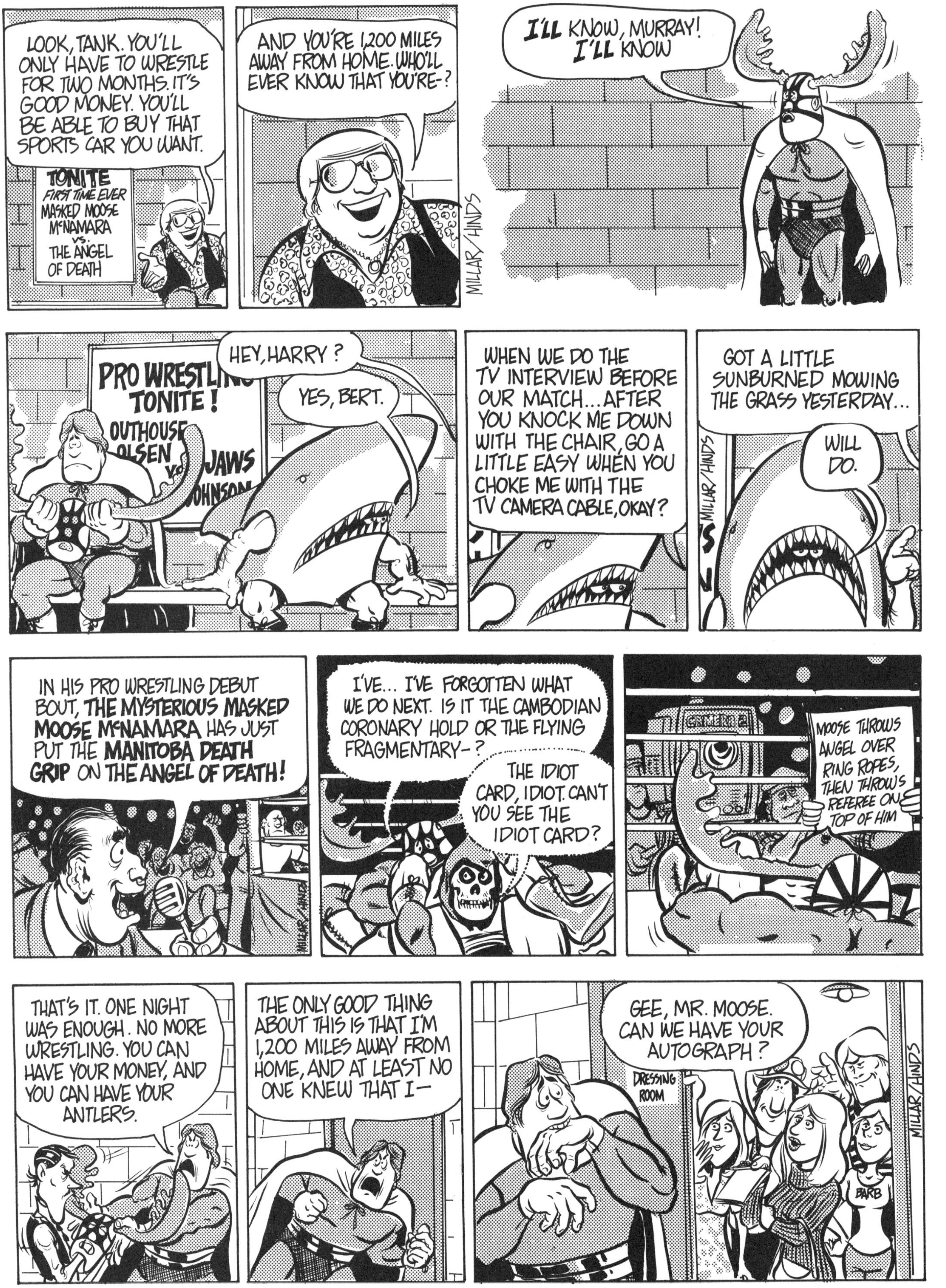
LOOK, TANK. YOU'LL ONLY HAVE TO WRESTLE FOR TWO MONTHS. IT'S GOOD MONEY. YOU'LL BE ABLE TO BUY THAT SPORTS CAR YOU WANT.
TONITE FIRST TIME EVER MASKED MOOSE McNAMARA vs. THE ANGEL OF DEATH
AND YOU'RE 1,200 MILES AWAY FROM HOME. WHO'LL EVER KNOW THAT YOU'RE-?
MILLAR/HINDS
I'LL KNOW, MURRAY! I'LL KNOW
PRO WRESTLING TONITE! OUTHOUSE OLSEN VS JAWS JOHNSON
HEY, HARRY?
YES, BERT.
WHEN WE DO THE TV INTERVIEW BEFORE OUR MATCH... AFTER YOU KNOCK ME DOWN WITH THE CHAIR, GO A LITTLE EASY WHEN YOU CHOKE ME WITH THE TV CAMERA CABLE, OKAY?
GOT A LITTLE SUNBURNED MOWING THE GRASS YESTERDAY...
MILLAR/HINDS
WILL DO.
IN HIS PRO WRESTLING DEBUT BOUT, THE MYSTERIOUS MASKED MOOSE McNAMARA HAS JUST PUT THE MANITOBA DEATH GRIP ON THE ANGEL OF DEATH!
MILLAR/HINDS
I'VE... I'VE FORGOTTEN WHAT WE DO NEXT. IS IT THE CAMBODIAN CORONARY HOLD OR THE FLYING FRAGMENTARY-?
THE IDIOT CARD, IDIOT. CAN'T YOU SEE THE IDIOT CARD?
CAMERA 2
MOOSE THROWS ANGEL OVER RING ROPES, THEN THROWS REFEREE ON TOP OF HIM
THAT'S IT. ONE NIGHT WAS ENOUGH. NO MORE WRESTLING. YOU CAN HAVE YOUR MONEY, AND YOU CAN HAVE YOUR ANTLERS.
THE ONLY GOOD THING ABOUT THIS IS THAT I'M 1,200 MILES AWAY FROM HOME, AND AT LEAST NO ONE KNEW THAT I—
GEE, MR. MOOSE. CAN WE HAVE YOUR AUTOGRAPH?
DRESSING ROOM
BARB
MILLAR/HINDS

TANK McNAMARA

by Jeff Millar & Bill Hinds

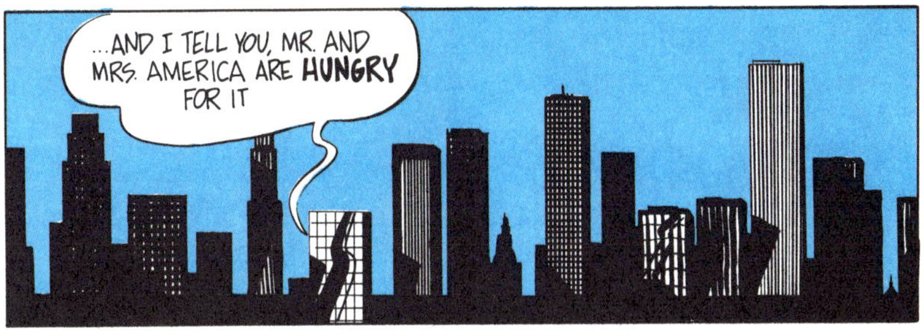

...AND I TELL YOU, MR. AND MRS. AMERICA ARE **HUNGRY** FOR IT

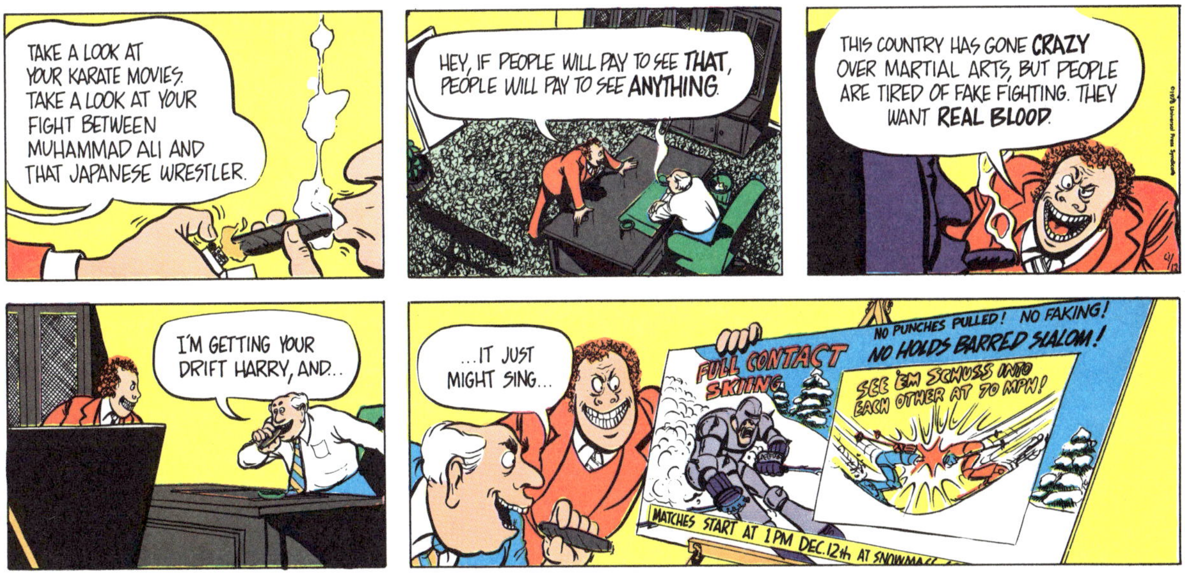

TAKE A LOOK AT YOUR KARATE MOVIES. TAKE A LOOK AT YOUR FIGHT BETWEEN MUHAMMAD ALI AND THAT JAPANESE WRESTLER.
HEY, IF PEOPLE WILL PAY TO SEE **THAT**, PEOPLE WILL PAY TO SEE **ANYTHING**.
THIS COUNTRY HAS GONE **CRAZY** OVER MARTIAL ARTS, BUT PEOPLE ARE TIRED OF FAKE FIGHTING. THEY WANT **REAL BLOOD**.
I'M GETTING YOUR DRIFT HARRY, AND...
...IT JUST MIGHT SING...
NO PUNCHES PULLED! NO FAKING!
NO HOLDS BARRED SLALOM!
FULL CONTACT SKIING
SEE 'EM SCHUSS INTO EACH OTHER AT 70 MPH!
MATCHES START AT 1 PM DEC. 12th AT SNOWMASS

TANK McNAMARA

by Jeff Millar & Bill Hinds

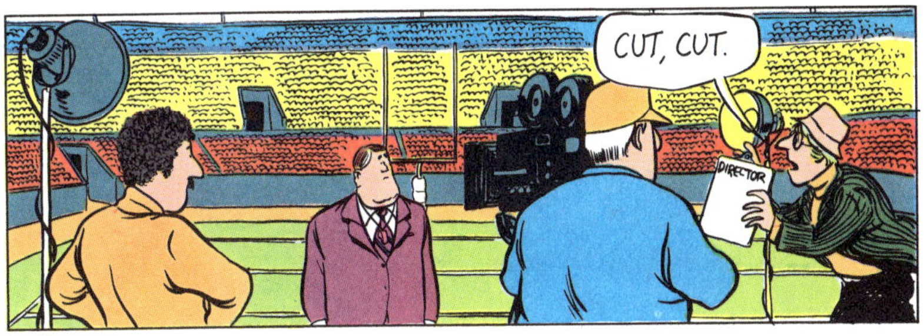

CUT, CUT.
DIRECTOR

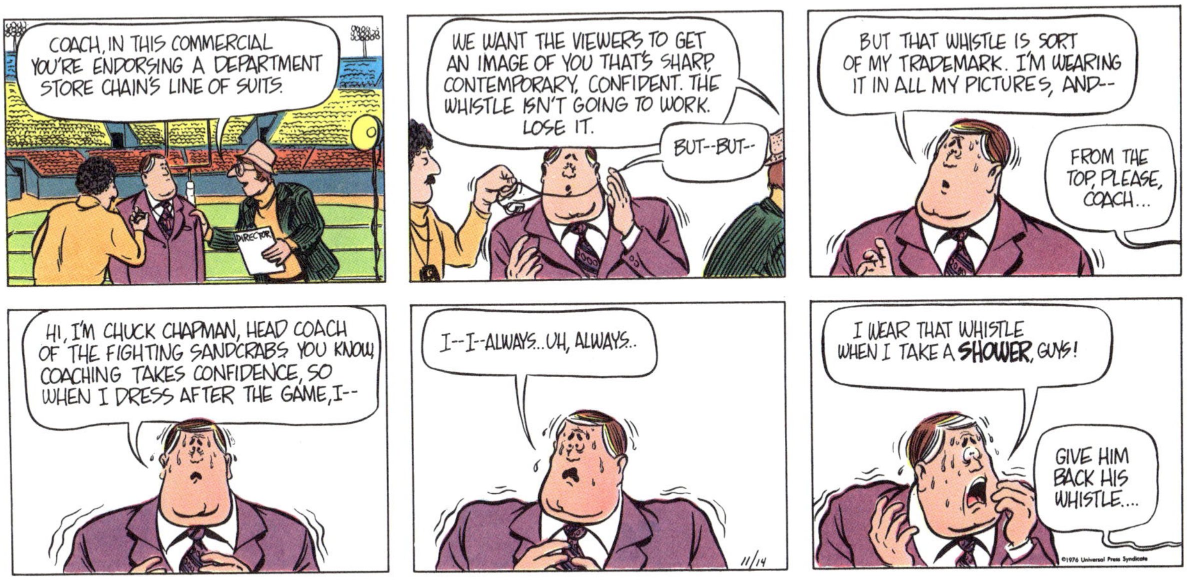

COACH, IN THIS COMMERCIAL YOU'RE ENDORSING A DEPARTMENT STORE CHAIN'S LINE OF SUITS.
DIRECTOR
WE WANT THE VIEWERS TO GET AN IMAGE OF YOU THAT'S SHARP, CONTEMPORARY, CONFIDENT. THE WHISTLE ISN'T GOING TO WORK. LOSE IT.
BUT--BUT--
BUT THAT WHISTLE IS SORT OF MY TRADEMARK. I'M WEARING IT IN ALL MY PICTURES, AND--
FROM THE TOP, PLEASE, COACH...
HI, I'M CHUCK CHAPMAN, HEAD COACH OF THE FIGHTING SANDCRABS. YOU KNOW, COACHING TAKES CONFIDENCE, SO WHEN I DRESS AFTER THE GAME, I--
I--I--ALWAYS...UH, ALWAYS..
I WEAR THAT WHISTLE WHEN I TAKE A **SHOWER**, GUYS!
GIVE HIM BACK HIS WHISTLE....
©1976 Universal Press Syndicate

TANK McNAMARA

by Jeff Millar & Bill Hinds

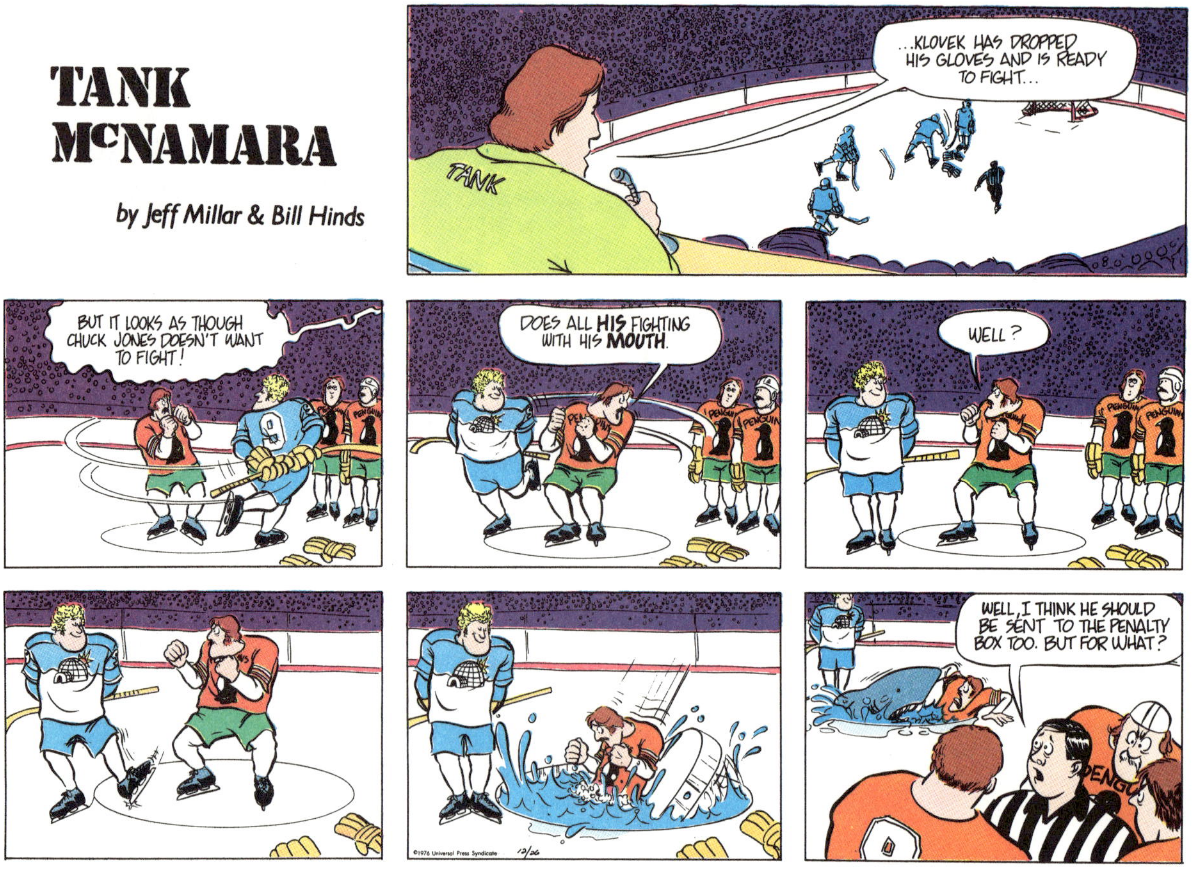

...KLOVEK HAS DROPPED HIS GLOVES AND IS READY TO FIGHT...
TANK
BUT IT LOOKS AS THOUGH CHUCK JONES DOESN'T WANT TO FIGHT!
DOES ALL HIS FIGHTING WITH HIS MOUTH.
WELL?
WELL, I THINK HE SHOULD BE SENT TO THE PENALTY BOX TOO. BUT FOR WHAT?
©1976 Universal Press Syndicate
12/26

TANK McNAMARA

by Jeff Millar & Bill Hinds

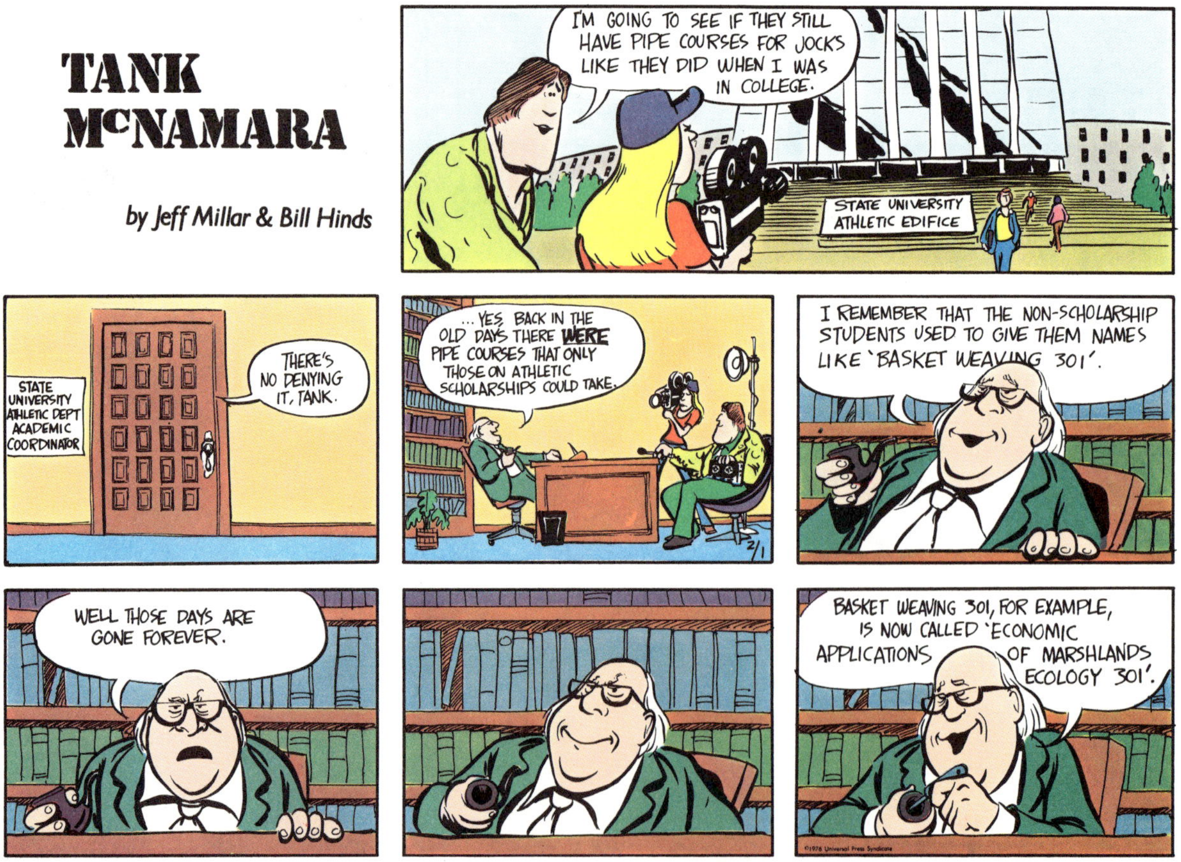

I'M GOING TO SEE IF THEY STILL HAVE PIPE COURSES FOR JOCKS LIKE THEY DID WHEN I WAS IN COLLEGE.
STATE UNIVERSITY ATHLETIC EDIFICE
STATE UNIVERSITY ATHLETIC DEPT ACADEMIC COORDINATOR
THERE'S NO DENYING IT, TANK.
...YES BACK IN THE OLD DAYS THERE WERE PIPE COURSES THAT ONLY THOSE ON ATHLETIC SCHOLARSHIPS COULD TAKE.
2/1
I REMEMBER THAT THE NON-SCHOLARSHIP STUDENTS USED TO GIVE THEM NAMES LIKE 'BASKET WEAVING 301'.
WELL THOSE DAYS ARE GONE FOREVER.
BASKET WEAVING 301, FOR EXAMPLE, IS NOW CALLED 'ECONOMIC APPLICATIONS OF MARSHLANDS ECOLOGY 301'.
©1976 Universal Press Syndicate

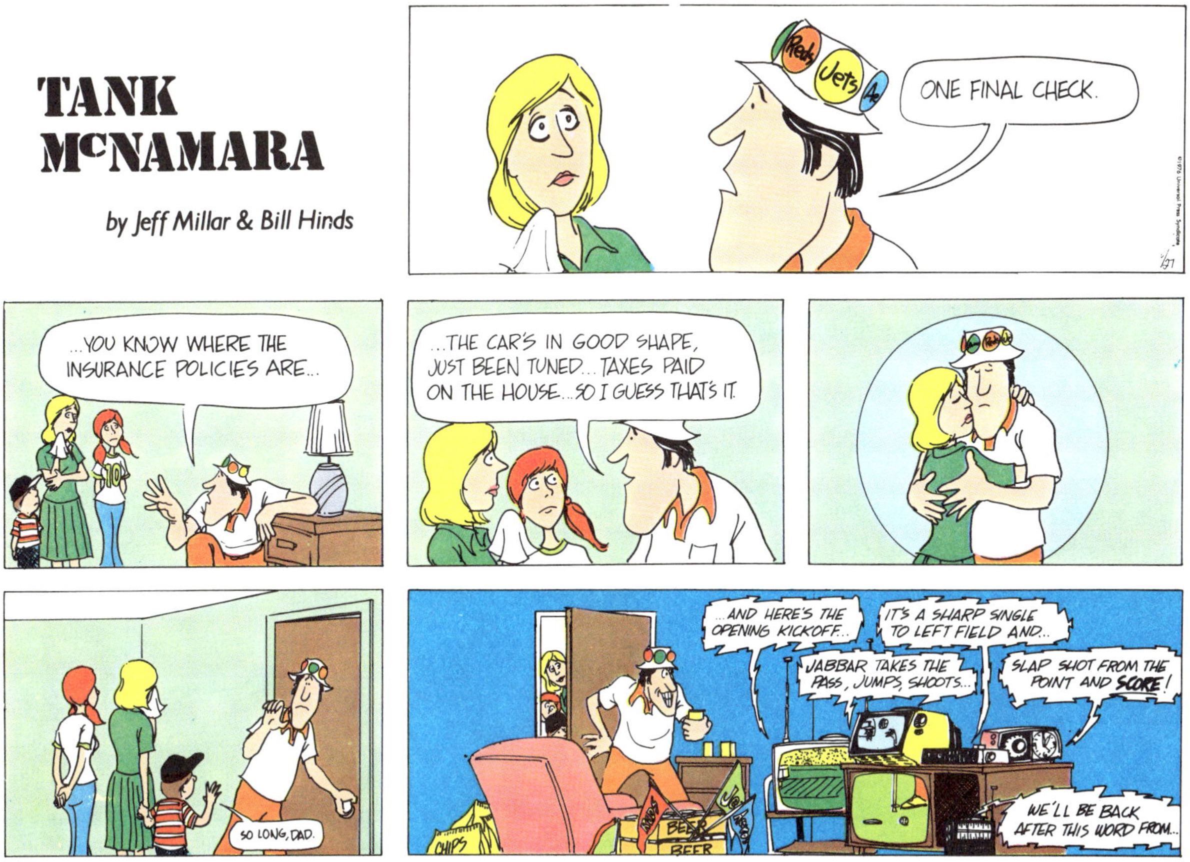
TANK McNAMARA
by Jeff Millar & Bill Hinds
ONE FINAL CHECK.
...YOU KNOW WHERE THE INSURANCE POLICIES ARE...
...THE CAR'S IN GOOD SHAPE, JUST BEEN TUNED... TAXES PAID ON THE HOUSE...SO I GUESS THAT'S IT.
SO LONG, DAD.
...AND HERE'S THE OPENING KICKOFF...
IT'S A SHARP SINGLE TO LEFT FIELD AND...
JABBAR TAKES THE PASS, JUMPS, SHOOTS...
SLAP SHOT FROM THE POINT AND SCORE!
WE'LL BE BACK AFTER THIS WORD FROM...
CHIPS
BEER
BEER

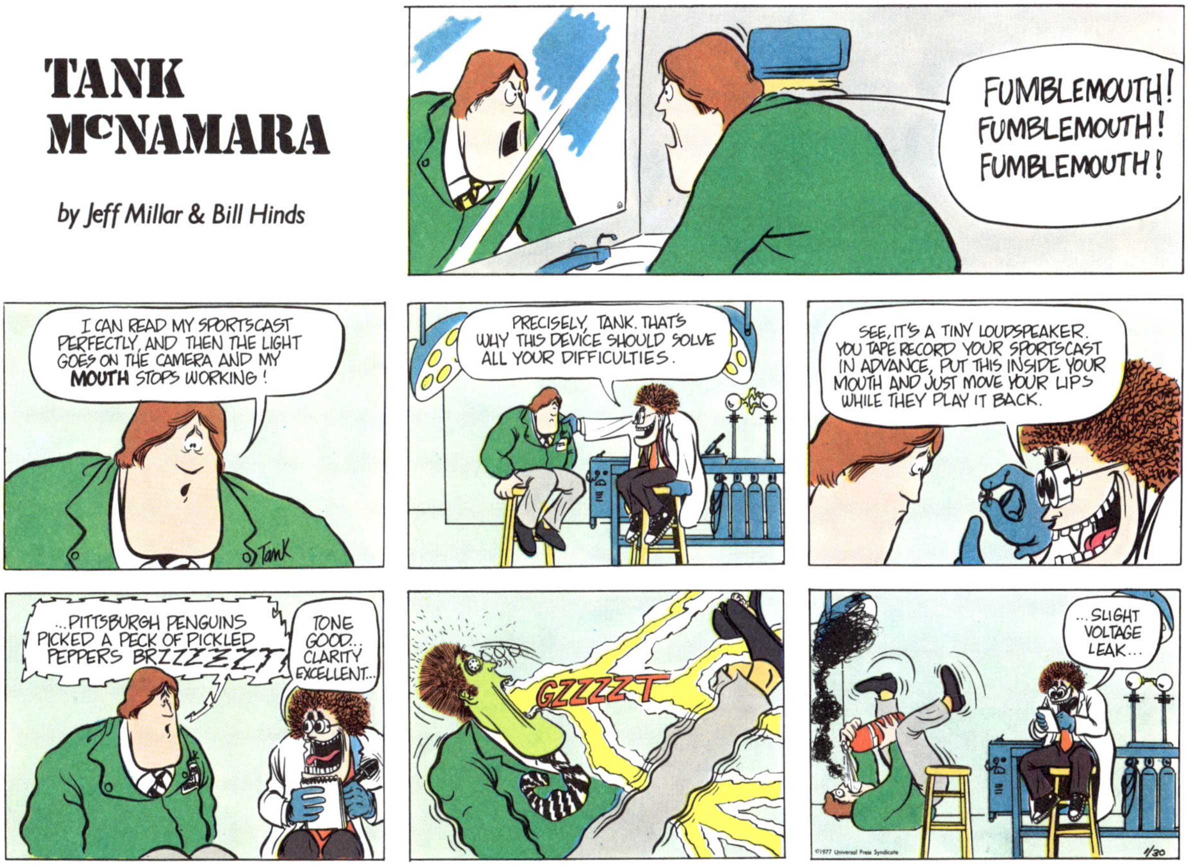
TANK McNAMARA
by Jeff Millar & Bill Hinds
FUMBLEMOUTH! FUMBLEMOUTH! FUMBLEMOUTH!
I CAN READ MY SPORTSCAST PERFECTLY, AND THEN THE LIGHT GOES ON THE CAMERA AND MY MOUTH STOPS WORKING!
Tank
PRECISELY, TANK. THAT'S WHY THIS DEVICE SHOULD SOLVE ALL YOUR DIFFICULTIES.
SEE, IT'S A TINY LOUDSPEAKER. YOU TAPE RECORD YOUR SPORTSCAST IN ADVANCE, PUT THIS INSIDE YOUR MOUTH AND JUST MOVE YOUR LIPS WHILE THEY PLAY IT BACK.
...PITTSBURGH PENGUINS PICKED A PECK OF PICKLED PEPPERS BRZZZZZT!
TONE GOOD... CLARITY EXCELLENT...
GZZZZT
...SLIGHT VOLTAGE LEAK...
©1977 Universal Press Syndicate
1/30

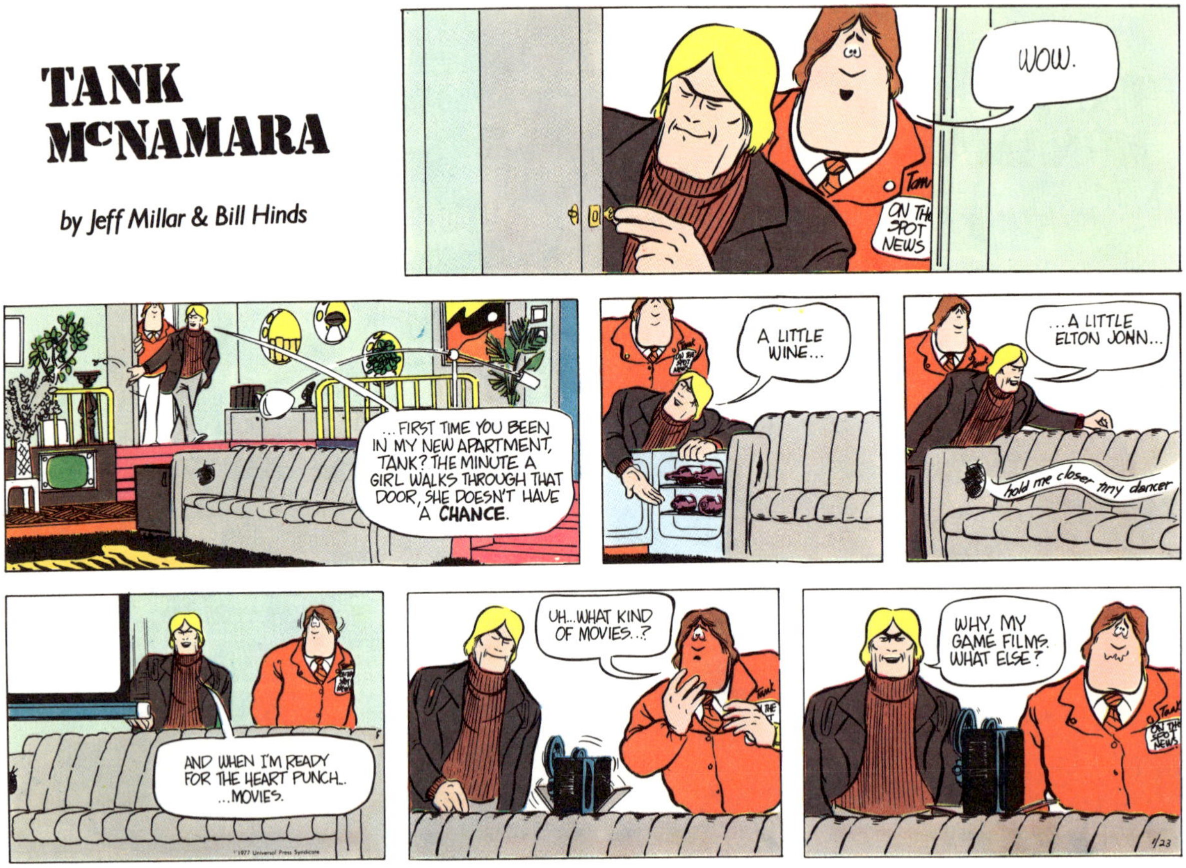
TANK McNAMARA
by Jeff Millar & Bill Hinds
WOW.
ON THE SPOT NEWS
...FIRST TIME YOU BEEN IN MY NEW APARTMENT, TANK? THE MINUTE A GIRL WALKS THROUGH THAT DOOR, SHE DOESN'T HAVE A **CHANCE**.
A LITTLE WINE...
...A LITTLE ELTON JOHN...
hold me closer tiny dancer
AND WHEN I'M READY FOR THE HEART PUNCH... ...MOVIES.
©1977 Universal Press Syndicate
UH...WHAT KIND OF MOVIES..?
WHY, MY GAME FILMS. WHAT ELSE?
1/23

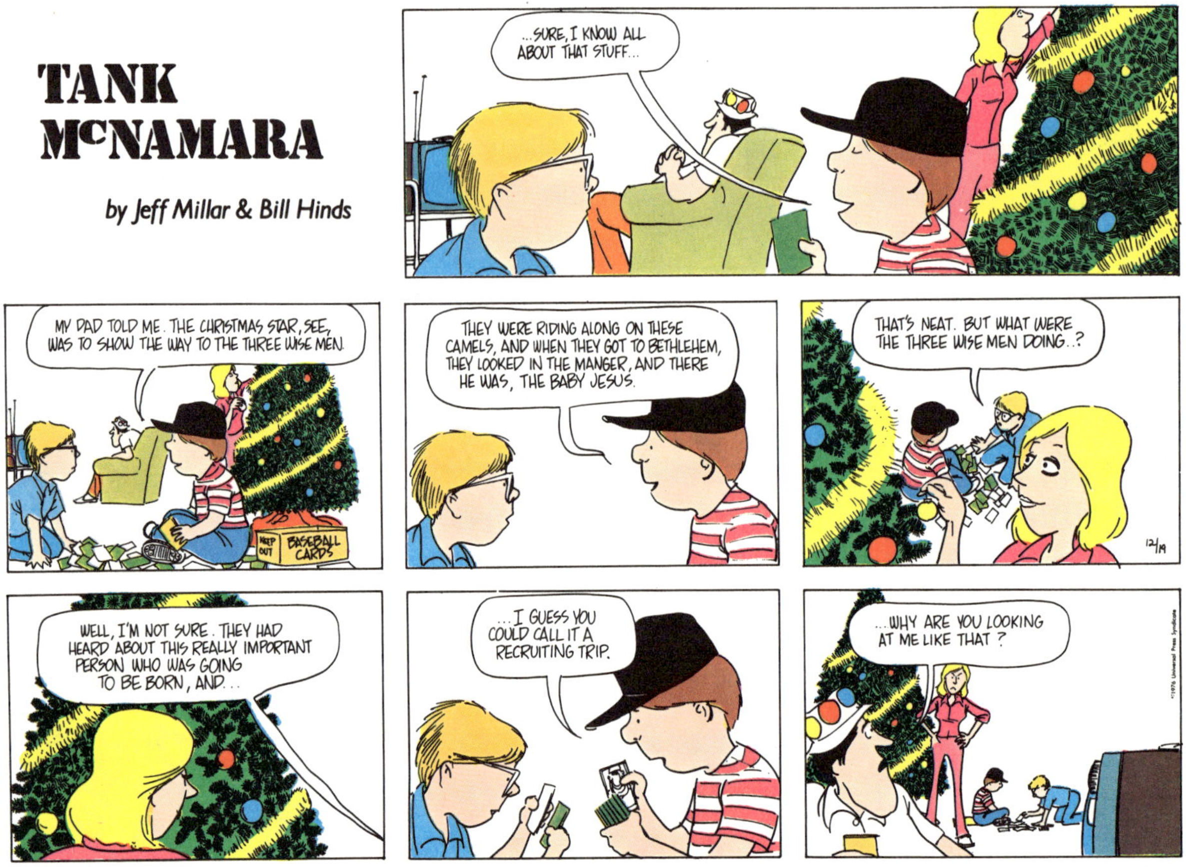
TANK McNAMARA
by Jeff Millar & Bill Hinds
...SURE, I KNOW ALL ABOUT THAT STUFF...
MY DAD TOLD ME. THE CHRISTMAS STAR, SEE, WAS TO SHOW THE WAY TO THE THREE WISE MEN.
KEEP OUT
BASEBALL CARDS
THEY WERE RIDING ALONG ON THESE CAMELS, AND WHEN THEY GOT TO BETHLEHEM, THEY LOOKED IN THE MANGER, AND THERE HE WAS, THE BABY JESUS.
THAT'S NEAT. BUT WHAT WERE THE THREE WISE MEN DOING..?
12/19
WELL, I'M NOT SURE. THEY HAD HEARD ABOUT THIS REALLY IMPORTANT PERSON WHO WAS GOING TO BE BORN, AND...
...I GUESS YOU COULD CALL IT A RECRUITING TRIP.
...WHY ARE YOU LOOKING AT ME LIKE THAT?

Bill and I don't have what you'd call exciting bios. I grew up in a small town on the Texas Gulf Coast and learned to be patient with people who say: "Reeely? You don't *talk* like a Texan...." I never shipped out on a tramp steamer or fought as a mercenary in a country with a funny name. I went to college and graduated and got married and got the same job I have today. I don't see Warner Bros. taking an option on my life story as a vehicle for Clint Eastwood. Sorry. I sit at a typewriter and type. Whoopee. I can fly an airplane. Best I can do for color.

If you thought athletics were important where you grew up, try growing up in a small Texas town in the fifties, where whether or not you were a football/basketball player *mattered*. Not that *I* cared that the prettiest girls in school wore the athletic letter jackets of their boyfriends. I had to wear my sweater myself (and it was just a sweater besides, no leather sleeves), and it had "drama" monogrammed into the school insignia so that you couldn't cut it off. I couldn't have cared less. Honest. (Ignore the drawing on page 185.)

I'm writing these notes because I'm the "words-guy" of the collaboration. Bill defers to me to talk about *Tank*. Like most artists, Bill thinks in images; he could probably *draw* how he feels about his work. He truly thinks in cartoons and apparently always has: Bill and I were being interviewed on radio at half-time during a football game. "We give our guests a sports coat for appearing on the show," said the host during a commercial. "What size should they send you?" Bill said: "Uh, well, I guess it'll have to be an 88 long with four sleeves...."

Bill was born in 1950 and is eight years younger than I. Big (about six-foot-two, two hundred pounds) and blond, he shares an apartment with a cranky yellow bird named Spot. He's a city kid, a doctor's son, grew up in a bland Houston suburb. He always remembers drawing. He told me once that his earliest, unvarying dream was to draw a syndicated comic strip. He had it by the time he was 23 years old. Neat, huh? When I told Bill that UPS had just offered us a syndication contract, I never saw a look of purer joy pass over any human face.

Tank exhibits only a small portion of Bill's abilities. Bill worked for a while as an artist at the *Chronicle,* where he did marvelous, inventive illustrations for the paper's Sunday magazines in an infinity of different styles. And he was one of the highlights of the guided tours the paper would give to busloads of kids. They'd crowd around his drawing board and would have to be dragged away to go look at the presses and more stable things. He would draw Tank for them, and then he would draw anything they called out — Mickey Mouse, Snoopy, Spiderman, the Incredible Hulk — while keeping up five simultaneous rushing conversations. For a finale, he would juggle three tennis balls (not very well) and draw a horse looking out at the kids with an exquisitely confused look upon its face while it floated off into the middle distance with a balloon tied around his middle.

"I get along with kids better than I do adults," Bill says. "I guess that doesn't say too much for me, huh?"

It says a lot for him.

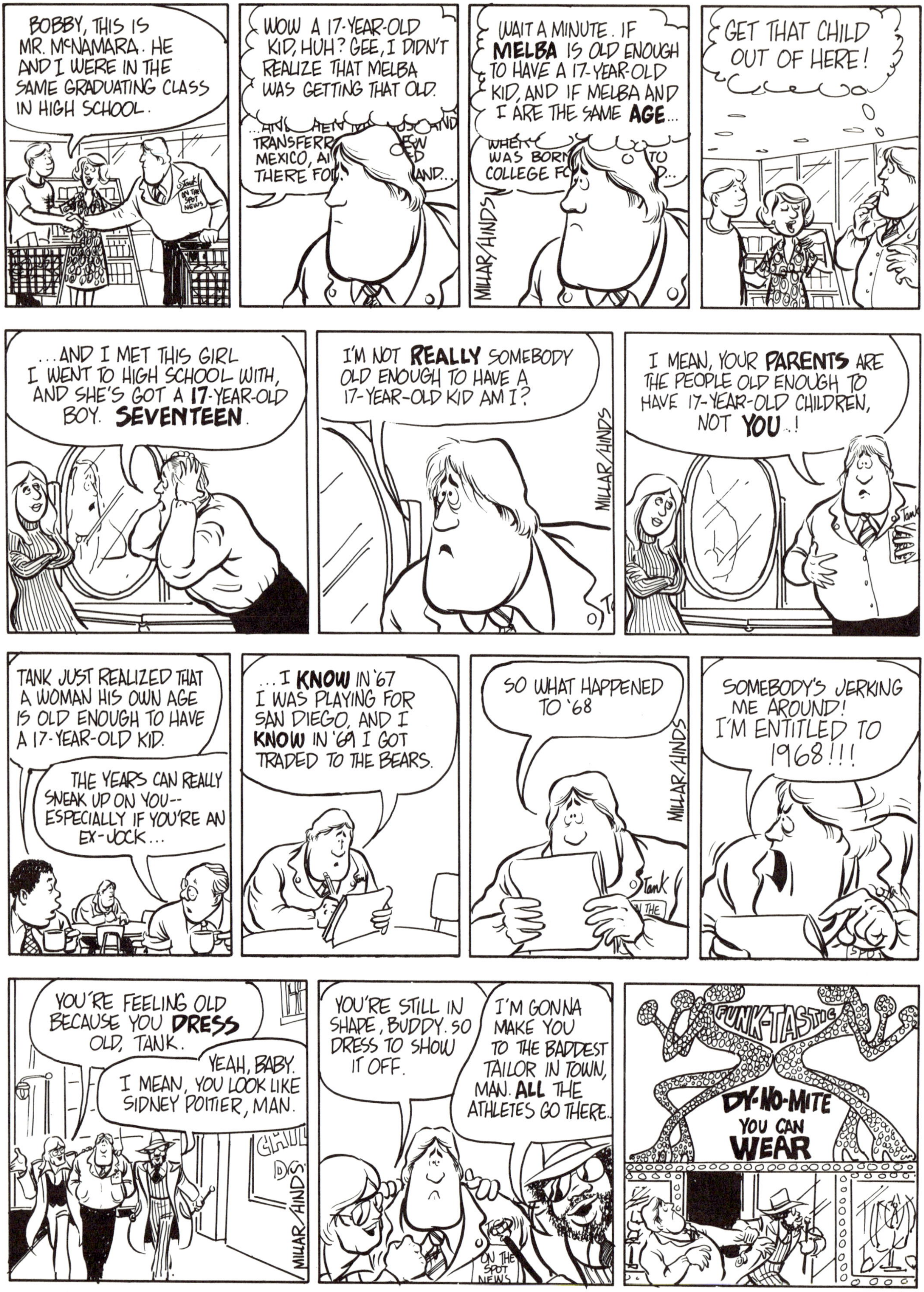
BOBBY, THIS IS MR. McNAMARA. HE AND I WERE IN THE SAME GRADUATING CLASS IN HIGH SCHOOL.
STAN ON THE SPOT NEWS
WOW A 17-YEAR-OLD KID, HUH? GEE, I DIDN'T REALIZE THAT MELBA WAS GETTING THAT OLD.
WAIT A MINUTE. IF MELBA IS OLD ENOUGH TO HAVE A 17-YEAR-OLD KID, AND IF MELBA AND I ARE THE SAME AGE...
MILLAR/HINDS
GET THAT CHILD OUT OF HERE!
...AND I MET THIS GIRL I WENT TO HIGH SCHOOL WITH, AND SHE'S GOT A 17-YEAR-OLD BOY. SEVENTEEN.
I'M NOT REALLY SOMEBODY OLD ENOUGH TO HAVE A 17-YEAR-OLD KID AM I?
MILLAR/HINDS
I MEAN, YOUR PARENTS ARE THE PEOPLE OLD ENOUGH TO HAVE 17-YEAR-OLD CHILDREN, NOT YOU..!
TANK JUST REALIZED THAT A WOMAN HIS OWN AGE IS OLD ENOUGH TO HAVE A 17-YEAR-OLD KID.
THE YEARS CAN REALLY SNEAK UP ON YOU-- ESPECIALLY IF YOU'RE AN EX-JOCK...
...I KNOW IN '67 I WAS PLAYING FOR SAN DIEGO, AND I KNOW IN '69 I GOT TRADED TO THE BEARS.
SO WHAT HAPPENED TO '68
MILLAR/HINDS
SOMEBODY'S JERKING ME AROUND! I'M ENTITLED TO 1968!!!
YOU'RE FEELING OLD BECAUSE YOU DRESS OLD, TANK.
YEAH, BABY. I MEAN, YOU LOOK LIKE SIDNEY POITIER, MAN.
MILLAR/HINDS
YOU'RE STILL IN SHAPE, BUDDY. SO DRESS TO SHOW IT OFF.
I'M GONNA MAKE YOU TO THE BADDEST TAILOR IN TOWN, MAN. ALL THE ATHLETES GO THERE..
ON THE SPOT NEWS
FUNK-TASTIC
DY-NO-MITE YOU CAN WEAR

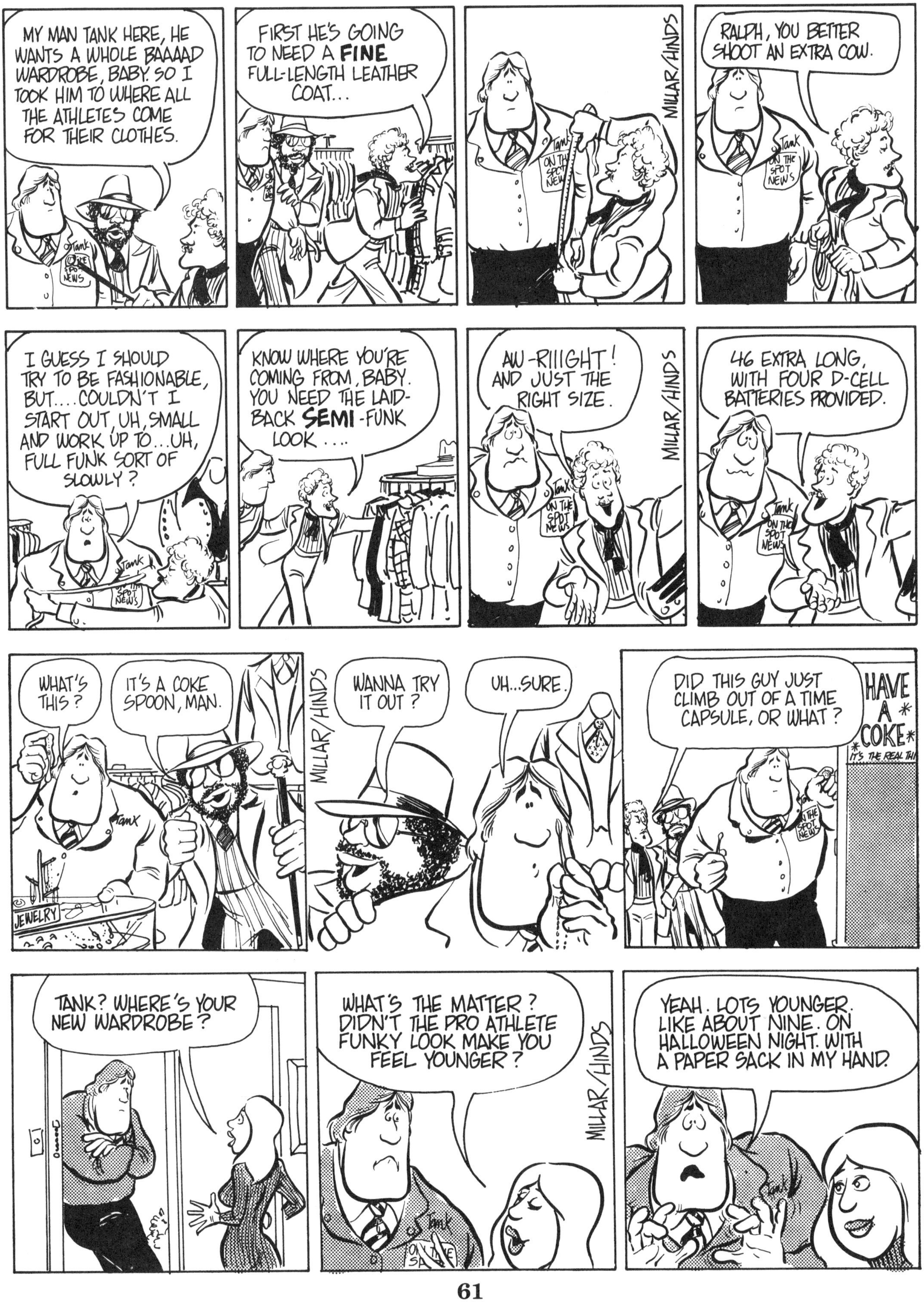
MY MAN TANK HERE, HE WANTS A WHOLE BAAAAD WARDROBE, BABY. SO I TOOK HIM TO WHERE ALL THE ATHLETES COME FOR THEIR CLOTHES.
FIRST HE'S GOING TO NEED A FINE FULL-LENGTH LEATHER COAT...
MILLAR/HINDS
RALPH, YOU BETTER SHOOT AN EXTRA COW.
I GUESS I SHOULD TRY TO BE FASHIONABLE, BUT.... COULDN'T I START OUT, UH, SMALL AND WORK UP TO...UH, FULL FUNK SORT OF SLOWLY?
KNOW WHERE YOU'RE COMING FROM, BABY. YOU NEED THE LAID-BACK SEMI-FUNK LOOK....
AW-RIIIGHT! AND JUST THE RIGHT SIZE.
MILLAR/HINDS
46 EXTRA LONG, WITH FOUR D-CELL BATTERIES PROVIDED.
WHAT'S THIS?
IT'S A COKE SPOON, MAN.
JEWELRY
MILLAR/HINDS
WANNA TRY IT OUT?
UH...SURE.
DID THIS GUY JUST CLIMB OUT OF A TIME CAPSULE, OR WHAT?
HAVE A COKE
TANK? WHERE'S YOUR NEW WARDROBE?
WHAT'S THE MATTER? DIDN'T THE PRO ATHLETE FUNKY LOOK MAKE YOU FEEL YOUNGER?
MILLAR/HINDS
YEAH. LOTS YOUNGER. LIKE ABOUT NINE. ON HALLOWEEN NIGHT. WITH A PAPER SACK IN MY HAND.

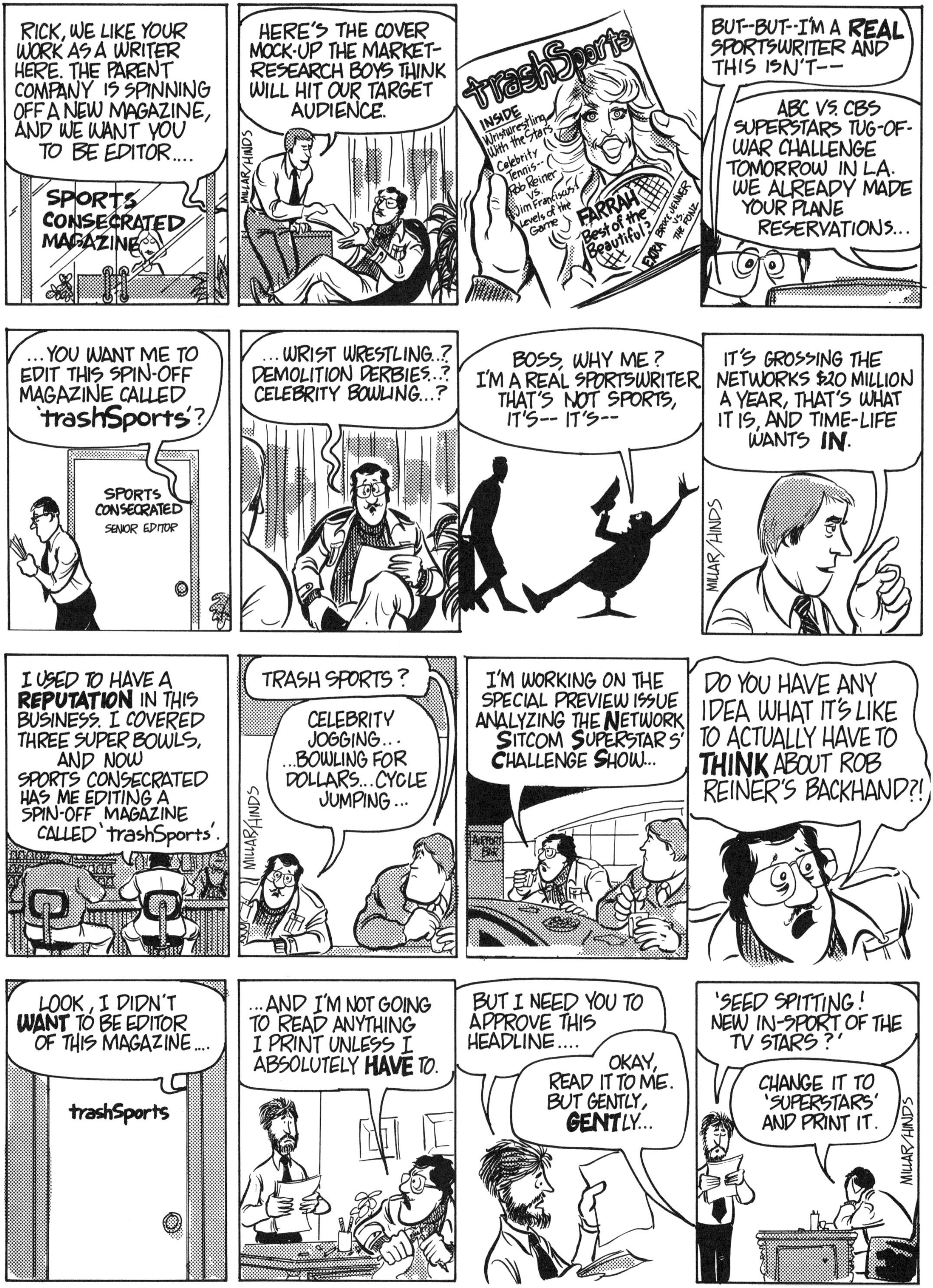
RICK, WE LIKE YOUR WORK AS A WRITER HERE. THE PARENT COMPANY IS SPINNING OFF A NEW MAGAZINE, AND WE WANT YOU TO BE EDITOR....
SPORTS CONSECRATED MAGAZINE
HERE'S THE COVER MOCK-UP THE MARKET-RESEARCH BOYS THINK WILL HIT OUR TARGET AUDIENCE.
MILLAR/HINDS
trashSports
INSIDE
Wristwrestling With the Stars
Celebrity Tennis-- Rob Reiner vs. Jim Franciscus! Levels of the Game
FARRAH Best of the Beautiful?
EXTRA BRUCE JENNER VS. THE FONZ
BUT--BUT--I'M A REAL SPORTSWRITER AND THIS ISN'T--
ABC VS. CBS SUPERSTARS TUG-OF-WAR CHALLENGE TOMORROW IN L.A. WE ALREADY MADE YOUR PLANE RESERVATIONS...
...YOU WANT ME TO EDIT THIS SPIN-OFF MAGAZINE CALLED 'trashSports'?
SPORTS CONSECRATED SENIOR EDITOR
...WRIST WRESTLING..? DEMOLITION DERBIES..? CELEBRITY BOWLING...?
BOSS, WHY ME? I'M A REAL SPORTSWRITER. THAT'S NOT SPORTS, IT'S-- IT'S--
IT'S GROSSING THE NETWORKS $20 MILLION A YEAR, THAT'S WHAT IT IS, AND TIME-LIFE WANTS IN.
MILLAR/HINDS
I USED TO HAVE A REPUTATION IN THIS BUSINESS. I COVERED THREE SUPER BOWLS, AND NOW SPORTS CONSECRATED HAS ME EDITING A SPIN-OFF MAGAZINE CALLED 'trashSports'.
TRASH SPORTS?
CELEBRITY JOGGING... ...BOWLING FOR DOLLARS...CYCLE JUMPING...
MILLAR/HINDS
I'M WORKING ON THE SPECIAL PREVIEW ISSUE ANALYZING THE NETWORK SITCOM SUPERSTARS' CHALLENGE SHOW...
DO YOU HAVE ANY IDEA WHAT IT'S LIKE TO ACTUALLY HAVE TO THINK ABOUT ROB REINER'S BACKHAND?!
LOOK, I DIDN'T WANT TO BE EDITOR OF THIS MAGAZINE....
trashSports
...AND I'M NOT GOING TO READ ANYTHING I PRINT UNLESS I ABSOLUTELY HAVE TO.
BUT I NEED YOU TO APPROVE THIS HEADLINE....
OKAY, READ IT TO ME. BUT GENTLY, GENTLY...
'SEED SPITTING! NEW IN-SPORT OF THE TV STARS?'
CHANGE IT TO 'SUPERSTARS' AND PRINT IT.
MILLAR/HINDS

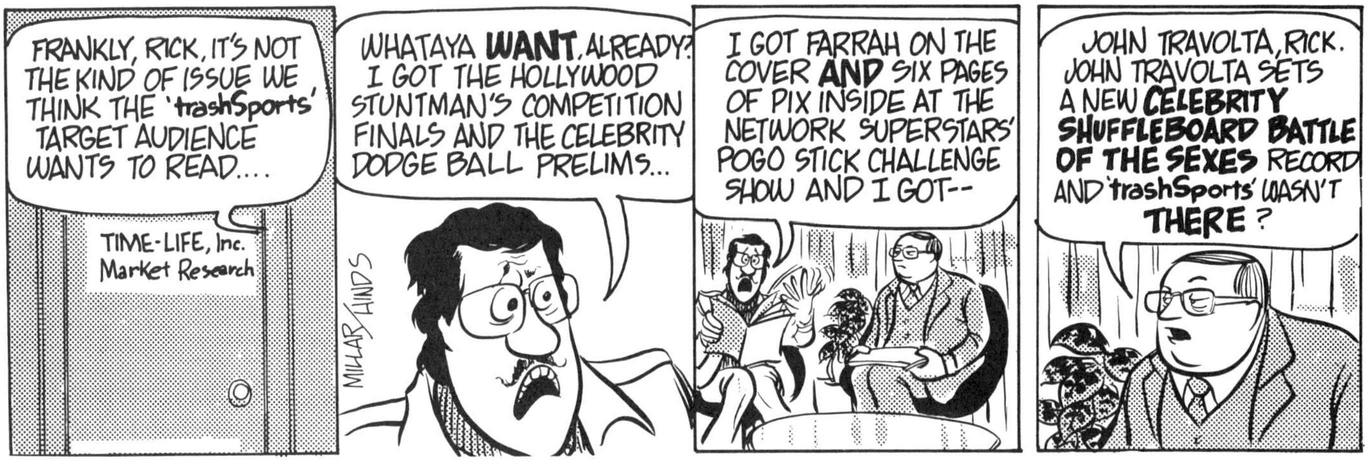
FRANKLY, RICK, IT'S NOT THE KIND OF ISSUE WE THINK THE 'trashSports' TARGET AUDIENCE WANTS TO READ....
TIME-LIFE, Inc. Market Research
WHATAYA WANT, ALREADY? I GOT THE HOLLYWOOD STUNTMAN'S COMPETITION FINALS AND THE CELEBRITY DODGE BALL PRELIMS...
MILLAR/HINDS
I GOT FARRAH ON THE COVER AND SIX PAGES OF PIX INSIDE AT THE NETWORK SUPERSTARS' POGO STICK CHALLENGE SHOW AND I GOT--
JOHN TRAVOLTA, RICK. JOHN TRAVOLTA SETS A NEW CELEBRITY SHUFFLEBOARD BATTLE OF THE SEXES RECORD AND 'trashSports' WASN'T THERE?

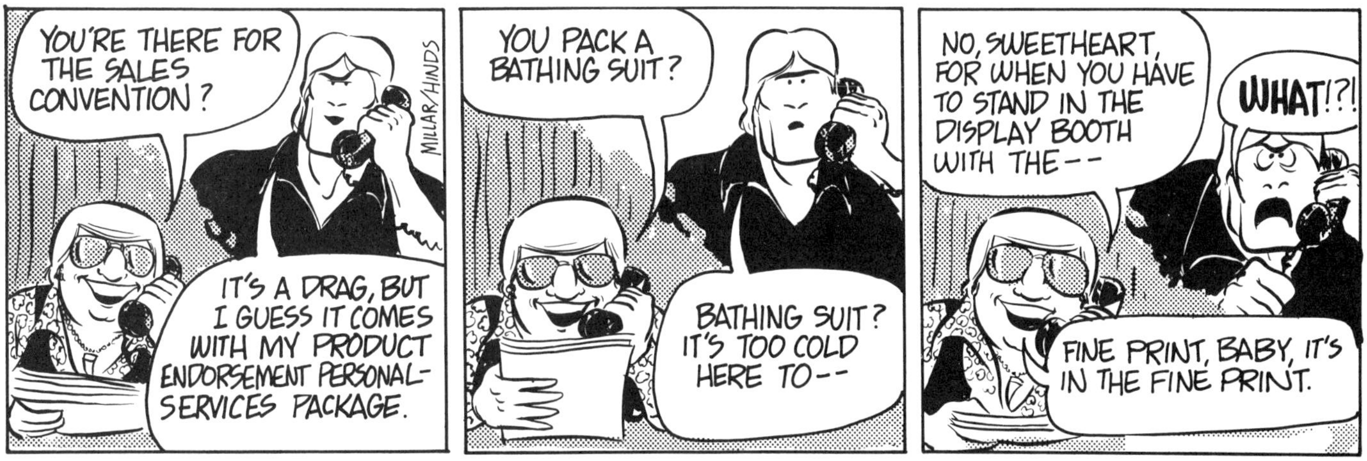
YOU'RE THERE FOR THE SALES CONVENTION?
MILLAR/HINDS
IT'S A DRAG, BUT I GUESS IT COMES WITH MY PRODUCT ENDORSEMENT PERSONAL-SERVICES PACKAGE.
YOU PACK A BATHING SUIT?
BATHING SUIT? IT'S TOO COLD HERE TO--
NO, SWEETHEART, FOR WHEN YOU HAVE TO STAND IN THE DISPLAY BOOTH WITH THE--
WHAT!?!
FINE PRINT, BABY, IT'S IN THE FINE PRINT.

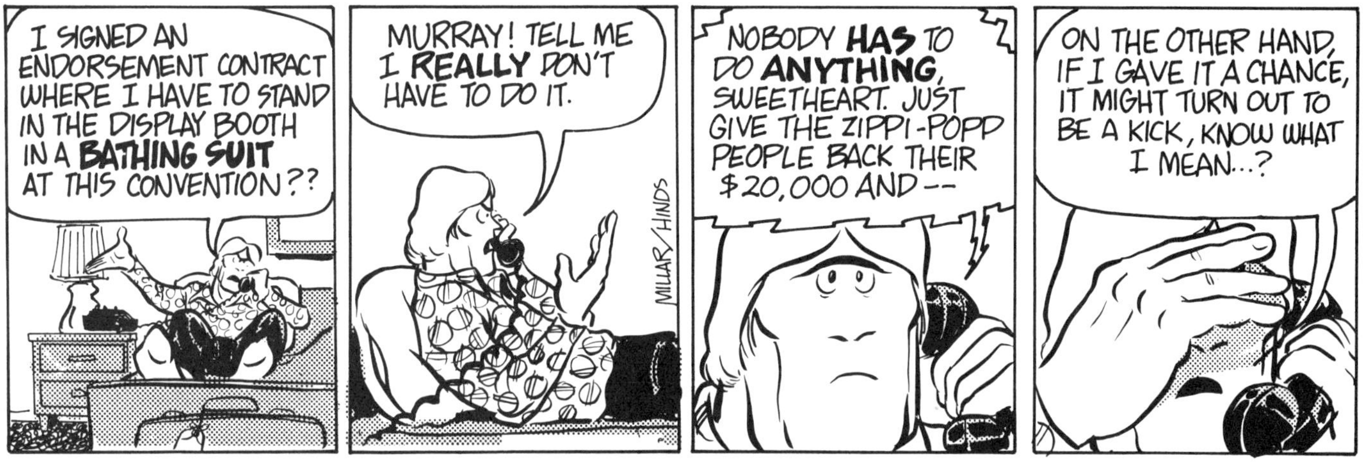
I SIGNED AN ENDORSEMENT CONTRACT WHERE I HAVE TO STAND IN THE DISPLAY BOOTH IN A BATHING SUIT AT THIS CONVENTION??
MURRAY! TELL ME I REALLY DON'T HAVE TO DO IT.
MILLAR/HINDS
NOBODY HAS TO DO ANYTHING, SWEETHEART. JUST GIVE THE ZIPPI-POPP PEOPLE BACK THEIR $20,000 AND--
ON THE OTHER HAND, IF I GAVE IT A CHANCE, IT MIGHT TURN OUT TO BE A KICK, KNOW WHAT I MEAN...?

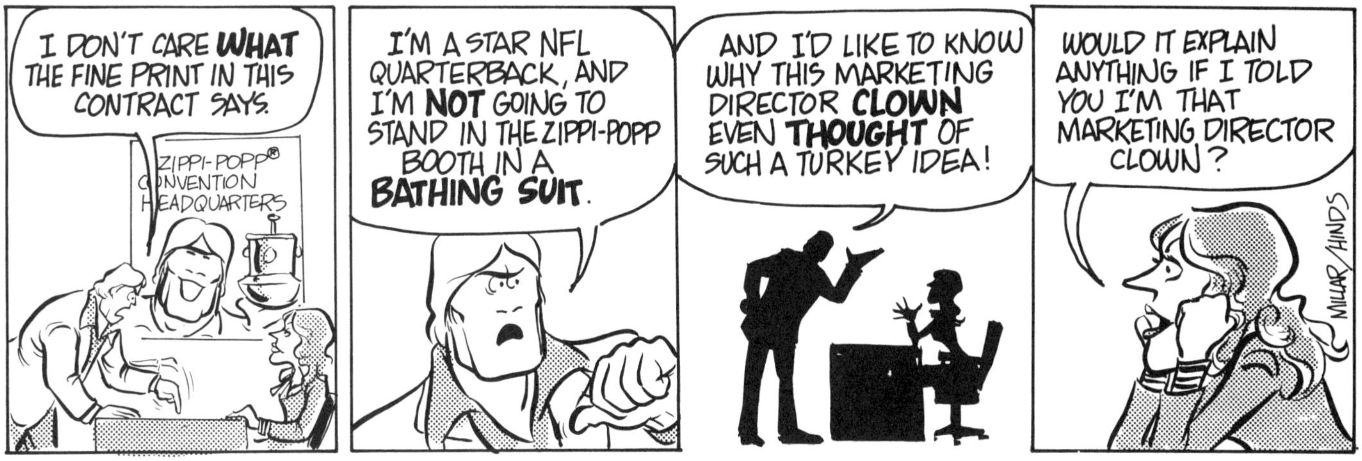
I DON'T CARE WHAT THE FINE PRINT IN THIS CONTRACT SAYS.
ZIPPI-POPP® CONVENTION HEADQUARTERS
I'M A STAR NFL QUARTERBACK, AND I'M NOT GOING TO STAND IN THE ZIPPI-POPP BOOTH IN A BATHING SUIT.
AND I'D LIKE TO KNOW WHY THIS MARKETING DIRECTOR CLOWN EVEN THOUGHT OF SUCH A TURKEY IDEA!
WOULD IT EXPLAIN ANYTHING IF I TOLD YOU I'M THAT MARKETING DIRECTOR CLOWN?
MILLAR/HINDS

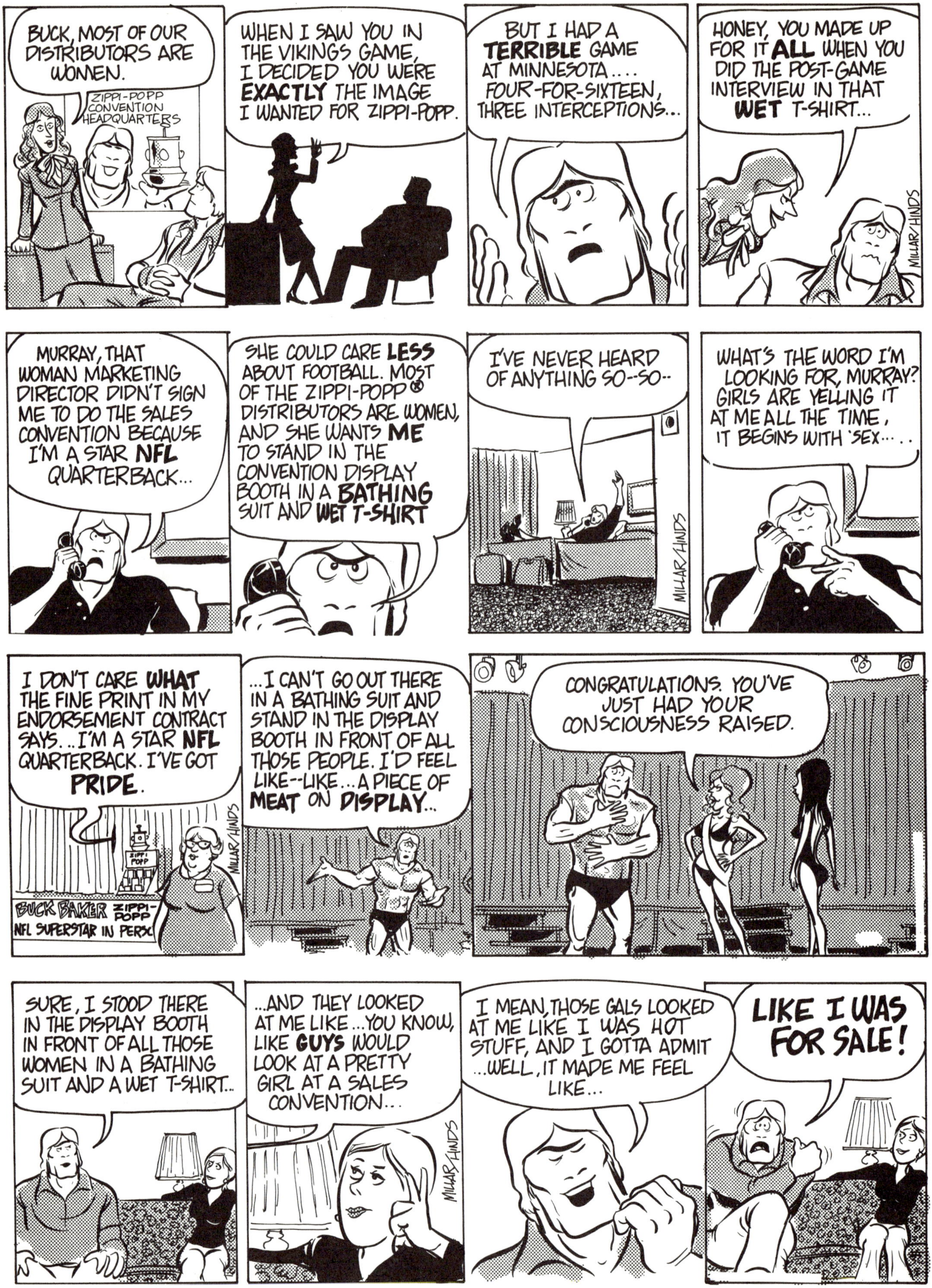
BUCK, MOST OF OUR DISTRIBUTORS ARE WOMEN.
ZIPPI-POPP CONVENTION HEADQUARTERS
WHEN I SAW YOU IN THE VIKINGS GAME, I DECIDED YOU WERE EXACTLY THE IMAGE I WANTED FOR ZIPPI-POPP.
BUT I HAD A TERRIBLE GAME AT MINNESOTA.... FOUR-FOR-SIXTEEN, THREE INTERCEPTIONS...
HONEY, YOU MADE UP FOR IT ALL WHEN YOU DID THE POST-GAME INTERVIEW IN THAT WET T-SHIRT...
MILLAR/HINDS
MURRAY, THAT WOMAN MARKETING DIRECTOR DIDN'T SIGN ME TO DO THE SALES CONVENTION BECAUSE I'M A STAR NFL QUARTERBACK...
SHE COULD CARE LESS ABOUT FOOTBALL. MOST OF THE ZIPPI-POPP® DISTRIBUTORS ARE WOMEN, AND SHE WANTS ME TO STAND IN THE CONVENTION DISPLAY BOOTH IN A BATHING SUIT AND WET T-SHIRT
I'VE NEVER HEARD OF ANYTHING SO--SO--
MILLAR/HINDS
WHAT'S THE WORD I'M LOOKING FOR, MURRAY? GIRLS ARE YELLING IT AT ME ALL THE TIME, IT BEGINS WITH 'SEX'....
I DON'T CARE WHAT THE FINE PRINT IN MY ENDORSEMENT CONTRACT SAYS... I'M A STAR NFL QUARTERBACK. I'VE GOT PRIDE.
ZIPPI-POPP
BUCK BAKER ZIPPI-POPP
NFL SUPERSTAR IN PERS
MILLAR/HINDS
...I CAN'T GO OUT THERE IN A BATHING SUIT AND STAND IN THE DISPLAY BOOTH IN FRONT OF ALL THOSE PEOPLE. I'D FEEL LIKE--LIKE... A PIECE OF MEAT ON DISPLAY...
CONGRATULATIONS. YOU'VE JUST HAD YOUR CONSCIOUSNESS RAISED.
SURE, I STOOD THERE IN THE DISPLAY BOOTH IN FRONT OF ALL THOSE WOMEN IN A BATHING SUIT AND A WET T-SHIRT...
...AND THEY LOOKED AT ME LIKE ...YOU KNOW, LIKE GUYS WOULD LOOK AT A PRETTY GIRL AT A SALES CONVENTION...
MILLAR/HINDS
I MEAN, THOSE GALS LOOKED AT ME LIKE I WAS HOT STUFF, AND I GOTTA ADMIT ...WELL, IT MADE ME FEEL LIKE...
LIKE I WAS FOR SALE!

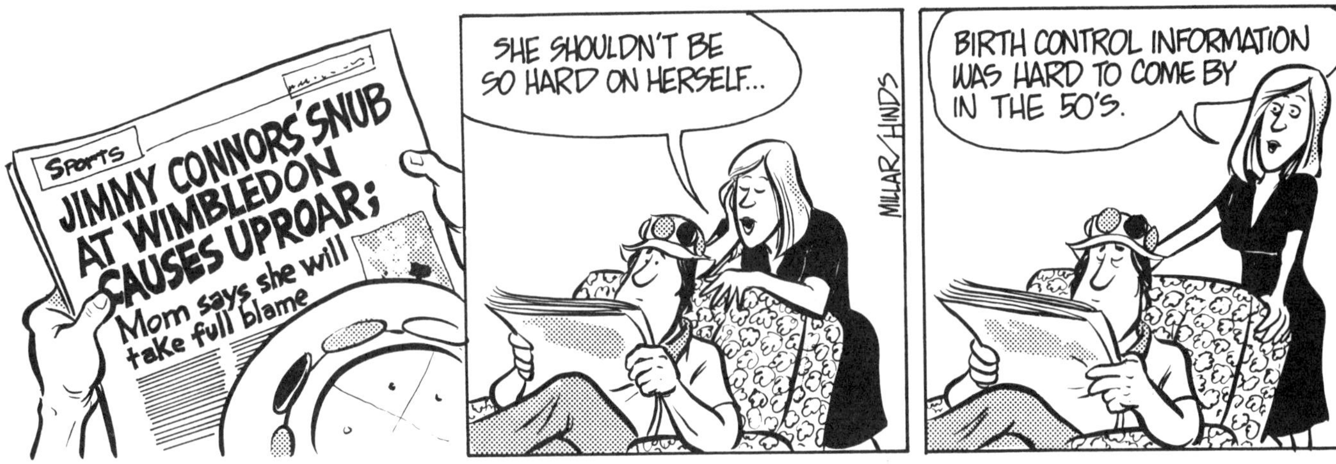
SPORTS
JIMMY CONNORS' SNUB AT WIMBLEDON CAUSES UPROAR;
Mom says she will take full blame
SHE SHOULDN'T BE SO HARD ON HERSELF...
MILLAR/HINDS
BIRTH CONTROL INFORMATION WAS HARD TO COME BY IN THE 50'S.

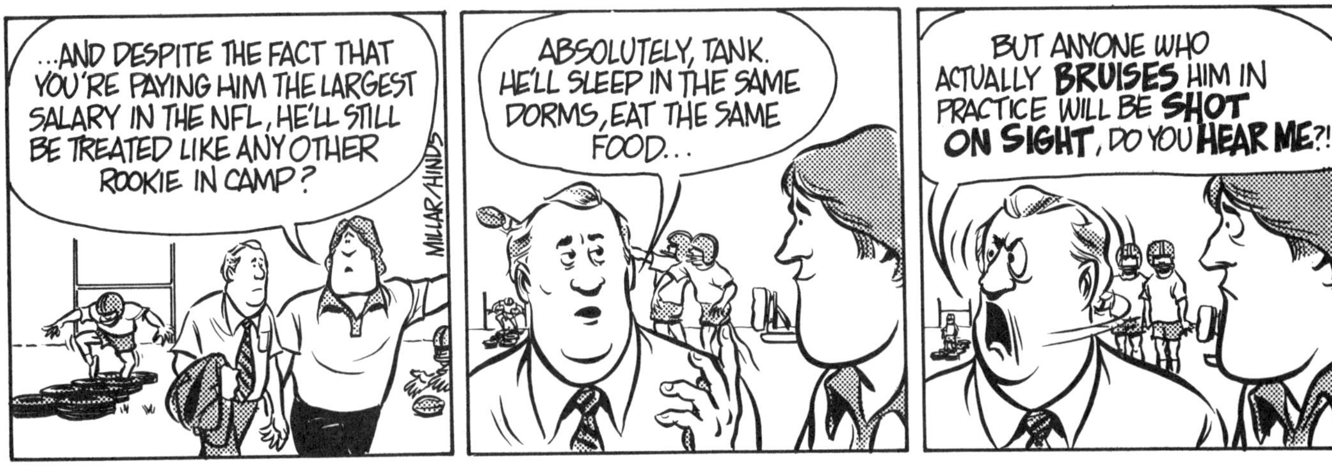
...AND DESPITE THE FACT THAT YOU'RE PAYING HIM THE LARGEST SALARY IN THE NFL, HE'LL STILL BE TREATED LIKE ANY OTHER ROOKIE IN CAMP?
MILLAR/HINDS
ABSOLUTELY, TANK. HE'LL SLEEP IN THE SAME DORMS, EAT THE SAME FOOD...
BUT ANYONE WHO ACTUALLY BRUISES HIM IN PRACTICE WILL BE SHOT ON SIGHT, DO YOU HEAR ME?!?!

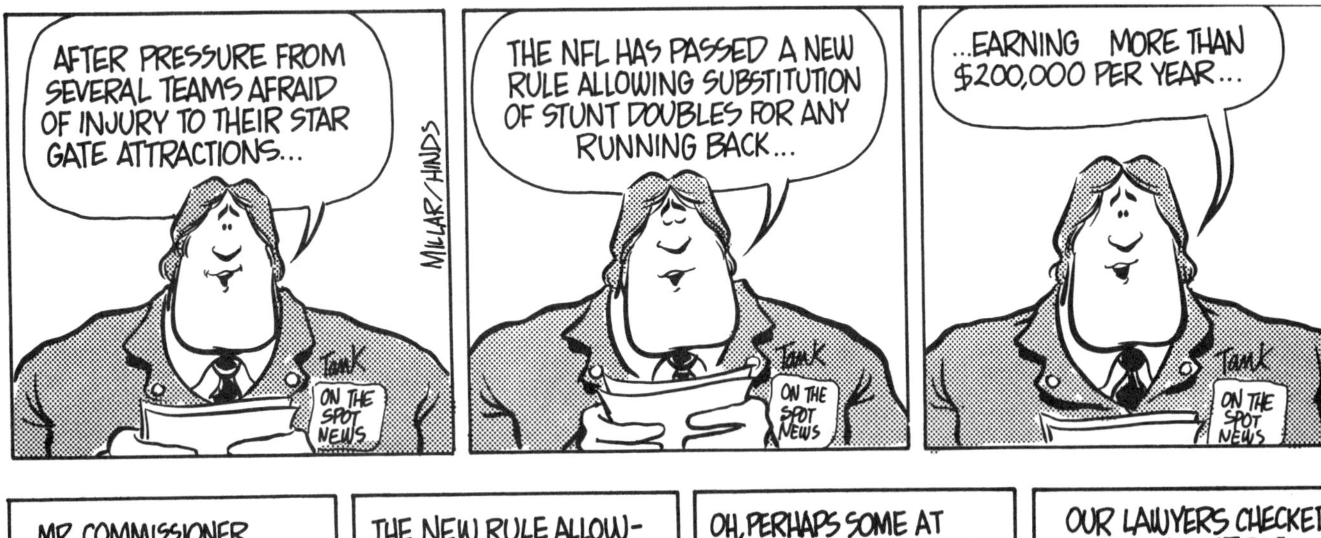
AFTER PRESSURE FROM SEVERAL TEAMS AFRAID OF INJURY TO THEIR STAR GATE ATTRACTIONS...
MILLAR/HINDS
TANK
ON THE SPOT NEWS
THE NFL HAS PASSED A NEW RULE ALLOWING SUBSTITUTION OF STUNT DOUBLES FOR ANY RUNNING BACK...
TANK
ON THE SPOT NEWS
...EARNING MORE THAN $200,000 PER YEAR...
TANK
ON THE SPOT NEWS

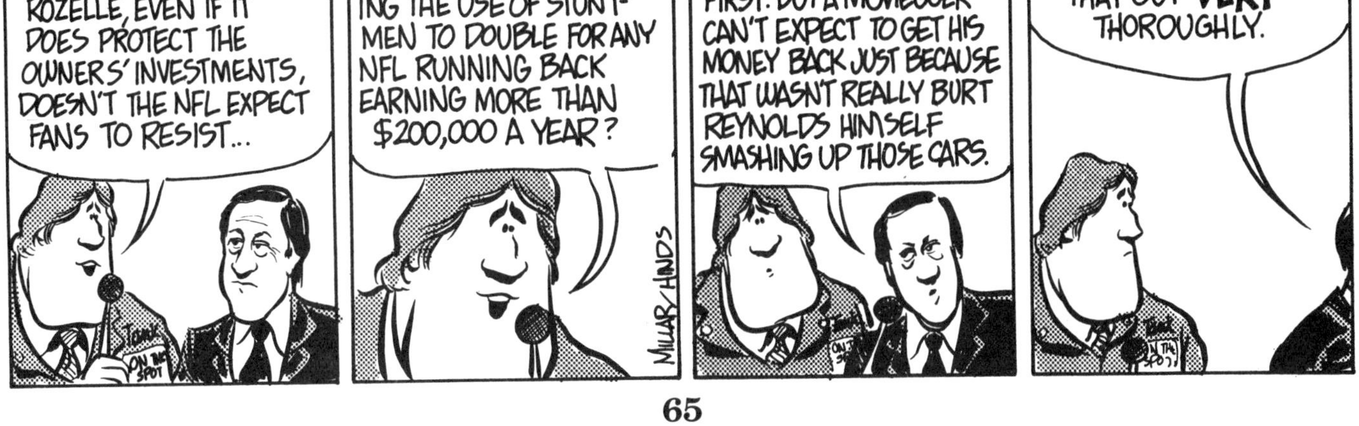
MR. COMMISSIONER ROZELLE, EVEN IF IT DOES PROTECT THE OWNERS' INVESTMENTS, DOESN'T THE NFL EXPECT FANS TO RESIST...
TANK
ON THE SPOT
...THE NEW RULE ALLOWING THE USE OF STUNTMEN TO DOUBLE FOR ANY NFL RUNNING BACK EARNING MORE THAN $200,000 A YEAR?
MILLAR/HINDS
OH, PERHAPS SOME AT FIRST. BUT A MOVIEGOER CAN'T EXPECT TO GET HIS MONEY BACK JUST BECAUSE THAT WASN'T REALLY BURT REYNOLDS HIMSELF SMASHING UP THOSE CARS.
OUR LAWYERS CHECKED THAT OUT VERY THOROUGHLY.

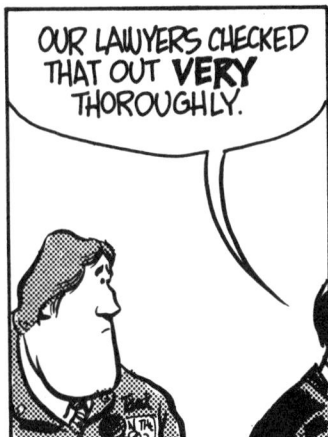

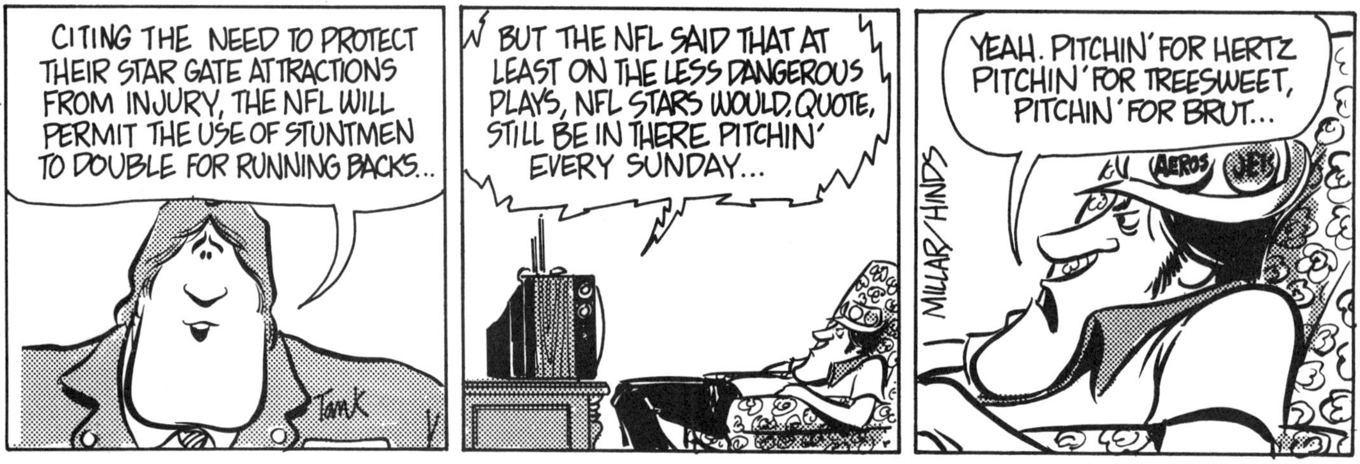
CITING THE NEED TO PROTECT THEIR STAR GATE ATTRACTIONS FROM INJURY, THE NFL WILL PERMIT THE USE OF STUNTMEN TO DOUBLE FOR RUNNING BACKS...
BUT THE NFL SAID THAT AT LEAST ON THE LESS DANGEROUS PLAYS, NFL STARS WOULD, QUOTE, STILL BE IN THERE PITCHIN' EVERY SUNDAY...
YEAH. PITCHIN' FOR HERTZ PITCHIN' FOR TREESWEET, PITCHIN' FOR BRUT...
AEROS
JETS
MILLAR/HINDS

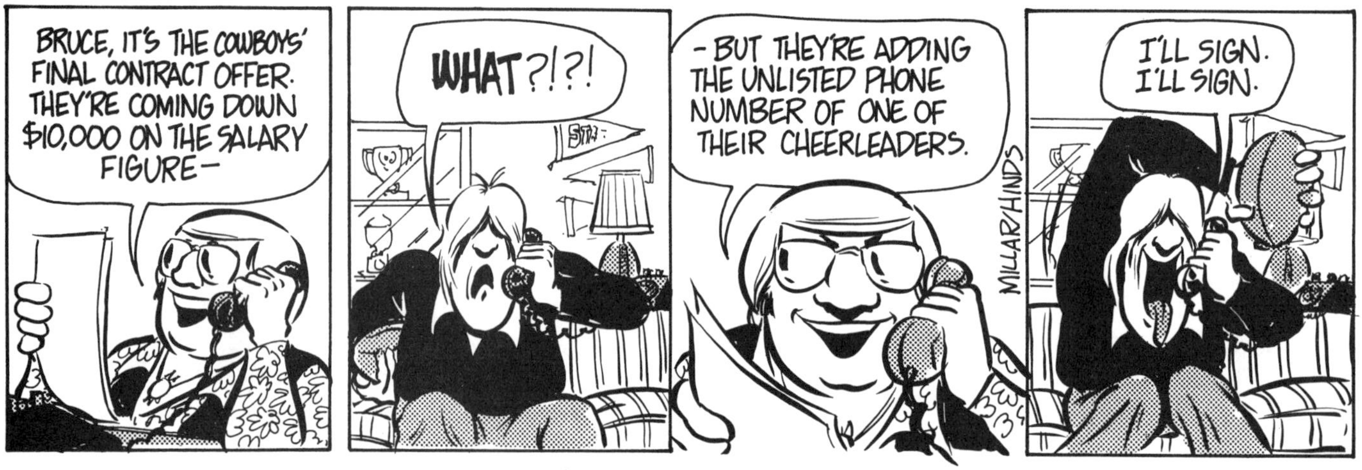
BRUCE, IT'S THE COWBOYS' FINAL CONTRACT OFFER. THEY'RE COMING DOWN $10,000 ON THE SALARY FIGURE—
WHAT?!?!
—BUT THEY'RE ADDING THE UNLISTED PHONE NUMBER OF ONE OF THEIR CHEERLEADERS.
I'LL SIGN. I'LL SIGN.
MILLAR/HINDS

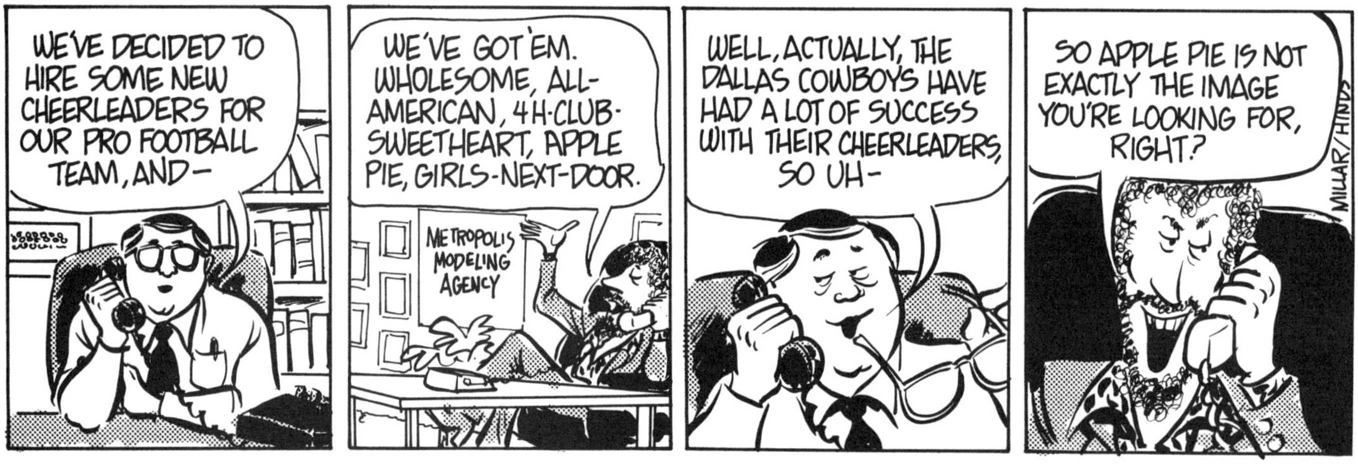
WE'VE DECIDED TO HIRE SOME NEW CHEERLEADERS FOR OUR PRO FOOTBALL TEAM, AND—
WE'VE GOT 'EM. WHOLESOME, ALL-AMERICAN, 4H-CLUB-SWEETHEART, APPLE PIE, GIRLS-NEXT-DOOR.
METROPOLIS MODELING AGENCY
WELL, ACTUALLY, THE DALLAS COWBOYS HAVE HAD A LOT OF SUCCESS WITH THEIR CHEERLEADERS, SO UH—
SO APPLE PIE IS NOT EXACTLY THE IMAGE YOU'RE LOOKING FOR, RIGHT?
MILLAR/HINDS

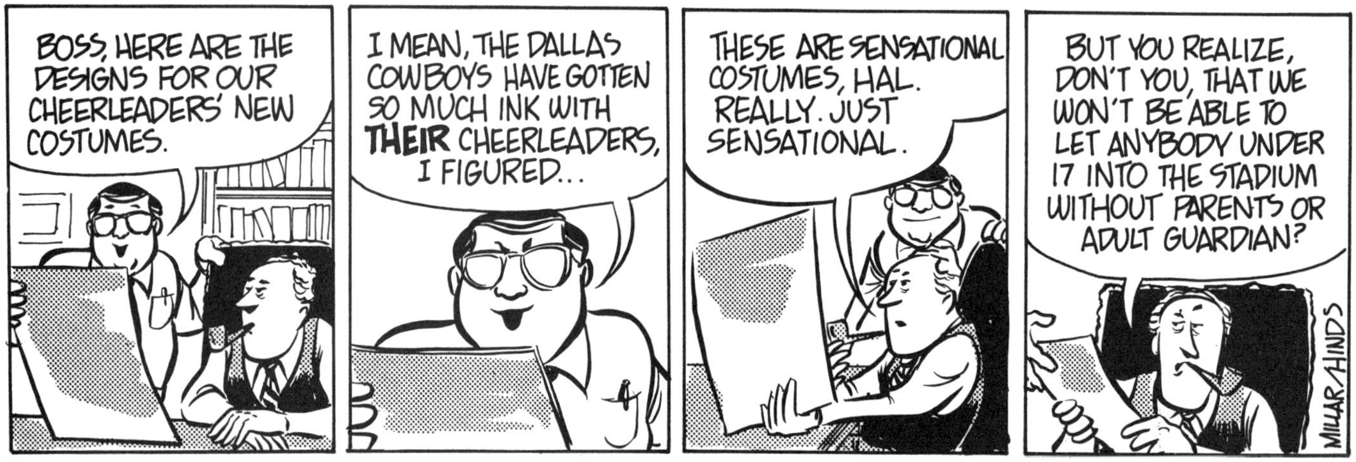
BOSS, HERE ARE THE DESIGNS FOR OUR CHEERLEADERS' NEW COSTUMES.
I MEAN, THE DALLAS COWBOYS HAVE GOTTEN SO MUCH INK WITH THEIR CHEERLEADERS, I FIGURED...
THESE ARE SENSATIONAL COSTUMES, HAL. REALLY. JUST SENSATIONAL.
BUT YOU REALIZE, DON'T YOU, THAT WE WON'T BE ABLE TO LET ANYBODY UNDER 17 INTO THE STADIUM WITHOUT PARENTS OR ADULT GUARDIAN?
MILLAR/HINDS

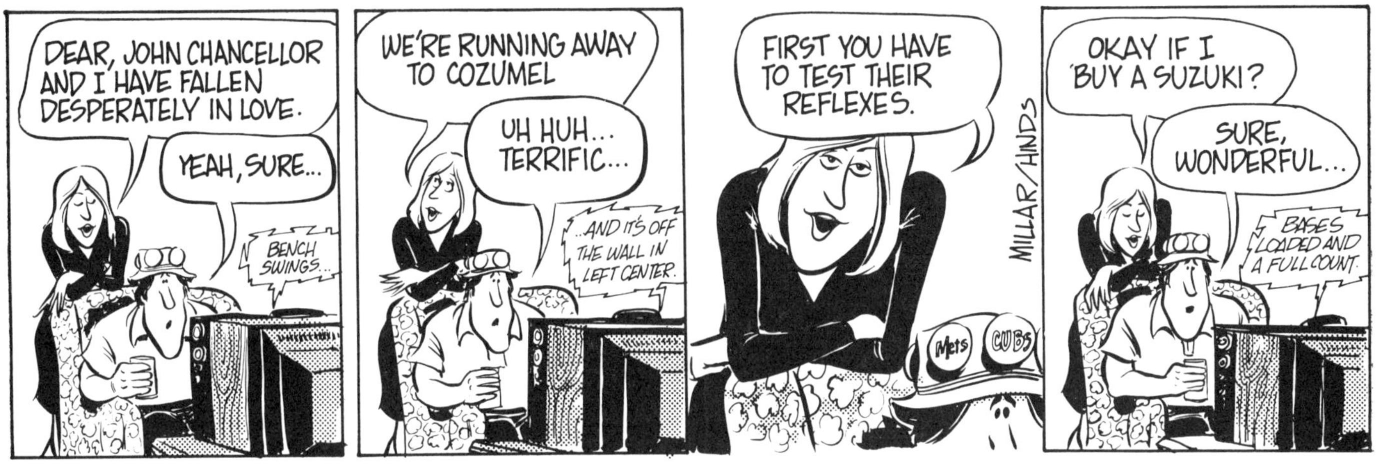
DEAR, JOHN CHANCELLOR AND I HAVE FALLEN DESPERATELY IN LOVE.
YEAH, SURE...
BENCH SWINGS...
WE'RE RUNNING AWAY TO COZUMEL
UH HUH... TERRIFIC...
...AND IT'S OFF THE WALL IN LEFT CENTER.
FIRST YOU HAVE TO TEST THEIR REFLEXES.
METS
CUBS
MILLAR/HINDS
OKAY IF I BUY A SUZUKI?
SURE, WONDERFUL...
BASES LOADED AND A FULL COUNT.

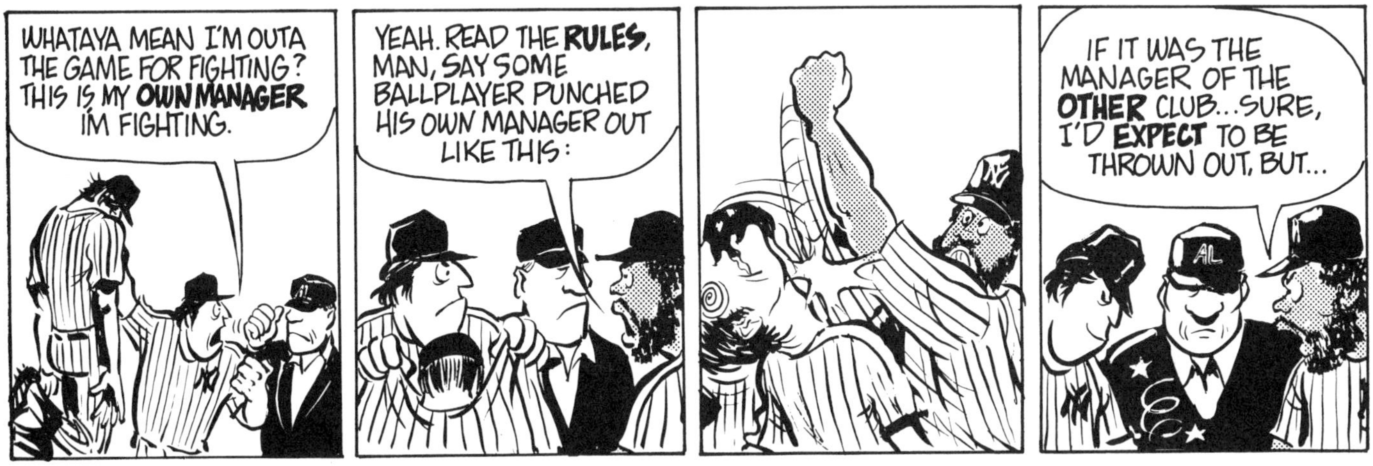
WHATAYA MEAN I'M OUTA THE GAME FOR FIGHTING? THIS IS MY **OWN MANAGER** I'M FIGHTING.
YEAH. READ THE **RULES**, MAN, SAY SOME BALLPLAYER PUNCHED HIS OWN MANAGER OUT LIKE THIS:
IF IT WAS THE MANAGER OF THE **OTHER** CLUB...SURE, I'D **EXPECT** TO BE THROWN OUT, BUT...
AL

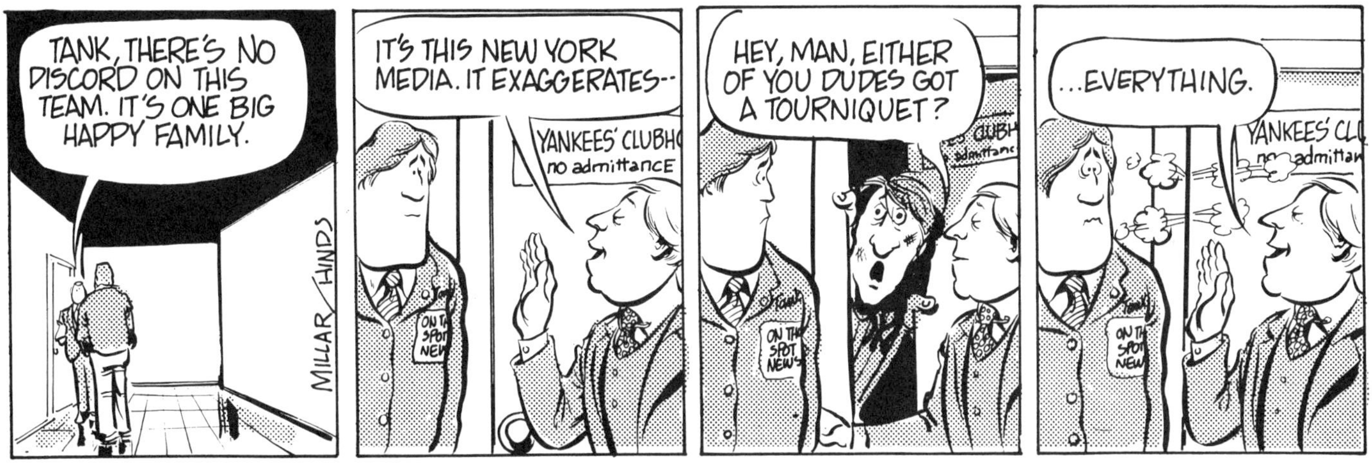
TANK, THERE'S NO DISCORD ON THIS TEAM. IT'S ONE BIG HAPPY FAMILY.
MILLAR/HINDS
IT'S THIS NEW YORK MEDIA. IT EXAGGERATES--
YANKEES' CLUBH
no admittance
HEY, MAN, EITHER OF YOU DUDES GOT A TOURNIQUET?
...EVERYTHING.

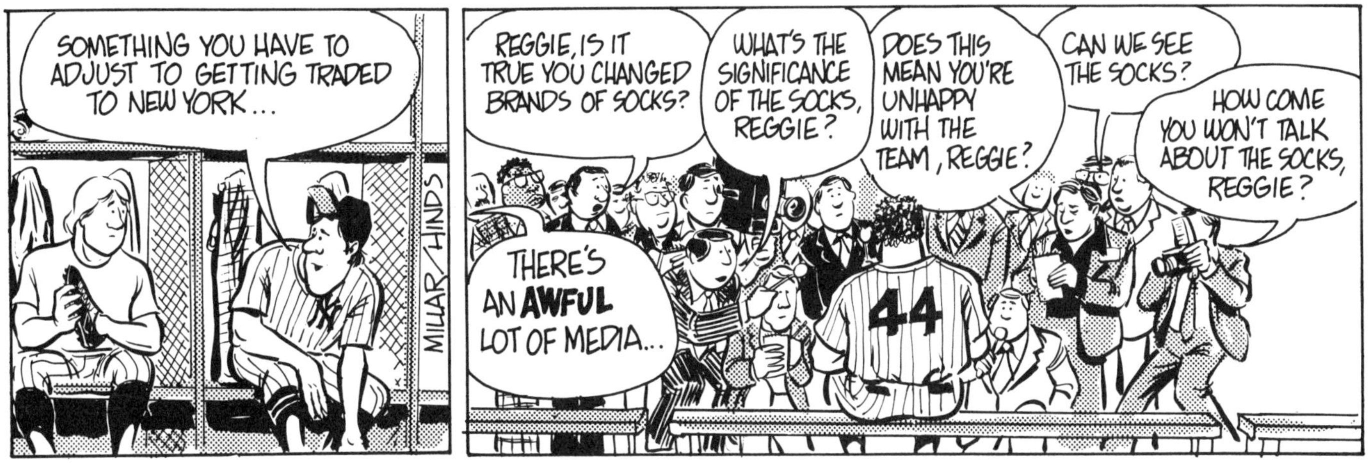
SOMETHING YOU HAVE TO ADJUST TO GETTING TRADED TO NEW YORK...
MILLAR/HINDS
REGGIE, IS IT TRUE YOU CHANGED BRANDS OF SOCKS?
WHAT'S THE SIGNIFICANCE OF THE SOCKS, REGGIE?
DOES THIS MEAN YOU'RE UNHAPPY WITH THE TEAM, REGGIE?
CAN WE SEE THE SOCKS?
HOW COME YOU WON'T TALK ABOUT THE SOCKS, REGGIE?
THERE'S AN **AWFUL** LOT OF MEDIA...
44

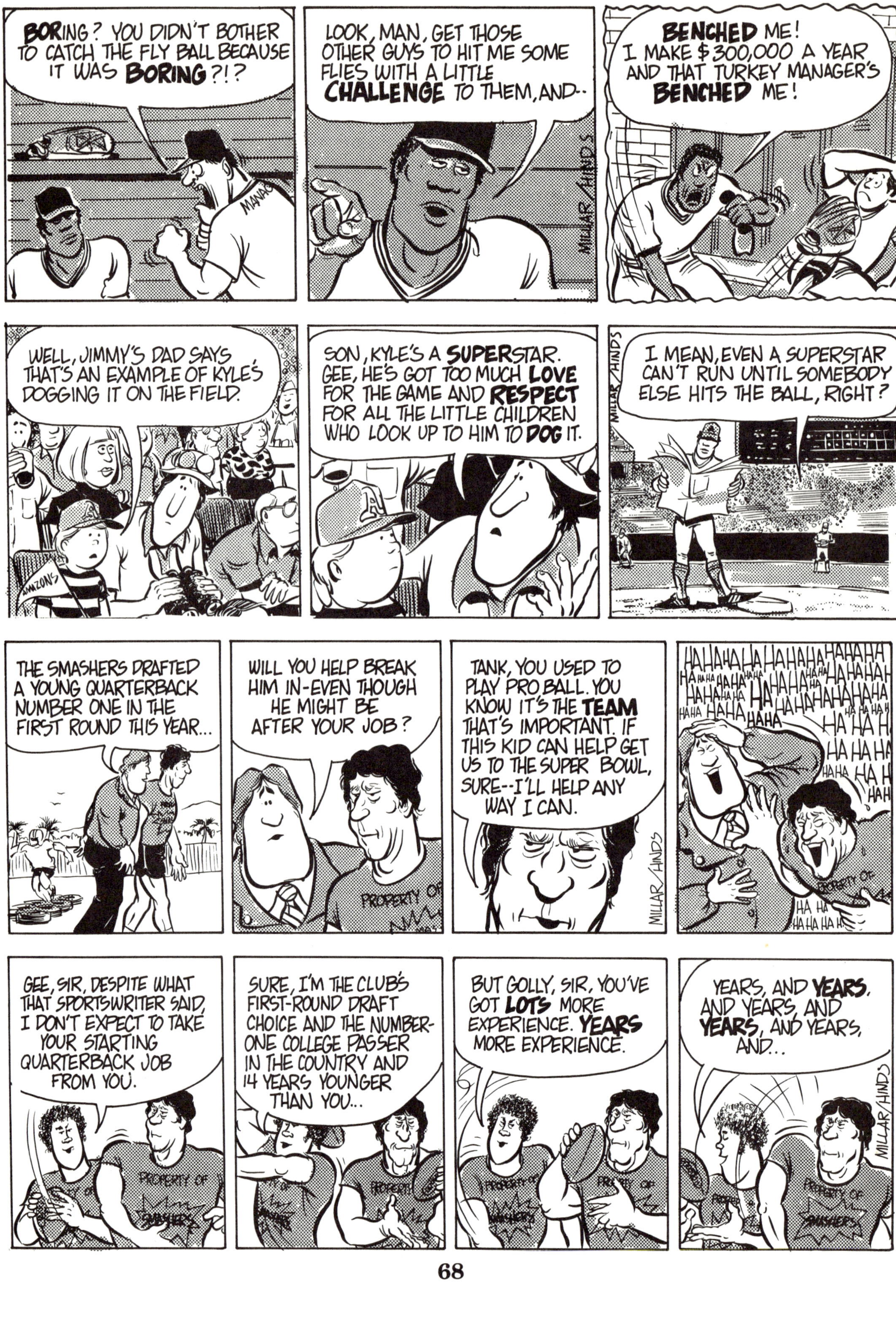
BORING? YOU DIDN'T BOTHER TO CATCH THE FLY BALL BECAUSE IT WAS BORING?!?
LOOK, MAN, GET THOSE OTHER GUYS TO HIT ME SOME FLIES WITH A LITTLE CHALLENGE TO THEM, AND--
MILLAR/HINDS
BENCHED ME! I MAKE $300,000 A YEAR AND THAT TURKEY MANAGER'S BENCHED ME!
WELL, JIMMY'S DAD SAYS THAT'S AN EXAMPLE OF KYLE'S DOGGING IT ON THE FIELD.
AMAZONS
SON, KYLE'S A SUPERSTAR. GEE, HE'S GOT TOO MUCH LOVE FOR THE GAME AND RESPECT FOR ALL THE LITTLE CHILDREN WHO LOOK UP TO HIM TO DOG IT.
MILLAR/HINDS
I MEAN, EVEN A SUPERSTAR CAN'T RUN UNTIL SOMEBODY ELSE HITS THE BALL, RIGHT?
THE SMASHERS DRAFTED A YOUNG QUARTERBACK NUMBER ONE IN THE FIRST ROUND THIS YEAR...
WILL YOU HELP BREAK HIM IN-EVEN THOUGH HE MIGHT BE AFTER YOUR JOB?
PROPERTY OF
TANK, YOU USED TO PLAY PRO BALL. YOU KNOW IT'S THE TEAM THAT'S IMPORTANT. IF THIS KID CAN HELP GET US TO THE SUPER BOWL, SURE--I'LL HELP ANY WAY I CAN.
MILLAR/HINDS
HAHAHA HA HAHAHA HAHAHA
PROPERTY OF
GEE, SIR, DESPITE WHAT THAT SPORTSWRITER SAID, I DON'T EXPECT TO TAKE YOUR STARTING QUARTERBACK JOB FROM YOU.
PROPERTY OF
SMASHERS
SURE, I'M THE CLUB'S FIRST-ROUND DRAFT CHOICE AND THE NUMBER-ONE COLLEGE PASSER IN THE COUNTRY AND 14 YEARS YOUNGER THAN YOU...
BUT GOLLY, SIR, YOU'VE GOT LOTS MORE EXPERIENCE. YEARS MORE EXPERIENCE.
PROPERTY OF
SMASHERS
YEARS, AND YEARS, AND YEARS, AND YEARS, AND YEARS, AND...
MILLAR/HINDS
PROPERTY OF
SMASHERS

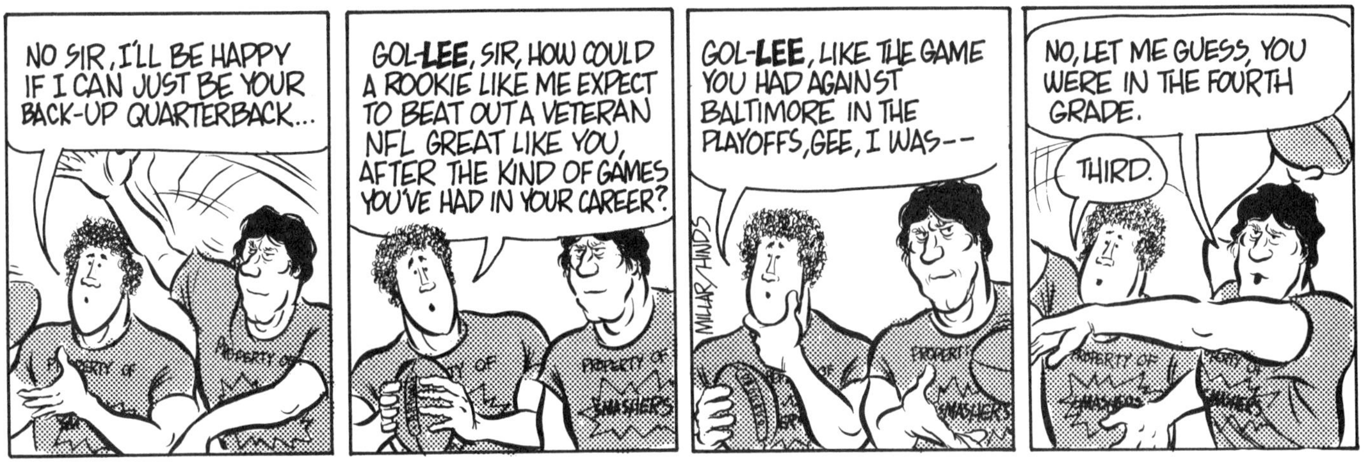
NO SIR, I'LL BE HAPPY IF I CAN JUST BE YOUR BACK-UP QUARTERBACK...
GOL-**LEE**, SIR, HOW COULD A ROOKIE LIKE ME EXPECT TO BEAT OUT A VETERAN NFL GREAT LIKE YOU, AFTER THE KIND OF GAMES YOU'VE HAD IN YOUR CAREER?
MILLAR/HINDS
GOL-**LEE**, LIKE THE GAME YOU HAD AGAINST BALTIMORE IN THE PLAYOFFS, GEE, I WAS--
NO, LET ME GUESS, YOU WERE IN THE FOURTH GRADE.
THIRD.

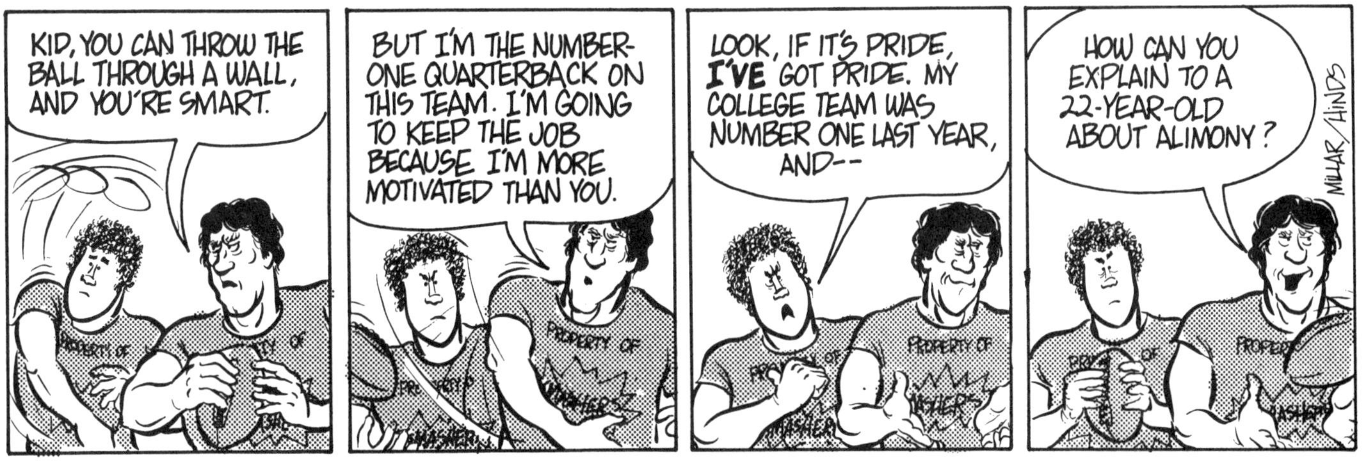
KID, YOU CAN THROW THE BALL THROUGH A WALL, AND YOU'RE SMART.
BUT I'M THE NUMBER-ONE QUARTERBACK ON THIS TEAM. I'M GOING TO KEEP THE JOB BECAUSE I'M MORE MOTIVATED THAN YOU.
LOOK, IF IT'S PRIDE, **I'VE** GOT PRIDE. MY COLLEGE TEAM WAS NUMBER ONE LAST YEAR, AND--
HOW CAN YOU EXPLAIN TO A 22-YEAR-OLD ABOUT ALIMONY?
MILLAR/HINDS

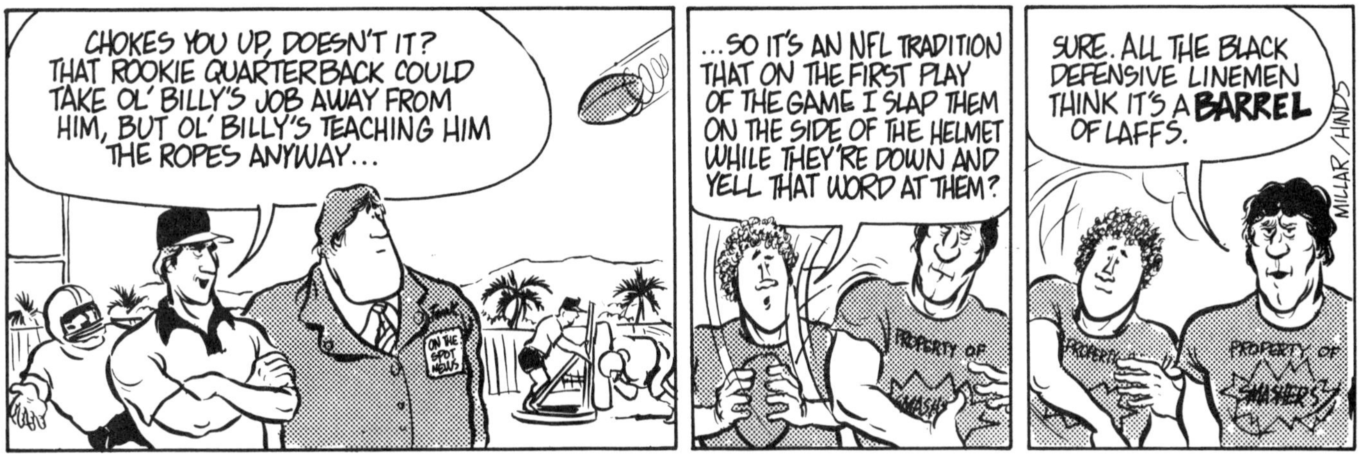
CHOKES YOU UP, DOESN'T IT? THAT ROOKIE QUARTERBACK COULD TAKE OL' BILLY'S JOB AWAY FROM HIM, BUT OL' BILLY'S TEACHING HIM THE ROPES ANYWAY...
ON THE SPOT NEWS
...SO IT'S AN NFL TRADITION THAT ON THE FIRST PLAY OF THE GAME I SLAP THEM ON THE SIDE OF THE HELMET WHILE THEY'RE DOWN AND YELL THAT WORD AT THEM?
SURE. ALL THE BLACK DEFENSIVE LINEMEN THINK IT'S A **BARREL** OF LAFFS.
MILLAR/HINDS

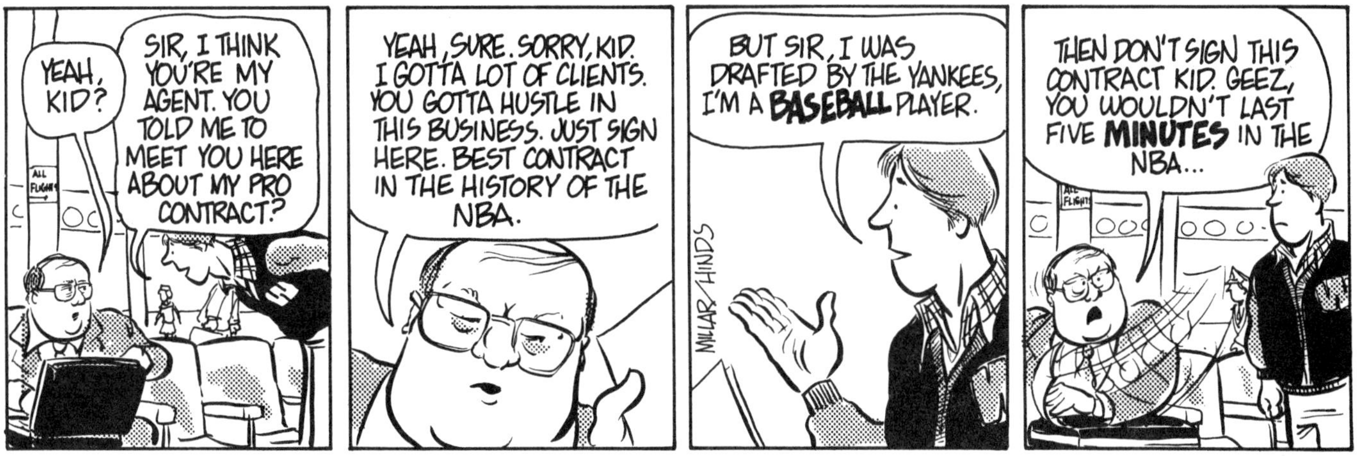
YEAH, KID?
SIR, I THINK YOU'RE MY AGENT. YOU TOLD ME TO MEET YOU HERE ABOUT MY PRO CONTRACT?
YEAH, SURE. SORRY, KID. I GOTTA LOT OF CLIENTS. YOU GOTTA HUSTLE IN THIS BUSINESS. JUST SIGN HERE. BEST CONTRACT IN THE HISTORY OF THE NBA.
MILLAR/HINDS
BUT SIR, I WAS DRAFTED BY THE YANKEES, I'M A **BASEBALL** PLAYER.
THEN DON'T SIGN THIS CONTRACT KID. GEEZ, YOU WOULDN'T LAST FIVE **MINUTES** IN THE NBA...

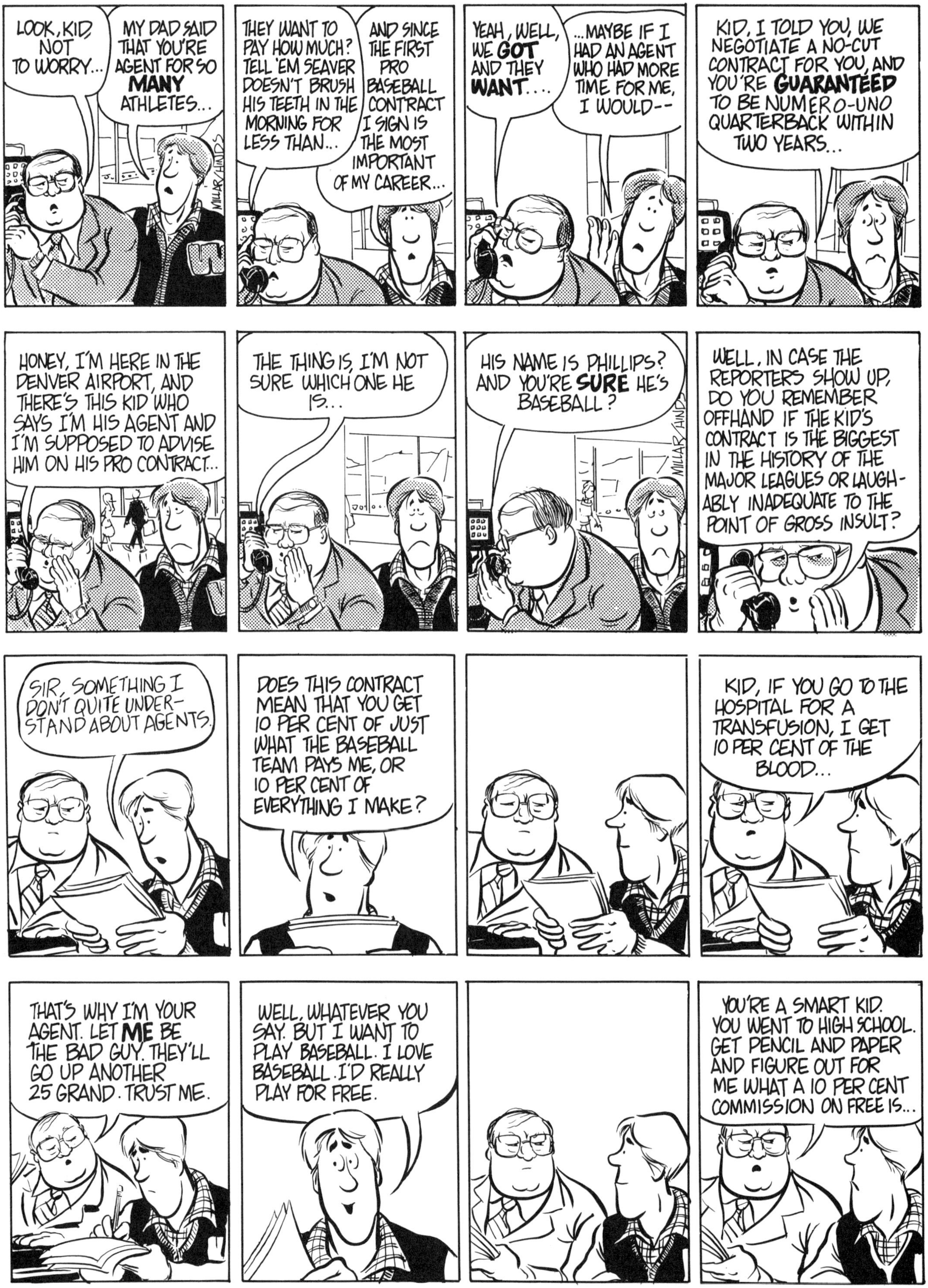
LOOK, KID, NOT TO WORRY...
MY DAD SAID THAT YOU'RE AGENT FOR SO **MANY** ATHLETES...
THEY WANT TO PAY HOW MUCH? TELL 'EM SEAVER DOESN'T BRUSH HIS TEETH IN THE MORNING FOR LESS THAN...
AND SINCE THE FIRST PRO BASEBALL CONTRACT I SIGN IS THE MOST IMPORTANT OF MY CAREER...
YEAH, WELL, WE **GOT** AND THEY **WANT**....
...MAYBE IF I HAD AN AGENT WHO HAD MORE TIME FOR ME, I WOULD--
KID, I TOLD YOU, WE NEGOTIATE A NO-CUT CONTRACT FOR YOU, AND YOU'RE **GUARANTEED** TO BE NUMERO-UNO QUARTERBACK WITHIN TWO YEARS...
HONEY, I'M HERE IN THE DENVER AIRPORT, AND THERE'S THIS KID WHO SAYS I'M HIS AGENT AND I'M SUPPOSED TO ADVISE HIM ON HIS PRO CONTRACT...
THE THING IS, I'M NOT SURE WHICH ONE HE IS...
HIS NAME IS PHILLIPS? AND YOU'RE **SURE** HE'S BASEBALL?
WELL, IN CASE THE REPORTERS SHOW UP, DO YOU REMEMBER OFFHAND IF THE KID'S CONTRACT IS THE BIGGEST IN THE HISTORY OF THE MAJOR LEAGUES OR LAUGHABLY INADEQUATE TO THE POINT OF GROSS INSULT?
SIR, SOMETHING I DON'T QUITE UNDERSTAND ABOUT AGENTS.
DOES THIS CONTRACT MEAN THAT YOU GET 10 PER CENT OF JUST WHAT THE BASEBALL TEAM PAYS ME, OR 10 PER CENT OF EVERYTHING I MAKE?
KID, IF YOU GO TO THE HOSPITAL FOR A TRANSFUSION, I GET 10 PER CENT OF THE BLOOD...
THAT'S WHY I'M YOUR AGENT. LET **ME** BE THE BAD GUY. THEY'LL GO UP ANOTHER 25 GRAND. TRUST ME.
WELL, WHATEVER YOU SAY. BUT I WANT TO PLAY BASEBALL. I LOVE BASEBALL. I'D REALLY PLAY FOR FREE.
YOU'RE A SMART KID. YOU WENT TO HIGH SCHOOL. GET PENCIL AND PAPER AND FIGURE OUT FOR ME WHAT A 10 PER CENT COMMISSION ON FREE IS...

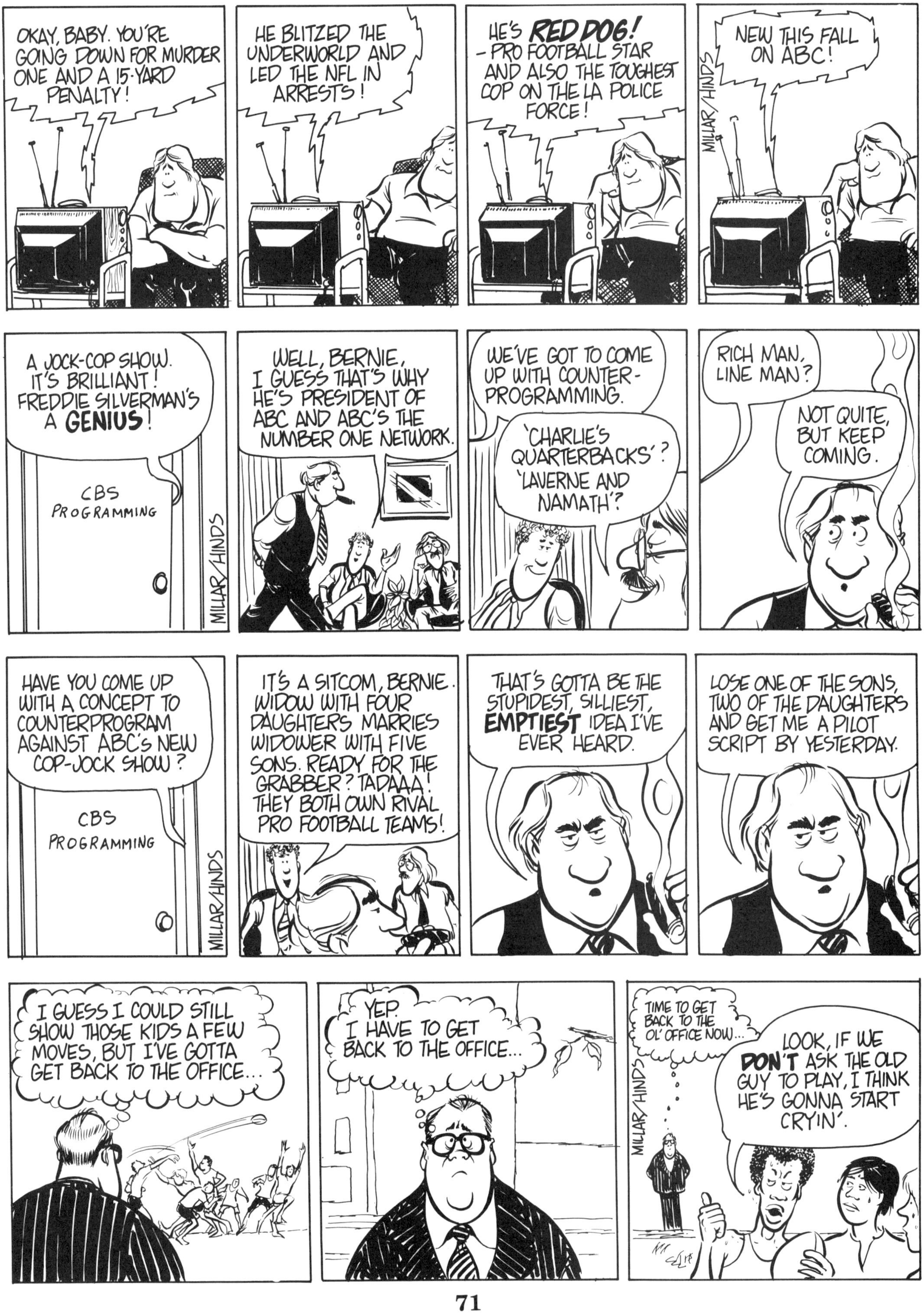
OKAY, BABY. YOU'RE GOING DOWN FOR MURDER ONE AND A 15-YARD PENALTY!
HE BLITZED THE UNDERWORLD AND LED THE NFL IN ARRESTS!
HE'S **RED DOG!** - PRO FOOTBALL STAR AND ALSO THE TOUGHEST COP ON THE LA POLICE FORCE!
MILLAR/HINDS
NEW THIS FALL ON ABC!
A JOCK-COP SHOW. IT'S BRILLIANT! FREDDIE SILVERMAN'S A **GENIUS**!
CBS PROGRAMMING
MILLAR/HINDS
WELL, BERNIE, I GUESS THAT'S WHY HE'S PRESIDENT OF ABC AND ABC'S THE NUMBER ONE NETWORK.
WE'VE GOT TO COME UP WITH COUNTER-PROGRAMMING.
'CHARLIE'S QUARTERBACKS'? 'LAVERNE AND NAMATH'?
RICH MAN, LINE MAN?
NOT QUITE, BUT KEEP COMING.
HAVE YOU COME UP WITH A CONCEPT TO COUNTERPROGRAM AGAINST ABC'S NEW COP-JOCK SHOW?
CBS PROGRAMMING
MILLAR/HINDS
IT'S A SITCOM, BERNIE. WIDOW WITH FOUR DAUGHTERS MARRIES WIDOWER WITH FIVE SONS. READY FOR THE GRABBER? TADAAA! THEY BOTH OWN RIVAL PRO FOOTBALL TEAMS!
THAT'S GOTTA BE THE STUPIDEST, SILLIEST, **EMPTIEST** IDEA I'VE EVER HEARD.
LOSE ONE OF THE SONS, TWO OF THE DAUGHTERS AND GET ME A PILOT SCRIPT BY YESTERDAY.
I GUESS I COULD STILL SHOW THOSE KIDS A FEW MOVES, BUT I'VE GOTTA GET BACK TO THE OFFICE...
YEP. I HAVE TO GET BACK TO THE OFFICE...
TIME TO GET BACK TO THE OL' OFFICE NOW...
MILLAR/HINDS
LOOK, IF WE **DON'T** ASK THE OLD GUY TO PLAY, I THINK HE'S GONNA START CRYIN'.

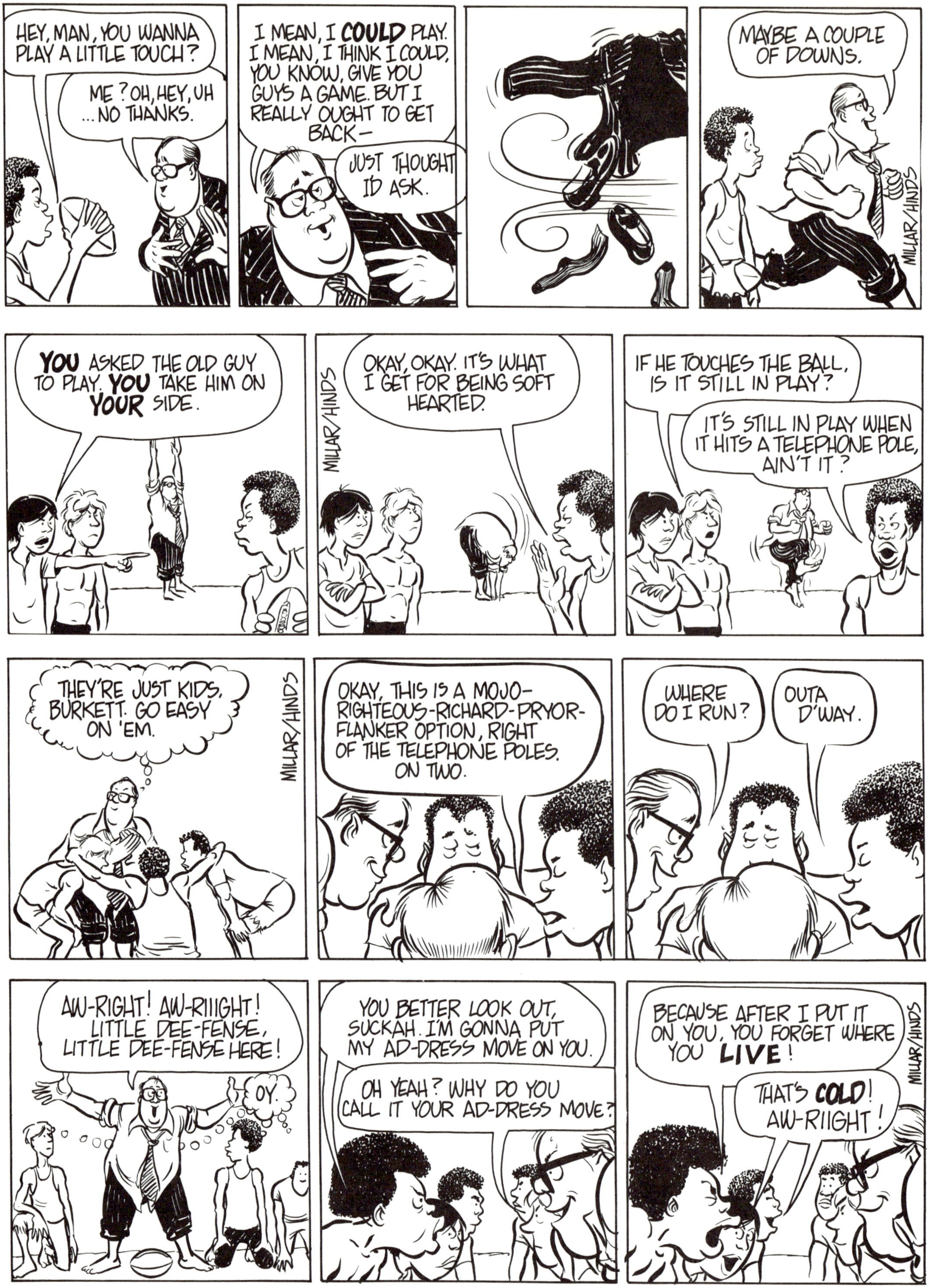
HEY, MAN, YOU WANNA PLAY A LITTLE TOUCH?
ME? OH, HEY, UH ... NO THANKS.
I MEAN, I COULD PLAY. I MEAN, I THINK I COULD, YOU KNOW, GIVE YOU GUYS A GAME. BUT I REALLY OUGHT TO GET BACK—
JUST THOUGHT I'D ASK.
MAYBE A COUPLE OF DOWNS.
MILLAR/HINDS
YOU ASKED THE OLD GUY TO PLAY. YOU TAKE HIM ON YOUR SIDE.
MILLAR/HINDS
OKAY, OKAY. IT'S WHAT I GET FOR BEING SOFT HEARTED.
IF HE TOUCHES THE BALL, IS IT STILL IN PLAY?
IT'S STILL IN PLAY WHEN IT HITS A TELEPHONE POLE, AIN'T IT?
THEY'RE JUST KIDS, BURKETT. GO EASY ON 'EM.
MILLAR/HINDS
OKAY, THIS IS A MOJO-RIGHTEOUS-RICHARD-PRYOR-FLANKER OPTION, RIGHT OF THE TELEPHONE POLES. ON TWO.
WHERE DO I RUN?
OUTA D'WAY.
AW-RIGHT! AW-RIIIGHT! LITTLE DEE-FENSE, LITTLE DEE-FENSE HERE!
OY.
YOU BETTER LOOK OUT, SUCKAH. I'M GONNA PUT MY AD-DRESS MOVE ON YOU.
OH YEAH? WHY DO YOU CALL IT YOUR AD-DRESS MOVE?
BECAUSE AFTER I PUT IT ON YOU, YOU FORGET WHERE YOU LIVE!
THAT'S COLD! AW-RIIGHT!
MILLAR/HINDS

TANK McNAMARA

by Jeff Millar & Bill Hinds

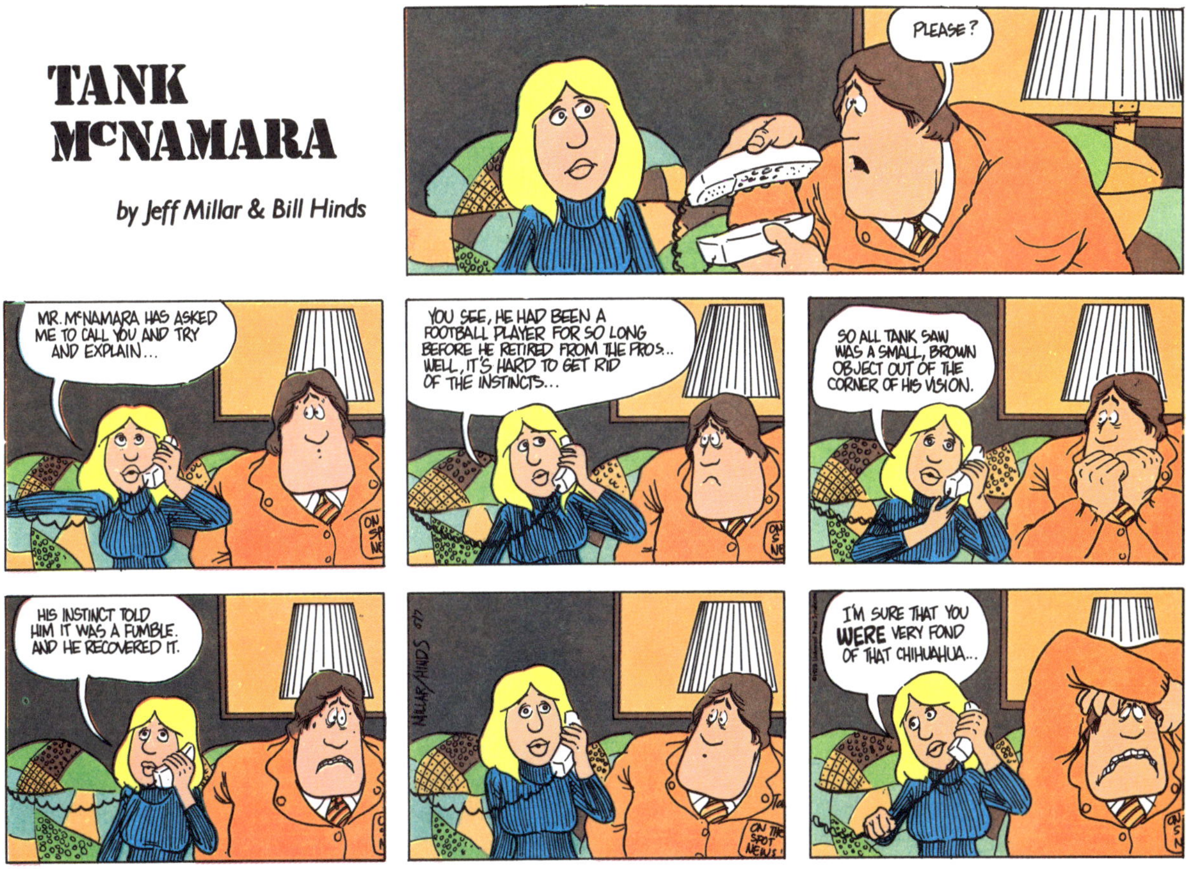

PLEASE?
MR. McNAMARA HAS ASKED ME TO CALL YOU AND TRY AND EXPLAIN...
YOU SEE, HE HAD BEEN A FOOTBALL PLAYER FOR SO LONG BEFORE HE RETIRED FROM THE PROS.. WELL, IT'S HARD TO GET RID OF THE INSTINCTS...
SO ALL TANK SAW WAS A SMALL, BROWN OBJECT OUT OF THE CORNER OF HIS VISION.
HIS INSTINCT TOLD HIM IT WAS A FUMBLE. AND HE RECOVERED IT.
I'M SURE THAT YOU WERE VERY FOND OF THAT CHIHUAHUA...

TANK McNAMARA

by Jeff Millar & Bill Hinds

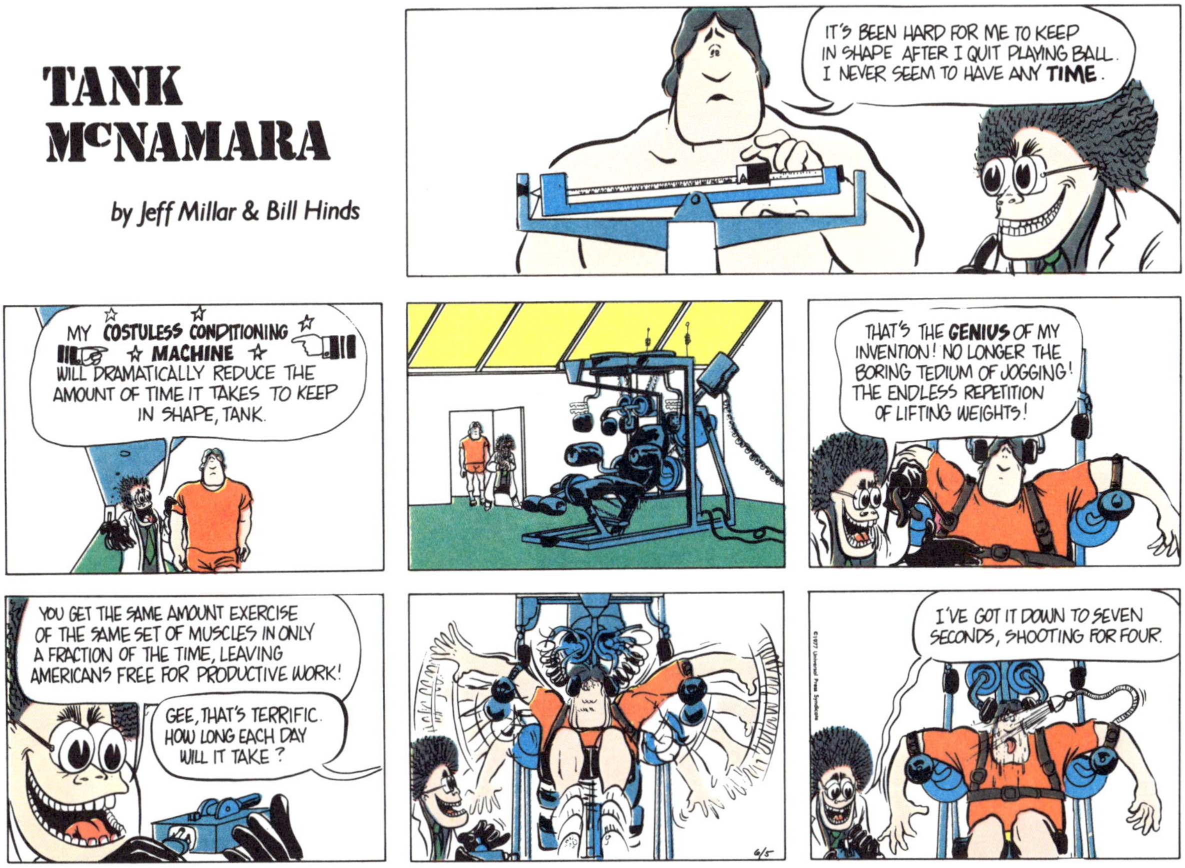

IT'S BEEN HARD FOR ME TO KEEP IN SHAPE AFTER I QUIT PLAYING BALL. I NEVER SEEM TO HAVE ANY TIME.
MY COSTULESS CONDITIONING MACHINE WILL DRAMATICALLY REDUCE THE AMOUNT OF TIME IT TAKES TO KEEP IN SHAPE, TANK.
THAT'S THE GENIUS OF MY INVENTION! NO LONGER THE BORING TEDIUM OF JOGGING! THE ENDLESS REPETITION OF LIFTING WEIGHTS!
YOU GET THE SAME AMOUNT EXERCISE OF THE SAME SET OF MUSCLES IN ONLY A FRACTION OF THE TIME, LEAVING AMERICANS FREE FOR PRODUCTIVE WORK!
GEE, THAT'S TERRIFIC. HOW LONG EACH DAY WILL IT TAKE?
I'VE GOT IT DOWN TO SEVEN SECONDS, SHOOTING FOR FOUR.

TANK McNAMARA

by Jeff Millar & Bill Hinds

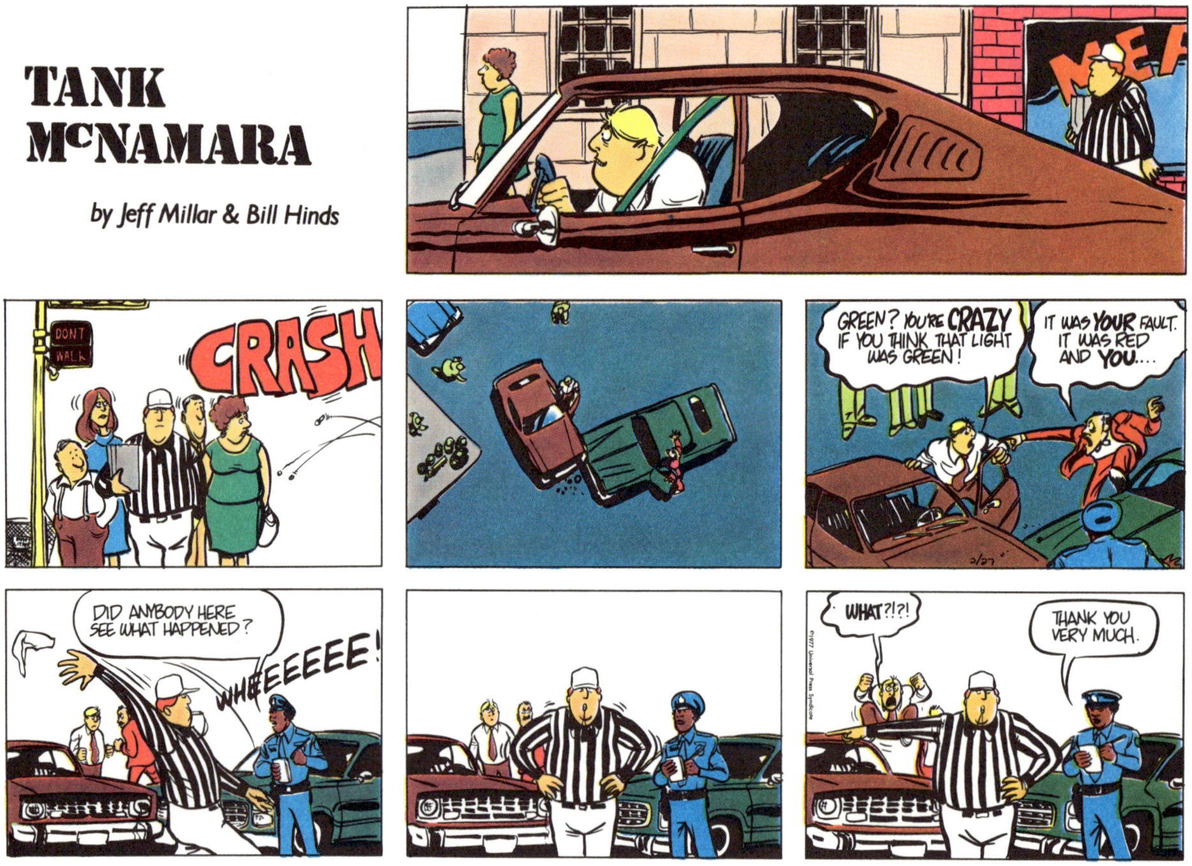
DONT WALK
CRASH
GREEN? YOU'RE CRAZY IF YOU THINK THAT LIGHT WAS GREEN!
IT WAS YOUR FAULT. IT WAS RED AND YOU....
DID ANYBODY HERE SEE WHAT HAPPENED?
WHEEEEEE!
WHAT?!?!
THANK YOU VERY MUCH.

TANK McNAMARA

by Jeff Millar & Bill Hinds

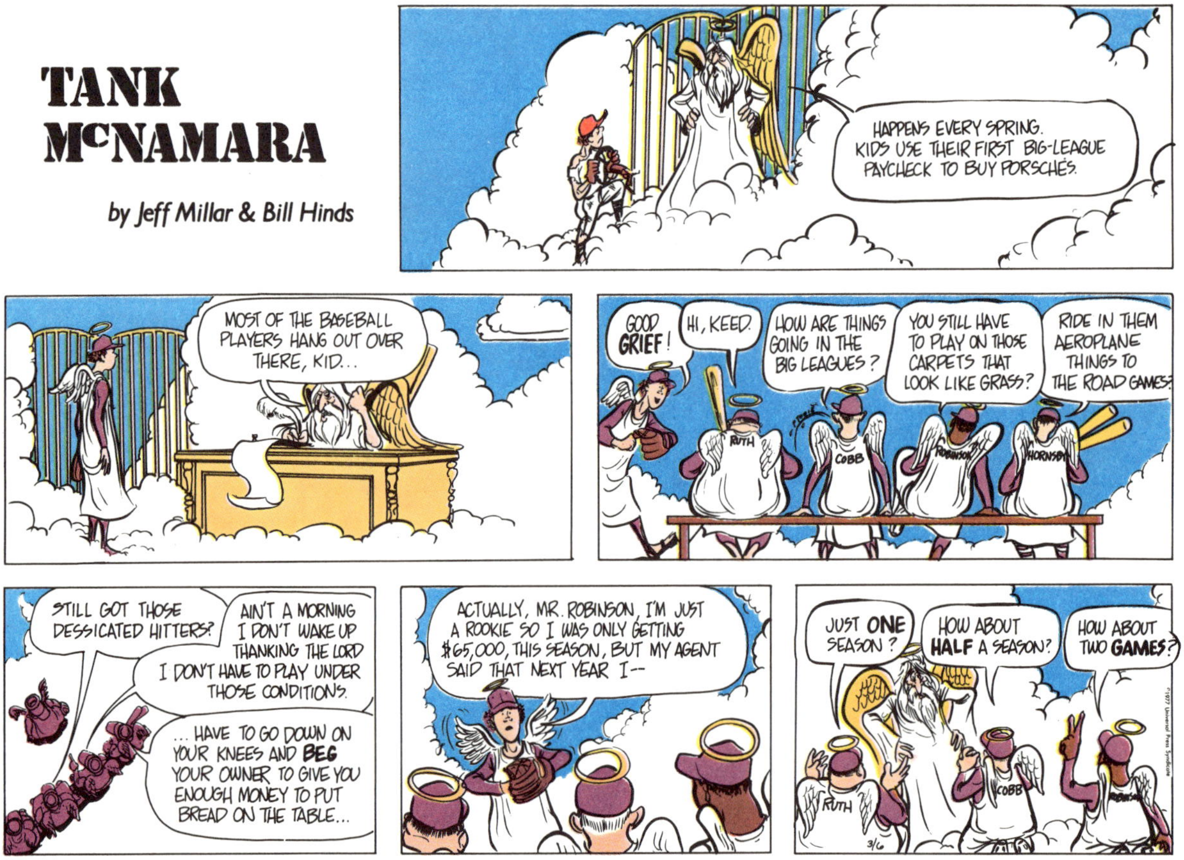
HAPPENS EVERY SPRING. KIDS USE THEIR FIRST BIG-LEAGUE PAYCHECK TO BUY PORSCHES.
MOST OF THE BASEBALL PLAYERS HANG OUT OVER THERE, KID...
GOOD GRIEF!
HI, KEED.
HOW ARE THINGS GOING IN THE BIG LEAGUES?
YOU STILL HAVE TO PLAY ON THOSE CARPETS THAT LOOK LIKE GRASS?
RIDE IN THEM AEROPLANE THINGS TO THE ROAD GAMES?
RUTH
COBB
ROBINSON
HORNSBY
STILL GOT THOSE DESSICATED HITTERS?
AIN'T A MORNING I DON'T WAKE UP THANKING THE LORD I DON'T HAVE TO PLAY UNDER THOSE CONDITIONS.
... HAVE TO GO DOWN ON YOUR KNEES AND BEG YOUR OWNER TO GIVE YOU ENOUGH MONEY TO PUT BREAD ON THE TABLE...
ACTUALLY, MR. ROBINSON, I'M JUST A ROOKIE SO I WAS ONLY GETTING $65,000 THIS SEASON, BUT MY AGENT SAID THAT NEXT YEAR I--
JUST ONE SEASON?
HOW ABOUT HALF A SEASON?
HOW ABOUT TWO GAMES?

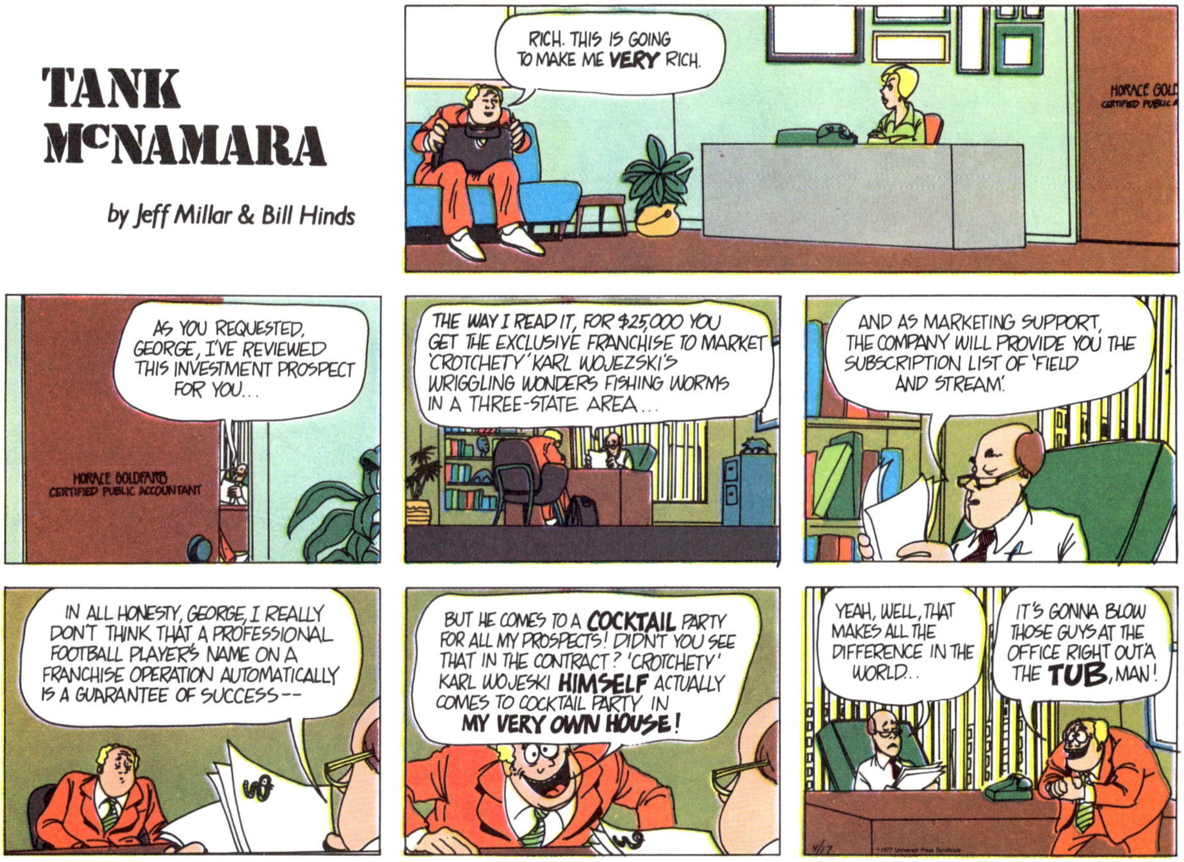
TANK McNAMARA
by Jeff Millar & Bill Hinds
RICH. THIS IS GOING TO MAKE ME **VERY** RICH.
HORACE GOLD... CERTIFIED PUBLIC A...
AS YOU REQUESTED, GEORGE, I'VE REVIEWED THIS INVESTMENT PROSPECT FOR YOU...
HORACE GOLDFARB CERTIFIED PUBLIC ACCOUNTANT
THE WAY I READ IT, FOR $25,000 YOU GET THE EXCLUSIVE FRANCHISE TO MARKET 'CROTCHETY' KARL WOJEZSKI'S WRIGGLING WONDERS FISHING WORMS IN A THREE-STATE AREA...
AND AS MARKETING SUPPORT, THE COMPANY WILL PROVIDE YOU THE SUBSCRIPTION LIST OF 'FIELD AND STREAM'.
IN ALL HONESTY, GEORGE, I REALLY DON'T THINK THAT A PROFESSIONAL FOOTBALL PLAYER'S NAME ON A FRANCHISE OPERATION AUTOMATICALLY IS A GUARANTEE OF SUCCESS--
BUT HE COMES TO A **COCKTAIL** PARTY FOR ALL MY PROSPECTS! DIDN'T YOU SEE THAT IN THE CONTRACT? 'CROTCHETY' KARL WOJESKI **HIMSELF** ACTUALLY COMES TO COCKTAIL PARTY IN **MY VERY OWN HOUSE!**
YEAH, WELL, THAT MAKES ALL THE DIFFERENCE IN THE WORLD...
IT'S GONNA BLOW THOSE GUYS AT THE OFFICE RIGHT OUT'A THE **TUB**, MAN!
4/17
©1977 Universal Press Syndicate

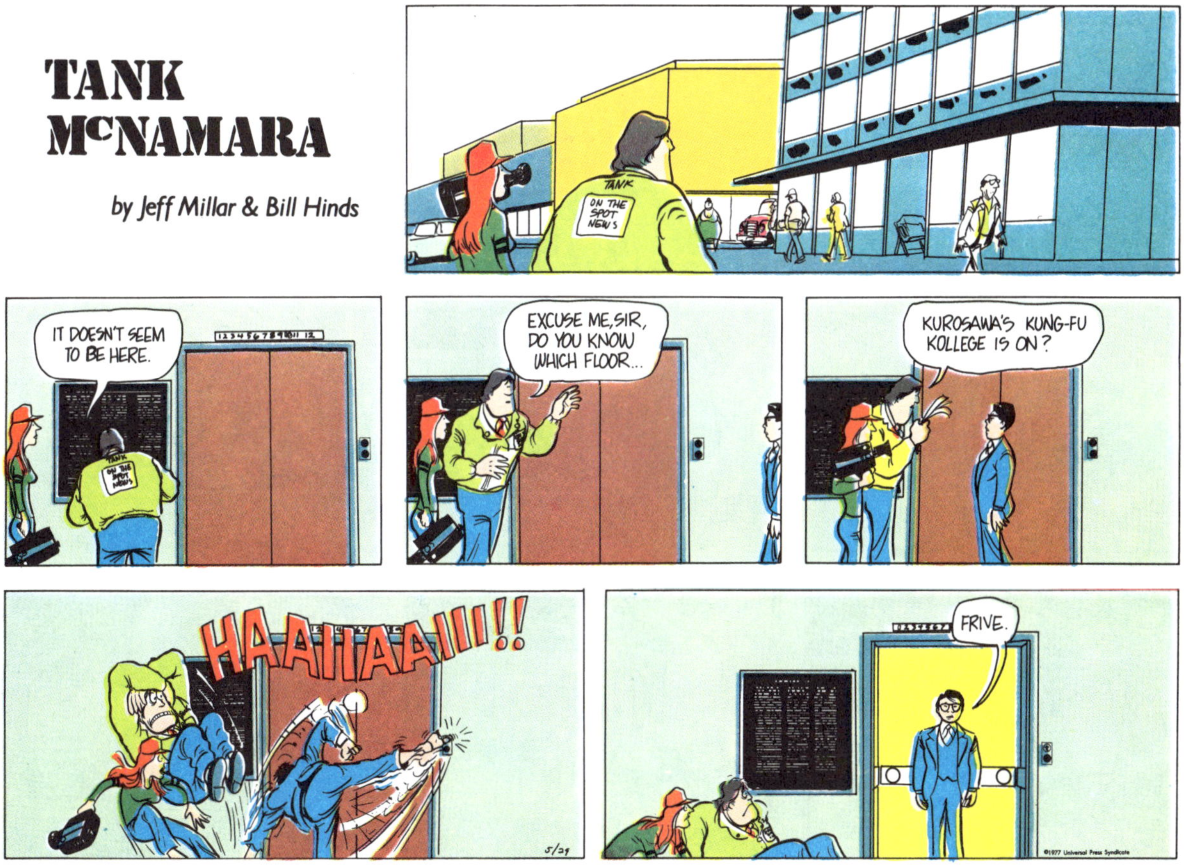
TANK McNAMARA
by Jeff Millar & Bill Hinds
TANK
ON THE SPOT NEWS
IT DOESN'T SEEM TO BE HERE.
EXCUSE ME, SIR, DO YOU KNOW WHICH FLOOR...
KUROSAWA'S KUNG-FU KOLLEGE IS ON?
HAAIIAAIII!!
FRIVE.
5/29
©1977 Universal Press Syndicate

TANK McNAMARA

by Jeff Millar & Bill Hinds

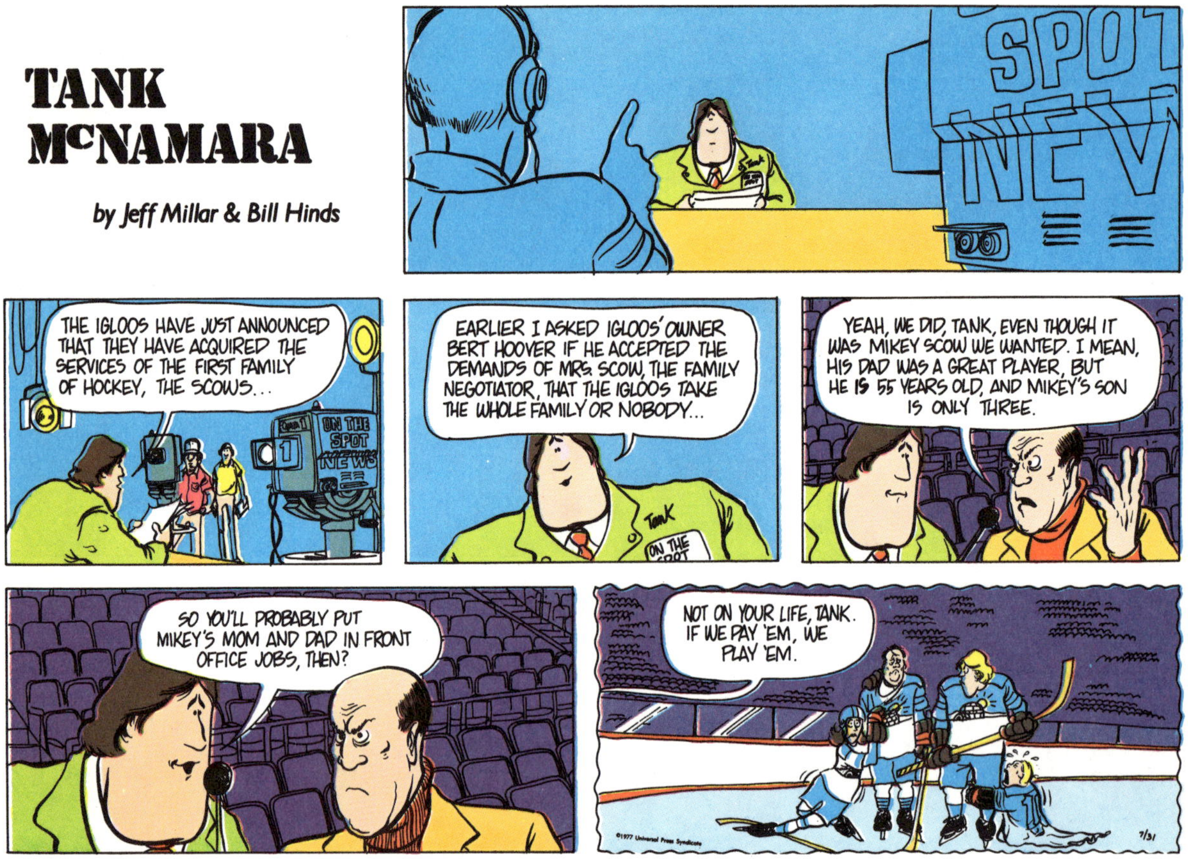
SPOT
NEW
ON THE SPOT NEWS
THE IGLOOS HAVE JUST ANNOUNCED THAT THEY HAVE ACQUIRED THE SERVICES OF THE FIRST FAMILY OF HOCKEY, THE SCOWS...
EARLIER I ASKED IGLOOS' OWNER BERT HOOVER IF HE ACCEPTED THE DEMANDS OF MRS. SCOW, THE FAMILY NEGOTIATOR, THAT THE IGLOOS TAKE THE WHOLE FAMILY OR NOBODY...
TANK
YEAH, WE DID, TANK, EVEN THOUGH IT WAS MIKEY SCOW WE WANTED. I MEAN, HIS DAD WAS A GREAT PLAYER, BUT HE IS 55 YEARS OLD, AND MIKEY'S SON IS ONLY THREE.
SO YOU'LL PROBABLY PUT MIKEY'S MOM AND DAD IN FRONT OFFICE JOBS, THEN?
NOT ON YOUR LIFE, TANK. IF WE PAY 'EM, WE PLAY 'EM.

TANK McNAMARA

by Jeff Millar & Bill Hinds

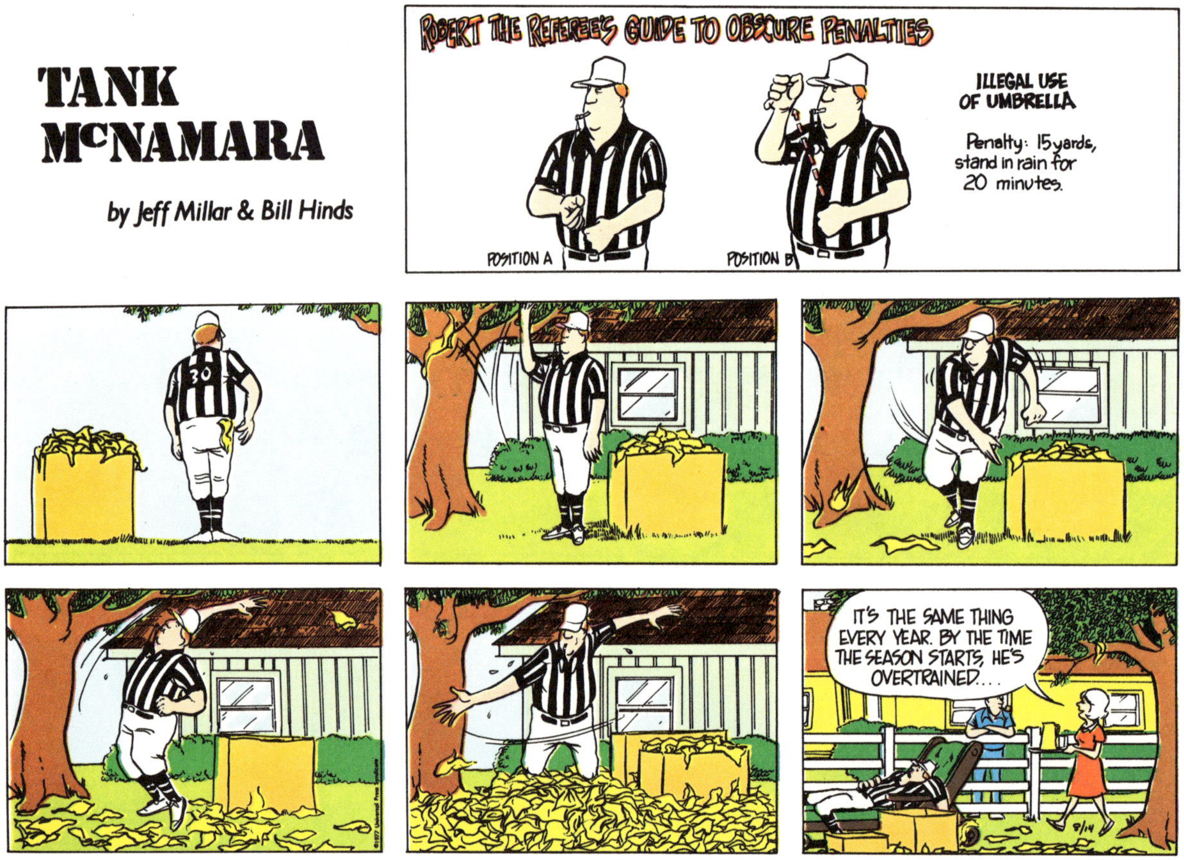
ROBERT THE REFEREE'S GUIDE TO OBSCURE PENALTIES
ILLEGAL USE OF UMBRELLA
Penalty: 15 yards, stand in rain for 20 minutes.
POSITION A
POSITION B
30
IT'S THE SAME THING EVERY YEAR. BY THE TIME THE SEASON STARTS, HE'S OVERTRAINED...

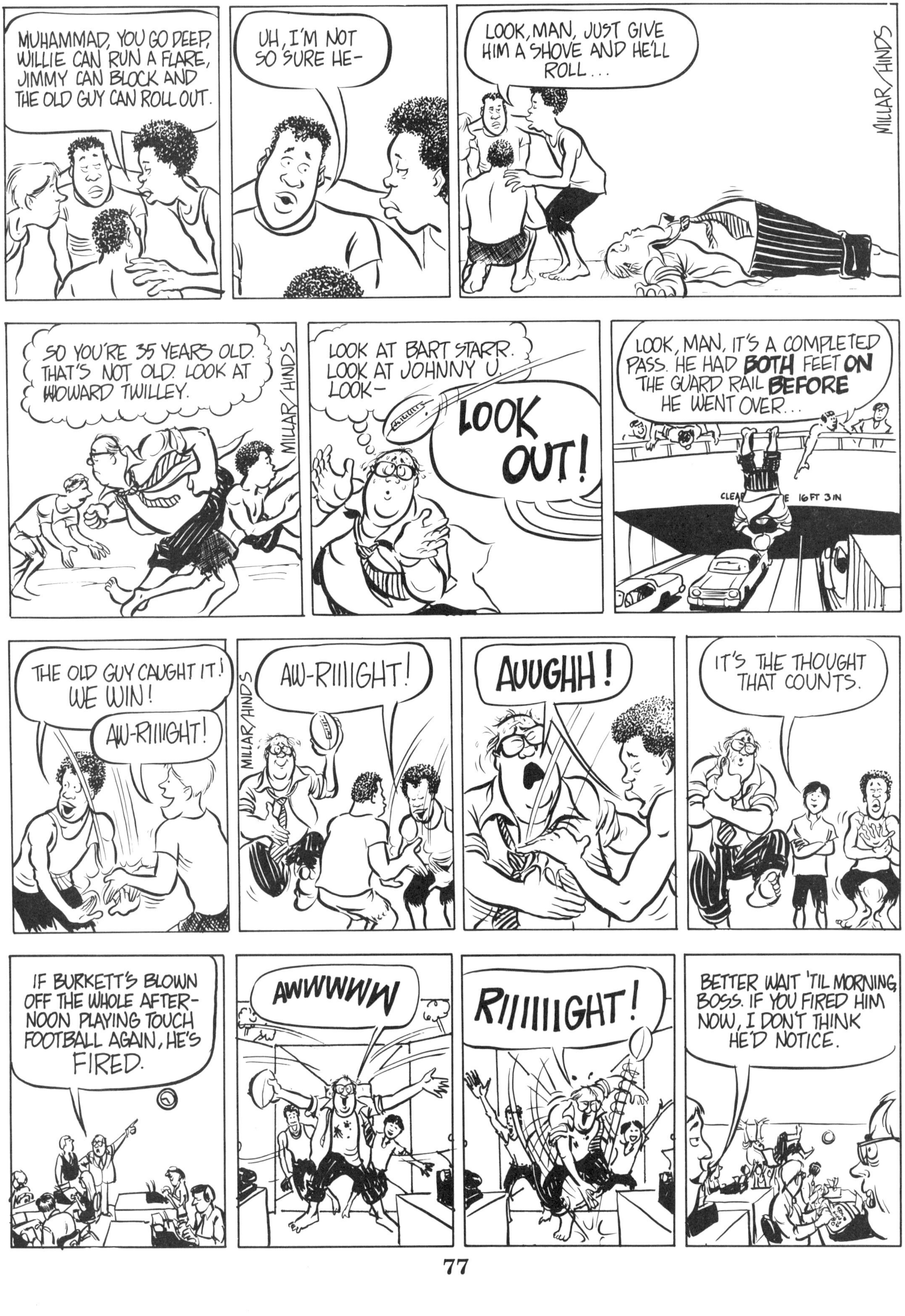
MUHAMMAD, YOU GO DEEP, WILLIE CAN RUN A FLARE, JIMMY CAN BLOCK AND THE OLD GUY CAN ROLL OUT.
UH, I'M NOT SO SURE HE-
LOOK, MAN, JUST GIVE HIM A SHOVE AND HE'LL ROLL...
MILLAR/HINDS
SO YOU'RE 35 YEARS OLD. THAT'S NOT OLD. LOOK AT HOWARD TWILLEY.
MILLAR/HINDS
LOOK AT BART STARR. LOOK AT JOHNNY U. LOOK-
LOOK OUT!
LOOK, MAN, IT'S A COMPLETED PASS. HE HAD **BOTH** FEET **ON** THE GUARD RAIL **BEFORE** HE WENT OVER...
THE OLD GUY CAUGHT IT! WE WIN!
AW-RIIIGHT!
MILLAR/HINDS
AW-RIIIGHT!
AUUGHH!
IT'S THE THOUGHT THAT COUNTS.
IF BURKETT'S BLOWN OFF THE WHOLE AFTERNOON PLAYING TOUCH FOOTBALL AGAIN, HE'S FIRED.
AWWWWW
RIIIIIIGHT!
BETTER WAIT 'TIL MORNING, BOSS. IF YOU FIRED HIM NOW, I DON'T THINK HE'D NOTICE.

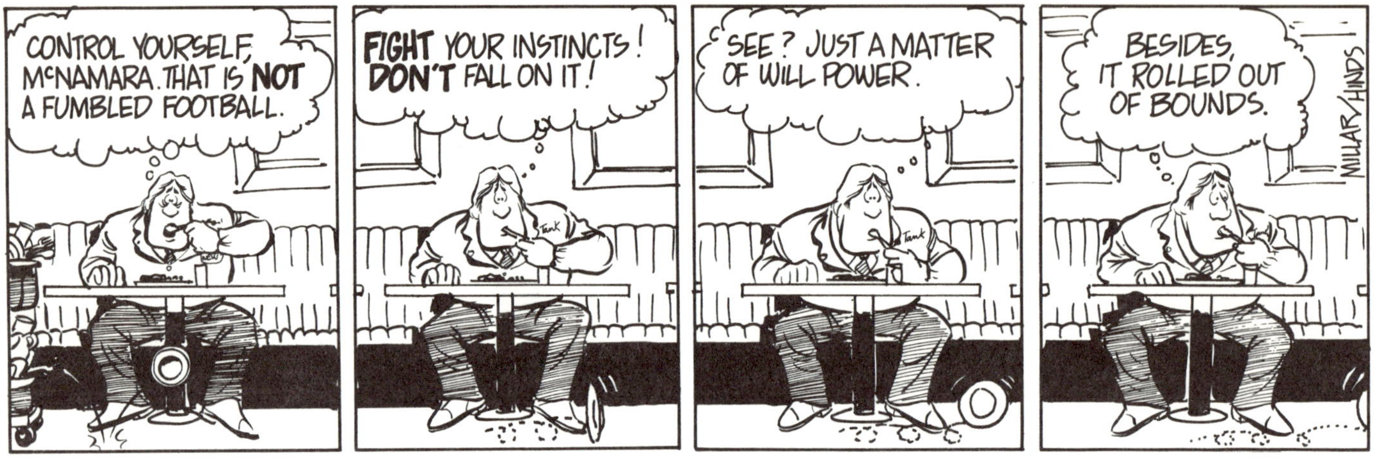
CONTROL YOURSELF, McNAMARA. THAT IS **NOT** A FUMBLED FOOTBALL.
FIGHT YOUR INSTINCTS! **DON'T** FALL ON IT!
SEE? JUST A MATTER OF WILL POWER.
BESIDES, IT ROLLED OUT OF BOUNDS.
MILLAR/HINDS

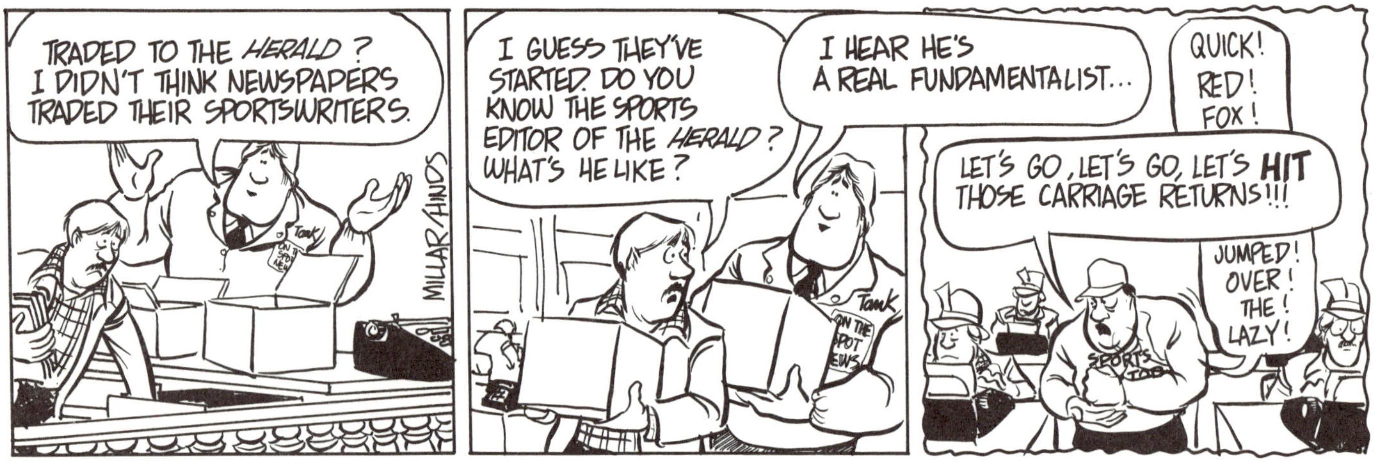
TRADED TO THE *HERALD*? I DIDN'T THINK NEWSPAPERS TRADED THEIR SPORTSWRITERS.
MILLAR/HINDS
I GUESS THEY'VE STARTED. DO YOU KNOW THE SPORTS EDITOR OF THE *HERALD*? WHAT'S HE LIKE?
I HEAR HE'S A REAL FUNDAMENTALIST...
ON THE SPOT NEWS
QUICK! RED! FOX!
LET'S GO, LET'S GO, LET'S **HIT** THOSE CARRIAGE RETURNS!!!
JUMPED! OVER! THE! LAZY!

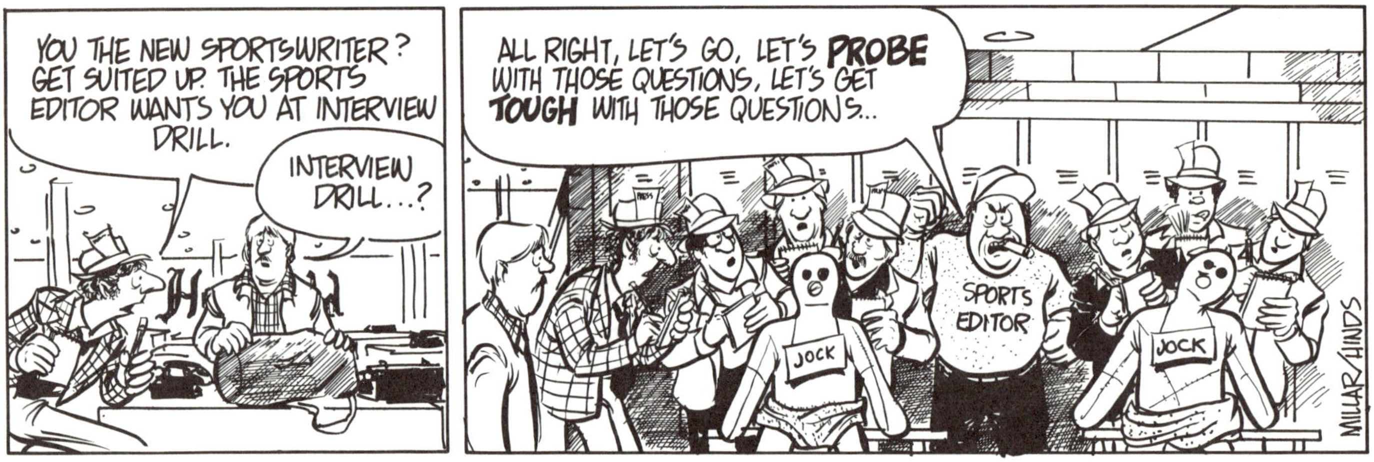
YOU THE NEW SPORTSWRITER? GET SUITED UP. THE SPORTS EDITOR WANTS YOU AT INTERVIEW DRILL.
INTERVIEW DRILL...?
ALL RIGHT, LET'S GO, LET'S **PROBE** WITH THOSE QUESTIONS, LET'S GET **TOUGH** WITH THOSE QUESTIONS...
SPORTS EDITOR
JOCK
JOCK
MILLAR/HINDS

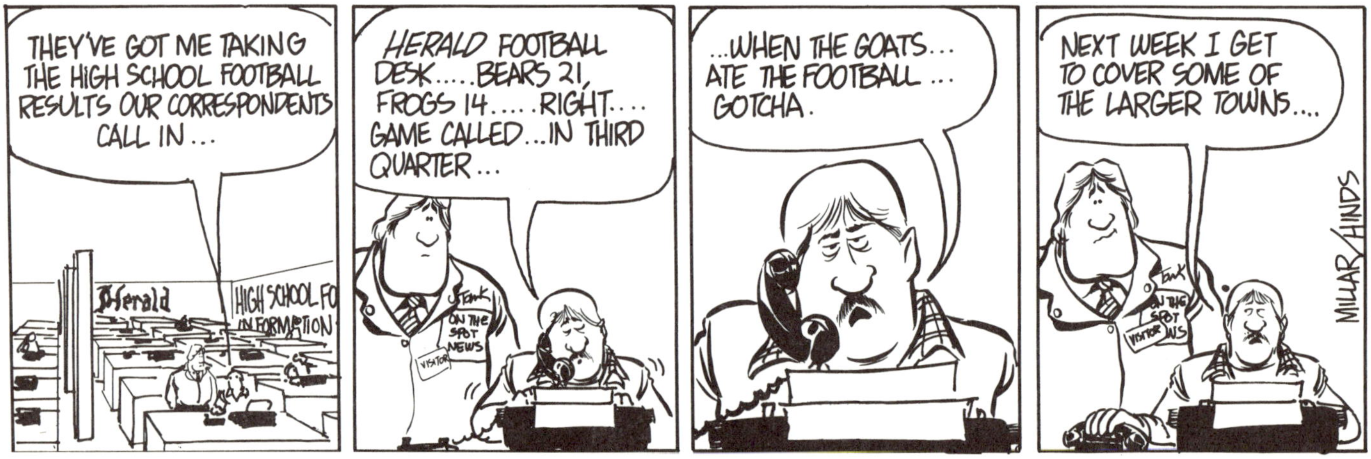
THEY'VE GOT ME TAKING THE HIGH SCHOOL FOOTBALL RESULTS OUR CORRESPONDENTS CALL IN...
Herald
HIGH SCHOOL FO INFORMATION
HERALD FOOTBALL DESK.....BEARS 21, FROGS 14.....RIGHT.... GAME CALLED...IN THIRD QUARTER...
ON THE SPOT NEWS
VISITOR
...WHEN THE GOATS... ATE THE FOOTBALL... GOTCHA.
NEXT WEEK I GET TO COVER SOME OF THE LARGER TOWNS....
MILLAR/HINDS

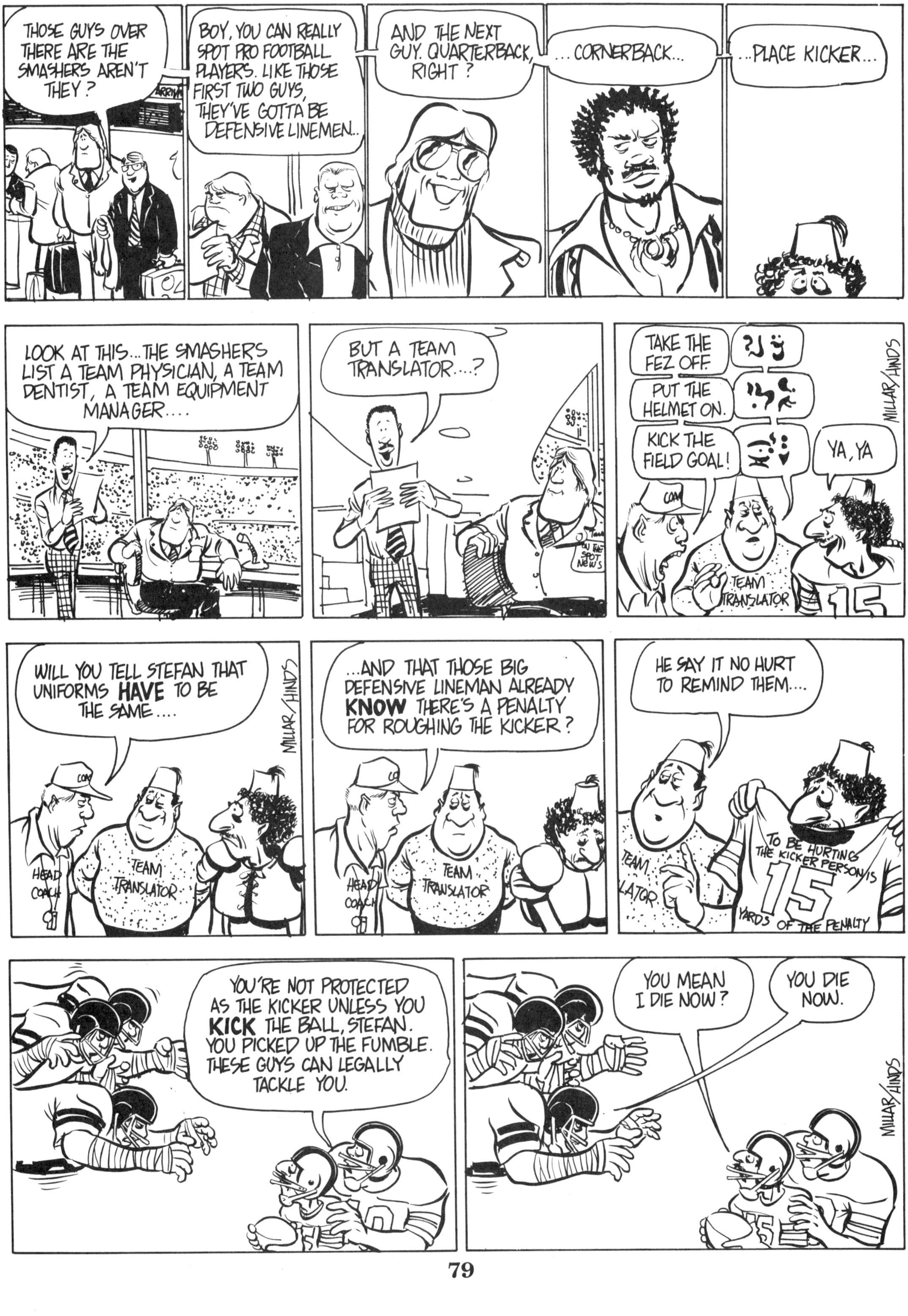
THOSE GUYS OVER THERE ARE THE SMASHERS AREN'T THEY?
BOY, YOU CAN REALLY SPOT PRO FOOTBALL PLAYERS. LIKE THOSE FIRST TWO GUYS, THEY'VE GOTTA BE DEFENSIVE LINEMEN..
AND THE NEXT GUY. QUARTERBACK, RIGHT?
...CORNERBACK...
...PLACE KICKER...
LOOK AT THIS...THE SMASHERS LIST A TEAM PHYSICIAN, A TEAM DENTIST, A TEAM EQUIPMENT MANAGER....
BUT A TEAM TRANSLATOR...?
ON THE SPOT NEWS
TAKE THE FEZ OFF.
PUT THE HELMET ON.
KICK THE FIELD GOAL!
YA, YA
TEAM TRANSLATOR
15
MILLAR/HINDS
WILL YOU TELL STEFAN THAT UNIFORMS **HAVE** TO BE THE SAME....
HEAD COACH
TEAM TRANSLATOR
MILLAR/HINDS
...AND THAT THOSE BIG DEFENSIVE LINEMAN ALREADY **KNOW** THERE'S A PENALTY FOR ROUGHING THE KICKER?
HEAD COACH
TEAM TRANSLATOR
HE SAY IT NO HURT TO REMIND THEM....
TO BE HURTING THE KICKER PERSON IS 15 YARDS OF THE PENALTY
YOU'RE NOT PROTECTED AS THE KICKER UNLESS YOU **KICK** THE BALL, STEFAN. YOU PICKED UP THE FUMBLE. THESE GUYS CAN LEGALLY TACKLE YOU.
YOU MEAN I DIE NOW?
YOU DIE NOW.
MILLAR/HINDS

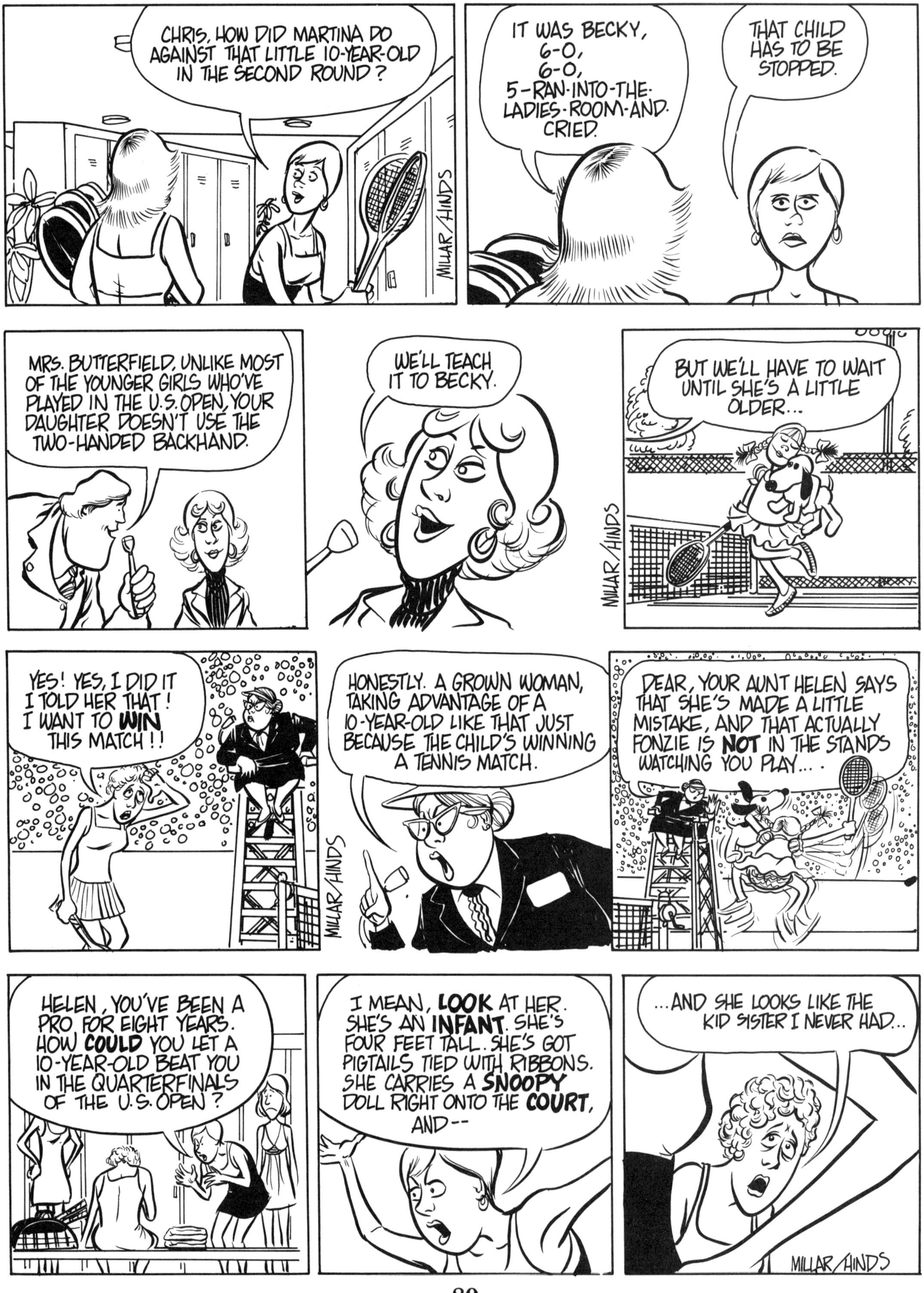
CHRIS, HOW DID MARTINA DO AGAINST THAT LITTLE 10-YEAR-OLD IN THE SECOND ROUND?
MILLAR/HINDS
IT WAS BECKY, 6-0, 6-0, 5-RAN-INTO-THE-LADIES-ROOM-AND-CRIED.
THAT CHILD HAS TO BE STOPPED.
MRS. BUTTERFIELD, UNLIKE MOST OF THE YOUNGER GIRLS WHO'VE PLAYED IN THE U.S. OPEN, YOUR DAUGHTER DOESN'T USE THE TWO-HANDED BACKHAND.
WE'LL TEACH IT TO BECKY.
BUT WE'LL HAVE TO WAIT UNTIL SHE'S A LITTLE OLDER...
MILLAR/HINDS
YES! YES, I DID IT I TOLD HER THAT! I WANT TO **WIN** THIS MATCH!!
MILLAR/HINDS
HONESTLY. A GROWN WOMAN, TAKING ADVANTAGE OF A 10-YEAR-OLD LIKE THAT JUST BECAUSE THE CHILD'S WINNING A TENNIS MATCH.
DEAR, YOUR AUNT HELEN SAYS THAT SHE'S MADE A LITTLE MISTAKE, AND THAT ACTUALLY FONZIE IS **NOT** IN THE STANDS WATCHING YOU PLAY...
HELEN, YOU'VE BEEN A PRO FOR EIGHT YEARS. HOW **COULD** YOU LET A 10-YEAR-OLD BEAT YOU IN THE QUARTERFINALS OF THE U.S. OPEN?
I MEAN, **LOOK** AT HER. SHE'S AN **INFANT**. SHE'S FOUR FEET TALL. SHE'S GOT PIGTAILS TIED WITH RIBBONS. SHE CARRIES A **SNOOPY** DOLL RIGHT ONTO THE **COURT**, AND--
...AND SHE LOOKS LIKE THE KID SISTER I NEVER HAD...
MILLAR/HINDS

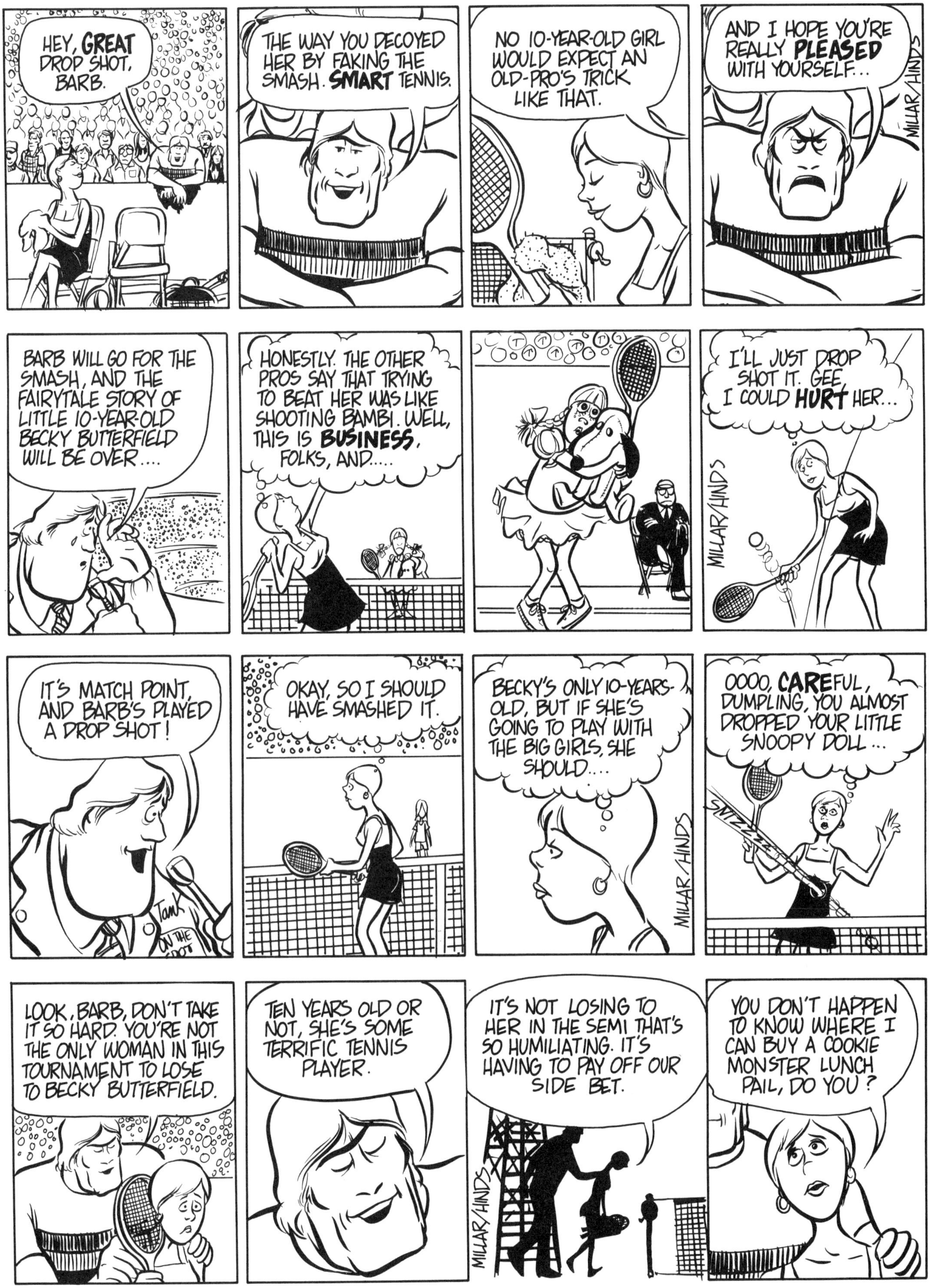
HEY, GREAT DROP SHOT, BARB.
THE WAY YOU DECOYED HER BY FAKING THE SMASH. SMART TENNIS.
NO 10-YEAR-OLD GIRL WOULD EXPECT AN OLD-PRO'S TRICK LIKE THAT.
AND I HOPE YOU'RE REALLY PLEASED WITH YOURSELF...
MILLAR/HINDS
BARB WILL GO FOR THE SMASH, AND THE FAIRYTALE STORY OF LITTLE 10-YEAR-OLD BECKY BUTTERFIELD WILL BE OVER....
HONESTLY. THE OTHER PROS SAY THAT TRYING TO BEAT HER WAS LIKE SHOOTING BAMBI. WELL, THIS IS BUSINESS, FOLKS, AND....
MILLAR/HINDS
I'LL JUST DROP SHOT IT. GEE, I COULD HURT HER...
IT'S MATCH POINT, AND BARB'S PLAYED A DROP SHOT!
OKAY, SO I SHOULD HAVE SMASHED IT.
BECKY'S ONLY 10-YEARS-OLD, BUT IF SHE'S GOING TO PLAY WITH THE BIG GIRLS, SHE SHOULD....
MILLAR/HINDS
OOOO, CAREFUL, DUMPLING, YOU ALMOST DROPPED YOUR LITTLE SNOOPY DOLL...
LOOK, BARB, DON'T TAKE IT SO HARD. YOU'RE NOT THE ONLY WOMAN IN THIS TOURNAMENT TO LOSE TO BECKY BUTTERFIELD.
TEN YEARS OLD OR NOT, SHE'S SOME TERRIFIC TENNIS PLAYER.
IT'S NOT LOSING TO HER IN THE SEMI THAT'S SO HUMILIATING. IT'S HAVING TO PAY OFF OUR SIDE BET.
MILLAR/HINDS
YOU DON'T HAPPEN TO KNOW WHERE I CAN BUY A COOKIE MONSTER LUNCH PAIL, DO YOU?

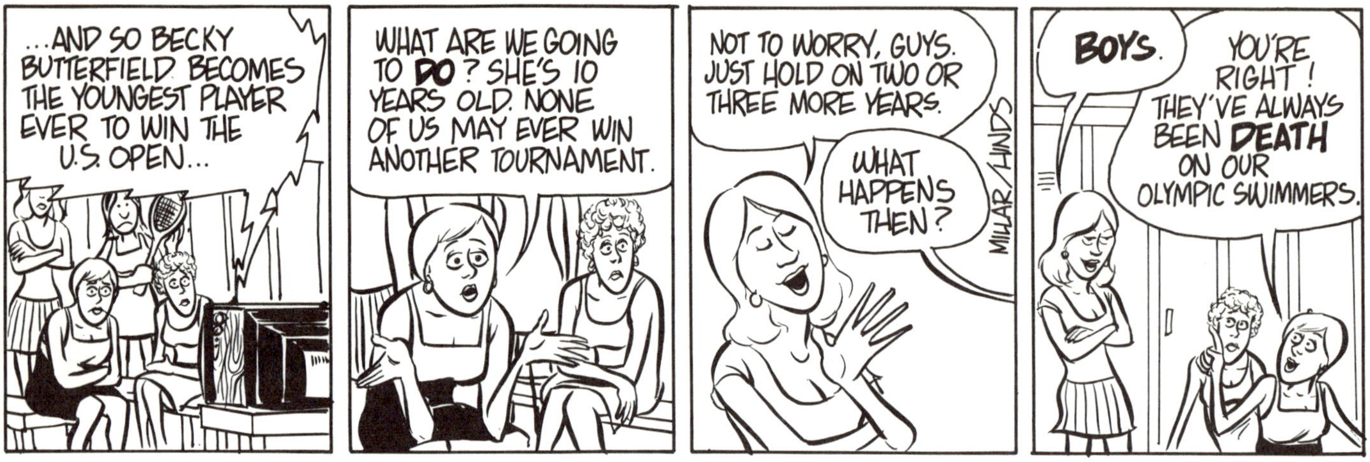
...AND SO BECKY BUTTERFIELD BECOMES THE YOUNGEST PLAYER EVER TO WIN THE U.S. OPEN...
WHAT ARE WE GOING TO **DO**? SHE'S 10 YEARS OLD. NONE OF US MAY EVER WIN ANOTHER TOURNAMENT.
NOT TO WORRY, GUYS. JUST HOLD ON TWO OR THREE MORE YEARS.
WHAT HAPPENS THEN?
MILLAR/HINDS
BOYS.
YOU'RE RIGHT! THEY'VE ALWAYS BEEN **DEATH** ON OUR OLYMPIC SWIMMERS.

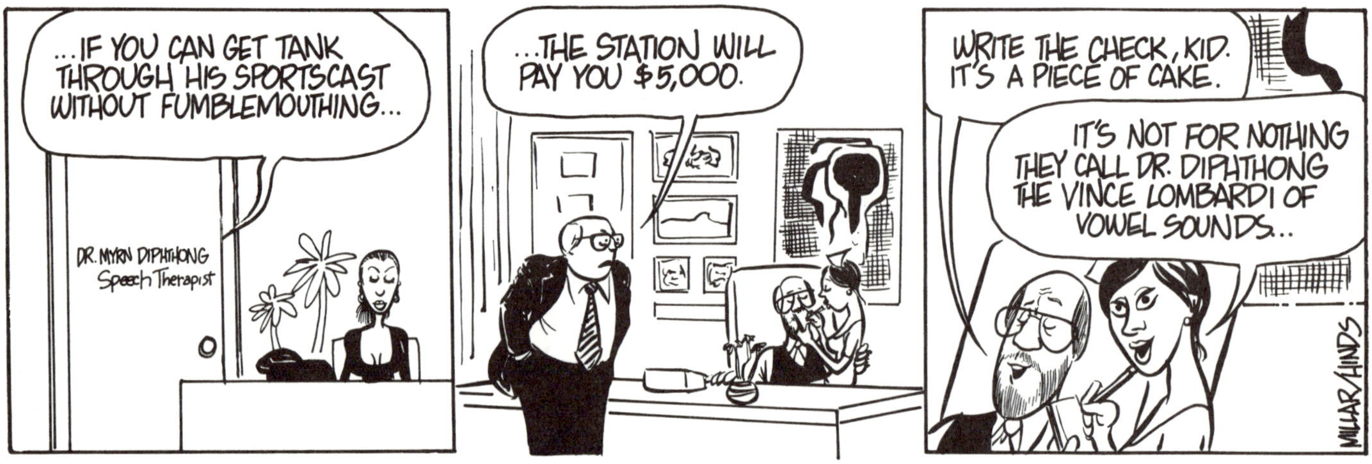
...IF YOU CAN GET TANK THROUGH HIS SPORTSCAST WITHOUT FUMBLEMOUTHING...
DR. MYRN DIPHTHONG
Speech Therapist
...THE STATION WILL PAY YOU $5,000.
WRITE THE CHECK, KID. IT'S A PIECE OF CAKE.
IT'S NOT FOR NOTHING THEY CALL DR. DIPHTHONG THE VINCE LOMBARDI OF VOWEL SOUNDS...
MILLAR/HINDS

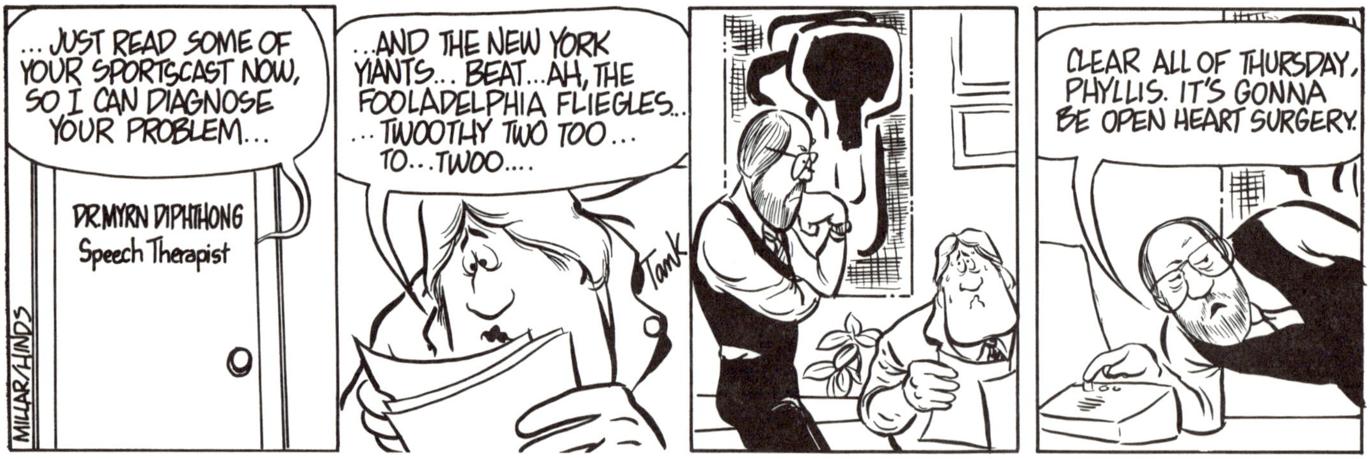
...JUST READ SOME OF YOUR SPORTSCAST NOW, SO I CAN DIAGNOSE YOUR PROBLEM...
DR. MYRN DIPHTHONG
Speech Therapist
MILLAR/HINDS
...AND THE NEW YORK YIANTS... BEAT...AH, THE FOOLADELPHIA FLIEGLES... ...TWOOTHY TWO TOO... TO...TWOO....
Tank
CLEAR ALL OF THURSDAY, PHYLLIS. IT'S GONNA BE OPEN HEART SURGERY.

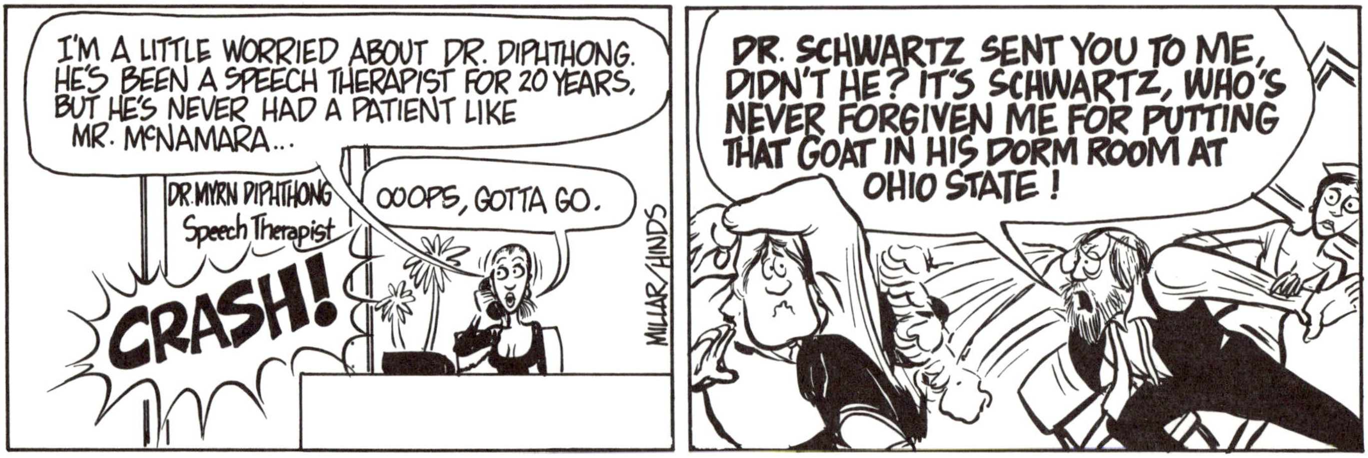
I'M A LITTLE WORRIED ABOUT DR. DIPHTHONG. HE'S BEEN A SPEECH THERAPIST FOR 20 YEARS, BUT HE'S NEVER HAD A PATIENT LIKE MR. McNAMARA...
DR. MYRN DIPHTHONG
Speech Therapist
OOOPS, GOTTA GO.
CRASH!
MILLAR/HINDS
DR. SCHWARTZ SENT YOU TO ME, DIDN'T HE? IT'S SCHWARTZ, WHO'S NEVER FORGIVEN ME FOR PUTTING THAT GOAT IN HIS DORM ROOM AT OHIO STATE!

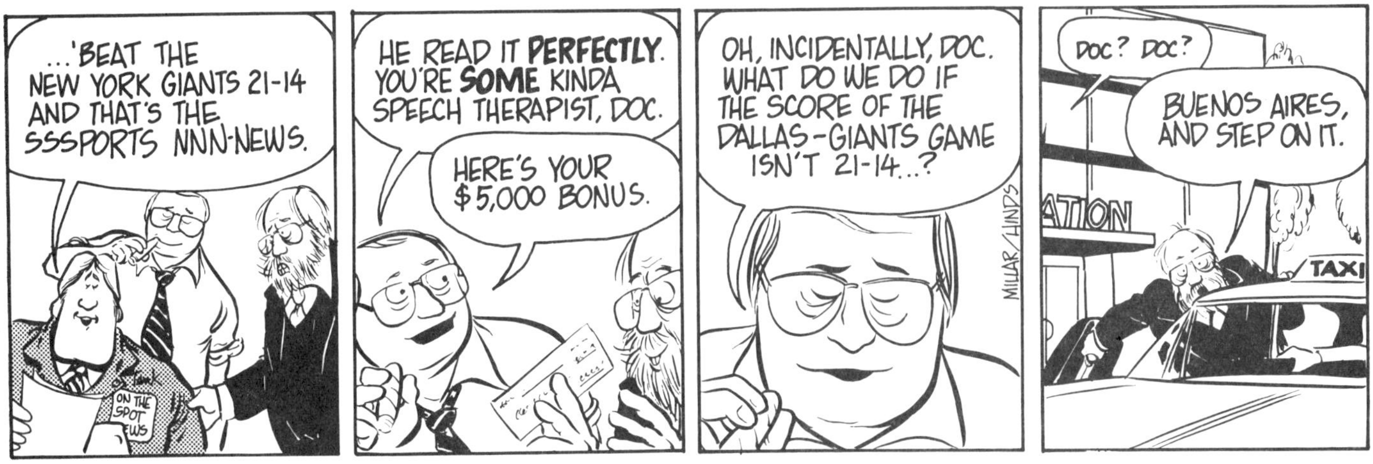
...'BEAT THE NEW YORK GIANTS 21-14 AND THAT'S THE SSSPORTS NNN-NEWS.
ON THE SPOT
HE READ IT **PERFECTLY**. YOU'RE **SOME** KINDA SPEECH THERAPIST, DOC.
HERE'S YOUR $5,000 BONUS.
OH, INCIDENTALLY, DOC. WHAT DO WE DO IF THE SCORE OF THE DALLAS-GIANTS GAME ISN'T 21-14...?
MILLAR/HINDS
DOC? DOC?
BUENOS AIRES, AND STEP ON IT.
ATION
TAXI

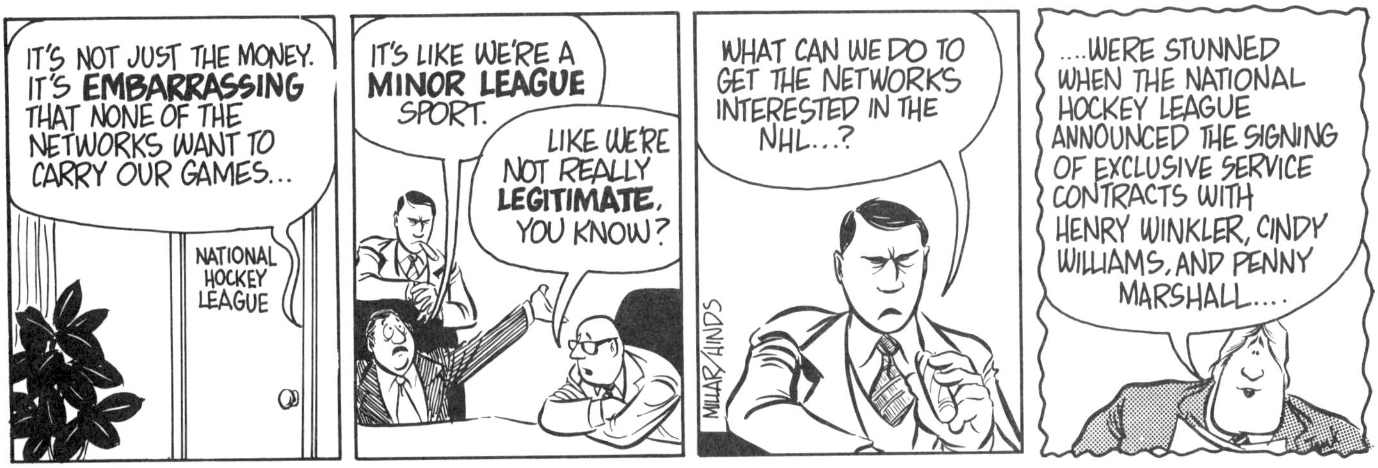
IT'S NOT JUST THE MONEY. IT'S **EMBARRASSING** THAT NONE OF THE NETWORKS WANT TO CARRY OUR GAMES...
NATIONAL HOCKEY LEAGUE
IT'S LIKE WE'RE A **MINOR LEAGUE** SPORT.
LIKE WE'RE NOT REALLY **LEGITIMATE**, YOU KNOW?
MILLAR/HINDS
WHAT CAN WE DO TO GET THE NETWORKS INTERESTED IN THE NHL...?
....WERE STUNNED WHEN THE NATIONAL HOCKEY LEAGUE ANNOUNCED THE SIGNING OF EXCLUSIVE SERVICE CONTRACTS WITH HENRY WINKLER, CINDY WILLIAMS, AND PENNY MARSHALL....

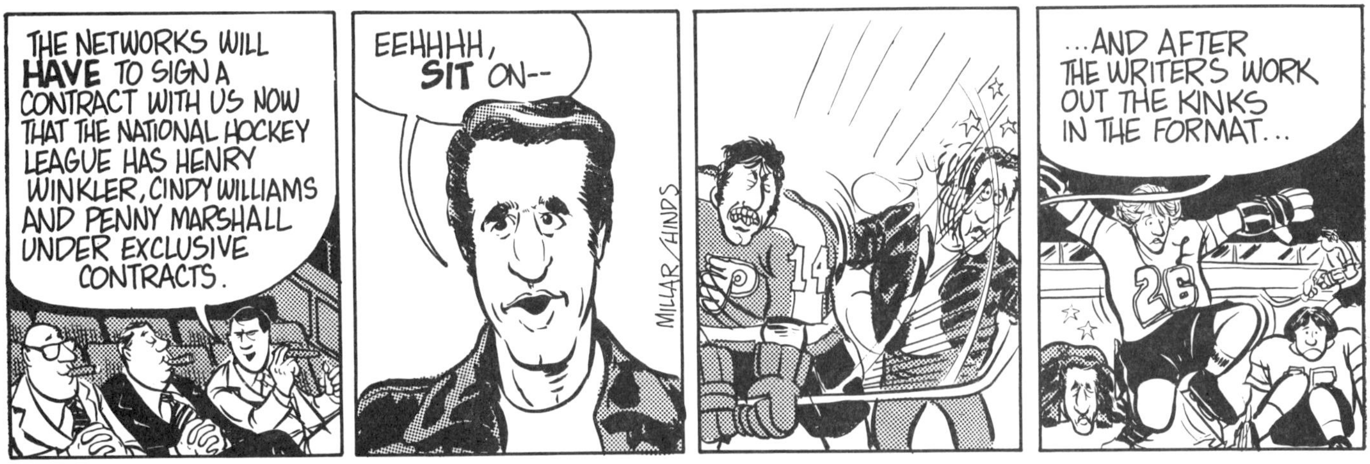
THE NETWORKS WILL **HAVE** TO SIGN A CONTRACT WITH US NOW THAT THE NATIONAL HOCKEY LEAGUE HAS HENRY WINKLER, CINDY WILLIAMS AND PENNY MARSHALL UNDER EXCLUSIVE CONTRACTS.
EEHHHH, **SIT** ON--
MILLAR/HINDS
...AND AFTER THE WRITERS WORK OUT THE KINKS IN THE FORMAT...

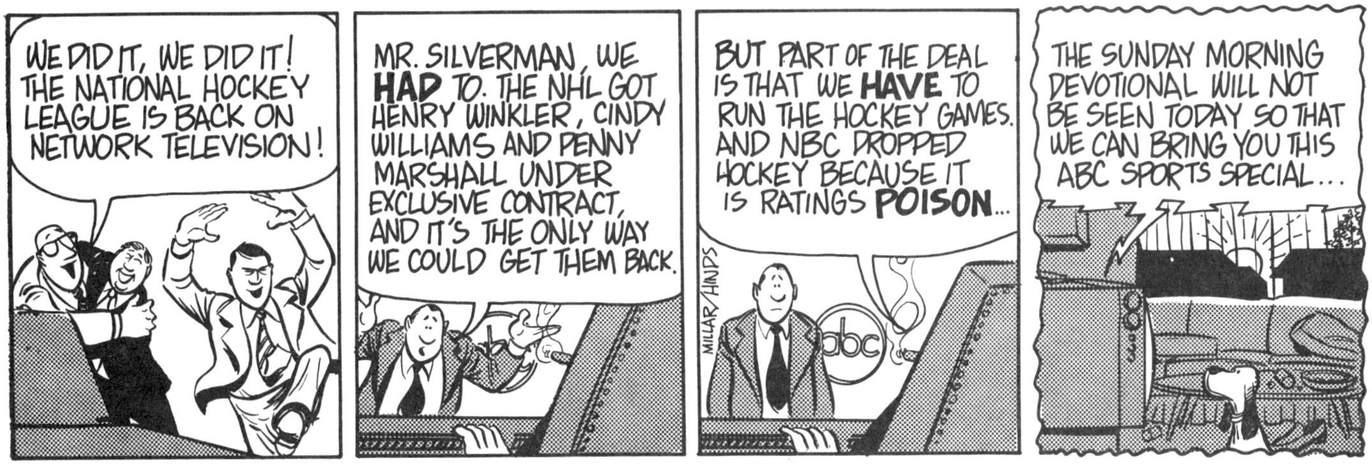
WE DID IT, WE DID IT! THE NATIONAL HOCKEY LEAGUE IS BACK ON NETWORK TELEVISION!
MR. SILVERMAN, WE **HAD** TO. THE NHL GOT HENRY WINKLER, CINDY WILLIAMS AND PENNY MARSHALL UNDER EXCLUSIVE CONTRACT, AND IT'S THE ONLY WAY WE COULD GET THEM BACK.
BUT PART OF THE DEAL IS THAT WE **HAVE** TO RUN THE HOCKEY GAMES. AND NBC DROPPED HOCKEY BECAUSE IT IS RATINGS **POISON**...
MILLAR/HINDS
abc
THE SUNDAY MORNING DEVOTIONAL WILL NOT BE SEEN TODAY SO THAT WE CAN BRING YOU THIS ABC SPORTS SPECIAL...

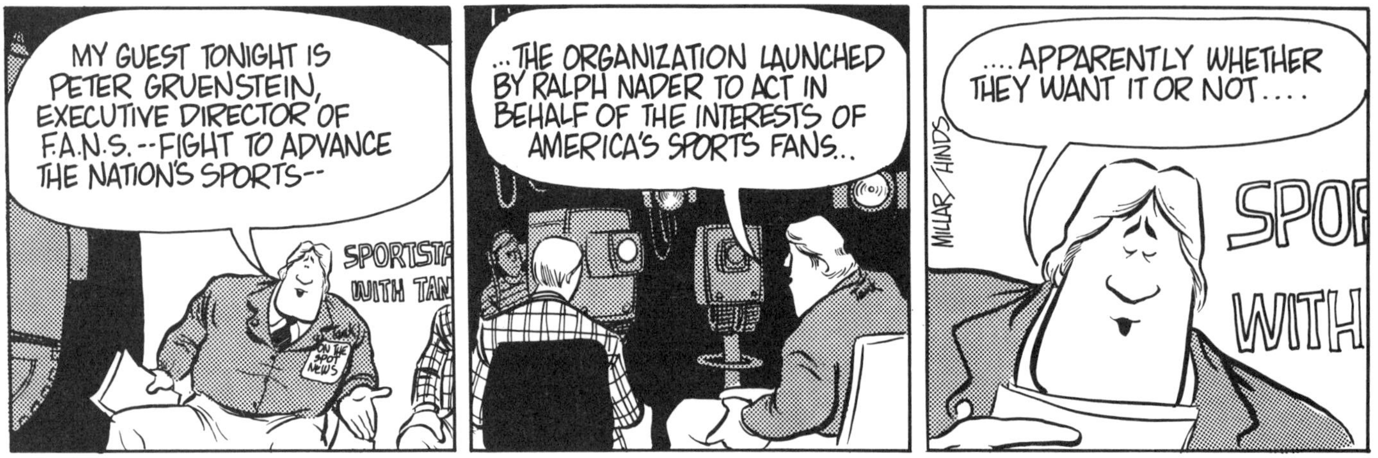
MY GUEST TONIGHT IS PETER GRUENSTEIN, EXECUTIVE DIRECTOR OF F.A.N.S.--FIGHT TO ADVANCE THE NATION'S SPORTS--
ON THE SPOT NEWS
...THE ORGANIZATION LAUNCHED BY RALPH NADER TO ACT IN BEHALF OF THE INTERESTS OF AMERICA'S SPORTS FANS...
....APPARENTLY WHETHER THEY WANT IT OR NOT....
MILLAR/HINDS

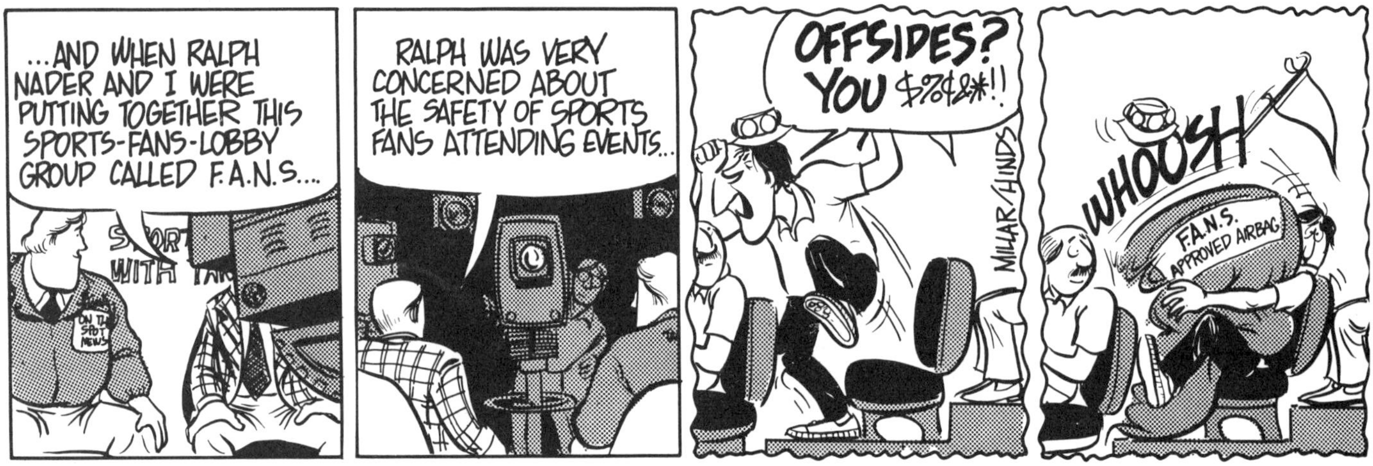
...AND WHEN RALPH NADER AND I WERE PUTTING TOGETHER THIS SPORTS-FANS-LOBBY GROUP CALLED F.A.N.S....
ON THE SPOT NEWS
RALPH WAS VERY CONCERNED ABOUT THE SAFETY OF SPORTS FANS ATTENDING EVENTS...
OFFSIDES? YOU $%¢&*!!
MILLAR/HINDS
WHOOSH
F.A.N.S. APPROVED AIRBAG

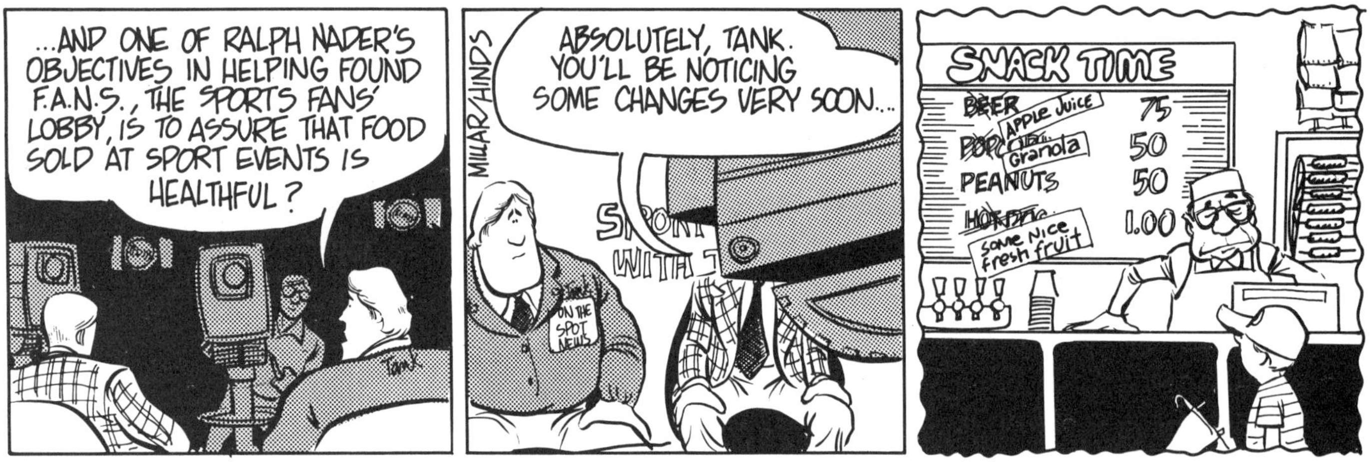
...AND ONE OF RALPH NADER'S OBJECTIVES IN HELPING FOUND F.A.N.S., THE SPORTS FANS' LOBBY, IS TO ASSURE THAT FOOD SOLD AT SPORT EVENTS IS HEALTHFUL?
MILLAR/HINDS
ABSOLUTELY, TANK. YOU'LL BE NOTICING SOME CHANGES VERY SOON...
ON THE SPOT NEWS
SNACK TIME
BEER Apple Juice 75
Granola 50
PEANUTS 50
Some Nice fresh fruit 1.00

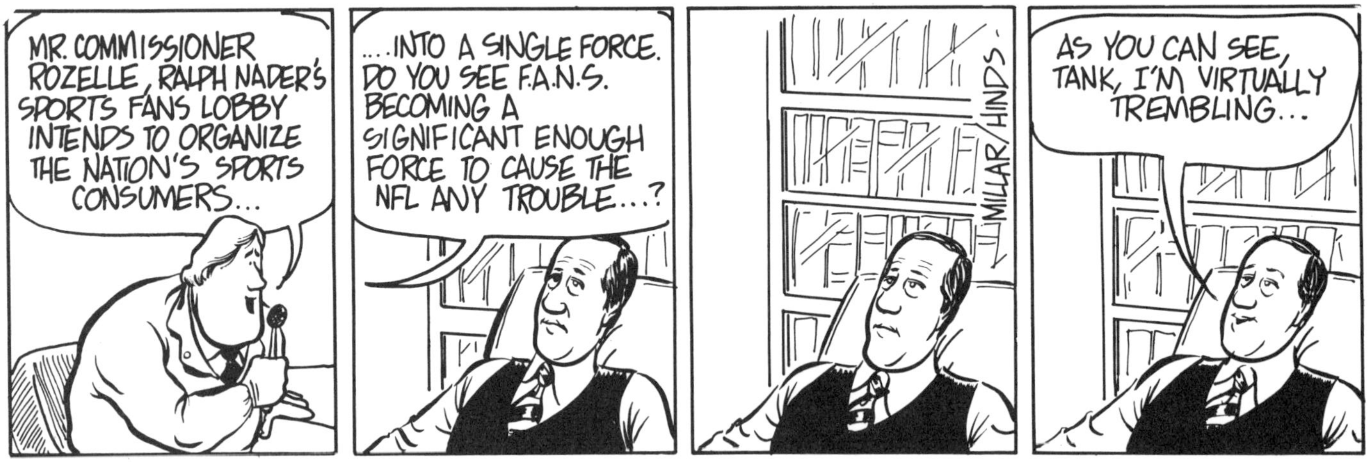
MR. COMMISSIONER ROZELLE, RALPH NADER'S SPORTS FANS LOBBY INTENDS TO ORGANIZE THE NATION'S SPORTS CONSUMERS...
....INTO A SINGLE FORCE. DO YOU SEE F.A.N.S. BECOMING A SIGNIFICANT ENOUGH FORCE TO CAUSE THE NFL ANY TROUBLE...?
MILLAR/HINDS
AS YOU CAN SEE, TANK, I'M VIRTUALLY TREMBLING...

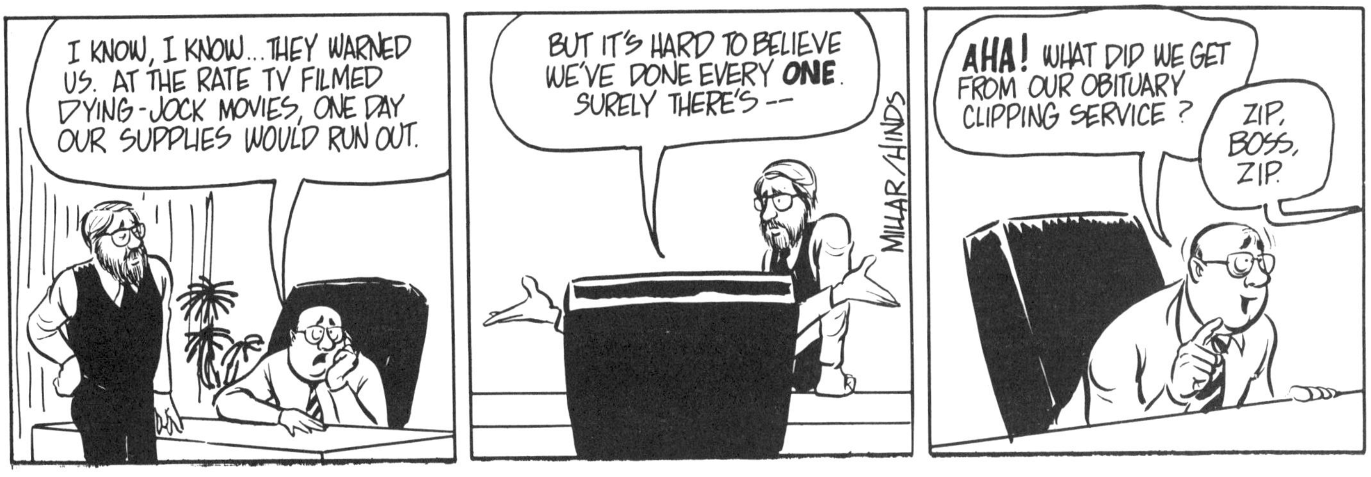
I KNOW, I KNOW...THEY WARNED US. AT THE RATE TV FILMED DYING-JOCK MOVIES, ONE DAY OUR SUPPLIES WOULD RUN OUT.
BUT IT'S HARD TO BELIEVE WE'VE DONE EVERY ONE. SURELY THERE'S --
MILLAR/HINDS
AHA! WHAT DID WE GET FROM OUR OBITUARY CLIPPING SERVICE?
ZIP, BOSS, ZIP.

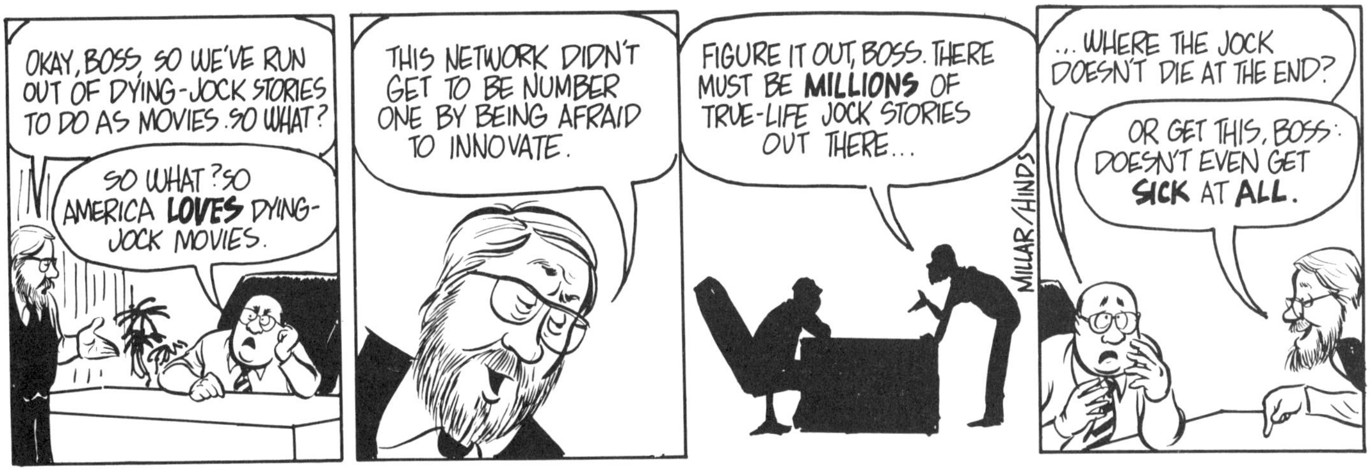
OKAY, BOSS, SO WE'VE RUN OUT OF DYING-JOCK STORIES TO DO AS MOVIES. SO WHAT?
SO WHAT? SO AMERICA LOVES DYING-JOCK MOVIES.
THIS NETWORK DIDN'T GET TO BE NUMBER ONE BY BEING AFRAID TO INNOVATE.
FIGURE IT OUT, BOSS. THERE MUST BE MILLIONS OF TRUE-LIFE JOCK STORIES OUT THERE...
MILLAR/HINDS
...WHERE THE JOCK DOESN'T DIE AT THE END?
OR GET THIS, BOSS: DOESN'T EVEN GET SICK AT ALL.

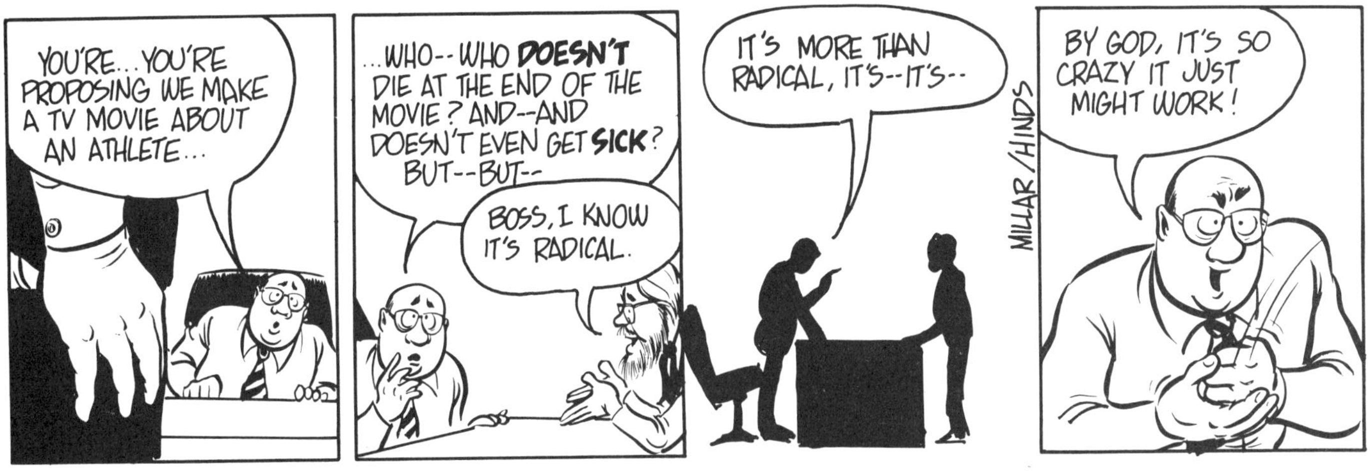
YOU'RE...YOU'RE PROPOSING WE MAKE A TV MOVIE ABOUT AN ATHLETE...
...WHO--WHO DOESN'T DIE AT THE END OF THE MOVIE? AND--AND DOESN'T EVEN GET SICK? BUT--BUT--
BOSS, I KNOW IT'S RADICAL.
IT'S MORE THAN RADICAL, IT'S--IT'S--
MILLAR/HINDS
BY GOD, IT'S SO CRAZY IT JUST MIGHT WORK!

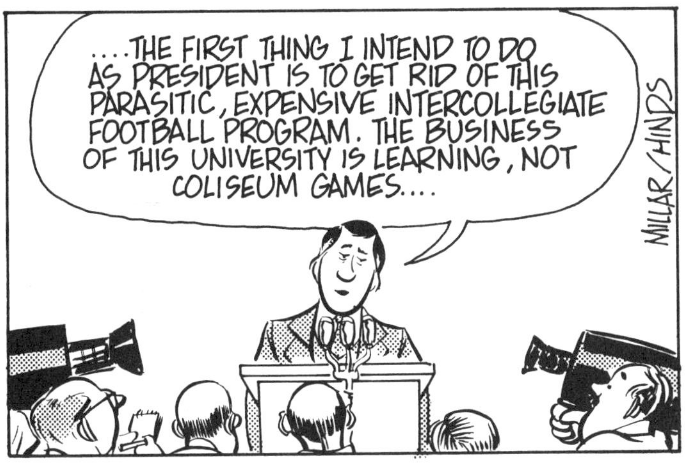
....THE FIRST THING I INTEND TO DO AS PRESIDENT IS TO GET RID OF THIS PARASITIC, EXPENSIVE INTERCOLLEGIATE FOOTBALL PROGRAM. THE BUSINESS OF THIS UNIVERSITY IS LEARNING, NOT COLISEUM GAMES....
MILLAR/HINDS

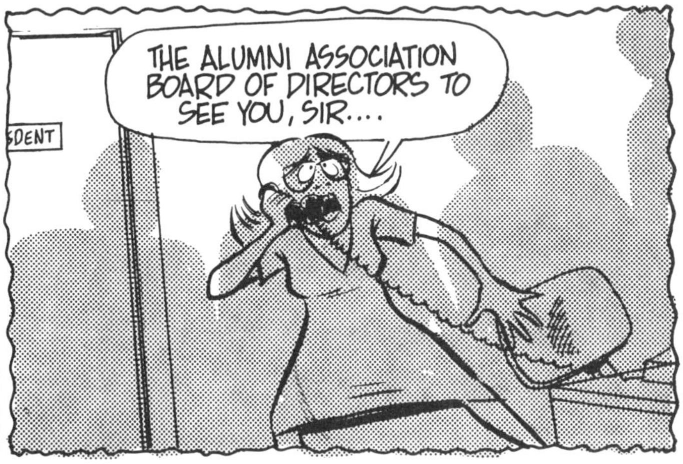
THE ALUMNI ASSOCIATION BOARD OF DIRECTORS TO SEE YOU, SIR....
SDENT

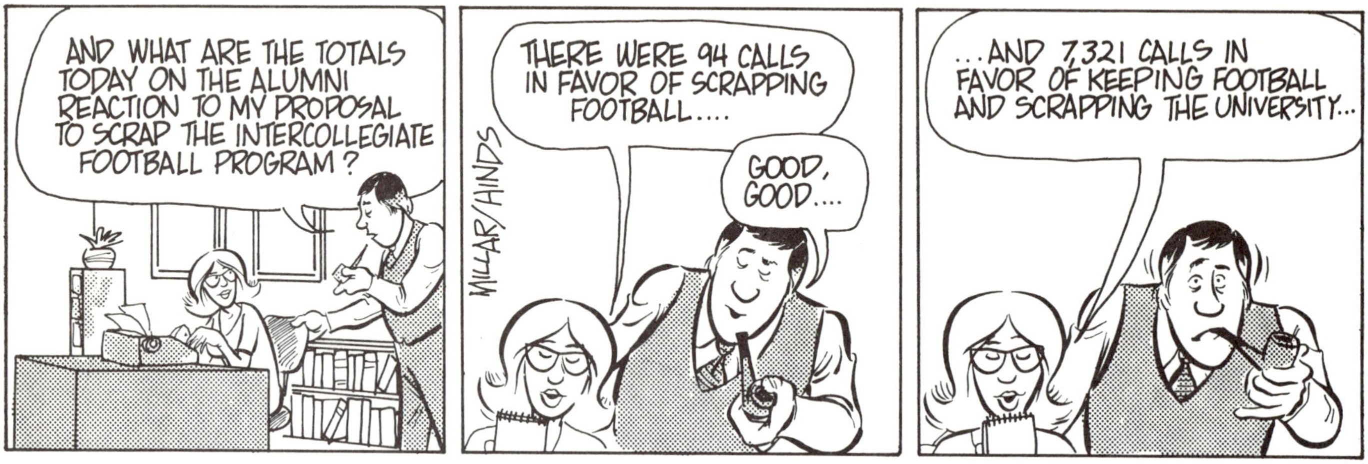
AND WHAT ARE THE TOTALS TODAY ON THE ALUMNI REACTION TO MY PROPOSAL TO SCRAP THE INTERCOLLEGIATE FOOTBALL PROGRAM?
MILLAR/HINDS
THERE WERE 94 CALLS IN FAVOR OF SCRAPPING FOOTBALL....
GOOD, GOOD....
...AND 7,321 CALLS IN FAVOR OF KEEPING FOOTBALL AND SCRAPPING THE UNIVERSITY...

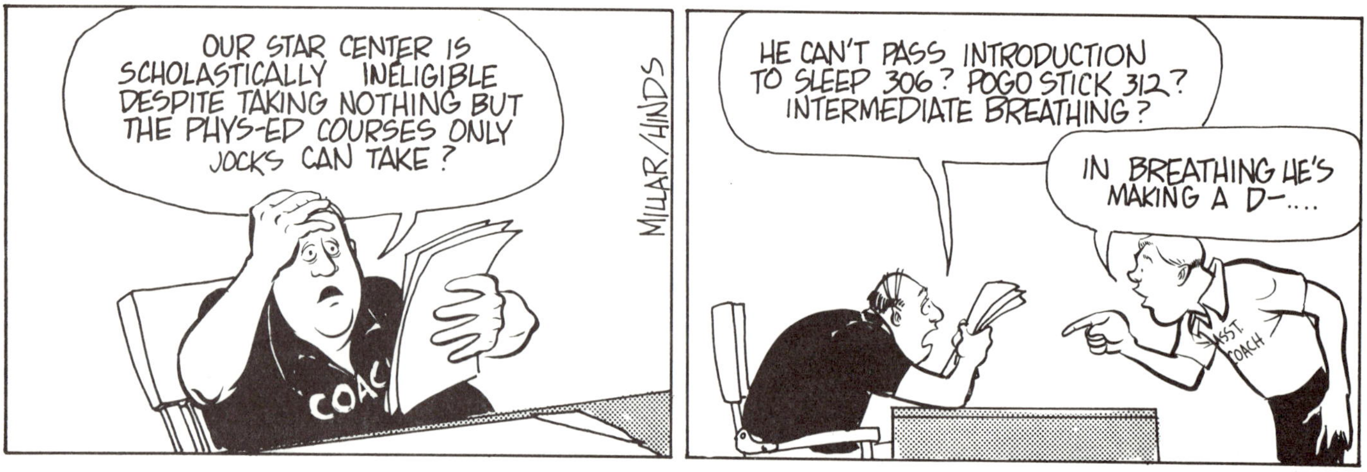
OUR STAR CENTER IS SCHOLASTICALLY INELIGIBLE DESPITE TAKING NOTHING BUT THE PHYS-ED COURSES ONLY JOCKS CAN TAKE?
COACH
MILLAR/HINDS
HE CAN'T PASS INTRODUCTION TO SLEEP 306? POGO STICK 312? INTERMEDIATE BREATHING?
IN BREATHING HE'S MAKING A D-....
ASST. COACH

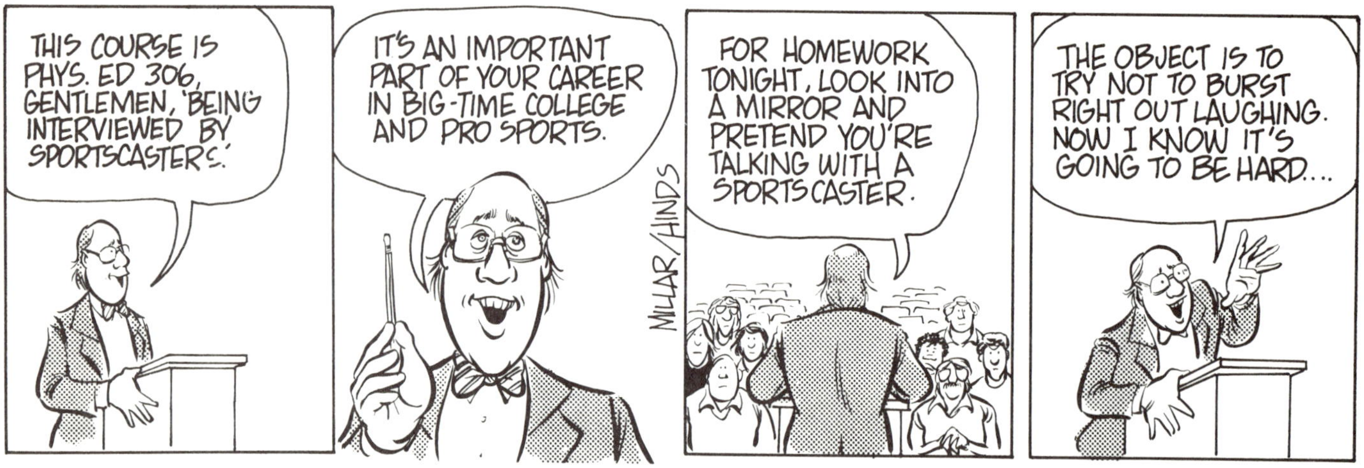
THIS COURSE IS PHYS. ED 306, GENTLEMEN, 'BEING INTERVIEWED BY SPORTSCASTERS.'
IT'S AN IMPORTANT PART OF YOUR CAREER IN BIG-TIME COLLEGE AND PRO SPORTS.
MILLAR/HINDS
FOR HOMEWORK TONIGHT, LOOK INTO A MIRROR AND PRETEND YOU'RE TALKING WITH A SPORTSCASTER.
THE OBJECT IS TO TRY NOT TO BURST RIGHT OUT LAUGHING. NOW I KNOW IT'S GOING TO BE HARD...

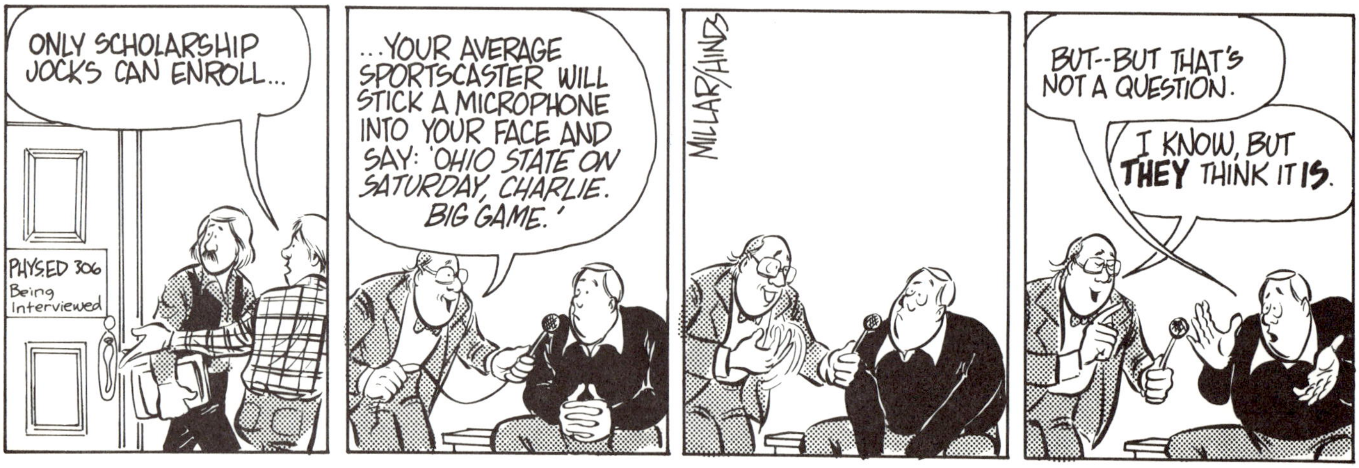
ONLY SCHOLARSHIP JOCKS CAN ENROLL...
PHYS.ED 306
Being Interviewed
...YOUR AVERAGE SPORTSCASTER WILL STICK A MICROPHONE INTO YOUR FACE AND SAY: 'OHIO STATE ON SATURDAY, CHARLIE. BIG GAME.'
MILLAR/HINDS
BUT--BUT THAT'S NOT A QUESTION.
I KNOW, BUT THEY THINK IT IS.

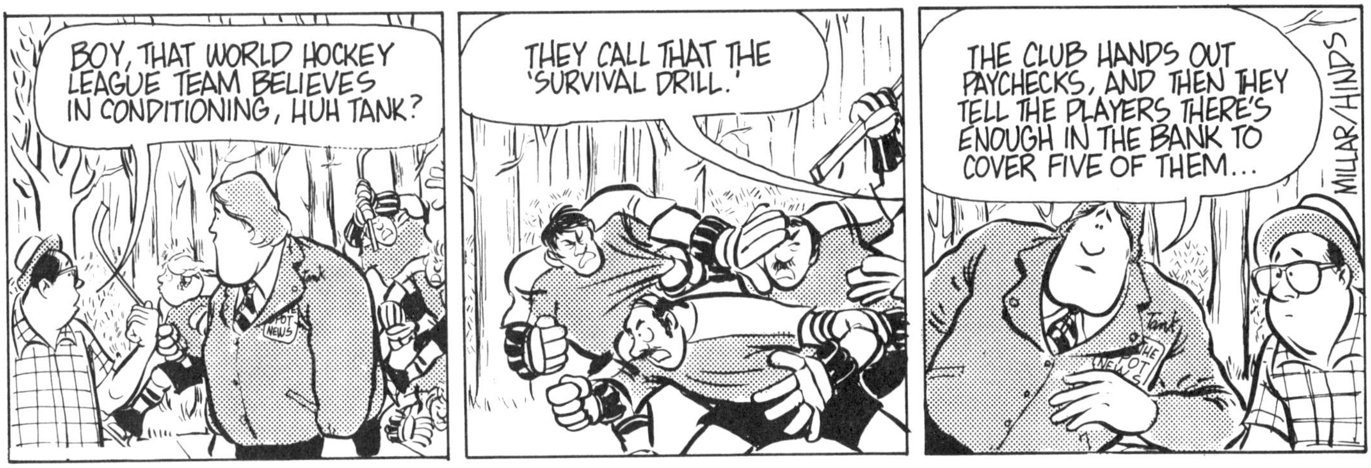
BOY, THAT WORLD HOCKEY LEAGUE TEAM BELIEVES IN CONDITIONING, HUH TANK?
THEY CALL THAT THE 'SURVIVAL DRILL.'
THE CLUB HANDS OUT PAYCHECKS, AND THEN THEY TELL THE PLAYERS THERE'S ENOUGH IN THE BANK TO COVER FIVE OF THEM...
MILLAR/HINDS

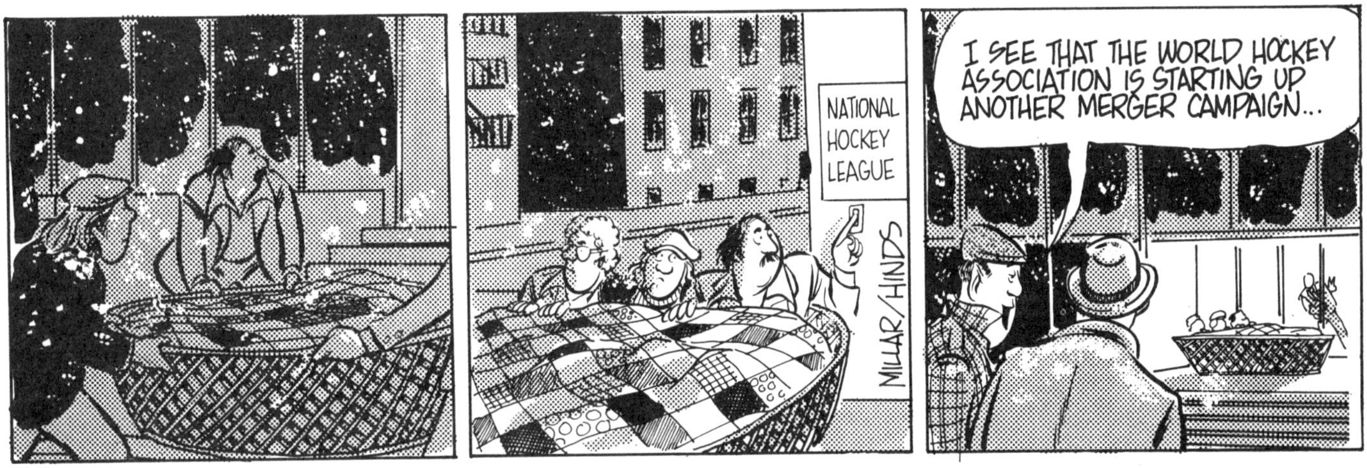
NATIONAL HOCKEY LEAGUE
MILLAR/HINDS
I SEE THAT THE WORLD HOCKEY ASSOCIATION IS STARTING UP ANOTHER MERGER CAMPAIGN...

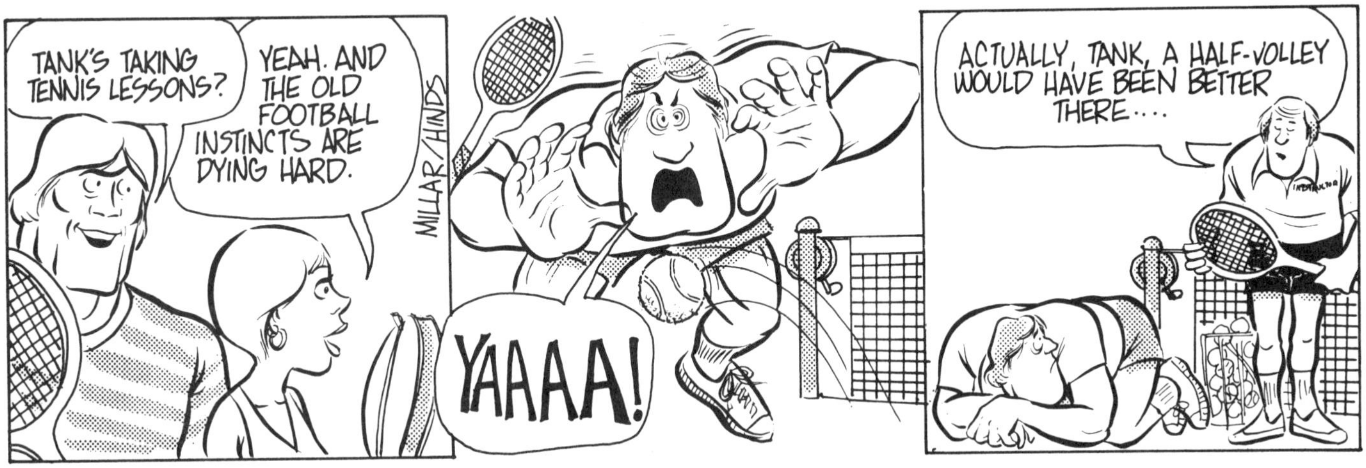
TANK'S TAKING TENNIS LESSONS?
YEAH. AND THE OLD FOOTBALL INSTINCTS ARE DYING HARD.
MILLAR/HINDS
YAAAA!
ACTUALLY, TANK, A HALF-VOLLEY WOULD HAVE BEEN BETTER THERE....

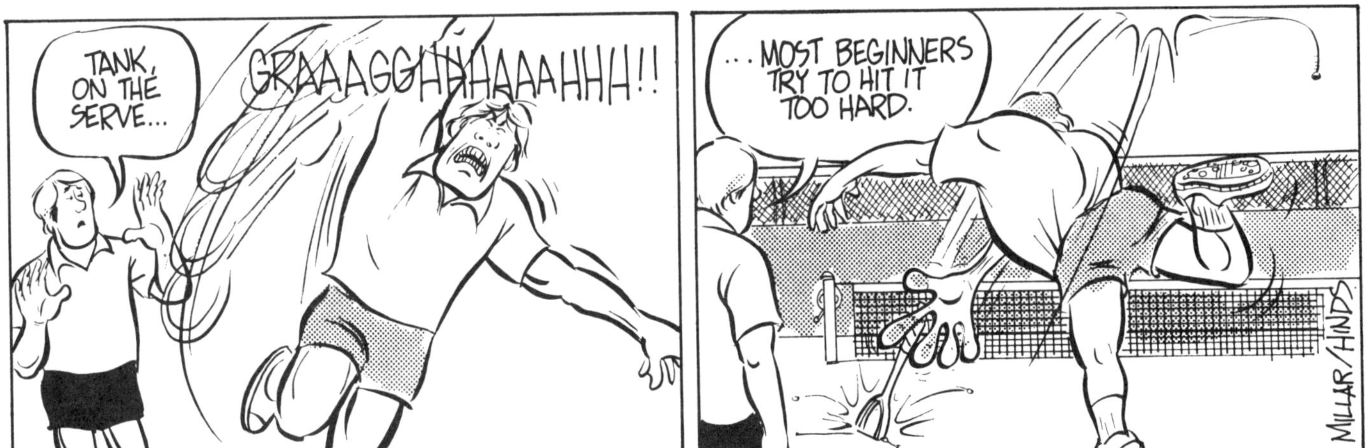
TANK, ON THE SERVE...
GRAAAGGHHHAAAAHHH!!
...MOST BEGINNERS TRY TO HIT IT TOO HARD.
MILLAR/HINDS

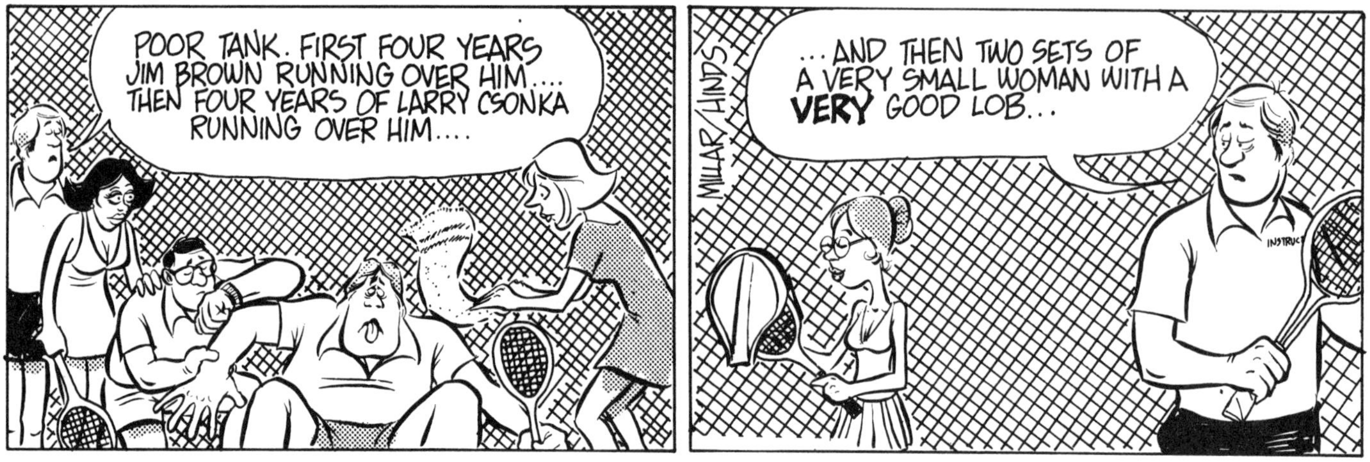
POOR TANK. FIRST FOUR YEARS JIM BROWN RUNNING OVER HIM.... THEN FOUR YEARS OF LARRY CSONKA RUNNING OVER HIM....
MILLAR/HINDS
...AND THEN TWO SETS OF A VERY SMALL WOMAN WITH A **VERY** GOOD LOB...

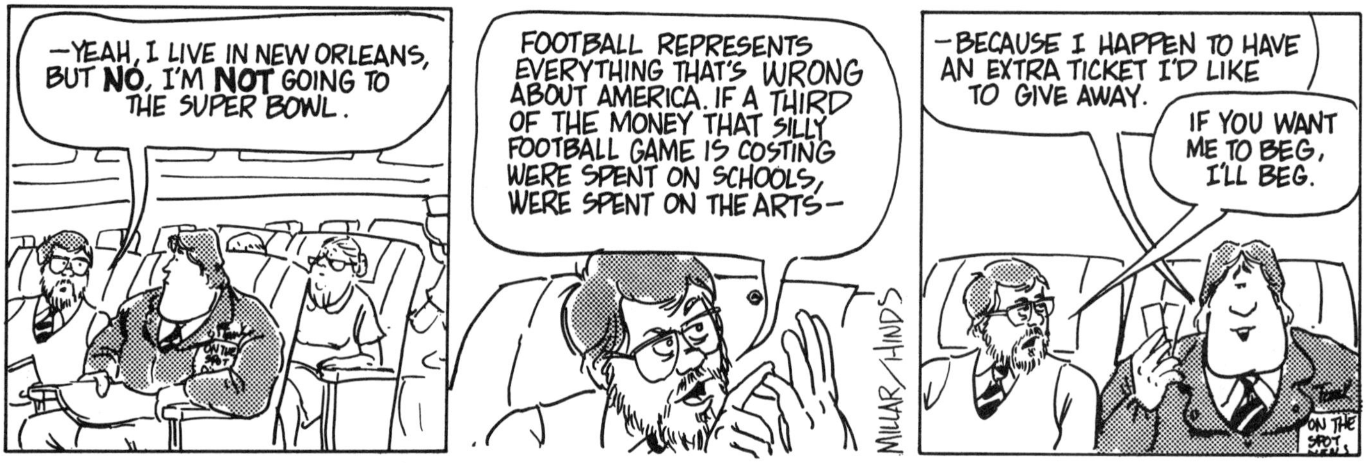
—YEAH, I LIVE IN NEW ORLEANS, BUT **NO**, I'M **NOT** GOING TO THE SUPER BOWL.
FOOTBALL REPRESENTS EVERYTHING THAT'S WRONG ABOUT AMERICA. IF A THIRD OF THE MONEY THAT SILLY FOOTBALL GAME IS COSTING WERE SPENT ON SCHOOLS, WERE SPENT ON THE ARTS—
MILLAR/HINDS
—BECAUSE I HAPPEN TO HAVE AN EXTRA TICKET I'D LIKE TO GIVE AWAY.
IF YOU WANT ME TO BEG, I'LL BEG.

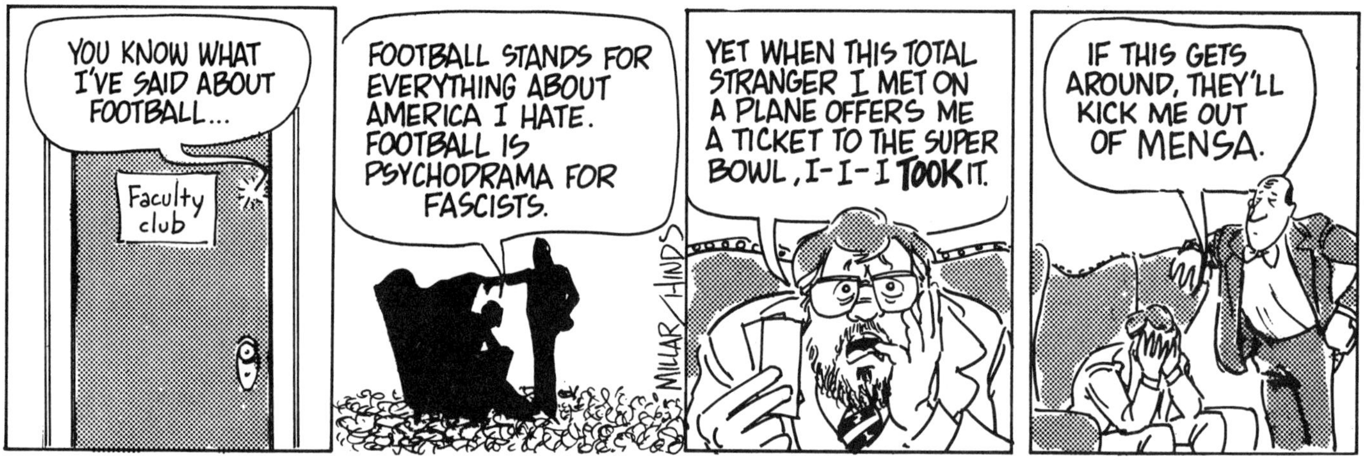
YOU KNOW WHAT I'VE SAID ABOUT FOOTBALL...
Faculty club
FOOTBALL STANDS FOR EVERYTHING ABOUT AMERICA I HATE. FOOTBALL IS PSYCHODRAMA FOR FASCISTS.
MILLAR/HINDS
YET WHEN THIS TOTAL STRANGER I MET ON A PLANE OFFERS ME A TICKET TO THE SUPER BOWL, I-I-I **TOOK** IT.
IF THIS GETS AROUND, THEY'LL KICK ME OUT OF MENSA.

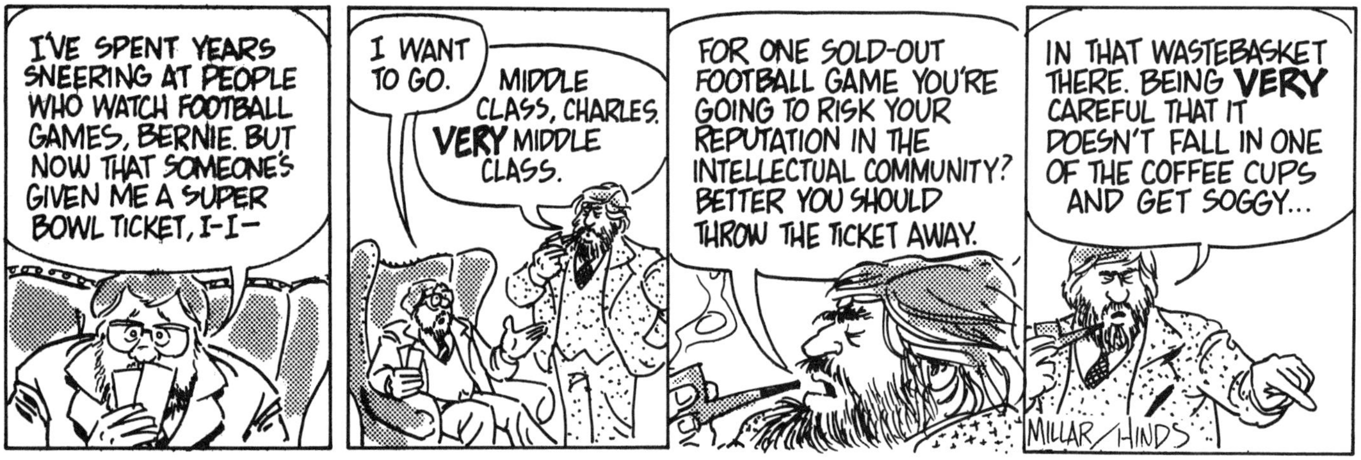
I'VE SPENT YEARS SNEERING AT PEOPLE WHO WATCH FOOTBALL GAMES, BERNIE. BUT NOW THAT SOMEONE'S GIVEN ME A SUPER BOWL TICKET, I-I—
I WANT TO GO.
MIDDLE CLASS, CHARLES. **VERY** MIDDLE CLASS.
FOR ONE SOLD-OUT FOOTBALL GAME YOU'RE GOING TO RISK YOUR REPUTATION IN THE INTELLECTUAL COMMUNITY? BETTER YOU SHOULD THROW THE TICKET AWAY.
IN THAT WASTEBASKET THERE. BEING **VERY** CAREFUL THAT IT DOESN'T FALL IN ONE OF THE COFFEE CUPS AND GET SOGGY...
MILLAR/HINDS

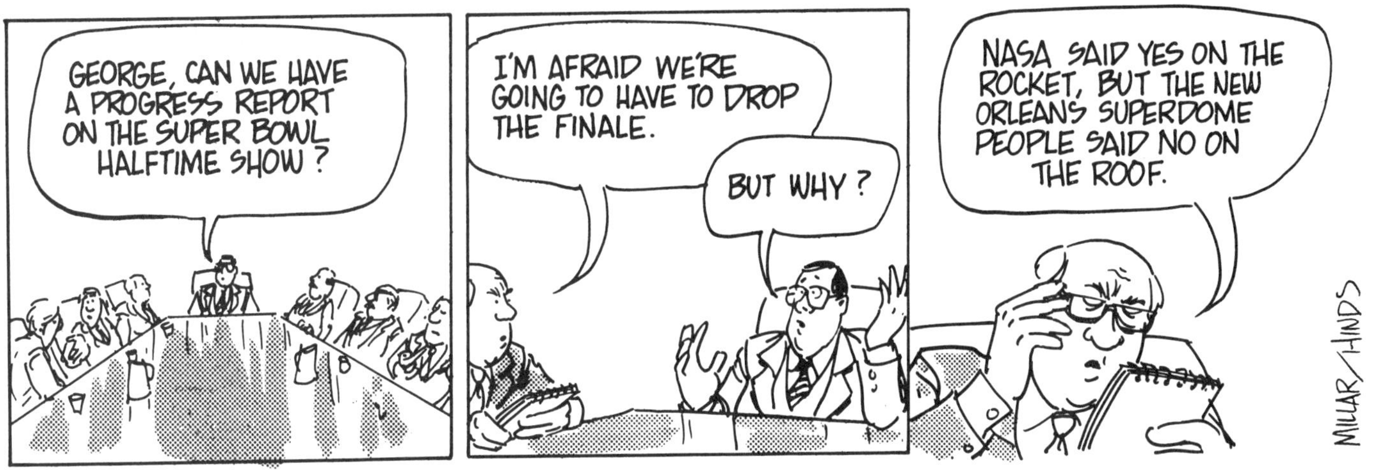
GEORGE, CAN WE HAVE A PROGRESS REPORT ON THE SUPER BOWL HALFTIME SHOW ?
I'M AFRAID WE'RE GOING TO HAVE TO DROP THE FINALE.
BUT WHY ?
NASA SAID YES ON THE ROCKET, BUT THE NEW ORLEANS SUPERDOME PEOPLE SAID NO ON THE ROOF.
MILLAR/HINDS

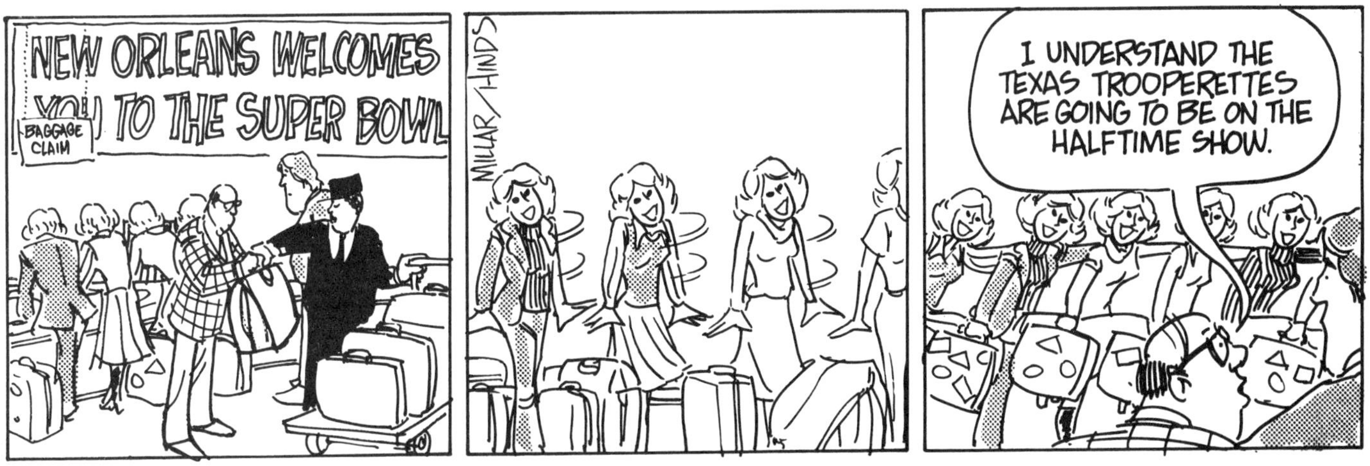
NEW ORLEANS WELCOMES YOU TO THE SUPER BOWL
BAGGAGE CLAIM
MILLAR/HINDS
I UNDERSTAND THE TEXAS TROOPERETTES ARE GOING TO BE ON THE HALFTIME SHOW.

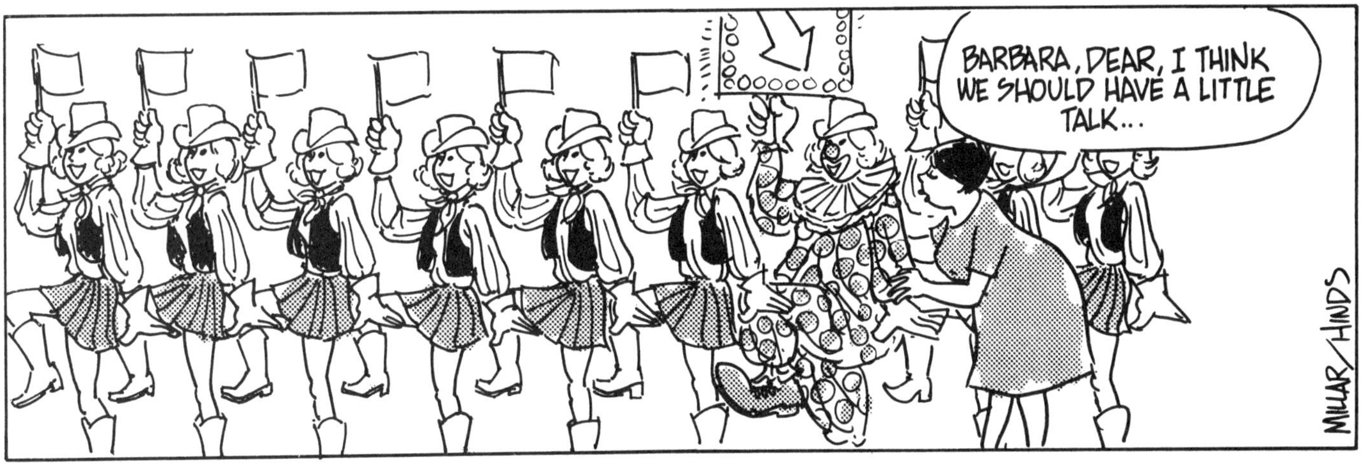
BARBARA, DEAR, I THINK WE SHOULD HAVE A LITTLE TALK...
MILLAR/HINDS

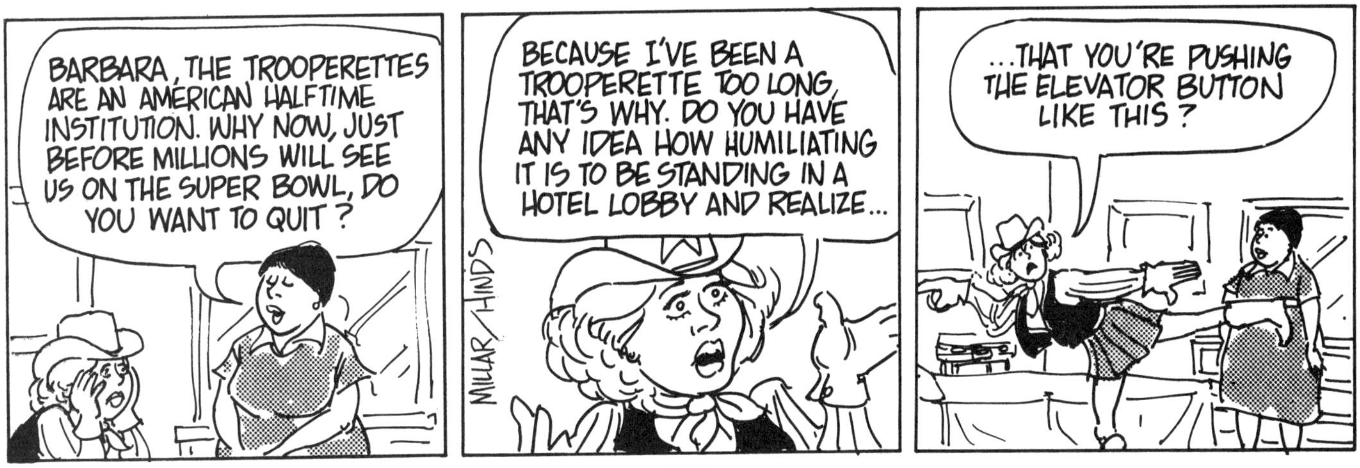
BARBARA, THE TROOPERETTES ARE AN AMERICAN HALFTIME INSTITUTION. WHY NOW, JUST BEFORE MILLIONS WILL SEE US ON THE SUPER BOWL, DO YOU WANT TO QUIT ?
BECAUSE I'VE BEEN A TROOPERETTE TOO LONG, THAT'S WHY. DO YOU HAVE ANY IDEA HOW HUMILIATING IT IS TO BE STANDING IN A HOTEL LOBBY AND REALIZE...
MILLAR/HINDS
...THAT YOU'RE PUSHING THE ELEVATOR BUTTON LIKE THIS ?

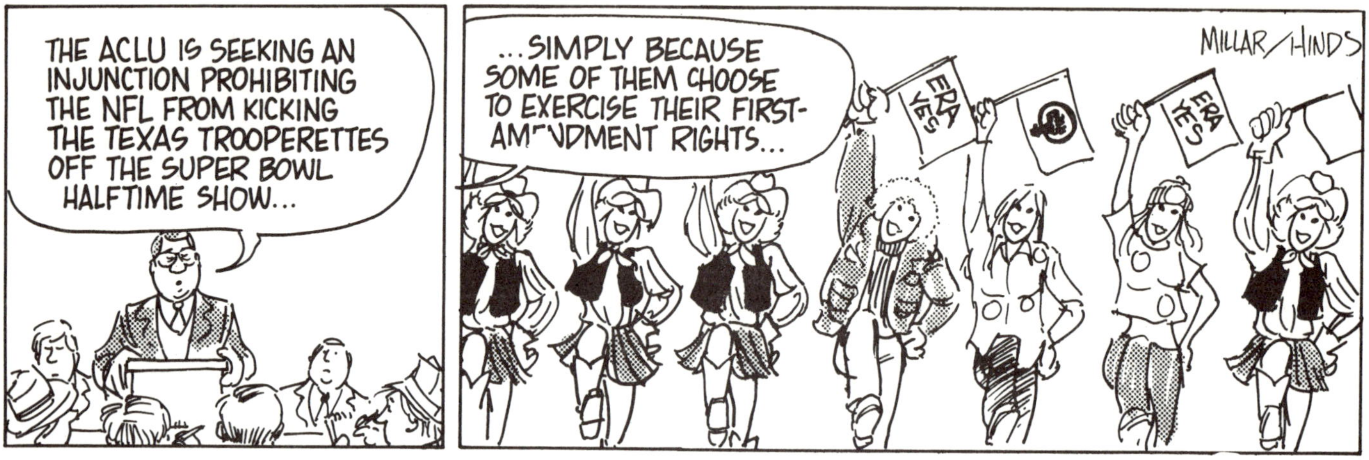
THE ACLU IS SEEKING AN INJUNCTION PROHIBITING THE NFL FROM KICKING THE TEXAS TROOPERETTES OFF THE SUPER BOWL HALFTIME SHOW...
...SIMPLY BECAUSE SOME OF THEM CHOOSE TO EXERCISE THEIR FIRST-AMENDMENT RIGHTS...
MILLAR/HINDS
ERA YES
ERA YES

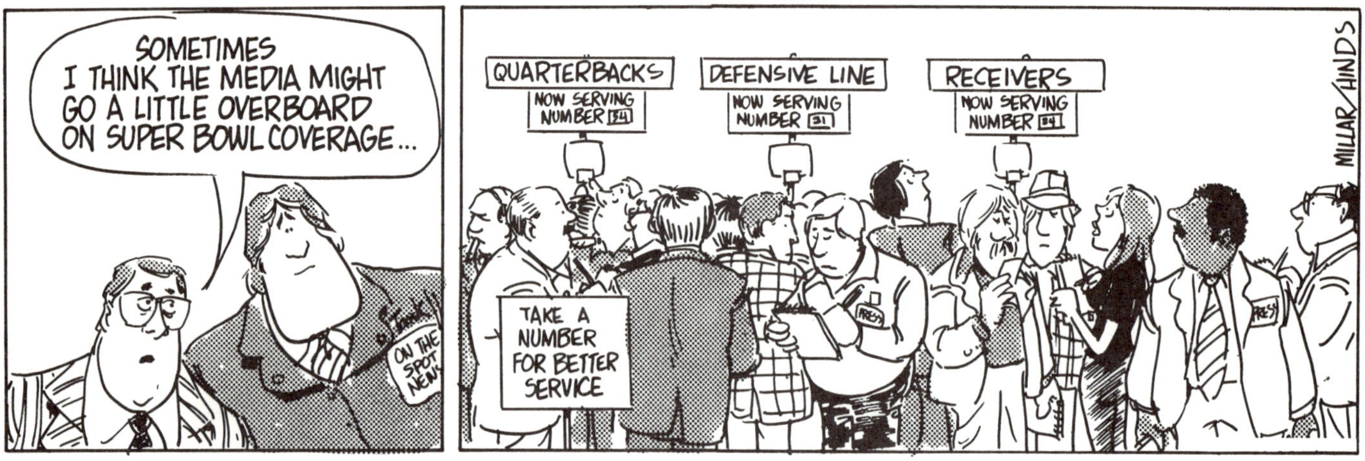
SOMETIMES I THINK THE MEDIA MIGHT GO A LITTLE OVERBOARD ON SUPER BOWL COVERAGE...
ON THE SPOT NEWS
QUARTERBACKS
NOW SERVING NUMBER 84
DEFENSIVE LINE
NOW SERVING NUMBER 31
RECEIVERS
NOW SERVING NUMBER 84
TAKE A NUMBER FOR BETTER SERVICE
PRESS
MILLAR/HINDS

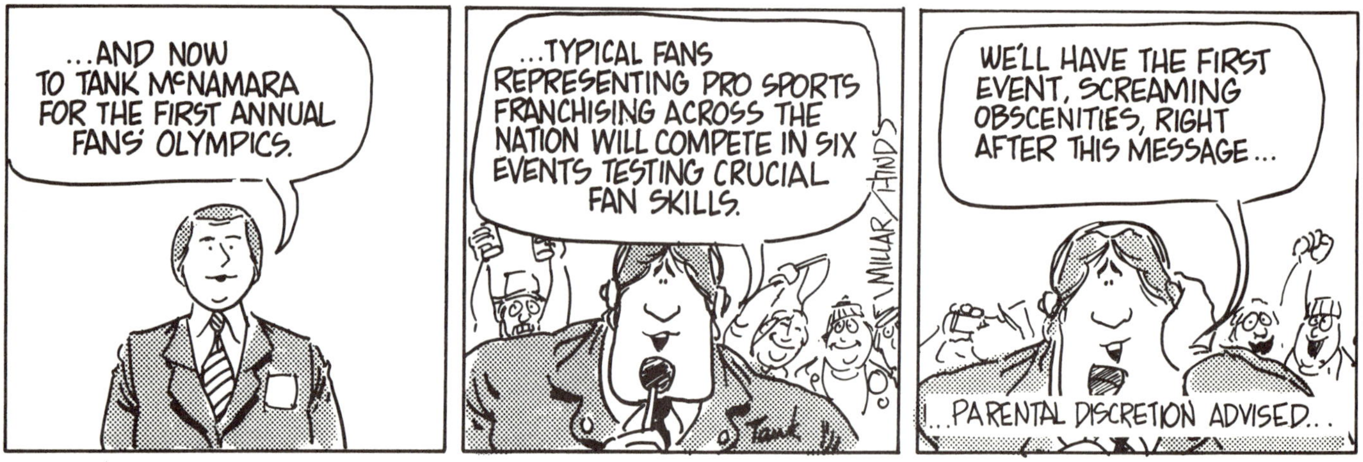
...AND NOW TO TANK McNAMARA FOR THE FIRST ANNUAL FANS' OLYMPICS.
...TYPICAL FANS REPRESENTING PRO SPORTS FRANCHISING ACROSS THE NATION WILL COMPETE IN SIX EVENTS TESTING CRUCIAL FAN SKILLS.
MILLAR/HINDS
WE'LL HAVE THE FIRST EVENT, SCREAMING OBSCENITIES, RIGHT AFTER THIS MESSAGE...
...PARENTAL DISCRETION ADVISED...

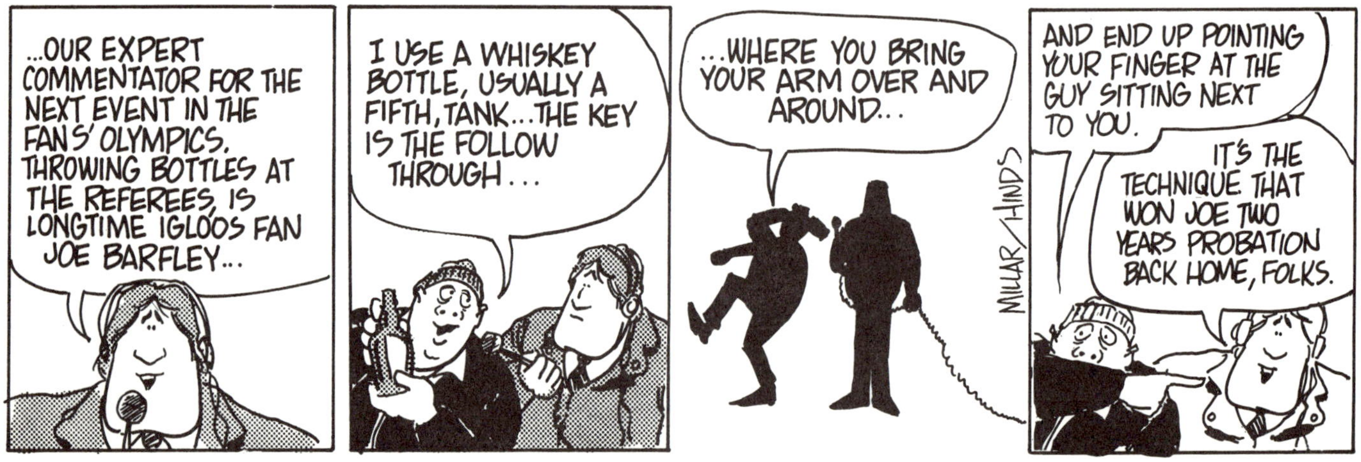
...OUR EXPERT COMMENTATOR FOR THE NEXT EVENT IN THE FAN'S OLYMPICS, THROWING BOTTLES AT THE REFEREES, IS LONGTIME IGLOOS FAN JOE BARFLEY...
I USE A WHISKEY BOTTLE, USUALLY A FIFTH, TANK...THE KEY IS THE FOLLOW THROUGH...
...WHERE YOU BRING YOUR ARM OVER AND AROUND...
MILLAR/HINDS
AND END UP POINTING YOUR FINGER AT THE GUY SITTING NEXT TO YOU.
IT'S THE TECHNIQUE THAT WON JOE TWO YEARS PROBATION BACK HOME, FOLKS.

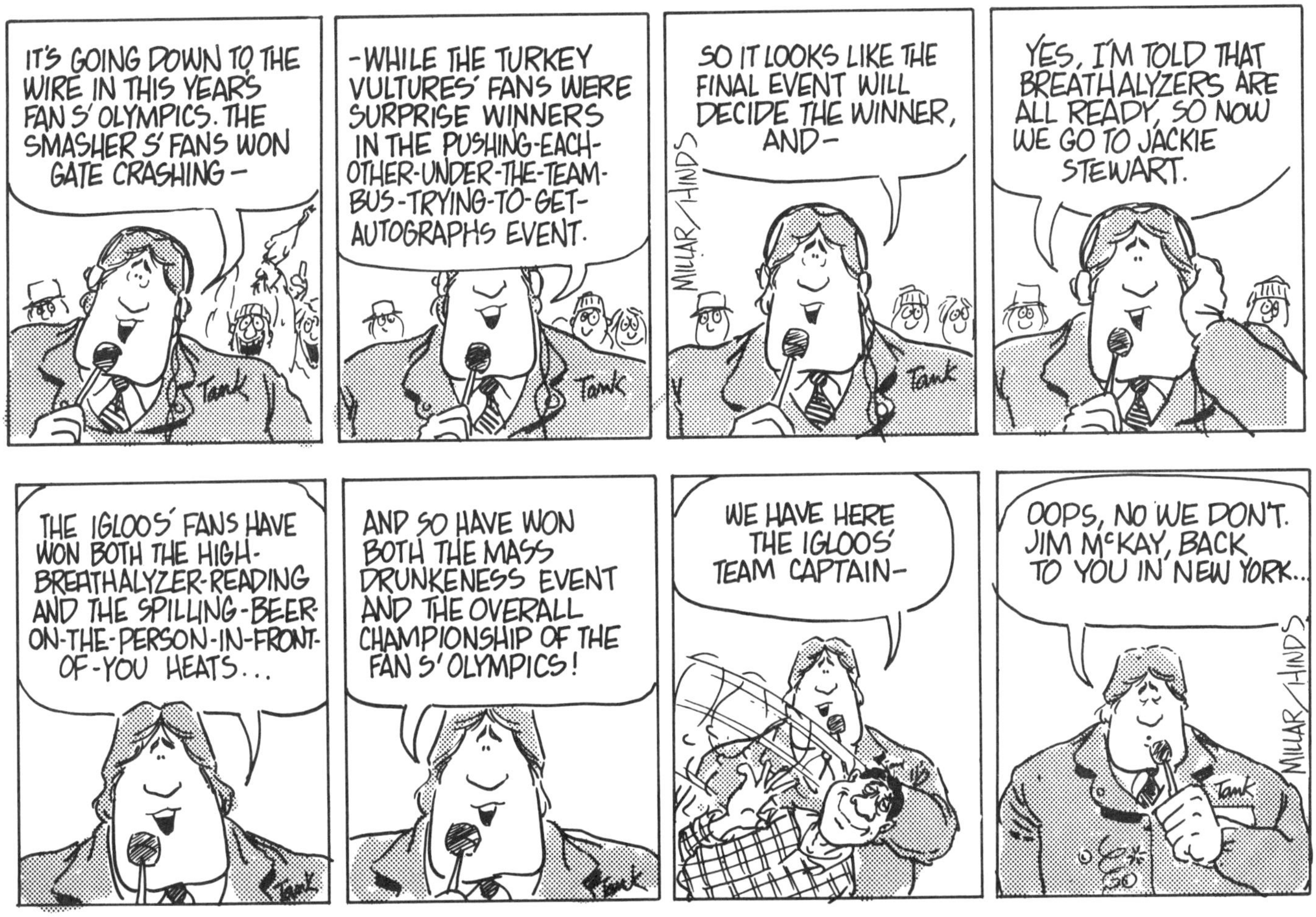
IT'S GOING DOWN TO THE WIRE IN THIS YEAR'S FAN S' OLYMPICS. THE SMASHER S' FANS WON GATE CRASHING –
– WHILE THE TURKEY VULTURES' FANS WERE SURPRISE WINNERS IN THE PUSHING-EACH-OTHER-UNDER-THE-TEAM-BUS-TRYING-TO-GET-AUTOGRAPHS EVENT.
SO IT LOOKS LIKE THE FINAL EVENT WILL DECIDE THE WINNER, AND –
MILLAR/HINDS
YES, I'M TOLD THAT BREATHALYZERS ARE ALL READY, SO NOW WE GO TO JACKIE STEWART.
THE IGLOOS' FANS HAVE WON BOTH THE HIGH-BREATHALYZER-READING AND THE SPILLING-BEER-ON-THE-PERSON-IN-FRONT-OF-YOU HEATS...
AND SO HAVE WON BOTH THE MASS DRUNKENESS EVENT AND THE OVERALL CHAMPIONSHIP OF THE FAN S' OLYMPICS!
WE HAVE HERE THE IGLOOS' TEAM CAPTAIN –
OOPS, NO WE DON'T. JIM McKAY, BACK TO YOU IN NEW YORK...
MILLAR/HINDS

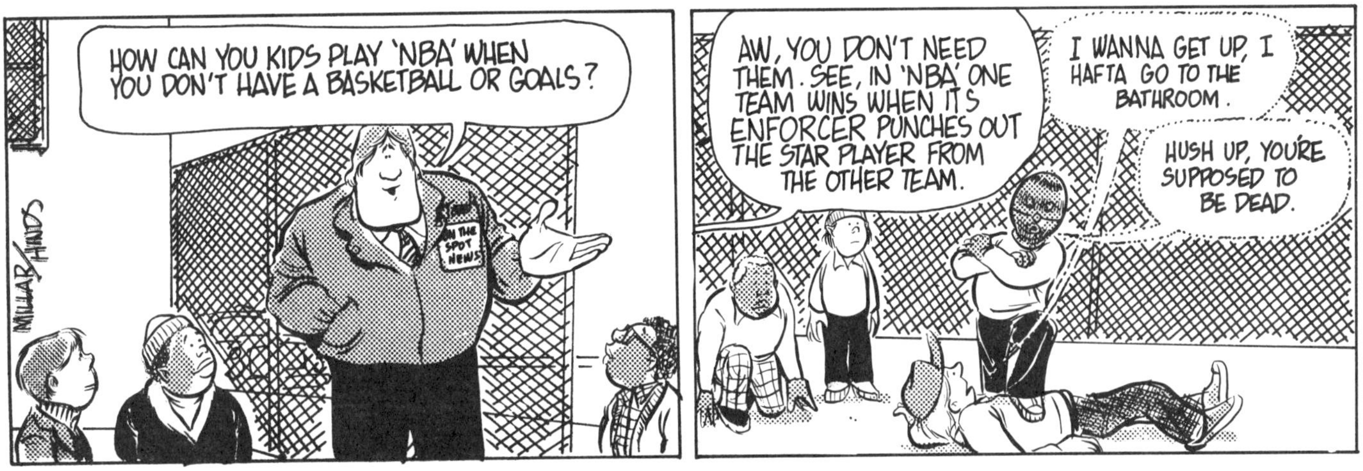
HOW CAN YOU KIDS PLAY 'NBA' WHEN YOU DON'T HAVE A BASKETBALL OR GOALS?
MILLAR/HINDS
AW, YOU DON'T NEED THEM. SEE, IN 'NBA' ONE TEAM WINS WHEN IT'S ENFORCER PUNCHES OUT THE STAR PLAYER FROM THE OTHER TEAM.
I WANNA GET UP, I HAFTA GO TO THE BATHROOM.
HUSH UP, YOU'RE SUPPOSED TO BE DEAD.

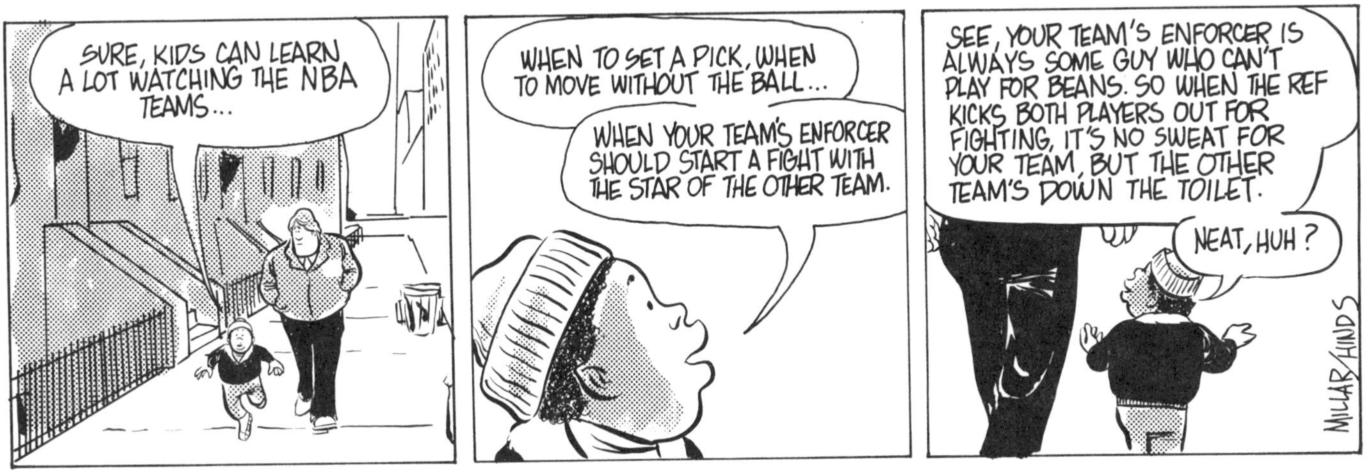
SURE, KIDS CAN LEARN A LOT WATCHING THE NBA TEAMS...
WHEN TO SET A PICK, WHEN TO MOVE WITHOUT THE BALL...
WHEN YOUR TEAM'S ENFORCER SHOULD START A FIGHT WITH THE STAR OF THE OTHER TEAM.
SEE, YOUR TEAM'S ENFORCER IS ALWAYS SOME GUY WHO CAN'T PLAY FOR BEANS. SO WHEN THE REF KICKS BOTH PLAYERS OUT FOR FIGHTING, IT'S NO SWEAT FOR YOUR TEAM, BUT THE OTHER TEAM'S DOWN THE TOILET.
NEAT, HUH?
MILLAR/HINDS

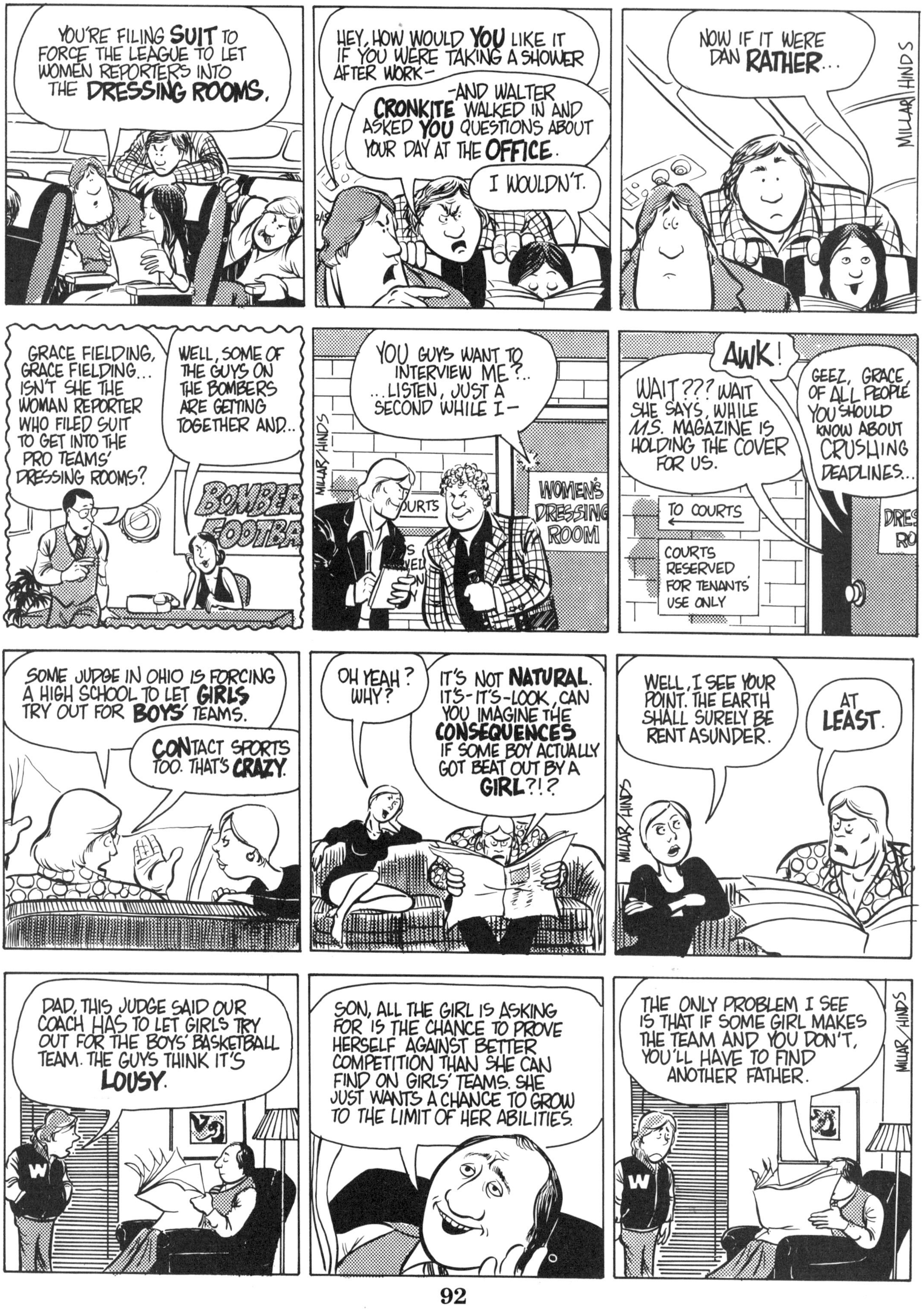
YOU'RE FILING SUIT TO FORCE THE LEAGUE TO LET WOMEN REPORTERS INTO THE DRESSING ROOMS.
HEY, HOW WOULD YOU LIKE IT IF YOU WERE TAKING A SHOWER AFTER WORK–
–AND WALTER CRONKITE WALKED IN AND ASKED YOU QUESTIONS ABOUT YOUR DAY AT THE OFFICE.
I WOULDN'T.
NOW IF IT WERE DAN RATHER...
MILLAR/HINDS
GRACE FIELDING, GRACE FIELDING... ISN'T SHE THE WOMAN REPORTER WHO FILED SUIT TO GET INTO THE PRO TEAMS' DRESSING ROOMS?
WELL, SOME OF THE GUYS ON THE BOMBERS ARE GETTING TOGETHER AND...
YOU GUYS WANT TO INTERVIEW ME?... ...LISTEN, JUST A SECOND WHILE I–
MILLAR/HINDS
WOMEN'S DRESSING ROOM
AWK!
WAIT??? WAIT SHE SAYS, WHILE MS. MAGAZINE IS HOLDING THE COVER FOR US.
GEEZ, GRACE, OF ALL PEOPLE YOU SHOULD KNOW ABOUT CRUSHING DEADLINES...
TO COURTS
COURTS RESERVED FOR TENANTS' USE ONLY
SOME JUDGE IN OHIO IS FORCING A HIGH SCHOOL TO LET GIRLS TRY OUT FOR BOYS' TEAMS.
CONTACT SPORTS TOO. THAT'S CRAZY.
OH YEAH? WHY?
IT'S NOT NATURAL. IT'S-IT'S-LOOK, CAN YOU IMAGINE THE CONSEQUENCES IF SOME BOY ACTUALLY GOT BEAT OUT BY A GIRL?!?
MILLAR/HINDS
WELL, I SEE YOUR POINT. THE EARTH SHALL SURELY BE RENT ASUNDER.
AT LEAST.
DAD, THIS JUDGE SAID OUR COACH HAS TO LET GIRLS TRY OUT FOR THE BOYS' BASKETBALL TEAM. THE GUYS THINK IT'S LOUSY.
SON, ALL THE GIRL IS ASKING FOR IS THE CHANCE TO PROVE HERSELF AGAINST BETTER COMPETITION THAN SHE CAN FIND ON GIRLS' TEAMS. SHE JUST WANTS A CHANCE TO GROW TO THE LIMIT OF HER ABILITIES.
THE ONLY PROBLEM I SEE IS THAT IF SOME GIRL MAKES THE TEAM AND YOU DON'T, YOU'LL HAVE TO FIND ANOTHER FATHER.
MILLAR/HINDS

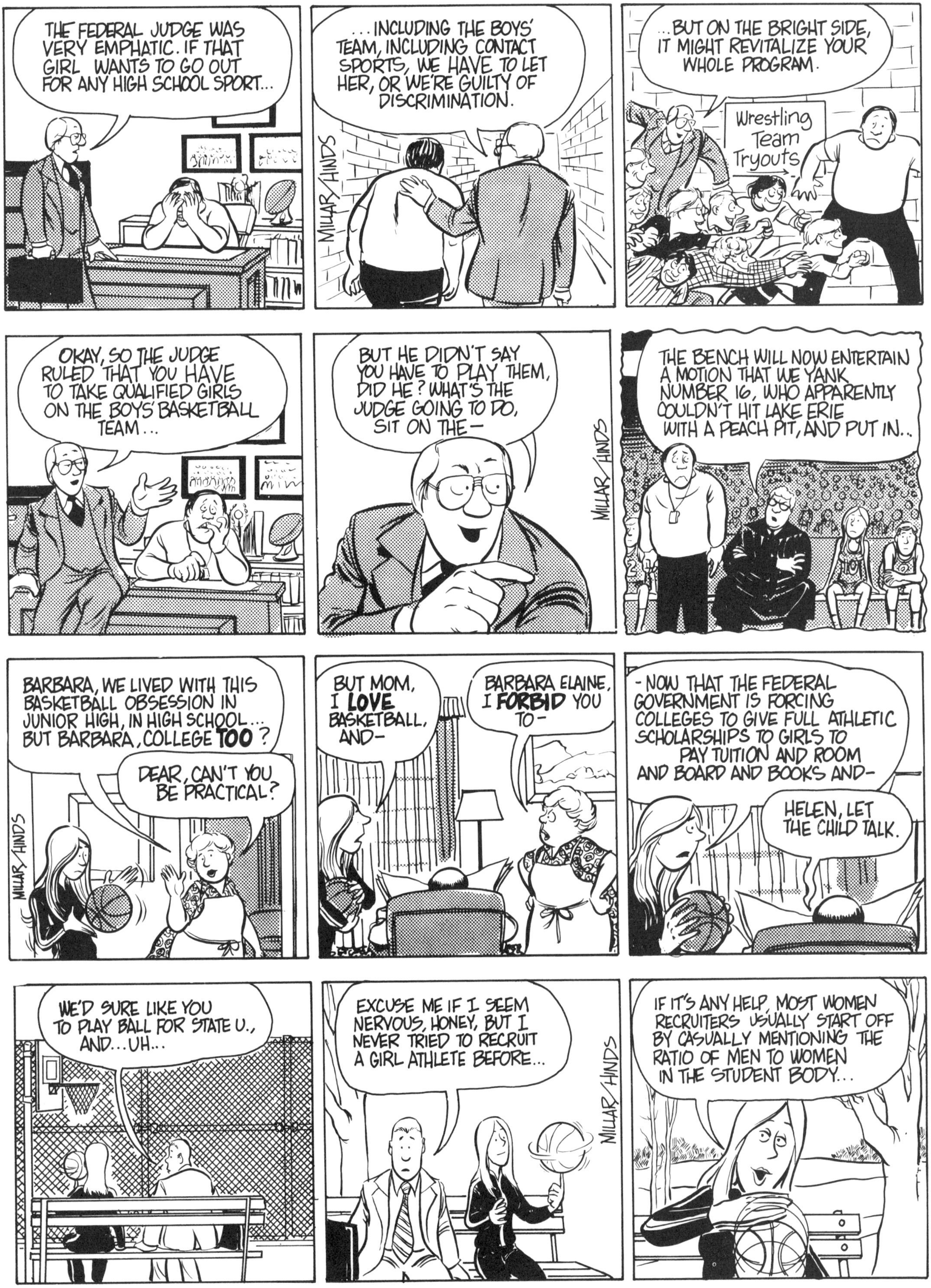
THE FEDERAL JUDGE WAS VERY EMPHATIC. IF THAT GIRL WANTS TO GO OUT FOR ANY HIGH SCHOOL SPORT...
...INCLUDING THE BOYS' TEAM, INCLUDING CONTACT SPORTS, WE HAVE TO LET HER, OR WE'RE GUILTY OF DISCRIMINATION.
MILLAR/HINDS
...BUT ON THE BRIGHT SIDE, IT MIGHT REVITALIZE YOUR WHOLE PROGRAM.
Wrestling Team Tryouts
OKAY, SO THE JUDGE RULED THAT YOU HAVE TO TAKE QUALIFIED GIRLS ON THE BOYS' BASKETBALL TEAM...
BUT HE DIDN'T SAY YOU HAVE TO PLAY THEM, DID HE? WHAT'S THE JUDGE GOING TO DO, SIT ON THE—
MILLAR/HINDS
THE BENCH WILL NOW ENTERTAIN A MOTION THAT WE YANK NUMBER 16, WHO APPARENTLY COULDN'T HIT LAKE ERIE WITH A PEACH PIT, AND PUT IN...
BARBARA, WE LIVED WITH THIS BASKETBALL OBSESSION IN JUNIOR HIGH, IN HIGH SCHOOL... BUT BARBARA, COLLEGE **TOO**?
DEAR, CAN'T YOU BE PRACTICAL?
MILLAR/HINDS
BUT MOM, I **LOVE** BASKETBALL, AND—
BARBARA ELAINE, I **FORBID** YOU TO—
-NOW THAT THE FEDERAL GOVERNMENT IS FORCING COLLEGES TO GIVE FULL ATHLETIC SCHOLARSHIPS TO GIRLS TO PAY TUITION AND ROOM AND BOARD AND BOOKS AND—
HELEN, LET THE CHILD TALK.
WE'D SURE LIKE YOU TO PLAY BALL FOR STATE U., AND...UH...
EXCUSE ME IF I SEEM NERVOUS, HONEY, BUT I NEVER TRIED TO RECRUIT A GIRL ATHLETE BEFORE...
MILLAR/HINDS
IF IT'S ANY HELP, MOST WOMEN RECRUITERS USUALLY START OFF BY CASUALLY MENTIONING THE RATIO OF MEN TO WOMEN IN THE STUDENT BODY...

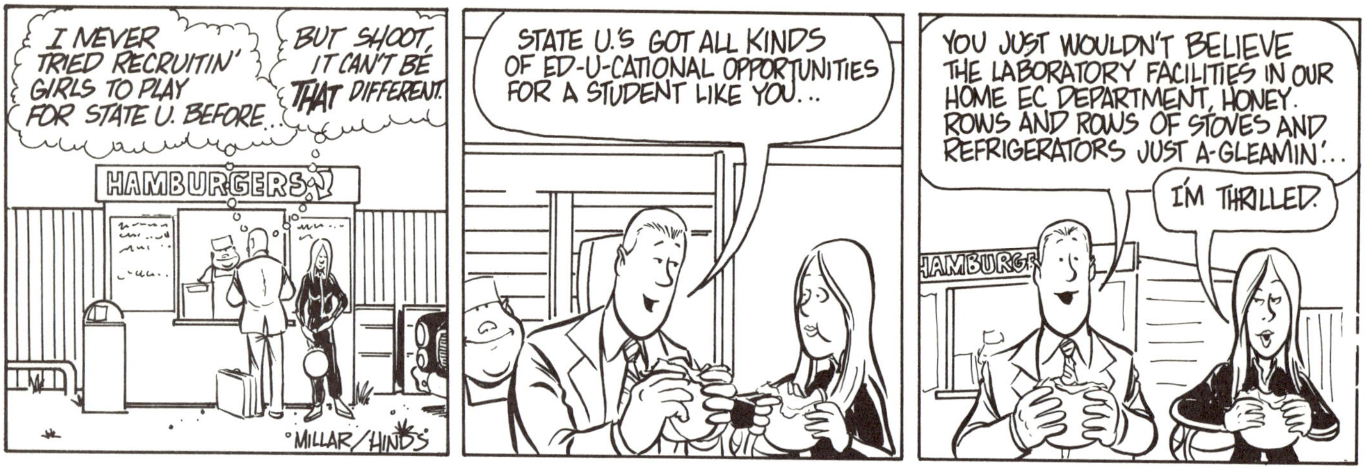
I NEVER TRIED RECRUITIN' GIRLS TO PLAY FOR STATE U. BEFORE...
BUT SHOOT, IT CAN'T BE THAT DIFFERENT.
HAMBURGERS
MILLAR/HINDS
STATE U.'S GOT ALL KINDS OF ED-U-CATIONAL OPPORTUNITIES FOR A STUDENT LIKE YOU...
YOU JUST WOULDN'T BELIEVE THE LABORATORY FACILITIES IN OUR HOME EC DEPARTMENT, HONEY. ROWS AND ROWS OF STOVES AND REFRIGERATORS JUST A-GLEAMIN'...
I'M THRILLED.

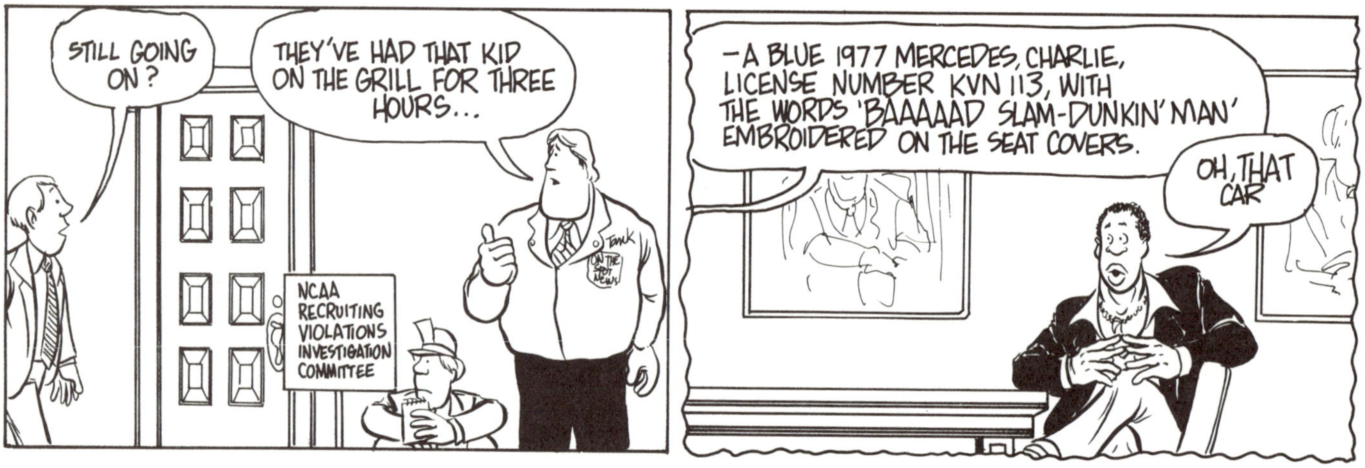
STILL GOING ON?
THEY'VE HAD THAT KID ON THE GRILL FOR THREE HOURS...
NCAA RECRUITING VIOLATIONS INVESTIGATION COMMITTEE
—A BLUE 1977 MERCEDES, CHARLIE, LICENSE NUMBER KVN 113, WITH THE WORDS 'BAAAAAD SLAM-DUNKIN' MAN' EMBROIDERED ON THE SEAT COVERS.
OH, THAT CAR

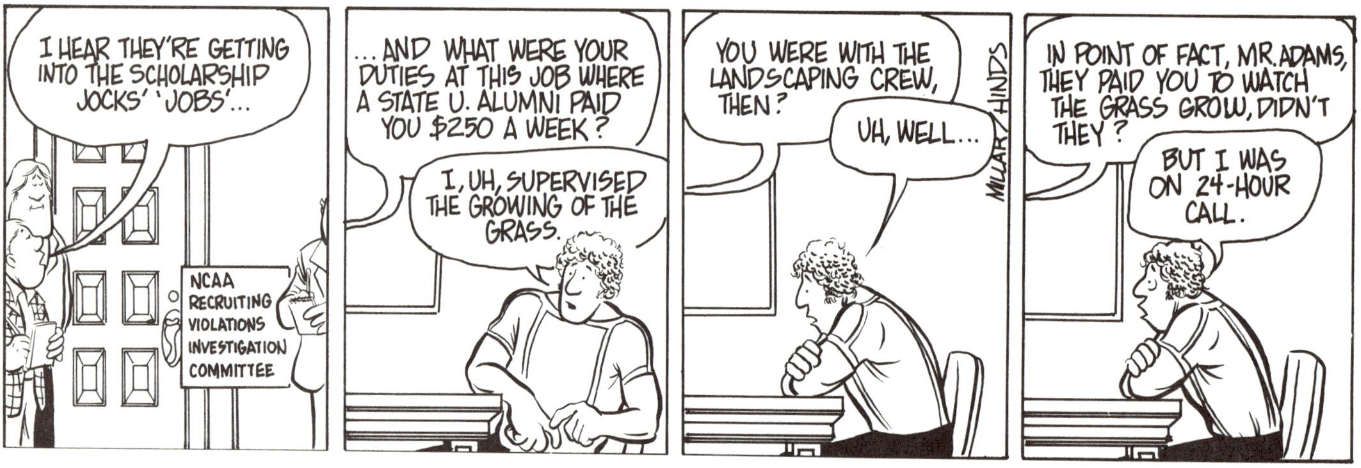
I HEAR THEY'RE GETTING INTO THE SCHOLARSHIP JOCKS' 'JOBS'...
NCAA RECRUITING VIOLATIONS INVESTIGATION COMMITTEE
...AND WHAT WERE YOUR DUTIES AT THIS JOB WHERE A STATE U. ALUMNI PAID YOU $250 A WEEK?
I, UH, SUPERVISED THE GROWING OF THE GRASS.
YOU WERE WITH THE LANDSCAPING CREW, THEN?
UH, WELL...
MILLAR/HINDS
IN POINT OF FACT, MR. ADAMS, THEY PAID YOU TO WATCH THE GRASS GROW, DIDN'T THEY?
BUT I WAS ON 24-HOUR CALL.

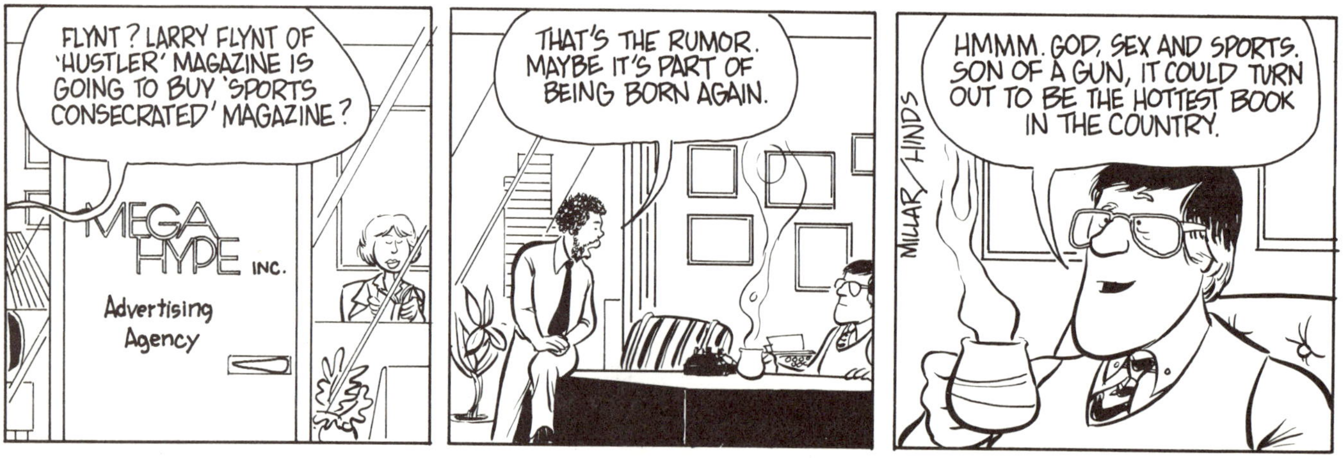
FLYNT? LARRY FLYNT OF 'HUSTLER' MAGAZINE IS GOING TO BUY 'SPORTS CONSECRATED' MAGAZINE?
MEGA HYPE INC.
Advertising Agency
THAT'S THE RUMOR. MAYBE IT'S PART OF BEING BORN AGAIN.
MILLAR/HINDS
HMMM. GOD, SEX AND SPORTS. SON OF A GUN, IT COULD TURN OUT TO BE THE HOTTEST BOOK IN THE COUNTRY.

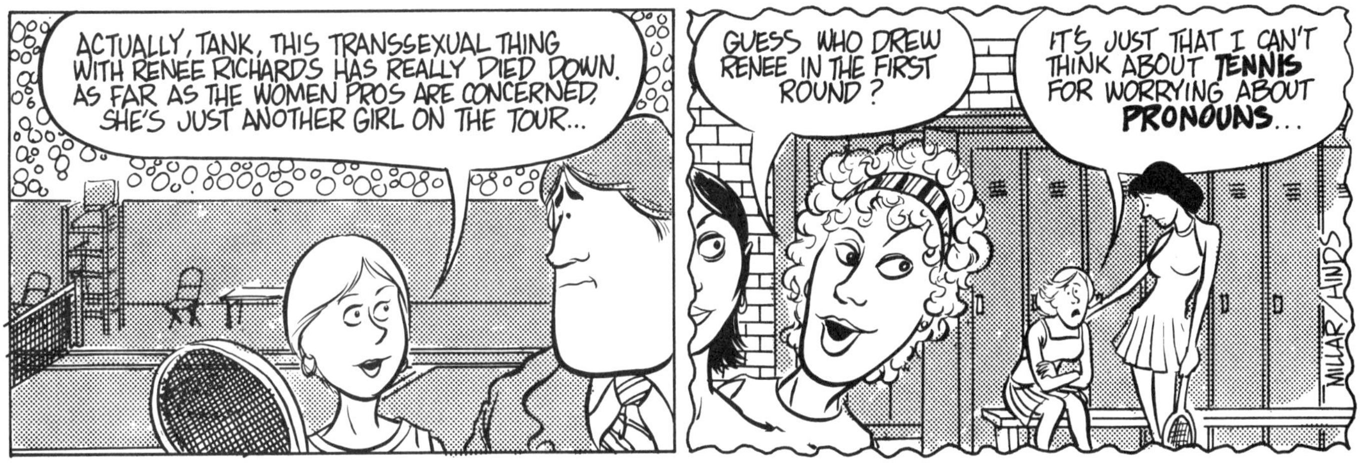
ACTUALLY, TANK, THIS TRANSSEXUAL THING WITH RENEE RICHARDS HAS REALLY DIED DOWN. AS FAR AS THE WOMEN PROS ARE CONCERNED, SHE'S JUST ANOTHER GIRL ON THE TOUR...
GUESS WHO DREW RENEE IN THE FIRST ROUND?
IT'S JUST THAT I CAN'T THINK ABOUT **TENNIS** FOR WORRYING ABOUT **PRONOUNS**...
MILLAR/HINDS

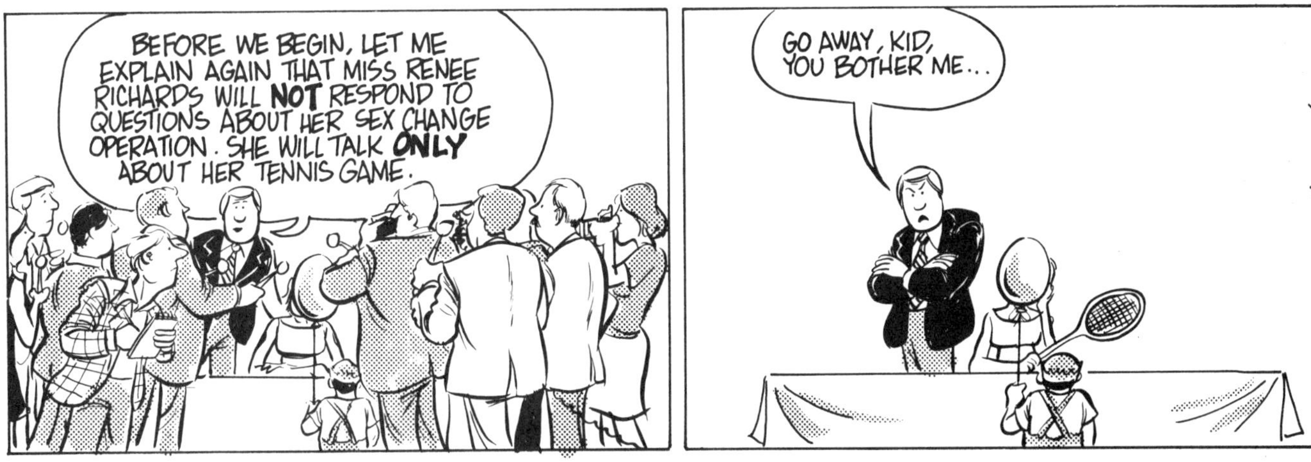
BEFORE WE BEGIN, LET ME EXPLAIN AGAIN THAT MISS RENEE RICHARDS WILL **NOT** RESPOND TO QUESTIONS ABOUT HER SEX CHANGE OPERATION. SHE WILL TALK **ONLY** ABOUT HER TENNIS GAME.
GO AWAY, KID, YOU BOTHER ME...
MILLAR/HINDS

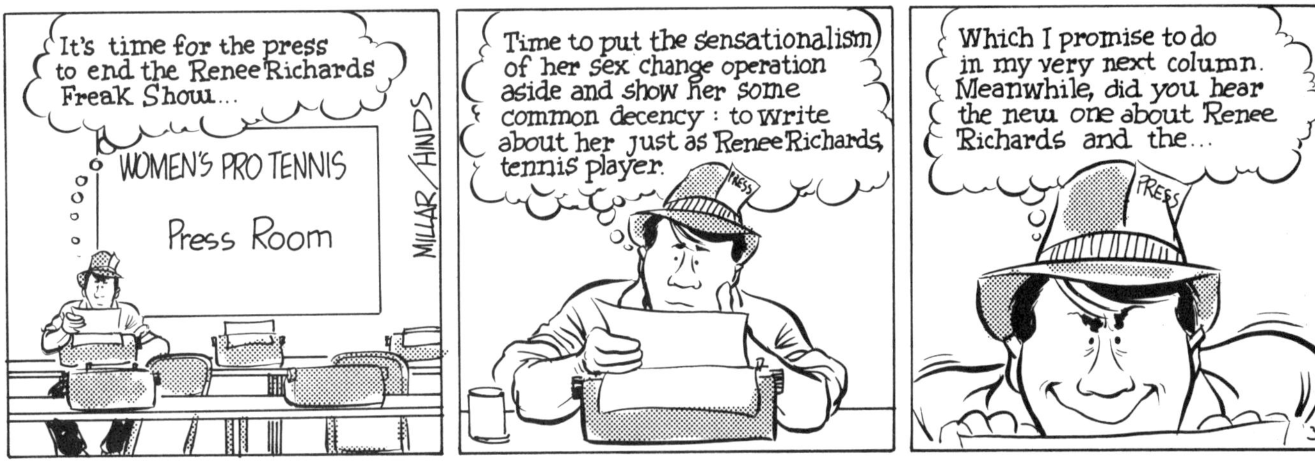
It's time for the press to end the Renee Richards Freak Show...
WOMEN'S PRO TENNIS
Press Room
MILLAR/HINDS
Time to put the sensationalism of her sex change operation aside and show her some common decency: to write about her just as Renee Richards, tennis player.
PRESS
Which I promise to do in my very next column. Meanwhile, did you hear the new one about Renee Richards and the...
PRESS
3/24

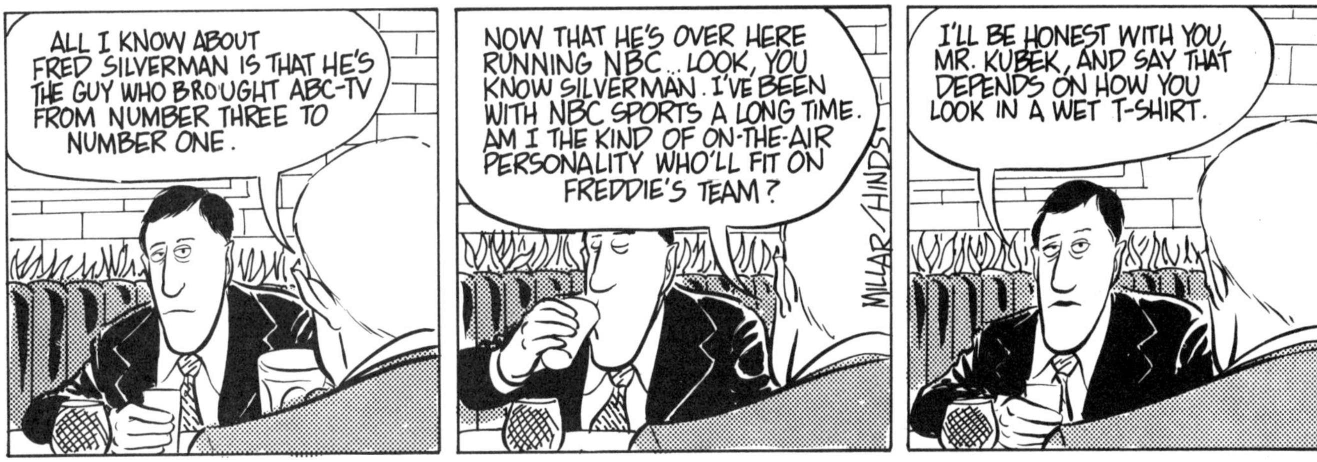
ALL I KNOW ABOUT FRED SILVERMAN IS THAT HE'S THE GUY WHO BROUGHT ABC-TV FROM NUMBER THREE TO NUMBER ONE.
NOW THAT HE'S OVER HERE RUNNING NBC... LOOK, YOU KNOW SILVERMAN. I'VE BEEN WITH NBC SPORTS A LONG TIME. AM I THE KIND OF ON-THE-AIR PERSONALITY WHO'LL FIT ON FREDDIE'S TEAM?
MILLAR/HINDS
I'LL BE HONEST WITH YOU, MR. KUBEK, AND SAY THAT DEPENDS ON HOW YOU LOOK IN A WET T-SHIRT.

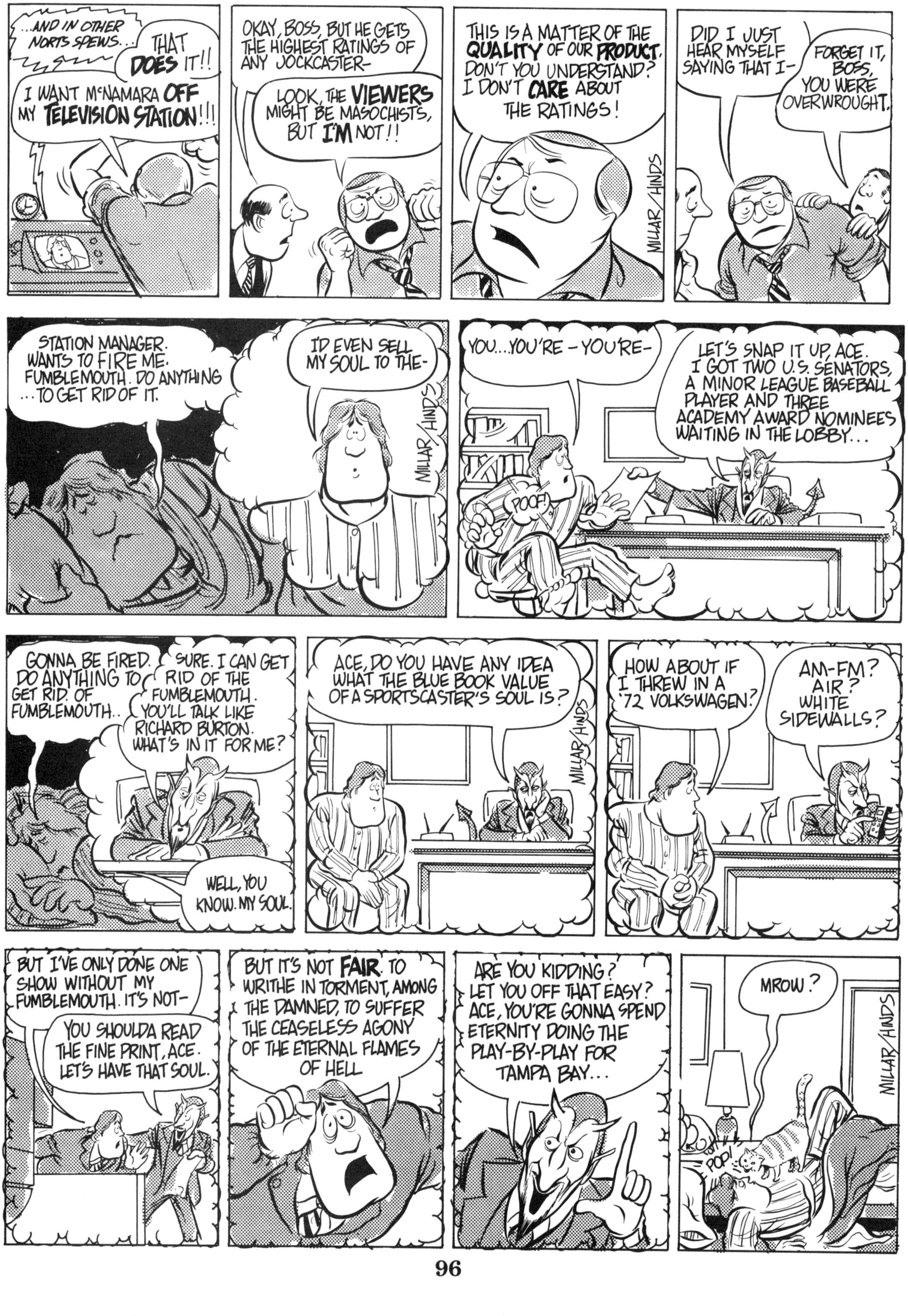
...AND IN OTHER NORTS SPEWS...
THAT DOES IT!!
I WANT McNAMARA OFF MY TELEVISION STATION!!!
OKAY, BOSS, BUT HE GETS THE HIGHEST RATINGS OF ANY JOCKCASTER-
LOOK, THE VIEWERS MIGHT BE MASOCHISTS, BUT I'M NOT!!
THIS IS A MATTER OF THE QUALITY OF OUR PRODUCT. DON'T YOU UNDERSTAND? I DON'T CARE ABOUT THE RATINGS!
MILLAR/HINDS
DID I JUST HEAR MYSELF SAYING THAT I-
FORGET IT, BOSS, YOU WERE OVERWROUGHT.
STATION MANAGER. WANTS TO FIRE ME. FUMBLEMOUTH. DO ANYTHING ...TO GET RID OF IT.
I'D EVEN SELL MY SOUL TO THE-
MILLAR/HINDS
YOU...YOU'RE - YOU'RE-
LET'S SNAP IT UP, ACE. I GOT TWO U.S. SENATORS, A MINOR LEAGUE BASEBALL PLAYER AND THREE ACADEMY AWARD NOMINEES WAITING IN THE LOBBY...
POOF!
GONNA BE FIRED. DO ANYTHING TO GET RID OF FUMBLEMOUTH..
SURE. I CAN GET RID OF THE FUMBLEMOUTH. YOU'LL TALK LIKE RICHARD BURTON. WHAT'S IN IT FOR ME?
WELL, YOU KNOW. MY SOUL.
ACE, DO YOU HAVE ANY IDEA WHAT THE BLUE BOOK VALUE OF A SPORTSCASTER'S SOUL IS?
MILLAR/HINDS
HOW ABOUT IF I THREW IN A '72 VOLKSWAGEN?
AM-FM? AIR? WHITE SIDEWALLS?
BUT I'VE ONLY DONE ONE SHOW WITHOUT MY FUMBLEMOUTH. IT'S NOT-
YOU SHOULDA READ THE FINE PRINT, ACE. LET'S HAVE THAT SOUL.
BUT IT'S NOT FAIR. TO WRITHE IN TORMENT, AMONG THE DAMNED, TO SUFFER THE CEASELESS AGONY OF THE ETERNAL FLAMES OF HELL
ARE YOU KIDDING? LET YOU OFF THAT EASY? ACE, YOU'RE GONNA SPEND ETERNITY DOING THE PLAY-BY-PLAY FOR TAMPA BAY...
MROW?
MILLAR/HINDS
POP!

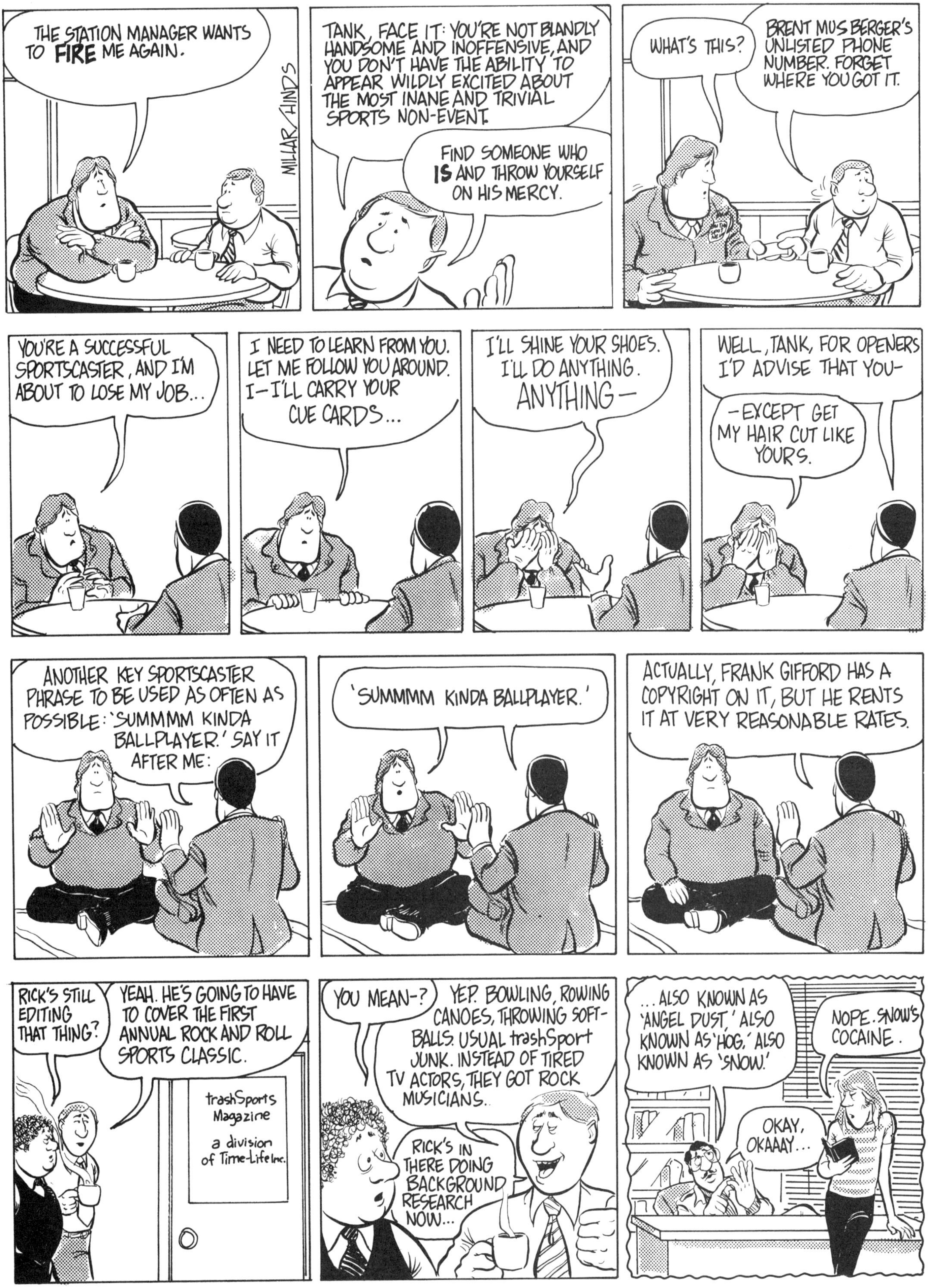
THE STATION MANAGER WANTS TO FIRE ME AGAIN.
MILLAR/HINDS
TANK, FACE IT: YOU'RE NOT BLANDLY HANDSOME AND INOFFENSIVE, AND YOU DON'T HAVE THE ABILITY TO APPEAR WILDLY EXCITED ABOUT THE MOST INANE AND TRIVIAL SPORTS NON-EVENT.
FIND SOMEONE WHO IS AND THROW YOURSELF ON HIS MERCY.
WHAT'S THIS?
BRENT MUS BERGER'S UNLISTED PHONE NUMBER. FORGET WHERE YOU GOT IT.
YOU'RE A SUCCESSFUL SPORTSCASTER, AND I'M ABOUT TO LOSE MY JOB...
I NEED TO LEARN FROM YOU. LET ME FOLLOW YOU AROUND. I—I'LL CARRY YOUR CUE CARDS...
I'LL SHINE YOUR SHOES. I'LL DO ANYTHING. ANYTHING—
WELL, TANK, FOR OPENERS I'D ADVISE THAT YOU-
-EXCEPT GET MY HAIR CUT LIKE YOURS.
ANOTHER KEY SPORTSCASTER PHRASE TO BE USED AS OFTEN AS POSSIBLE: 'SUMMMM KINDA BALLPLAYER.' SAY IT AFTER ME:
'SUMMMM KINDA BALLPLAYER.'
ACTUALLY, FRANK GIFFORD HAS A COPYRIGHT ON IT, BUT HE RENTS IT AT VERY REASONABLE RATES.
RICK'S STILL EDITING THAT THING?
YEAH. HE'S GOING TO HAVE TO COVER THE FIRST ANNUAL ROCK AND ROLL SPORTS CLASSIC.
trashSports Magazine
a division of Time-Life Inc.
YOU MEAN-?
YEP. BOWLING, ROWING CANOES, THROWING SOFT-BALLS. USUAL trashSport JUNK. INSTEAD OF TIRED TV ACTORS, THEY GOT ROCK MUSICIANS.
RICK'S IN THERE DOING BACKGROUND RESEARCH NOW...
...ALSO KNOWN AS 'ANGEL DUST,' ALSO KNOWN AS 'HOG,' ALSO KNOWN AS 'SNOW.'
NOPE. SNOW'S COCAINE.
OKAY, OKAAAY...

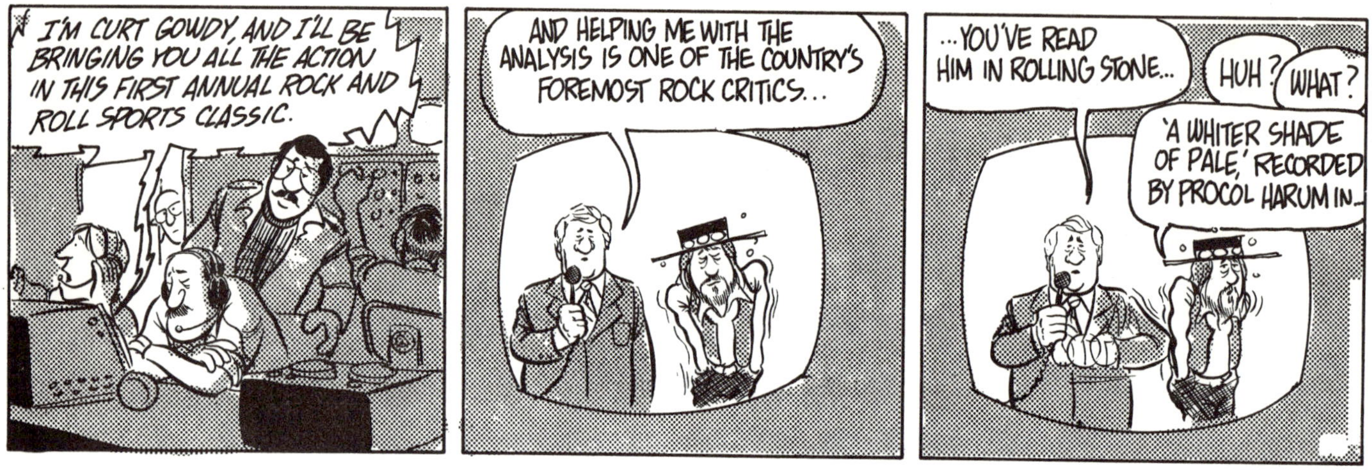
I'M CURT GOWDY, AND I'LL BE BRINGING YOU ALL THE ACTION IN THIS FIRST ANNUAL ROCK AND ROLL SPORTS CLASSIC.
AND HELPING ME WITH THE ANALYSIS IS ONE OF THE COUNTRY'S FOREMOST ROCK CRITICS...
...YOU'VE READ HIM IN ROLLING STONE...
HUH?
WHAT?
'A WHITER SHADE OF PALE,' RECORDED BY PROCOL HARUM IN...

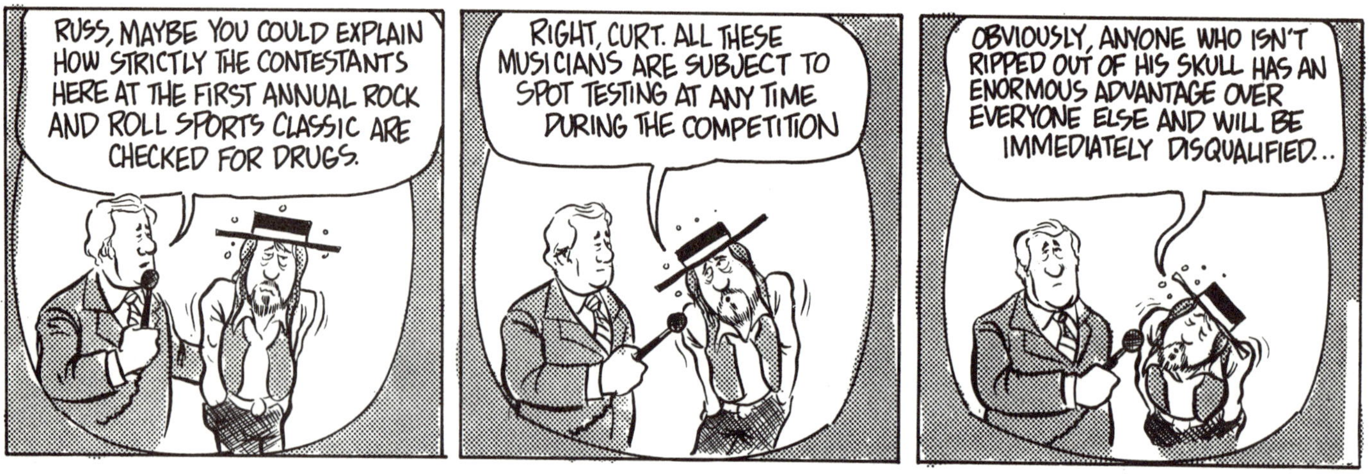
RUSS, MAYBE YOU COULD EXPLAIN HOW STRICTLY THE CONTESTANTS HERE AT THE FIRST ANNUAL ROCK AND ROLL SPORTS CLASSIC ARE CHECKED FOR DRUGS.
RIGHT, CURT. ALL THESE MUSICIANS ARE SUBJECT TO SPOT TESTING AT ANY TIME DURING THE COMPETITION
OBVIOUSLY, ANYONE WHO ISN'T RIPPED OUT OF HIS SKULL HAS AN ENORMOUS ADVANTAGE OVER EVERYONE ELSE AND WILL BE IMMEDIATELY DISQUALIFIED...

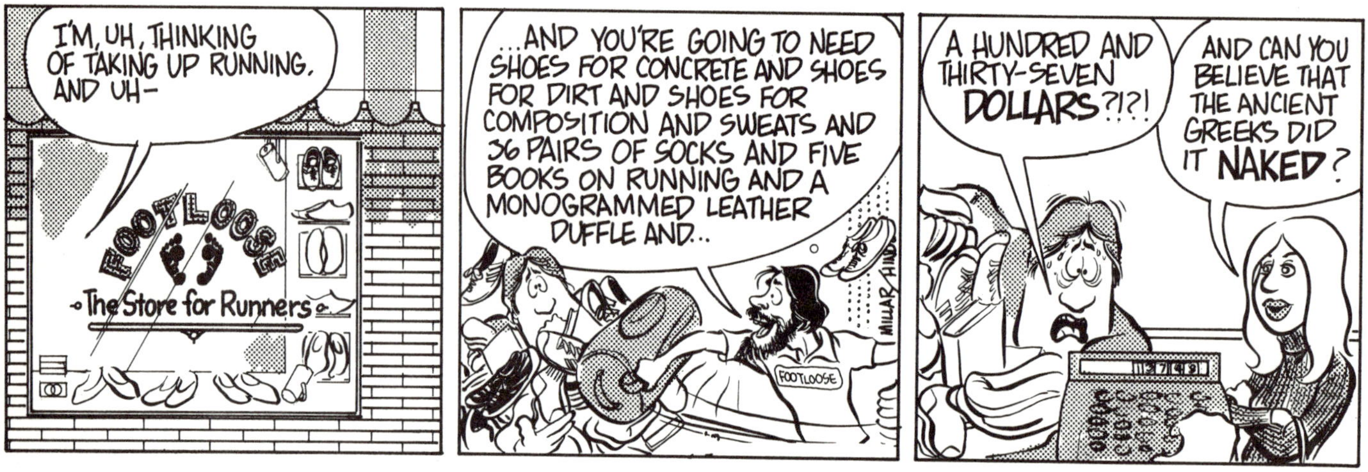
I'M, UH, THINKING OF TAKING UP RUNNING, AND UH-
FOOTLOOSE
The Store for Runners
...AND YOU'RE GOING TO NEED SHOES FOR CONCRETE AND SHOES FOR DIRT AND SHOES FOR COMPOSITION AND SWEATS AND 36 PAIRS OF SOCKS AND FIVE BOOKS ON RUNNING AND A MONOGRAMMED LEATHER DUFFLE AND...
FOOTLOOSE
MILLAR/HINDS
A HUNDRED AND THIRTY-SEVEN DOLLARS?!?!
AND CAN YOU BELIEVE THAT THE ANCIENT GREEKS DID IT NAKED?

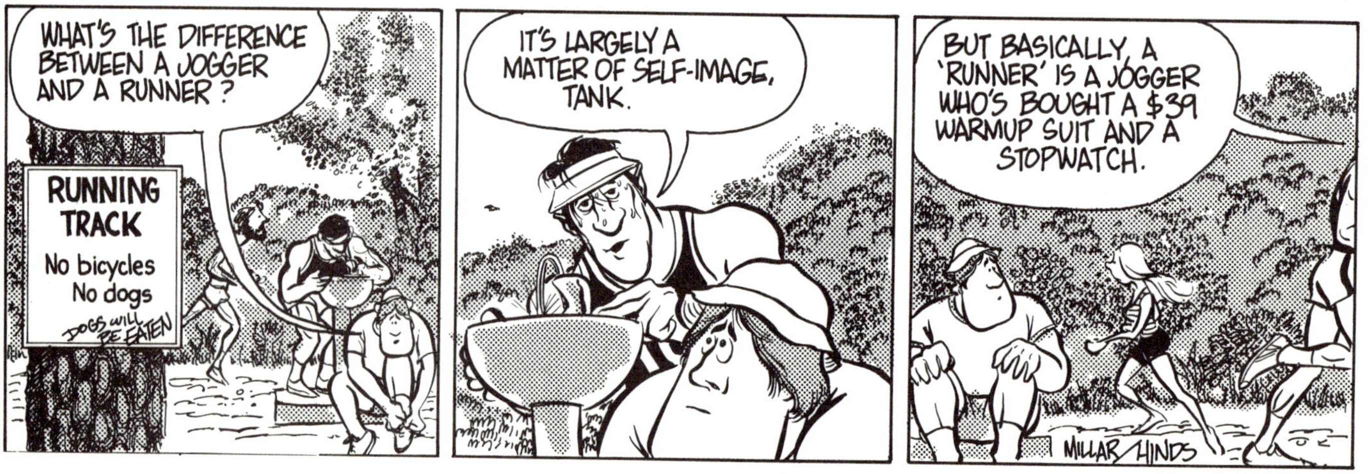
WHAT'S THE DIFFERENCE BETWEEN A JOGGER AND A RUNNER?
RUNNING TRACK
No bicycles
No dogs
DOGS WILL BE EATEN
IT'S LARGELY A MATTER OF SELF-IMAGE, TANK.
BUT BASICALLY, A 'RUNNER' IS A JOGGER WHO'S BOUGHT A $39 WARMUP SUIT AND A STOPWATCH.
MILLAR/HINDS

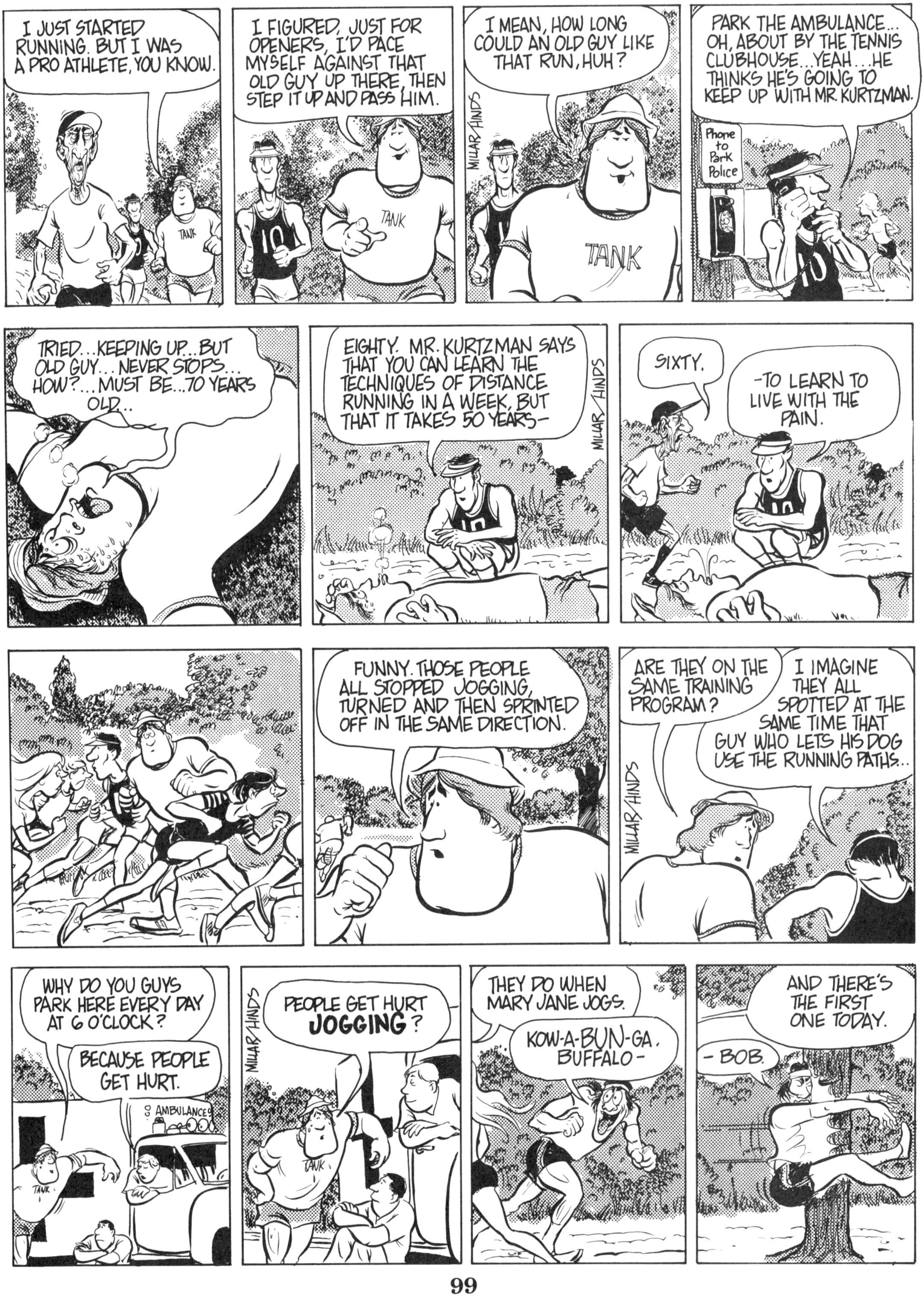
I JUST STARTED RUNNING. BUT I WAS A PRO ATHLETE, YOU KNOW.
TANK
I FIGURED, JUST FOR OPENERS, I'D PACE MYSELF AGAINST THAT OLD GUY UP THERE, THEN STEP IT UP AND PASS HIM.
TANK
MILLAR/HINDS
I MEAN, HOW LONG COULD AN OLD GUY LIKE THAT RUN, HUH?
TANK
PARK THE AMBULANCE... OH, ABOUT BY THE TENNIS CLUBHOUSE... YEAH... HE THINKS HE'S GOING TO KEEP UP WITH MR. KURTZMAN.
Phone to Park Police
TRIED... KEEPING UP... BUT OLD GUY... NEVER STOPS... HOW?... MUST BE... 70 YEARS OLD...
EIGHTY. MR. KURTZMAN SAYS THAT YOU CAN LEARN THE TECHNIQUES OF DISTANCE RUNNING IN A WEEK, BUT THAT IT TAKES 50 YEARS—
MILLAR/HINDS
SIXTY.
—TO LEARN TO LIVE WITH THE PAIN.
FUNNY. THOSE PEOPLE ALL STOPPED JOGGING, TURNED AND THEN SPRINTED OFF IN THE SAME DIRECTION.
ARE THEY ON THE SAME TRAINING PROGRAM?
I IMAGINE THEY ALL SPOTTED AT THE SAME TIME THAT GUY WHO LETS HIS DOG USE THE RUNNING PATHS...
MILLAR/HINDS
WHY DO YOU GUYS PARK HERE EVERY DAY AT 6 O'CLOCK?
BECAUSE PEOPLE GET HURT.
AMBULANCE
TANK
MILLAR/HINDS
PEOPLE GET HURT **JOGGING**?
TANK
THEY DO WHEN MARY JANE JOGS.
KOW-A-BUN-GA, BUFFALO—
—BOB.
AND THERE'S THE FIRST ONE TODAY.

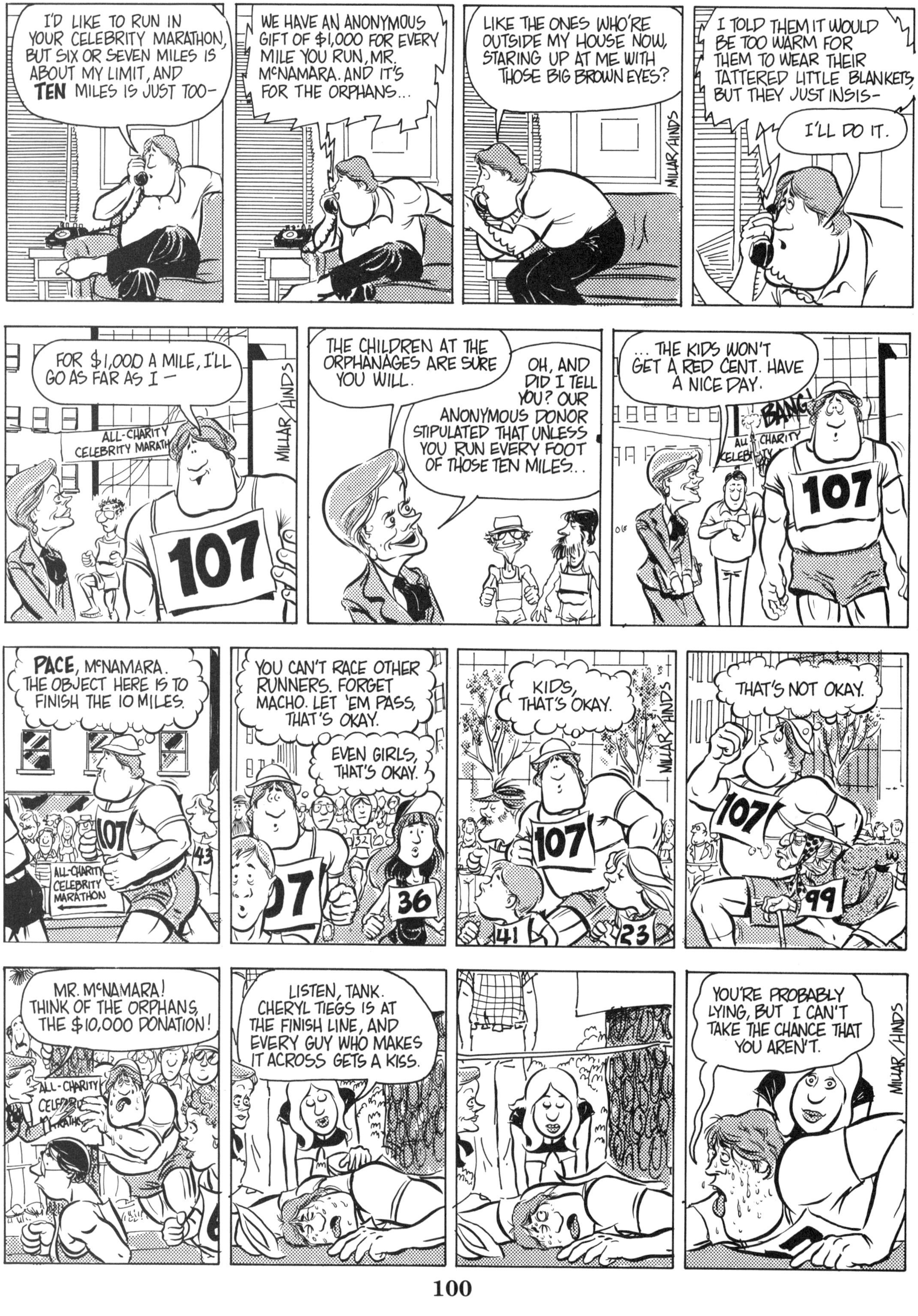
I'D LIKE TO RUN IN YOUR CELEBRITY MARATHON, BUT SIX OR SEVEN MILES IS ABOUT MY LIMIT, AND TEN MILES IS JUST TOO-
WE HAVE AN ANONYMOUS GIFT OF $1,000 FOR EVERY MILE YOU RUN, MR. McNAMARA. AND IT'S FOR THE ORPHANS...
LIKE THE ONES WHO'RE OUTSIDE MY HOUSE NOW, STARING UP AT ME WITH THOSE BIG BROWN EYES?
MILLAR/HINDS
I TOLD THEM IT WOULD BE TOO WARM FOR THEM TO WEAR THEIR TATTERED LITTLE BLANKETS, BUT THEY JUST INSIS-
I'LL DO IT.
FOR $1,000 A MILE, I'LL GO AS FAR AS I —
ALL-CHARITY CELEBRITY MARATH
107
MILLAR/HINDS
THE CHILDREN AT THE ORPHANAGES ARE SURE YOU WILL.
OH, AND DID I TELL YOU? OUR ANONYMOUS DONOR STIPULATED THAT UNLESS YOU RUN EVERY FOOT OF THOSE TEN MILES...
... THE KIDS WON'T GET A RED CENT. HAVE A NICE DAY.
BANG!
107
PACE, McNAMARA. THE OBJECT HERE IS TO FINISH THE 10 MILES.
ALL-CHARITY CELEBRITY MARATHON
107
43
YOU CAN'T RACE OTHER RUNNERS. FORGET MACHO. LET 'EM PASS, THAT'S OKAY.
EVEN GIRLS, THAT'S OKAY.
36
KIDS, THAT'S OKAY.
MILLAR/HINDS
107
41
23
THAT'S NOT OKAY.
107
99
MR. McNAMARA! THINK OF THE ORPHANS, THE $10,000 DONATION!
ALL-CHARITY
LISTEN, TANK. CHERYL TIEGS IS AT THE FINISH LINE, AND EVERY GUY WHO MAKES IT ACROSS GETS A KISS.
YOU'RE PROBABLY LYING, BUT I CAN'T TAKE THE CHANCE THAT YOU AREN'T.
MILLAR/HINDS

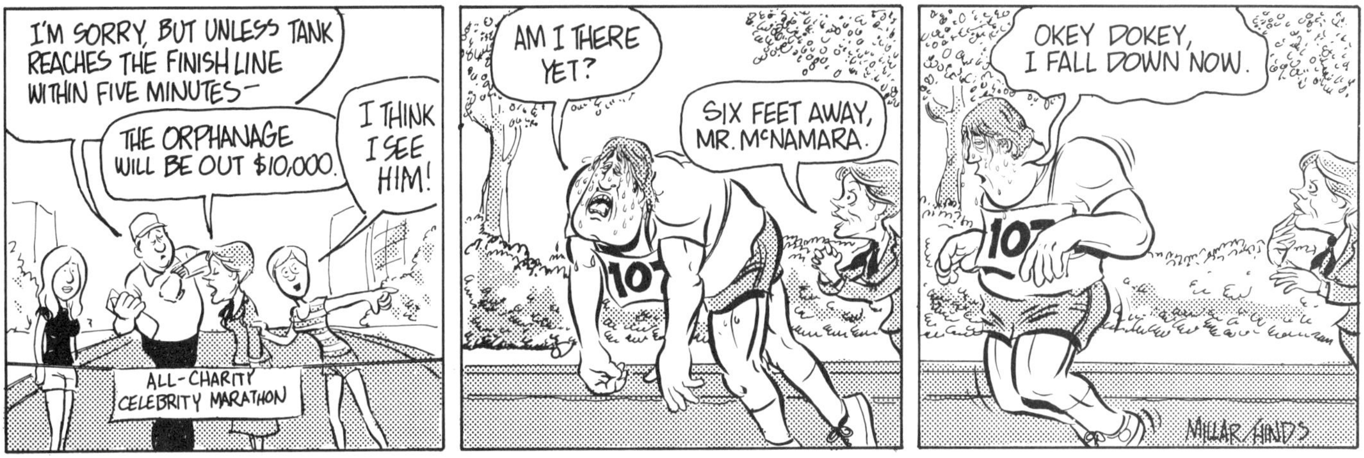
I'M SORRY, BUT UNLESS TANK REACHES THE FINISH LINE WITHIN FIVE MINUTES—
THE ORPHANAGE WILL BE OUT $10,000.
I THINK I SEE HIM!
ALL-CHARITY CELEBRITY MARATHON
AM I THERE YET?
SIX FEET AWAY, MR. McNAMARA.
107
OKEY DOKEY, I FALL DOWN NOW.
MILLAR/HINDS

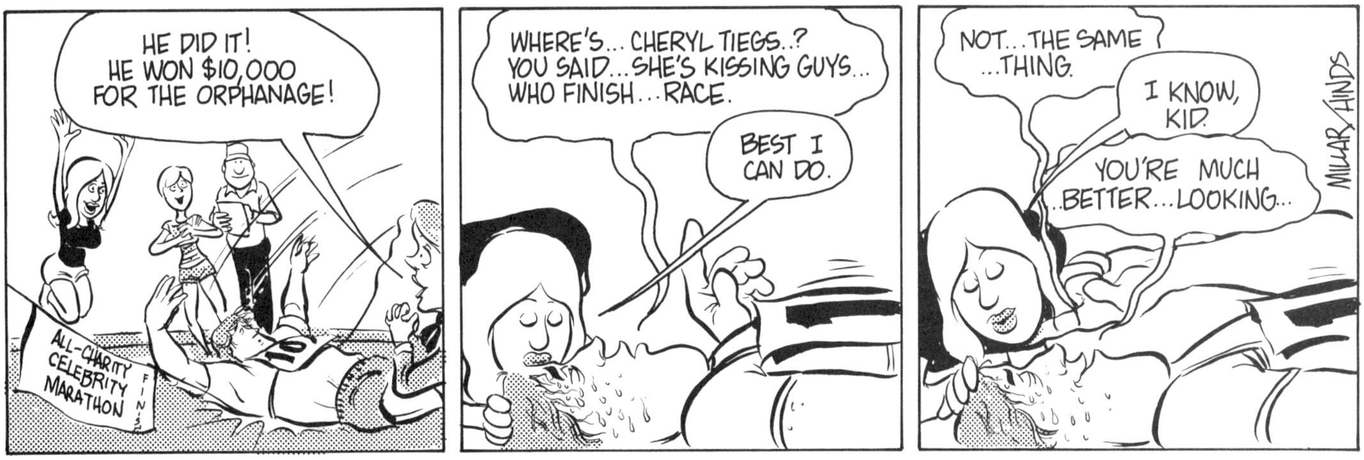
HE DID IT! HE WON $10,000 FOR THE ORPHANAGE!
ALL-CHARITY CELEBRITY MARATHON
WHERE'S... CHERYL TIEGS..? YOU SAID...SHE'S KISSING GUYS... WHO FINISH...RACE.
BEST I CAN DO.
NOT...THE SAME ...THING.
I KNOW, KID.
YOU'RE MUCH ..BETTER...LOOKING...
MILLAR/HINDS

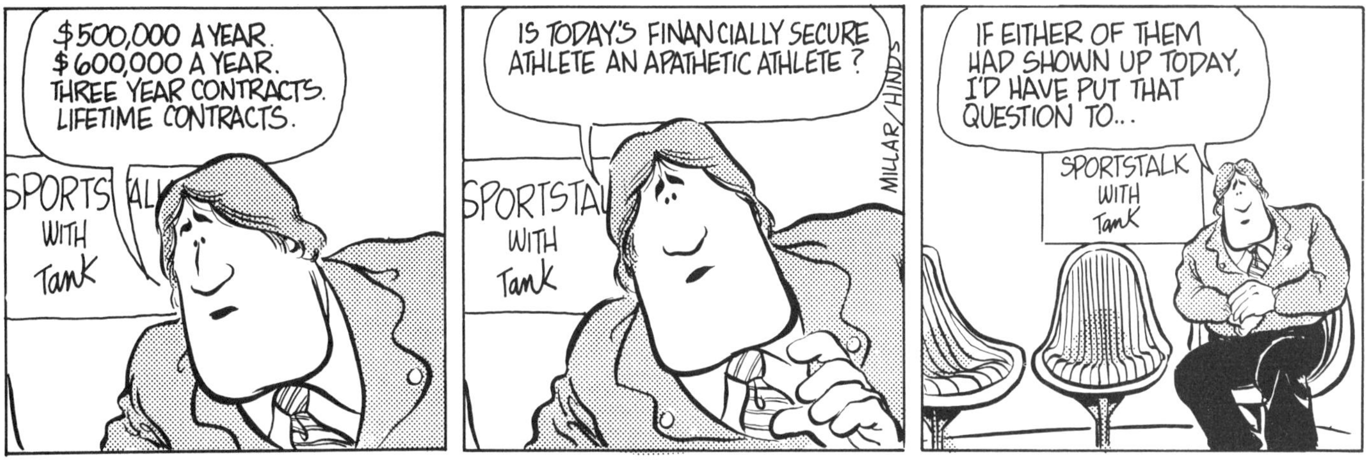
$500,000 A YEAR. $600,000 A YEAR. THREE YEAR CONTRACTS. LIFETIME CONTRACTS.
SPORTSTALK WITH Tank
IS TODAY'S FINANCIALLY SECURE ATHLETE AN APATHETIC ATHLETE?
MILLAR/HINDS
IF EITHER OF THEM HAD SHOWN UP TODAY, I'D HAVE PUT THAT QUESTION TO...
SPORTSTALK WITH Tank

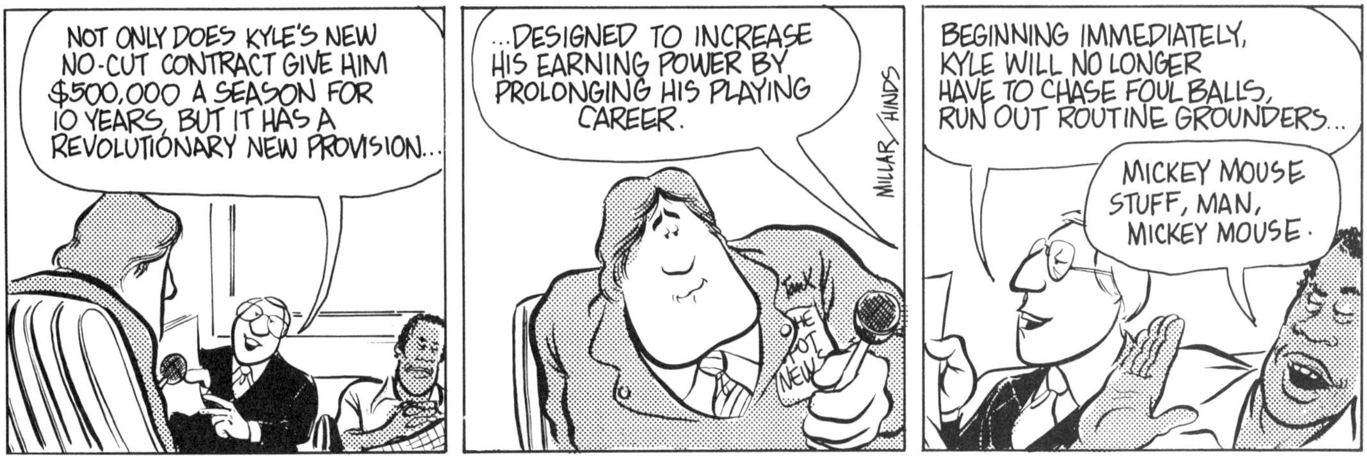
NOT ONLY DOES KYLE'S NEW NO-CUT CONTRACT GIVE HIM $500,000 A SEASON FOR 10 YEARS, BUT IT HAS A REVOLUTIONARY NEW PROVISION...
...DESIGNED TO INCREASE HIS EARNING POWER BY PROLONGING HIS PLAYING CAREER.
MILLAR/HINDS
BEGINNING IMMEDIATELY, KYLE WILL NO LONGER HAVE TO CHASE FOUL BALLS, RUN OUT ROUTINE GROUNDERS...
MICKEY MOUSE STUFF, MAN, MICKEY MOUSE.

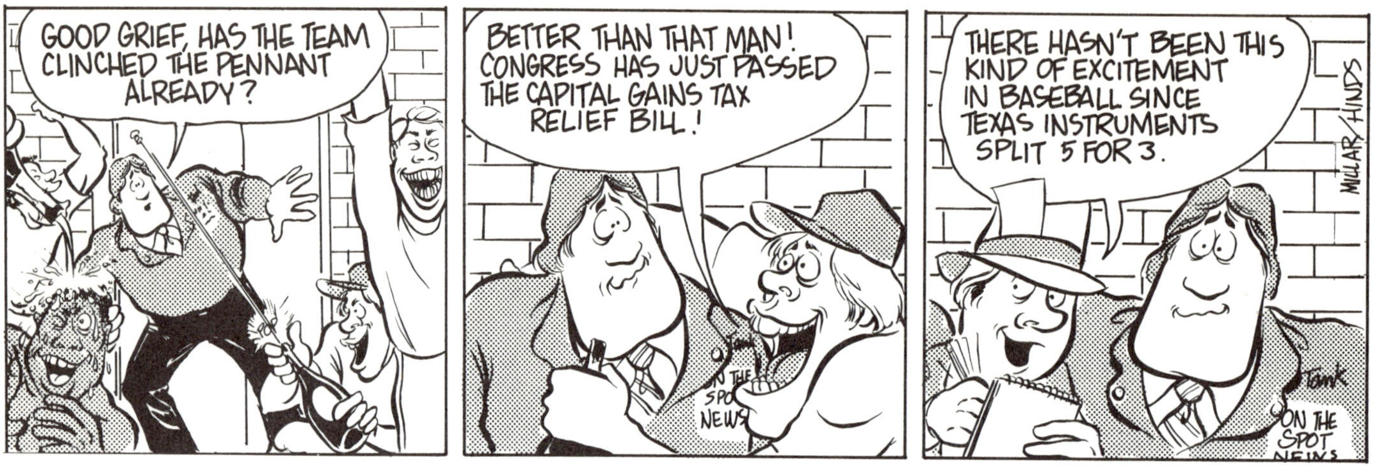
GOOD GRIEF, HAS THE TEAM CLINCHED THE PENNANT ALREADY?
BETTER THAN THAT MAN! CONGRESS HAS JUST PASSED THE CAPITAL GAINS TAX RELIEF BILL!
THERE HASN'T BEEN THIS KIND OF EXCITEMENT IN BASEBALL SINCE TEXAS INSTRUMENTS SPLIT 5 FOR 3.
ON THE SPOT NEWS
MILLAR/HINDS

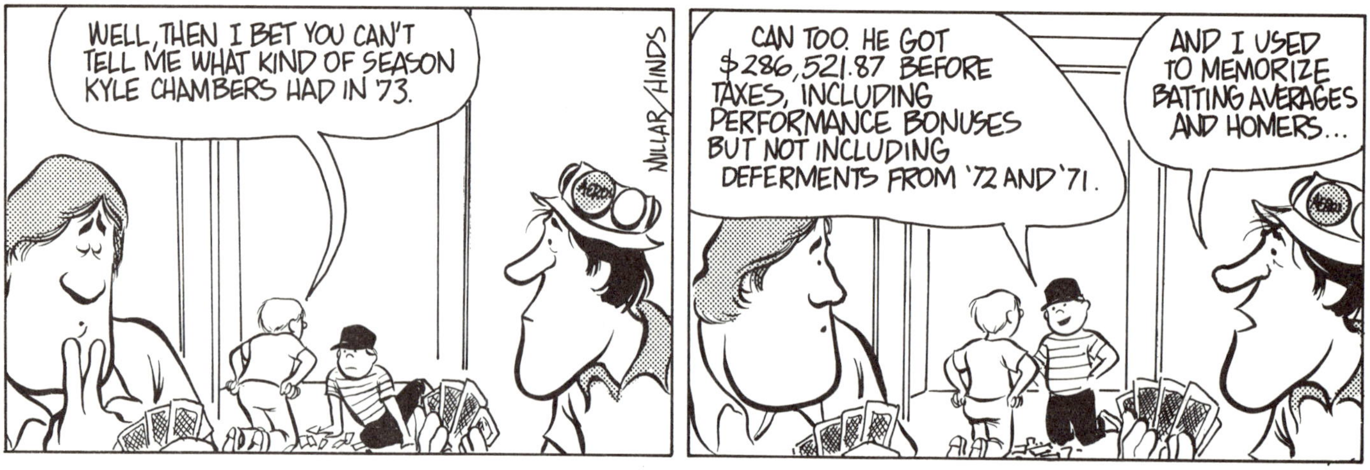
WELL, THEN I BET YOU CAN'T TELL ME WHAT KIND OF SEASON KYLE CHAMBERS HAD IN '73.
MILLAR/HINDS
CAN TOO. HE GOT $286,521.87 BEFORE TAXES, INCLUDING PERFORMANCE BONUSES BUT NOT INCLUDING DEFERMENTS FROM '72 AND '71.
AND I USED TO MEMORIZE BATTING AVERAGES AND HOMERS...

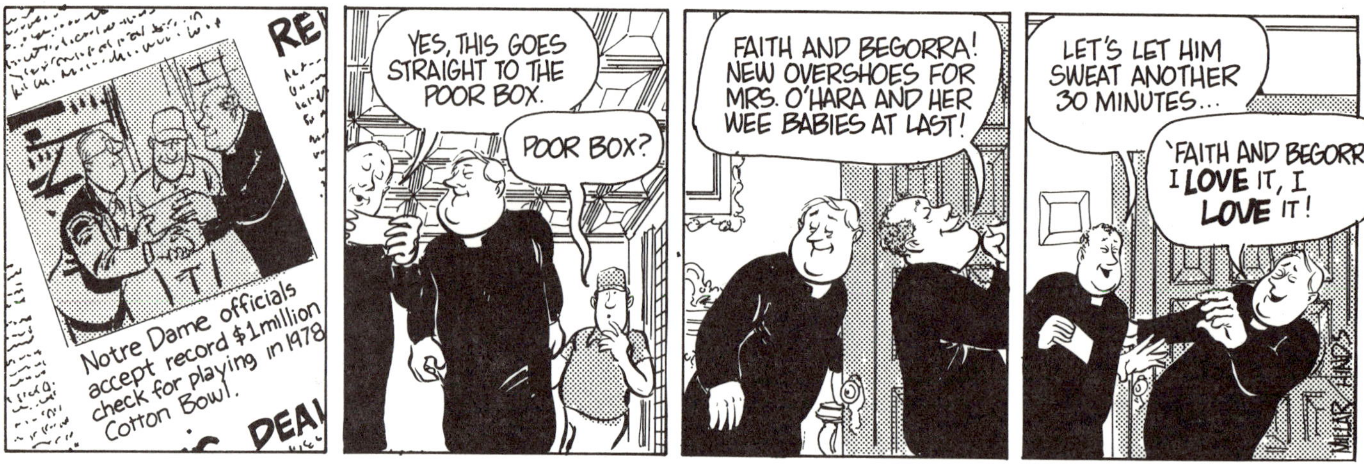
RE
Notre Dame officials accept record $1 million check for playing in 1978 Cotton Bowl.
DEA
YES, THIS GOES STRAIGHT TO THE POOR BOX.
POOR BOX?
FAITH AND BEGORRA! NEW OVERSHOES FOR MRS. O'HARA AND HER WEE BABIES AT LAST!
LET'S LET HIM SWEAT ANOTHER 30 MINUTES...
'FAITH AND BEGORRA.' I LOVE IT, I LOVE IT!
MILLAR/HINDS

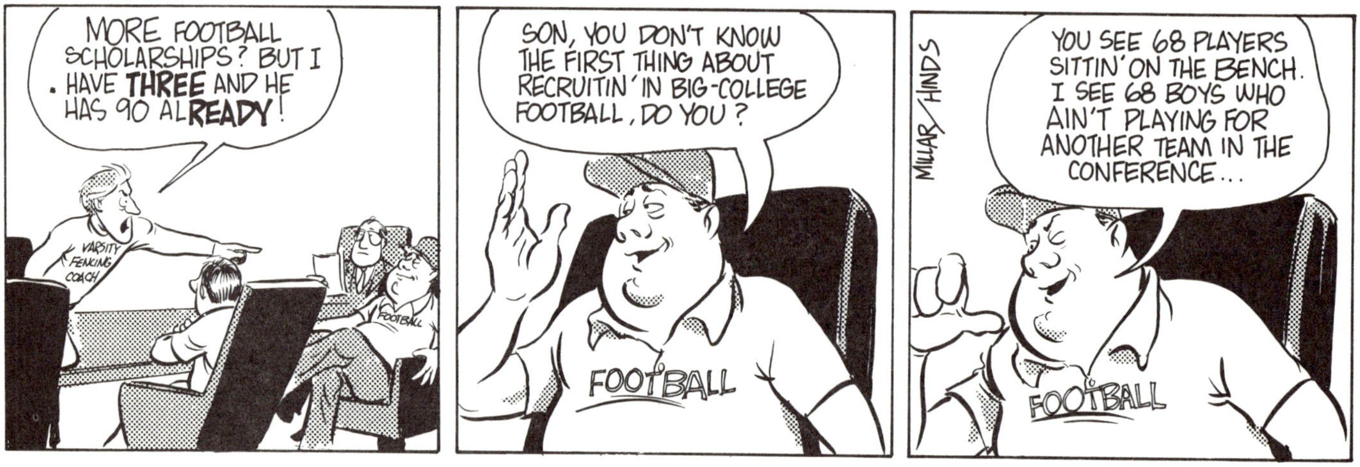
MORE FOOTBALL SCHOLARSHIPS? BUT I HAVE THREE AND HE HAS 90 ALREADY!
VARSITY FENCING COACH
FOOTBALL
SON, YOU DON'T KNOW THE FIRST THING ABOUT RECRUITIN' IN BIG-COLLEGE FOOTBALL, DO YOU?
FOOTBALL
MILLAR/HINDS
YOU SEE 68 PLAYERS SITTIN' ON THE BENCH. I SEE 68 BOYS WHO AIN'T PLAYING FOR ANOTHER TEAM IN THE CONFERENCE...
FOOTBALL

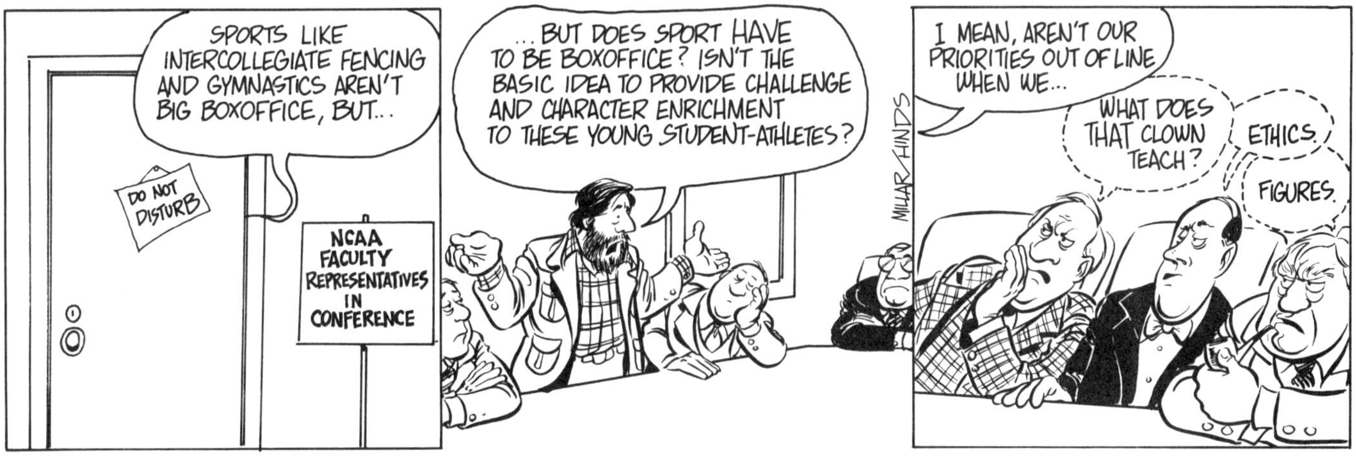
SPORTS LIKE INTERCOLLEGIATE FENCING AND GYMNASTICS AREN'T BIG BOXOFFICE, BUT...
DO NOT DISTURB
NCAA FACULTY REPRESENTATIVES IN CONFERENCE
...BUT DOES SPORT HAVE TO BE BOXOFFICE? ISN'T THE BASIC IDEA TO PROVIDE CHALLENGE AND CHARACTER ENRICHMENT TO THESE YOUNG STUDENT-ATHLETES?
MILLAR/HINDS
I MEAN, AREN'T OUR PRIORITIES OUT OF LINE WHEN WE...
WHAT DOES THAT CLOWN TEACH?
ETHICS.
FIGURES.

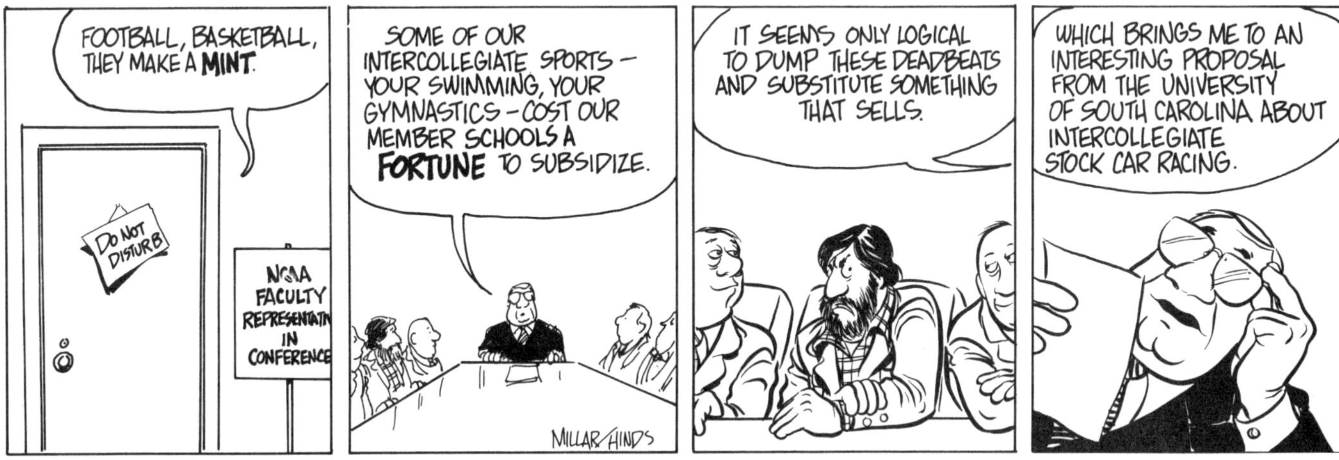
FOOTBALL, BASKETBALL, THEY MAKE A MINT.
DO NOT DISTURB
NCAA FACULTY REPRESENTATI IN CONFERENCE
SOME OF OUR INTERCOLLEGIATE SPORTS — YOUR SWIMMING, YOUR GYMNASTICS — COST OUR MEMBER SCHOOLS A FORTUNE TO SUBSIDIZE.
MILLAR/HINDS
IT SEEMS ONLY LOGICAL TO DUMP THESE DEADBEATS AND SUBSTITUTE SOMETHING THAT SELLS.
WHICH BRINGS ME TO AN INTERESTING PROPOSAL FROM THE UNIVERSITY OF SOUTH CAROLINA ABOUT INTERCOLLEGIATE STOCK CAR RACING.

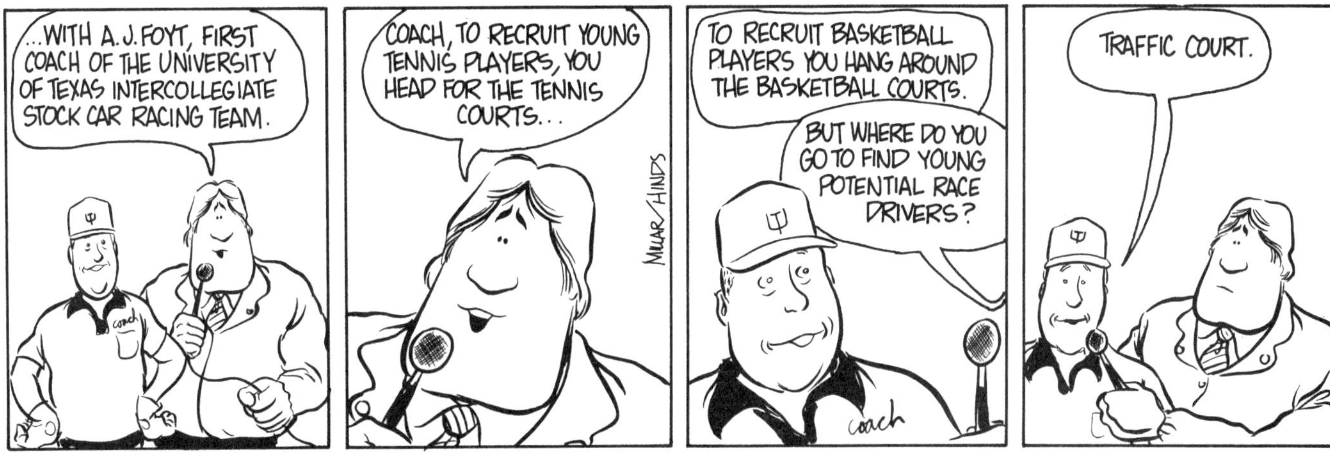
...WITH A. J. FOYT, FIRST COACH OF THE UNIVERSITY OF TEXAS INTERCOLLEGIATE STOCK CAR RACING TEAM.
COACH
COACH, TO RECRUIT YOUNG TENNIS PLAYERS, YOU HEAD FOR THE TENNIS COURTS...
MILLAR/HINDS
TO RECRUIT BASKETBALL PLAYERS YOU HANG AROUND THE BASKETBALL COURTS.
BUT WHERE DO YOU GO TO FIND YOUNG POTENTIAL RACE DRIVERS?
COACH
TRAFFIC COURT.

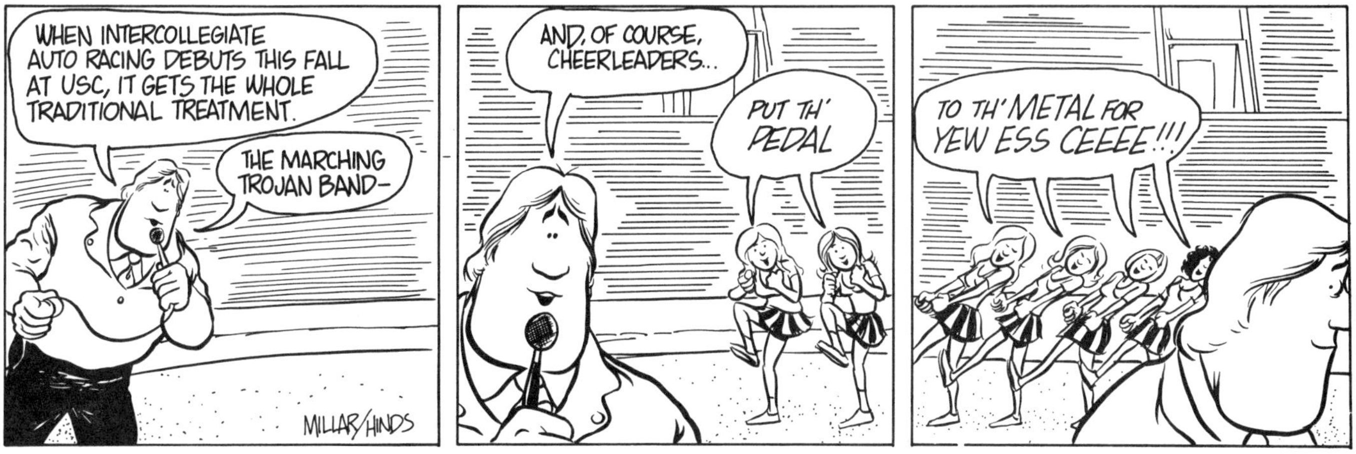
WHEN INTERCOLLEGIATE AUTO RACING DEBUTS THIS FALL AT USC, IT GETS THE WHOLE TRADITIONAL TREATMENT.
THE MARCHING TROJAN BAND—
MILLAR/HINDS
AND, OF COURSE, CHEERLEADERS...
PUT TH' PEDAL
TO TH' METAL FOR YEW ESS CEEEE!!!

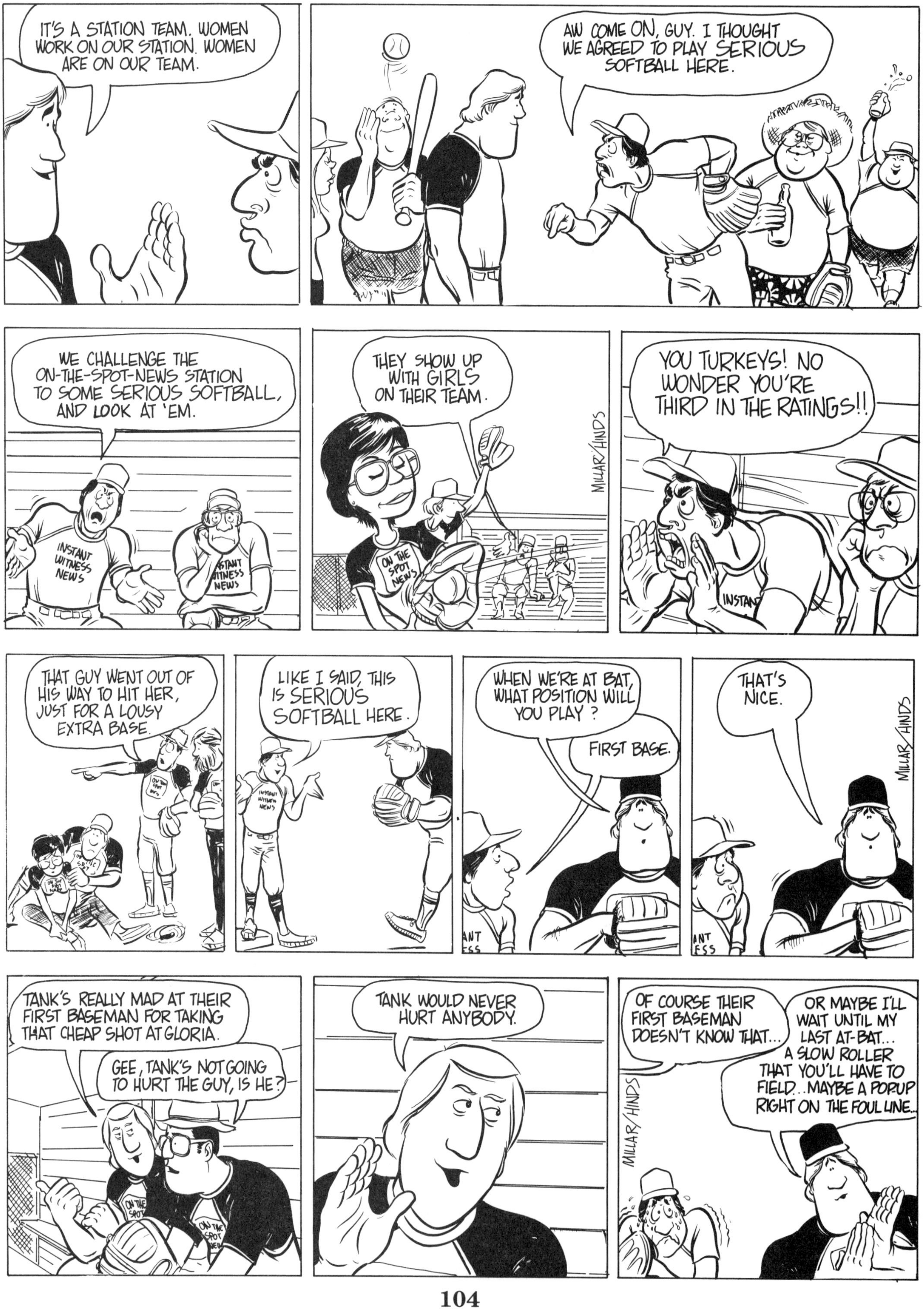
IT'S A STATION TEAM. WOMEN WORK ON OUR STATION. WOMEN ARE ON OUR TEAM.
AW COME ON, GUY. I THOUGHT WE AGREED TO PLAY SERIOUS SOFTBALL HERE.
WE CHALLENGE THE ON-THE-SPOT-NEWS STATION TO SOME SERIOUS SOFTBALL, AND LOOK AT 'EM.
INSTANT WITNESS NEWS
INSTANT WITNESS NEWS
THEY SHOW UP WITH GIRLS ON THEIR TEAM.
ON THE SPOT NEWS
MILLAR/HINDS
YOU TURKEYS! NO WONDER YOU'RE THIRD IN THE RATINGS!!
THAT GUY WENT OUT OF HIS WAY TO HIT HER, JUST FOR A LOUSY EXTRA BASE.
LIKE I SAID, THIS IS SERIOUS SOFTBALL HERE.
WHEN WE'RE AT BAT, WHAT POSITION WILL YOU PLAY ?
FIRST BASE.
THAT'S NICE.
MILLAR/HINDS
TANK'S REALLY MAD AT THEIR FIRST BASEMAN FOR TAKING THAT CHEAP SHOT AT GLORIA.
GEE, TANK'S NOT GOING TO HURT THE GUY, IS HE?
TANK WOULD NEVER HURT ANYBODY.
OF COURSE THEIR FIRST BASEMAN DOESN'T KNOW THAT...
OR MAYBE I'LL WAIT UNTIL MY LAST AT-BAT... A SLOW ROLLER THAT YOU'LL HAVE TO FIELD...MAYBE A POPUP RIGHT ON THE FOUL LINE...
MILLAR/HINDS

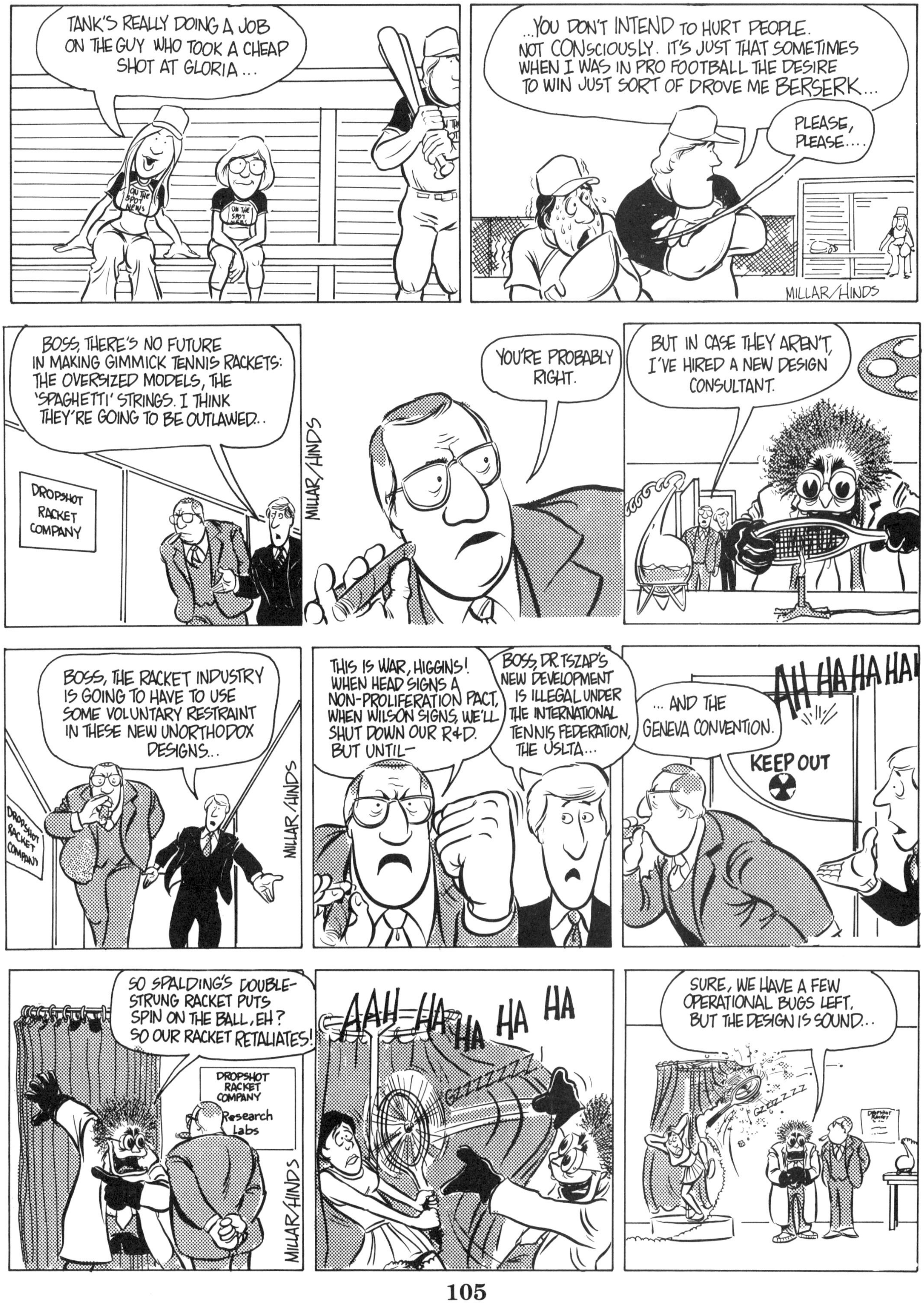

TANK'S REALLY DOING A JOB ON THE GUY WHO TOOK A CHEAP SHOT AT GLORIA...
ON THE SPOT NEWS
ON THE SPOT NEWS
...YOU DON'T INTEND TO HURT PEOPLE. NOT CONSCIOUSLY. IT'S JUST THAT SOMETIMES WHEN I WAS IN PRO FOOTBALL THE DESIRE TO WIN JUST SORT OF DROVE ME BERSERK...
PLEASE, PLEASE....
MILLAR/HINDS
BOSS, THERE'S NO FUTURE IN MAKING GIMMICK TENNIS RACKETS: THE OVERSIZED MODELS, THE 'SPAGHETTI' STRINGS. I THINK THEY'RE GOING TO BE OUTLAWED..
DROPSHOT RACKET COMPANY
MILLAR/HINDS
YOU'RE PROBABLY RIGHT.
BUT IN CASE THEY AREN'T, I'VE HIRED A NEW DESIGN CONSULTANT.
BOSS, THE RACKET INDUSTRY IS GOING TO HAVE TO USE SOME VOLUNTARY RESTRAINT IN THESE NEW UNORTHODOX DESIGNS...
DROPSHOT RACKET COMPANY
MILLAR/HINDS
THIS IS WAR, HIGGINS! WHEN HEAD SIGNS A NON-PROLIFERATION PACT, WHEN WILSON SIGNS, WE'LL SHUT DOWN OUR R&D. BUT UNTIL-
BOSS, DR. TSZAP'S NEW DEVELOPMENT IS ILLEGAL UNDER THE INTERNATIONAL TENNIS FEDERATION, THE USLTA...
... AND THE GENEVA CONVENTION.
AH HA HA HA HA
KEEP OUT
SO SPALDING'S DOUBLE-STRUNG RACKET PUTS SPIN ON THE BALL, EH? SO OUR RACKET RETALIATES!
DROPSHOT RACKET COMPANY Research Labs
MILLAR/HINDS
AAH HA HA HA HA HA
GZZZZZZZ
SURE, WE HAVE A FEW OPERATIONAL BUGS LEFT, BUT THE DESIGN IS SOUND...
GZZZZZZ

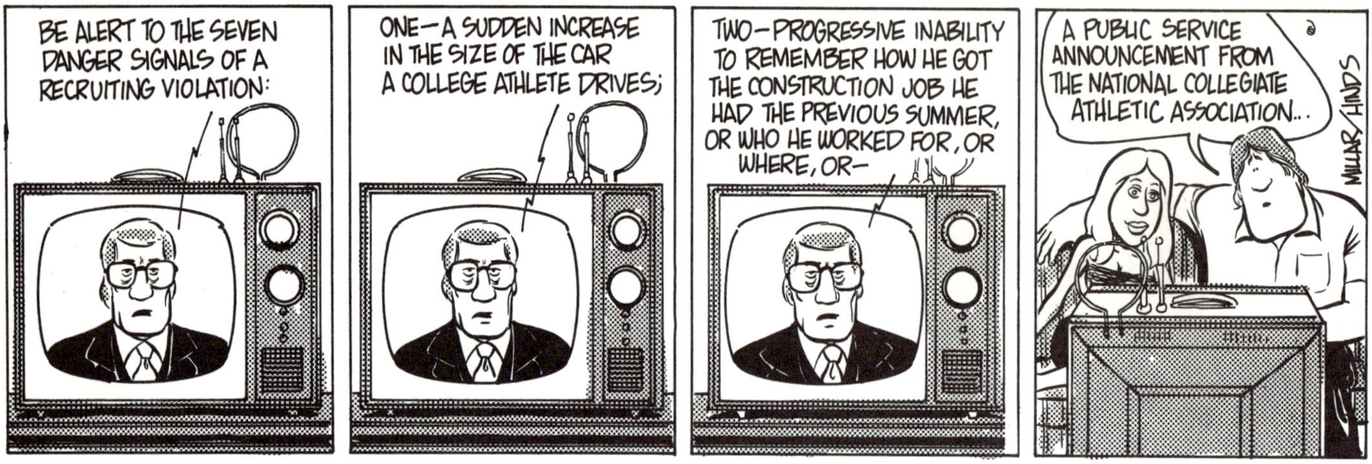
BE ALERT TO THE SEVEN DANGER SIGNALS OF A RECRUITING VIOLATION:
ONE—A SUDDEN INCREASE IN THE SIZE OF THE CAR A COLLEGE ATHLETE DRIVES;
TWO—PROGRESSIVE INABILITY TO REMEMBER HOW HE GOT THE CONSTRUCTION JOB HE HAD THE PREVIOUS SUMMER, OR WHO HE WORKED FOR, OR WHERE, OR—
A PUBLIC SERVICE ANNOUNCEMENT FROM THE NATIONAL COLLEGIATE ATHLETIC ASSOCIATION...
MILLAR/HINDS

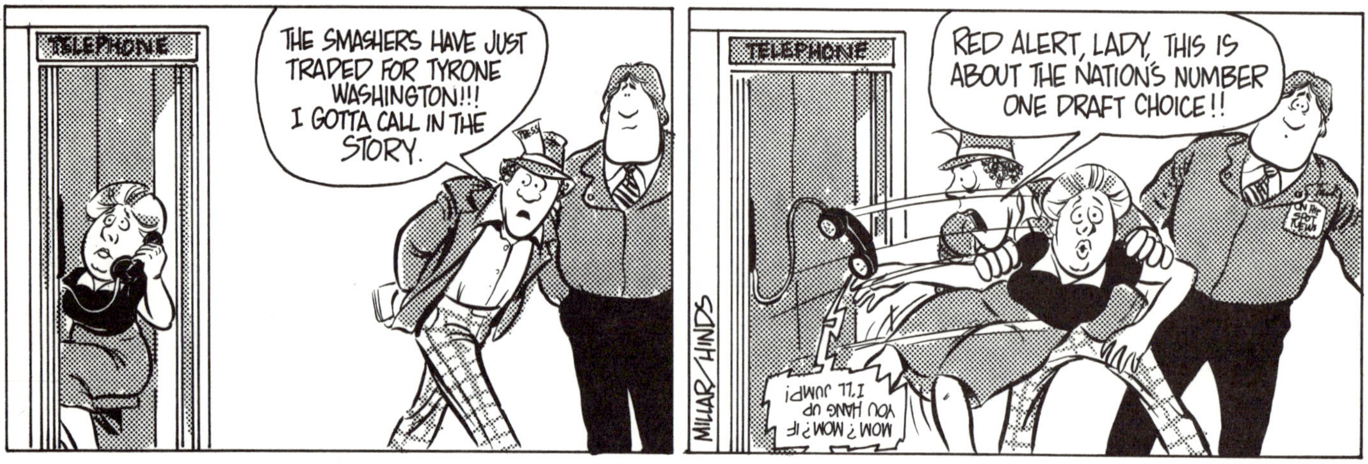
TELEPHONE
THE SMASHERS HAVE JUST TRADED FOR TYRONE WASHINGTON!!! I GOTTA CALL IN THE STORY.
MILLAR/HINDS
TELEPHONE
RED ALERT, LADY, THIS IS ABOUT THE NATION'S NUMBER ONE DRAFT CHOICE!!
MOM? MOM? IF YOU HANG UP I'LL JUMP!

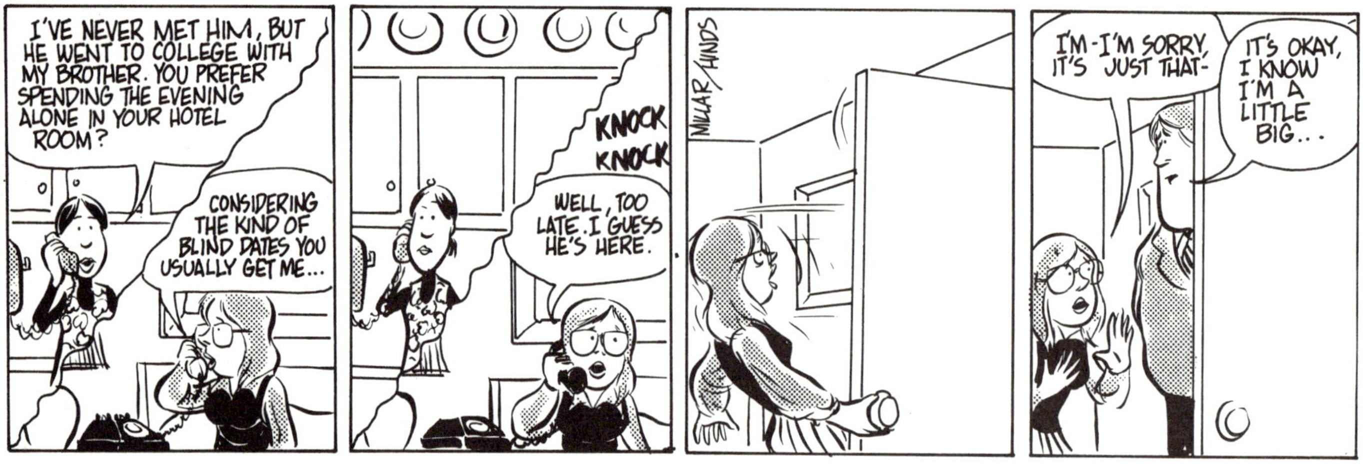
I'VE NEVER MET HIM, BUT HE WENT TO COLLEGE WITH MY BROTHER. YOU PREFER SPENDING THE EVENING ALONE IN YOUR HOTEL ROOM?
CONSIDERING THE KIND OF BLIND DATES YOU USUALLY GET ME...
KNOCK KNOCK
WELL, TOO LATE. I GUESS HE'S HERE.
MILLAR/HINDS
I'M-I'M SORRY, IT'S JUST THAT-
IT'S OKAY, I KNOW I'M A LITTLE BIG...

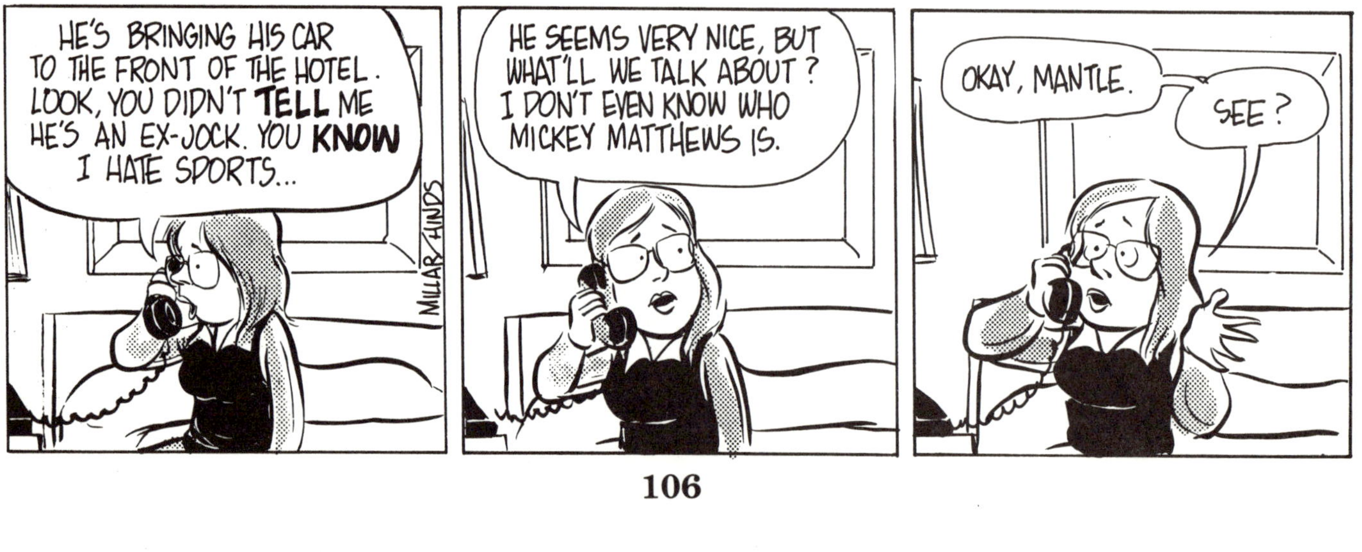
HE'S BRINGING HIS CAR TO THE FRONT OF THE HOTEL. LOOK, YOU DIDN'T TELL ME HE'S AN EX-JOCK. YOU KNOW I HATE SPORTS...
MILLAR/HINDS
HE SEEMS VERY NICE, BUT WHAT'LL WE TALK ABOUT? I DON'T EVEN KNOW WHO MICKEY MATTHEWS IS.
OKAY, MANTLE.
SEE?

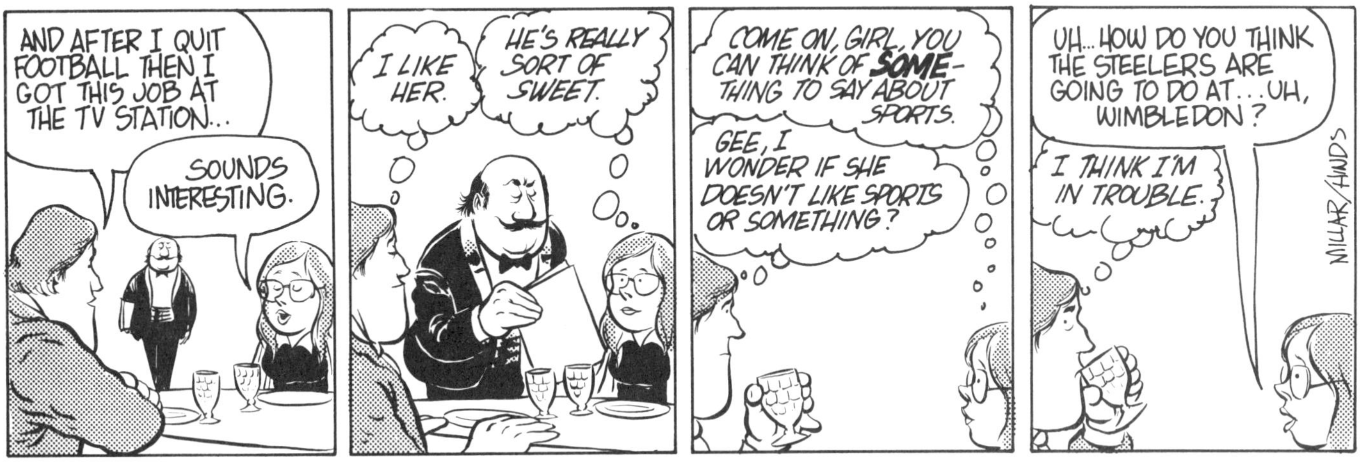
AND AFTER I QUIT FOOTBALL THEN I GOT THIS JOB AT THE TV STATION...
SOUNDS INTERESTING.
I LIKE HER.
HE'S REALLY SORT OF SWEET.
COME ON, GIRL, YOU CAN THINK OF SOME-THING TO SAY ABOUT SPORTS.
GEE, I WONDER IF SHE DOESN'T LIKE SPORTS OR SOMETHING?
UH... HOW DO YOU THINK THE STEELERS ARE GOING TO DO AT... UH, WIMBLEDON?
I THINK I'M IN TROUBLE.
MILLAR/HINDS

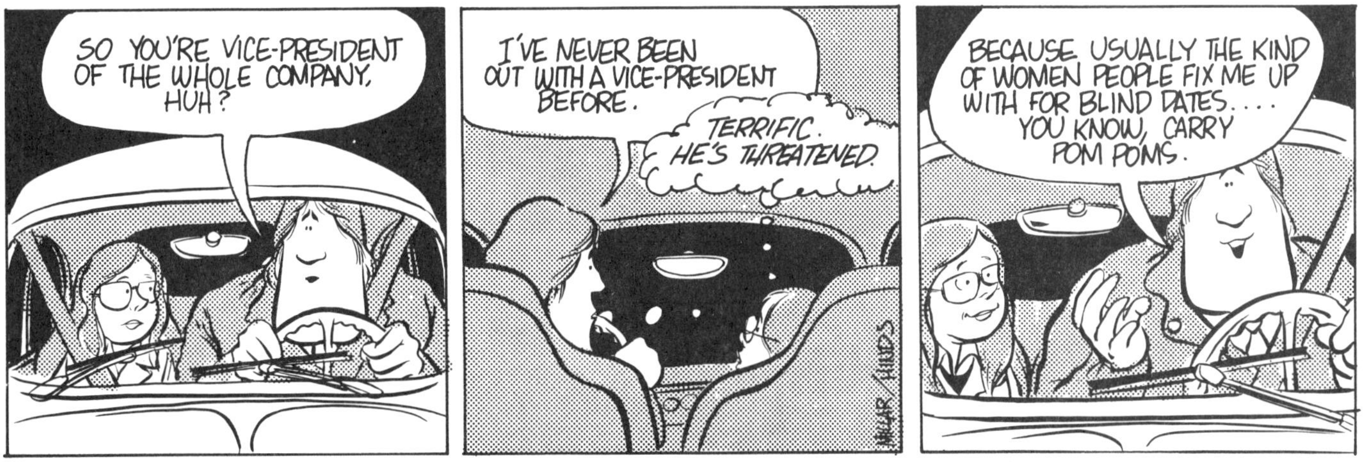
SO YOU'RE VICE-PRESIDENT OF THE WHOLE COMPANY, HUH?
I'VE NEVER BEEN OUT WITH A VICE-PRESIDENT BEFORE.
TERRIFIC. HE'S THREATENED.
MILLAR/HINDS
BECAUSE USUALLY THE KIND OF WOMEN PEOPLE FIX ME UP WITH FOR BLIND DATES.... YOU KNOW, CARRY POM POMS.

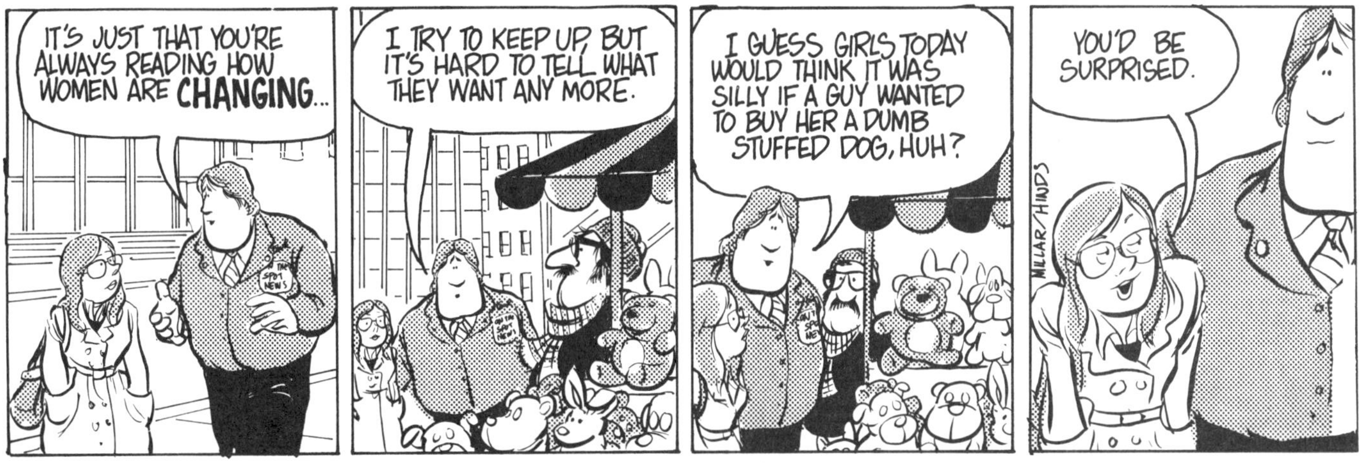
IT'S JUST THAT YOU'RE ALWAYS READING HOW WOMEN ARE CHANGING...
I TRY TO KEEP UP, BUT IT'S HARD TO TELL WHAT THEY WANT ANY MORE.
I GUESS GIRLS TODAY WOULD THINK IT WAS SILLY IF A GUY WANTED TO BUY HER A DUMB STUFFED DOG, HUH?
MILLAR/HINDS
YOU'D BE SURPRISED.

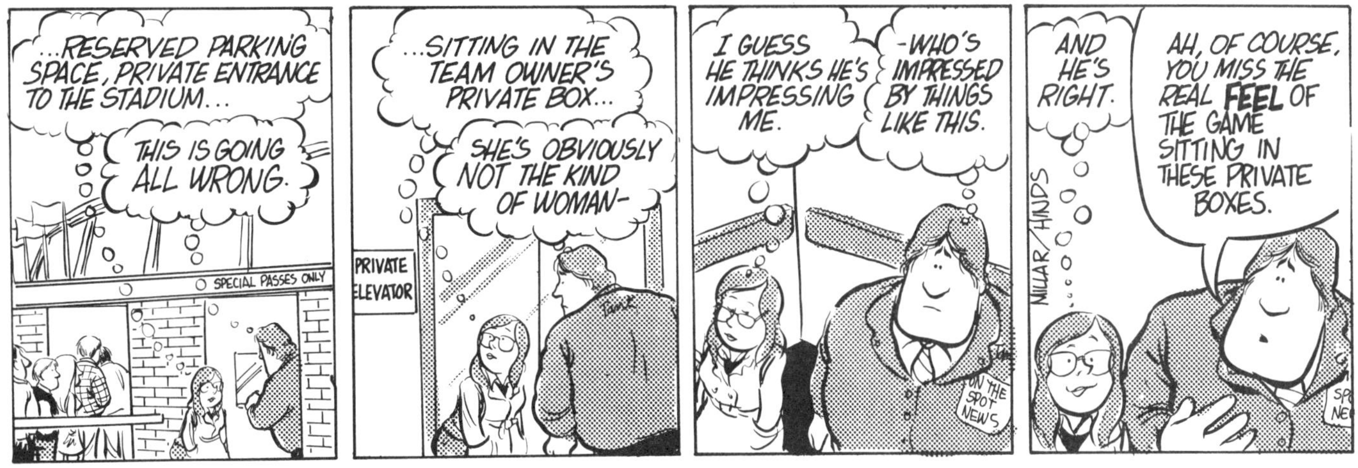
...RESERVED PARKING SPACE, PRIVATE ENTRANCE TO THE STADIUM...
THIS IS GOING ALL WRONG.
SPECIAL PASSES ONLY
...SITTING IN THE TEAM OWNER'S PRIVATE BOX...
SHE'S OBVIOUSLY NOT THE KIND OF WOMAN-
PRIVATE ELEVATOR
I GUESS HE THINKS HE'S IMPRESSING ME.
-WHO'S IMPRESSED BY THINGS LIKE THIS.
ON THE SPOT NEWS
AND HE'S RIGHT.
MILLAR/HINDS
AH, OF COURSE, YOU MISS THE REAL FEEL OF THE GAME SITTING IN THESE PRIVATE BOXES.

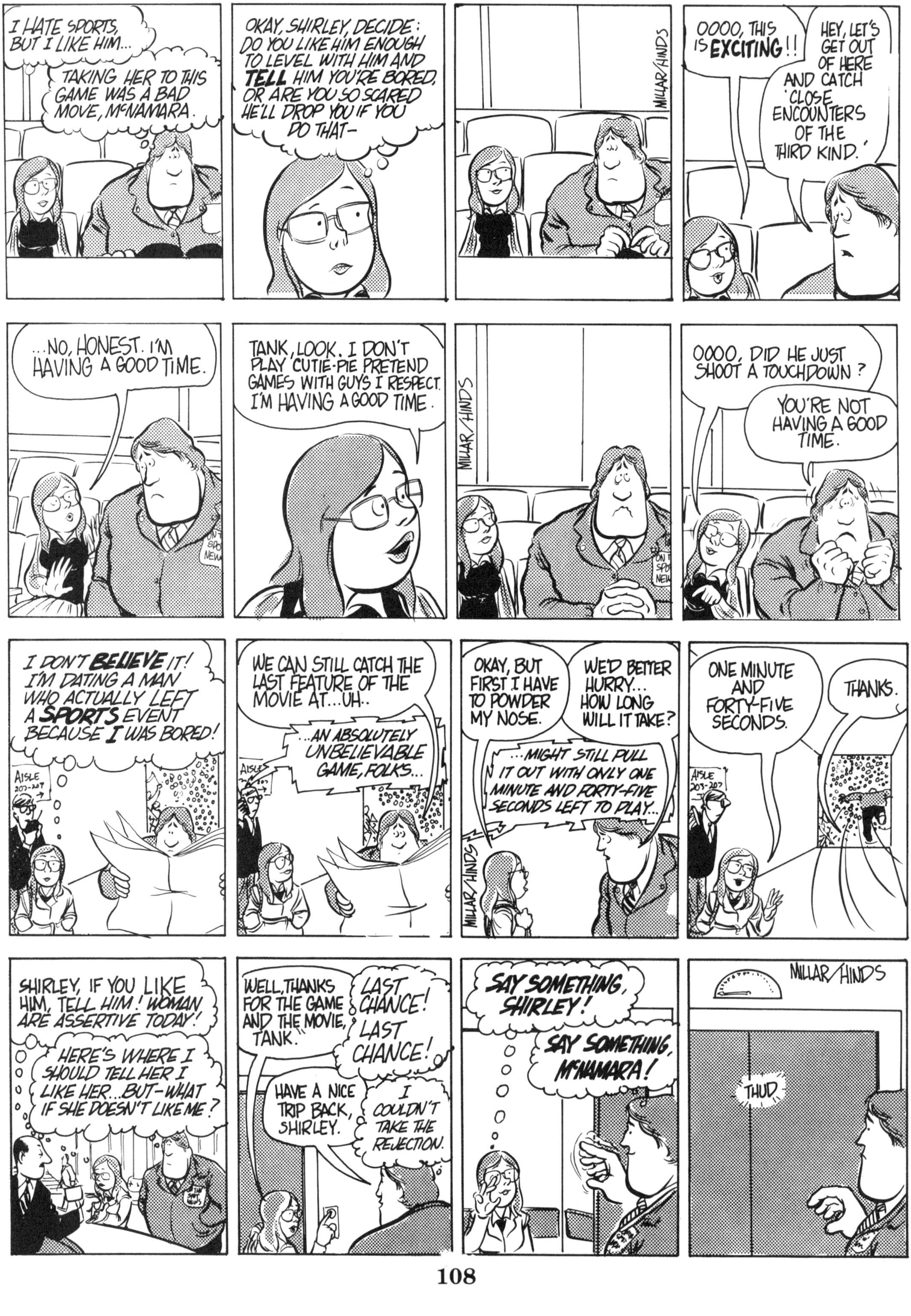
I HATE SPORTS, BUT I LIKE HIM...
TAKING HER TO THIS GAME WAS A BAD MOVE, McNAMARA.
OKAY, SHIRLEY, DECIDE: DO YOU LIKE HIM ENOUGH TO LEVEL WITH HIM AND TELL HIM YOU'RE BORED, OR ARE YOU SO SCARED HE'LL DROP YOU IF YOU DO THAT–
MILLAR/HINDS
OOOO, THIS IS EXCITING!!
HEY, LET'S GET OUT OF HERE AND CATCH 'CLOSE ENCOUNTERS OF THE THIRD KIND.'
...NO, HONEST. I'M HAVING A GOOD TIME.
TANK, LOOK. I DON'T PLAY CUTIE-PIE PRETEND GAMES WITH GUYS I RESPECT. I'M HAVING A GOOD TIME.
MILLAR/HINDS
OOOO, DID HE JUST SHOOT A TOUCHDOWN?
YOU'RE NOT HAVING A GOOD TIME.
I DON'T BELIEVE IT! I'M DATING A MAN WHO ACTUALLY LEFT A SPORTS EVENT BECAUSE I WAS BORED!
WE CAN STILL CATCH THE LAST FEATURE OF THE MOVIE AT...UH..
...AN ABSOLUTELY UNBELIEVABLE GAME, FOLKS...
OKAY, BUT FIRST I HAVE TO POWDER MY NOSE.
WE'D BETTER HURRY... HOW LONG WILL IT TAKE?
...MIGHT STILL PULL IT OUT WITH ONLY ONE MINUTE AND FORTY-FIVE SECONDS LEFT TO PLAY...
MILLAR/HINDS
ONE MINUTE AND FORTY-FIVE SECONDS.
THANKS.
SHIRLEY, IF YOU LIKE HIM, TELL HIM! WOMAN ARE ASSERTIVE TODAY!
HERE'S WHERE I SHOULD TELL HER I LIKE HER...BUT–WHAT IF SHE DOESN'T LIKE ME?
WELL, THANKS FOR THE GAME AND THE MOVIE, TANK.
LAST CHANCE! LAST CHANCE!
HAVE A NICE TRIP BACK, SHIRLEY.
I COULDN'T TAKE THE REJECTION.
SAY SOMETHING, SHIRLEY!
SAY SOMETHING, McNAMARA!
MILLAR/HINDS
THUD

TANK McNAMARA

by Jeff Millar & Bill Hinds

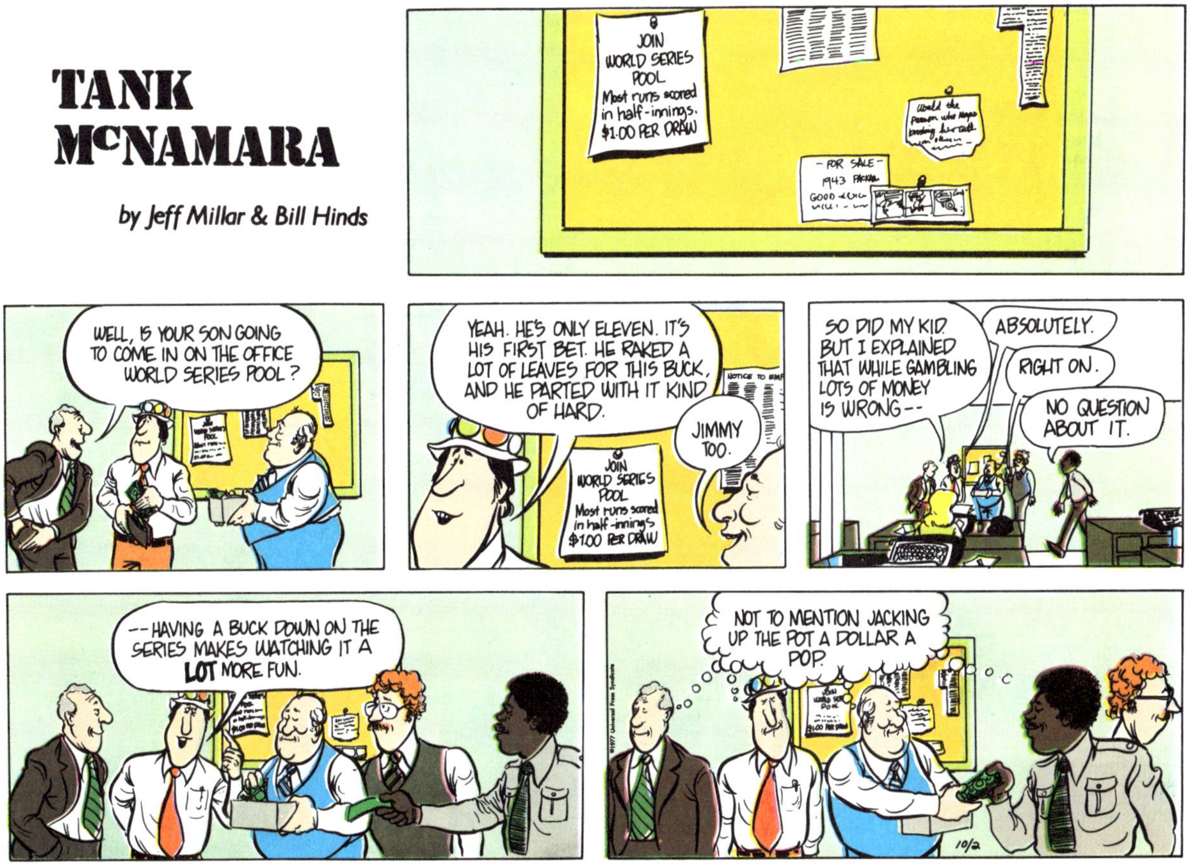

JOIN WORLD SERIES POOL Most runs scored in half-innings. $1.00 PER DRAW
— FOR SALE — 1943
WELL, IS YOUR SON GOING TO COME IN ON THE OFFICE WORLD SERIES POOL?
YEAH. HE'S ONLY ELEVEN. IT'S HIS FIRST BET. HE RAKED A LOT OF LEAVES FOR THIS BUCK, AND HE PARTED WITH IT KIND OF HARD.
JOIN WORLD SERIES POOL Most runs scored in half-innings $1.00 PER DRAW
JIMMY TOO.
SO DID MY KID. BUT I EXPLAINED THAT WHILE GAMBLING LOTS OF MONEY IS WRONG--
ABSOLUTELY.
RIGHT ON.
NO QUESTION ABOUT IT.
--HAVING A BUCK DOWN ON THE SERIES MAKES WATCHING IT A LOT MORE FUN.
NOT TO MENTION JACKING UP THE POT A DOLLAR A POP.
10/2

TANK McNAMARA

by Jeff Millar & Bill Hinds

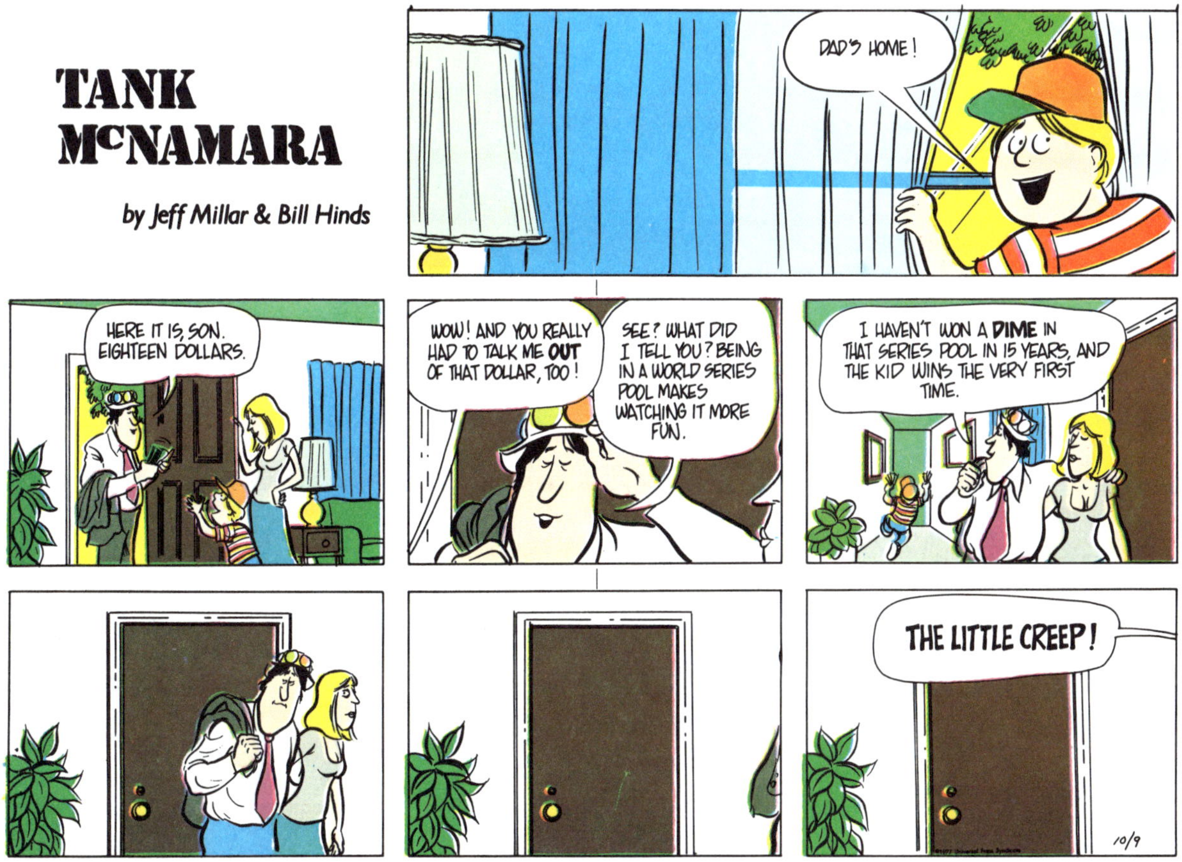

DAD'S HOME!
HERE IT IS, SON. EIGHTEEN DOLLARS.
WOW! AND YOU REALLY HAD TO TALK ME OUT OF THAT DOLLAR, TOO!
SEE? WHAT DID I TELL YOU? BEING IN A WORLD SERIES POOL MAKES WATCHING IT MORE FUN.
I HAVEN'T WON A DIME IN THAT SERIES POOL IN 15 YEARS, AND THE KID WINS THE VERY FIRST TIME.
THE LITTLE CREEP!
10/9

TANK McNAMARA

by Jeff Millar & Bill Hinds

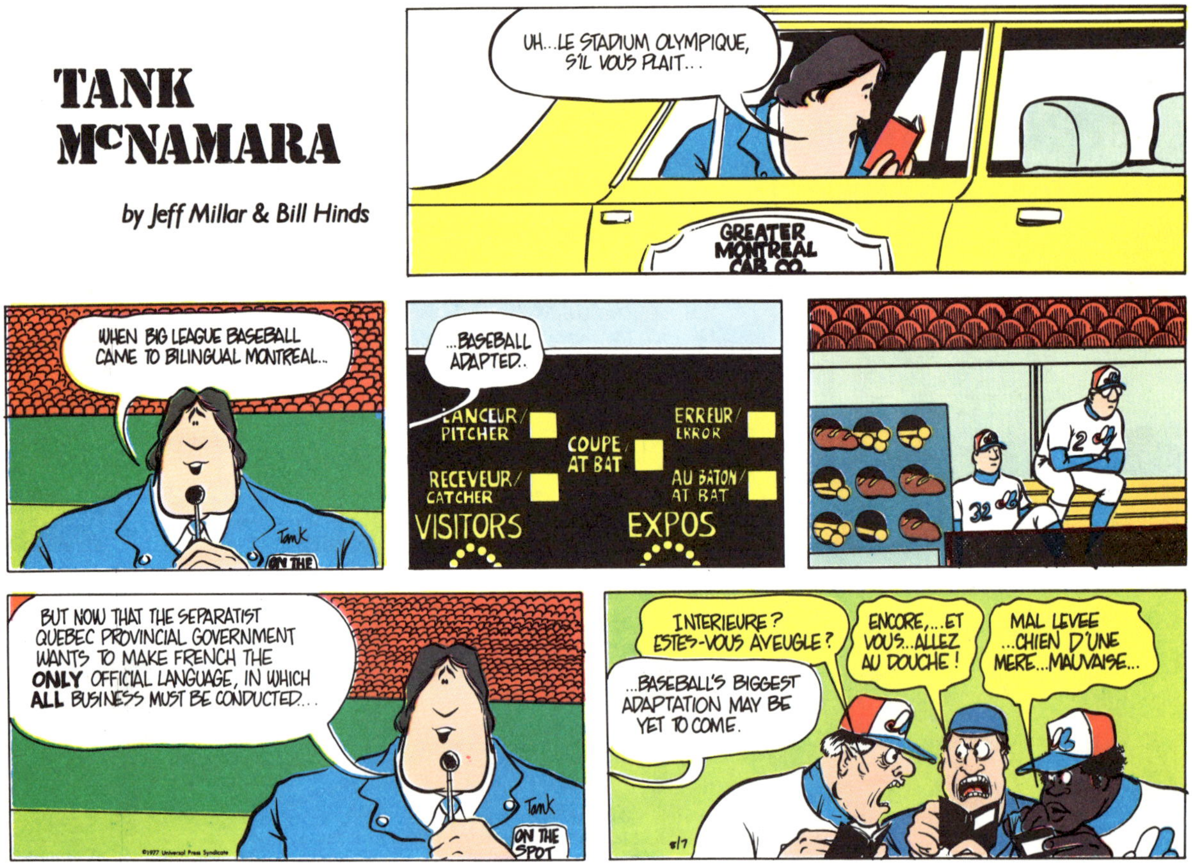

UH...LE STADIUM OLYMPIQUE, S'IL VOUS PLAIT...
GREATER MONTREAL CAB CO.
WHEN BIG LEAGUE BASEBALL CAME TO BILINGUAL MONTREAL...
TANK
...BASEBALL ADAPTED...
LANCEUR/ PITCHER
COUPE/ AT BAT
ERREUR/ ERROR
RECEVEUR/ CATCHER
AU BATON/ AT BAT
VISITORS
EXPOS
BUT NOW THAT THE SEPARATIST QUEBEC PROVINCIAL GOVERNMENT WANTS TO MAKE FRENCH THE **ONLY** OFFICIAL LANGUAGE, IN WHICH **ALL** BUSINESS MUST BE CONDUCTED...
TANK
ON THE SPOT
©1977 Universal Press Syndicate
...BASEBALL'S BIGGEST ADAPTATION MAY BE YET TO COME.
INTERIEURE? ESTES-VOUS AVEUGLE?
ENCORE,...ET VOUS...ALLEZ AU DOUCHE!
MAL LEVEE ...CHIEN D'UNE MERE...MAUVAISE...
8/7

TANK McNAMARA

by Jeff Millar & Bill Hinds

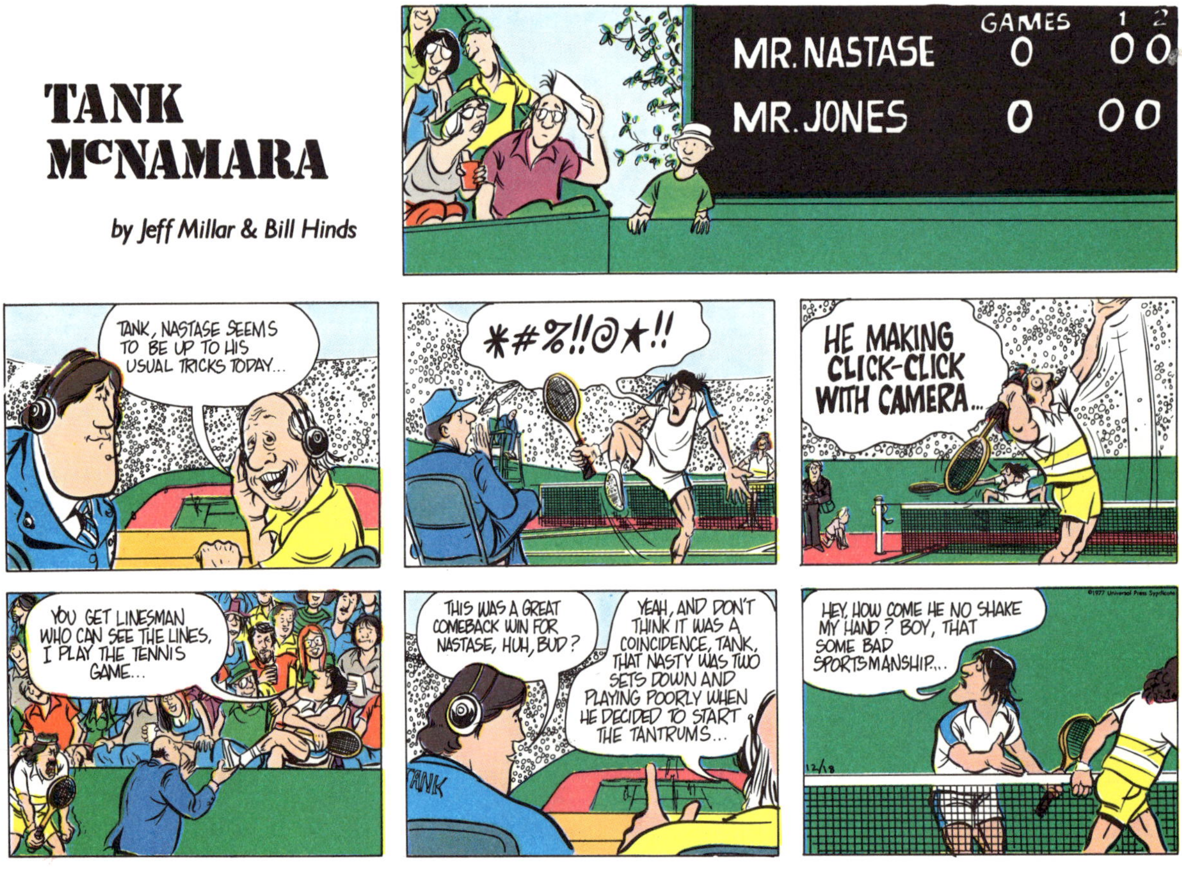

GAMES 1 2
MR. NASTASE 0 0 0
MR. JONES 0 0 0
TANK, NASTASE SEEMS TO BE UP TO HIS USUAL TRICKS TODAY...
*#%!!@★!!
HE MAKING CLICK-CLICK WITH CAMERA...
YOU GET LINESMAN WHO CAN SEE THE LINES, I PLAY THE TENNIS GAME...
THIS WAS A GREAT COMEBACK WIN FOR NASTASE, HUH, BUD?
YEAH, AND DON'T THINK IT WAS A COINCIDENCE, TANK. THAT NASTY WAS TWO SETS DOWN AND PLAYING POORLY WHEN HE DECIDED TO START THE TANTRUMS...
TANK
12/18
©1977 Universal Press Syndicate
HEY, HOW COME HE NO SHAKE MY HAND? BOY, THAT SOME BAD SPORTSMANSHIP...

TANK McNAMARA

by Jeff Millar & Bill Hinds

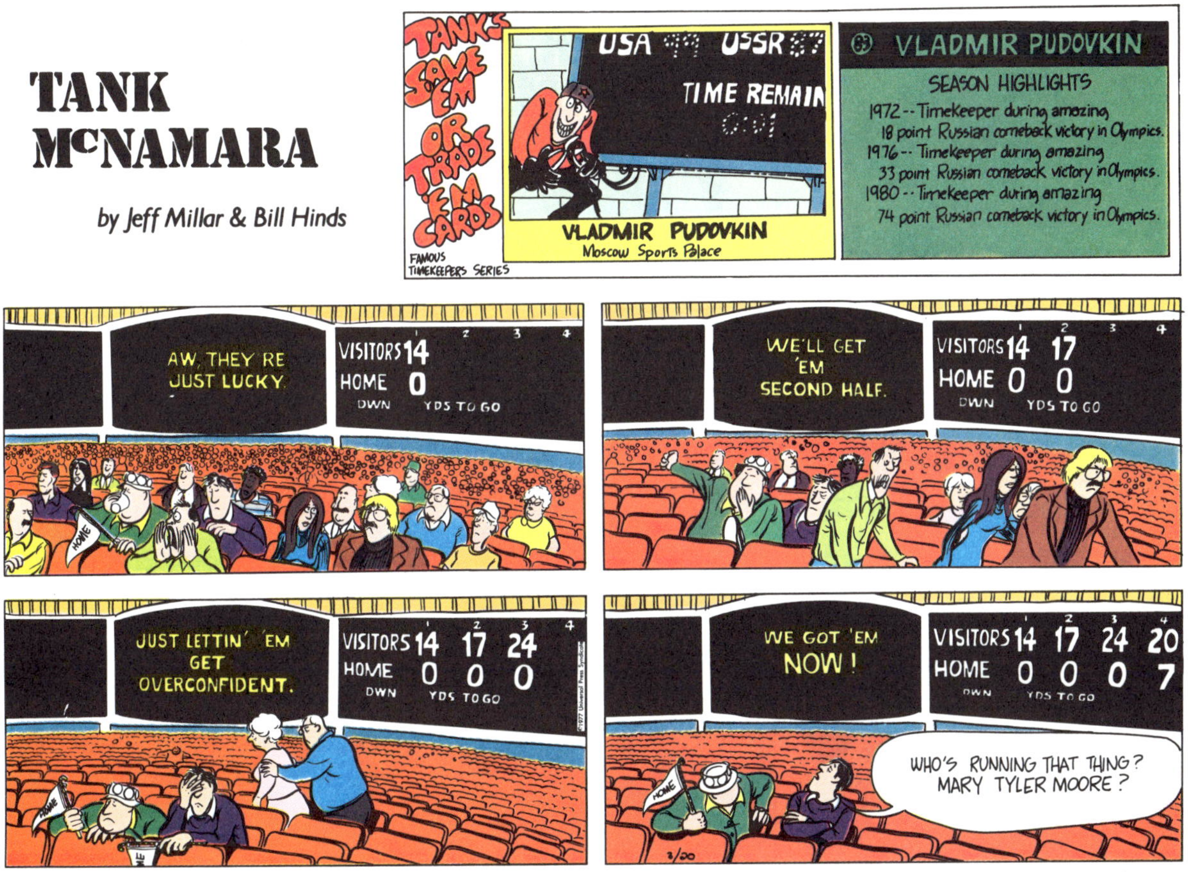
TANK'S SAVE 'EM OR TRADE 'EM CARDS
FAMOUS TIMEKEEPERS SERIES
USA 99 USSR 87
TIME REMAIN
VLADMIR PUDOVKIN
Moscow Sports Palace
VLADMIR PUDOVKIN
SEASON HIGHLIGHTS
1972 -- Timekeeper during amazing 18 point Russian comeback victory in Olympics.
1976 -- Timekeeper during amazing 33 point Russian comeback victory in Olympics.
1980 -- Timekeeper during amazing 74 point Russian comeback victory in Olympics.
AW, THEY'RE JUST LUCKY.
VISITORS 14
HOME 0
DWN YDS TO GO
WE'LL GET 'EM SECOND HALF.
VISITORS 14 17
HOME 0 0
JUST LETTIN' 'EM GET OVERCONFIDENT.
VISITORS 14 17 24
HOME 0 0 0
WE GOT 'EM NOW!
VISITORS 14 17 24 20
HOME 0 0 0 7
WHO'S RUNNING THAT THING? MARY TYLER MOORE?

TANK McNAMARA

by Jeff Millar & Bill Hinds

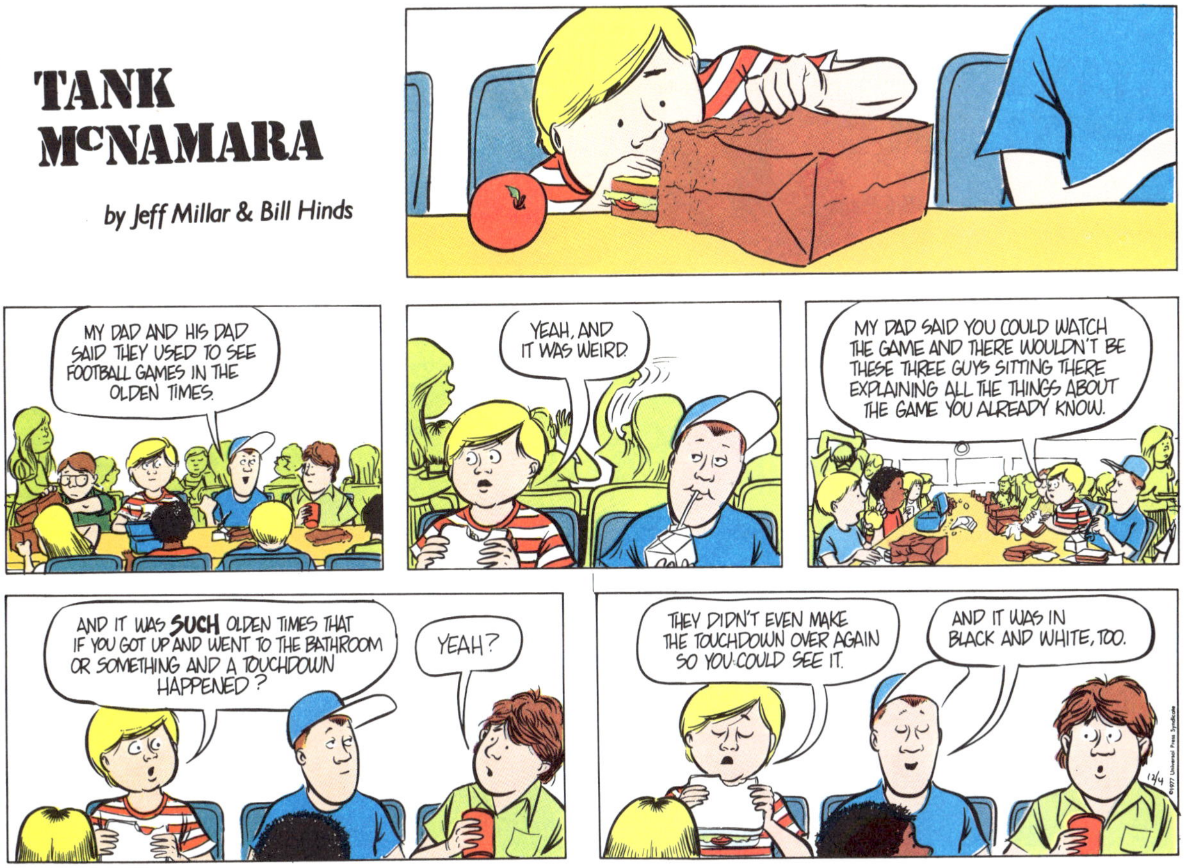
MY DAD AND HIS DAD SAID THEY USED TO SEE FOOTBALL GAMES IN THE OLDEN TIMES.
YEAH, AND IT WAS WEIRD.
MY DAD SAID YOU COULD WATCH THE GAME AND THERE WOULDN'T BE THESE THREE GUYS SITTING THERE EXPLAINING ALL THE THINGS ABOUT THE GAME YOU ALREADY KNOW.
AND IT WAS SUCH OLDEN TIMES THAT IF YOU GOT UP AND WENT TO THE BATHROOM OR SOMETHING AND A TOUCHDOWN HAPPENED?
YEAH?
THEY DIDN'T EVEN MAKE THE TOUCHDOWN OVER AGAIN SO YOU COULD SEE IT.
AND IT WAS IN BLACK AND WHITE, TOO.

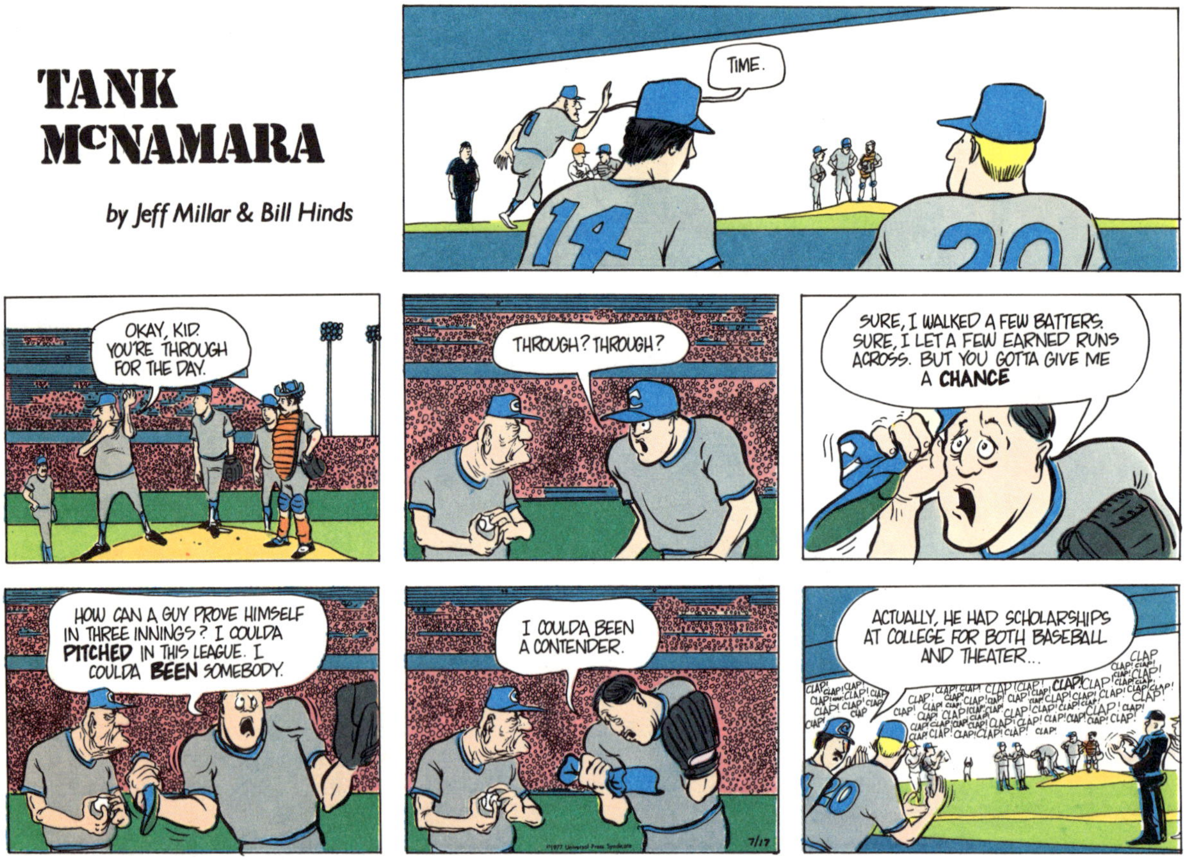
TANK McNAMARA
by Jeff Millar & Bill Hinds
TIME.
OKAY, KID. YOU'RE THROUGH FOR THE DAY.
THROUGH? THROUGH?
SURE, I WALKED A FEW BATTERS. SURE, I LET A FEW EARNED RUNS ACROSS. BUT YOU GOTTA GIVE ME A CHANCE
HOW CAN A GUY PROVE HIMSELF IN THREE INNINGS? I COULDA PITCHED IN THIS LEAGUE. I COULDA BEEN SOMEBODY.
I COULDA BEEN A CONTENDER.
©1977 Universal Press Syndicate
7/17
ACTUALLY, HE HAD SCHOLARSHIPS AT COLLEGE FOR BOTH BASEBALL AND THEATER...
CLAP! CLAP! CLAP! CLAP! CLAP! CLAP!

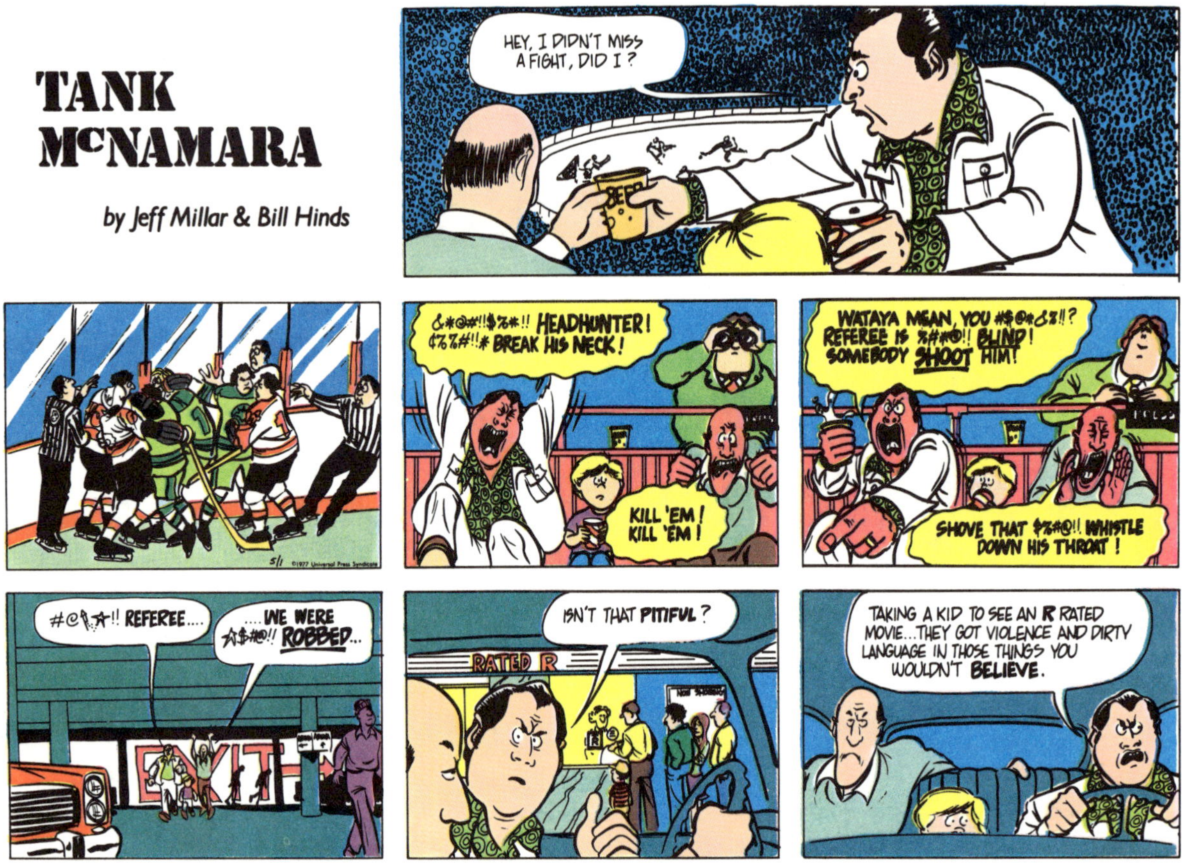
TANK McNAMARA
by Jeff Millar & Bill Hinds
HEY, I DIDN'T MISS A FIGHT, DID I?
BEER
5/1 ©1977 Universal Press Syndicate
&*@#!!$%*!! HEADHUNTER! ¢%%#!!* BREAK HIS NECK!
KILL 'EM! KILL 'EM!
WATAYA MEAN, YOU #$@*&%!!? REFEREE IS %#*@!! BLIND! SOMEBODY SHOOT HIM!
SHOVE THAT $%#@!! WHISTLE DOWN HIS THROAT!
#@!☆!! REFEREE....
....WE WERE ☆$#@!! ROBBED...
EXIT
ISN'T THAT PITIFUL?
RATED R
TAKING A KID TO SEE AN R RATED MOVIE...THEY GOT VIOLENCE AND DIRTY LANGUAGE IN THOSE THINGS YOU WOULDN'T BELIEVE.

So. How do collaborators on a comic strip get out the product? Do we lock ourselves in a room and snap out funny lines, spraying each other with seltzer bottles from time to time?

No. We work separately. **MILLAR/HINDS** live only about five miles apart, but we'll go stretches without more contact than maybe one phone call a week. Not that we don't like each other; the collaboration didn't evolve into a Laurel & Hardy, professional-marriage kind of thing.

My stuff comes first (you'd be surprised how often people ask us: "Bill, do you make the drawings first and then Jeff writes the words to go in the little circles . . . ?") I write what we call copy, which is like a miniature movie script for each strip. Here's what I wrote for the Sunday panel which appears on page 224 . . .

Logo line: in the station, a coworker is asking Tank: "Tank, I was wondering . . ."

1. *(i.e., first panel)* "When you were a kid, did you ever think about doing anything except becoming a pro football player?"

2. Tank has a small neutral smile on his face. His eyes cut toward a THINK balloon which grows into a flashback effect at the right side of the panel. A school bus is pulling up in front of a place like Jones Hall. On the marquee: BALLET: SPECIAL STUDENT MATINEE.

3. *(Keep borders which signify flashback is still on.)* Close on Tank — about 14 years old (he'd probably have a flat-top haircut and be wearing a letter jacket) — who is in the audience. He's holding a ballet program and is looking at what he sees with utter amazement.

4. *(still flashback)* We see teenage Tank peeking out a door, looking both ways down the hall to make sure no one's seeing him.

5. *(flashback)* Tank's inside the bathroom. Holding on to the towel rack for balance, he tries doing one of the ballet positions in imitation of what he'd seen. He's smiling.

6. *(The flashback effect returns to the present.)* Reverse orientation of the first panel as the adult Tank is

113

thinking this scene (which should be drawn very broadly): 14-year-old Tank is in the kitchen of his house, wincing, as his father has half-fallen over on the kitchen table, scattering breakfast dishes. The father is clutching at his chest and screaming: "You want to quit football practice and do WHAT?!?!?!"

The adult Tank, as he thinks this scene, has a nostalgic smile on his face (if Tank has any real regrets about not taking up dance, he's gotten over them long ago). Tank says, in response to the coworker's question: "Not seriously..."

The "logo line" refers to the top tier of panels, which many papers do not run and must be written so that they can be dropped without affecting the sense of the rest of the strip.

Usually my copy for Bill is less detailed than this. We've developed a shorthand communication over the years based upon a sense of how the other thinks. And I deliberately keep the instructions in the copy as minimal as I can. The idea is to allow Bill — force upon him, more than allow him — the freedom to bring as much of his imagination and observation to the product as possible.

I could, I guess, describe what each character's wearing and what the doorknobs should look like. But Bill is my collaborator, not my illustrator. So when I write that two characters are eating "in a ludicrously gaudy fast-food franchise restaurant with a baseball motif," I leave what it looks like to Bill. He almost always thinks of things that I never would, so I get a laugh from the drawings just as if it were new to me. It's my material and yet it isn't; it surprises me. *Tank* is the product of a truly symbiotic relationship: It is something that neither of us — assuming that I could draw and Bill had my verbal skills — would do individually. I'm so comfortable with what Bill does with what I write that I no longer see Bill's drawings before they're sent off to the Syndicate.

I usually deliver the copy to Bill in batches of three weeks' worth at a time, about two weeks ahead of the deadline the Syndicate imposes upon us, which is three weeks ahead of the publication of the first one in the batch. We're talking about the Monday-Saturday strips, the "dailies," as they're known in the trade. The Sundays are done on a different schedule; the deadlines are longer.

I carry around a little green notebook in which I write down ideas which may or may not become strips. Examples: "TV spots about recruiting violations furnished by the NCAA" . . . "Steve Ford — pro team rodeo" . . . "soccer voodoo" . . . "first round draft choice coyly says he'll sign for $50 a week." The first and last became strips. The second and third didn't. Usable ideas are more precious than the unlisted phone numbers of the Dallas Cowboys' Cheerleaders. They cannot be bought nor manufactured. They have to happen. Prowling for them seems to occupy more of my waking moments than I care to think about.

I try to write three weeks' worth as quickly as possible. Newspaper reporter's instincts, I guess. I work just as well fast as I do slowly. I can do it in one day, if I'm hot. I'm a big believer in the theory that one has good days and one has bad days. If I make writing the copy one brief but intense experience at a time when I feel productive, I don't have to force myself to work on days when it's just not coming.

Bill . . . ah, changes his work habits pretty regularly. Okay: He doesn't *have* any work habits. He is not an organized person. Nothing is delivered into his hands which has not been cloned in the Xerox machine, because things have a way of getting into the corners of his apartment, where they are consumed by a time warp.

He starts by drawing the borders. Then, having mentally mapped out how he'll draw it, he letters the balloons; *Tank* is a word-oriented strip, and the dialogue is accommodated first. Bill has made remarks on that subject to me in the strip: He's drawn Tank a couple of times with the balloon obscuring half his face, or had him leaning over, moving out of the balloon's way.

Then, after the most rudimentary pencil guidelines, he's inking. He now uses a fine brush dipped in India ink. He feels it gives him a more expressive and better-controlled line than a pen; and it's faster, always a consideration. In addition to *Tank,* Bill draws another feature syndicated by Universal Press: *According to Guinness.* I am continually amazed, when I have occasion to watch him work, how few strokes of his brush define objects, establish spaces, become faces with precise expression. My envy of his skills approaches Biblical proportions.

Okay. Moving right along. The next section may be an eye-opener. It was to me: How much Tank's changed since August 5, 1974. . . .

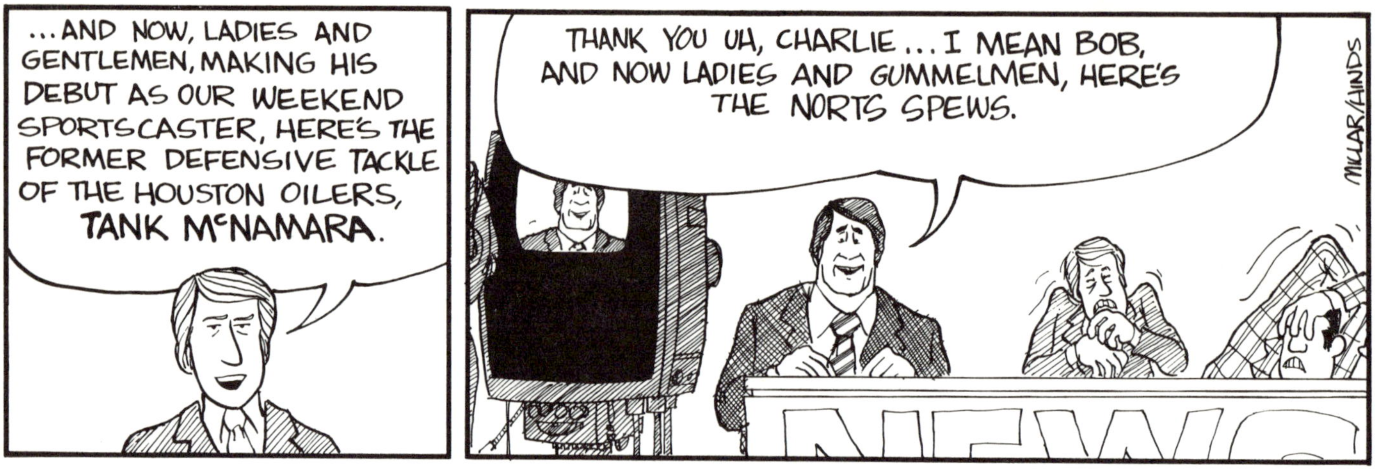
...AND NOW, LADIES AND GENTLEMEN, MAKING HIS DEBUT AS OUR WEEKEND SPORTSCASTER, HERE'S THE FORMER DEFENSIVE TACKLE OF THE HOUSTON OILERS, TANK McNAMARA.
THANK YOU UH, CHARLIE... I MEAN BOB, AND NOW LADIES AND GUMMELMEN, HERE'S THE NORTS SPEWS.
MILLAR/HINDS

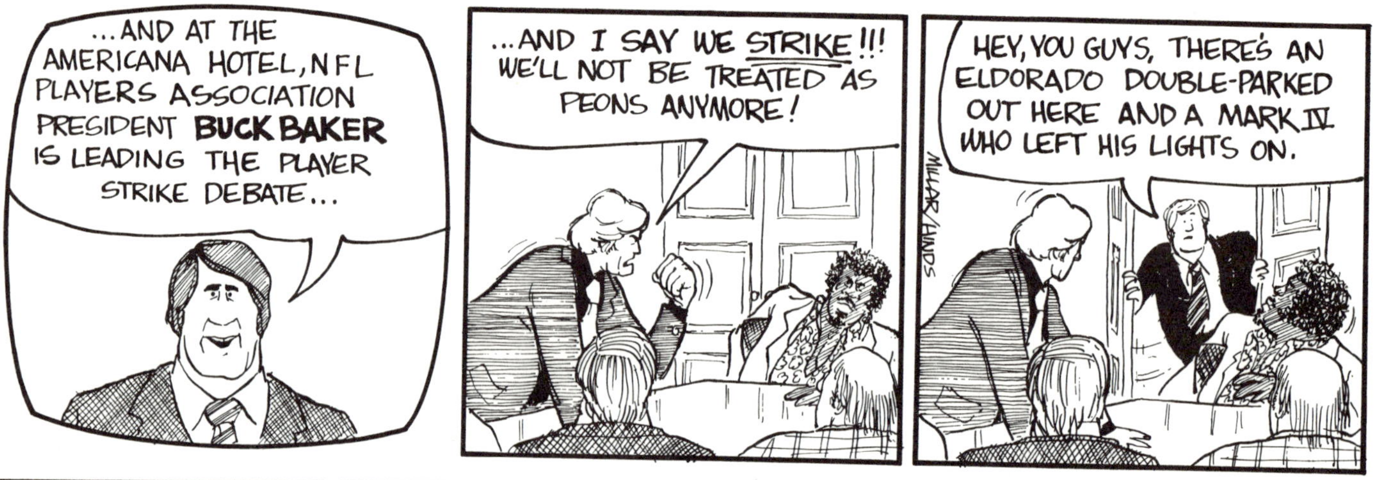
...AND AT THE AMERICANA HOTEL, NFL PLAYERS ASSOCIATION PRESIDENT BUCK BAKER IS LEADING THE PLAYER STRIKE DEBATE...
...AND I SAY WE STRIKE!!! WE'LL NOT BE TREATED AS PEONS ANYMORE!
MILLAR/HINDS
HEY, YOU GUYS, THERE'S AN ELDORADO DOUBLE-PARKED OUT HERE AND A MARK IV WHO LEFT HIS LIGHTS ON.

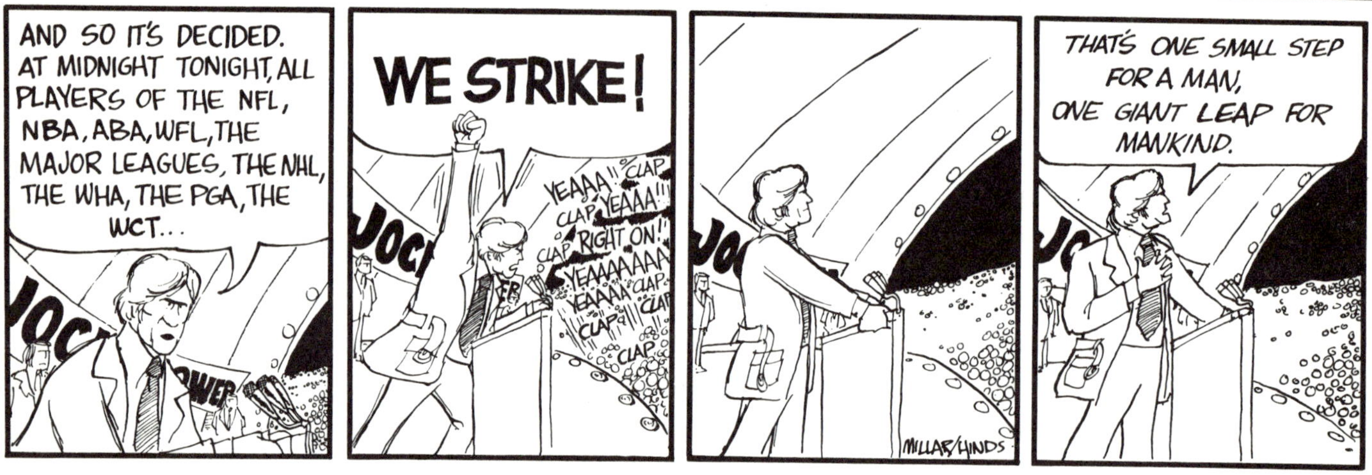
AND SO IT'S DECIDED. AT MIDNIGHT TONIGHT, ALL PLAYERS OF THE NFL, NBA, ABA, WFL, THE MAJOR LEAGUES, THE NHL, THE WHA, THE PGA, THE WCT...
WE STRIKE!
YEAAA!! CLAP CLAP YEAAA!!! RIGHT ON! CLAP YEAAAAAAA YEAAAA CLAP CLAP CLAP CLAP
MILLAR/HINDS
THAT'S ONE SMALL STEP FOR A MAN, ONE GIANT LEAP FOR MANKIND.

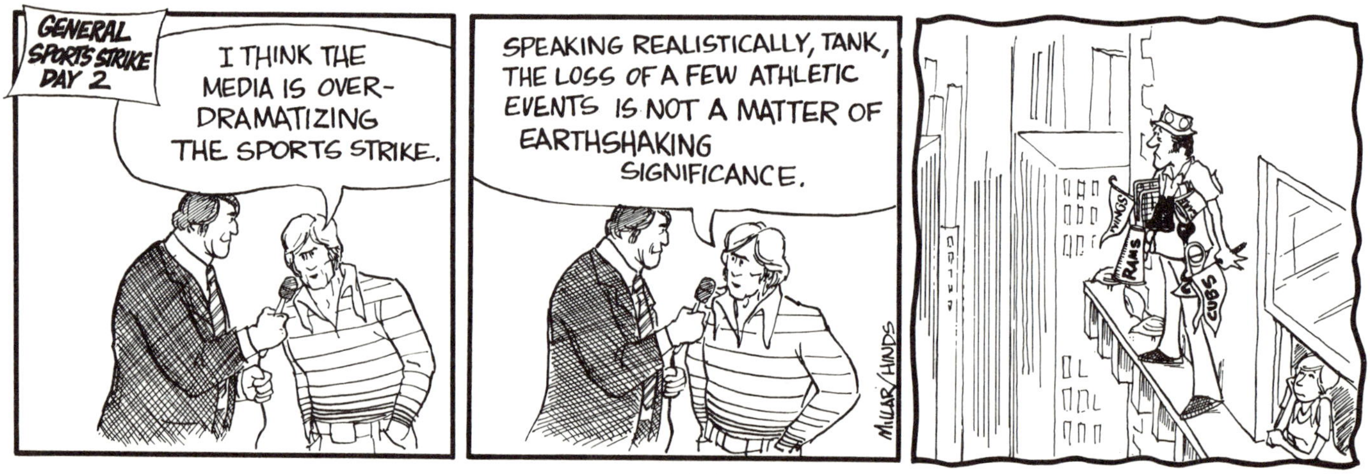
GENERAL SPORTS STRIKE DAY 2
I THINK THE MEDIA IS OVER-DRAMATIZING THE SPORTS STRIKE.
SPEAKING REALISTICALLY, TANK, THE LOSS OF A FEW ATHLETIC EVENTS IS NOT A MATTER OF EARTHSHAKING SIGNIFICANCE.
MILLAR/HINDS
RAMS
CUBS

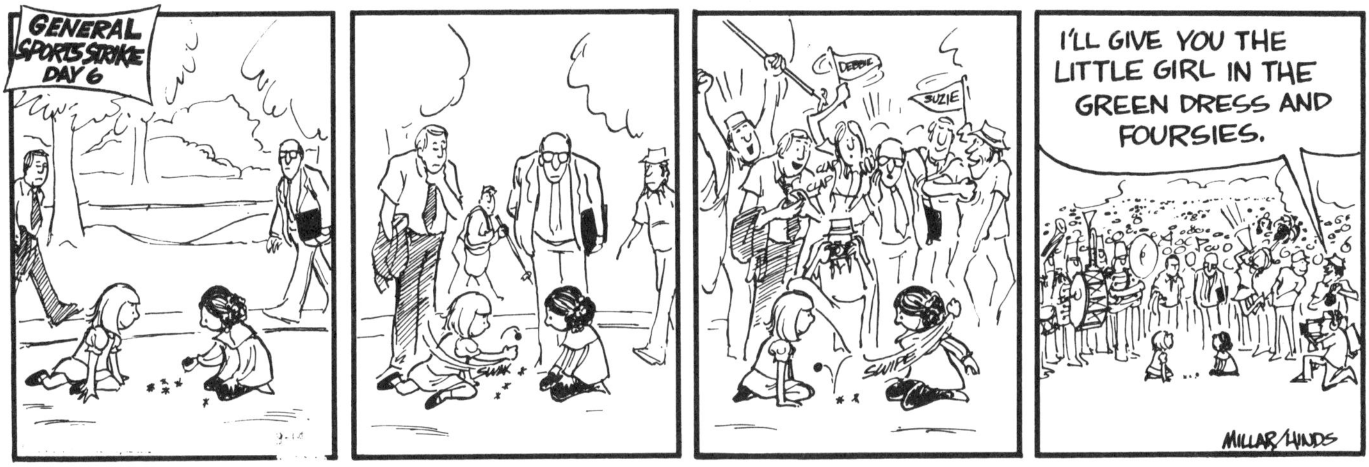
GENERAL SPORTS STRIKE DAY 6
DEBBIE
SUZIE
I'LL GIVE YOU THE LITTLE GIRL IN THE GREEN DRESS AND FOURSIES.
MILLAR/HINDS

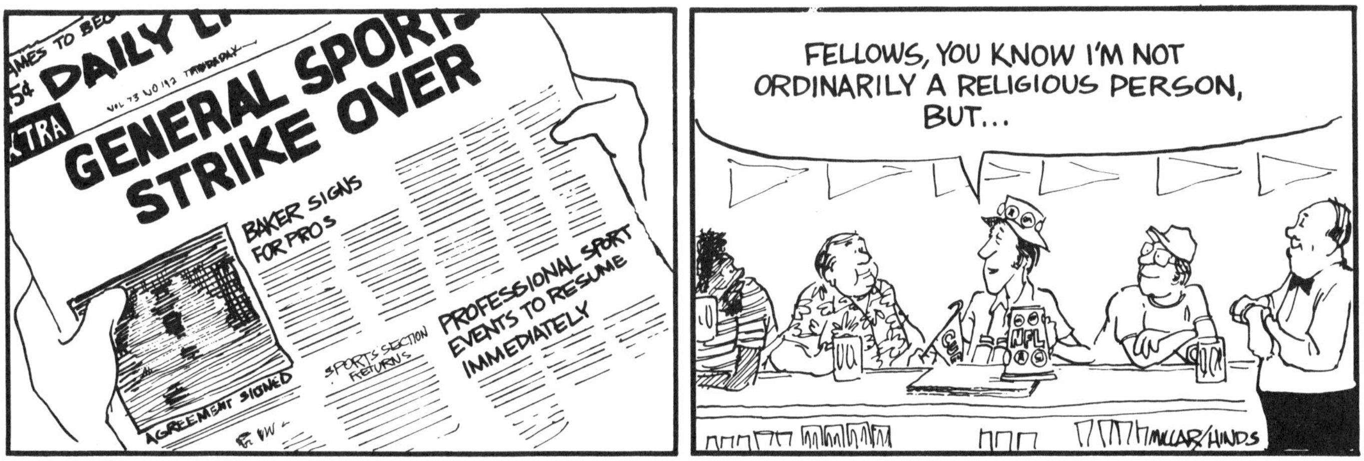
DAILY
GENERAL SPORTS STRIKE OVER
BAKER SIGNS FOR PROS
PROFESSIONAL SPORT EVENTS TO RESUME IMMEDIATELY
SPORTS SECTION RETURNS
AGREEMENT SIGNED
FELLOWS, YOU KNOW I'M NOT ORDINARILY A RELIGIOUS PERSON, BUT...
NFL
MILLAR/HINDS

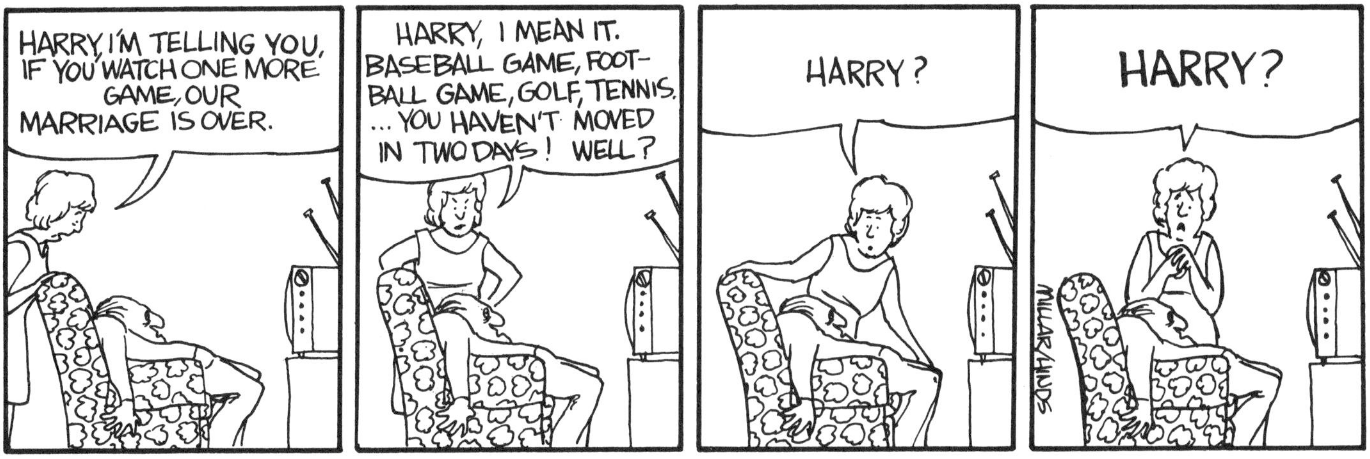
HARRY, I'M TELLING YOU, IF YOU WATCH ONE MORE GAME, OUR MARRIAGE IS OVER.
HARRY, I MEAN IT. BASEBALL GAME, FOOTBALL GAME, GOLF, TENNIS. ...YOU HAVEN'T MOVED IN TWO DAYS! WELL?
HARRY?
MILLAR/HINDS
HARRY?

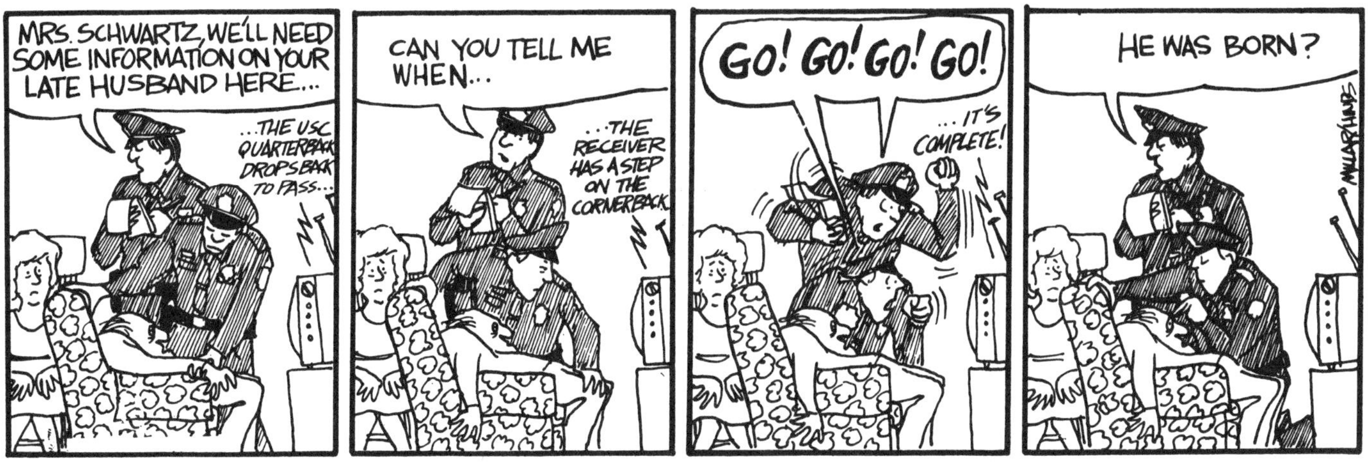
MRS. SCHWARTZ, WE'LL NEED SOME INFORMATION ON YOUR LATE HUSBAND HERE...
...THE USC QUARTERBACK DROPS BACK TO PASS...
CAN YOU TELL ME WHEN...
...THE RECEIVER HAS A STEP ON THE CORNERBACK
GO! GO! GO! GO!
...IT'S COMPLETE!
HE WAS BORN?
MILLAR/HINDS

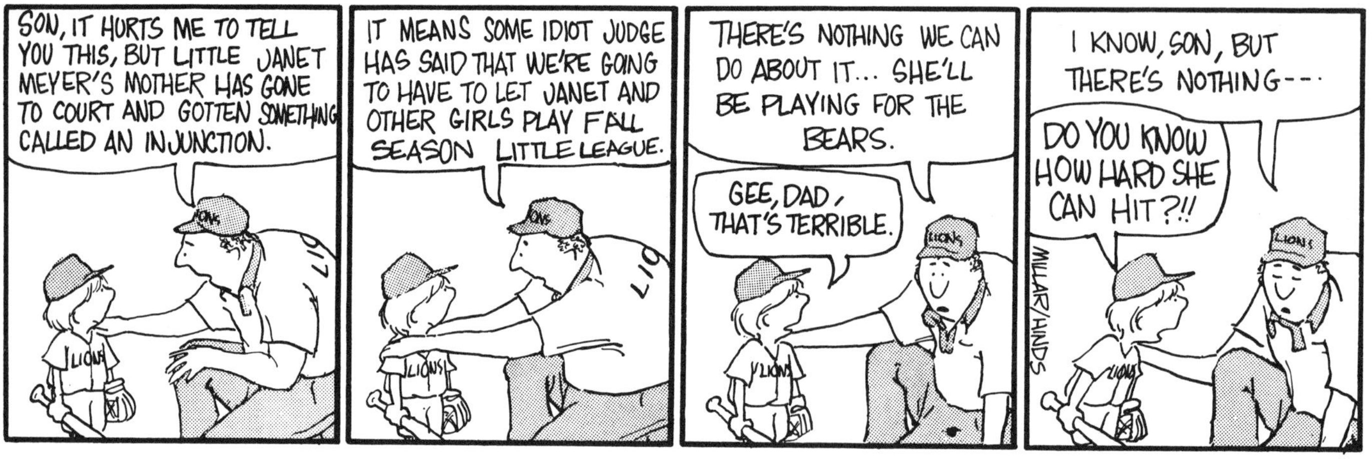
SON, IT HURTS ME TO TELL YOU THIS, BUT LITTLE JANET MEYER'S MOTHER HAS GONE TO COURT AND GOTTEN SOMETHING CALLED AN INJUNCTION.
IT MEANS SOME IDIOT JUDGE HAS SAID THAT WE'RE GOING TO HAVE TO LET JANET AND OTHER GIRLS PLAY FALL SEASON LITTLE LEAGUE.
THERE'S NOTHING WE CAN DO ABOUT IT... SHE'LL BE PLAYING FOR THE BEARS.
GEE, DAD, THAT'S TERRIBLE.
I KNOW, SON, BUT THERE'S NOTHING---
DO YOU KNOW HOW HARD SHE CAN HIT?!!
MILLAR/HINDS

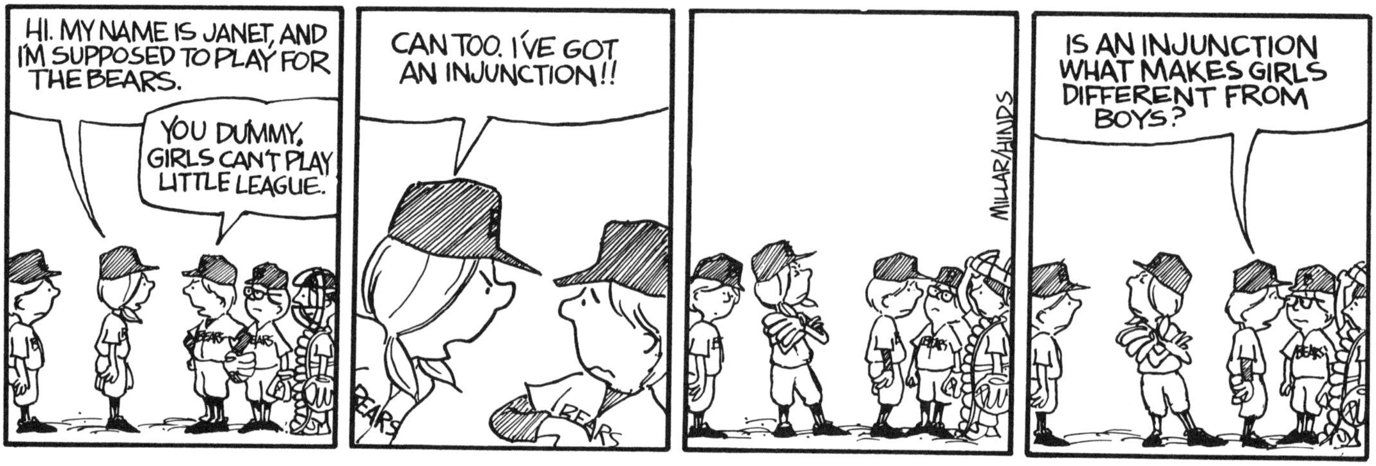
HI. MY NAME IS JANET, AND I'M SUPPOSED TO PLAY FOR THE BEARS.
YOU DUMMY. GIRLS CAN'T PLAY LITTLE LEAGUE.
CAN TOO. I'VE GOT AN INJUNCTION!!
MILLAR/HINDS
IS AN INJUNCTION WHAT MAKES GIRLS DIFFERENT FROM BOYS?

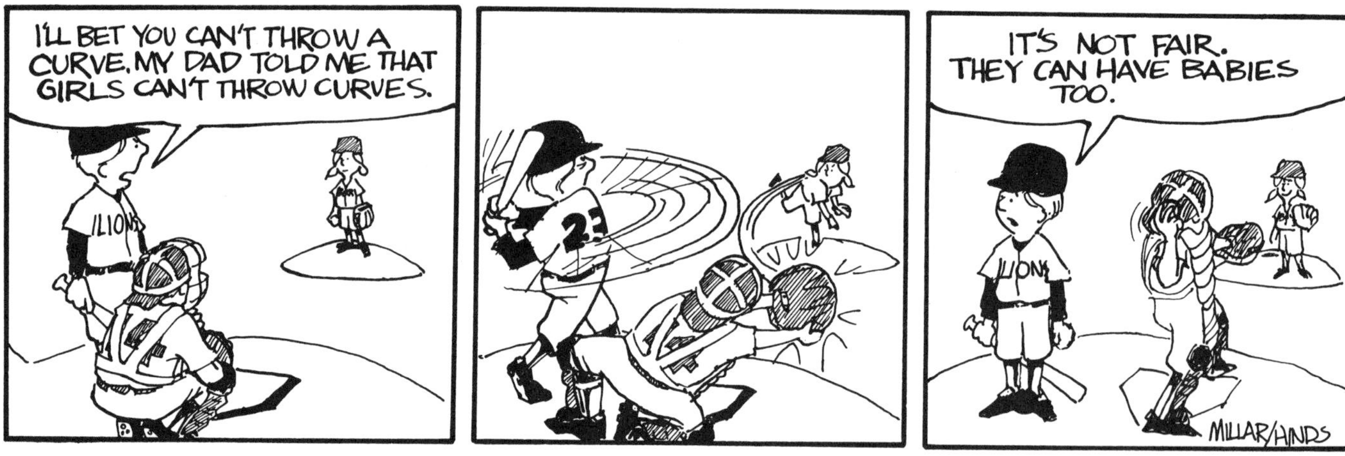
I'LL BET YOU CAN'T THROW A CURVE. MY DAD TOLD ME THAT GIRLS CAN'T THROW CURVES.
IT'S NOT FAIR. THEY CAN HAVE BABIES TOO.
MILLAR/HINDS

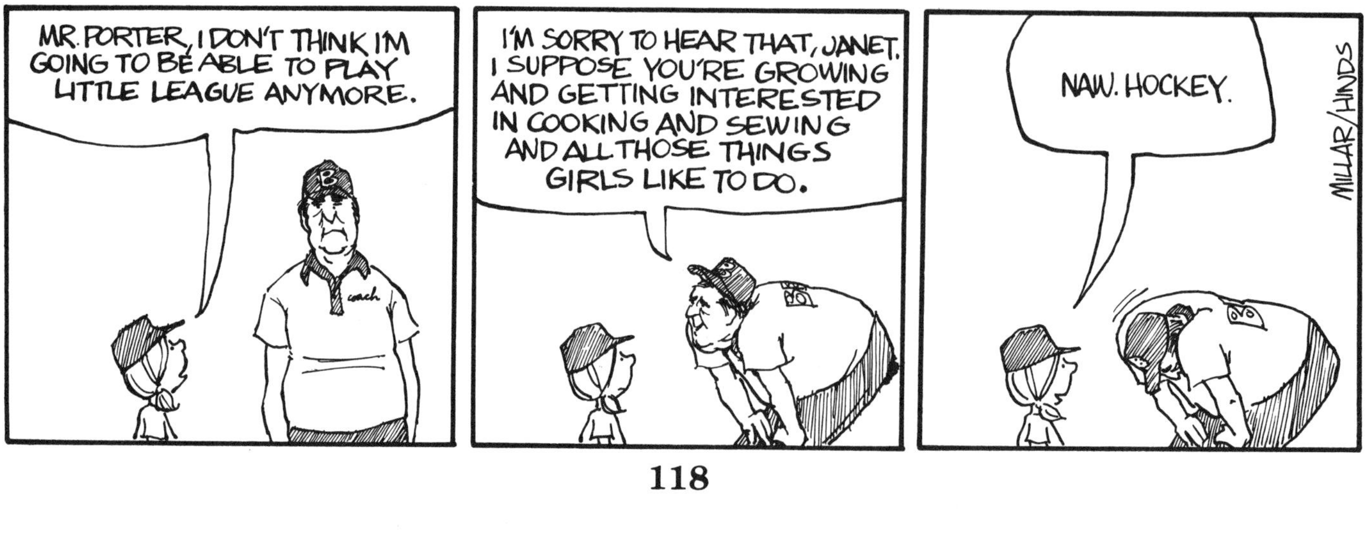
MR. PORTER, I DON'T THINK I'M GOING TO BE ABLE TO PLAY LITTLE LEAGUE ANYMORE.
I'M SORRY TO HEAR THAT, JANET. I SUPPOSE YOU'RE GROWING AND GETTING INTERESTED IN COOKING AND SEWING AND ALL THOSE THINGS GIRLS LIKE TO DO.
NAW. HOCKEY.
MILLAR/HINDS

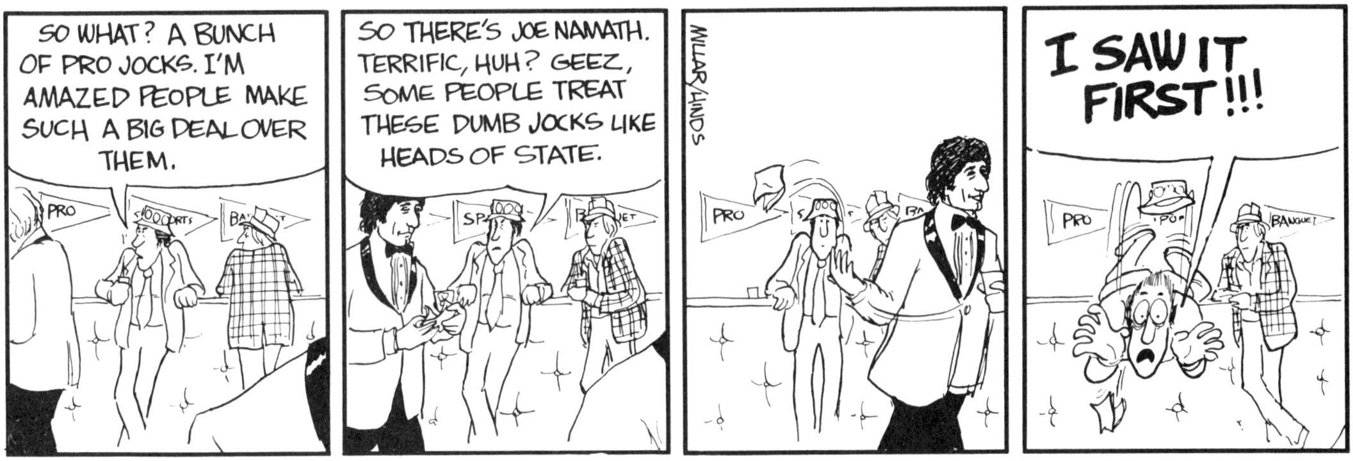
SO WHAT? A BUNCH OF PRO JOCKS. I'M AMAZED PEOPLE MAKE SUCH A BIG DEAL OVER THEM.
SO THERE'S JOE NAMATH. TERRIFIC, HUH? GEEZ, SOME PEOPLE TREAT THESE DUMB JOCKS LIKE HEADS OF STATE.
MILLAR/HINDS
I SAW IT FIRST!!!

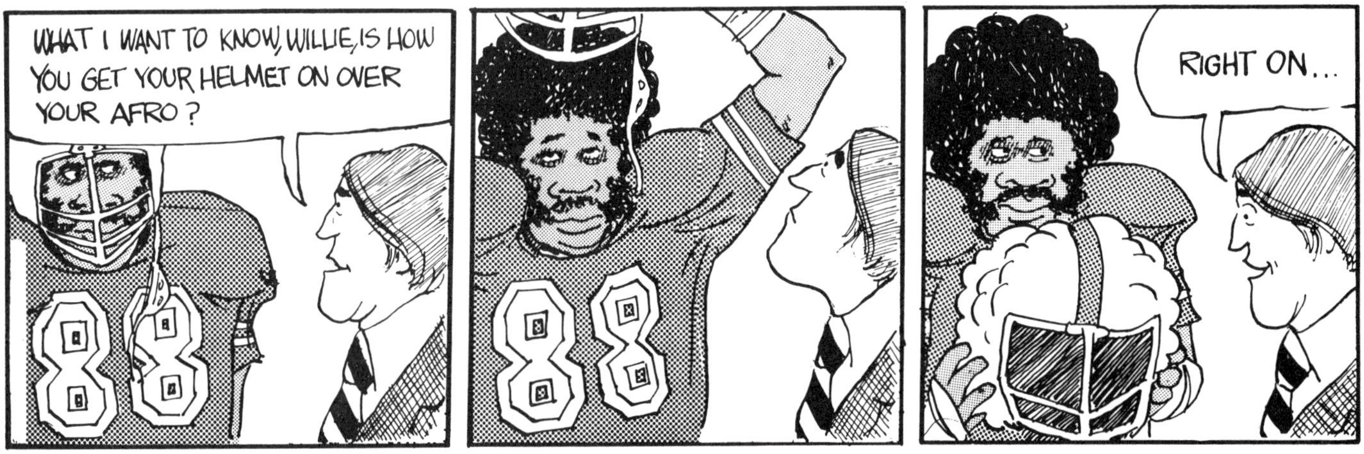
WHAT I WANT TO KNOW, WILLIE, IS HOW YOU GET YOUR HELMET ON OVER YOUR AFRO?
RIGHT ON...

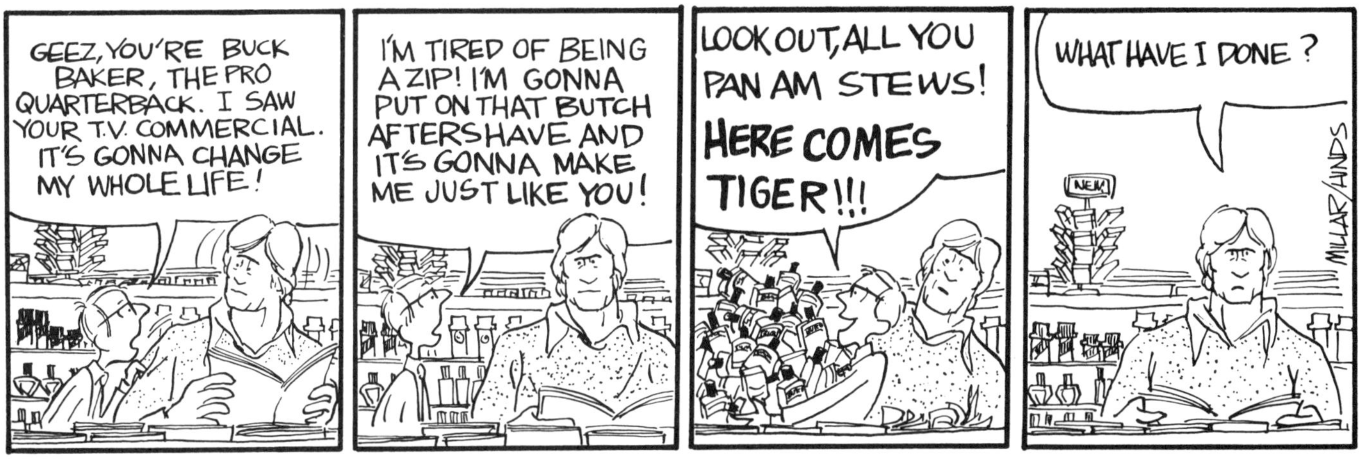
GEEZ, YOU'RE BUCK BAKER, THE PRO QUARTERBACK. I SAW YOUR T.V. COMMERCIAL. IT'S GONNA CHANGE MY WHOLE LIFE!
I'M TIRED OF BEING A ZIP! I'M GONNA PUT ON THAT BUTCH AFTERSHAVE AND IT'S GONNA MAKE ME JUST LIKE YOU!
LOOK OUT, ALL YOU PAN AM STEWS! HERE COMES TIGER!!!
WHAT HAVE I DONE?
NEW
MILLAR/HINDS

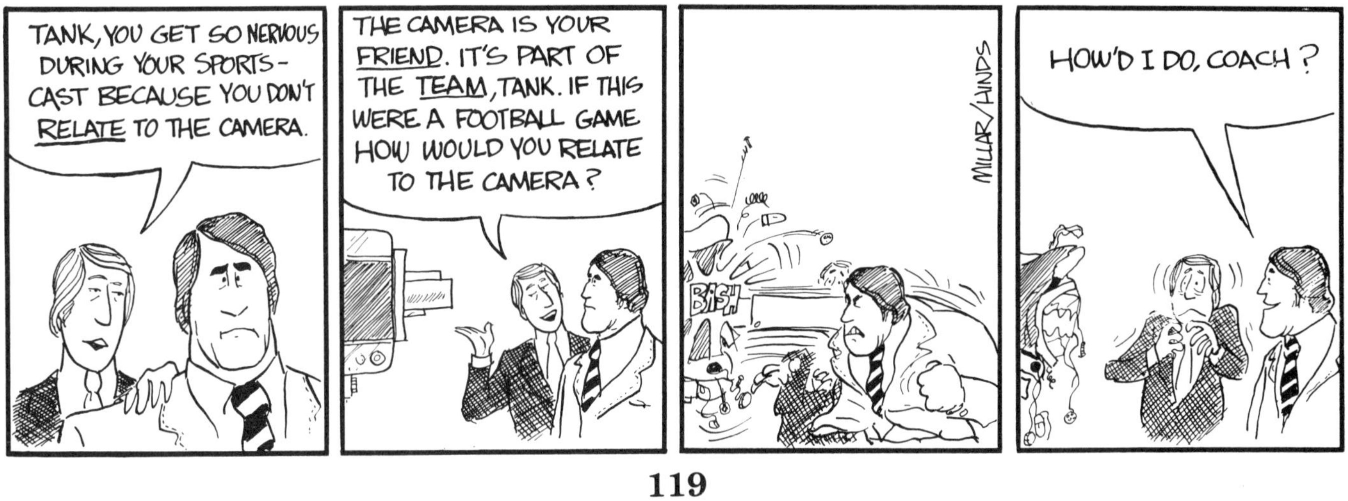
TANK, YOU GET SO NERVOUS DURING YOUR SPORTS-CAST BECAUSE YOU DON'T RELATE TO THE CAMERA.
THE CAMERA IS YOUR FRIEND. IT'S PART OF THE TEAM, TANK. IF THIS WERE A FOOTBALL GAME HOW WOULD YOU RELATE TO THE CAMERA?
MILLAR/HINDS
BASH
HOW'D I DO, COACH?

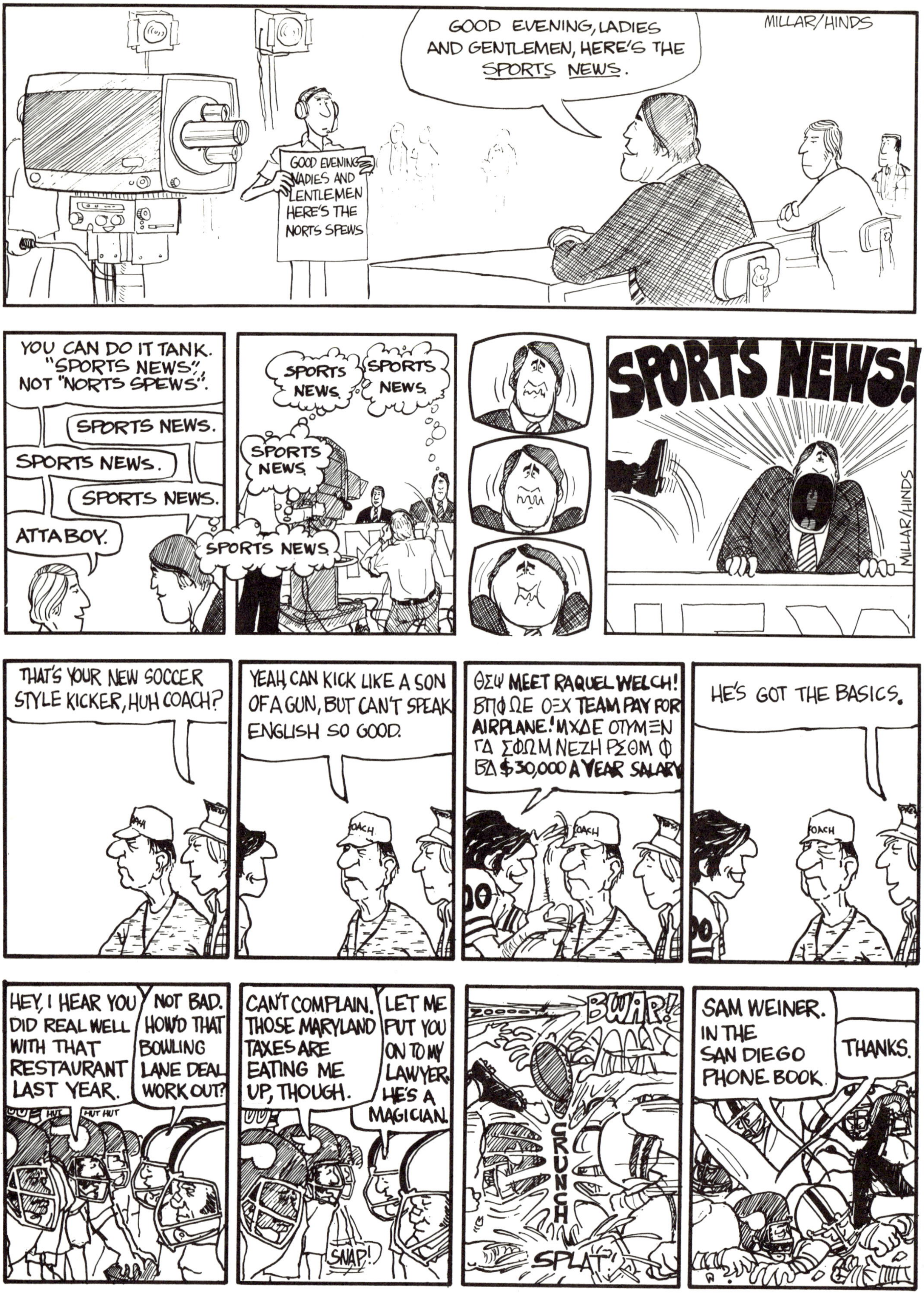
MILLAR/HINDS
GOOD EVENING, LADIES AND GENTLEMEN, HERE'S THE SPORTS NEWS.
GOOD EVENING LADIES AND GENTLEMEN HERE'S THE NORTS SPEWS
YOU CAN DO IT TANK. "SPORTS NEWS", NOT "NORTS SPEWS".
SPORTS NEWS.
SPORTS NEWS.
SPORTS NEWS.
ATTABOY.
SPORTS NEWS
SPORTS NEWS
SPORTS NEWS
SPORTS NEWS
SPORTS NEWS
SPORTS NEWS!
MILLAR/HINDS
THAT'S YOUR NEW SOCCER STYLE KICKER, HUH COACH?
YEAH, CAN KICK LIKE A SON OF A GUN, BUT CAN'T SPEAK ENGLISH SO GOOD.
ΘΣΨ MEET RAQUEL WELCH! ΒΠΦ ΩΕ ΘΞΧ TEAM PAY FOR AIRPLANE! ΜΧΔΕ ΟΤΥΜΞΝ ΓΔ ΣΦΩΜ ΝΕΖΗ ΡΣΘΜ Φ ΒΔ $30,000 A YEAR SALARY
HE'S GOT THE BASICS.
HEY, I HEAR YOU DID REAL WELL WITH THAT RESTAURANT LAST YEAR.
NOT BAD. HOW'D THAT BOWLING LANE DEAL WORK OUT?
HUT HUT HUT
CAN'T COMPLAIN. THOSE MARYLAND TAXES ARE EATING ME UP, THOUGH.
LET ME PUT YOU ON TO MY LAWYER. HE'S A MAGICIAN.
SNAP!
ZOOOOT
BWAP!
CRUNCH
SPLAT!
SAM WEINER. IN THE SAN DIEGO PHONE BOOK.
THANKS.

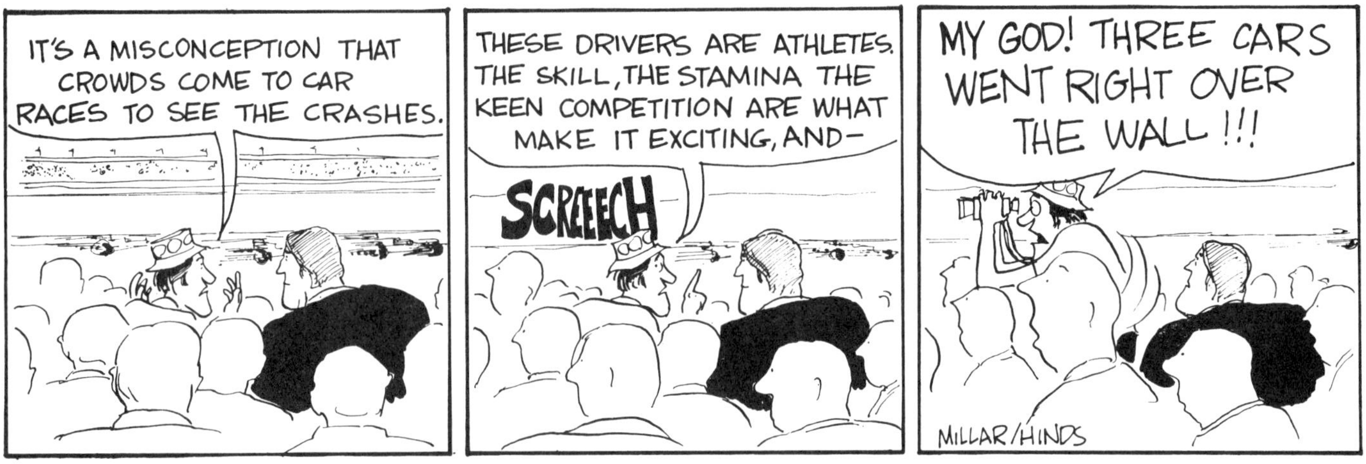
IT'S A MISCONCEPTION THAT CROWDS COME TO CAR RACES TO SEE THE CRASHES.
THESE DRIVERS ARE ATHLETES. THE SKILL, THE STAMINA THE KEEN COMPETITION ARE WHAT MAKE IT EXCITING, AND—
SCREEECH
MY GOD! THREE CARS WENT RIGHT OVER THE WALL!!!
MILLAR/HINDS

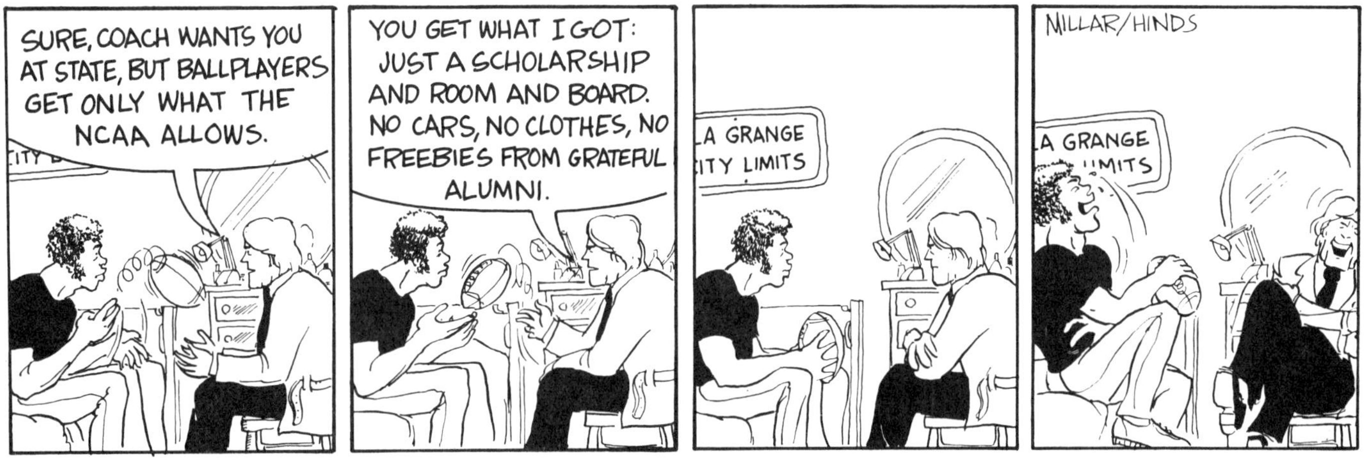
SURE, COACH WANTS YOU AT STATE, BUT BALLPLAYERS GET ONLY WHAT THE NCAA ALLOWS.
YOU GET WHAT I GOT: JUST A SCHOLARSHIP AND ROOM AND BOARD. NO CARS, NO CLOTHES, NO FREEBIES FROM GRATEFUL ALUMNI.
LA GRANGE CITY LIMITS
MILLAR/HINDS

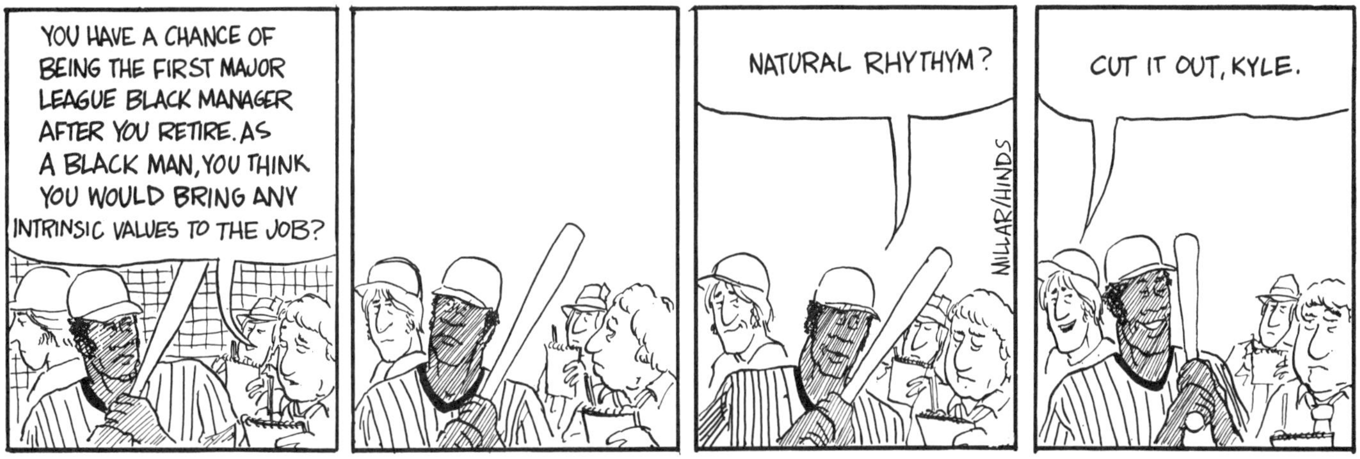
YOU HAVE A CHANCE OF BEING THE FIRST MAJOR LEAGUE BLACK MANAGER AFTER YOU RETIRE. AS A BLACK MAN, YOU THINK YOU WOULD BRING ANY INTRINSIC VALUES TO THE JOB?
NATURAL RHYTHYM?
MILLAR/HINDS
CUT IT OUT, KYLE.

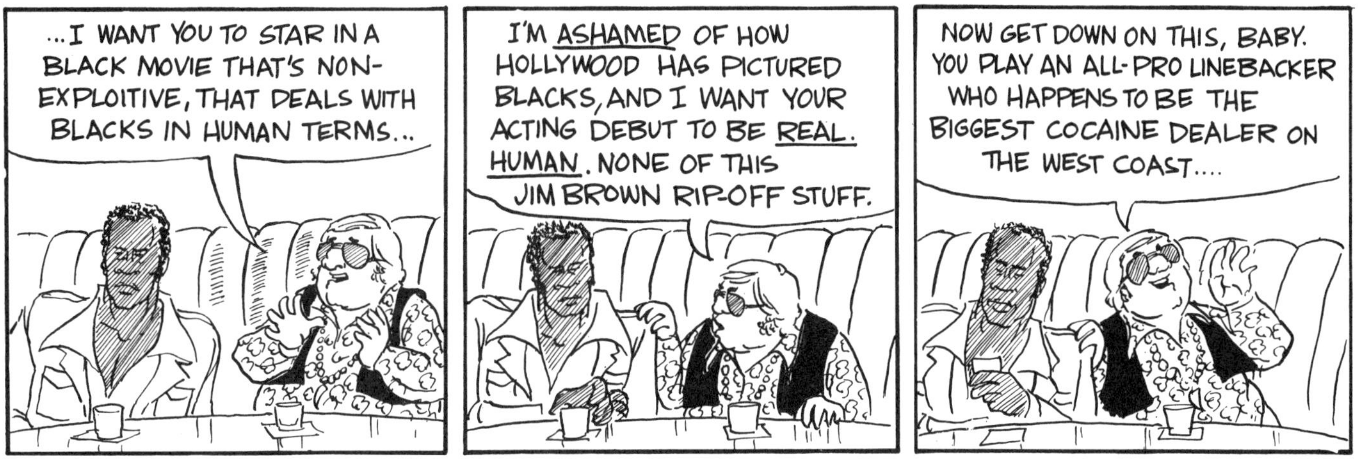
...I WANT YOU TO STAR IN A BLACK MOVIE THAT'S NON-EXPLOITIVE, THAT DEALS WITH BLACKS IN HUMAN TERMS...
I'M ASHAMED OF HOW HOLLYWOOD HAS PICTURED BLACKS, AND I WANT YOUR ACTING DEBUT TO BE REAL. HUMAN. NONE OF THIS JIM BROWN RIP-OFF STUFF.
NOW GET DOWN ON THIS, BABY. YOU PLAY AN ALL-PRO LINEBACKER WHO HAPPENS TO BE THE BIGGEST COCAINE DEALER ON THE WEST COAST....

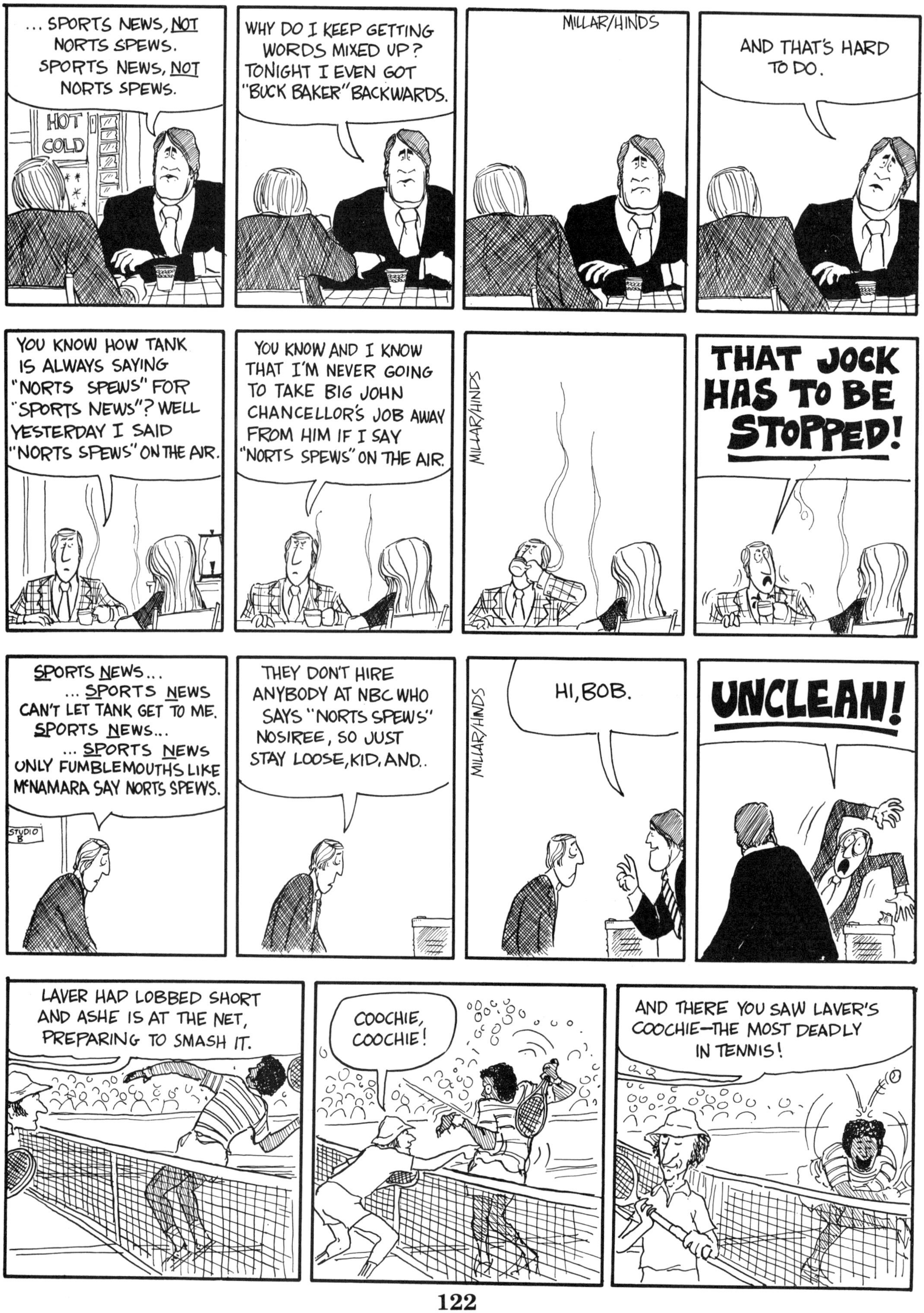
... SPORTS NEWS, NOT NORTS SPEWS. SPORTS NEWS, NOT NORTS SPEWS.
HOT
COLD
WHY DO I KEEP GETTING WORDS MIXED UP? TONIGHT I EVEN GOT "BUCK BAKER" BACKWARDS.
MILLAR/HINDS
AND THAT'S HARD TO DO.
YOU KNOW HOW TANK IS ALWAYS SAYING "NORTS SPEWS" FOR "SPORTS NEWS"? WELL YESTERDAY I SAID "NORTS SPEWS" ON THE AIR.
YOU KNOW AND I KNOW THAT I'M NEVER GOING TO TAKE BIG JOHN CHANCELLOR'S JOB AWAY FROM HIM IF I SAY "NORTS SPEWS" ON THE AIR.
MILLAR/HINDS
THAT JOCK HAS TO BE STOPPED!
SPORTS NEWS... ... SPORTS NEWS CAN'T LET TANK GET TO ME. SPORTS NEWS... ... SPORTS NEWS ONLY FUMBLEMOUTHS LIKE McNAMARA SAY NORTS SPEWS.
STUDIO B
THEY DON'T HIRE ANYBODY AT NBC WHO SAYS "NORTS SPEWS" NOSIREE, SO JUST STAY LOOSE, KID, AND..
MILLAR/HINDS
HI, BOB.
UNCLEAN!
LAVER HAD LOBBED SHORT AND ASHE IS AT THE NET, PREPARING TO SMASH IT.
COOCHIE, COOCHIE!
AND THERE YOU SAW LAVER'S COOCHIE—THE MOST DEADLY IN TENNIS!

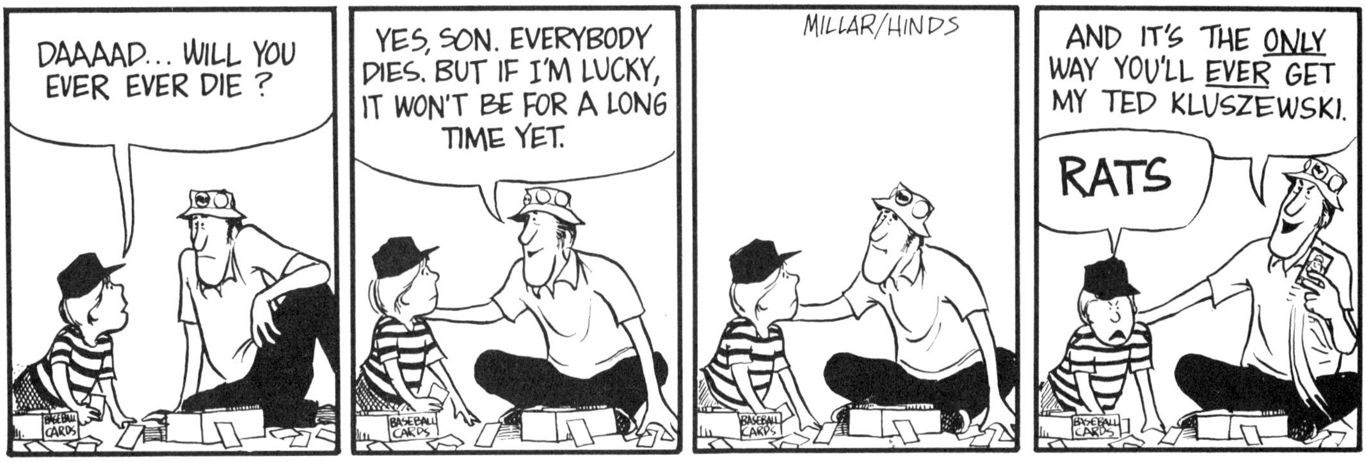
DAAAAD... WILL YOU EVER EVER DIE ?
BASEBALL CARDS
YES, SON. EVERYBODY DIES. BUT IF I'M LUCKY, IT WON'T BE FOR A LONG TIME YET.
MILLAR/HINDS
AND IT'S THE ONLY WAY YOU'LL EVER GET MY TED KLUSZEWSKI.
RATS

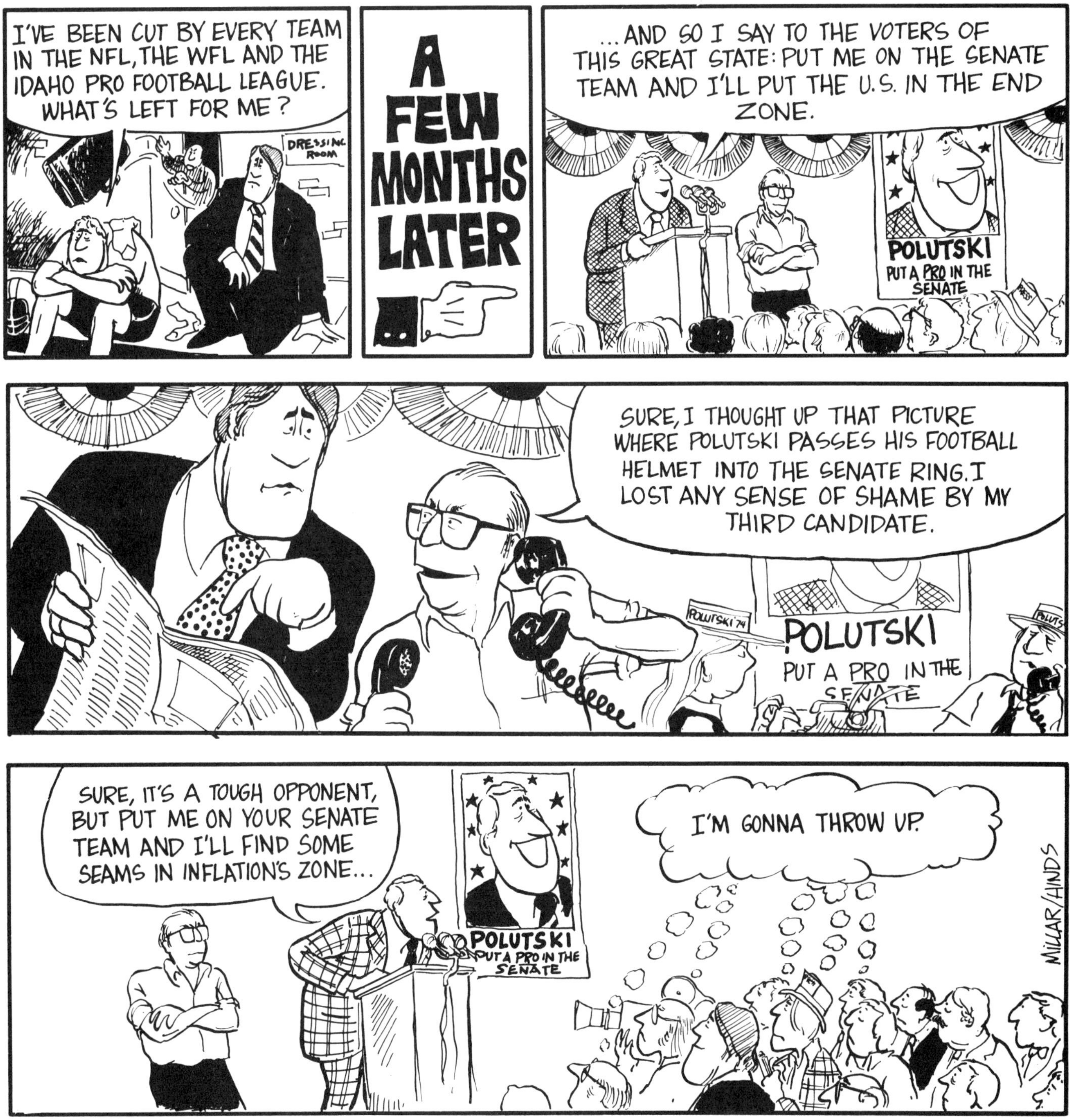
I'VE BEEN CUT BY EVERY TEAM IN THE NFL, THE WFL AND THE IDAHO PRO FOOTBALL LEAGUE. WHAT'S LEFT FOR ME ?
DRESSING ROOM
A FEW MONTHS LATER
...AND SO I SAY TO THE VOTERS OF THIS GREAT STATE: PUT ME ON THE SENATE TEAM AND I'LL PUT THE U.S. IN THE END ZONE.
POLUTSKI
PUT A PRO IN THE SENATE
PRESS
SURE, I THOUGHT UP THAT PICTURE WHERE POLUTSKI PASSES HIS FOOTBALL HELMET INTO THE SENATE RING. I LOST ANY SENSE OF SHAME BY MY THIRD CANDIDATE.
POLUTSKI '74
POLUTSKI
PUT A PRO IN THE SENATE
SURE, IT'S A TOUGH OPPONENT, BUT PUT ME ON YOUR SENATE TEAM AND I'LL FIND SOME SEAMS IN INFLATION'S ZONE...
POLUTSKI
PUT A PRO IN THE SENATE
I'M GONNA THROW UP.
MILLAR/HINDS

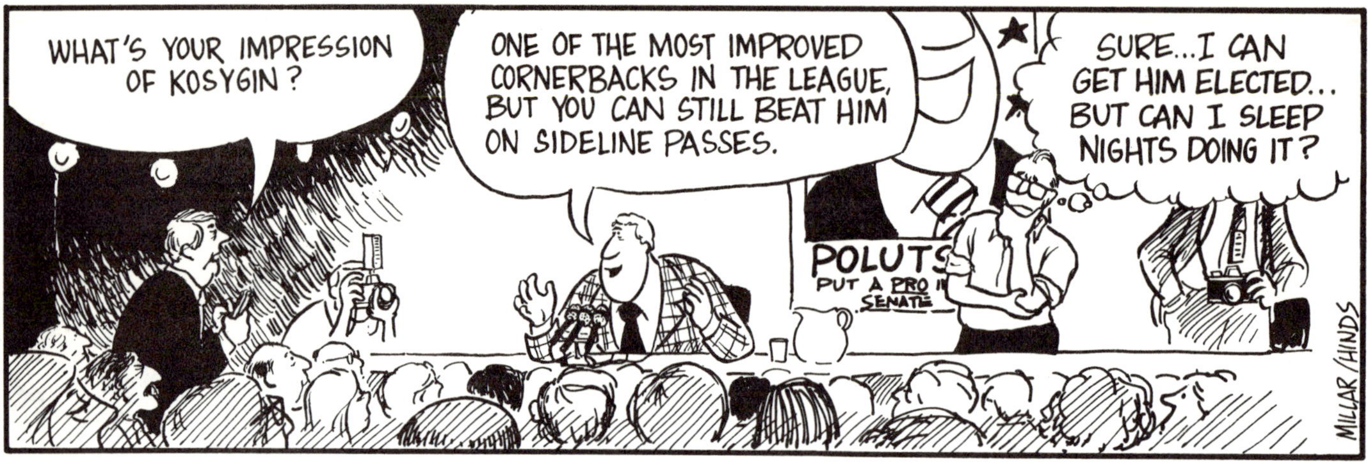
WHAT'S YOUR IMPRESSION OF KOSYGIN?
ONE OF THE MOST IMPROVED CORNERBACKS IN THE LEAGUE, BUT YOU CAN STILL BEAT HIM ON SIDELINE PASSES.
SURE...I CAN GET HIM ELECTED... BUT CAN I SLEEP NIGHTS DOING IT?
POLUTS
PUT A PRO I
SENATE
MILLAR/HINDS

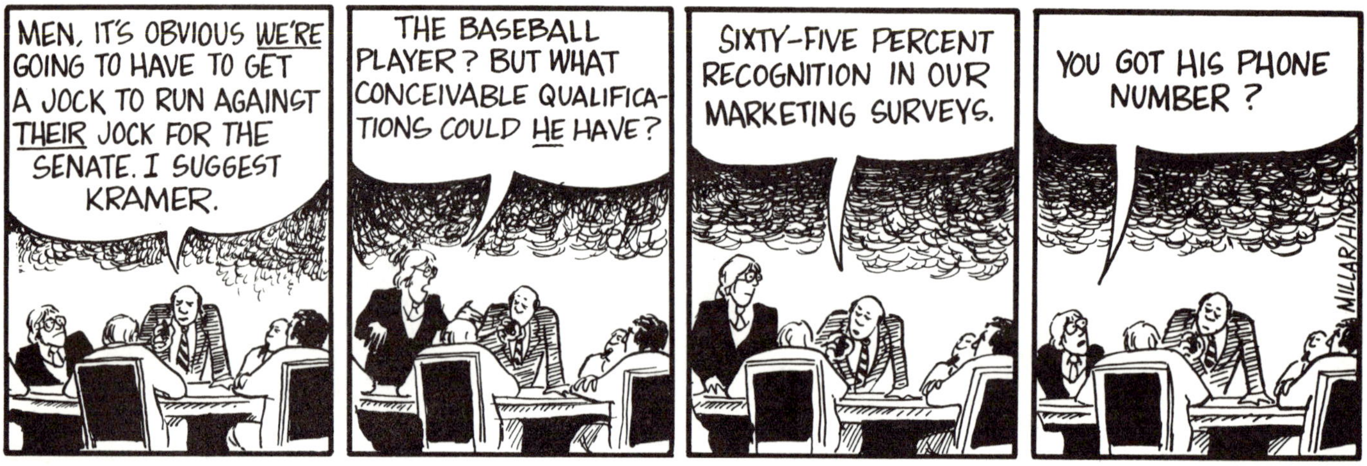
MEN, IT'S OBVIOUS WE'RE GOING TO HAVE TO GET A JOCK TO RUN AGAINST THEIR JOCK FOR THE SENATE. I SUGGEST KRAMER.
THE BASEBALL PLAYER? BUT WHAT CONCEIVABLE QUALIFICATIONS COULD HE HAVE?
SIXTY-FIVE PERCENT RECOGNITION IN OUR MARKETING SURVEYS.
YOU GOT HIS PHONE NUMBER?
MILLAR/HINDS

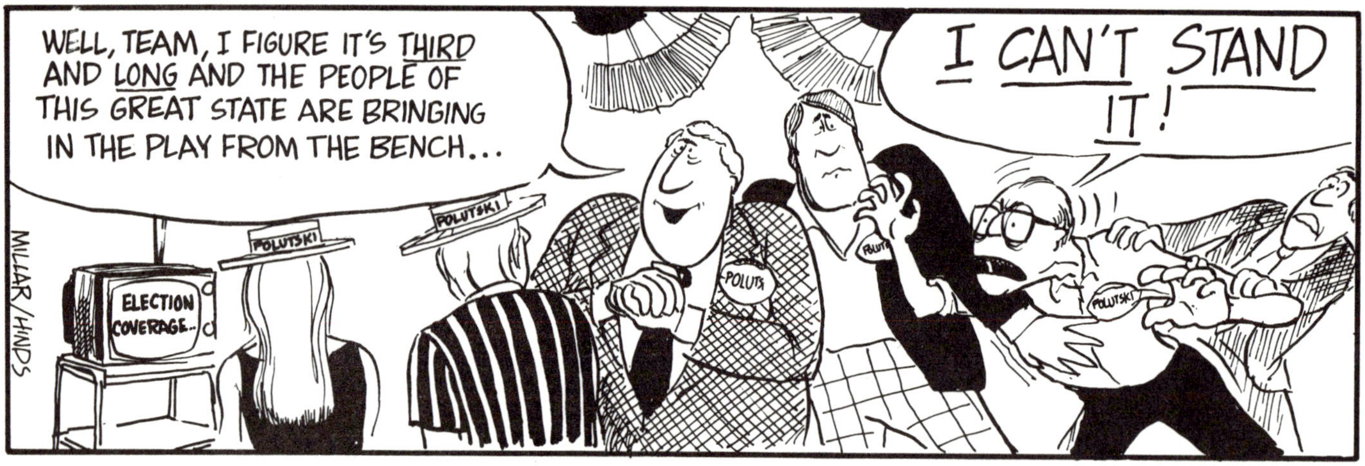
WELL, TEAM, I FIGURE IT'S THIRD AND LONG AND THE PEOPLE OF THIS GREAT STATE ARE BRINGING IN THE PLAY FROM THE BENCH...
I CAN'T STAND IT!
MILLAR/HINDS
POLUTSKI
POLUTSKI
ELECTION COVERAGE...
POLUTS
POLUTSKI

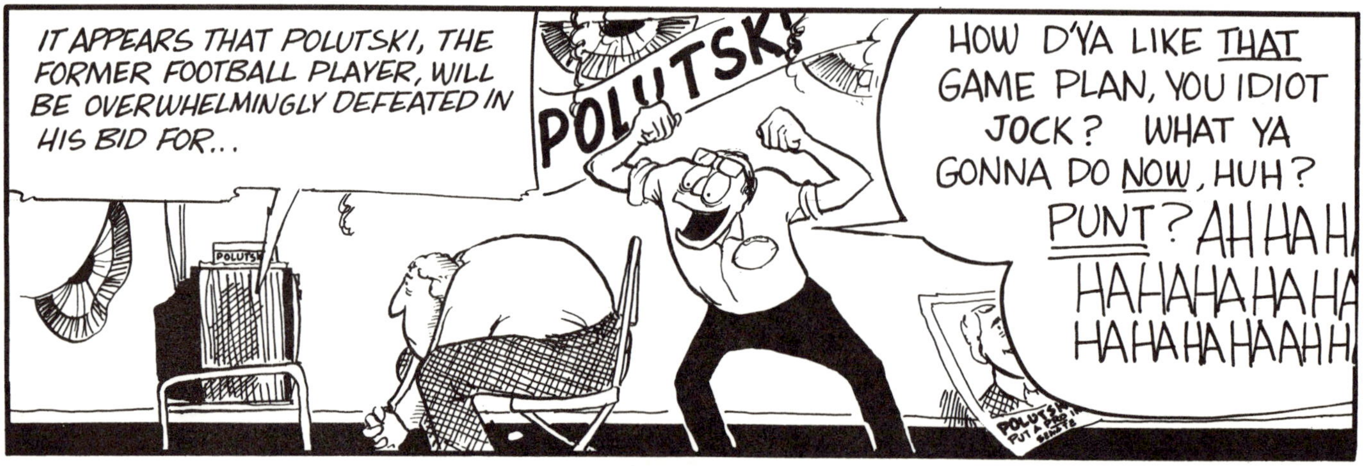
IT APPEARS THAT POLUTSKI, THE FORMER FOOTBALL PLAYER, WILL BE OVERWHELMINGLY DEFEATED IN HIS BID FOR...
POLUTSKI
HOW D'YA LIKE THAT GAME PLAN, YOU IDIOT JOCK? WHAT YA GONNA DO NOW, HUH? PUNT? AH HA HA HAHAHAHAHAHA HAHAHAHAAHH

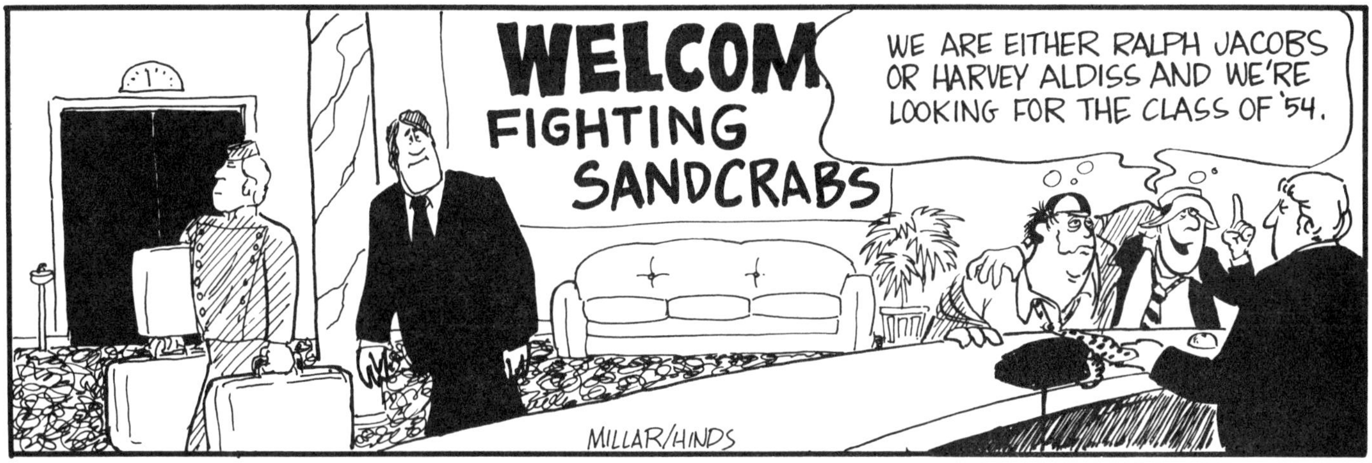
WELCOM
FIGHTING
SANDCRABS
WE ARE EITHER RALPH JACOBS OR HARVEY ALDISS AND WE'RE LOOKING FOR THE CLASS OF '54.
MILLAR/HINDS

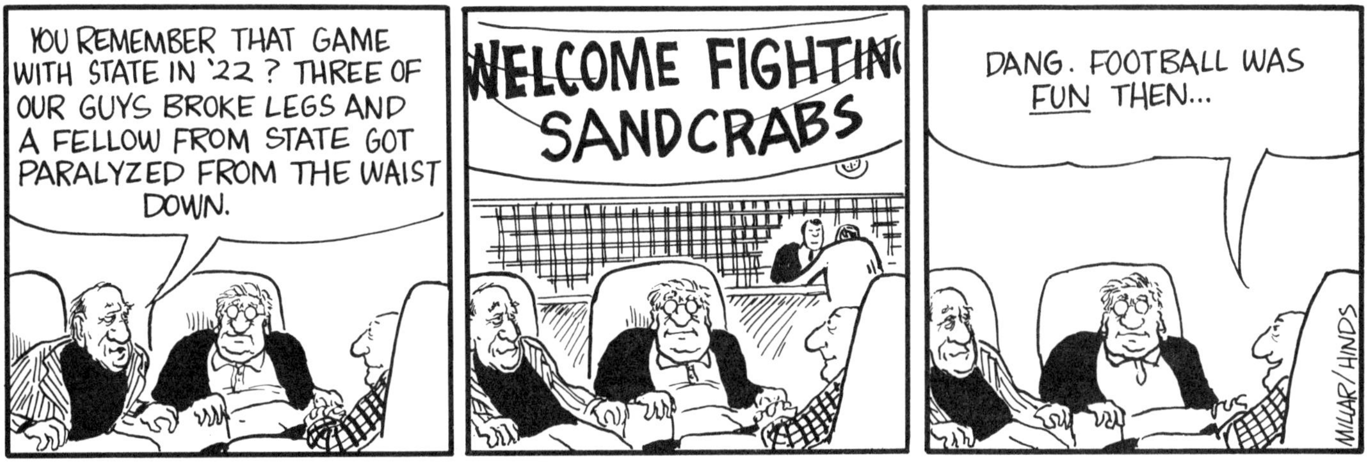
YOU REMEMBER THAT GAME WITH STATE IN '22 ? THREE OF OUR GUYS BROKE LEGS AND A FELLOW FROM STATE GOT PARALYZED FROM THE WAIST DOWN.
WELCOME FIGHTIN
SANDCRABS
DANG. FOOTBALL WAS FUN THEN...
MILLAR/HINDS

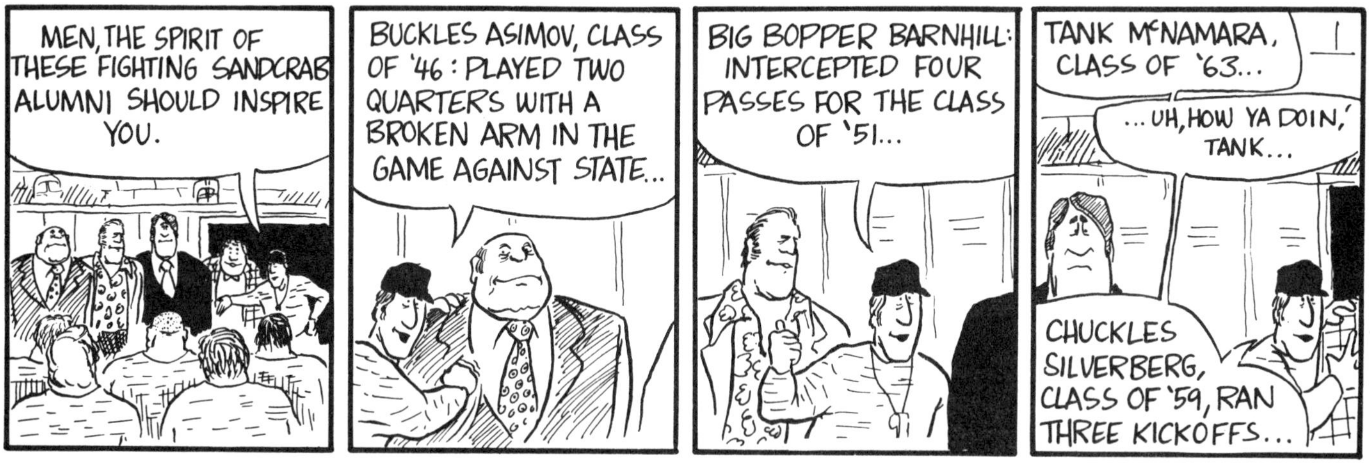
MEN, THE SPIRIT OF THESE FIGHTING SANDCRAB ALUMNI SHOULD INSPIRE YOU.
BUCKLES ASIMOV, CLASS OF '46 : PLAYED TWO QUARTERS WITH A BROKEN ARM IN THE GAME AGAINST STATE...
BIG BOPPER BARNHILL: INTERCEPTED FOUR PASSES FOR THE CLASS OF '51...
TANK McNAMARA, CLASS OF '63...
...UH, HOW YA DOIN,' TANK...
CHUCKLES SILVERBERG, CLASS OF '59, RAN THREE KICKOFFS...

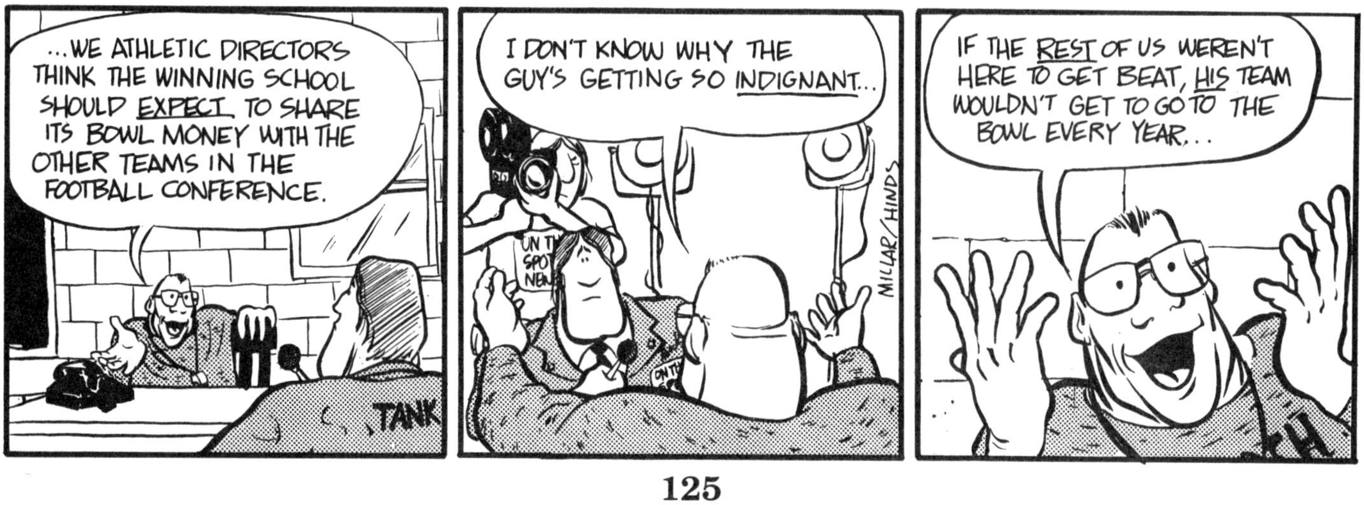
...WE ATHLETIC DIRECTORS THINK THE WINNING SCHOOL SHOULD EXPECT TO SHARE ITS BOWL MONEY WITH THE OTHER TEAMS IN THE FOOTBALL CONFERENCE.
TANK
I DON'T KNOW WHY THE GUY'S GETTING SO INDIGNANT...
MILLAR/HINDS
IF THE REST OF US WEREN'T HERE TO GET BEAT, HIS TEAM WOULDN'T GET TO GO TO THE BOWL EVERY YEAR...

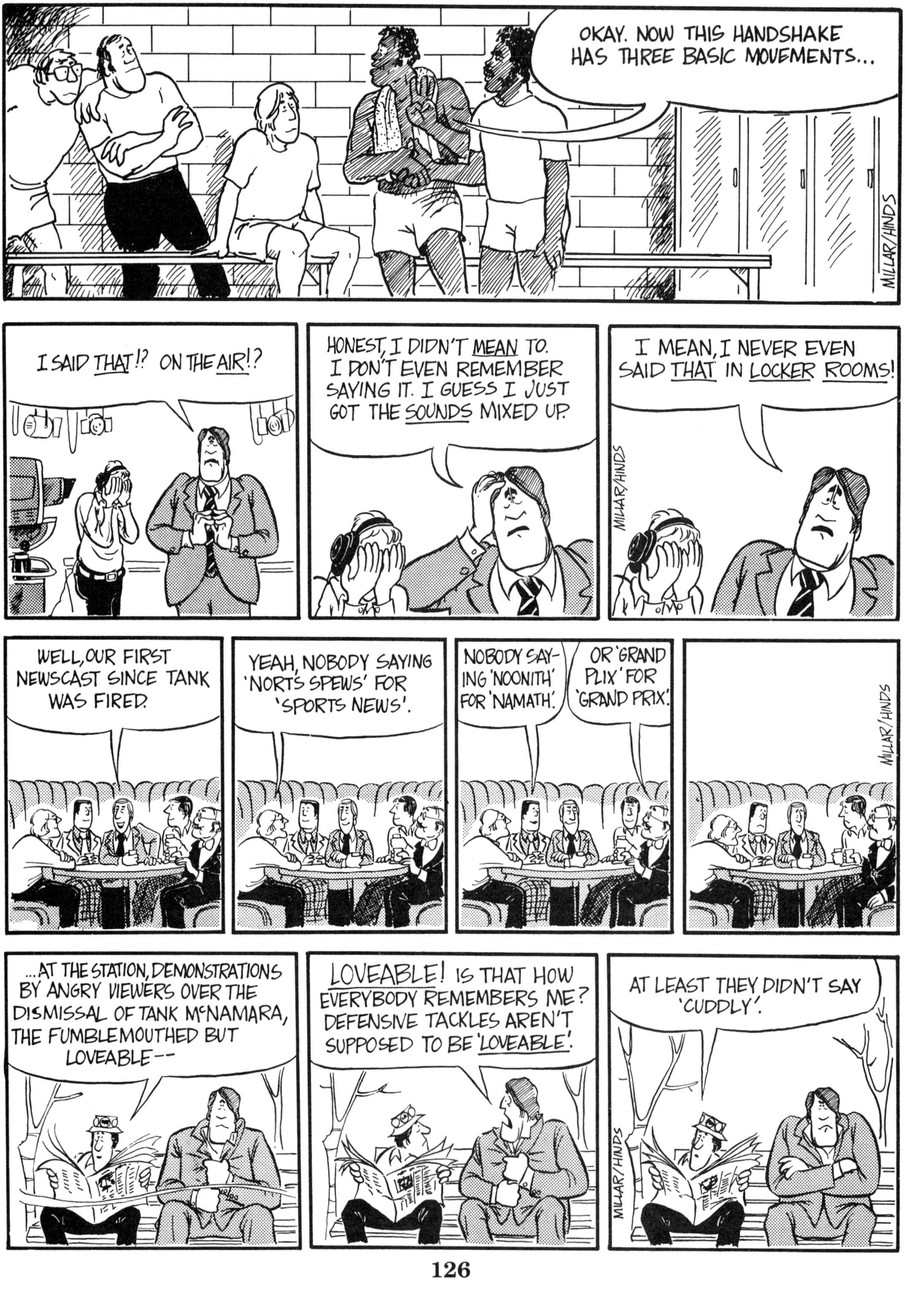
OKAY. NOW THIS HANDSHAKE HAS THREE BASIC MOVEMENTS...
MILLAR/HINDS
I SAID THAT!? ON THE AIR!?
HONEST, I DIDN'T MEAN TO. I DON'T EVEN REMEMBER SAYING IT. I GUESS I JUST GOT THE SOUNDS MIXED UP.
MILLAR/HINDS
I MEAN, I NEVER EVEN SAID THAT IN LOCKER ROOMS!
WELL, OUR FIRST NEWSCAST SINCE TANK WAS FIRED.
YEAH, NOBODY SAYING 'NORTS SPEWS' FOR 'SPORTS NEWS'.
NOBODY SAY-ING 'NOONITH' FOR 'NAMATH'.
OR 'GRAND PLIX' FOR 'GRAND PRIX'.
MILLAR/HINDS
...AT THE STATION, DEMONSTRATIONS BY ANGRY VIEWERS OVER THE DISMISSAL OF TANK McNAMARA, THE FUMBLEMOUTHED BUT LOVEABLE--
LOVEABLE! IS THAT HOW EVERYBODY REMEMBERS ME? DEFENSIVE TACKLES AREN'T SUPPOSED TO BE 'LOVEABLE'.
MILLAR/HINDS
AT LEAST THEY DIDN'T SAY 'CUDDLY'.

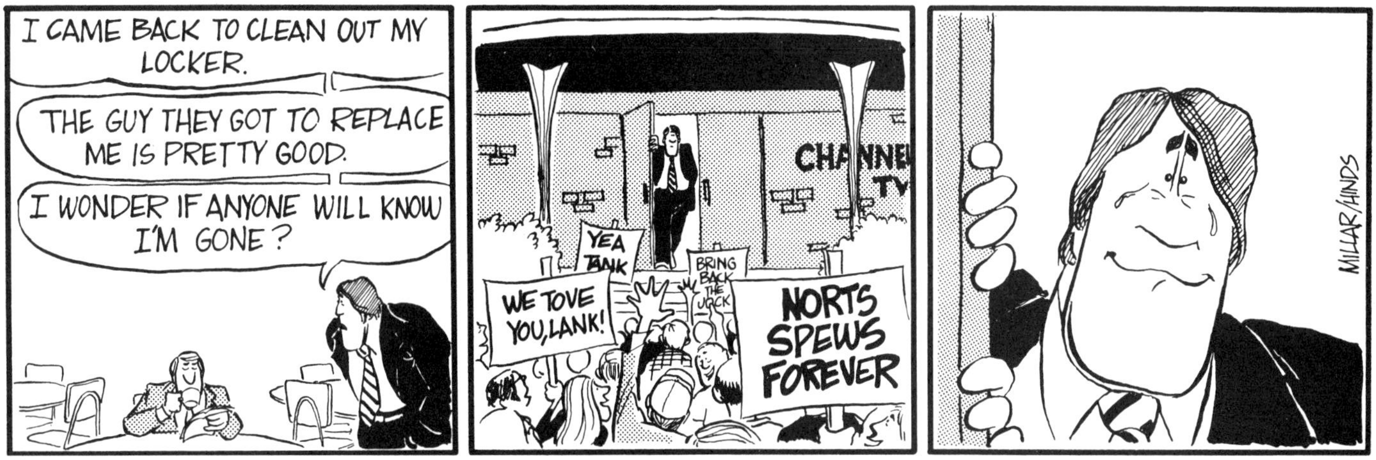
I CAME BACK TO CLEAN OUT MY LOCKER.
THE GUY THEY GOT TO REPLACE ME IS PRETTY GOOD.
I WONDER IF ANYONE WILL KNOW I'M GONE?
YEA TANK
WE TOVE YOU, LANK!
BRING BACK THE JOCK
NORTS SPEWS FOREVER
MILLAR/HINDS

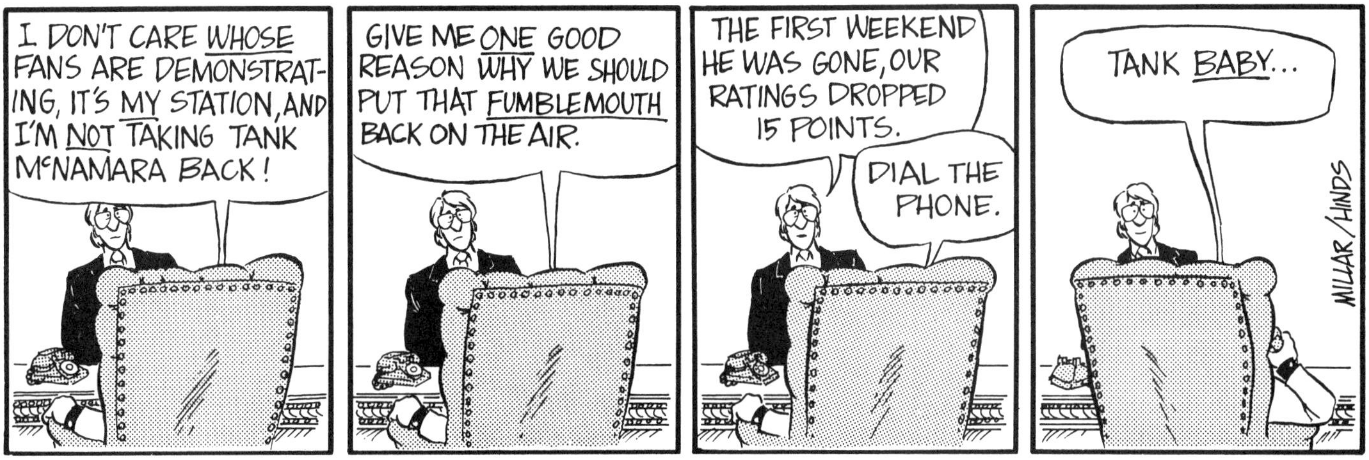
I DON'T CARE WHOSE FANS ARE DEMONSTRATING, IT'S MY STATION, AND I'M NOT TAKING TANK McNAMARA BACK!
GIVE ME ONE GOOD REASON WHY WE SHOULD PUT THAT FUMBLEMOUTH BACK ON THE AIR.
THE FIRST WEEKEND HE WAS GONE, OUR RATINGS DROPPED 15 POINTS.
DIAL THE PHONE.
TANK BABY...
MILLAR/HINDS

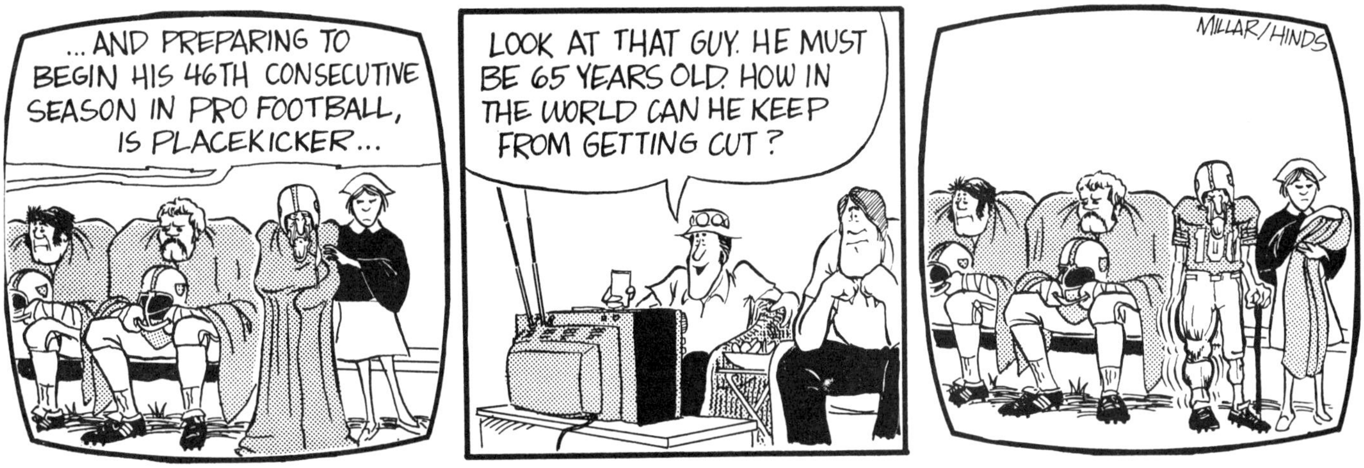
...AND PREPARING TO BEGIN HIS 46TH CONSECUTIVE SEASON IN PRO FOOTBALL, IS PLACEKICKER...
LOOK AT THAT GUY. HE MUST BE 65 YEARS OLD. HOW IN THE WORLD CAN HE KEEP FROM GETTING CUT?
MILLAR/HINDS

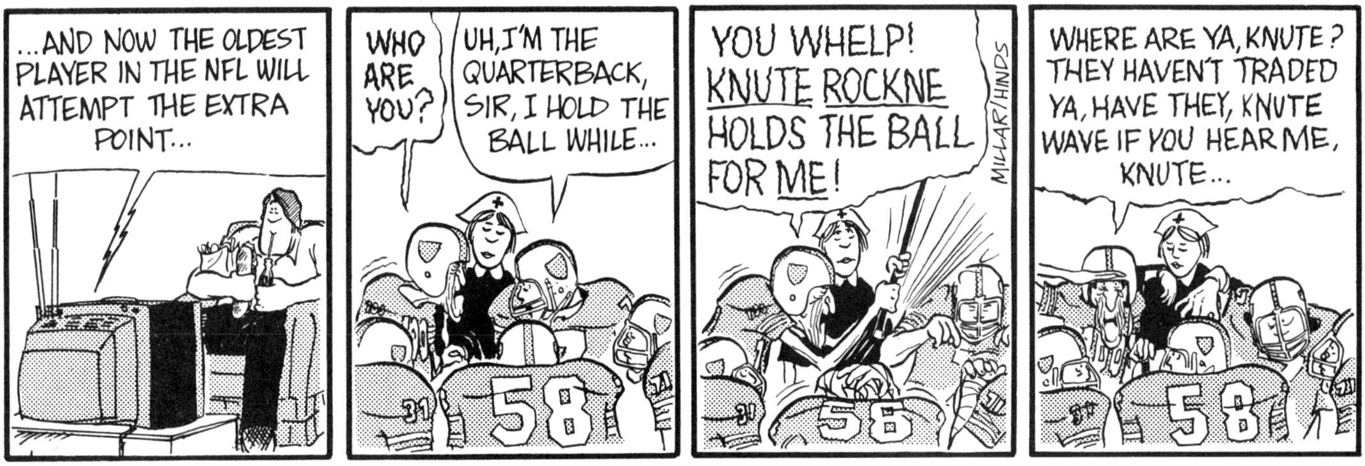
...AND NOW THE OLDEST PLAYER IN THE NFL WILL ATTEMPT THE EXTRA POINT...
WHO ARE YOU?
UH, I'M THE QUARTERBACK, SIR, I HOLD THE BALL WHILE...
YOU WHELP! KNUTE ROCKNE HOLDS THE BALL FOR ME!
MILLAR/HINDS
WHERE ARE YA, KNUTE? THEY HAVEN'T TRADED YA, HAVE THEY, KNUTE WAVE IF YOU HEAR ME, KNUTE...

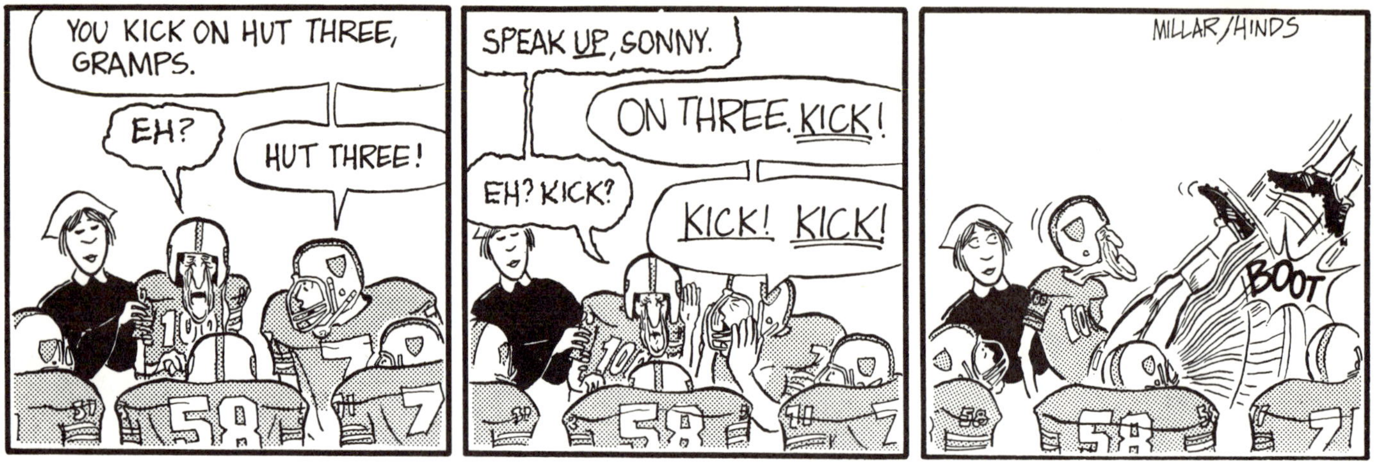
YOU KICK ON HUT THREE, GRAMPS.
EH?
HUT THREE!
SPEAK UP, SONNY.
ON THREE. KICK!
EH? KICK?
KICK! KICK!
MILLAR/HINDS
BOOT

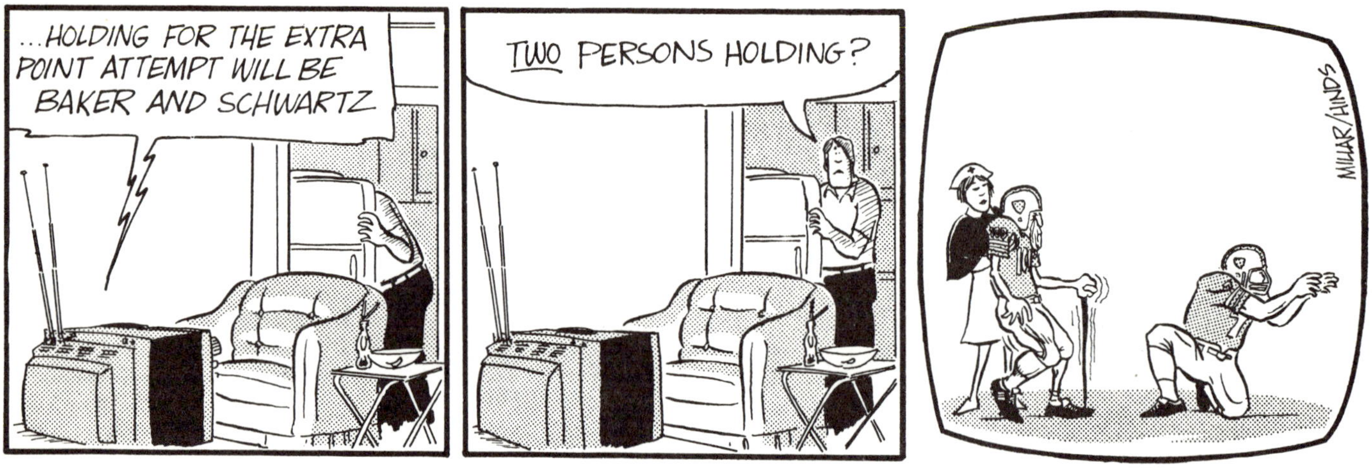
...HOLDING FOR THE EXTRA POINT ATTEMPT WILL BE BAKER AND SCHWARTZ
TWO PERSONS HOLDING?
MILLAR/HINDS

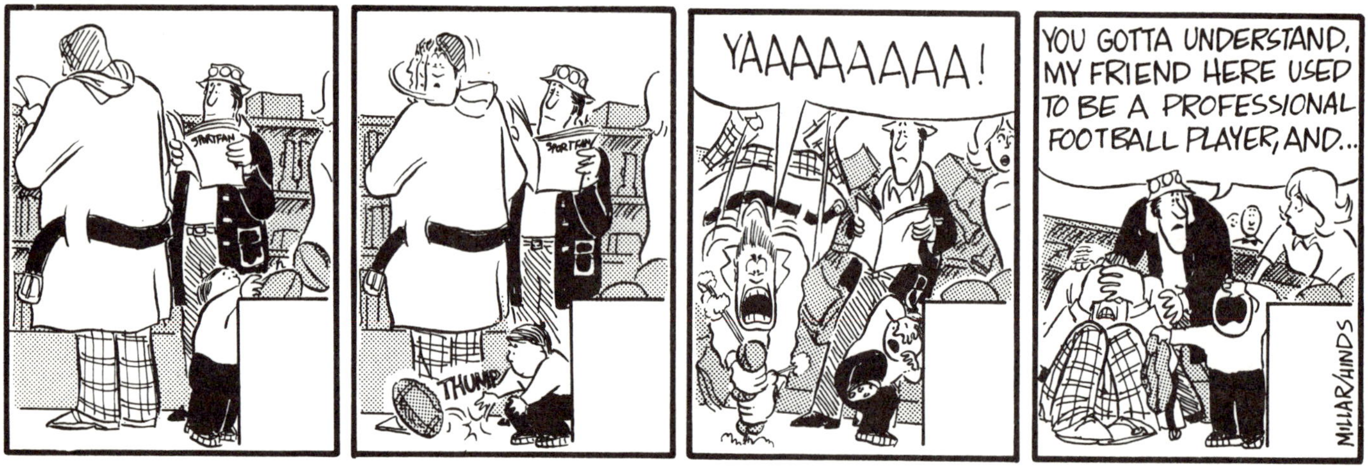
SPORTFAN
THUMP
YAAAAAAAA!
YOU GOTTA UNDERSTAND, MY FRIEND HERE USED TO BE A PROFESSIONAL FOOTBALL PLAYER, AND...
MILLAR/HINDS

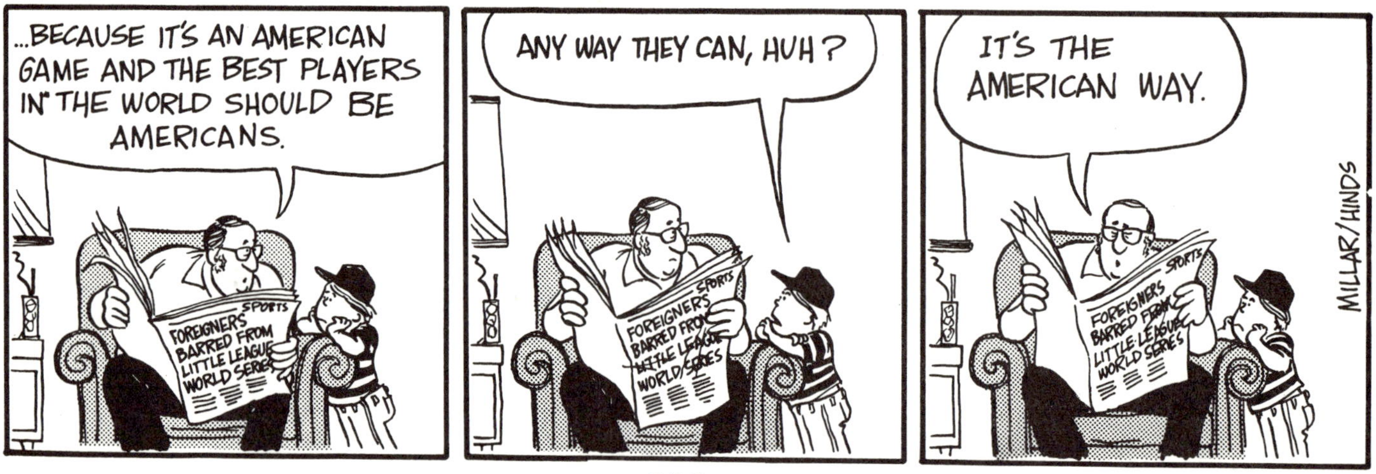
...BECAUSE IT'S AN AMERICAN GAME AND THE BEST PLAYERS IN THE WORLD SHOULD BE AMERICANS.
SPORTS
FOREIGNERS BARRED FROM LITTLE LEAGUE WORLD SERIES
ANY WAY THEY CAN, HUH?
IT'S THE AMERICAN WAY.
MILLAR/HINDS

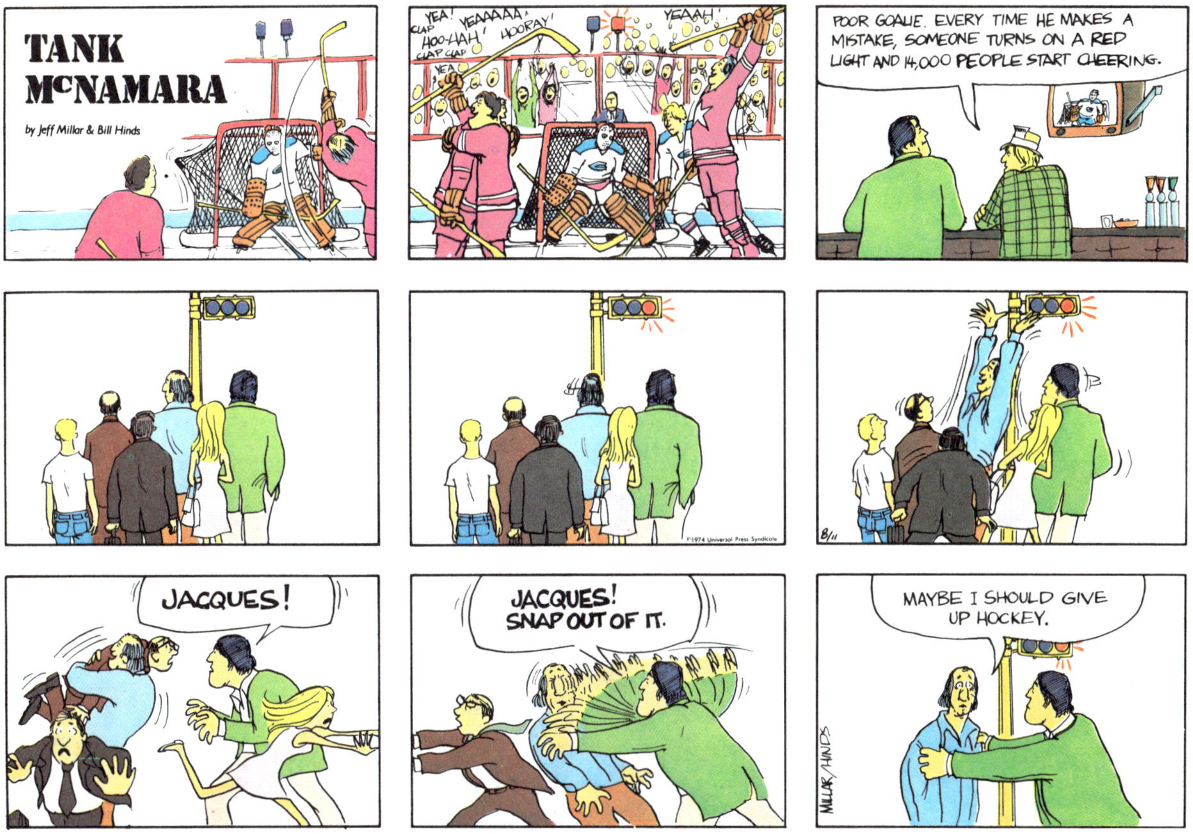
TANK McNAMARA
by Jeff Millar & Bill Hinds
YEA! YEAAAAA! HOO-HAH! HOORAY! YEAAH!
CLAP CLAP CLAP CLAP
POOR GOALIE. EVERY TIME HE MAKES A MISTAKE, SOMEONE TURNS ON A RED LIGHT AND 14,000 PEOPLE START CHEERING.
©1974 Universal Press Syndicate
8/11
JACQUES!
JACQUES! SNAP OUT OF IT.
MAYBE I SHOULD GIVE UP HOCKEY.
MILLAR/HINDS

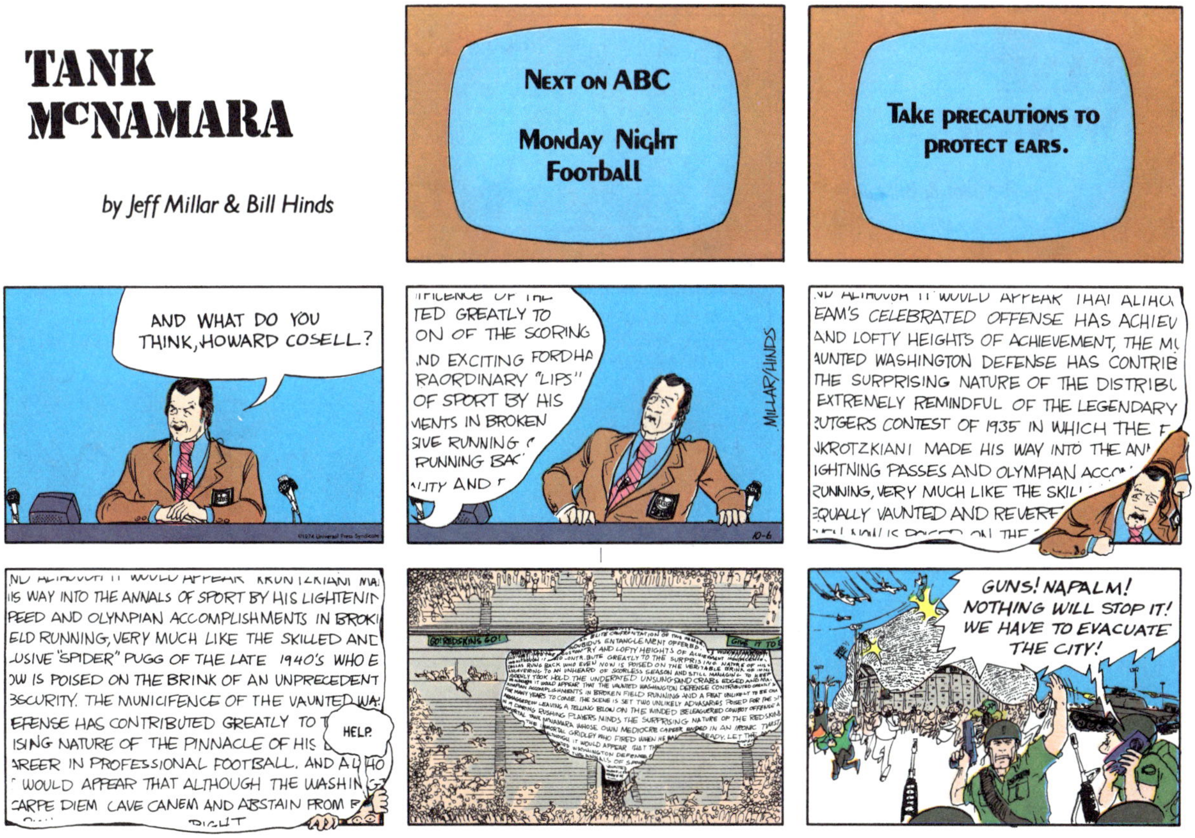
TANK McNAMARA
by Jeff Millar & Bill Hinds
Next on ABC
Monday Night Football
Take precautions to protect ears.
AND WHAT DO YOU THINK, HOWARD COSELL?
MILLAR/HINDS
10-6
TED GREATLY TO
ON OF THE SCORING
ND EXCITING FORDHA
RAORDINARY "LIPS"
OF SPORT BY HIS
MENTS IN BROKEN
SIVE RUNNING
RUNNING BAC
EAM'S CELEBRATED OFFENSE HAS ACHIEV
AND LOFTY HEIGHTS OF ACHIEVEMENT, THE M
AUNTED WASHINGTON DEFENSE HAS CONTRIB
THE SURPRISING NATURE OF THE DISTRIBU
EXTREMELY REMINDFUL OF THE LEGENDARY
UTGERS CONTEST OF 1935 IN WHICH THE
KROTZKIANI MADE HIS WAY INTO THE AN
IGHTNING PASSES AND OLYMPIAN ACCO
RUNNING, VERY MUCH LIKE THE SKIL
EQUALLY VAUNTED AND REVERE
IS WAY INTO THE ANNALS OF SPORT BY HIS LIGHTENIN
PEED AND OLYMPIAN ACCOMPLISHMENTS IN BROKI
ELD RUNNING, VERY MUCH LIKE THE SKILLED AND
USIVE "SPIDER" PUGG OF THE LATE 1940'S WHO E
OW IS POISED ON THE BRINK OF AN UNPRECEDENT
BSCURITY. THE MUNICIFENCE OF THE VAUNTED WA
EFENSE HAS CONTRIBUTED GREATLY TO T
ISING NATURE OF THE PINNACLE OF HIS
AREER IN PROFESSIONAL FOOTBALL, AND AL
WOULD APPEAR THAT ALTHOUGH THE WASHIN
CARPE DIEM CAVE CANEM AND ABSTAIN FROM
HELP.
GO! REDSKINS GO!
GIVE IT TO
GUNS! NAPALM! NOTHING WILL STOP IT! WE HAVE TO EVACUATE THE CITY!

TANK McNAMARA

by Jeff Millar & Bill Hinds

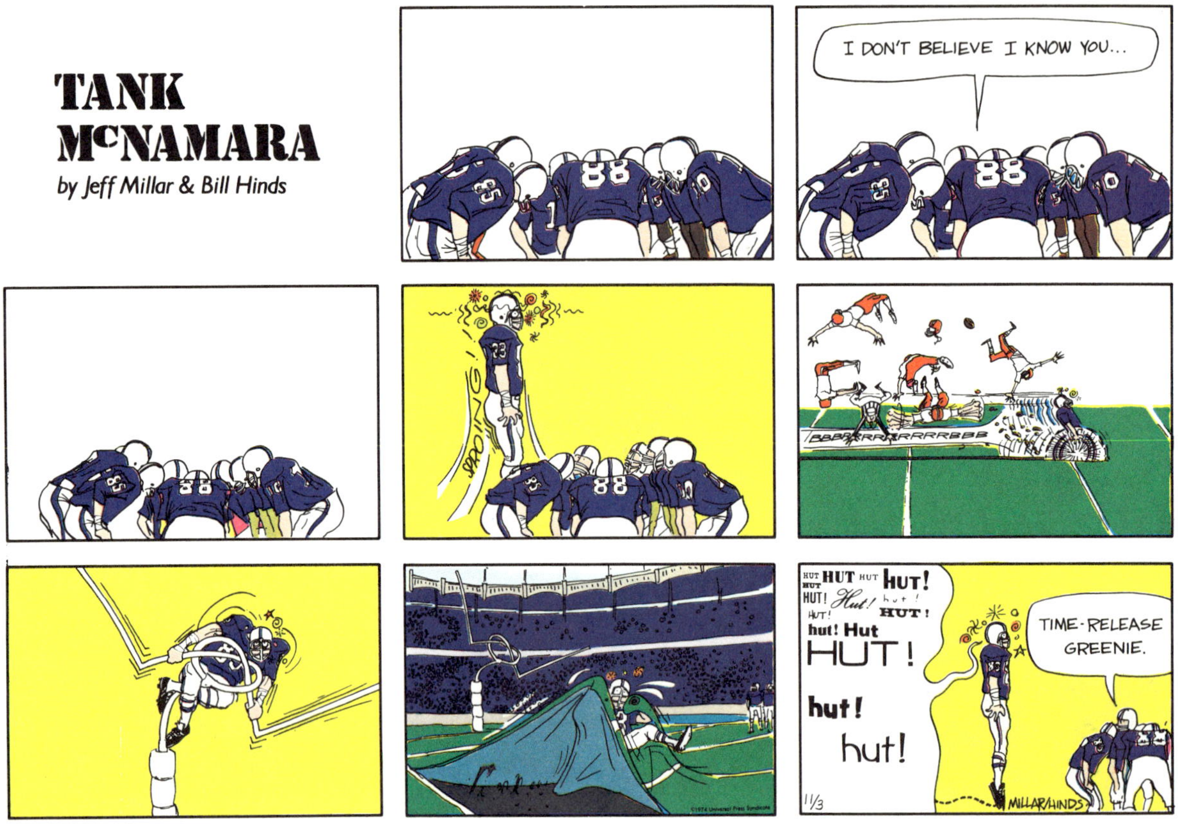

I DON'T BELIEVE I KNOW YOU...
SPROING!
BBBBRRRRRRRRRRBBB
HUT HUT HUT HUT HUT! HUT! Hut! hut! HUT! HUT! hut! Hut HUT! hut! hut!
TIME-RELEASE GREENIE.
11/3
MILLAR/HINDS

TANK McNAMARA

by Jeff Millar & Bill Hinds

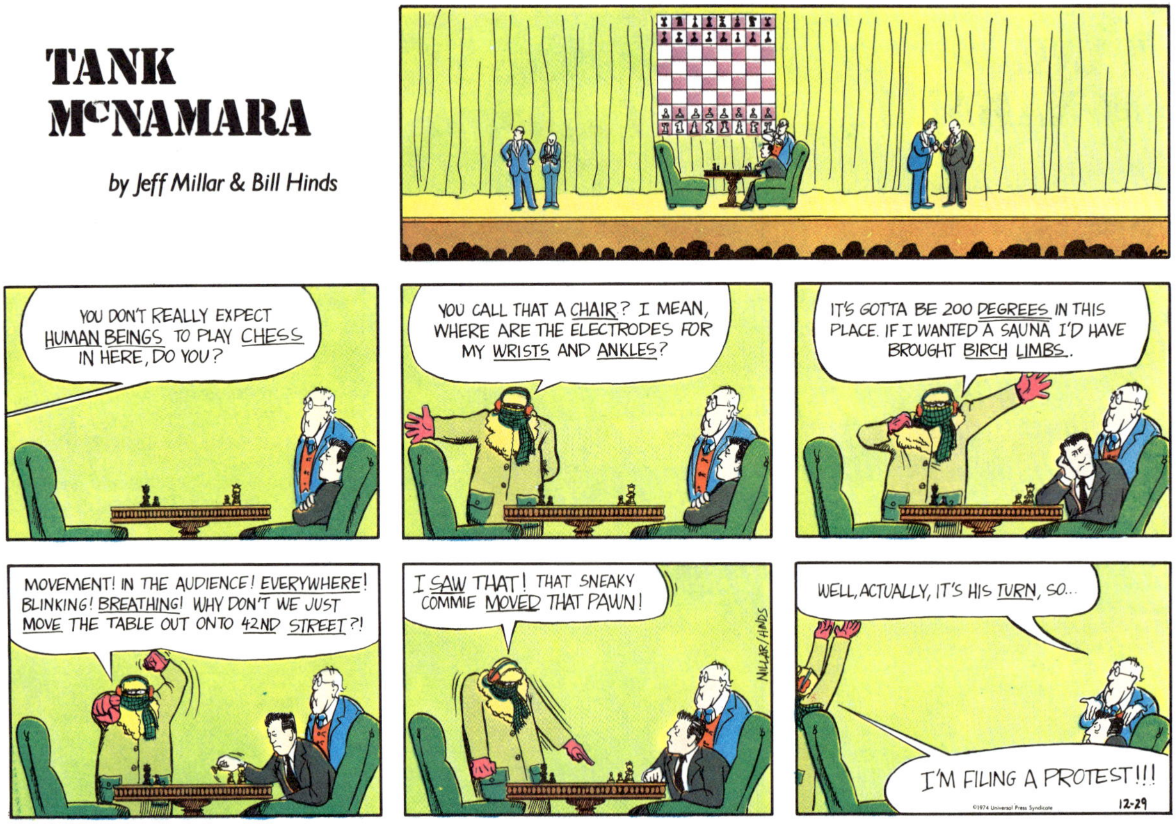

YOU DON'T REALLY EXPECT HUMAN BEINGS TO PLAY CHESS IN HERE, DO YOU?
YOU CALL THAT A CHAIR? I MEAN, WHERE ARE THE ELECTRODES FOR MY WRISTS AND ANKLES?
IT'S GOTTA BE 200 DEGREES IN THIS PLACE. IF I WANTED A SAUNA I'D HAVE BROUGHT BIRCH LIMBS.
MOVEMENT! IN THE AUDIENCE! EVERYWHERE! BLINKING! BREATHING! WHY DON'T WE JUST MOVE THE TABLE OUT ONTO 42ND STREET?!
I SAW THAT! THAT SNEAKY COMMIE MOVED THAT PAWN!
MILLAR/HINDS
WELL, ACTUALLY, IT'S HIS TURN, SO...
I'M FILING A PROTEST!!!
12-29

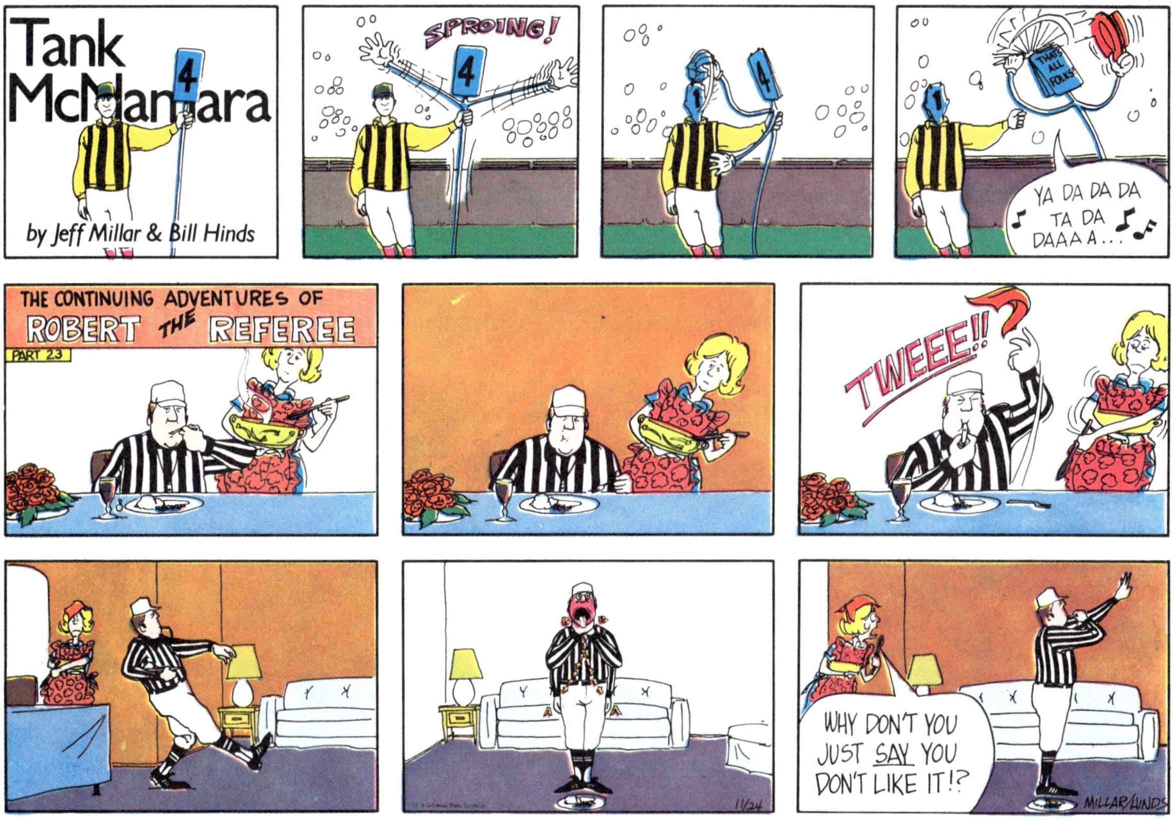
Tank McNamara
by Jeff Millar & Bill Hinds
SPROING!
THAT'S ALL FOLKS
YA DA DA DA TA DA DAAA A...
THE CONTINUING ADVENTURES OF ROBERT THE REFEREE
PART 23
TWEEE!!
WHY DON'T YOU JUST SAY YOU DON'T LIKE IT!?
11/24
MILLAR/HINDS

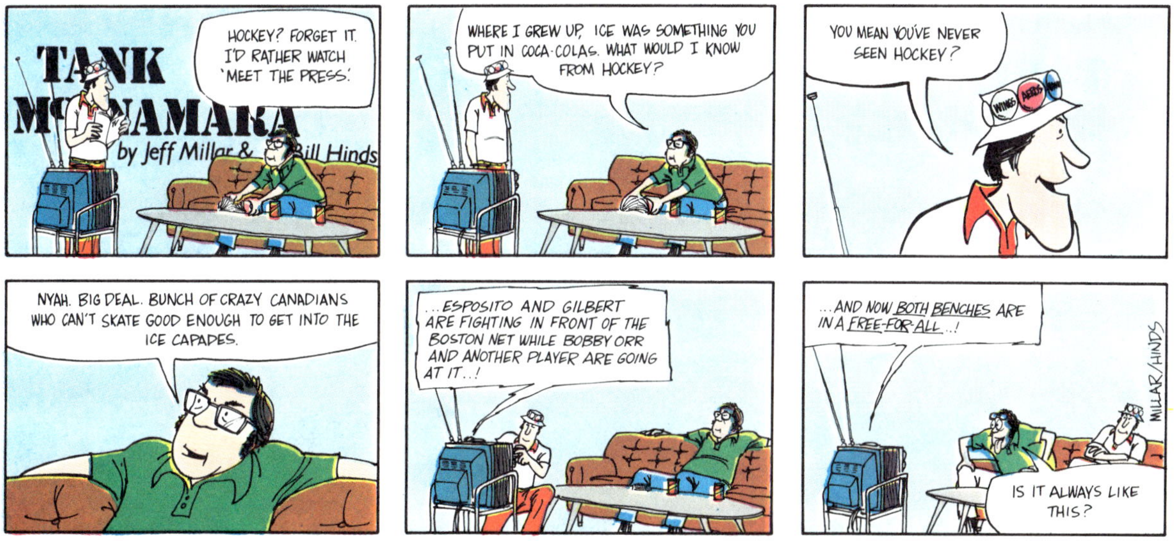
TANK McNAMARA
by Jeff Millar & Bill Hinds
HOCKEY? FORGET IT. I'D RATHER WATCH 'MEET THE PRESS.'
WHERE I GREW UP, ICE WAS SOMETHING YOU PUT IN COCA-COLAS. WHAT WOULD I KNOW FROM HOCKEY?
YOU MEAN YOU'VE NEVER SEEN HOCKEY?
WINGS
NYAH. BIG DEAL. BUNCH OF CRAZY CANADIANS WHO CAN'T SKATE GOOD ENOUGH TO GET INTO THE ICE CAPADES.
...ESPOSITO AND GILBERT ARE FIGHTING IN FRONT OF THE BOSTON NET WHILE BOBBY ORR AND ANOTHER PLAYER ARE GOING AT IT...!
...AND NOW BOTH BENCHES ARE IN A FREE-FOR-ALL...!
MILLAR/HINDS
IS IT ALWAYS LIKE THIS?

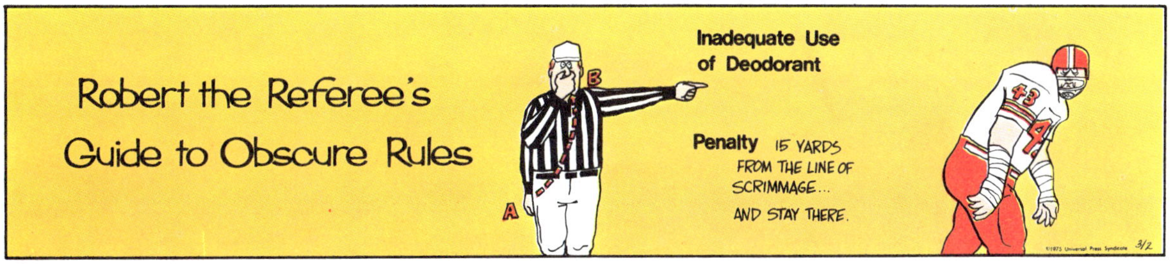
Robert the Referee's Guide to Obscure Rules
Inadequate Use of Deodorant
Penalty 15 YARDS FROM THE LINE OF SCRIMMAGE... AND STAY THERE.
A
B
43
3/2

TANK McNAMARA

by Jeff Millar & Bill Hinds

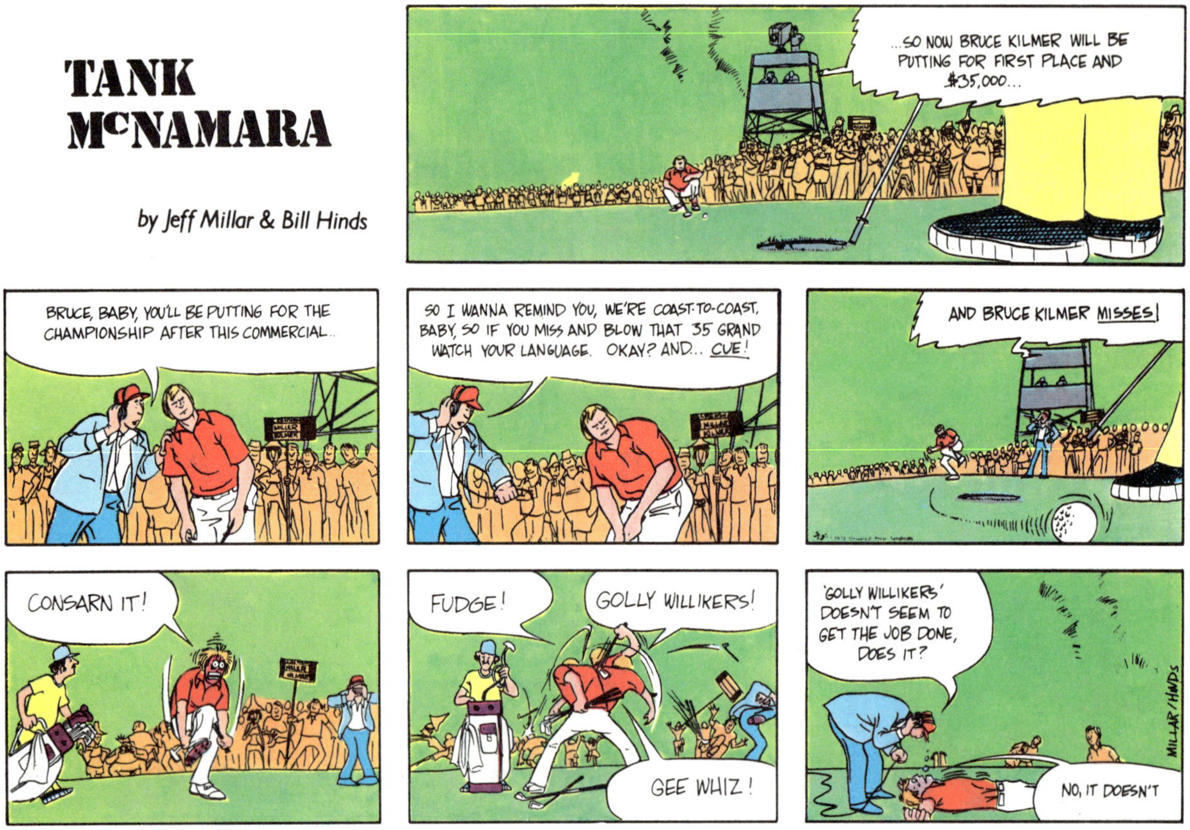

...SO NOW BRUCE KILMER WILL BE PUTTING FOR FIRST PLACE AND $35,000...
BRUCE, BABY, YOU'LL BE PUTTING FOR THE CHAMPIONSHIP AFTER THIS COMMERCIAL...
SO I WANNA REMIND YOU, WE'RE COAST-TO-COAST, BABY, SO IF YOU MISS AND BLOW THAT 35 GRAND WATCH YOUR LANGUAGE. OKAY? AND... CUE!
AND BRUCE KILMER MISSES!
CONSARN IT!
FUDGE!
GOLLY WILLIKERS!
GEE WHIZ!
'GOLLY WILLIKERS' DOESN'T SEEM TO GET THE JOB DONE, DOES IT?
NO, IT DOESN'T
MILLAR/HINDS

TANK McNAMARA

by Jeff Millar & Bill Hinds

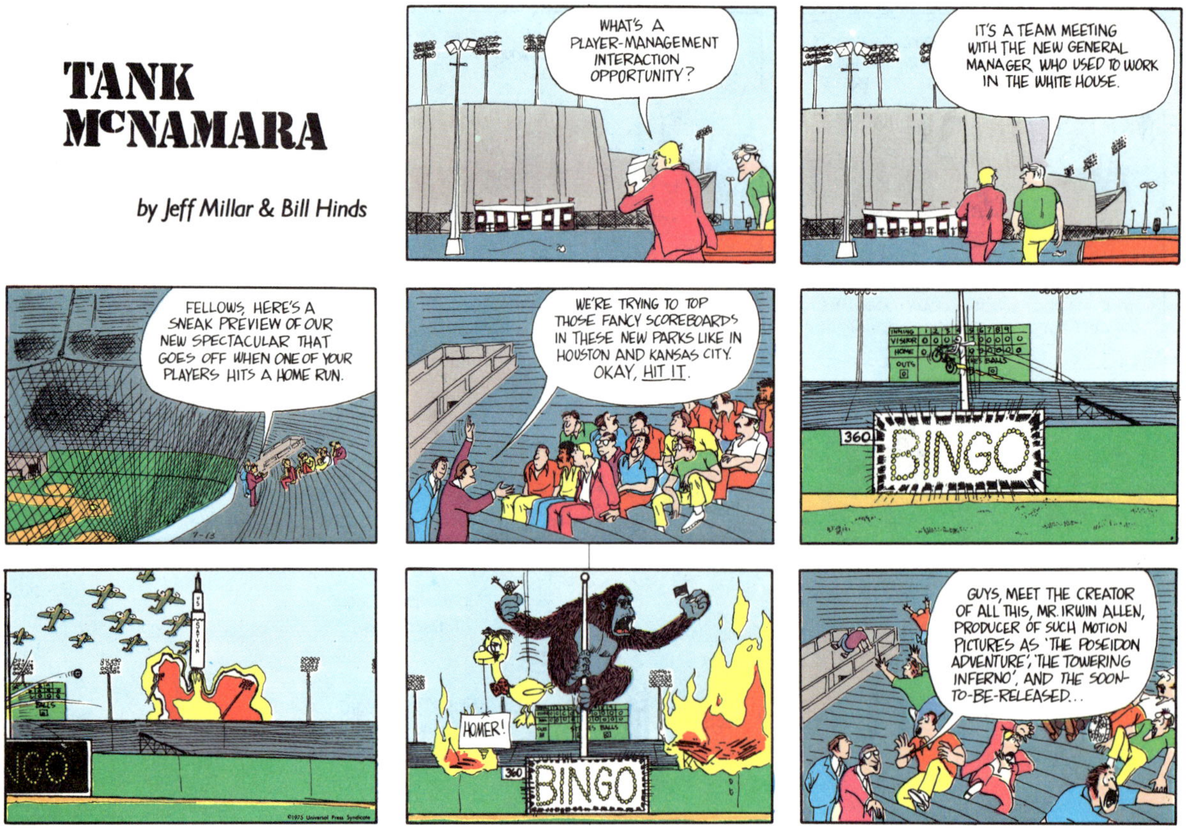

WHAT'S A PLAYER-MANAGEMENT INTERACTION OPPORTUNITY?
IT'S A TEAM MEETING WITH THE NEW GENERAL MANAGER, WHO USED TO WORK IN THE WHITE HOUSE.
FELLOWS, HERE'S A SNEAK PREVIEW OF OUR NEW SPECTACULAR THAT GOES OFF WHEN ONE OF YOUR PLAYERS HITS A HOME RUN.
WE'RE TRYING TO TOP THOSE FANCY SCOREBOARDS IN THESE NEW PARKS LIKE IN HOUSTON AND KANSAS CITY. OKAY, HIT IT.
360
BINGO
HOMER!
360
BINGO
GUYS, MEET THE CREATOR OF ALL THIS, MR. IRWIN ALLEN, PRODUCER OF SUCH MOTION PICTURES AS 'THE POSEIDON ADVENTURE', 'THE TOWERING INFERNO', AND THE SOON-TO-BE-RELEASED...

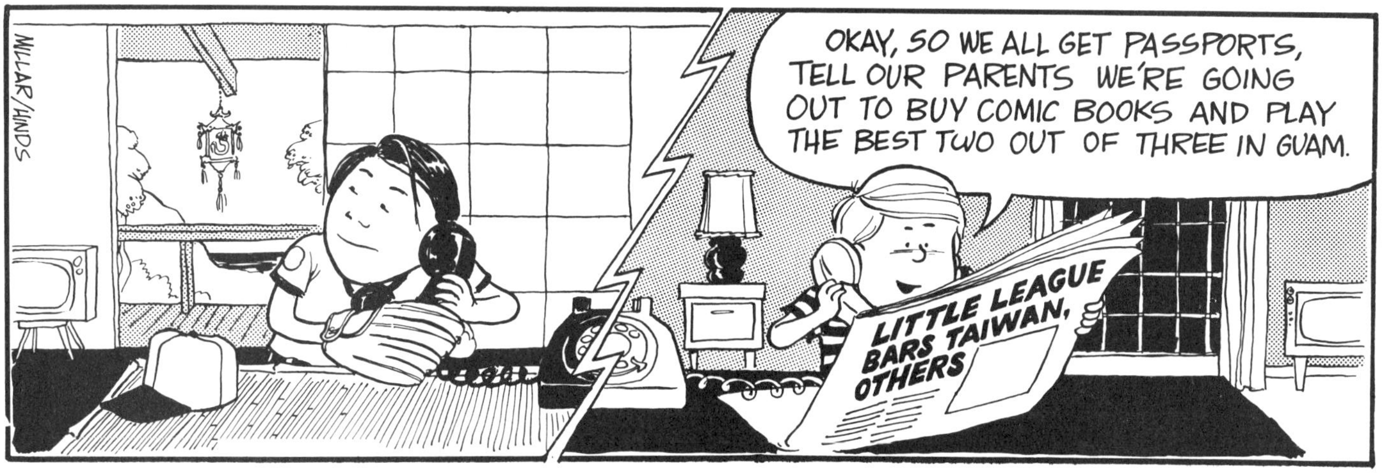
MILLAR/HINDS
OKAY, SO WE ALL GET PASSPORTS, TELL OUR PARENTS WE'RE GOING OUT TO BUY COMIC BOOKS AND PLAY THE BEST TWO OUT OF THREE IN GUAM.
LITTLE LEAGUE BARS TAIWAN, OTHERS

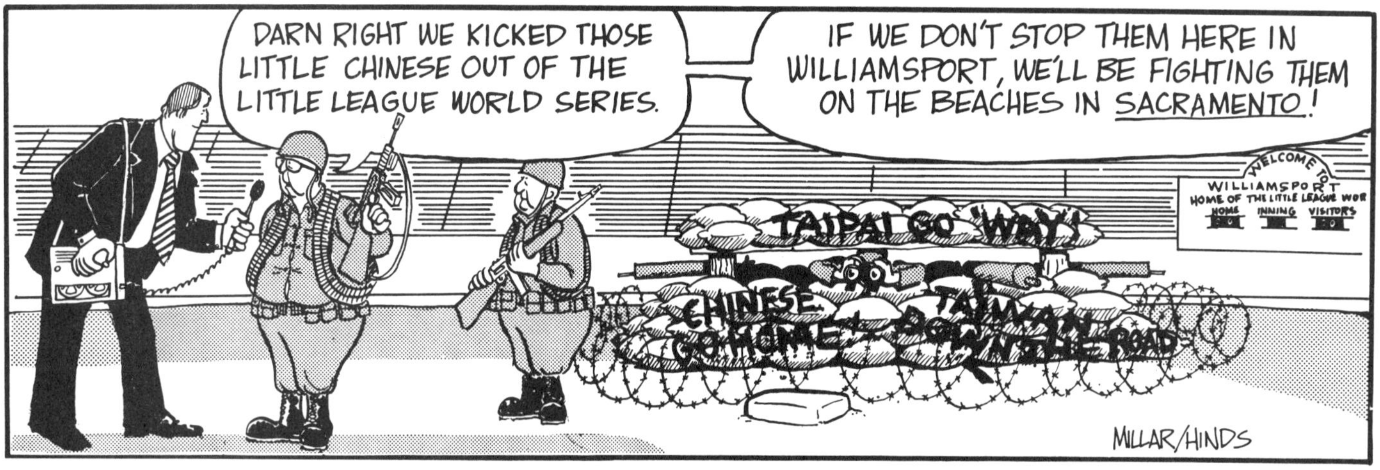
DARN RIGHT WE KICKED THOSE LITTLE CHINESE OUT OF THE LITTLE LEAGUE WORLD SERIES.
IF WE DON'T STOP THEM HERE IN WILLIAMSPORT, WE'LL BE FIGHTING THEM ON THE BEACHES IN SACRAMENTO!
WELCOME TO WILLIAMSPORT HOME OF THE LITTLE LEAGUE WOR
HOME INNING VISITORS
TAIPAI GO 'WAY!
CHINESE GO HOME
TAIWAN DOWN THE ROAD
MILLAR/HINDS

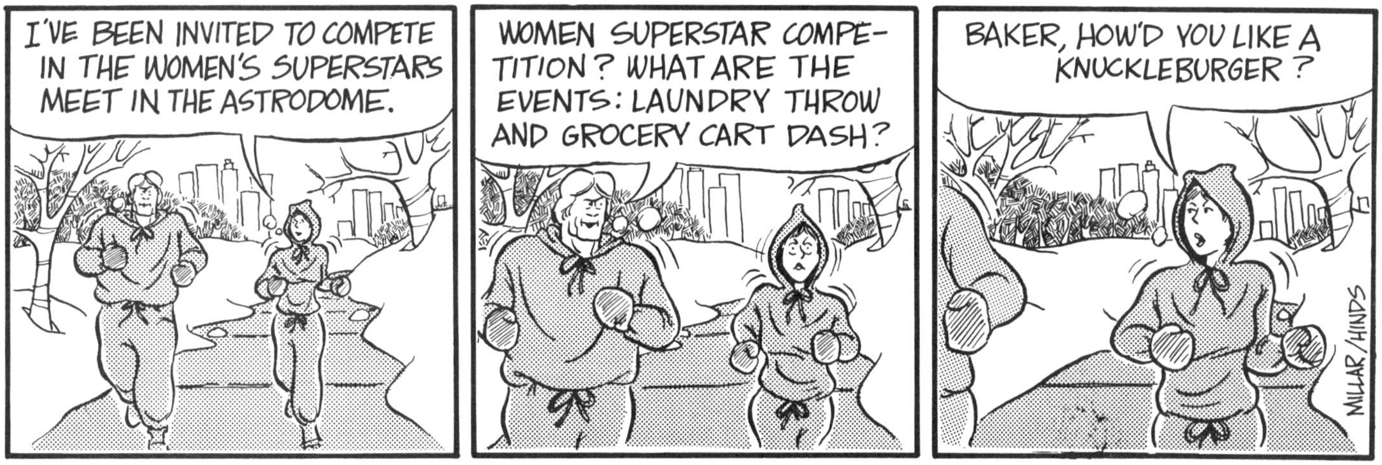
I'VE BEEN INVITED TO COMPETE IN THE WOMEN'S SUPERSTARS MEET IN THE ASTRODOME.
WOMEN SUPERSTAR COMPETITION? WHAT ARE THE EVENTS: LAUNDRY THROW AND GROCERY CART DASH?
BAKER, HOW'D YOU LIKE A KNUCKLEBURGER?
MILLAR/HINDS

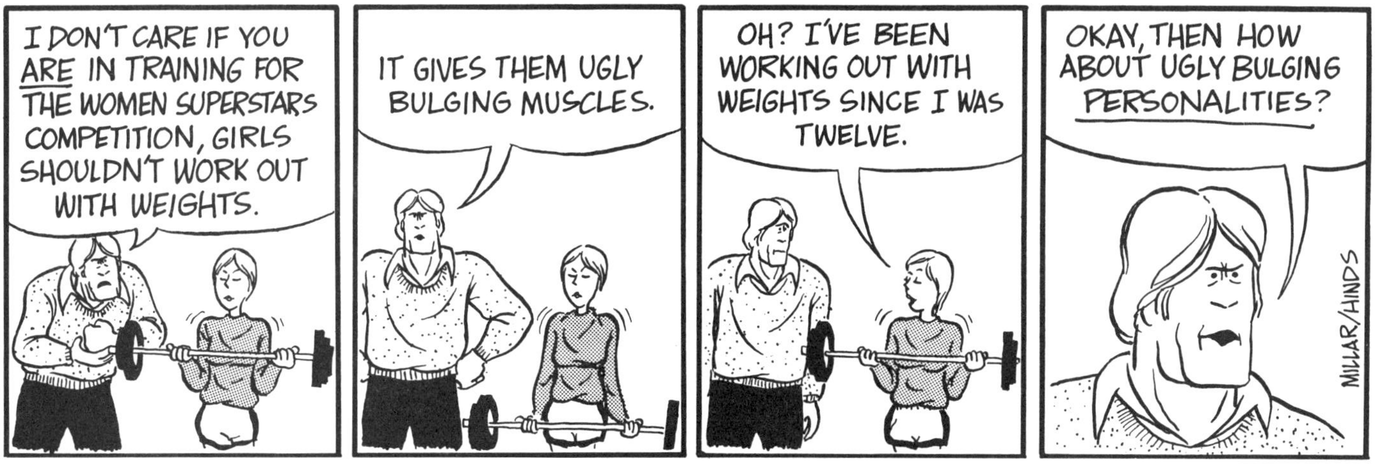
I DON'T CARE IF YOU ARE IN TRAINING FOR THE WOMEN SUPERSTARS COMPETITION, GIRLS SHOULDN'T WORK OUT WITH WEIGHTS.
IT GIVES THEM UGLY BULGING MUSCLES.
OH? I'VE BEEN WORKING OUT WITH WEIGHTS SINCE I WAS TWELVE.
OKAY, THEN HOW ABOUT UGLY BULGING PERSONALITIES?
MILLAR/HINDS

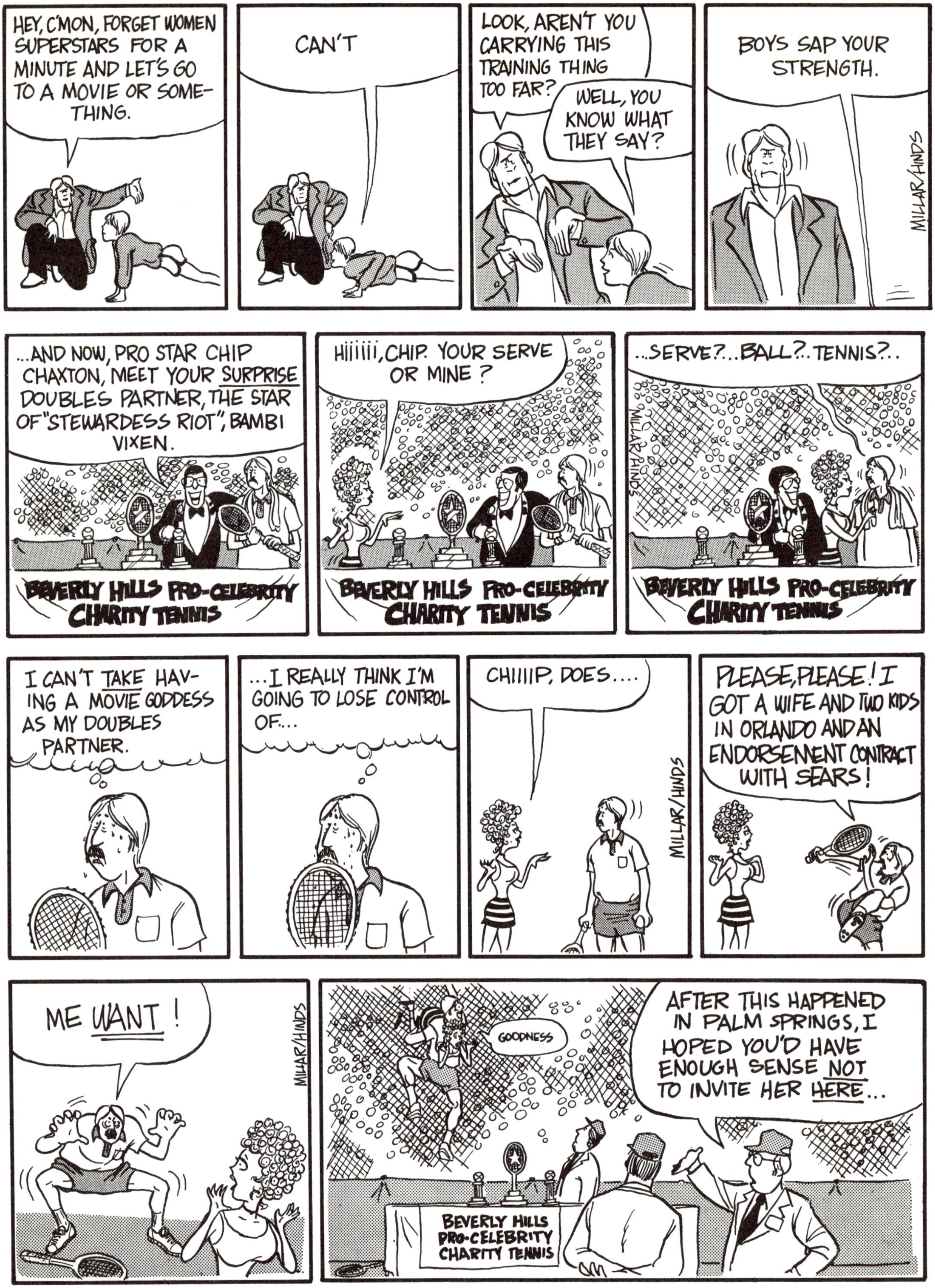
HEY, C'MON, FORGET WOMEN SUPERSTARS FOR A MINUTE AND LET'S GO TO A MOVIE OR SOMETHING.
CAN'T
LOOK, AREN'T YOU CARRYING THIS TRAINING THING TOO FAR?
WELL, YOU KNOW WHAT THEY SAY?
BOYS SAP YOUR STRENGTH.
MILLAR/HINDS
...AND NOW, PRO STAR CHIP CHAXTON, MEET YOUR SURPRISE DOUBLES PARTNER, THE STAR OF "STEWARDESS RIOT", BAMBI VIXEN.
BEVERLY HILLS PRO-CELEBRITY CHARITY TENNIS
HIIIIII, CHIP. YOUR SERVE OR MINE ?
BEVERLY HILLS PRO-CELEBRITY CHARITY TENNIS
...SERVE?...BALL?...TENNIS?..
MILLAR/HINDS
BEVERLY HILLS PRO-CELEBRITY CHARITY TENNIS
I CAN'T TAKE HAVING A MOVIE GODDESS AS MY DOUBLES PARTNER.
...I REALLY THINK I'M GOING TO LOSE CONTROL OF...
CHIIIIP, DOES....
MILLAR/HINDS
PLEASE, PLEASE! I GOT A WIFE AND TWO KIDS IN ORLANDO AND AN ENDORSEMENT CONTRACT WITH SEARS!
ME WANT !
MILLAR/HINDS
GOODNESS
AFTER THIS HAPPENED IN PALM SPRINGS, I HOPED YOU'D HAVE ENOUGH SENSE NOT TO INVITE HER HERE...
BEVERLY HILLS PRO-CELEBRITY CHARITY TENNIS

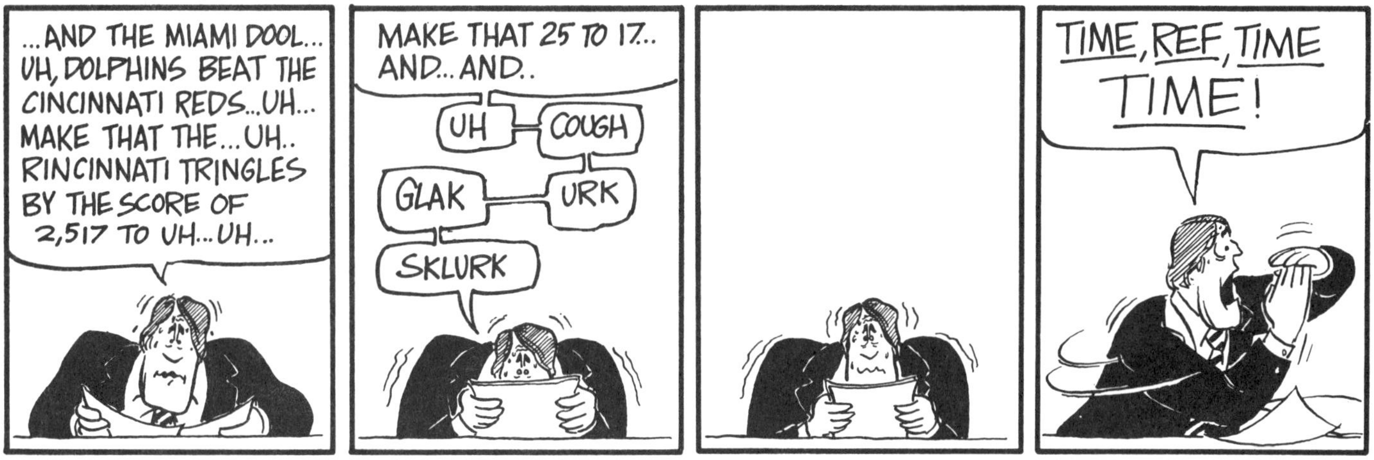
...AND THE MIAMI DOOL... UH, DOLPHINS BEAT THE CINCINNATI REDS...UH... MAKE THAT THE...UH.. RINCINNATI TRINGLES BY THE SCORE OF 2,517 TO UH...UH...
MAKE THAT 25 TO 17.. AND...AND..
UH
COUGH
GLAK
URK
SKLURK
TIME, REF, TIME TIME!

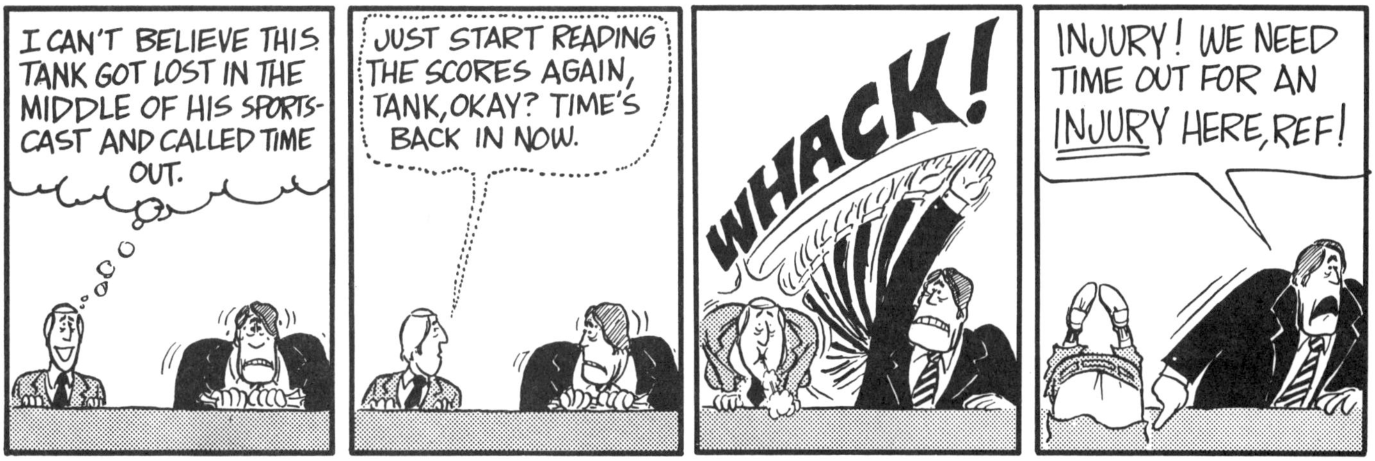
I CAN'T BELIEVE THIS. TANK GOT LOST IN THE MIDDLE OF HIS SPORTSCAST AND CALLED TIME OUT.
JUST START READING THE SCORES AGAIN, TANK, OKAY? TIME'S BACK IN NOW.
WHACK!
INJURY! WE NEED TIME OUT FOR AN INJURY HERE, REF!

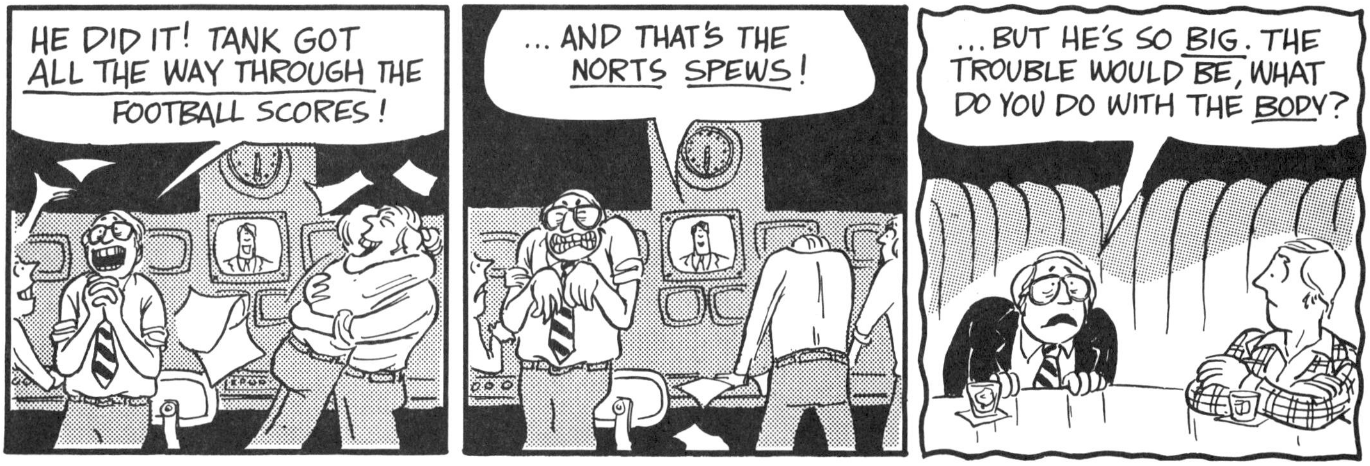
HE DID IT! TANK GOT ALL THE WAY THROUGH THE FOOTBALL SCORES!
... AND THAT'S THE NORTS SPEWS!
... BUT HE'S SO BIG. THE TROUBLE WOULD BE, WHAT DO YOU DO WITH THE BODY?

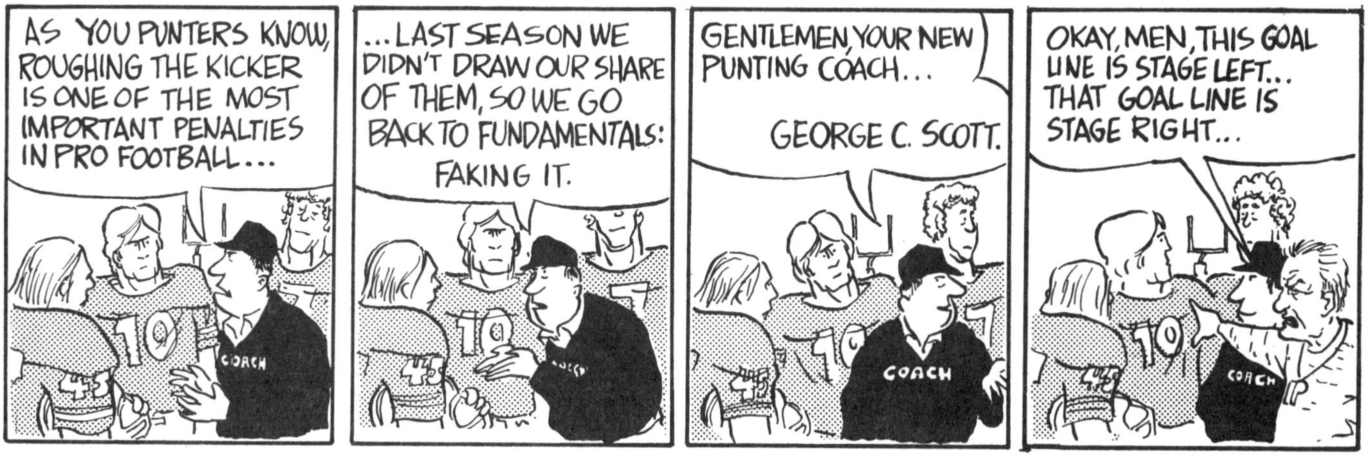
AS YOU PUNTERS KNOW, ROUGHING THE KICKER IS ONE OF THE MOST IMPORTANT PENALTIES IN PRO FOOTBALL...
COACH
...LAST SEASON WE DIDN'T DRAW OUR SHARE OF THEM, SO WE GO BACK TO FUNDAMENTALS: FAKING IT.
GENTLEMEN, YOUR NEW PUNTING COACH... GEORGE C. SCOTT.
COACH
OKAY, MEN, THIS GOAL LINE IS STAGE LEFT... THAT GOAL LINE IS STAGE RIGHT...
COACH

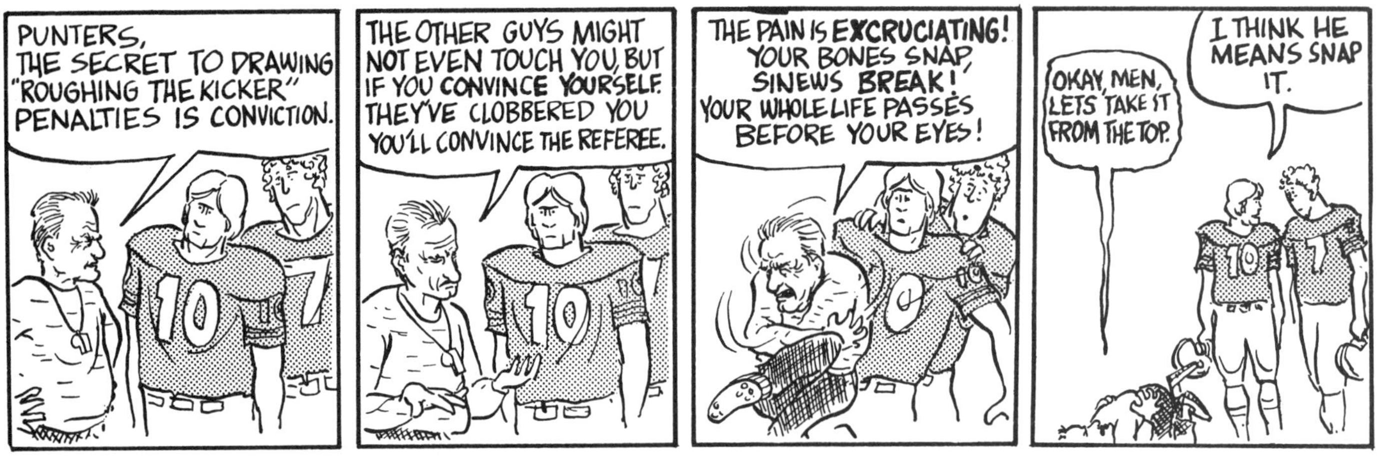
PUNTERS, THE SECRET TO DRAWING "ROUGHING THE KICKER" PENALTIES IS CONVICTION.
THE OTHER GUYS MIGHT NOT EVEN TOUCH YOU, BUT IF YOU CONVINCE YOURSELF THEY'VE CLOBBERED YOU YOU'LL CONVINCE THE REFEREE.
THE PAIN IS EXCRUCIATING! YOUR BONES SNAP, SINEWS BREAK! YOUR WHOLE LIFE PASSES BEFORE YOUR EYES!
OKAY, MEN, LETS TAKE IT FROM THE TOP.
I THINK HE MEANS SNAP IT.

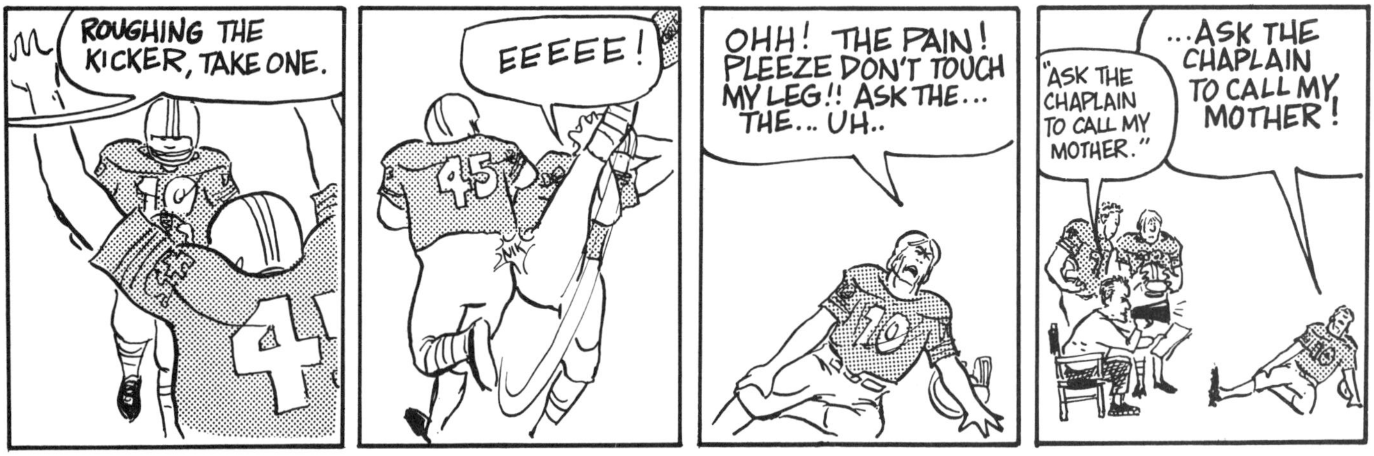
ROUGHING THE KICKER, TAKE ONE.
EEEEE!
OHH! THE PAIN! PLEEZE DON'T TOUCH MY LEG!! ASK THE... THE... UH..
"ASK THE CHAPLAIN TO CALL MY MOTHER."
...ASK THE CHAPLAIN TO CALL MY MOTHER!

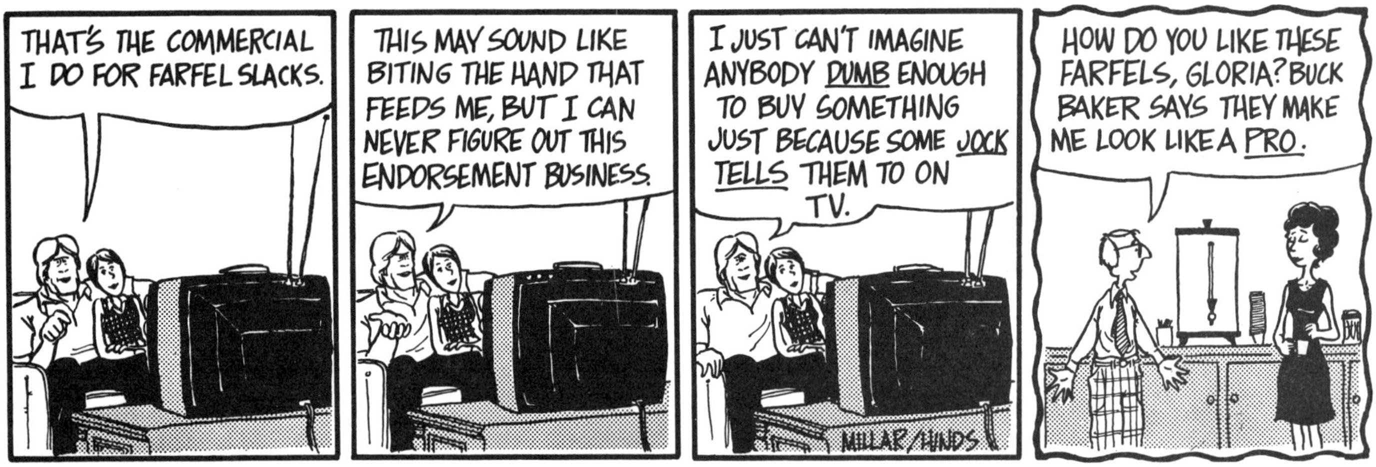
THAT'S THE COMMERCIAL I DO FOR FARFEL SLACKS.
THIS MAY SOUND LIKE BITING THE HAND THAT FEEDS ME, BUT I CAN NEVER FIGURE OUT THIS ENDORSEMENT BUSINESS.
I JUST CAN'T IMAGINE ANYBODY DUMB ENOUGH TO BUY SOMETHING JUST BECAUSE SOME JOCK TELLS THEM TO ON TV.
MILLAR/HINDS
HOW DO YOU LIKE THESE FARFELS, GLORIA? BUCK BAKER SAYS THEY MAKE ME LOOK LIKE A PRO.

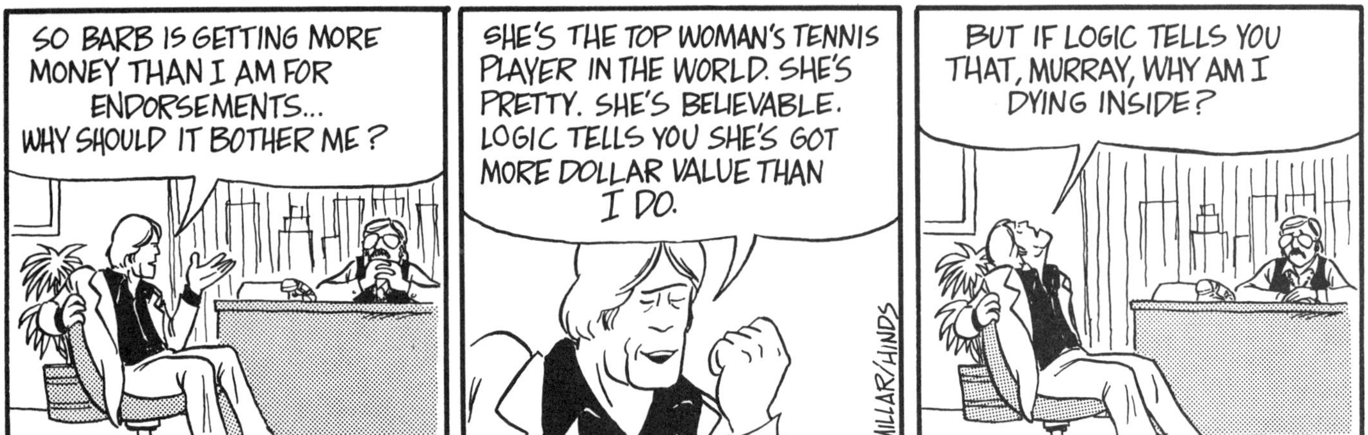
SO BARB IS GETTING MORE MONEY THAN I AM FOR ENDORSEMENTS... WHY SHOULD IT BOTHER ME?
SHE'S THE TOP WOMAN'S TENNIS PLAYER IN THE WORLD. SHE'S PRETTY. SHE'S BELIEVABLE. LOGIC TELLS YOU SHE'S GOT MORE DOLLAR VALUE THAN I DO.
MILLAR/HINDS
BUT IF LOGIC TELLS YOU THAT, MURRAY, WHY AM I DYING INSIDE?

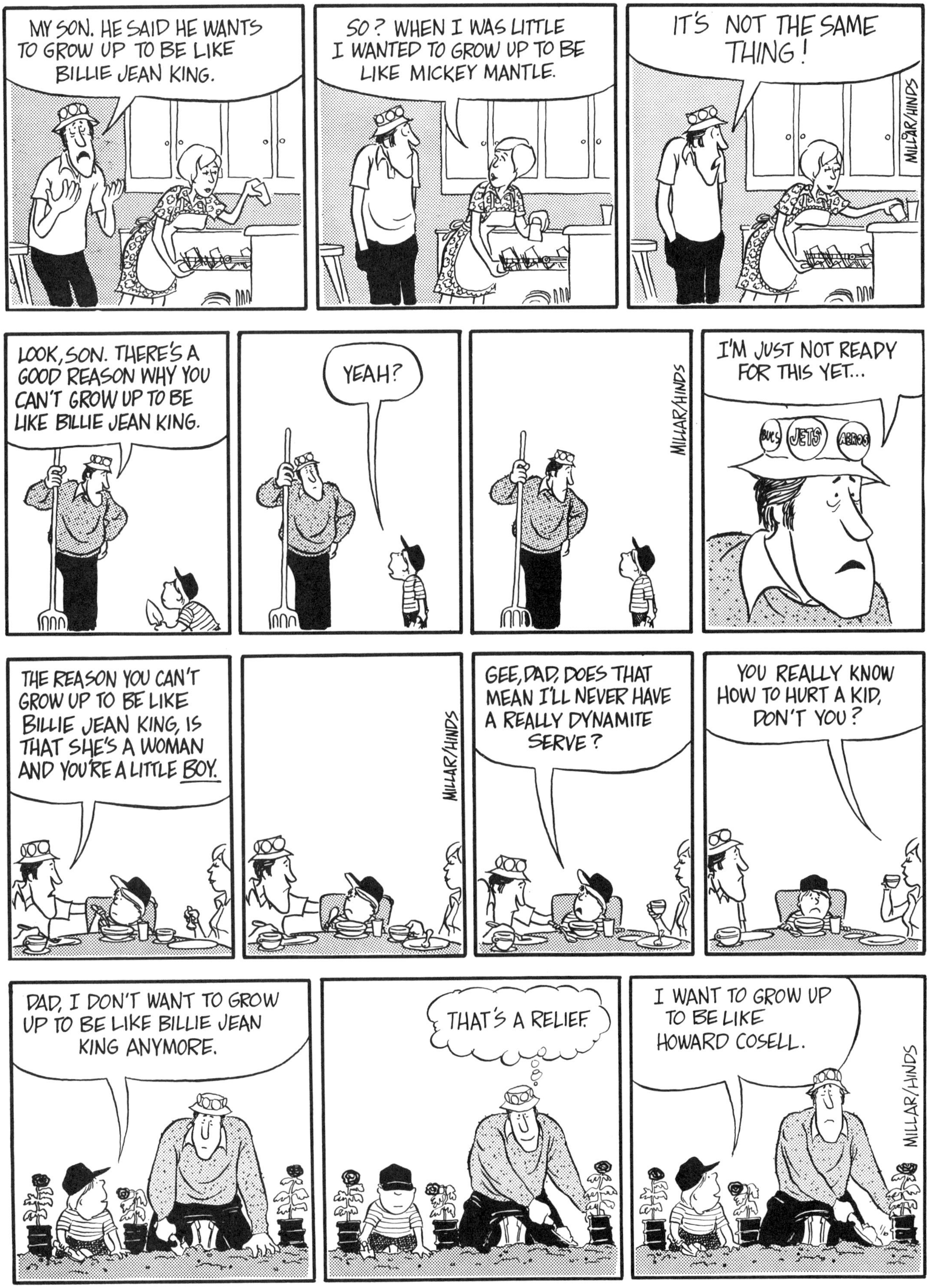

MY SON. HE SAID HE WANTS TO GROW UP TO BE LIKE BILLIE JEAN KING.
SO? WHEN I WAS LITTLE I WANTED TO GROW UP TO BE LIKE MICKEY MANTLE.
IT'S NOT THE SAME THING!
MILLAR/HINDS
LOOK, SON. THERE'S A GOOD REASON WHY YOU CAN'T GROW UP TO BE LIKE BILLIE JEAN KING.
YEAH?
MILLAR/HINDS
I'M JUST NOT READY FOR THIS YET...
BUCS
JETS
ABROS
THE REASON YOU CAN'T GROW UP TO BE LIKE BILLIE JEAN KING, IS THAT SHE'S A WOMAN AND YOU'RE A LITTLE BOY.
MILLAR/HINDS
GEE, DAD, DOES THAT MEAN I'LL NEVER HAVE A REALLY DYNAMITE SERVE?
YOU REALLY KNOW HOW TO HURT A KID, DON'T YOU?
DAD, I DON'T WANT TO GROW UP TO BE LIKE BILLIE JEAN KING ANYMORE.
THAT'S A RELIEF.
I WANT TO GROW UP TO BE LIKE HOWARD COSELL.
MILLAR/HINDS

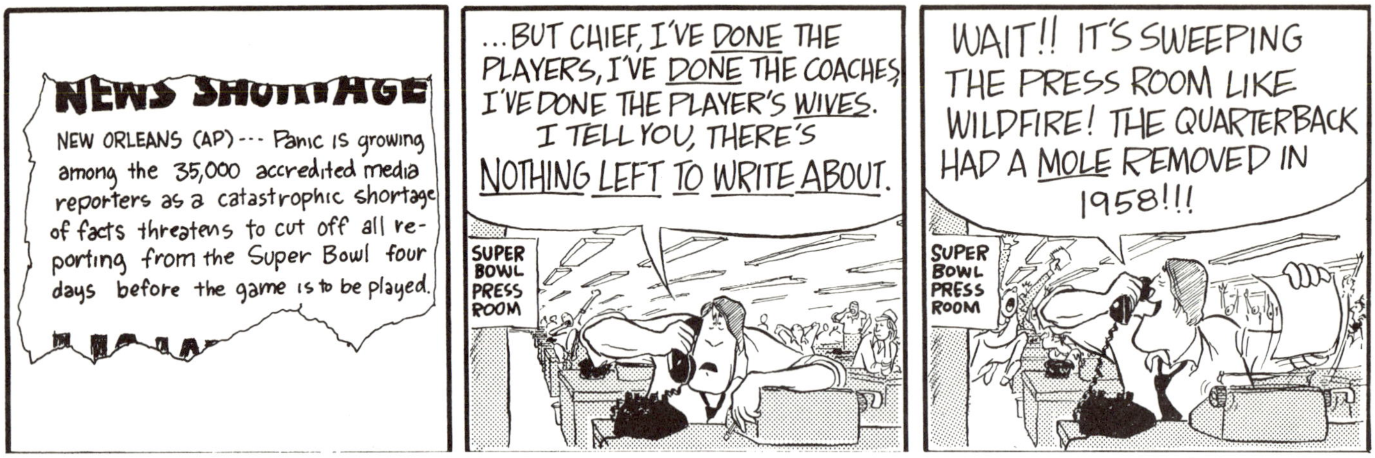
NEWS SHORTAGE
NEW ORLEANS (AP) --- Panic is growing among the 35,000 accredited media reporters as a catastrophic shortage of facts threatens to cut off all reporting from the Super Bowl four days before the game is to be played.
...BUT CHIEF, I'VE DONE THE PLAYERS, I'VE DONE THE COACHES, I'VE DONE THE PLAYER'S WIVES. I TELL YOU, THERE'S NOTHING LEFT TO WRITE ABOUT.
SUPER BOWL PRESS ROOM
WAIT!! IT'S SWEEPING THE PRESS ROOM LIKE WILDFIRE! THE QUARTERBACK HAD A MOLE REMOVED IN 1958!!!
SUPER BOWL PRESS ROOM

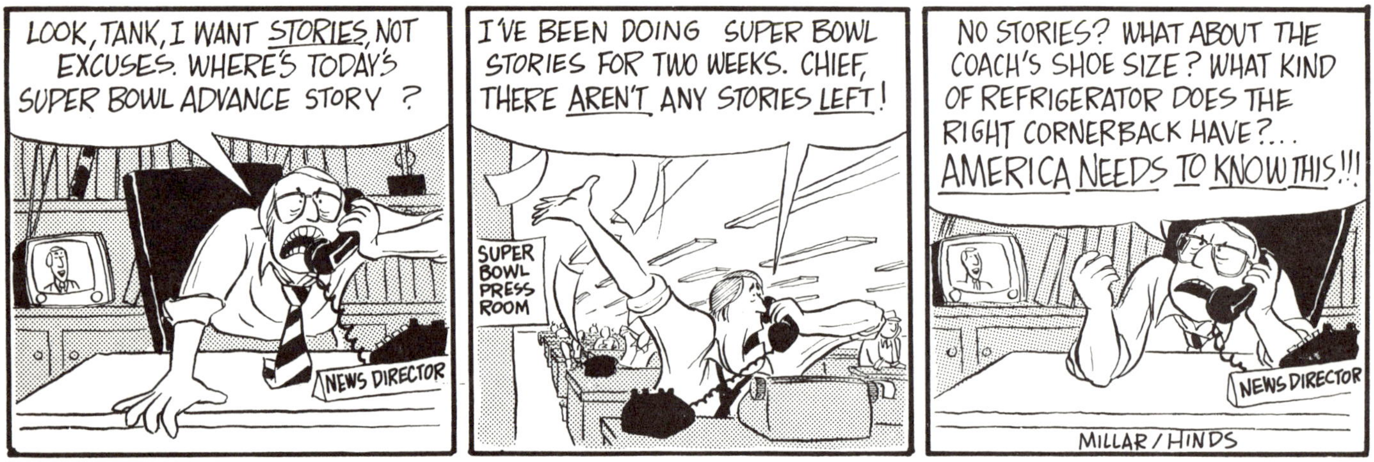
LOOK, TANK, I WANT STORIES, NOT EXCUSES. WHERE'S TODAY'S SUPER BOWL ADVANCE STORY ?
NEWS DIRECTOR
I'VE BEEN DOING SUPER BOWL STORIES FOR TWO WEEKS. CHIEF, THERE AREN'T ANY STORIES LEFT!
SUPER BOWL PRESS ROOM
NO STORIES? WHAT ABOUT THE COACH'S SHOE SIZE? WHAT KIND OF REFRIGERATOR DOES THE RIGHT CORNERBACK HAVE?... AMERICA NEEDS TO KNOW THIS!!!
NEWS DIRECTOR
MILLAR/HINDS

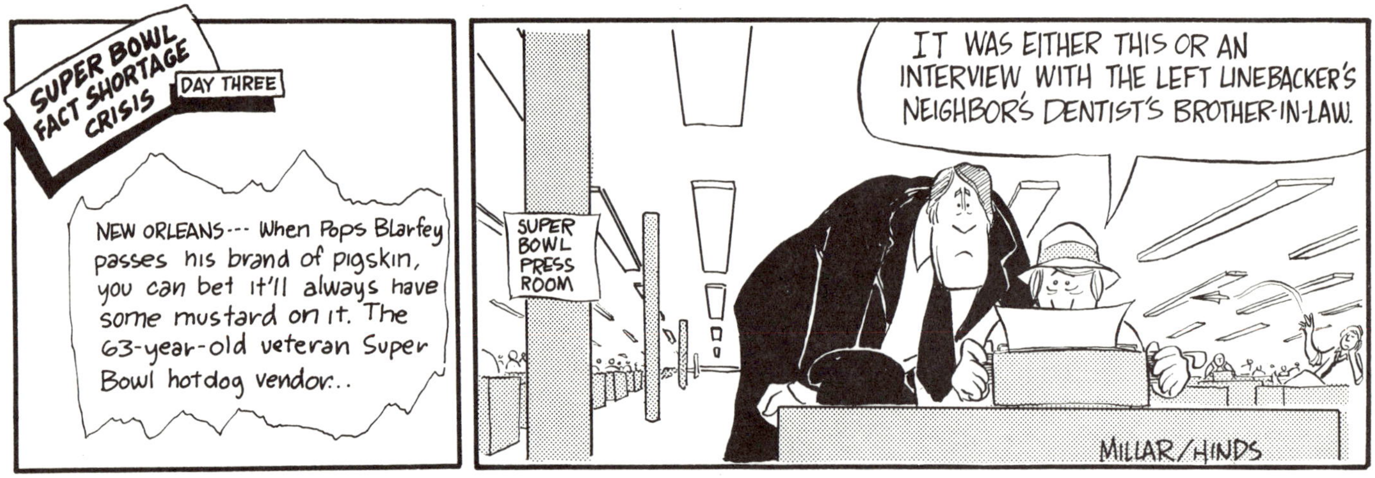
SUPER BOWL FACT SHORTAGE CRISIS
DAY THREE
NEW ORLEANS--- When Pops Blarfey passes his brand of pigskin, you can bet it'll always have some mustard on it. The 63-year-old veteran Super Bowl hotdog vendor..
IT WAS EITHER THIS OR AN INTERVIEW WITH THE LEFT LINEBACKER'S NEIGHBOR'S DENTIST'S BROTHER-IN-LAW.
SUPER BOWL PRESS ROOM
MILLAR/HINDS

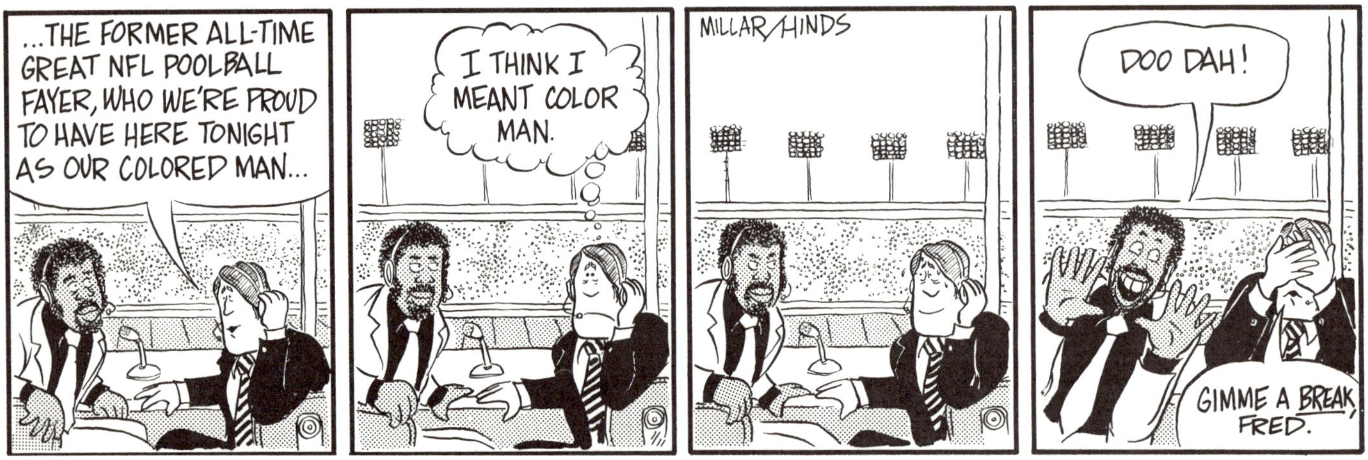
...THE FORMER ALL-TIME GREAT NFL POOLBALL FAYER, WHO WE'RE PROUD TO HAVE HERE TONIGHT AS OUR COLORED MAN...
I THINK I MEANT COLOR MAN.
MILLAR/HINDS
DOO DAH!
GIMME A BREAK, FRED.

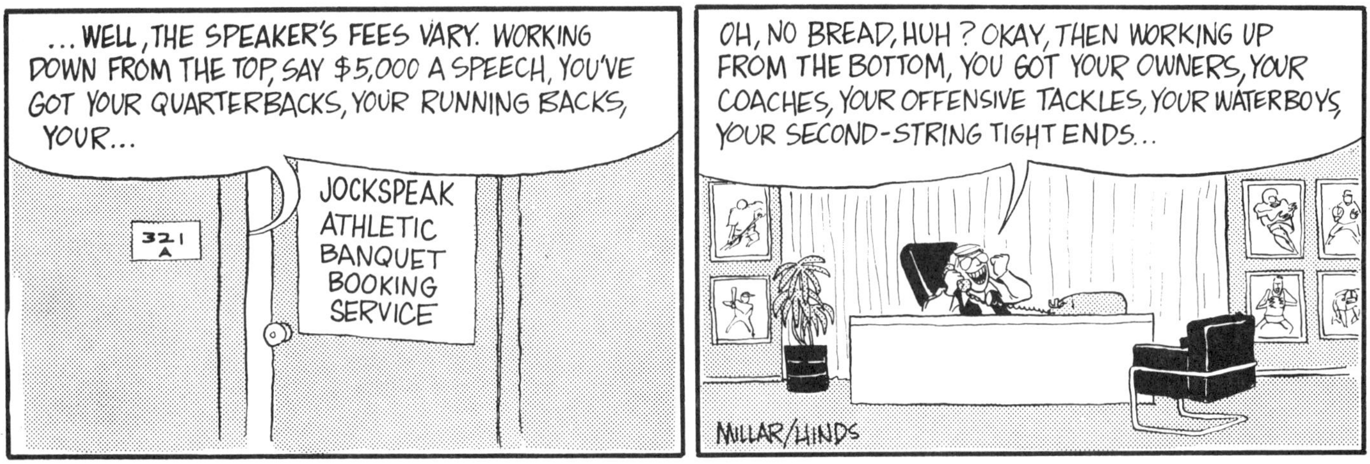
...WELL, THE SPEAKER'S FEES VARY. WORKING DOWN FROM THE TOP, SAY $5,000 A SPEECH, YOU'VE GOT YOUR QUARTERBACKS, YOUR RUNNING BACKS, YOUR...
321 A
JOCKSPEAK ATHLETIC BANQUET BOOKING SERVICE
OH, NO BREAD, HUH? OKAY, THEN WORKING UP FROM THE BOTTOM, YOU GOT YOUR OWNERS, YOUR COACHES, YOUR OFFENSIVE TACKLES, YOUR WATERBOYS, YOUR SECOND-STRING TIGHT ENDS...
MILLAR/HINDS

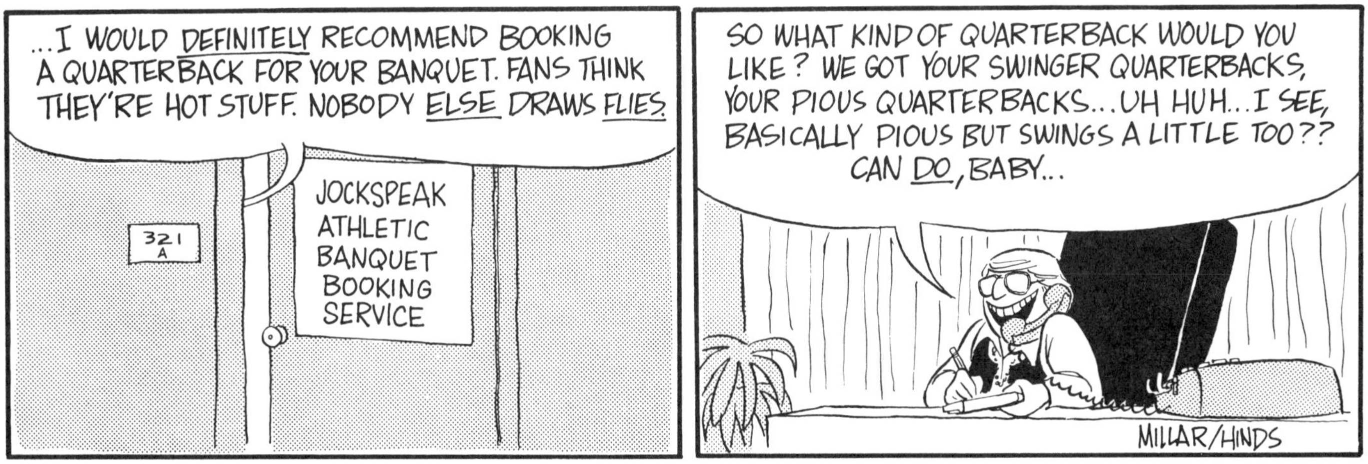
...I WOULD DEFINITELY RECOMMEND BOOKING A QUARTERBACK FOR YOUR BANQUET. FANS THINK THEY'RE HOT STUFF. NOBODY ELSE DRAWS FLIES.
321 A
JOCKSPEAK ATHLETIC BANQUET BOOKING SERVICE
SO WHAT KIND OF QUARTERBACK WOULD YOU LIKE? WE GOT YOUR SWINGER QUARTERBACKS, YOUR PIOUS QUARTERBACKS...UH HUH...I SEE, BASICALLY PIOUS BUT SWINGS A LITTLE TOO?? CAN DO, BABY...
MILLAR/HINDS

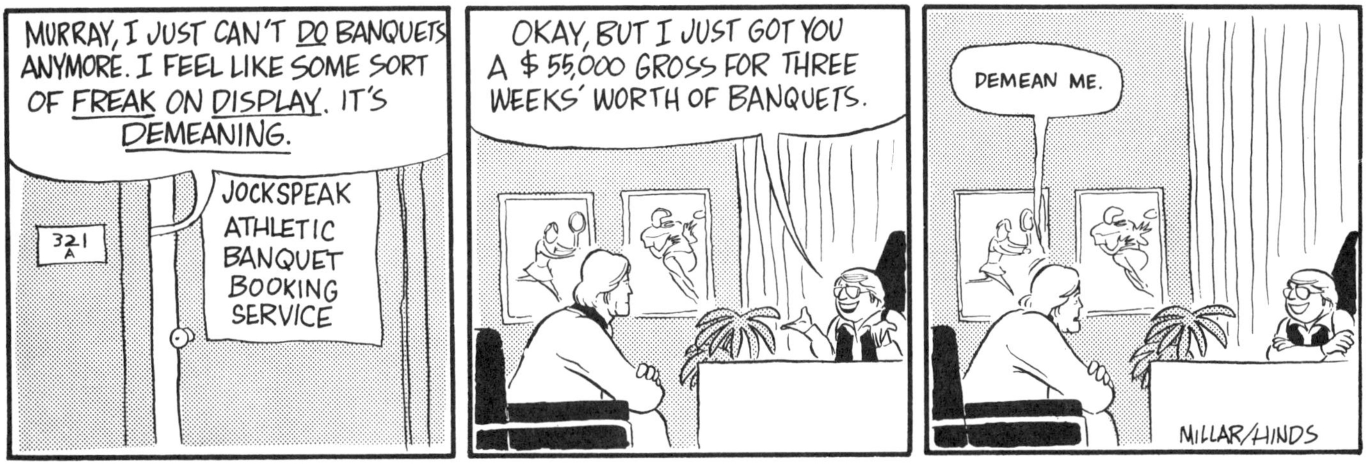
MURRAY, I JUST CAN'T DO BANQUETS ANYMORE. I FEEL LIKE SOME SORT OF FREAK ON DISPLAY. IT'S DEMEANING.
321 A
JOCKSPEAK ATHLETIC BANQUET BOOKING SERVICE
OKAY, BUT I JUST GOT YOU A $55,000 GROSS FOR THREE WEEKS' WORTH OF BANQUETS.
DEMEAN ME.
MILLAR/HINDS

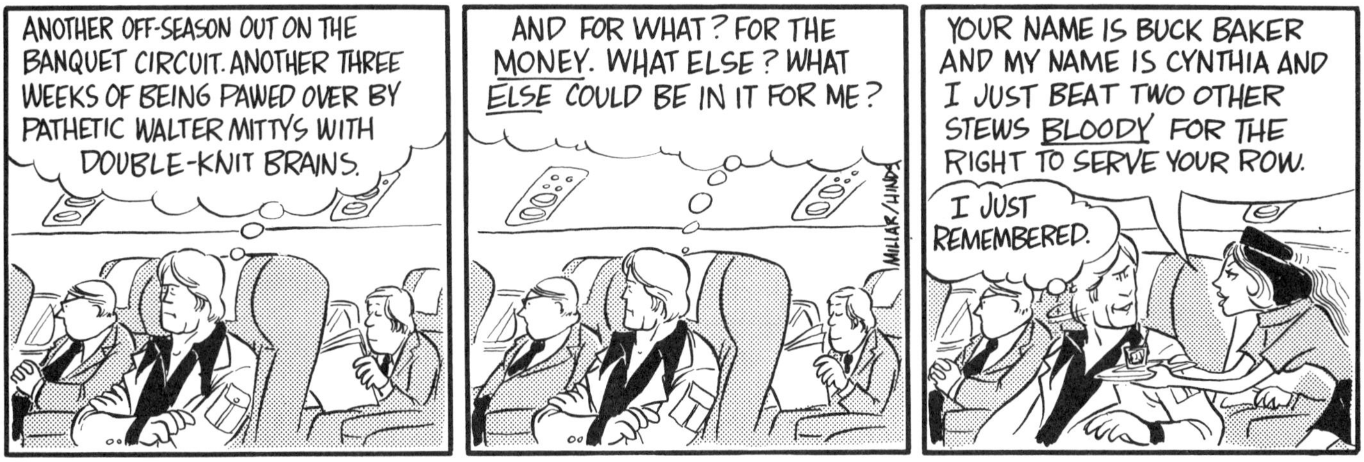
ANOTHER OFF-SEASON OUT ON THE BANQUET CIRCUIT. ANOTHER THREE WEEKS OF BEING PAWED OVER BY PATHETIC WALTER MITTYS WITH DOUBLE-KNIT BRAINS.
AND FOR WHAT? FOR THE MONEY. WHAT ELSE? WHAT ELSE COULD BE IN IT FOR ME?
MILLAR/HINDS
YOUR NAME IS BUCK BAKER AND MY NAME IS CYNTHIA AND I JUST BEAT TWO OTHER STEWS BLOODY FOR THE RIGHT TO SERVE YOUR ROW.
I JUST REMEMBERED.

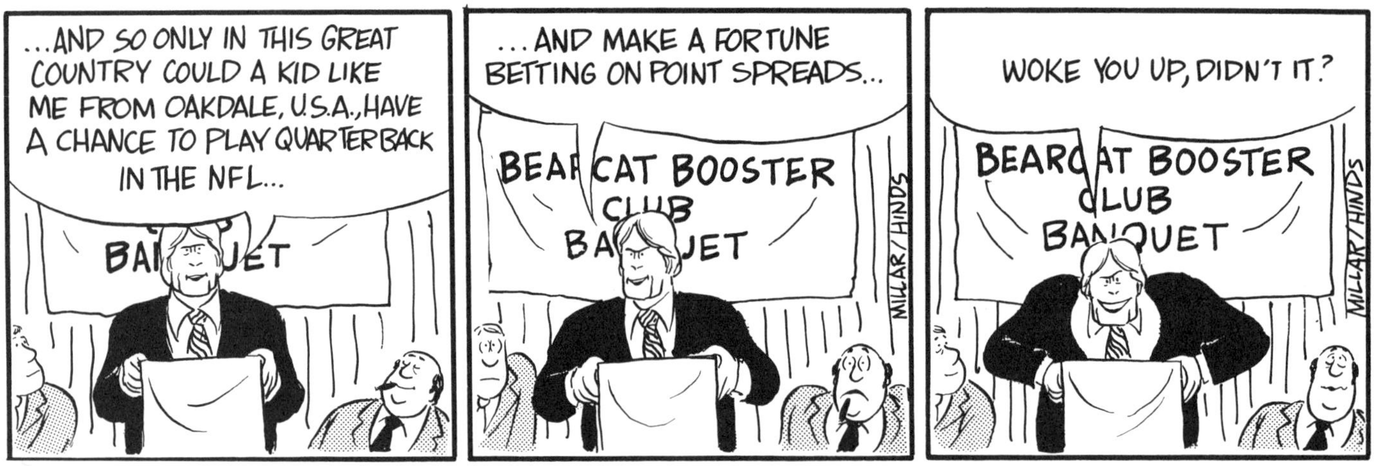
...AND SO ONLY IN THIS GREAT COUNTRY COULD A KID LIKE ME FROM OAKDALE, U.S.A., HAVE A CHANCE TO PLAY QUARTERBACK IN THE NFL...
...AND MAKE A FORTUNE BETTING ON POINT SPREADS...
WOKE YOU UP, DIDN'T IT?
BEARCAT BOOSTER CLUB BANQUET
MILLAR/HINDS

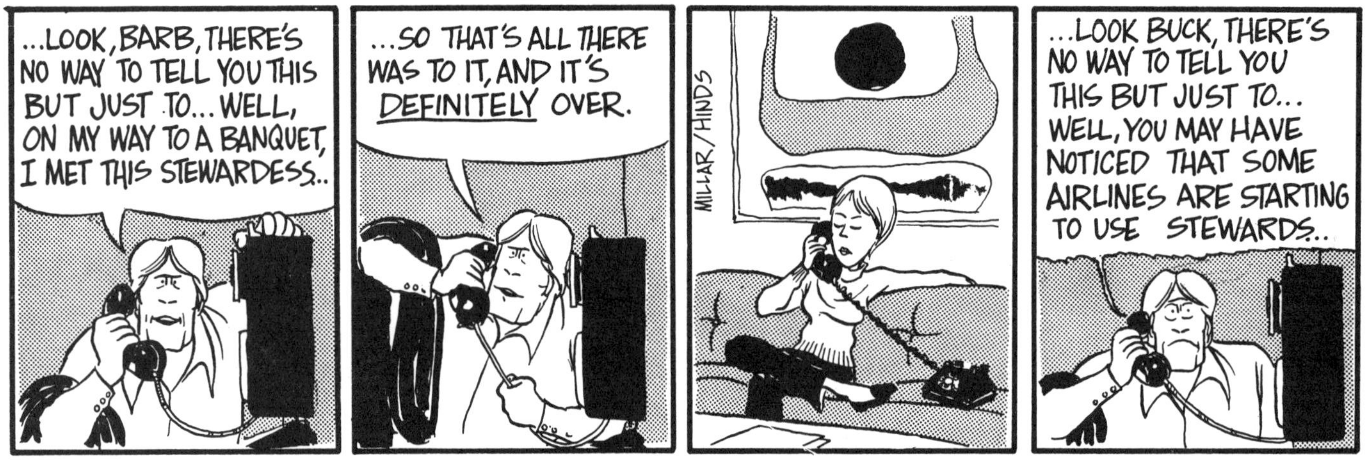
...LOOK, BARB, THERE'S NO WAY TO TELL YOU THIS BUT JUST TO... WELL, ON MY WAY TO A BANQUET, I MET THIS STEWARDESS..
...SO THAT'S ALL THERE WAS TO IT, AND IT'S DEFINITELY OVER.
...LOOK BUCK, THERE'S NO WAY TO TELL YOU THIS BUT JUST TO... WELL, YOU MAY HAVE NOTICED THAT SOME AIRLINES ARE STARTING TO USE STEWARDS..
MILLAR/HINDS

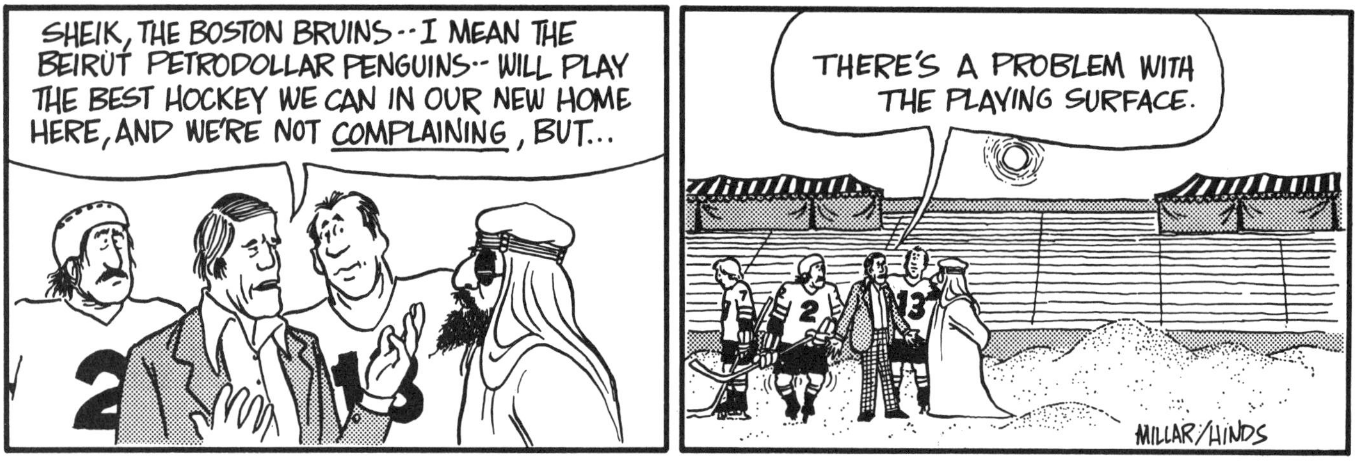
SHEIK, THE BOSTON BRUINS -- I MEAN THE BEIRUT PETRODOLLAR PENGUINS -- WILL PLAY THE BEST HOCKEY WE CAN IN OUR NEW HOME HERE, AND WE'RE NOT COMPLAINING, BUT...
THERE'S A PROBLEM WITH THE PLAYING SURFACE.
MILLAR/HINDS

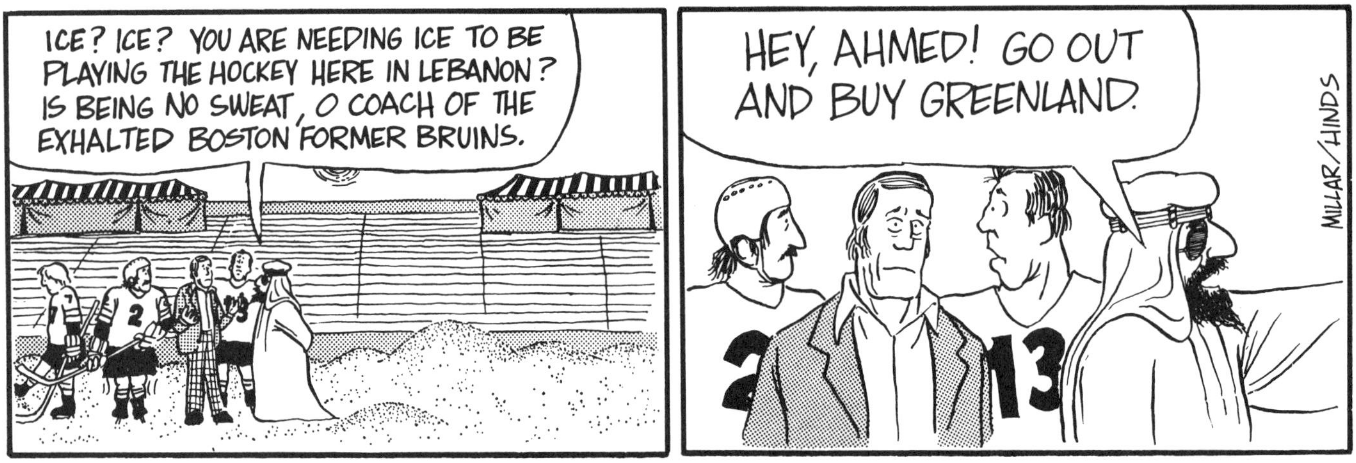
ICE? ICE? YOU ARE NEEDING ICE TO BE PLAYING THE HOCKEY HERE IN LEBANON? IS BEING NO SWEAT, O COACH OF THE EXHALTED BOSTON FORMER BRUINS.
HEY, AHMED! GO OUT AND BUY GREENLAND.
MILLAR/HINDS

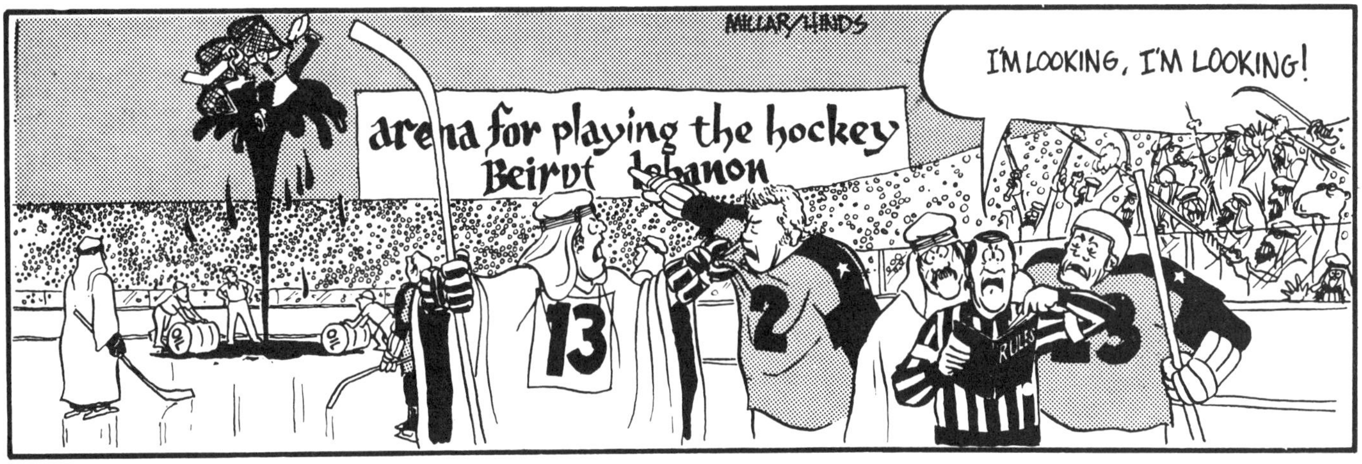
MILLAR/HINDS
arena for playing the hockey
Beirut Lebanon
I'M LOOKING, I'M LOOKING!
RULES

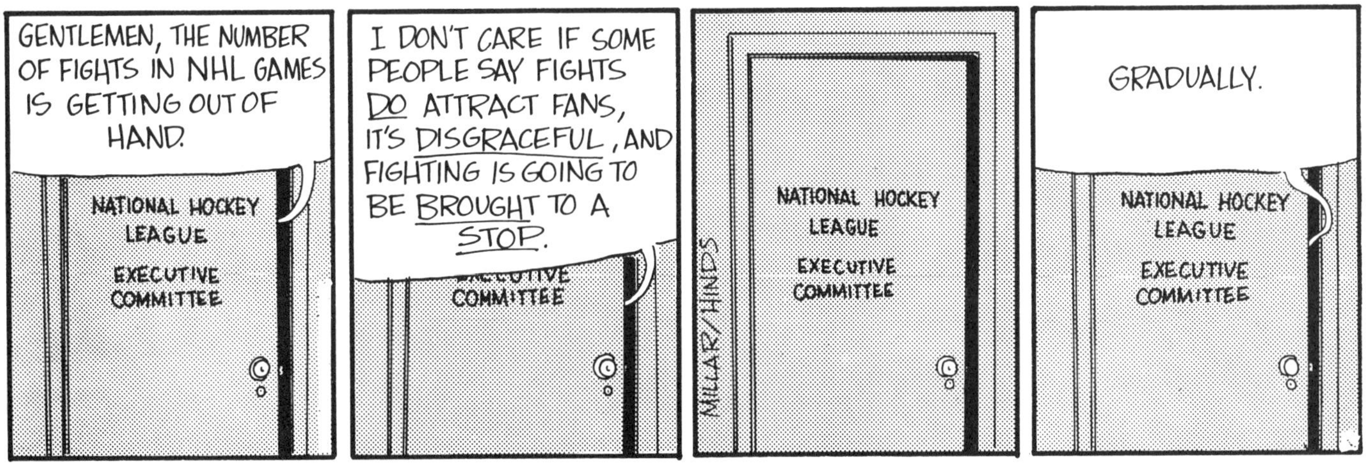
GENTLEMEN, THE NUMBER OF FIGHTS IN NHL GAMES IS GETTING OUT OF HAND.
NATIONAL HOCKEY LEAGUE EXECUTIVE COMMITTEE
I DON'T CARE IF SOME PEOPLE SAY FIGHTS DO ATTRACT FANS, IT'S DISGRACEFUL, AND FIGHTING IS GOING TO BE BROUGHT TO A STOP.
MILLAR/HINDS
NATIONAL HOCKEY LEAGUE EXECUTIVE COMMITTEE
GRADUALLY.
NATIONAL HOCKEY LEAGUE EXECUTIVE COMMITTEE

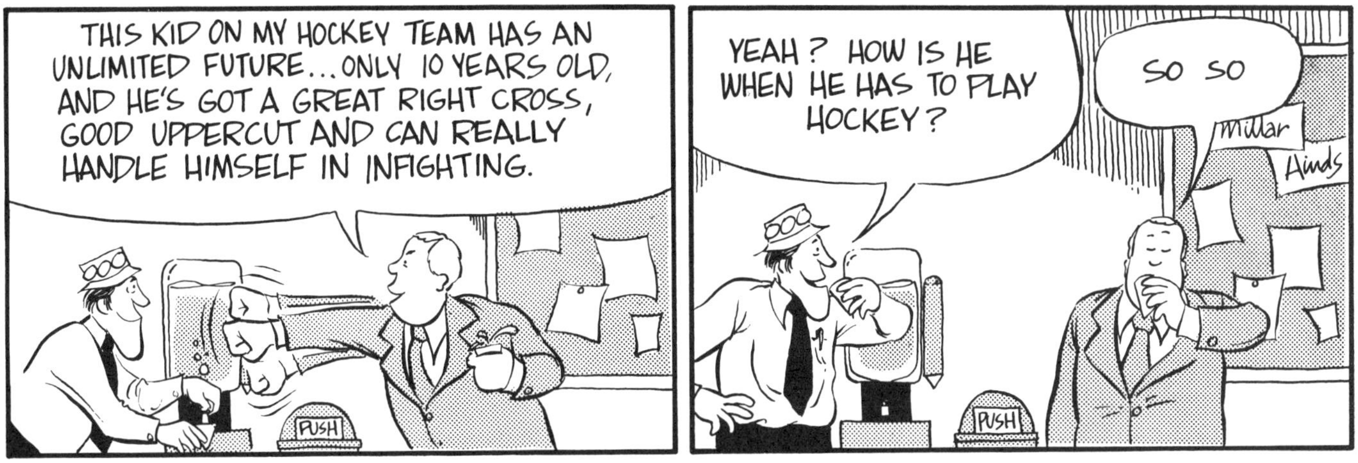
THIS KID ON MY HOCKEY TEAM HAS AN UNLIMITED FUTURE... ONLY 10 YEARS OLD, AND HE'S GOT A GREAT RIGHT CROSS, GOOD UPPERCUT AND CAN REALLY HANDLE HIMSELF IN INFIGHTING.
PUSH
YEAH? HOW IS HE WHEN HE HAS TO PLAY HOCKEY?
SO SO
Millar Hinds
PUSH

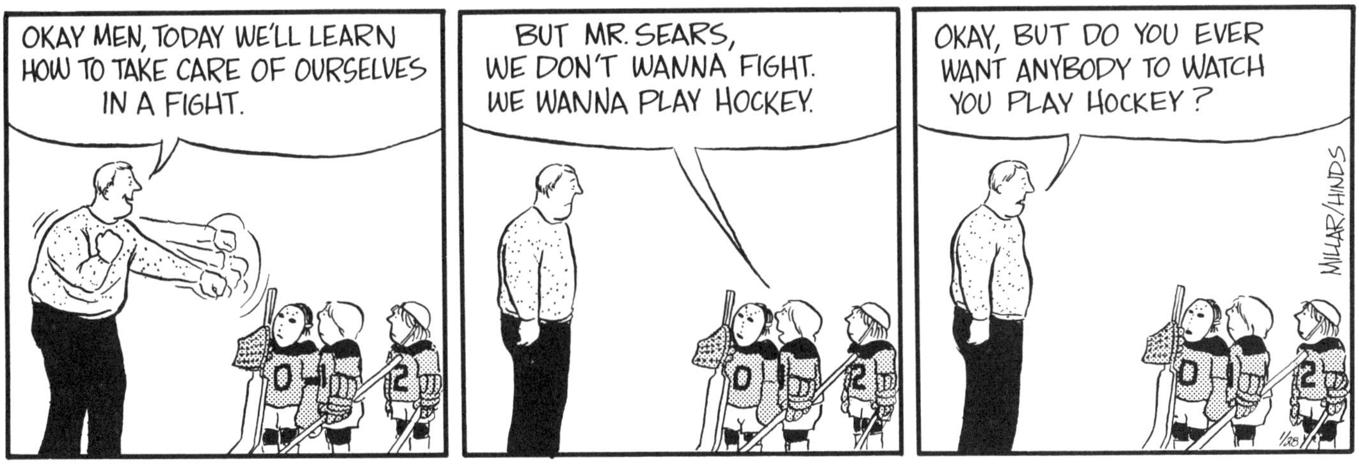
OKAY MEN, TODAY WE'LL LEARN HOW TO TAKE CARE OF OURSELVES IN A FIGHT.
BUT MR. SEARS, WE DON'T WANNA FIGHT. WE WANNA PLAY HOCKEY.
OKAY, BUT DO YOU EVER WANT ANYBODY TO WATCH YOU PLAY HOCKEY?
MILLAR/HINDS

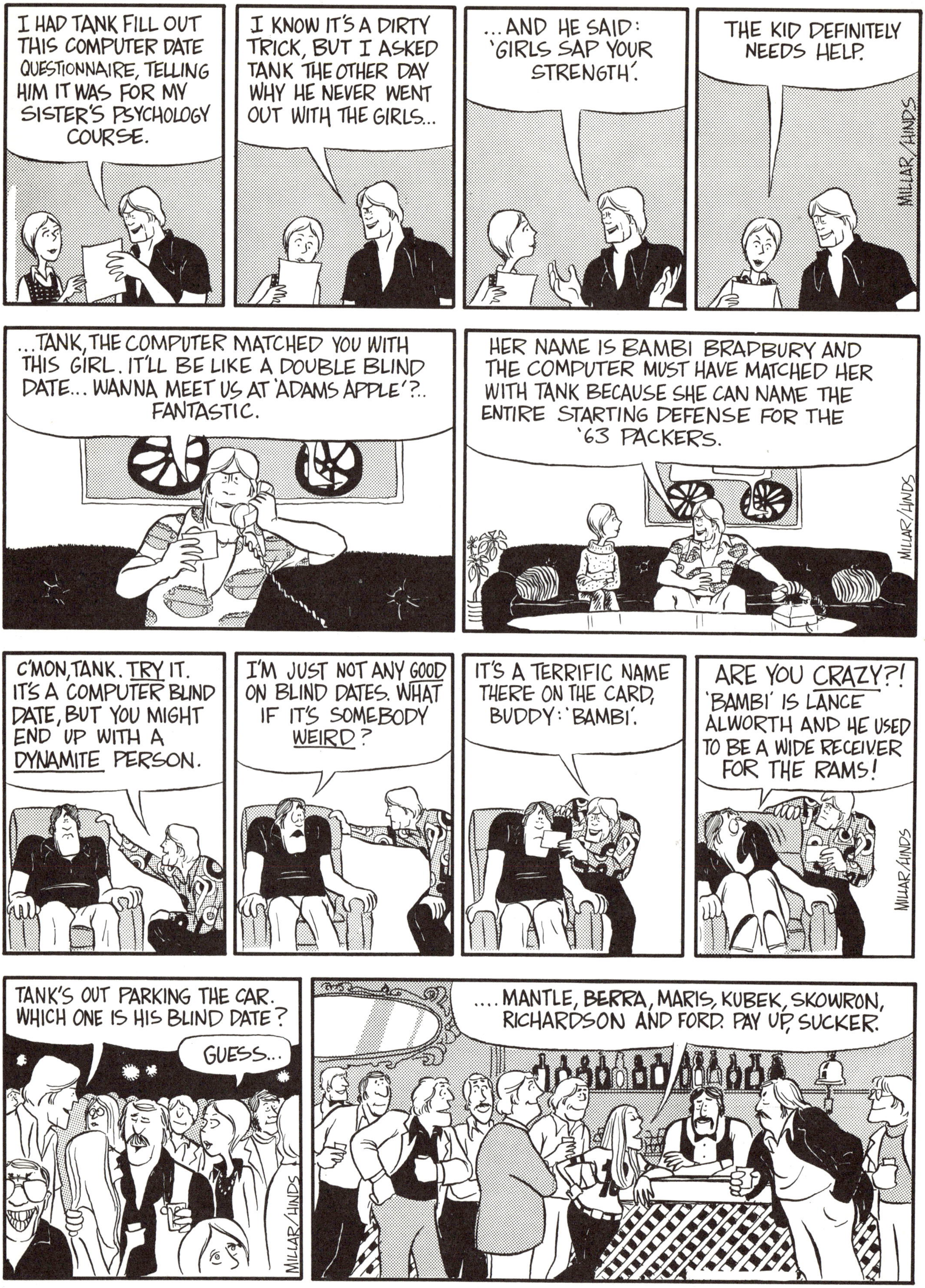
I HAD TANK FILL OUT THIS COMPUTER DATE QUESTIONNAIRE, TELLING HIM IT WAS FOR MY SISTER'S PSYCHOLOGY COURSE.
I KNOW IT'S A DIRTY TRICK, BUT I ASKED TANK THE OTHER DAY WHY HE NEVER WENT OUT WITH THE GIRLS...
...AND HE SAID: 'GIRLS SAP YOUR STRENGTH'.
THE KID DEFINITELY NEEDS HELP.
MILLAR/HINDS
...TANK, THE COMPUTER MATCHED YOU WITH THIS GIRL. IT'LL BE LIKE A DOUBLE BLIND DATE... WANNA MEET US AT 'ADAMS APPLE'?.. FANTASTIC.
HER NAME IS BAMBI BRADBURY AND THE COMPUTER MUST HAVE MATCHED HER WITH TANK BECAUSE SHE CAN NAME THE ENTIRE STARTING DEFENSE FOR THE '63 PACKERS.
MILLAR/HINDS
C'MON, TANK. TRY IT. IT'S A COMPUTER BLIND DATE, BUT YOU MIGHT END UP WITH A DYNAMITE PERSON.
I'M JUST NOT ANY GOOD ON BLIND DATES. WHAT IF IT'S SOMEBODY WEIRD?
IT'S A TERRIFIC NAME THERE ON THE CARD, BUDDY: 'BAMBI'.
ARE YOU CRAZY?! 'BAMBI' IS LANCE ALWORTH AND HE USED TO BE A WIDE RECEIVER FOR THE RAMS!
MILLAR/HINDS
TANK'S OUT PARKING THE CAR. WHICH ONE IS HIS BLIND DATE?
GUESS...
MILLAR/HINDS
....MANTLE, BERRA, MARIS, KUBEK, SKOWRON, RICHARDSON AND FORD. PAY UP, SUCKER.

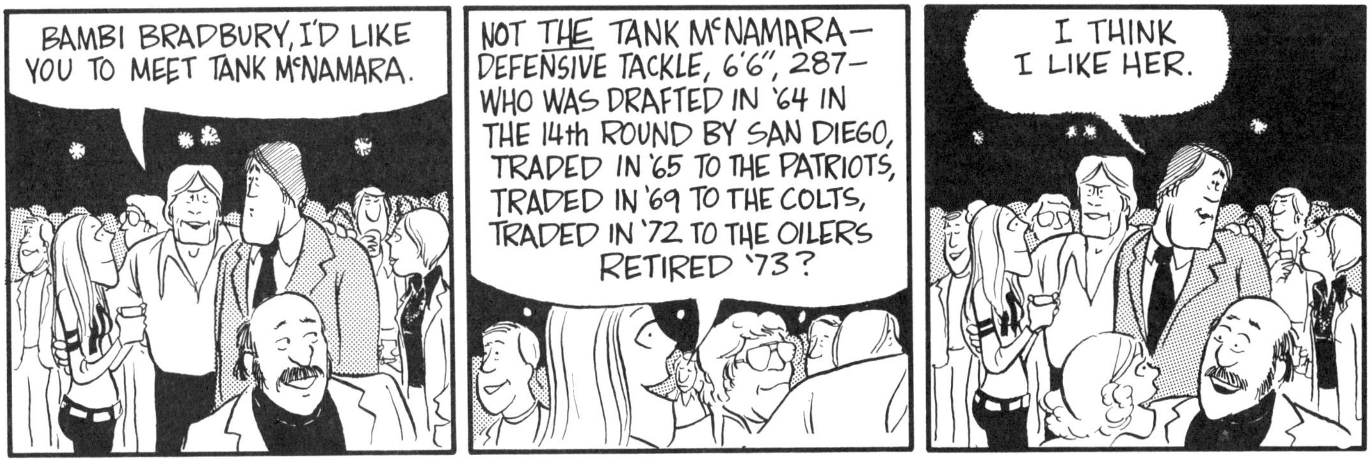
BAMBI BRADBURY, I'D LIKE YOU TO MEET TANK McNAMARA.
NOT THE TANK McNAMARA— DEFENSIVE TACKLE, 6'6", 287— WHO WAS DRAFTED IN '64 IN THE 14th ROUND BY SAN DIEGO, TRADED IN '65 TO THE PATRIOTS, TRADED IN '69 TO THE COLTS, TRADED IN '72 TO THE OILERS RETIRED '73?
I THINK I LIKE HER.

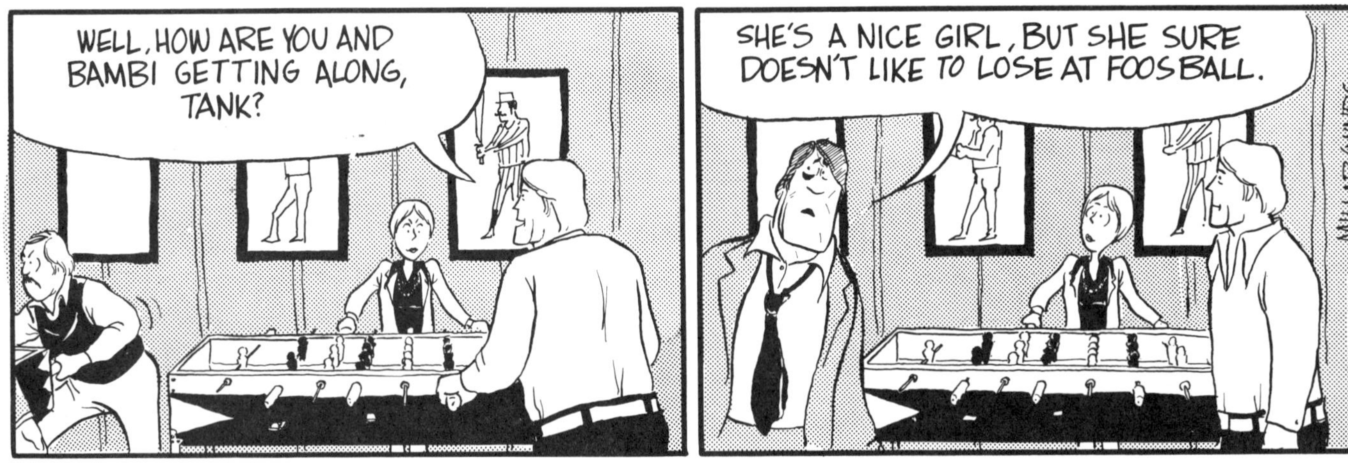
WELL, HOW ARE YOU AND BAMBI GETTING ALONG, TANK?
SHE'S A NICE GIRL, BUT SHE SURE DOESN'T LIKE TO LOSE AT FOOSBALL.
MILLAR/HINDS

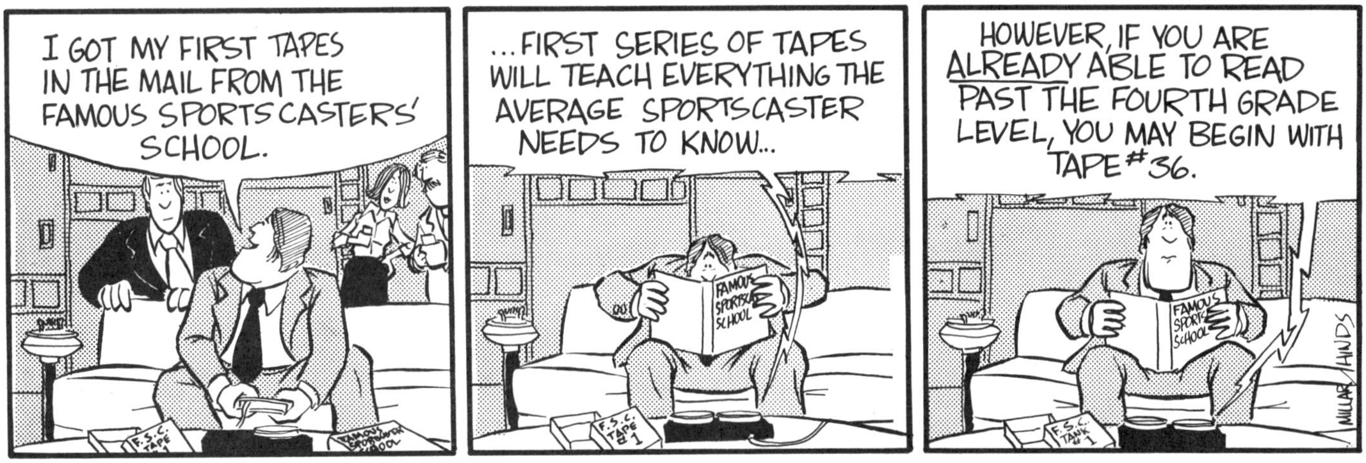
I GOT MY FIRST TAPES IN THE MAIL FROM THE FAMOUS SPORTSCASTERS' SCHOOL.
...FIRST SERIES OF TAPES WILL TEACH EVERYTHING THE AVERAGE SPORTSCASTER NEEDS TO KNOW...
FAMOUS SPORTSCASTER SCHOOL
HOWEVER, IF YOU ARE ALREADY ABLE TO READ PAST THE FOURTH GRADE LEVEL, YOU MAY BEGIN WITH TAPE #36.
F.S.C. TAPE #1
MILLAR/HINDS

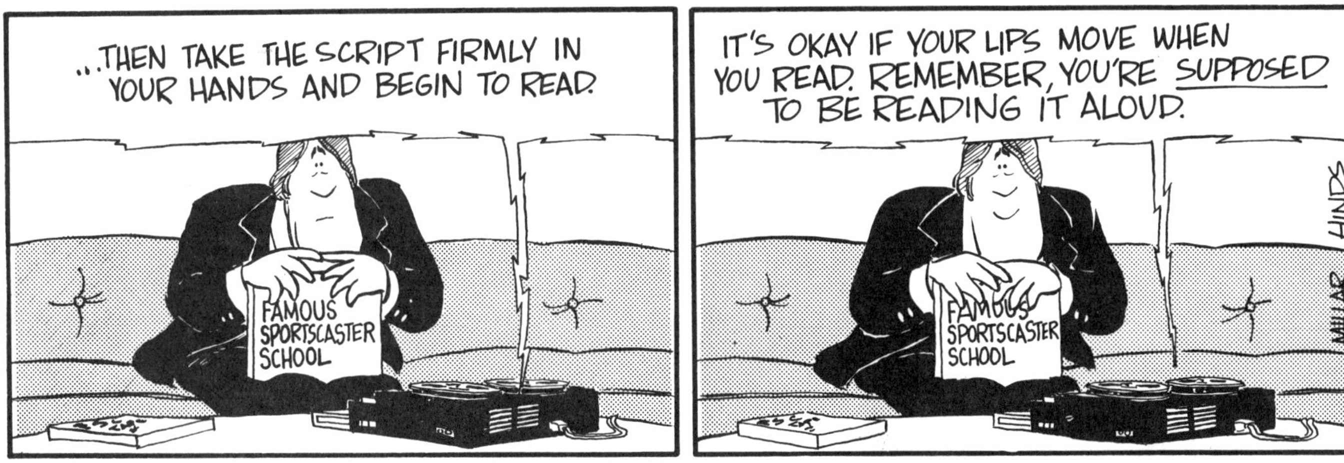
...THEN TAKE THE SCRIPT FIRMLY IN YOUR HANDS AND BEGIN TO READ.
FAMOUS SPORTSCASTER SCHOOL
IT'S OKAY IF YOUR LIPS MOVE WHEN YOU READ. REMEMBER, YOU'RE SUPPOSED TO BE READING IT ALOUD.
FAMOUS SPORTSCASTER SCHOOL
MILLAR HINDS

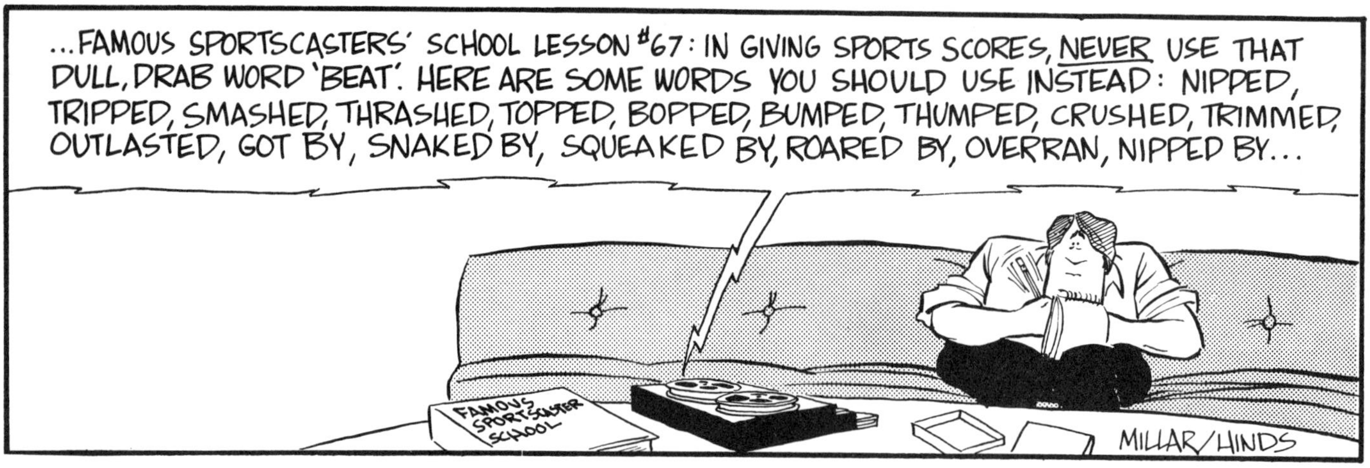
...FAMOUS SPORTSCASTERS' SCHOOL LESSON #67: IN GIVING SPORTS SCORES, NEVER USE THAT DULL, DRAB WORD 'BEAT'. HERE ARE SOME WORDS YOU SHOULD USE INSTEAD: NIPPED, TRIPPED, SMASHED, THRASHED, TOPPED, BOPPED, BUMPED, THUMPED, CRUSHED, TRIMMED, OUTLASTED, GOT BY, SNAKED BY, SQUEAKED BY, ROARED BY, OVERRAN, NIPPED BY...
FAMOUS SPORTSCASTER SCHOOL
MILLAR/HINDS

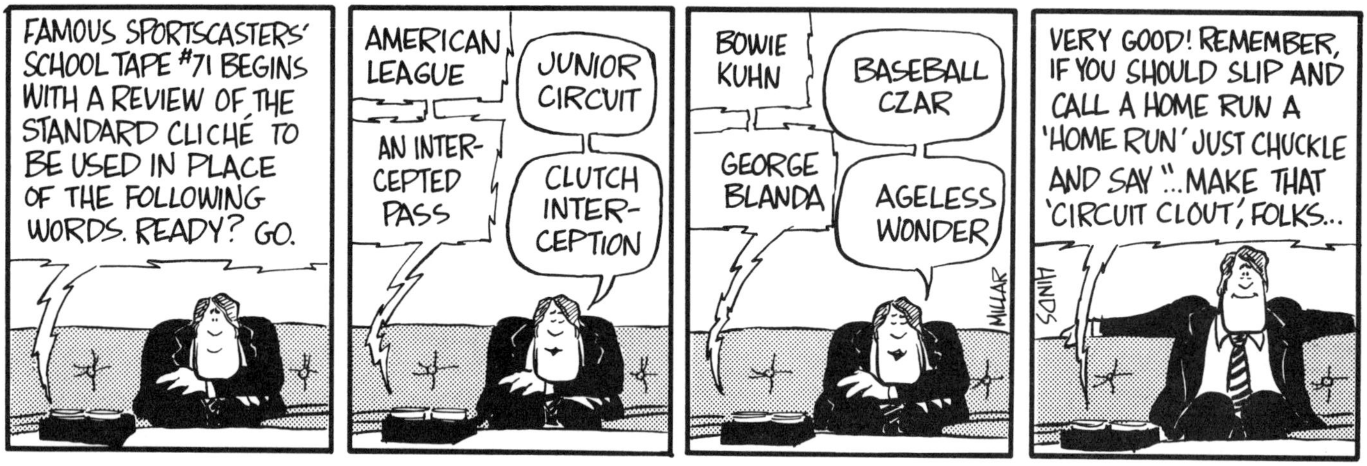
FAMOUS SPORTSCASTERS' SCHOOL TAPE #71 BEGINS WITH A REVIEW OF THE STANDARD CLICHÉ TO BE USED IN PLACE OF THE FOLLOWING WORDS. READY? GO.
AMERICAN LEAGUE
JUNIOR CIRCUIT
AN INTERCEPTED PASS
CLUTCH INTERCEPTION
BOWIE KUHN
BASEBALL CZAR
GEORGE BLANDA
AGELESS WONDER
MILLAR
HINDS
VERY GOOD! REMEMBER, IF YOU SHOULD SLIP AND CALL A HOME RUN A 'HOME RUN' JUST CHUCKLE AND SAY "...MAKE THAT 'CIRCUIT CLOUT,' FOLKS...

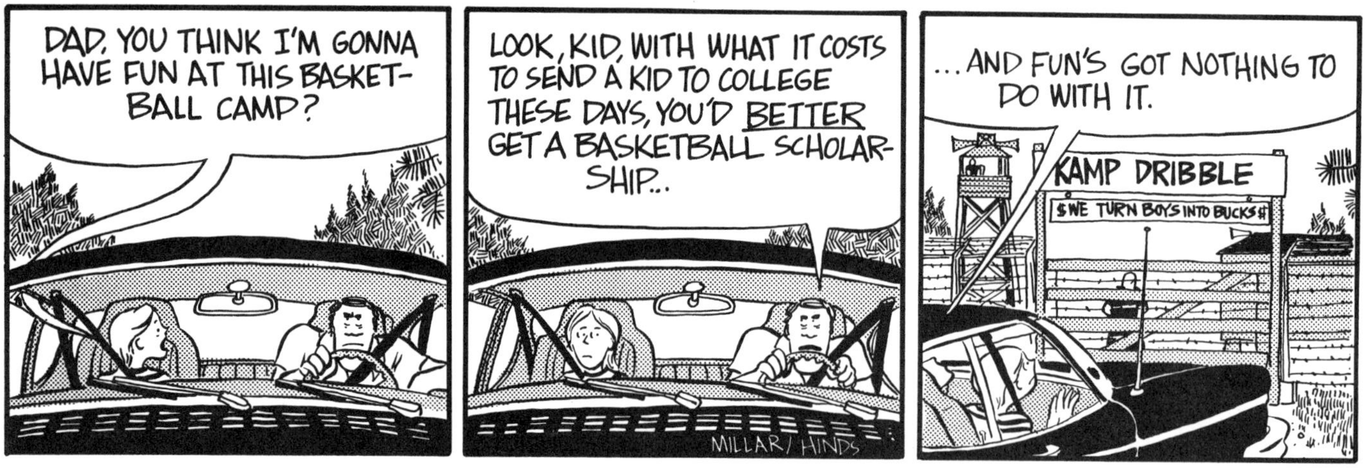
DAD, YOU THINK I'M GONNA HAVE FUN AT THIS BASKETBALL CAMP?
LOOK, KID, WITH WHAT IT COSTS TO SEND A KID TO COLLEGE THESE DAYS, YOU'D BETTER GET A BASKETBALL SCHOLARSHIP...
MILLAR/HINDS
...AND FUN'S GOT NOTHING TO DO WITH IT.
KAMP DRIBBLE
$WE TURN BOYS INTO BUCKS$

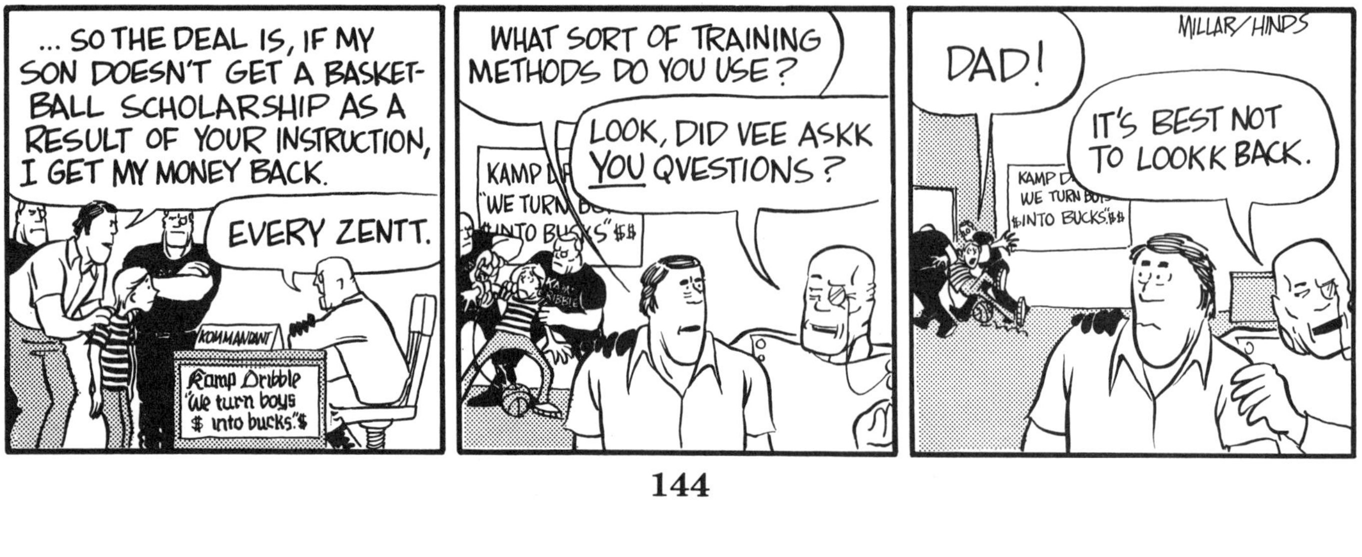
...SO THE DEAL IS, IF MY SON DOESN'T GET A BASKETBALL SCHOLARSHIP AS A RESULT OF YOUR INSTRUCTION, I GET MY MONEY BACK.
EVERY ZENTT.
KOMMANDANT
Kamp Dribble "We turn boys $ into bucks."$
WHAT SORT OF TRAINING METHODS DO YOU USE?
LOOK, DID VEE ASKK YOU QVESTIONS?
MILLAR/HINDS
DAD!
IT'S BEST NOT TO LOOKK BACK.

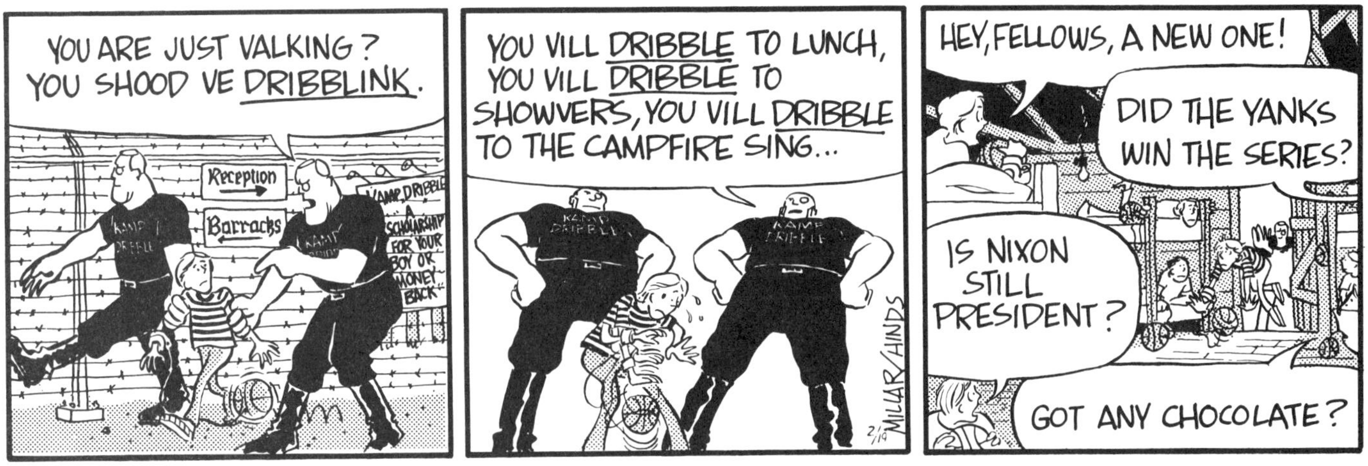
YOU ARE JUST VALKING? YOU SHOOD VE DRIBBLINK.
Reception
Barracks
KAMP DRIBBLE A SCHOLARSHIP FOR YOUR BOY OR MONEY BACK
YOU VILL DRIBBLE TO LUNCH, YOU VILL DRIBBLE TO SHOWVERS, YOU VILL DRIBBLE TO THE CAMPFIRE SING...
MILLAR/HINDS
HEY, FELLOWS, A NEW ONE!
DID THE YANKS WIN THE SERIES?
IS NIXON STILL PRESIDENT?
GOT ANY CHOCOLATE?

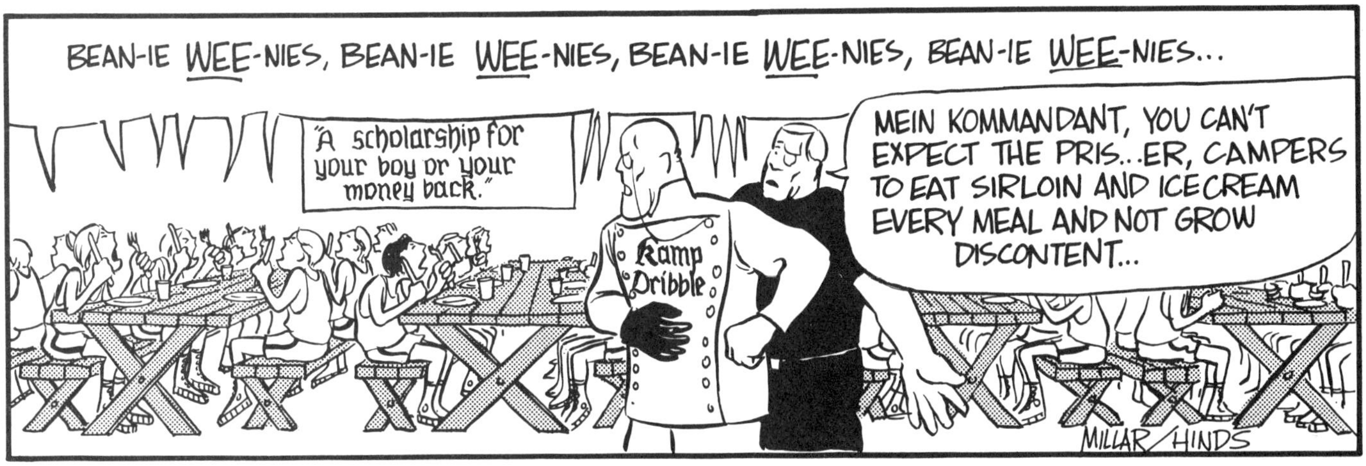
BEAN-IE WEE-NIES, BEAN-IE WEE-NIES, BEAN-IE WEE-NIES, BEAN-IE WEE-NIES...
"A scholarship for your boy or your money back."
MEIN KOMMANDANT, YOU CAN'T EXPECT THE PRIS...ER, CAMPERS TO EAT SIRLOIN AND ICE CREAM EVERY MEAL AND NOT GROW DISCONTENT...
Kamp Dribble
MILLAR/HINDS

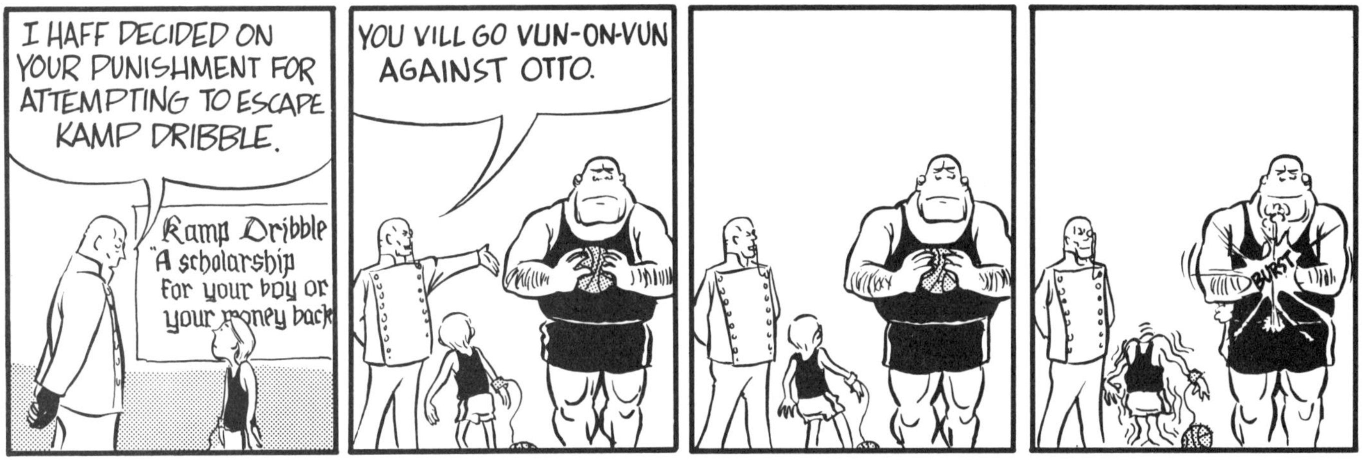
I HAFF DECIDED ON YOUR PUNISHMENT FOR ATTEMPTING TO ESCAPE KAMP DRIBBLE.
Kamp Dribble "A scholarship for your boy or your money back
YOU VILL GO VUN-ON-VUN AGAINST OTTO.
BURST

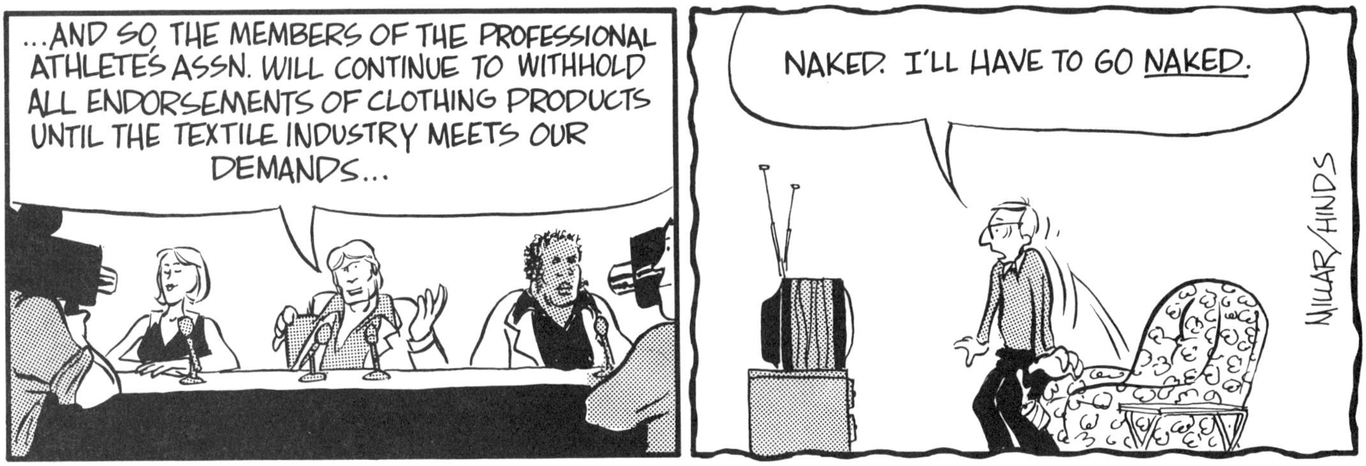
...AND SO, THE MEMBERS OF THE PROFESSIONAL ATHLETES ASSN. WILL CONTINUE TO WITHHOLD ALL ENDORSEMENTS OF CLOTHING PRODUCTS UNTIL THE TEXTILE INDUSTRY MEETS OUR DEMANDS...
NAKED. I'LL HAVE TO GO NAKED.
MILLAR/HINDS

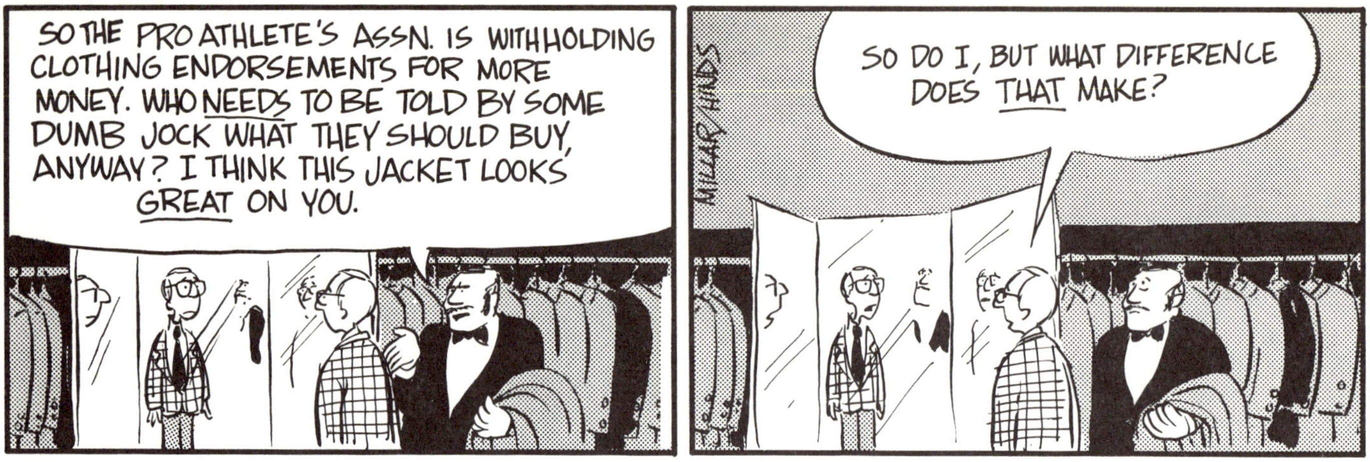
SO THE PRO ATHLETE'S ASSN. IS WITHHOLDING CLOTHING ENDORSEMENTS FOR MORE MONEY. WHO NEEDS TO BE TOLD BY SOME DUMB JOCK WHAT THEY SHOULD BUY, ANYWAY? I THINK THIS JACKET LOOKS GREAT ON YOU.
MILLAR/HINDS
SO DO I, BUT WHAT DIFFERENCE DOES THAT MAKE?

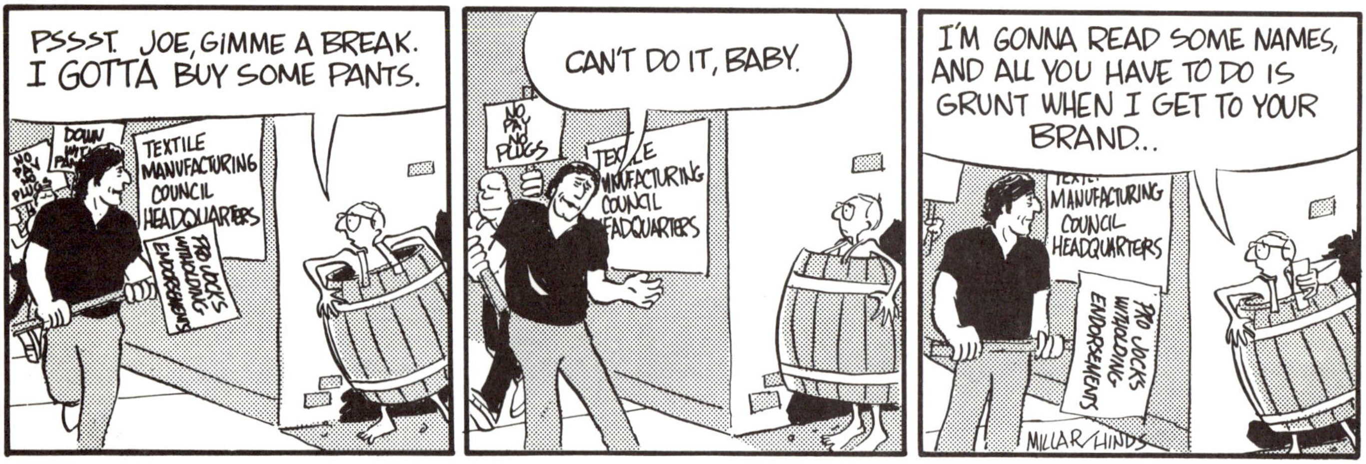
PSSST. JOE, GIMME A BREAK. I GOTTA BUY SOME PANTS.
NO PAY NO PLUGS
TEXTILE MANUFACTURING COUNCIL HEADQUARTERS
PRO JOCKS WITHOLDING ENDORSEMENTS
CAN'T DO IT, BABY.
NO PAY NO PLUGS
TEXTILE MANUFACTURING COUNCIL HEADQUARTERS
I'M GONNA READ SOME NAMES, AND ALL YOU HAVE TO DO IS GRUNT WHEN I GET TO YOUR BRAND...
MANUFACTURING COUNCIL HEADQUARTERS
PRO JOCKS WITHOLDING ENDORSEMENTS
MILLAR/HINDS

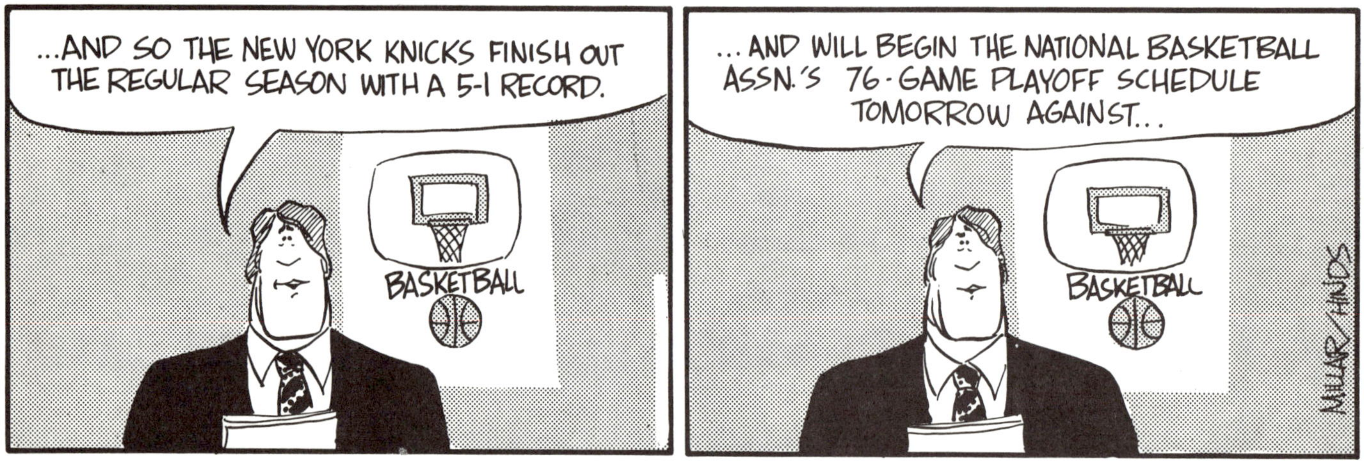
...AND SO THE NEW YORK KNICKS FINISH OUT THE REGULAR SEASON WITH A 5-1 RECORD.
BASKETBALL
...AND WILL BEGIN THE NATIONAL BASKETBALL ASSN.'S 76-GAME PLAYOFF SCHEDULE TOMORROW AGAINST...
BASKETBALL
MILLAR/HINDS

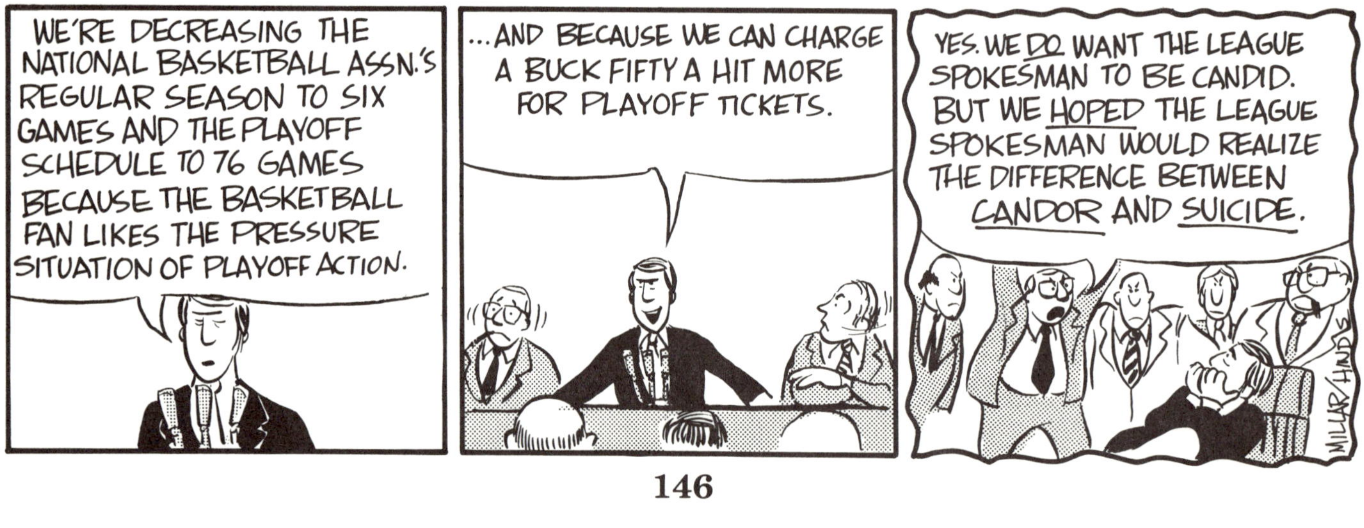
WE'RE DECREASING THE NATIONAL BASKETBALL ASSN.'S REGULAR SEASON TO SIX GAMES AND THE PLAYOFF SCHEDULE TO 76 GAMES BECAUSE THE BASKETBALL FAN LIKES THE PRESSURE SITUATION OF PLAYOFF ACTION.
...AND BECAUSE WE CAN CHARGE A BUCK FIFTY A HIT MORE FOR PLAYOFF TICKETS.
YES. WE DO WANT THE LEAGUE SPOKESMAN TO BE CANDID. BUT WE HOPED THE LEAGUE SPOKESMAN WOULD REALIZE THE DIFFERENCE BETWEEN CANDOR AND SUICIDE.
MILLAR/HINDS

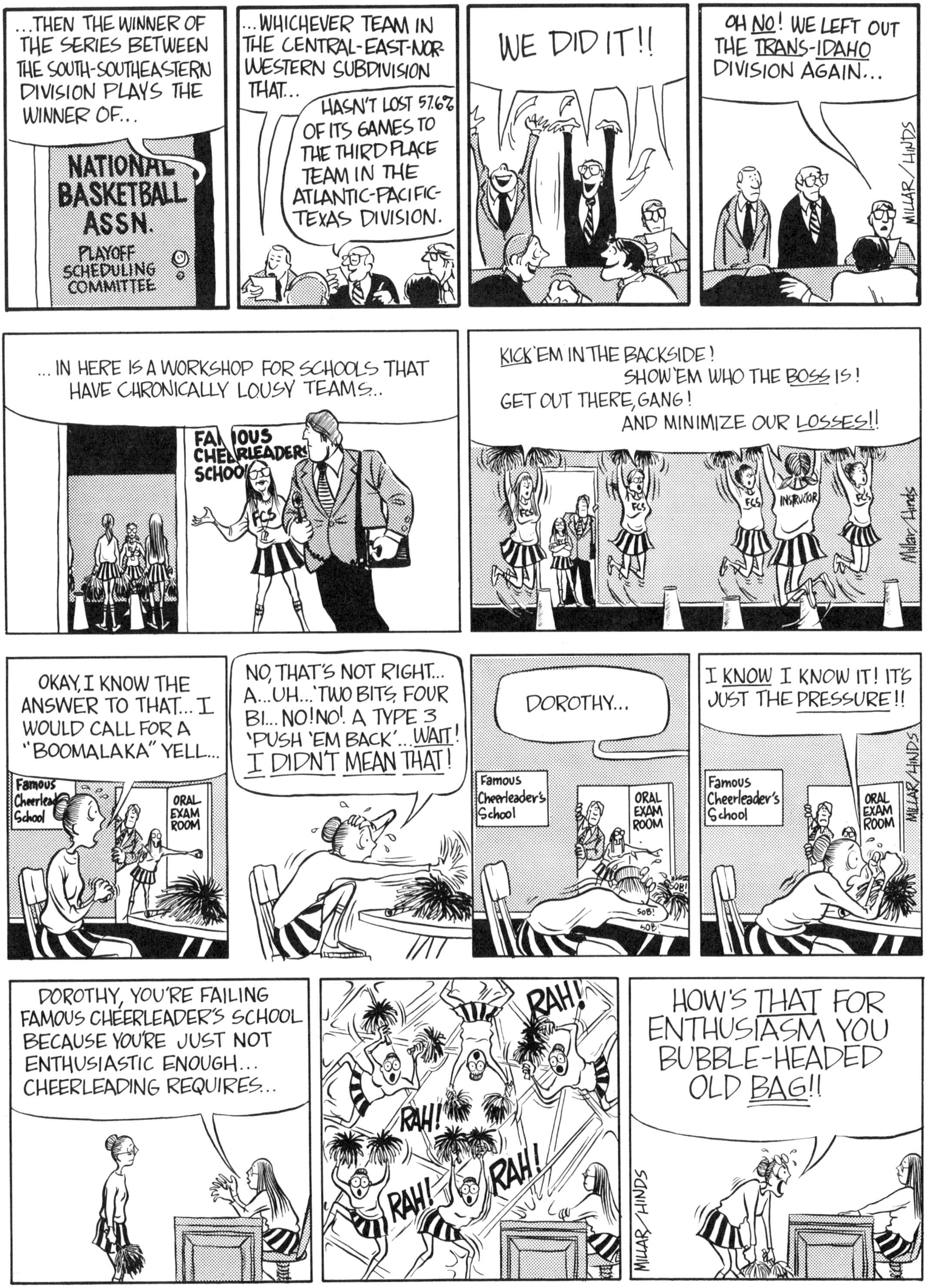
...THEN THE WINNER OF THE SERIES BETWEEN THE SOUTH-SOUTHEASTERN DIVISION PLAYS THE WINNER OF...
NATIONAL BASKETBALL ASSN.
PLAYOFF SCHEDULING COMMITTEE
...WHICHEVER TEAM IN THE CENTRAL-EAST-NOR-WESTERN SUBDIVISION THAT...
HASN'T LOST 57.6% OF ITS GAMES TO THE THIRD PLACE TEAM IN THE ATLANTIC-PACIFIC-TEXAS DIVISION.
WE DID IT!!
OH NO! WE LEFT OUT THE TRANS-IDAHO DIVISION AGAIN...
MILLAR/HINDS
...IN HERE IS A WORKSHOP FOR SCHOOLS THAT HAVE CHRONICALLY LOUSY TEAMS...
FAMOUS CHEERLEADERS SCHOOL
FCS
KICK 'EM IN THE BACKSIDE!
SHOW 'EM WHO THE BOSS IS!
GET OUT THERE, GANG!
AND MINIMIZE OUR LOSSES!!
FCS
FCS
FCS
INSTRUCTOR
FCS
Millar Hinds
OKAY, I KNOW THE ANSWER TO THAT... I WOULD CALL FOR A "BOOMALAKA" YELL...
Famous Cheerleader's School
ORAL EXAM ROOM
NO, THAT'S NOT RIGHT... A...UH...'TWO BITS, FOUR BI... NO! NO!. A TYPE 3 'PUSH 'EM BACK'...WAIT! I DIDN'T MEAN THAT!
DOROTHY...
Famous Cheerleader's School
ORAL EXAM ROOM
SOB!
SOB!
SOB!
I KNOW I KNOW IT! IT'S JUST THE PRESSURE!!
Famous Cheerleader's School
ORAL EXAM ROOM
MILLAR/HINDS
DOROTHY, YOU'RE FAILING FAMOUS CHEERLEADER'S SCHOOL BECAUSE YOU'RE JUST NOT ENTHUSIASTIC ENOUGH... CHEERLEADING REQUIRES...
RAH!
RAH!
RAH!
RAH!
MILLAR/HINDS
HOW'S THAT FOR ENTHUSIASM YOU BUBBLE-HEADED OLD BAG!!

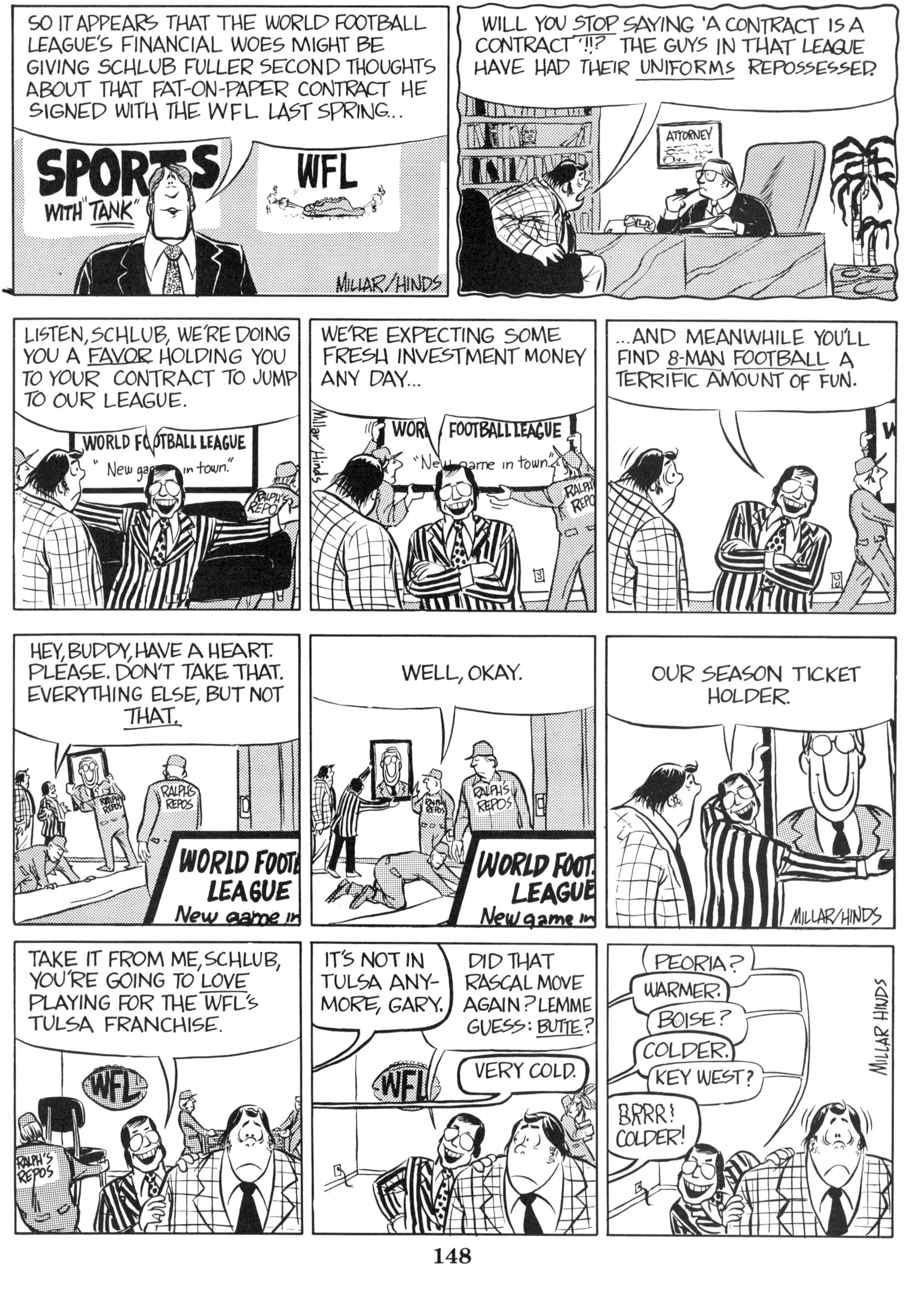
SO IT APPEARS THAT THE WORLD FOOTBALL LEAGUE'S FINANCIAL WOES MIGHT BE GIVING SCHLUB FULLER SECOND THOUGHTS ABOUT THAT FAT-ON-PAPER CONTRACT HE SIGNED WITH THE WFL LAST SPRING...
SPORTS WITH "TANK"
WFL
MILLAR/HINDS
WILL YOU STOP SAYING 'A CONTRACT IS A CONTRACT'!!? THE GUYS IN THAT LEAGUE HAVE HAD THEIR UNIFORMS REPOSSESSED.
ATTORNEY
LISTEN, SCHLUB, WE'RE DOING YOU A FAVOR HOLDING YOU TO YOUR CONTRACT TO JUMP TO OUR LEAGUE.
WORLD FOOTBALL LEAGUE "New game in town."
RALPH'S REPOS
WE'RE EXPECTING SOME FRESH INVESTMENT MONEY ANY DAY...
Millar/Hinds
...AND MEANWHILE YOU'LL FIND 8-MAN FOOTBALL A TERRIFIC AMOUNT OF FUN.
HEY, BUDDY, HAVE A HEART. PLEASE. DON'T TAKE THAT. EVERYTHING ELSE, BUT NOT THAT.
RALPH'S REPOS
WORLD FOOTB LEAGUE New game in
WELL, OKAY.
OUR SEASON TICKET HOLDER.
MILLAR/HINDS
TAKE IT FROM ME, SCHLUB, YOU'RE GOING TO LOVE PLAYING FOR THE WFL'S TULSA FRANCHISE.
WFL
RALPH'S REPOS
IT'S NOT IN TULSA ANYMORE, GARY.
DID THAT RASCAL MOVE AGAIN? LEMME GUESS: BUTTE?
VERY COLD.
PEORIA?
WARMER.
BOISE?
COLDER.
KEY WEST?
BRRR! COLDER!
MILLAR HINDS

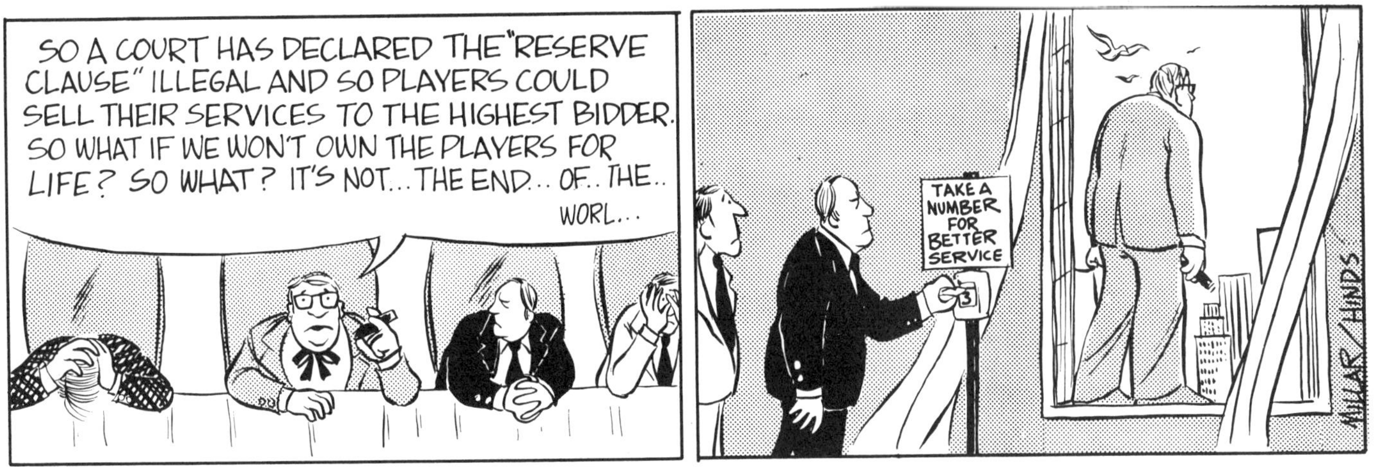
SO A COURT HAS DECLARED THE "RESERVE CLAUSE" ILLEGAL AND SO PLAYERS COULD SELL THEIR SERVICES TO THE HIGHEST BIDDER. SO WHAT IF WE WON'T OWN THE PLAYERS FOR LIFE? SO WHAT? IT'S NOT... THE END... OF.. THE.. WORL...
TAKE A NUMBER FOR BETTER SERVICE
3
MILLAR/HINDS

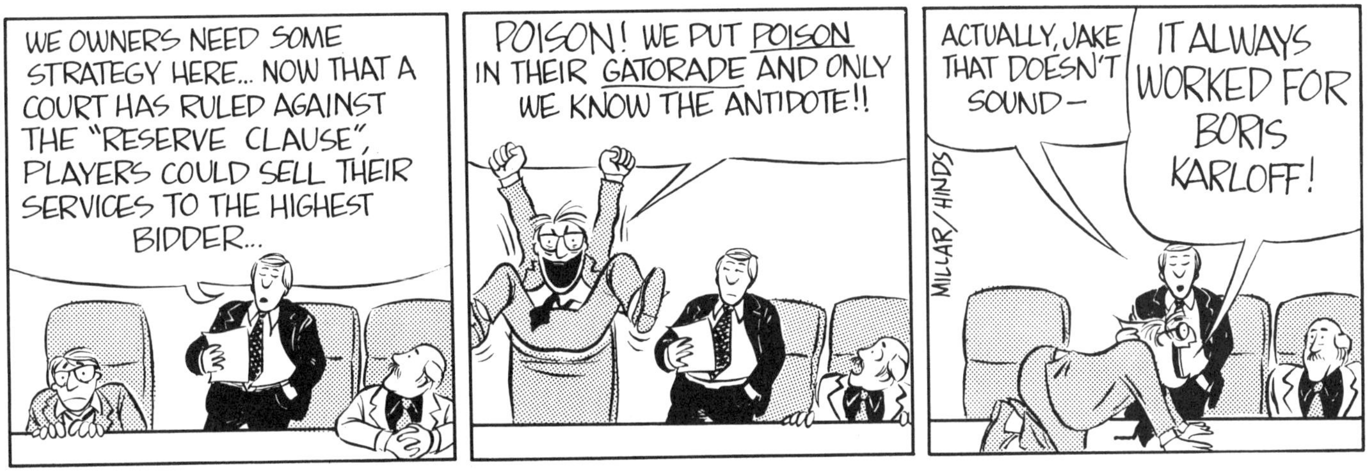
WE OWNERS NEED SOME STRATEGY HERE... NOW THAT A COURT HAS RULED AGAINST THE "RESERVE CLAUSE", PLAYERS COULD SELL THEIR SERVICES TO THE HIGHEST BIDDER...
POISON! WE PUT POISON IN THEIR GATORADE AND ONLY WE KNOW THE ANTIDOTE!!
MILLAR/HINDS
ACTUALLY, JAKE THAT DOESN'T SOUND—
IT ALWAYS WORKED FOR BORIS KARLOFF!

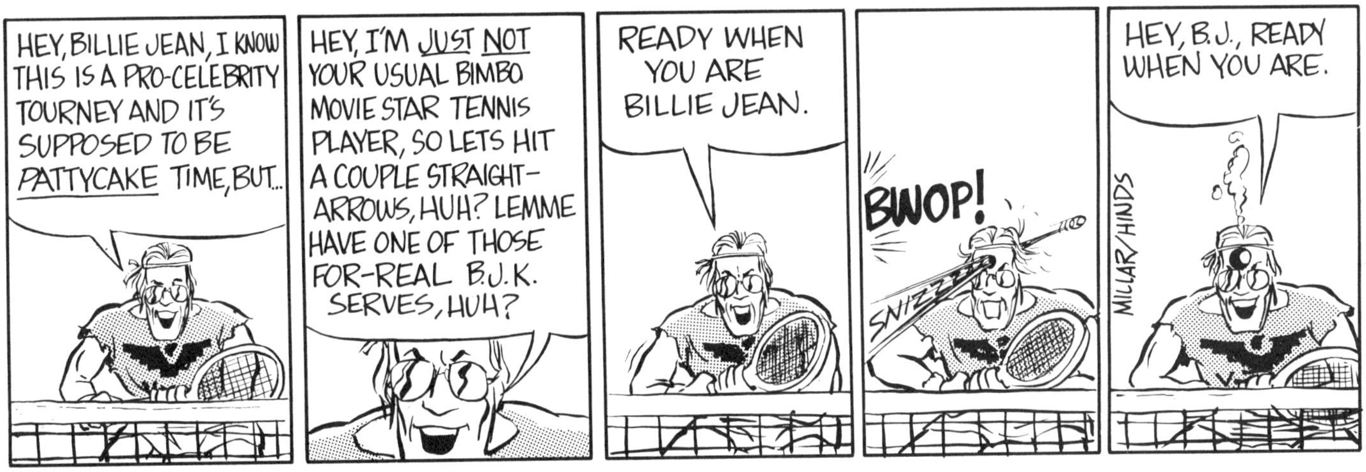
HEY, BILLIE JEAN, I KNOW THIS IS A PRO-CELEBRITY TOURNEY AND IT'S SUPPOSED TO BE PATTYCAKE TIME, BUT...
HEY, I'M JUST NOT YOUR USUAL BIMBO MOVIE STAR TENNIS PLAYER, SO LETS HIT A COUPLE STRAIGHT-ARROWS, HUH? LEMME HAVE ONE OF THOSE FOR-REAL B.J.K. SERVES, HUH?
READY WHEN YOU ARE BILLIE JEAN.
BWOP!
SNIZZZ
MILLAR/HINDS
HEY, B.J., READY WHEN YOU ARE.

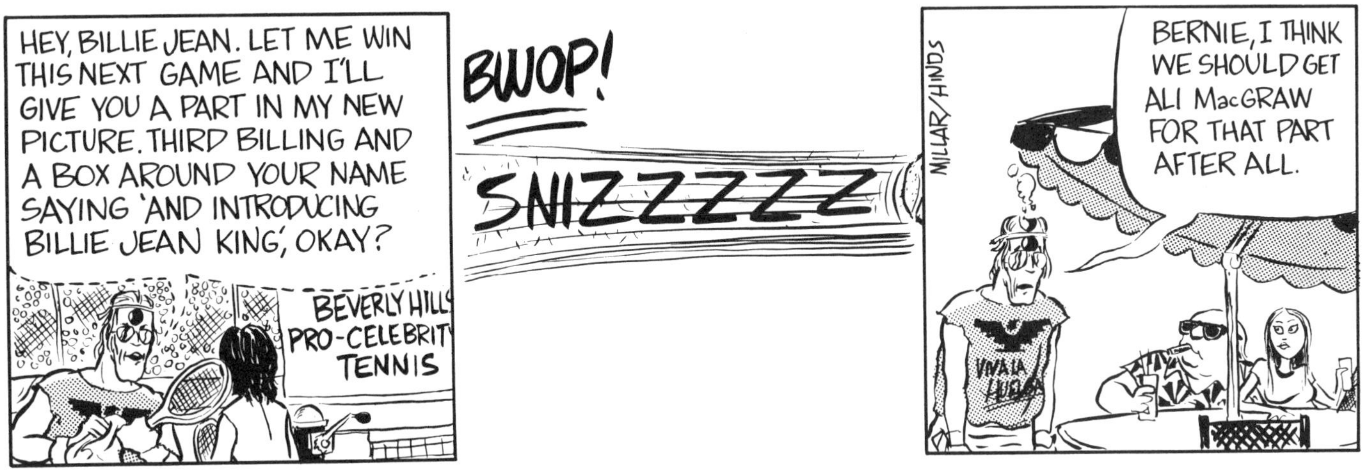
HEY, BILLIE JEAN. LET ME WIN THIS NEXT GAME AND I'LL GIVE YOU A PART IN MY NEW PICTURE. THIRD BILLING AND A BOX AROUND YOUR NAME SAYING 'AND INTRODUCING BILLIE JEAN KING', OKAY?
BEVERLY HILLS PRO-CELEBRITY TENNIS
BWOP!
SNIZZZZZZ
MILLAR/HINDS
BERNIE, I THINK WE SHOULD GET ALI MacGRAW FOR THAT PART AFTER ALL.

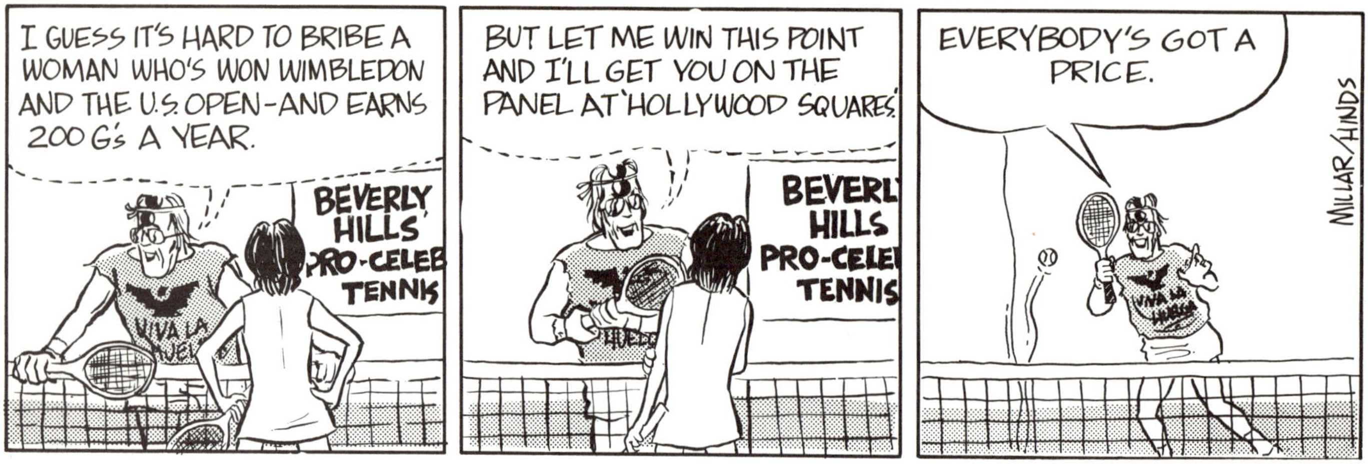
I GUESS IT'S HARD TO BRIBE A WOMAN WHO'S WON WIMBLEDON AND THE U.S. OPEN—AND EARNS 200 G's A YEAR.
BUT LET ME WIN THIS POINT AND I'LL GET YOU ON THE PANEL AT 'HOLLYWOOD SQUARES.'
EVERYBODY'S GOT A PRICE.
MILLAR/HINDS

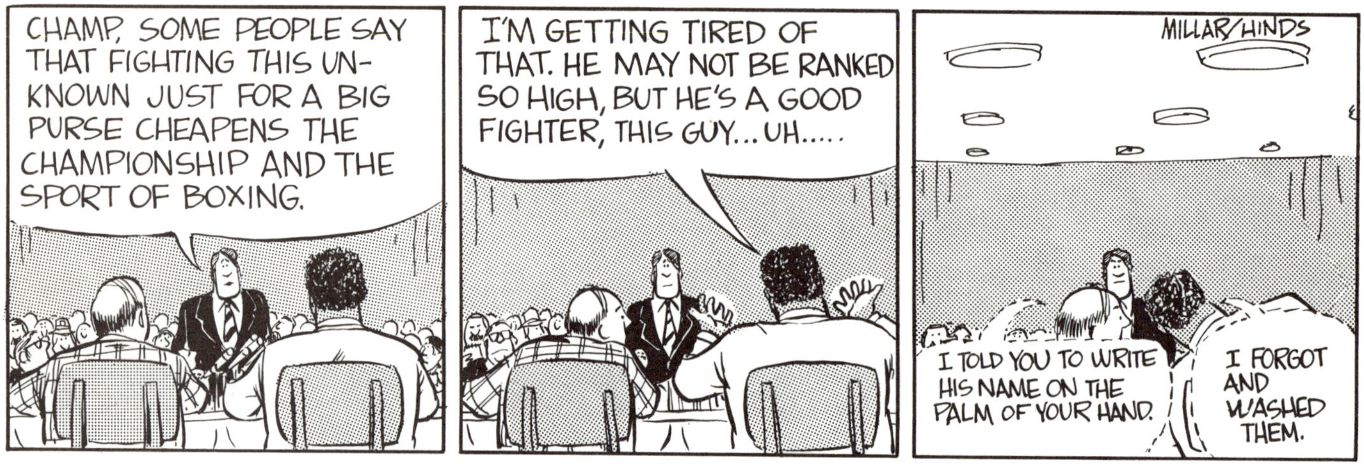
CHAMP, SOME PEOPLE SAY THAT FIGHTING THIS UNKNOWN JUST FOR A BIG PURSE CHEAPENS THE CHAMPIONSHIP AND THE SPORT OF BOXING.
I'M GETTING TIRED OF THAT. HE MAY NOT BE RANKED SO HIGH, BUT HE'S A GOOD FIGHTER, THIS GUY... UH.....
MILLAR/HINDS
I TOLD YOU TO WRITE HIS NAME ON THE PALM OF YOUR HAND.
I FORGOT AND WASHED THEM.

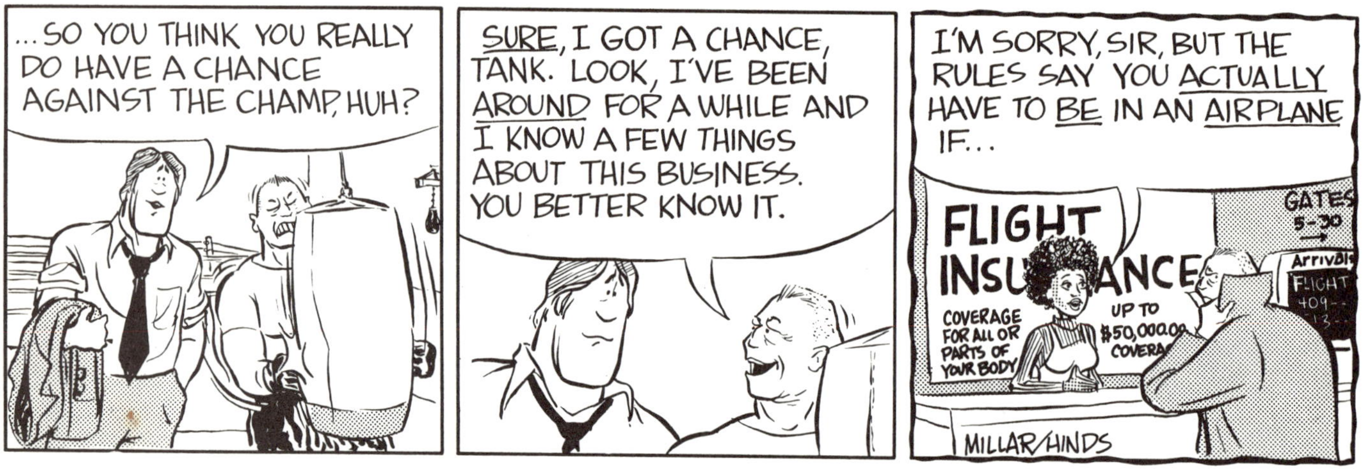
...SO YOU THINK YOU REALLY DO HAVE A CHANCE AGAINST THE CHAMP, HUH?
SURE, I GOT A CHANCE, TANK. LOOK, I'VE BEEN AROUND FOR A WHILE AND I KNOW A FEW THINGS ABOUT THIS BUSINESS. YOU BETTER KNOW IT.
I'M SORRY, SIR, BUT THE RULES SAY YOU ACTUALLY HAVE TO BE IN AN AIRPLANE IF...
COVERAGE FOR ALL OR PARTS OF YOUR BODY
MILLAR/HINDS

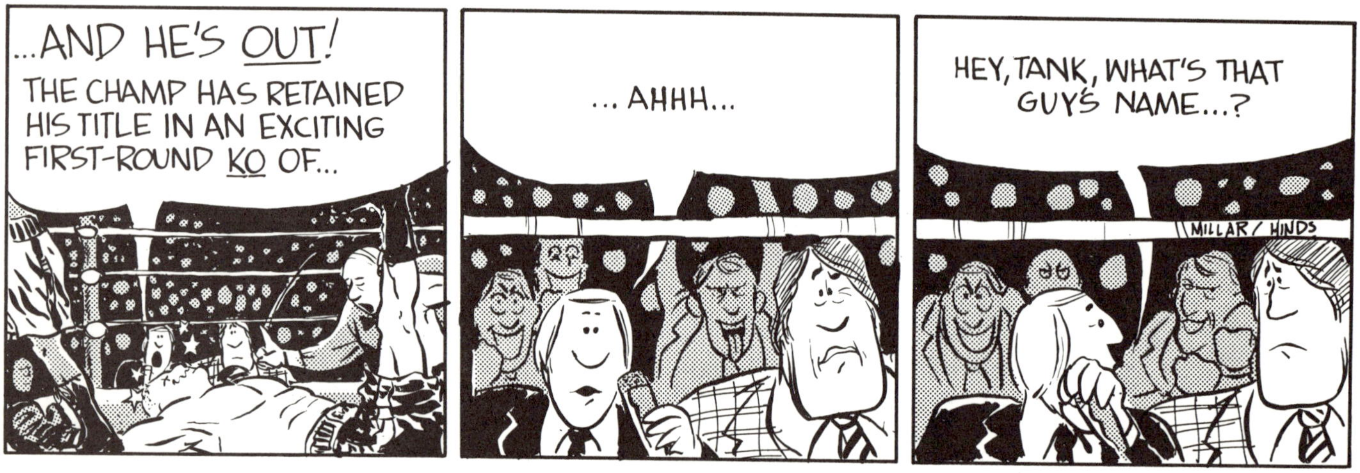
...AND HE'S OUT! THE CHAMP HAS RETAINED HIS TITLE IN AN EXCITING FIRST-ROUND KO OF...
... AHHH...
HEY, TANK, WHAT'S THAT GUY'S NAME...?
MILLAR/HINDS

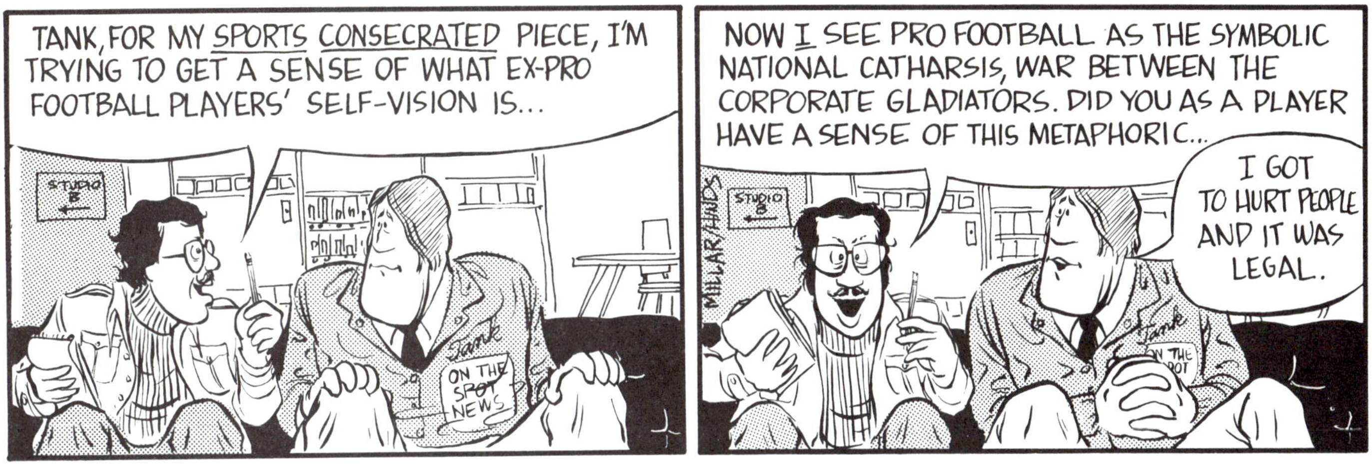
TANK, FOR MY SPORTS CONSECRATED PIECE, I'M TRYING TO GET A SENSE OF WHAT EX-PRO FOOTBALL PLAYERS' SELF-VISION IS...
STUDIO B
Tank
ON THE SPOT NEWS
NOW I SEE PRO FOOTBALL AS THE SYMBOLIC NATIONAL CATHARSIS, WAR BETWEEN THE CORPORATE GLADIATORS. DID YOU AS A PLAYER HAVE A SENSE OF THIS METAPHORIC...
I GOT TO HURT PEOPLE AND IT WAS LEGAL.
MILLAR/HINDS

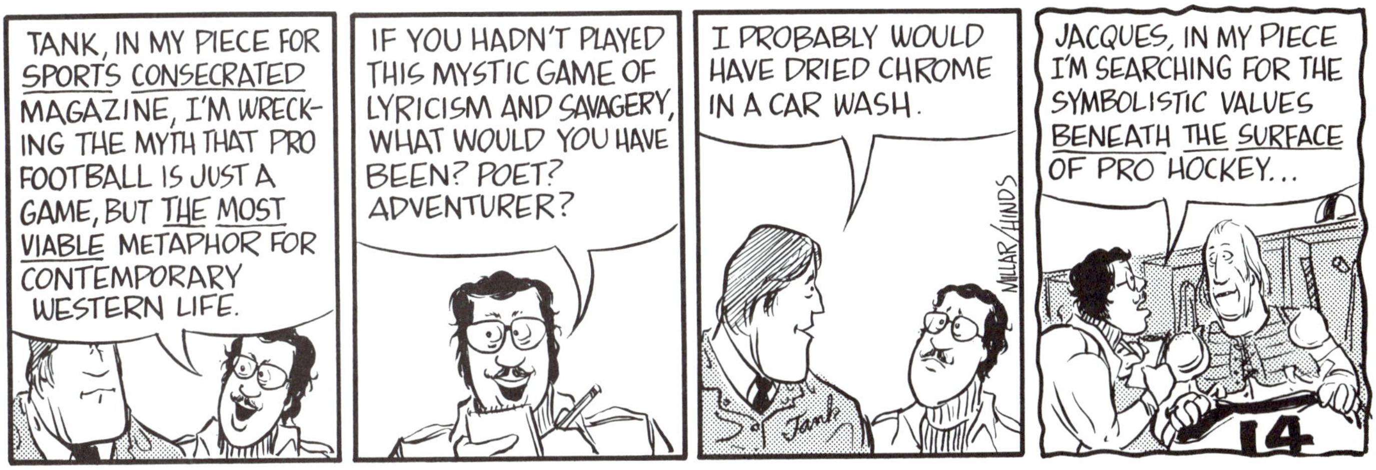
TANK, IN MY PIECE FOR SPORTS CONSECRATED MAGAZINE, I'M WRECKING THE MYTH THAT PRO FOOTBALL IS JUST A GAME, BUT THE MOST VIABLE METAPHOR FOR CONTEMPORARY WESTERN LIFE.
IF YOU HADN'T PLAYED THIS MYSTIC GAME OF LYRICISM AND SAVAGERY, WHAT WOULD YOU HAVE BEEN? POET? ADVENTURER?
I PROBABLY WOULD HAVE DRIED CHROME IN A CAR WASH.
MILLAR/HINDS
JACQUES, IN MY PIECE I'M SEARCHING FOR THE SYMBOLISTIC VALUES BENEATH THE SURFACE OF PRO HOCKEY...
14

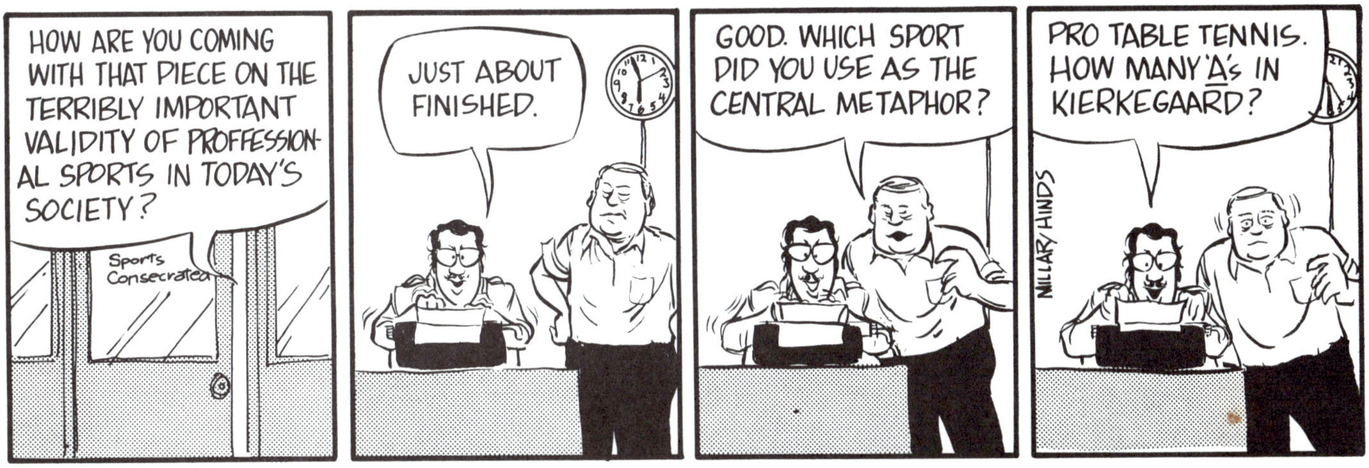
HOW ARE YOU COMING WITH THAT PIECE ON THE TERRIBLY IMPORTANT VALIDITY OF PROFFESSIONAL SPORTS IN TODAY'S SOCIETY?
Sports Consecrated
JUST ABOUT FINISHED.
GOOD. WHICH SPORT DID YOU USE AS THE CENTRAL METAPHOR?
PRO TABLE TENNIS. HOW MANY 'A's IN KIERKEGAARD?
MILLAR/HINDS

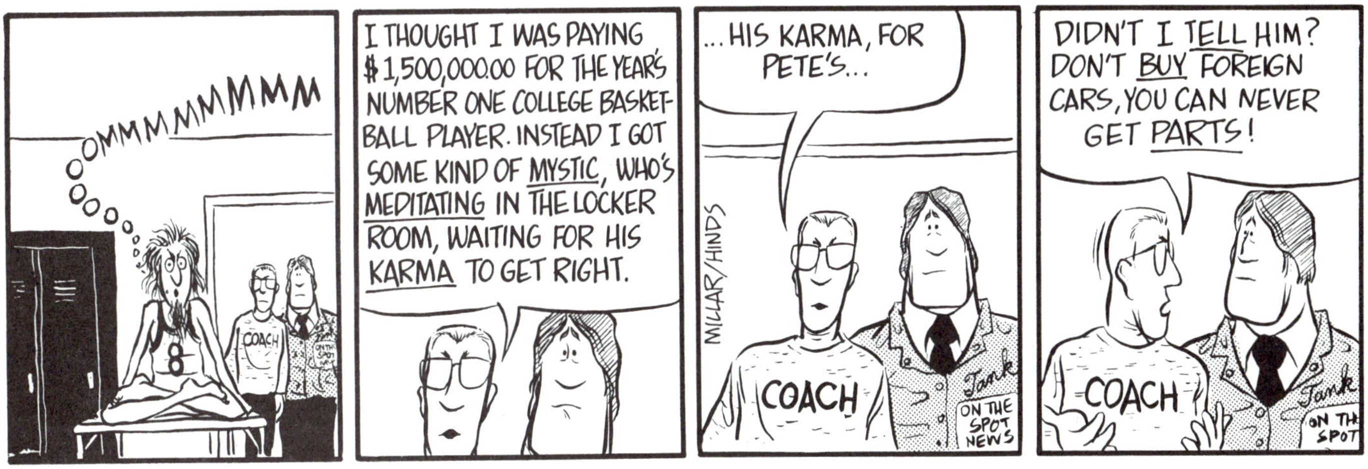
OOMMMMMMMMM
COACH
I THOUGHT I WAS PAYING $1,500,000.00 FOR THE YEAR'S NUMBER ONE COLLEGE BASKETBALL PLAYER. INSTEAD I GOT SOME KIND OF MYSTIC, WHO'S MEDITATING IN THE LOCKER ROOM, WAITING FOR HIS KARMA TO GET RIGHT.
...HIS KARMA, FOR PETE'S...
MILLAR/HINDS
COACH
Tank
ON THE SPOT NEWS
DIDN'T I TELL HIM? DON'T BUY FOREIGN CARS, YOU CAN NEVER GET PARTS!
COACH

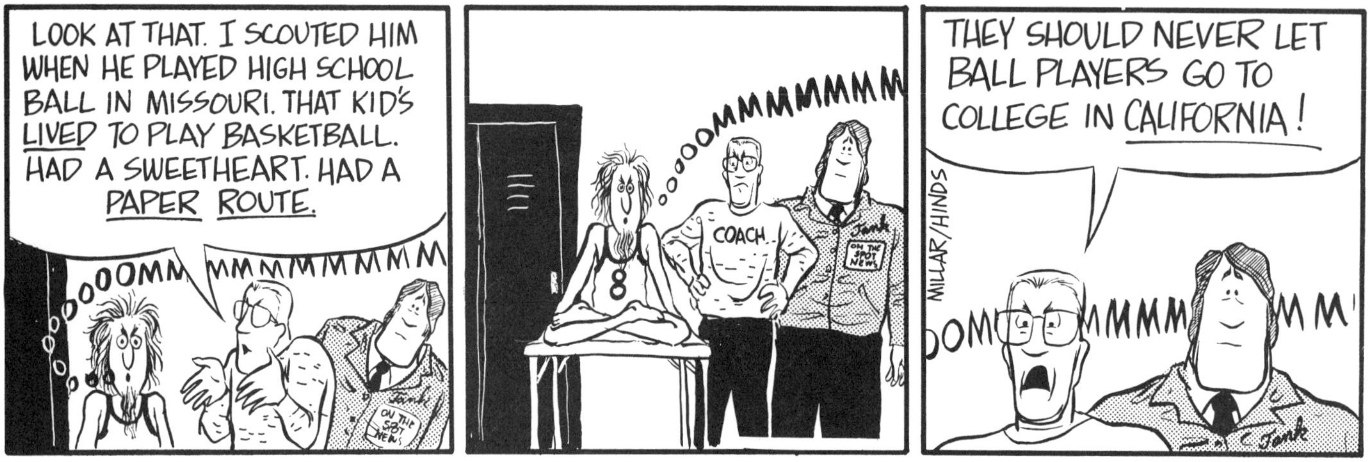
LOOK AT THAT. I SCOUTED HIM WHEN HE PLAYED HIGH SCHOOL BALL IN MISSOURI. THAT KID'S LIVED TO PLAY BASKETBALL. HAD A SWEETHEART. HAD A PAPER ROUTE.
oooOOMMMMMMMMMMM
ON THE SPOT NEWS
oooOOMMMMMMMMMM
COACH
ON THE SPOT NEWS
MILLAR/HINDS
THEY SHOULD NEVER LET BALL PLAYERS GO TO COLLEGE IN CALIFORNIA!
OOMMMMMMMM

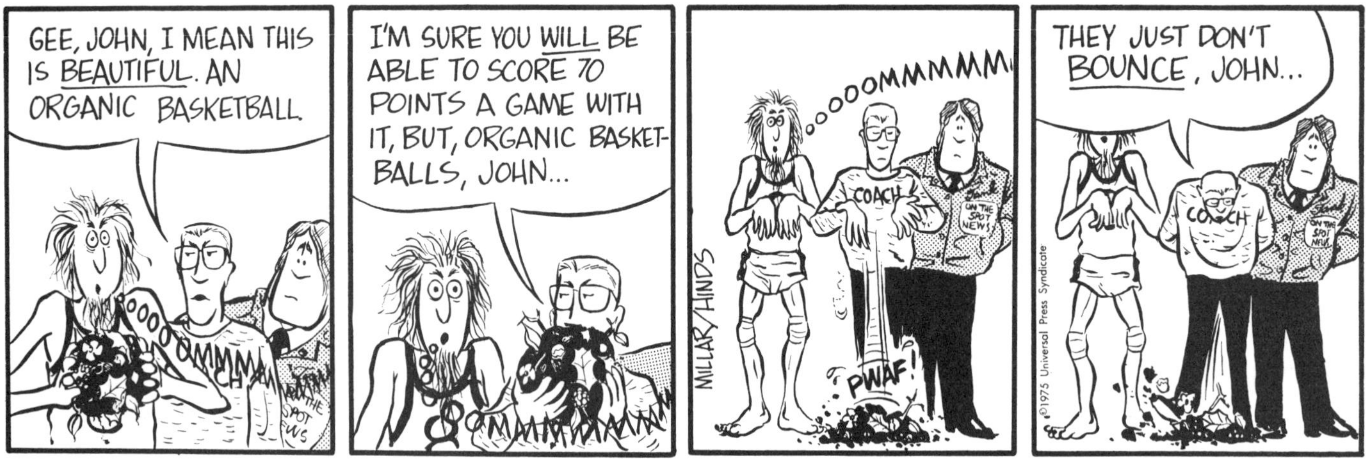
GEE, JOHN, I MEAN THIS IS BEAUTIFUL. AN ORGANIC BASKETBALL.
oOOOMMMM
I'M SURE YOU WILL BE ABLE TO SCORE 70 POINTS A GAME WITH IT, BUT, ORGANIC BASKETBALLS, JOHN...
OOMMMMMMM
MILLAR/HINDS
ooOOOMMMMMM
COACH
ON THE SPOT NEWS
PWAF!
©1975 Universal Press Syndicate
THEY JUST DON'T BOUNCE, JOHN...
COACH

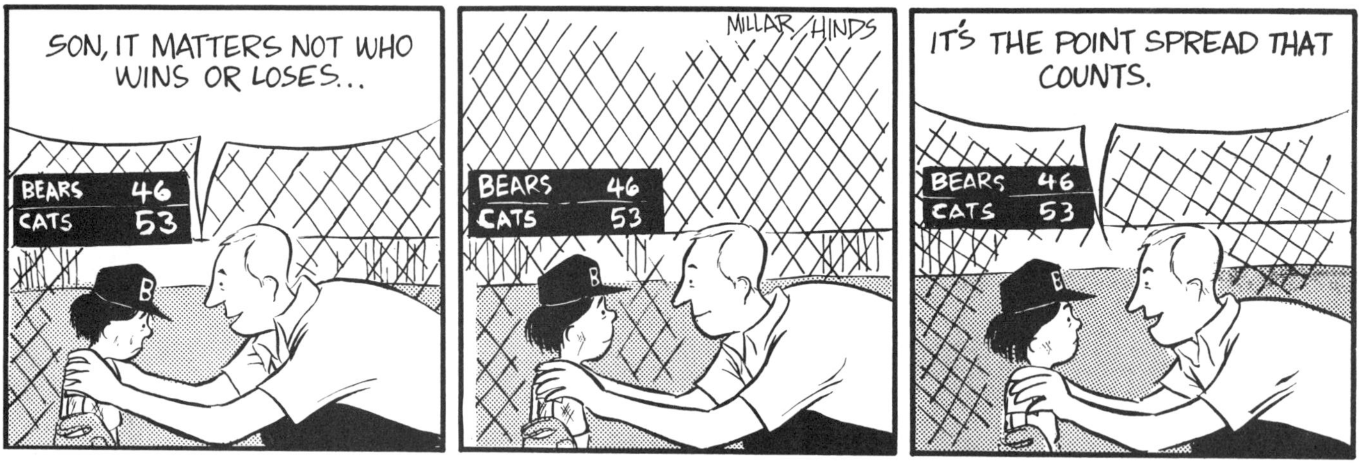
SON, IT MATTERS NOT WHO WINS OR LOSES...
BEARS 46
CATS 53
MILLAR/HINDS
BEARS 46
CATS 53
IT'S THE POINT SPREAD THAT COUNTS.
BEARS 46
CATS 53

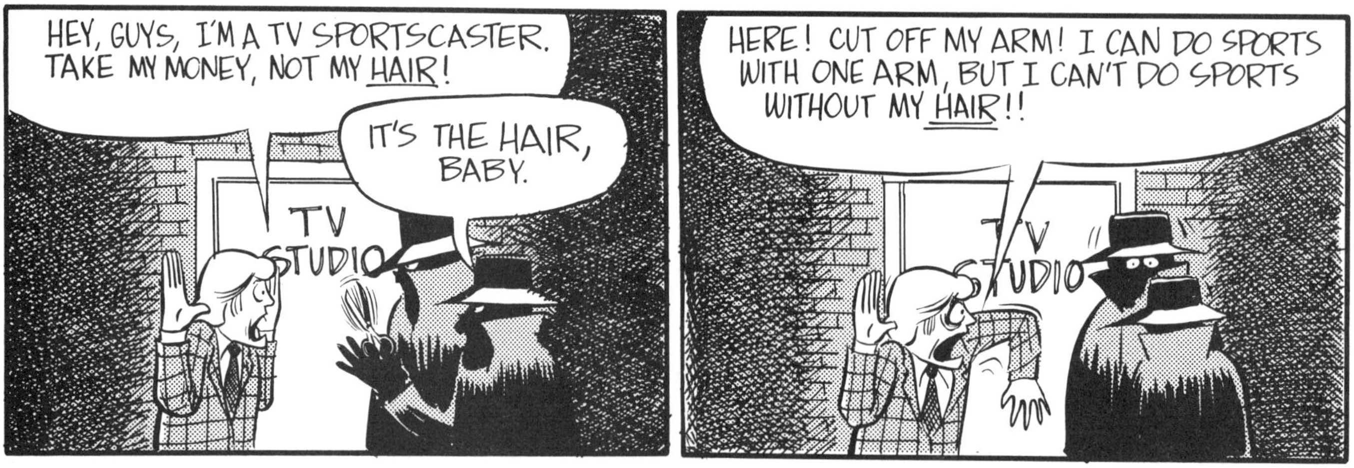
HEY, GUYS, I'M A TV SPORTSCASTER. TAKE MY MONEY, NOT MY HAIR!
IT'S THE HAIR, BABY.
TV STUDIO
HERE! CUT OFF MY ARM! I CAN DO SPORTS WITH ONE ARM, BUT I CAN'T DO SPORTS WITHOUT MY HAIR!!
TV STUDIO

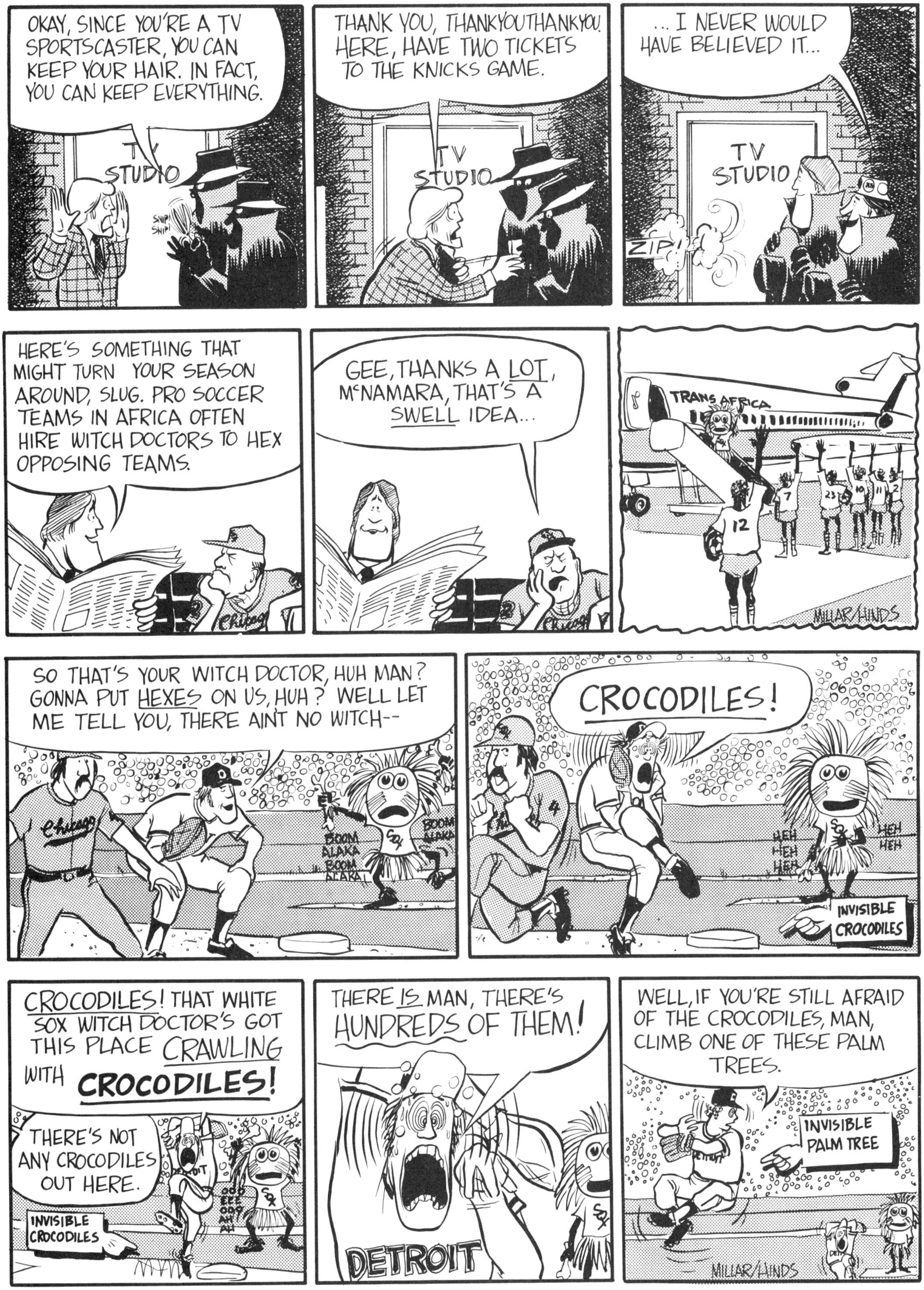
OKAY, SINCE YOU'RE A TV SPORTSCASTER, YOU CAN KEEP YOUR HAIR. IN FACT, YOU CAN KEEP EVERYTHING.
TV STUDIO
SNIP! SNIP!
THANK YOU, THANKYOUTHANKYOU. HERE, HAVE TWO TICKETS TO THE KNICKS GAME.
TV STUDIO
...I NEVER WOULD HAVE BELIEVED IT...
TV STUDIO
ZIP!
HERE'S SOMETHING THAT MIGHT TURN YOUR SEASON AROUND, SLUG. PRO SOCCER TEAMS IN AFRICA OFTEN HIRE WITCH DOCTORS TO HEX OPPOSING TEAMS.
GEE, THANKS A LOT, McNAMARA, THAT'S A SWELL IDEA...
TRANS AFRICA
MILLAR/HINDS
SO THAT'S YOUR WITCH DOCTOR, HUH MAN? GONNA PUT HEXES ON US, HUH? WELL LET ME TELL YOU, THERE AIN'T NO WITCH--
BOOM ALAKA BOOM ALAKA
BOOM ALAKA
CROCODILES!
HEH HEH HEH
HEH HEH
INVISIBLE CROCODILES
CROCODILES! THAT WHITE SOX WITCH DOCTOR'S GOT THIS PLACE CRAWLING WITH CROCODILES!
THERE'S NOT ANY CROCODILES OUT HERE.
INVISIBLE CROCODILES
THERE IS MAN, THERE'S HUNDREDS OF THEM!
DETROIT
WELL, IF YOU'RE STILL AFRAID OF THE CROCODILES, MAN, CLIMB ONE OF THESE PALM TREES.
INVISIBLE PALM TREE
MILLAR/HINDS

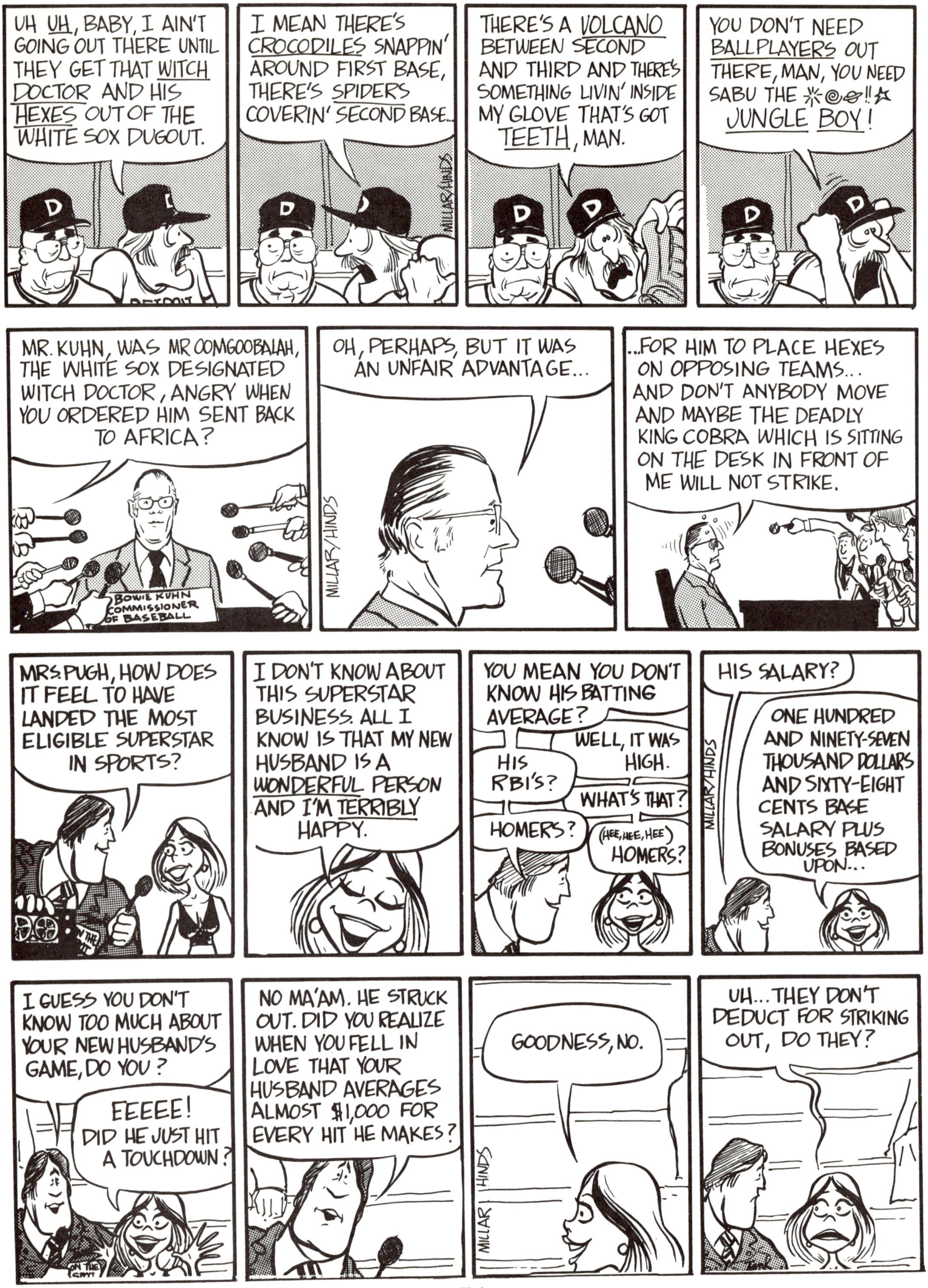

UH UH, BABY, I AIN'T GOING OUT THERE UNTIL THEY GET THAT WITCH DOCTOR AND HIS HEXES OUT OF THE WHITE SOX DUGOUT.
I MEAN THERE'S CROCODILES SNAPPIN' AROUND FIRST BASE, THERE'S SPIDERS COVERIN' SECOND BASE...
MILLAR/HINDS
THERE'S A VOLCANO BETWEEN SECOND AND THIRD AND THERE'S SOMETHING LIVIN' INSIDE MY GLOVE THAT'S GOT TEETH, MAN.
YOU DON'T NEED BALLPLAYERS OUT THERE, MAN, YOU NEED SABU THE JUNGLE BOY!
MR. KUHN, WAS MR. OOMGOOBALAH, THE WHITE SOX DESIGNATED WITCH DOCTOR, ANGRY WHEN YOU ORDERED HIM SENT BACK TO AFRICA?
BOWIE KUHN COMMISSIONER OF BASEBALL
OH, PERHAPS, BUT IT WAS AN UNFAIR ADVANTAGE...
MILLAR/HINDS
...FOR HIM TO PLACE HEXES ON OPPOSING TEAMS... AND DON'T ANYBODY MOVE AND MAYBE THE DEADLY KING COBRA WHICH IS SITTING ON THE DESK IN FRONT OF ME WILL NOT STRIKE.
MRS. PUGH, HOW DOES IT FEEL TO HAVE LANDED THE MOST ELIGIBLE SUPERSTAR IN SPORTS?
I DON'T KNOW ABOUT THIS SUPERSTAR BUSINESS. ALL I KNOW IS THAT MY NEW HUSBAND IS A WONDERFUL PERSON AND I'M TERRIBLY HAPPY.
YOU MEAN YOU DON'T KNOW HIS BATTING AVERAGE?
WELL, IT WAS HIGH.
HIS RBI'S?
WHAT'S THAT?
HOMERS?
(HEE, HEE, HEE) HOMERS?
HIS SALARY?
MILLAR/HINDS
ONE HUNDRED AND NINETY-SEVEN THOUSAND DOLLARS AND SIXTY-EIGHT CENTS BASE SALARY PLUS BONUSES BASED UPON...
I GUESS YOU DON'T KNOW TOO MUCH ABOUT YOUR NEW HUSBAND'S GAME, DO YOU?
EEEEE! DID HE JUST HIT A TOUCHDOWN?
ON THE SPOT
NO MA'AM. HE STRUCK OUT. DID YOU REALIZE WHEN YOU FELL IN LOVE THAT YOUR HUSBAND AVERAGES ALMOST $1,000 FOR EVERY HIT HE MAKES?
GOODNESS, NO.
MILLAR/HINDS
UH... THEY DON'T DEDUCT FOR STRIKING OUT, DO THEY?

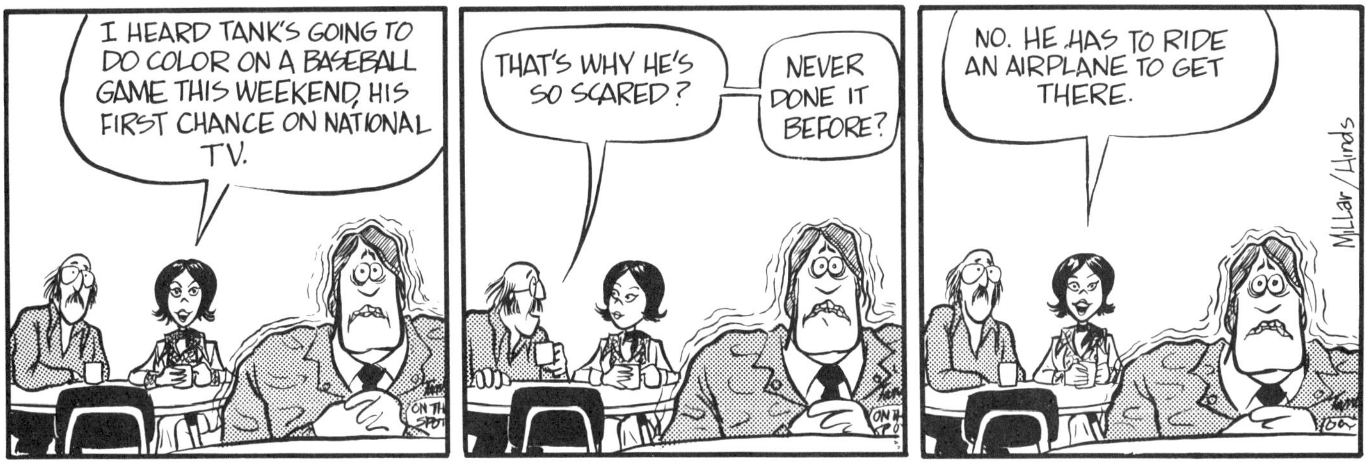
I HEARD TANK'S GOING TO DO COLOR ON A BASEBALL GAME THIS WEEKEND, HIS FIRST CHANCE ON NATIONAL TV.
THAT'S WHY HE'S SO SCARED?
NEVER DONE IT BEFORE?
NO. HE HAS TO RIDE AN AIRPLANE TO GET THERE.
Millar/Hinds

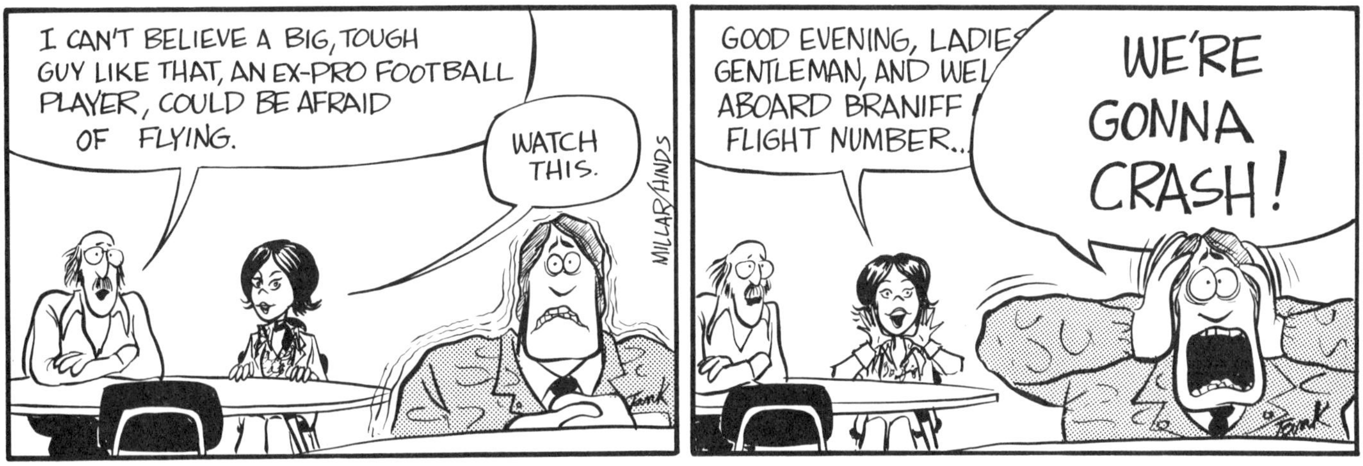
I CAN'T BELIEVE A BIG, TOUGH GUY LIKE THAT, AN EX-PRO FOOTBALL PLAYER, COULD BE AFRAID OF FLYING.
WATCH THIS.
MILLAR/HINDS
GOOD EVENING, LADIES GENTLEMAN, AND WEL ABOARD BRANIFF FLIGHT NUMBER...
WE'RE GONNA CRASH!

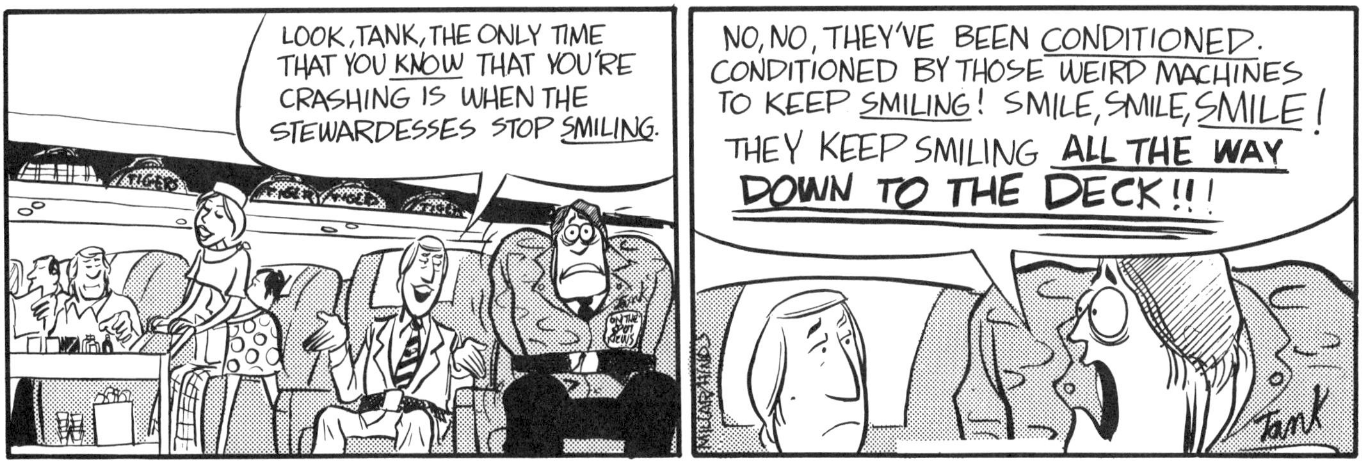
LOOK, TANK, THE ONLY TIME THAT YOU KNOW THAT YOU'RE CRASHING IS WHEN THE STEWARDESSES STOP SMILING.
TIGERS
NO, NO, THEY'VE BEEN CONDITIONED. CONDITIONED BY THOSE WEIRD MACHINES TO KEEP SMILING! SMILE, SMILE, SMILE!
THEY KEEP SMILING ALL THE WAY DOWN TO THE DECK!!!

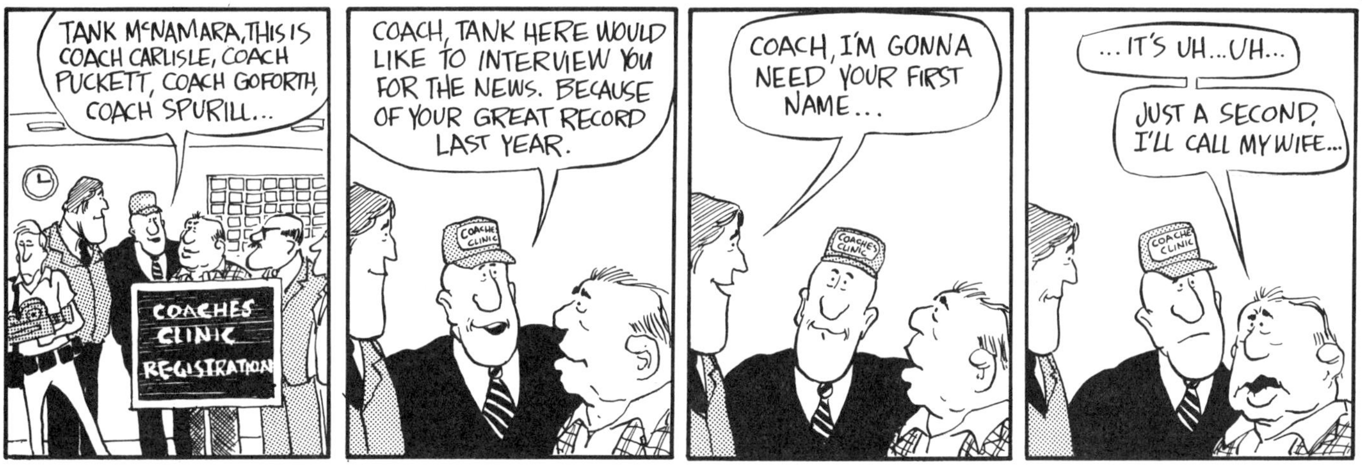
TANK McNAMARA, THIS IS COACH CARLISLE, COACH PUCKETT, COACH GOFORTH, COACH SPURILL...
COACHES CLINIC REGISTRATION
COACH, TANK HERE WOULD LIKE TO INTERVIEW YOU FOR THE NEWS. BECAUSE OF YOUR GREAT RECORD LAST YEAR.
COACH, I'M GONNA NEED YOUR FIRST NAME...
... IT'S UH...UH...
JUST A SECOND, I'LL CALL MY WIFE...

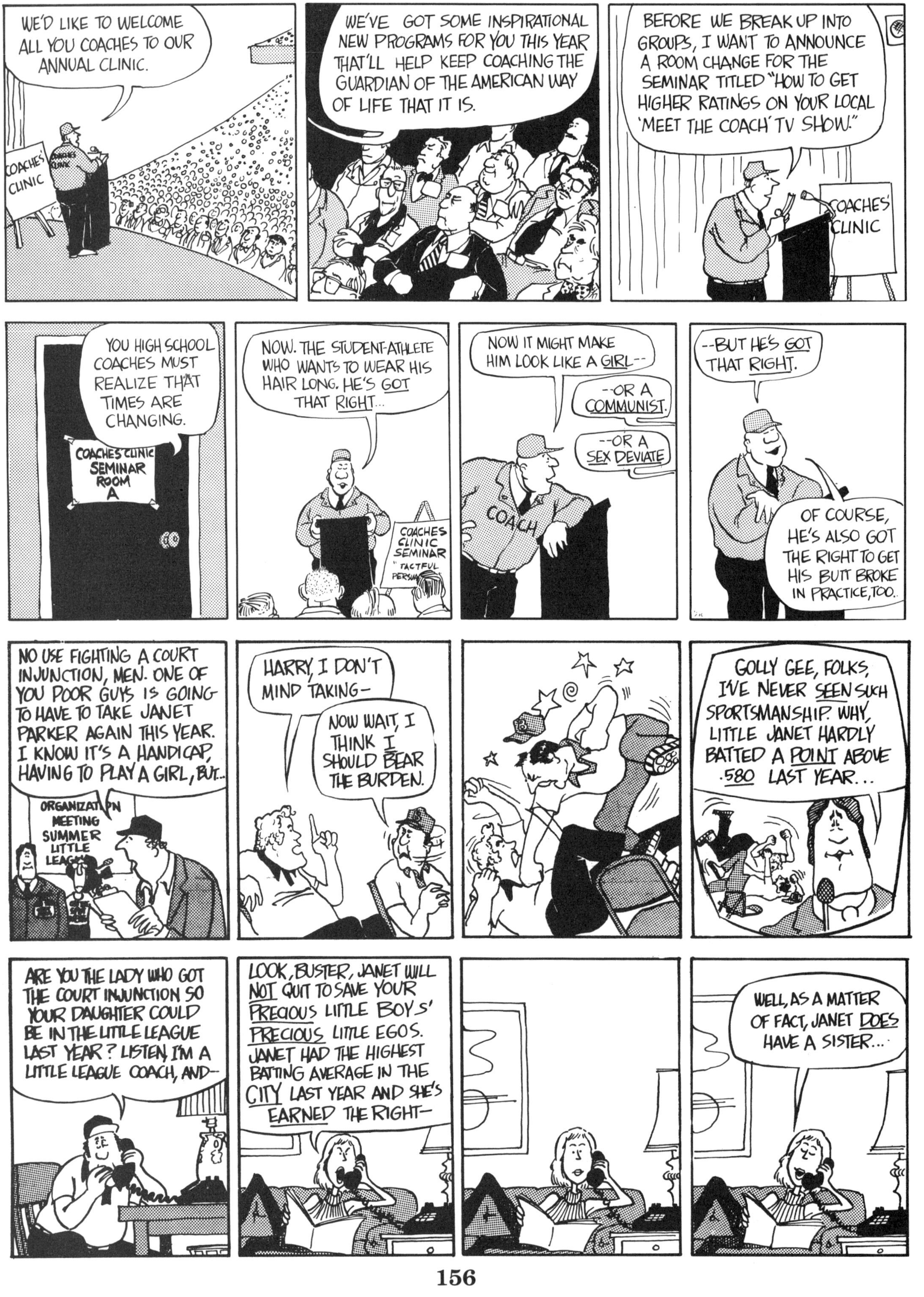

WE'D LIKE TO WELCOME ALL YOU COACHES TO OUR ANNUAL CLINIC.
COACHES' CLINIC
WE'VE GOT SOME INSPIRATIONAL NEW PROGRAMS FOR YOU THIS YEAR THAT'LL HELP KEEP COACHING THE GUARDIAN OF THE AMERICAN WAY OF LIFE THAT IT IS.
BEFORE WE BREAK UP INTO GROUPS, I WANT TO ANNOUNCE A ROOM CHANGE FOR THE SEMINAR TITLED "HOW TO GET HIGHER RATINGS ON YOUR LOCAL 'MEET THE COACH' TV SHOW."
COACHES' CLINIC
YOU HIGH SCHOOL COACHES MUST REALIZE THAT TIMES ARE CHANGING.
COACHES CLINIC SEMINAR ROOM A
NOW. THE STUDENT-ATHLETE WHO WANTS TO WEAR HIS HAIR LONG. HE'S GOT THAT RIGHT...
COACHES CLINIC SEMINAR "TACTFUL PERSUA
NOW IT MIGHT MAKE HIM LOOK LIKE A GIRL--
--OR A COMMUNIST.
--OR A SEX DEVIATE
COACH
--BUT HE'S GOT THAT RIGHT.
OF COURSE, HE'S ALSO GOT THE RIGHT TO GET HIS BUTT BROKE IN PRACTICE, TOO.
NO USE FIGHTING A COURT INJUNCTION, MEN. ONE OF YOU POOR GUYS IS GOING TO HAVE TO TAKE JANET PARKER AGAIN THIS YEAR. I KNOW IT'S A HANDICAP, HAVING TO PLAY A GIRL, BUT...
ORGANIZATION MEETING SUMMER LITTLE LEAG
HARRY, I DON'T MIND TAKING—
NOW WAIT, I THINK I SHOULD BEAR THE BURDEN.
GOLLY GEE, FOLKS, I'VE NEVER SEEN SUCH SPORTSMANSHIP. WHY, LITTLE JANET HARDLY BATTED A POINT ABOVE .580 LAST YEAR...
ARE YOU THE LADY WHO GOT THE COURT INJUNCTION SO YOUR DAUGHTER COULD BE IN THE LITTLE LEAGUE LAST YEAR? LISTEN, I'M A LITTLE LEAGUE COACH, AND—
LOOK, BUSTER, JANET WILL NOT QUIT TO SAVE YOUR PRECIOUS LITTLE BOYS' PRECIOUS LITTLE EGOS. JANET HAD THE HIGHEST BATTING AVERAGE IN THE CITY LAST YEAR AND SHE'S EARNED THE RIGHT—
WELL, AS A MATTER OF FACT, JANET DOES HAVE A SISTER...

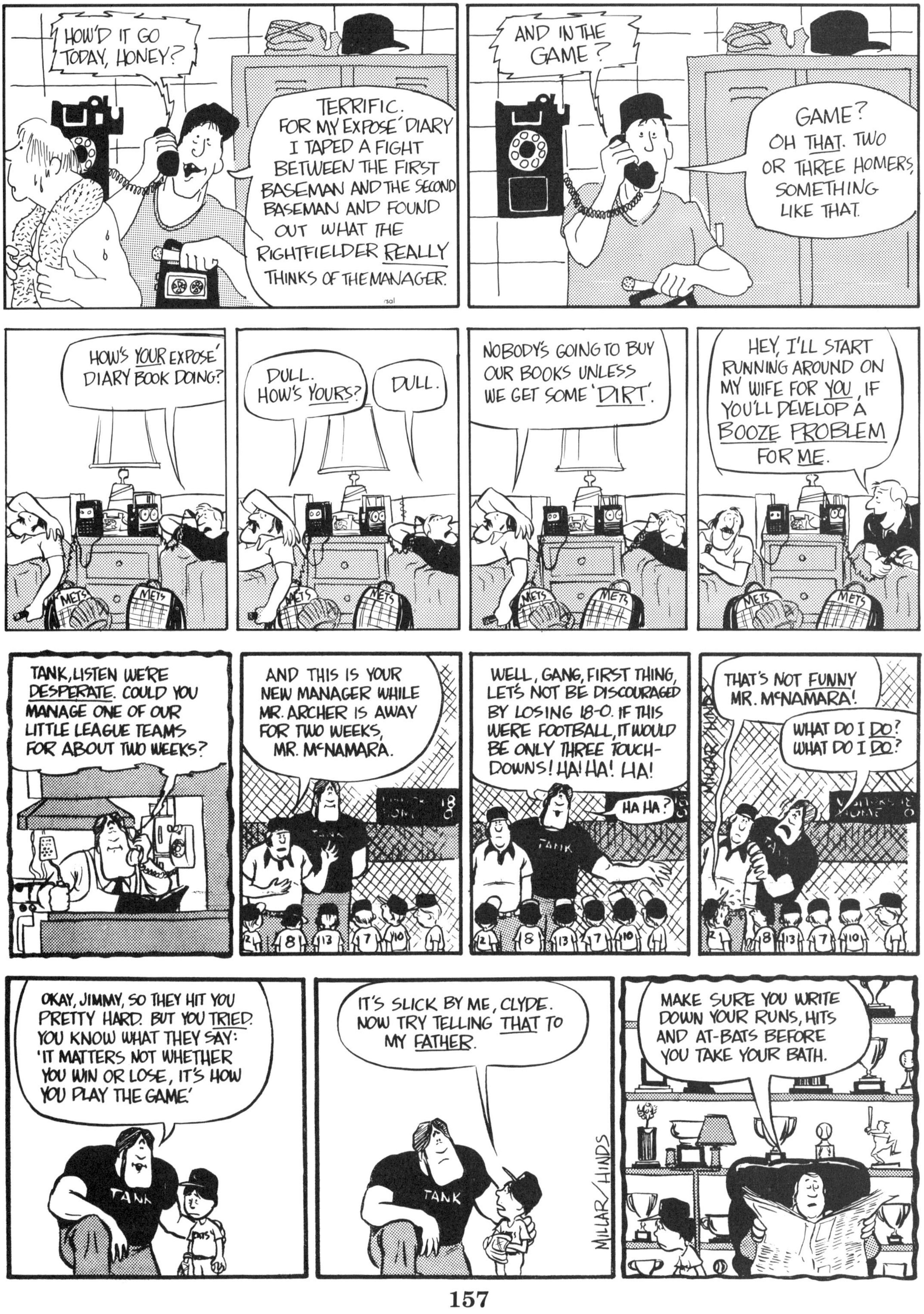
HOW'D IT GO TODAY, HONEY?
TERRIFIC. FOR MY EXPOSE' DIARY I TAPED A FIGHT BETWEEN THE FIRST BASEMAN AND THE SECOND BASEMAN AND FOUND OUT WHAT THE RIGHTFIELDER REALLY THINKS OF THE MANAGER.
AND IN THE GAME?
GAME? OH THAT. TWO OR THREE HOMERS, SOMETHING LIKE THAT.
HOW'S YOUR EXPOSE' DIARY BOOK DOING?
DULL. HOW'S YOURS?
DULL.
NOBODY'S GOING TO BUY OUR BOOKS UNLESS WE GET SOME 'DIRT'.
HEY, I'LL START RUNNING AROUND ON MY WIFE FOR YOU, IF YOU'LL DEVELOP A BOOZE PROBLEM FOR ME.
METS
METS
TANK, LISTEN WE'RE DESPERATE. COULD YOU MANAGE ONE OF OUR LITTLE LEAGUE TEAMS FOR ABOUT TWO WEEKS?
AND THIS IS YOUR NEW MANAGER WHILE MR. ARCHER IS AWAY FOR TWO WEEKS, MR. McNAMARA.
TANK
WELL, GANG, FIRST THING, LET'S NOT BE DISCOURAGED BY LOSING 18-0. IF THIS WERE FOOTBALL, IT WOULD BE ONLY THREE TOUCH-DOWNS! HA! HA! HA!
HA HA?
THAT'S NOT FUNNY MR. McNAMARA!
WHAT DO I DO? WHAT DO I DO?
OKAY, JIMMY, SO THEY HIT YOU PRETTY HARD. BUT YOU TRIED. YOU KNOW WHAT THEY SAY: 'IT MATTERS NOT WHETHER YOU WIN OR LOSE, IT'S HOW YOU PLAY THE GAME.'
TANK
IT'S SLICK BY ME, CLYDE. NOW TRY TELLING THAT TO MY FATHER.
MILLAR/HINDS
MAKE SURE YOU WRITE DOWN YOUR RUNS, HITS AND AT-BATS BEFORE YOU TAKE YOUR BATH.

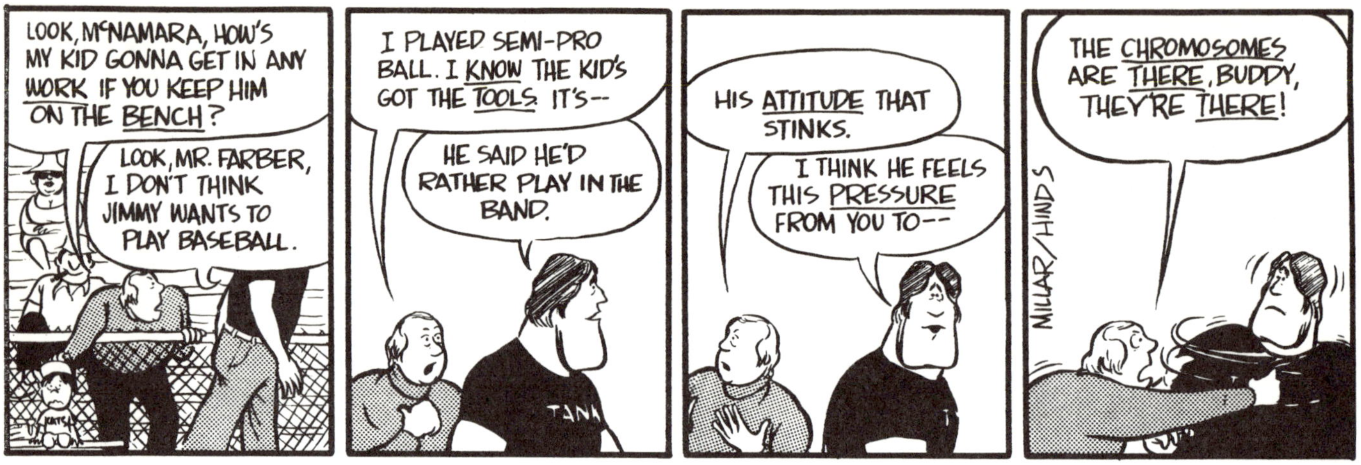
LOOK, McNAMARA, HOW'S MY KID GONNA GET IN ANY WORK IF YOU KEEP HIM ON THE BENCH?
LOOK, MR. FARBER, I DON'T THINK JIMMY WANTS TO PLAY BASEBALL.
I PLAYED SEMI-PRO BALL. I KNOW THE KID'S GOT THE TOOLS. IT'S--
HE SAID HE'D RATHER PLAY IN THE BAND.
HIS ATTITUDE THAT STINKS.
I THINK HE FEELS THIS PRESSURE FROM YOU TO--
THE CHROMOSOMES ARE THERE, BUDDY, THEY'RE THERE!
MILLAR/HINDS

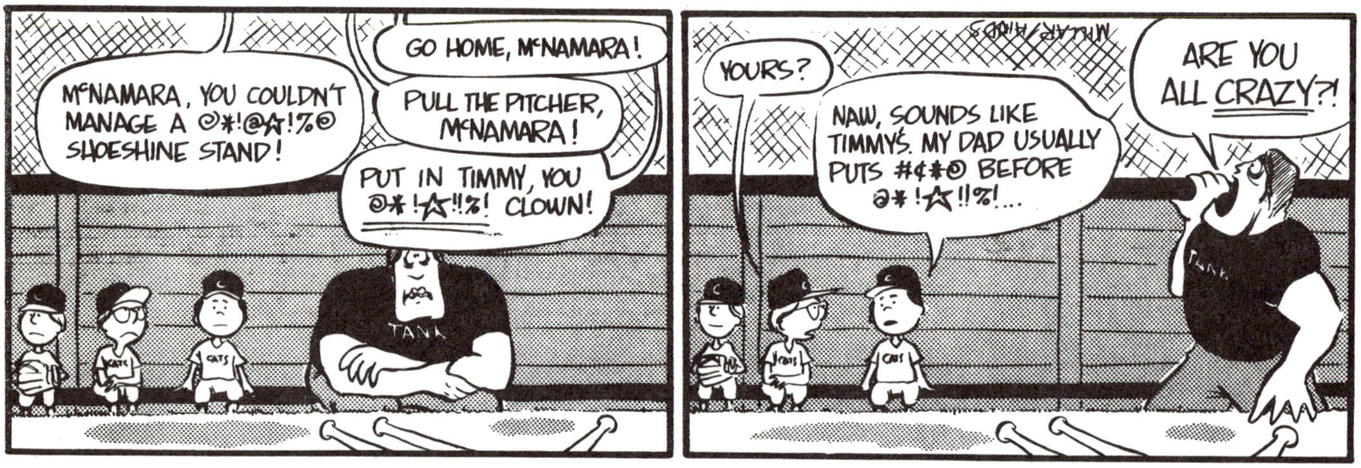
McNAMARA, YOU COULDN'T MANAGE A @*!@☆!%@ SHOESHINE STAND!
GO HOME, McNAMARA!
PULL THE PITCHER, McNAMARA!
PUT IN TIMMY, YOU @*!☆!!%! CLOWN!
YOURS?
NAW, SOUNDS LIKE TIMMY'S. MY DAD USUALLY PUTS #¢*@ BEFORE @*!☆!!%!...
ARE YOU ALL CRAZY?!
MILLAR/HINDS

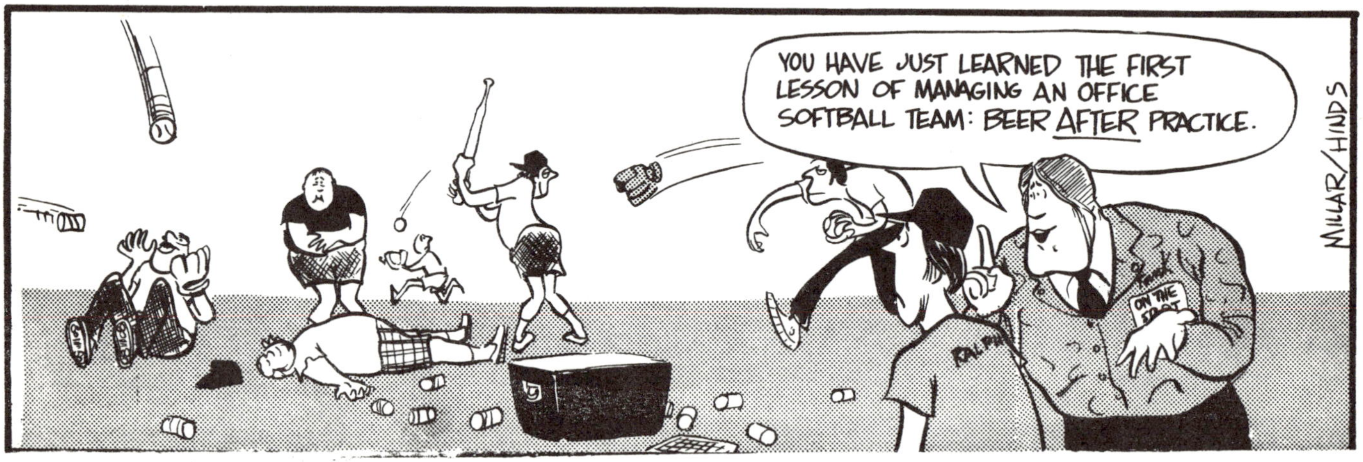
YOU HAVE JUST LEARNED THE FIRST LESSON OF MANAGING AN OFFICE SOFTBALL TEAM: BEER AFTER PRACTICE.
MILLAR/HINDS

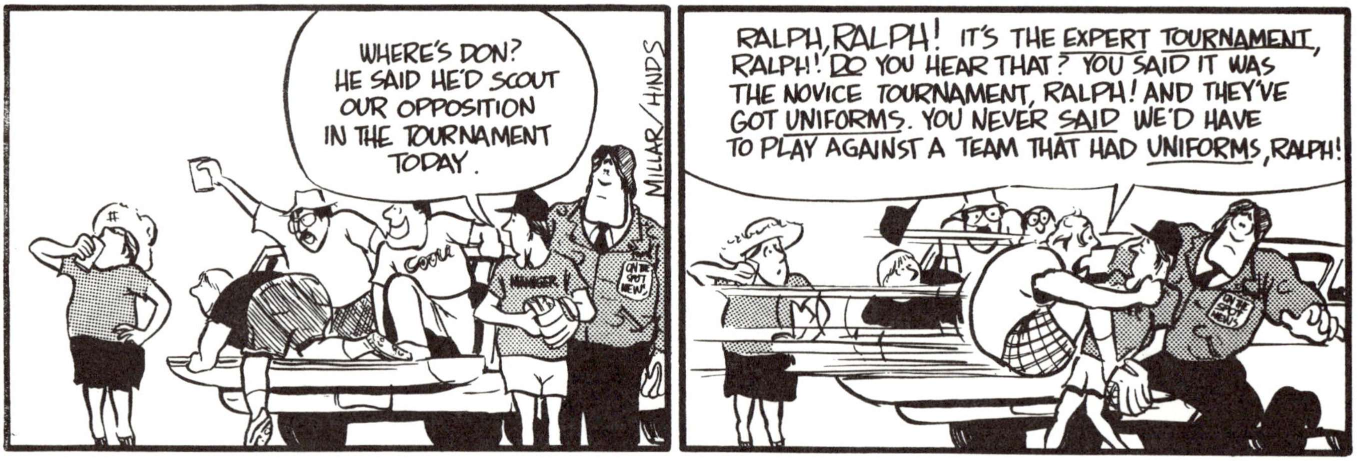
WHERE'S DON? HE SAID HE'D SCOUT OUR OPPOSITION IN THE TOURNAMENT TODAY.
MILLAR/HINDS
RALPH, RALPH! IT'S THE EXPERT TOURNAMENT, RALPH! DO YOU HEAR THAT? YOU SAID IT WAS THE NOVICE TOURNAMENT, RALPH! AND THEY'VE GOT UNIFORMS. YOU NEVER SAID WE'D HAVE TO PLAY AGAINST A TEAM THAT HAD UNIFORMS, RALPH!

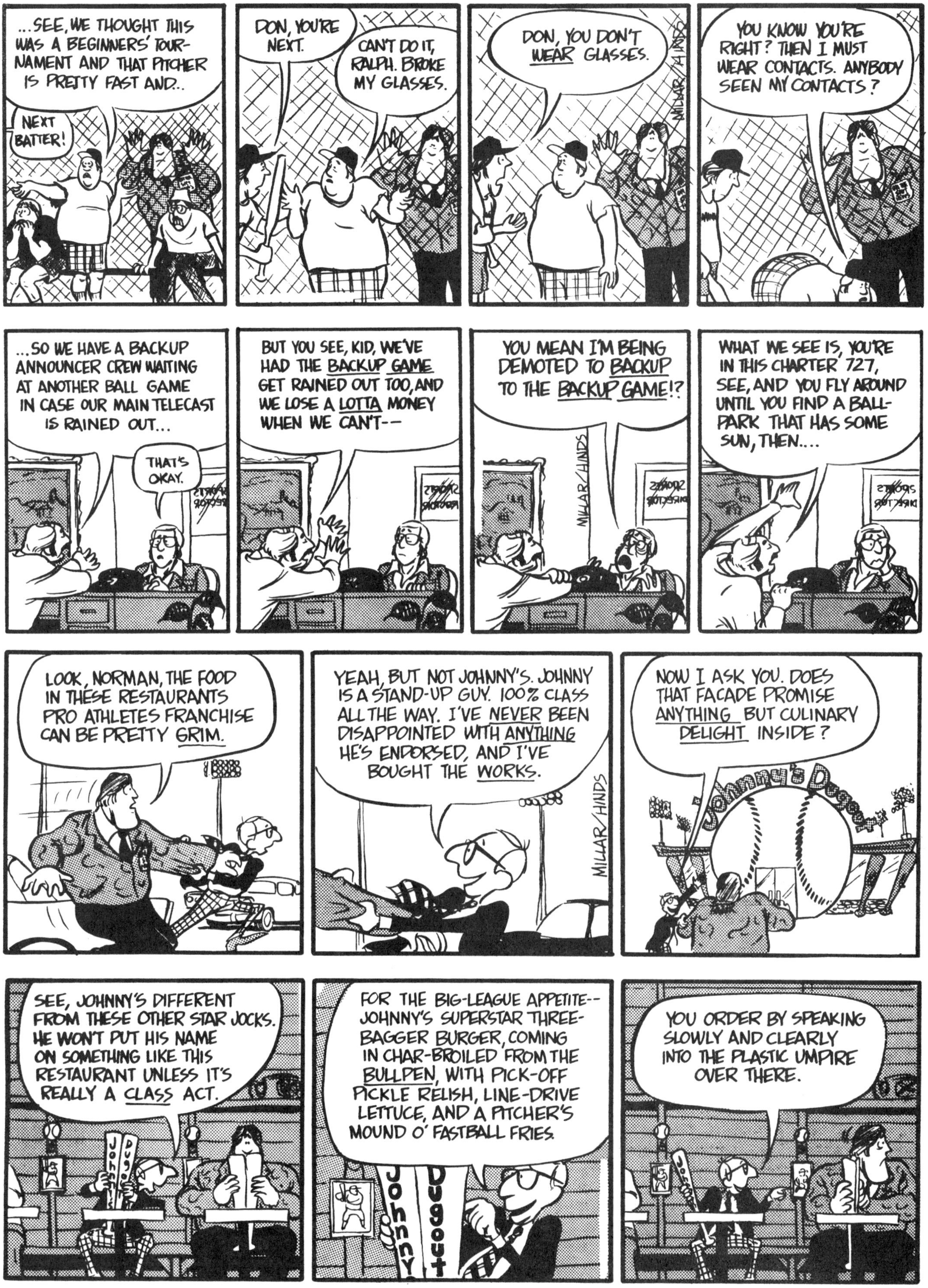
...SEE, WE THOUGHT THIS WAS A BEGINNERS' TOURNAMENT AND THAT PITCHER IS PRETTY FAST AND..
NEXT BATTER!
DON, YOU'RE NEXT.
CAN'T DO IT, RALPH. BROKE MY GLASSES.
DON, YOU DON'T WEAR GLASSES.
MILLAR/HINDS
YOU KNOW YOU'RE RIGHT? THEN I MUST WEAR CONTACTS. ANYBODY SEEN MY CONTACTS?
...SO WE HAVE A BACKUP ANNOUNCER CREW WAITING AT ANOTHER BALL GAME IN CASE OUR MAIN TELECAST IS RAINED OUT...
THAT'S OKAY.
BUT YOU SEE, KID, WE'VE HAD THE BACKUP GAME GET RAINED OUT TOO, AND WE LOSE A LOTTA MONEY WHEN WE CAN'T--
YOU MEAN I'M BEING DEMOTED TO BACKUP TO THE BACKUP GAME!?
MILLAR/HINDS
WHAT WE SEE IS, YOU'RE IN THIS CHARTER 727, SEE, AND YOU FLY AROUND UNTIL YOU FIND A BALLPARK THAT HAS SOME SUN, THEN....
LOOK, NORMAN, THE FOOD IN THESE RESTAURANTS PRO ATHLETES FRANCHISE CAN BE PRETTY GRIM.
YEAH, BUT NOT JOHNNY'S. JOHNNY IS A STAND-UP GUY. 100% CLASS ALL THE WAY. I'VE NEVER BEEN DISAPPOINTED WITH ANYTHING HE'S ENDORSED, AND I'VE BOUGHT THE WORKS.
MILLAR/HINDS
NOW I ASK YOU. DOES THAT FACADE PROMISE ANYTHING BUT CULINARY DELIGHT INSIDE?
Johnny's Dugout
SEE, JOHNNY'S DIFFERENT FROM THESE OTHER STAR JOCKS. HE WON'T PUT HIS NAME ON SOMETHING LIKE THIS RESTAURANT UNLESS IT'S REALLY A CLASS ACT.
FOR THE BIG-LEAGUE APPETITE-- JOHNNY'S SUPERSTAR THREE-BAGGER BURGER, COMING IN CHAR-BROILED FROM THE BULLPEN, WITH PICK-OFF PICKLE RELISH, LINE-DRIVE LETTUCE, AND A PITCHER'S MOUND O' FASTBALL FRIES.
Johnny Dugout
YOU ORDER BY SPEAKING SLOWLY AND CLEARLY INTO THE PLASTIC UMPIRE OVER THERE.

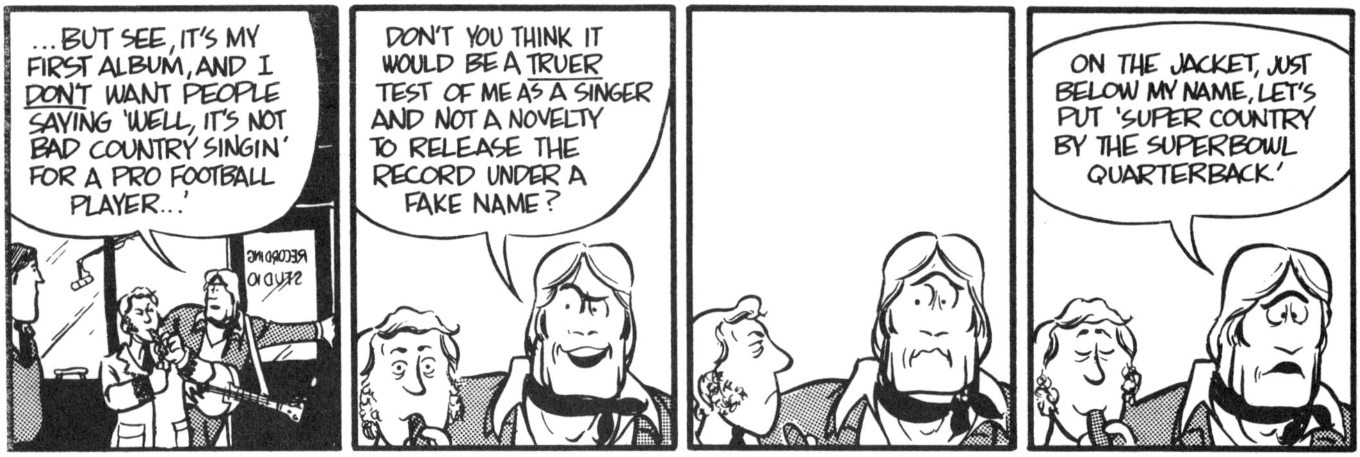
...BUT SEE, IT'S MY FIRST ALBUM, AND I DON'T WANT PEOPLE SAYING 'WELL, IT'S NOT BAD COUNTRY SINGIN' FOR A PRO FOOTBALL PLAYER...'
DON'T YOU THINK IT WOULD BE A TRUER TEST OF ME AS A SINGER AND NOT A NOVELTY TO RELEASE THE RECORD UNDER A FAKE NAME?
ON THE JACKET, JUST BELOW MY NAME, LET'S PUT 'SUPER COUNTRY BY THE SUPERBOWL QUARTERBACK.'

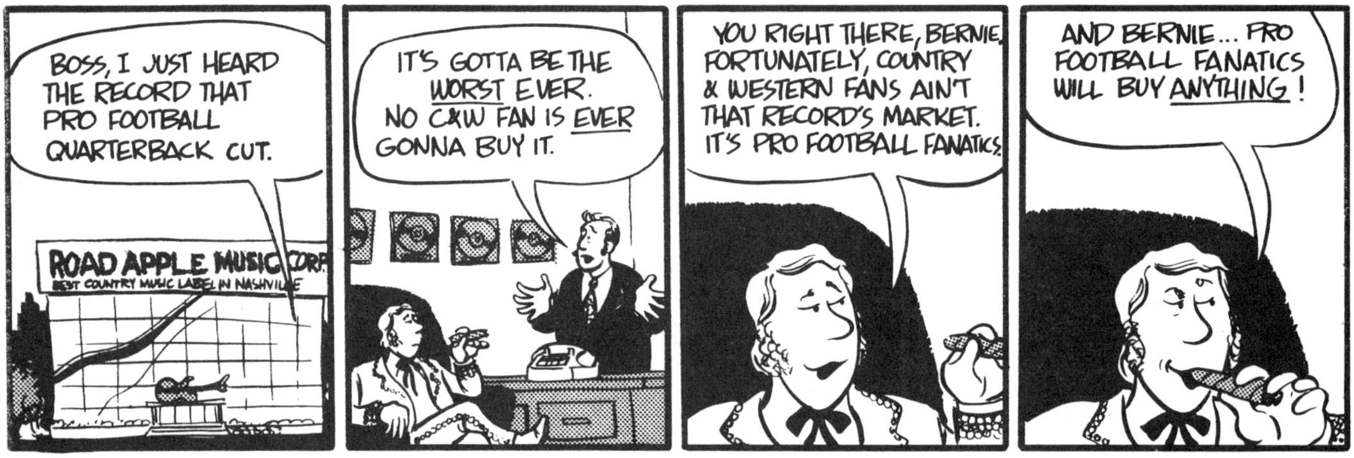
BOSS, I JUST HEARD THE RECORD THAT PRO FOOTBALL QUARTERBACK CUT.
ROAD APPLE MUSIC CORP.
BEST COUNTRY MUSIC LABEL IN NASHVILLE
IT'S GOTTA BE THE WORST EVER. NO C&W FAN IS EVER GONNA BUY IT.
YOU RIGHT THERE, BERNIE, FORTUNATELY, COUNTRY & WESTERN FANS AIN'T THAT RECORD'S MARKET. IT'S PRO FOOTBALL FANATICS.
AND BERNIE... PRO FOOTBALL FANATICS WILL BUY ANYTHING!

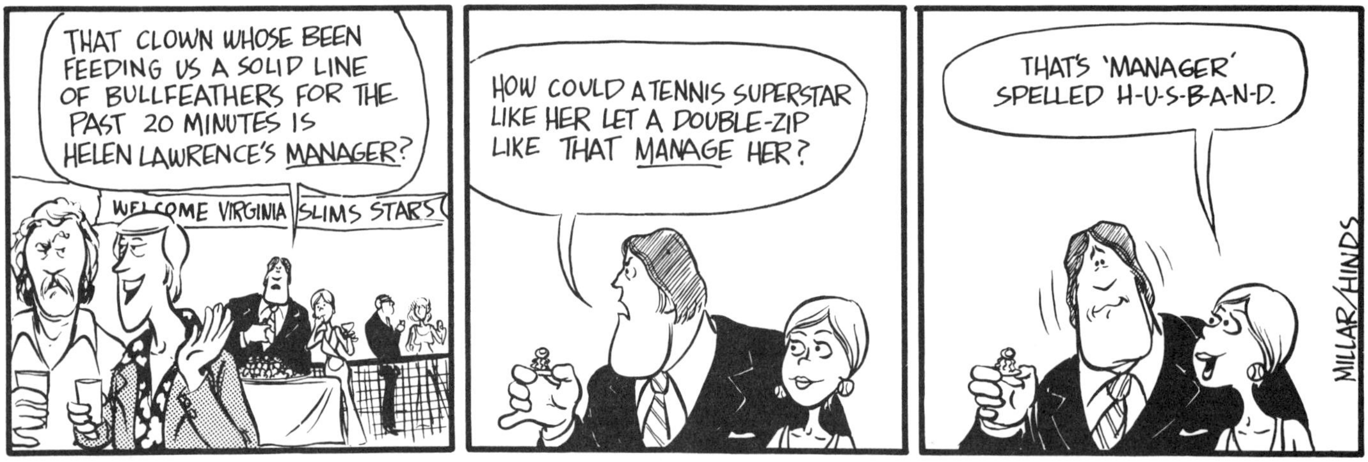
THAT CLOWN WHOSE BEEN FEEDING US A SOLID LINE OF BULLFEATHERS FOR THE PAST 20 MINUTES IS HELEN LAWRENCE'S MANAGER?
WELCOME VIRGINIA SLIMS STARS
HOW COULD A TENNIS SUPERSTAR LIKE HER LET A DOUBLE-ZIP LIKE THAT MANAGE HER?
THAT'S 'MANAGER' SPELLED H-U-S-B-A-N-D.
MILLAR/HINDS

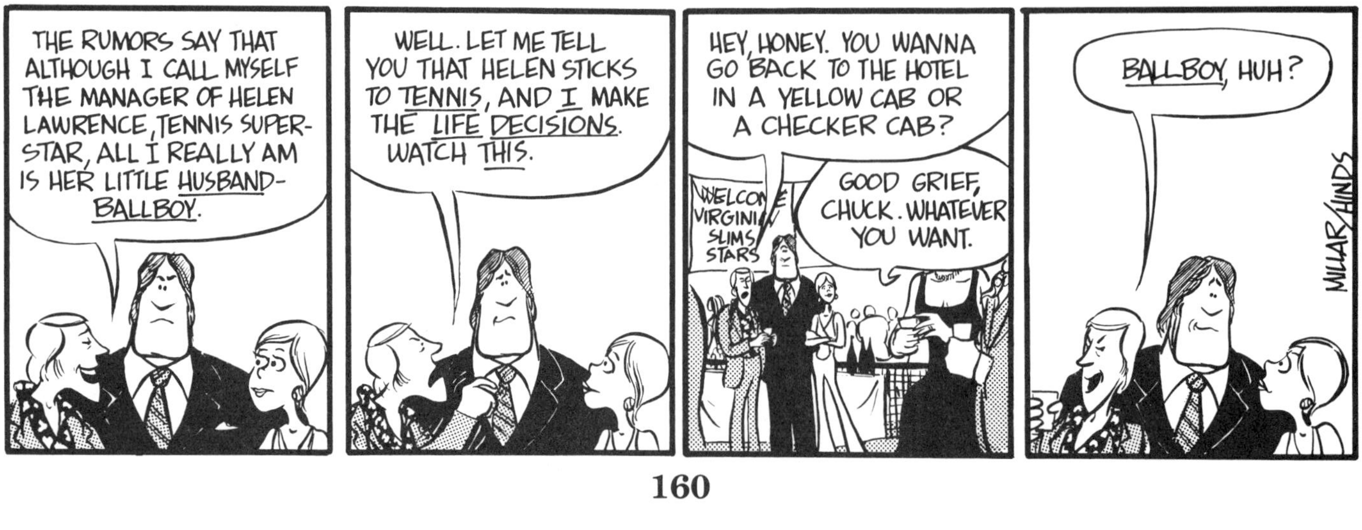
THE RUMORS SAY THAT ALTHOUGH I CALL MYSELF THE MANAGER OF HELEN LAWRENCE, TENNIS SUPERSTAR, ALL I REALLY AM IS HER LITTLE HUSBAND-BALLBOY.
WELL. LET ME TELL YOU THAT HELEN STICKS TO TENNIS, AND I MAKE THE LIFE DECISIONS. WATCH THIS.
HEY, HONEY. YOU WANNA GO BACK TO THE HOTEL IN A YELLOW CAB OR A CHECKER CAB?
WELCOME VIRGINIA SLIMS STARS
GOOD GRIEF, CHUCK. WHATEVER YOU WANT.
BALLBOY, HUH?
MILLAR/HINDS

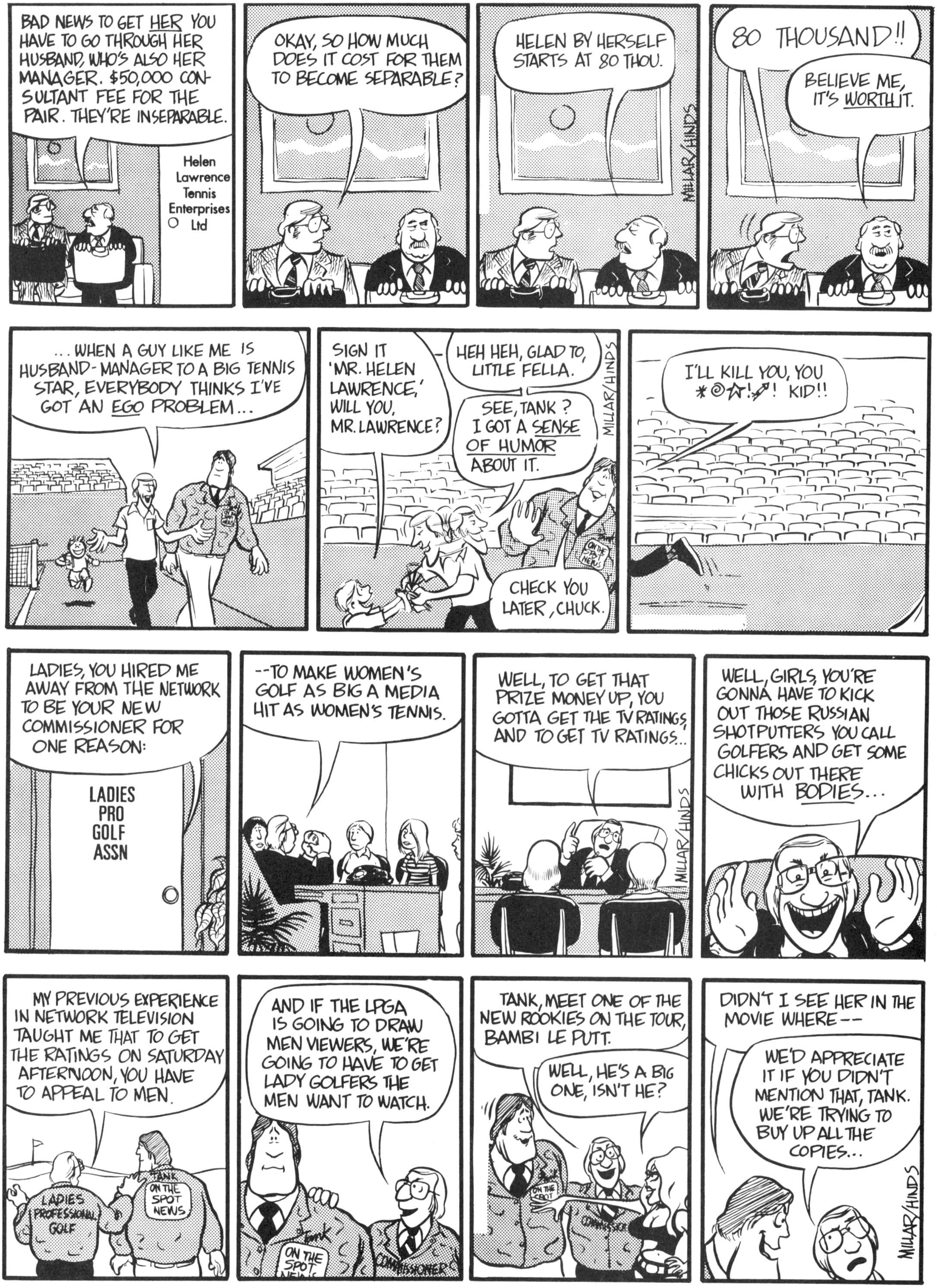
BAD NEWS TO GET HER YOU HAVE TO GO THROUGH HER HUSBAND, WHO'S ALSO HER MANAGER. $50,000 CONSULTANT FEE FOR THE PAIR. THEY'RE INSEPARABLE.
Helen Lawrence Tennis Enterprises Ltd
OKAY, SO HOW MUCH DOES IT COST FOR THEM TO BECOME SEPARABLE?
HELEN BY HERSELF STARTS AT 80 THOU.
MILLAR/HINDS
80 THOUSAND!!
BELIEVE ME, IT'S WORTH IT.
...WHEN A GUY LIKE ME IS HUSBAND-MANAGER TO A BIG TENNIS STAR, EVERYBODY THINKS I'VE GOT AN EGO PROBLEM...
SIGN IT 'MR. HELEN LAWRENCE,' WILL YOU, MR. LAWRENCE?
HEH HEH, GLAD TO, LITTLE FELLA.
SEE, TANK? I GOT A SENSE OF HUMOR ABOUT IT.
CHECK YOU LATER, CHUCK.
MILLAR/HINDS
I'LL KILL YOU, YOU *@☆!! KID!!
LADIES, YOU HIRED ME AWAY FROM THE NETWORK TO BE YOUR NEW COMMISSIONER FOR ONE REASON:
LADIES PRO GOLF ASSN
--TO MAKE WOMEN'S GOLF AS BIG A MEDIA HIT AS WOMEN'S TENNIS.
WELL, TO GET THAT PRIZE MONEY UP, YOU GOTTA GET THE TV RATINGS, AND TO GET TV RATINGS...
MILLAR/HINDS
WELL, GIRLS, YOU'RE GONNA HAVE TO KICK OUT THOSE RUSSIAN SHOTPUTTERS YOU CALL GOLFERS AND GET SOME CHICKS OUT THERE WITH BODIES...
MY PREVIOUS EXPERIENCE IN NETWORK TELEVISION TAUGHT ME THAT TO GET THE RATINGS ON SATURDAY AFTERNOON, YOU HAVE TO APPEAL TO MEN.
LADIES PROFESSIONAL GOLF
TANK ON THE SPOT NEWS
AND IF THE LPGA IS GOING TO DRAW MEN VIEWERS, WE'RE GOING TO HAVE TO GET LADY GOLFERS THE MEN WANT TO WATCH.
COMMISSIONER
TANK, MEET ONE OF THE NEW ROOKIES ON THE TOUR, BAMBI LE PUTT.
WELL, HE'S A BIG ONE, ISN'T HE?
DIDN'T I SEE HER IN THE MOVIE WHERE--
WE'D APPRECIATE IT IF YOU DIDN'T MENTION THAT, TANK. WE'RE TRYING TO BUY UP ALL THE COPIES...
MILLAR/HINDS

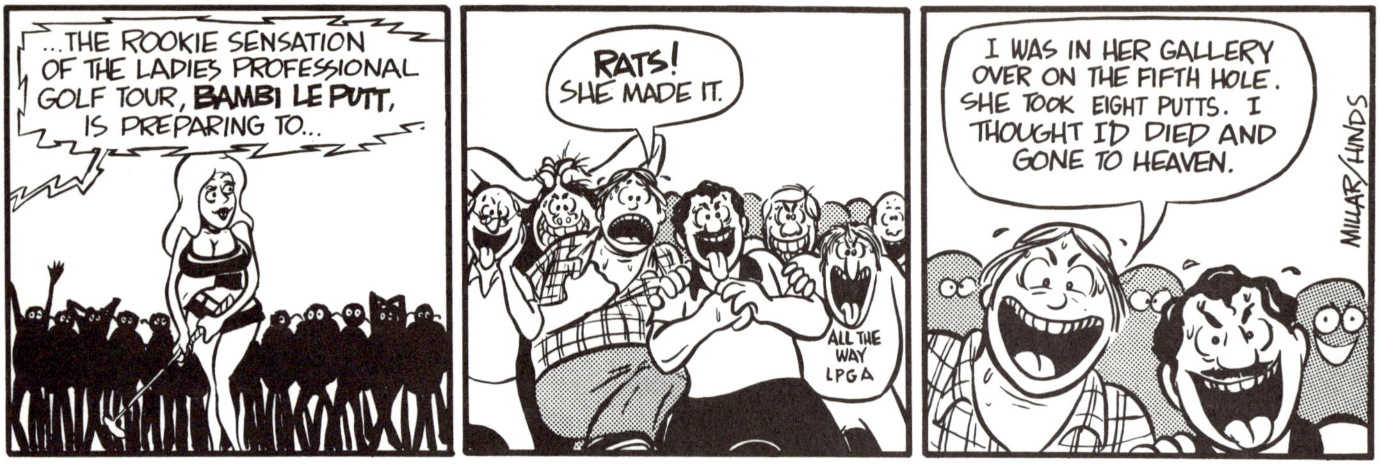
...THE ROOKIE SENSATION OF THE LADIES PROFESSIONAL GOLF TOUR, BAMBI LE PUTT, IS PREPARING TO...
RATS! SHE MADE IT.
ALL THE WAY LPGA
I WAS IN HER GALLERY OVER ON THE FIFTH HOLE. SHE TOOK EIGHT PUTTS. I THOUGHT I'D DIED AND GONE TO HEAVEN.
MILLAR/HINDS

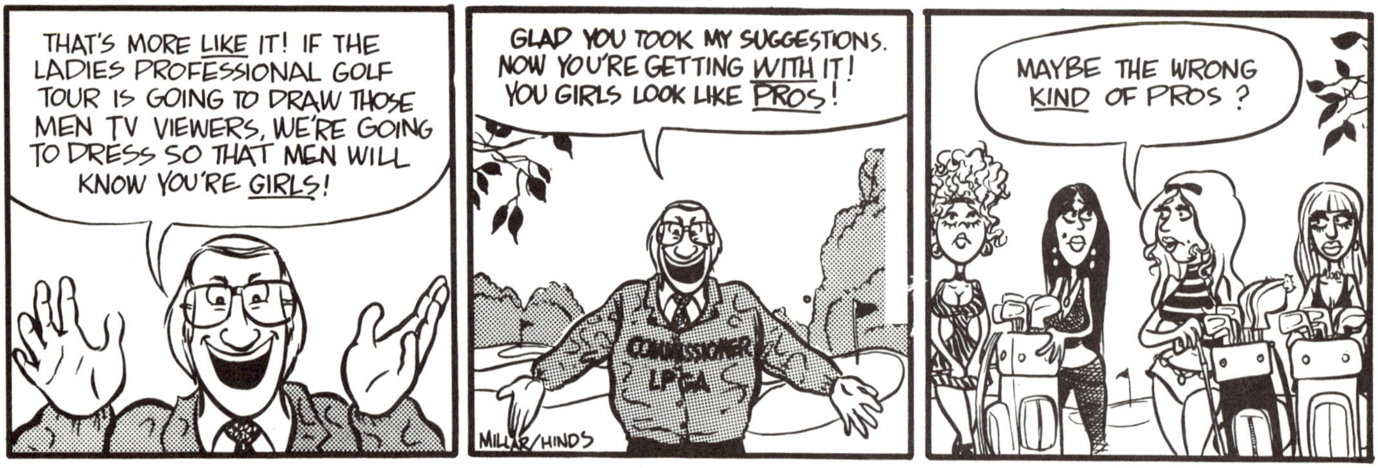
THAT'S MORE LIKE IT! IF THE LADIES PROFESSIONAL GOLF TOUR IS GOING TO DRAW THOSE MEN TV VIEWERS, WE'RE GOING TO DRESS SO THAT MEN WILL KNOW YOU'RE GIRLS!
GLAD YOU TOOK MY SUGGESTIONS. NOW YOU'RE GETTING WITH IT! YOU GIRLS LOOK LIKE PROS!
COMMISSIONER LPGA
MILLAR/HINDS
MAYBE THE WRONG KIND OF PROS?

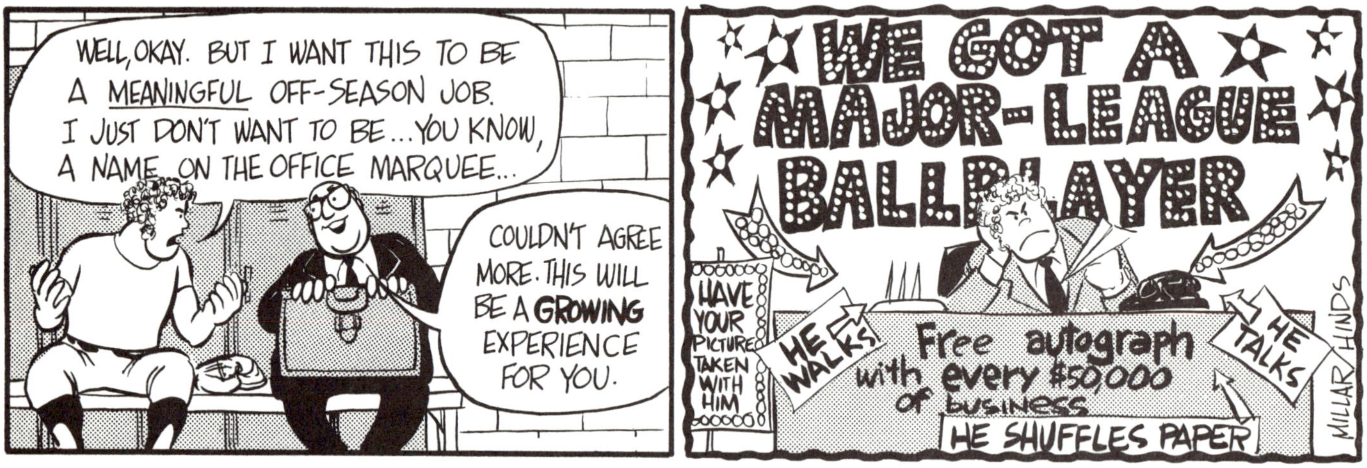
WELL, OKAY. BUT I WANT THIS TO BE A MEANINGFUL OFF-SEASON JOB. I JUST DON'T WANT TO BE...YOU KNOW, A NAME ON THE OFFICE MARQUEE...
COULDN'T AGREE MORE. THIS WILL BE A GROWING EXPERIENCE FOR YOU.
WE GOT A MAJOR-LEAGUE BALLPLAYER
HAVE YOUR PICTURE TAKEN WITH HIM
HE WALKS
HE TALKS
Free autograph with every $50,000 of business
HE SHUFFLES PAPER
MILLAR/HINDS

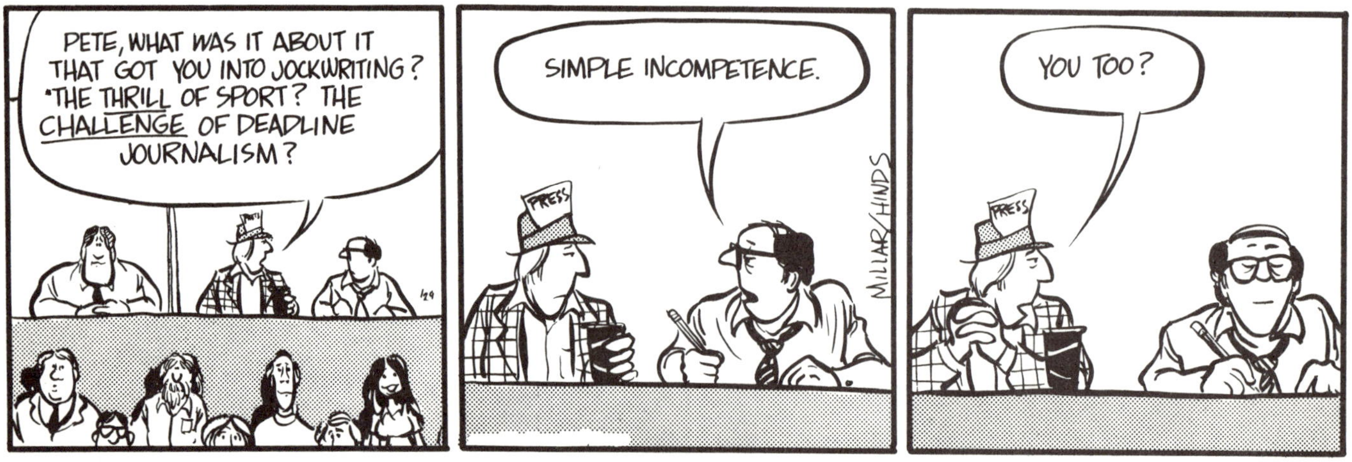
PETE, WHAT WAS IT ABOUT IT THAT GOT YOU INTO JOCKWRITING? THE THRILL OF SPORT? THE CHALLENGE OF DEADLINE JOURNALISM?
SIMPLE INCOMPETENCE.
PRESS
MILLAR/HINDS
YOU TOO?
PRESS

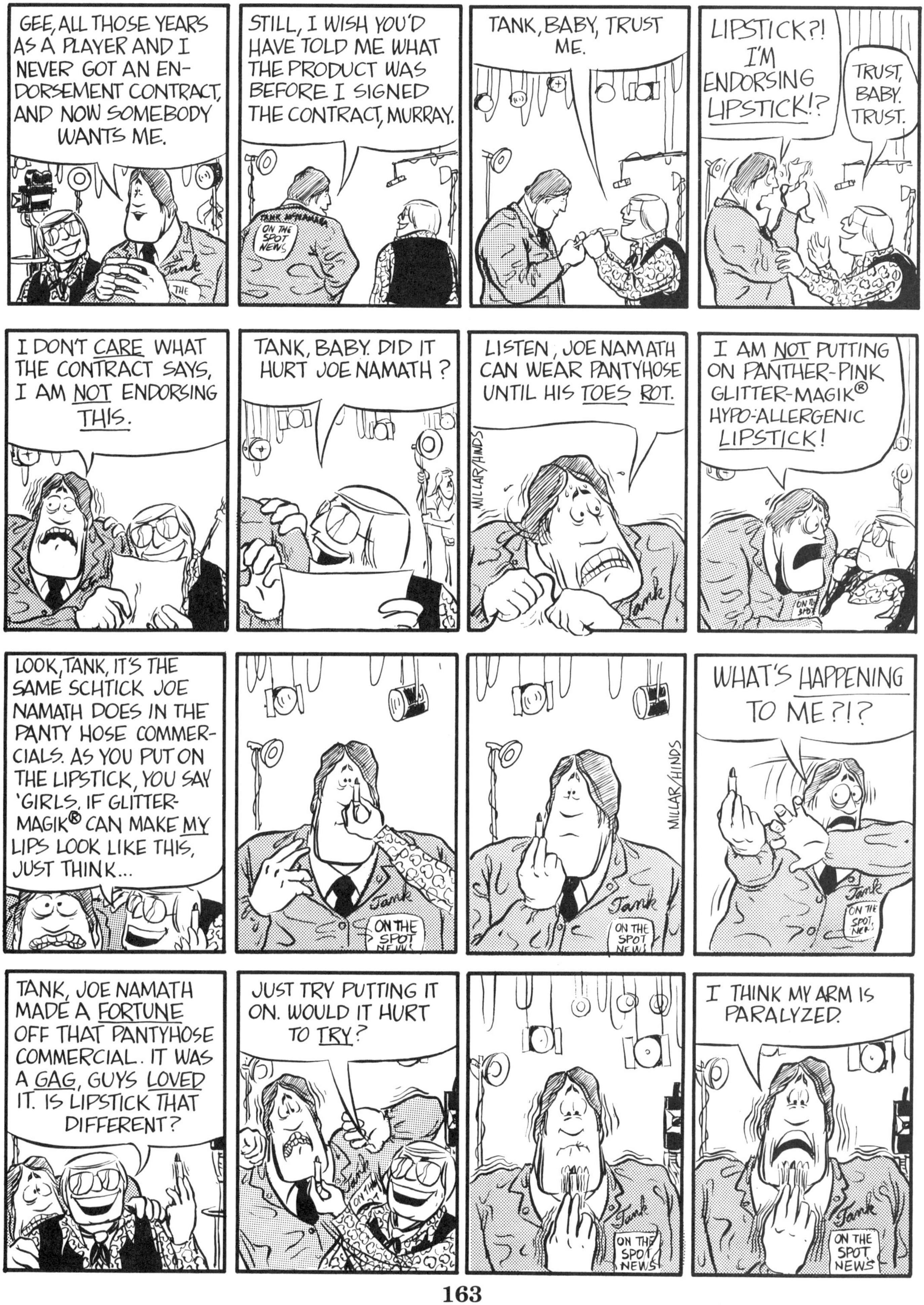
GEE, ALL THOSE YEARS AS A PLAYER AND I NEVER GOT AN ENDORSEMENT CONTRACT, AND NOW SOMEBODY WANTS ME.
STILL, I WISH YOU'D HAVE TOLD ME WHAT THE PRODUCT WAS BEFORE I SIGNED THE CONTRACT, MURRAY.
TANK, BABY, TRUST ME.
LIPSTICK?! I'M ENDORSING LIPSTICK!?
TRUST, BABY. TRUST.
I DON'T CARE WHAT THE CONTRACT SAYS, I AM NOT ENDORSING THIS.
TANK, BABY. DID IT HURT JOE NAMATH?
LISTEN, JOE NAMATH CAN WEAR PANTYHOSE UNTIL HIS TOES ROT.
MILLAR/HINDS
I AM NOT PUTTING ON PANTHER-PINK GLITTER-MAGIK® HYPO-ALLERGENIC LIPSTICK!
LOOK, TANK, IT'S THE SAME SCHTICK JOE NAMATH DOES IN THE PANTY HOSE COMMERCIALS. AS YOU PUT ON THE LIPSTICK, YOU SAY 'GIRLS, IF GLITTER-MAGIK® CAN MAKE MY LIPS LOOK LIKE THIS, JUST THINK...
MILLAR/HINDS
WHAT'S HAPPENING TO ME?!?
TANK, JOE NAMATH MADE A FORTUNE OFF THAT PANTYHOSE COMMERCIAL. IT WAS A GAG, GUYS LOVED IT. IS LIPSTICK THAT DIFFERENT?
JUST TRY PUTTING IT ON. WOULD IT HURT TO TRY?
I THINK MY ARM IS PARALYZED.

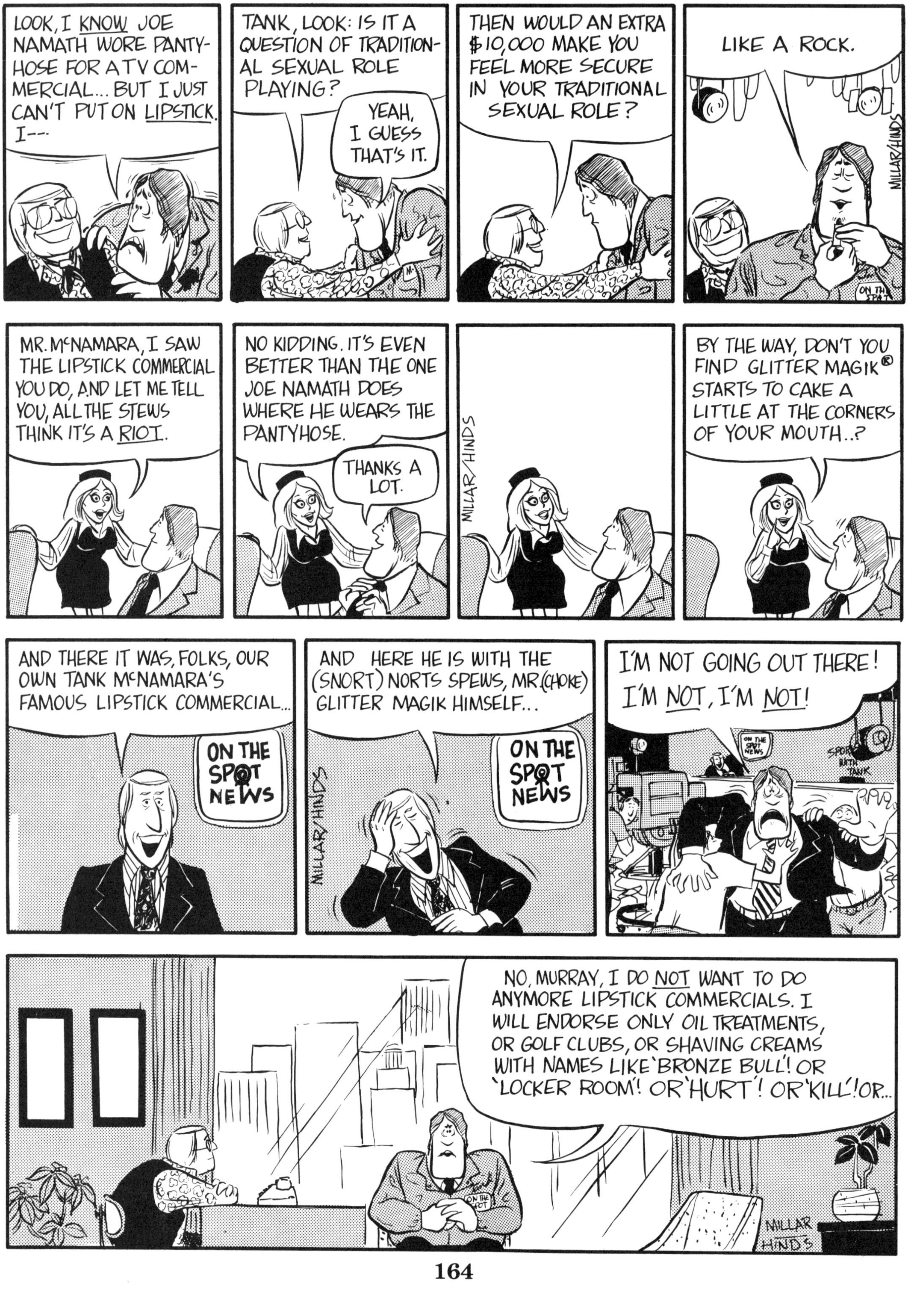
LOOK, I KNOW JOE NAMATH WORE PANTY-HOSE FOR A TV COMMERCIAL... BUT I JUST CAN'T PUT ON LIPSTICK. I---
TANK, LOOK: IS IT A QUESTION OF TRADITIONAL SEXUAL ROLE PLAYING?
YEAH, I GUESS THAT'S IT.
THEN WOULD AN EXTRA $10,000 MAKE YOU FEEL MORE SECURE IN YOUR TRADITIONAL SEXUAL ROLE?
LIKE A ROCK.
MILLAR/HINDS
MR. McNAMARA, I SAW THE LIPSTICK COMMERCIAL YOU DO, AND LET ME TELL YOU, ALL THE STEWS THINK IT'S A RIOT.
NO KIDDING. IT'S EVEN BETTER THAN THE ONE JOE NAMATH DOES WHERE HE WEARS THE PANTYHOSE.
THANKS A LOT.
MILLAR/HINDS
BY THE WAY, DON'T YOU FIND GLITTER MAGIK® STARTS TO CAKE A LITTLE AT THE CORNERS OF YOUR MOUTH..?
AND THERE IT WAS, FOLKS, OUR OWN TANK McNAMARA'S FAMOUS LIPSTICK COMMERCIAL...
ON THE SPOT NEWS
AND HERE HE IS WITH THE (SNORT) NORTS SPEWS, MR. (CHOKE) GLITTER MAGIK HIMSELF...
ON THE SPOT NEWS
MILLAR/HINDS
I'M NOT GOING OUT THERE! I'M NOT, I'M NOT!
NO, MURRAY, I DO NOT WANT TO DO ANYMORE LIPSTICK COMMERCIALS. I WILL ENDORSE ONLY OIL TREATMENTS, OR GOLF CLUBS, OR SHAVING CREAMS WITH NAMES LIKE 'BRONZE BULL'! OR 'LOCKER ROOM'! OR 'HURT'! OR 'KILL'! OR...
ON THE SPOT
MILLAR HINDS

TANK McNAMARA

by Jeff Millar & Bill Hinds

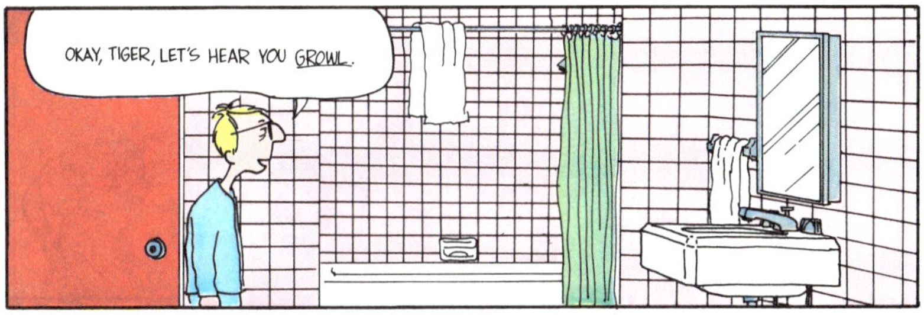

OKAY, TIGER, LET'S HEAR YOU GROWL.

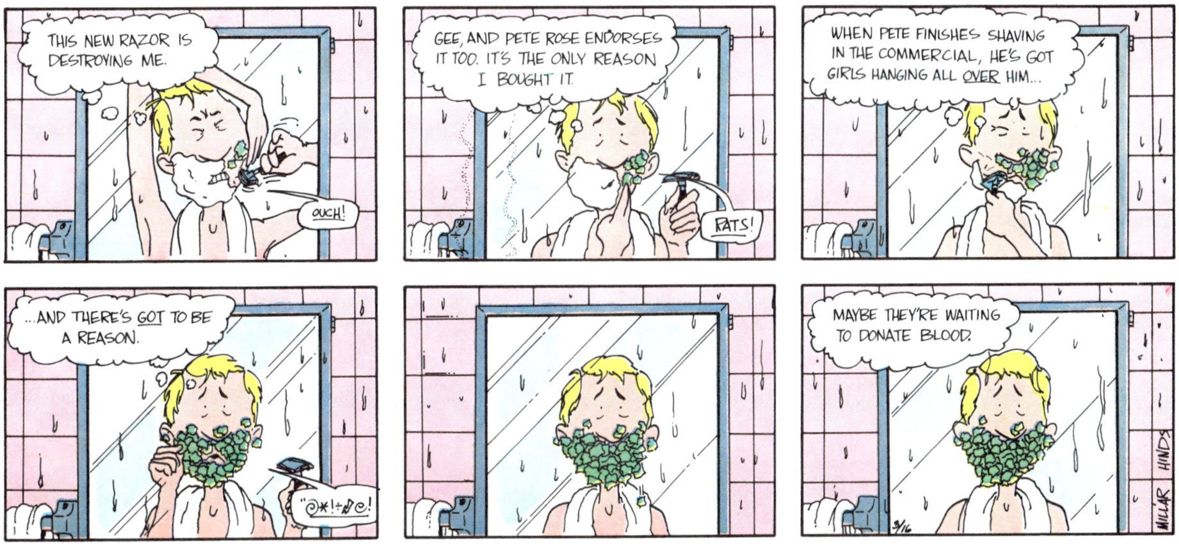

THIS NEW RAZOR IS DESTROYING ME.
OUCH!
GEE, AND PETE ROSE ENDORSES IT TOO. IT'S THE ONLY REASON I BOUGHT IT.
RATS!
WHEN PETE FINISHES SHAVING IN THE COMMERCIAL, HE'S GOT GIRLS HANGING ALL OVER HIM...
...AND THERE'S GOT TO BE A REASON.
"@*!÷#@!
MAYBE THEY'RE WAITING TO DONATE BLOOD.
3/16
MILLAR HINDS

TANK McNAMARA

by Jeff Millar & Bill Hinds

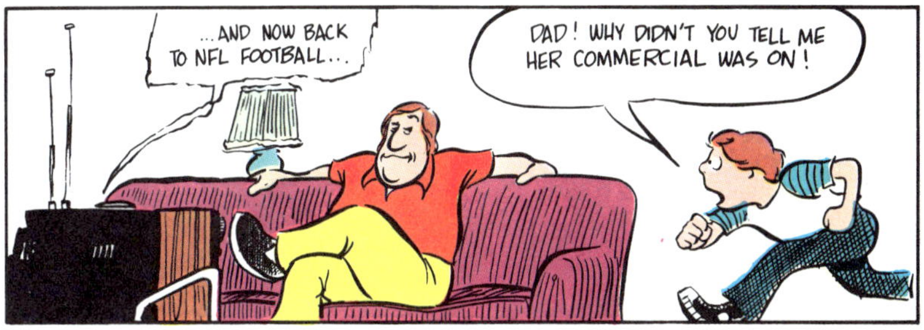

...AND NOW BACK TO NFL FOOTBALL...
DAD! WHY DIDN'T YOU TELL ME HER COMMERCIAL WAS ON!

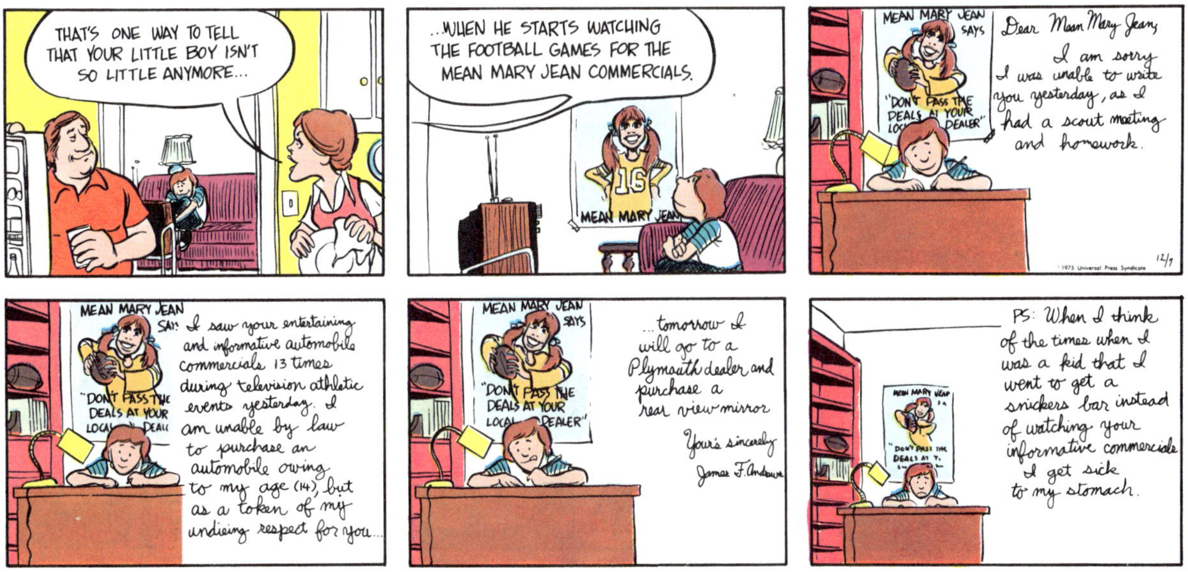

THAT'S ONE WAY TO TELL THAT YOUR LITTLE BOY ISN'T SO LITTLE ANYMORE...
...WHEN HE STARTS WATCHING THE FOOTBALL GAMES FOR THE MEAN MARY JEAN COMMERCIALS.
16
MEAN MARY JEAN
MEAN MARY JEAN SAYS
"DON'T PASS THE DEALS AT YOUR LOCAL DEALER"
Dear Mean Mary Jean,
I am sorry I was unable to write you yesterday, as I had a scout meeting and homework.
© 1975 Universal Press Syndicate
12/7
I saw your entertaining and informative automobile commercials 13 times during television athletic events yesterday. I am unable by law to purchase an automobile owing to my age (14), but as a token of my undieing respect for you...
...tomorrow I will go to a Plymouth dealer and purchase a rear view mirror
Your's sincerely
James F. Andrews
PS: When I think of the times when I was a kid that I went to get a snickers bar instead of watching your informative commercials I get sick to my stomach.

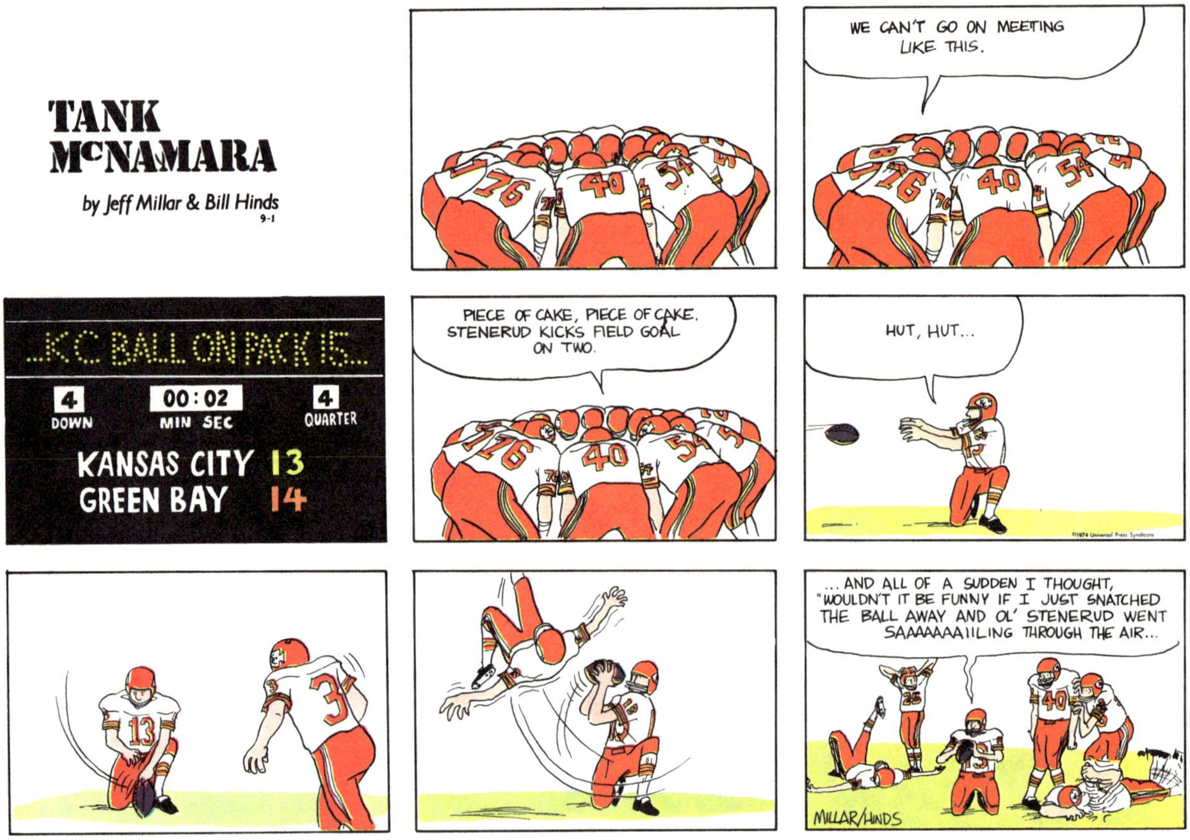
TANK McNAMARA
by Jeff Millar & Bill Hinds
9-1
WE CAN'T GO ON MEETING LIKE THIS.
...K.C. BALL ON PACK 15...
4 DOWN
00:02 MIN SEC
4 QUARTER
KANSAS CITY 13
GREEN BAY 14
PIECE OF CAKE, PIECE OF CAKE. STENERUD KICKS FIELD GOAL ON TWO.
HUT, HUT...
...AND ALL OF A SUDDEN I THOUGHT, "WOULDN'T IT BE FUNNY IF I JUST SNATCHED THE BALL AWAY AND OL' STENERUD WENT SAAAAAAAIILING THROUGH THE AIR...
MILLAR/HINDS

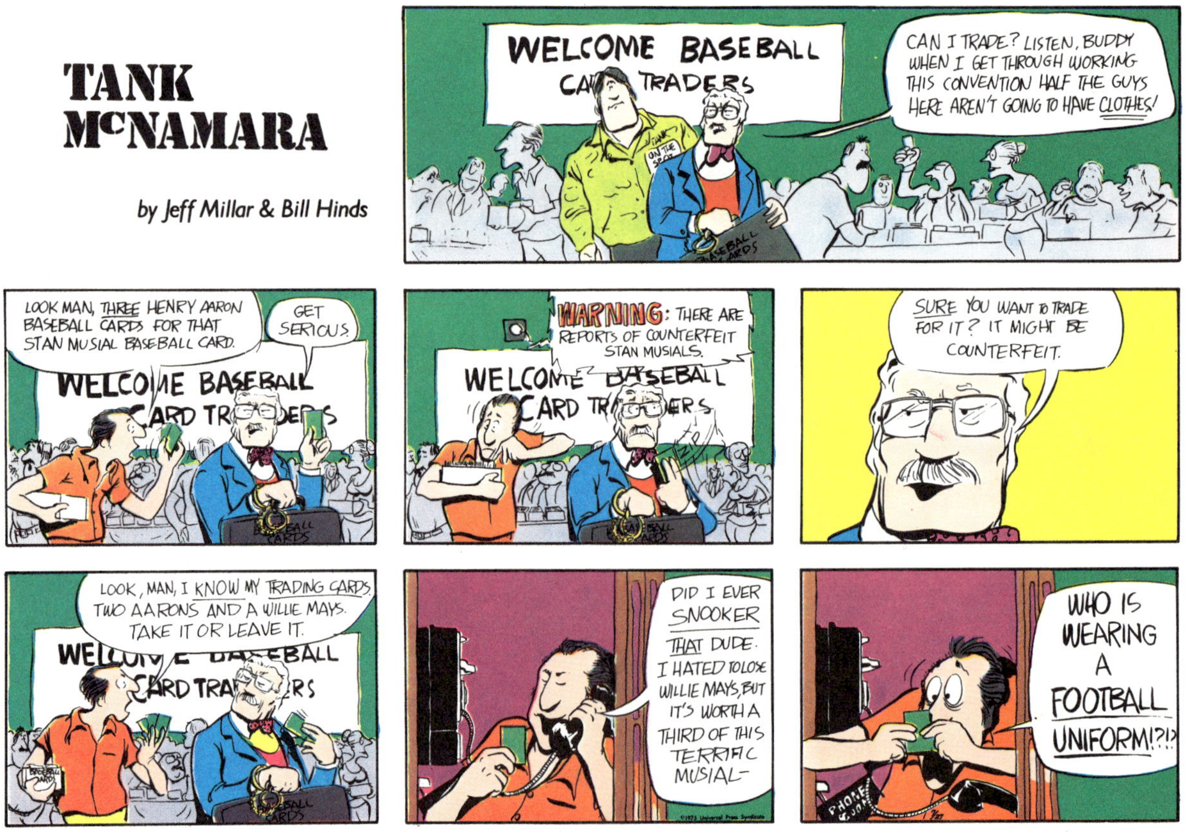
TANK McNAMARA
by Jeff Millar & Bill Hinds
WELCOME BASEBALL
CAN I TRADE? LISTEN, BUDDY WHEN I GET THROUGH WORKING THIS CONVENTION HALF THE GUYS HERE AREN'T GOING TO HAVE CLOTHES!
BASEBALL CARDS
LOOK MAN, THREE HENRY AARON BASEBALL CARDS FOR THAT STAN MUSIAL BASEBALL CARD.
GET SERIOUS.
WARNING: THERE ARE REPORTS OF COUNTERFEIT STAN MUSIALS.
SURE YOU WANT TO TRADE FOR IT? IT MIGHT BE COUNTERFEIT.
LOOK, MAN, I KNOW MY TRADING CARDS. TWO AARONS AND A WILLIE MAYS. TAKE IT OR LEAVE IT.
DID I EVER SNOOKER THAT DUDE. I HATED TO LOSE WILLIE MAYS, BUT IT'S WORTH A THIRD OF THIS TERRIFIC MUSIAL–
WHO IS WEARING A FOOTBALL UNIFORM!?!?

TANK McNAMARA

by Jeff Millar & Bill Hinds

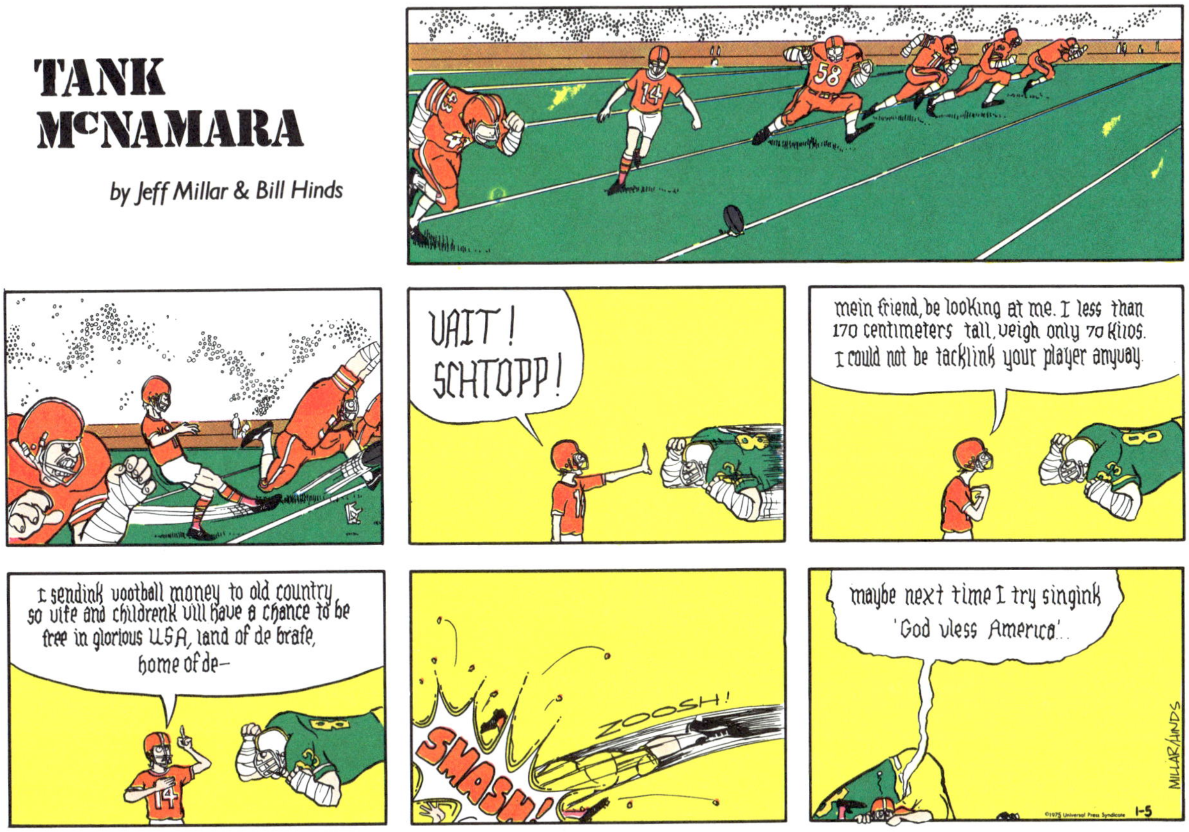

VAIT! SCHTOPP!
mein friend, be looking at me. I less than 170 centimeters tall, veigh only 70 kilos. I could not be tacklink your player anyvay.
I sendink vootball money to old country so vife and childrenk vill have a chance to be free in glorious U.S.A, land of de brafe, home of de—
SMASH!
ZOOSH!
maybe next time I try singink 'God vless America'..
MILLAR/HINDS
1-5

TANK McNAMARA

by Jeff Millar & Bill Hinds

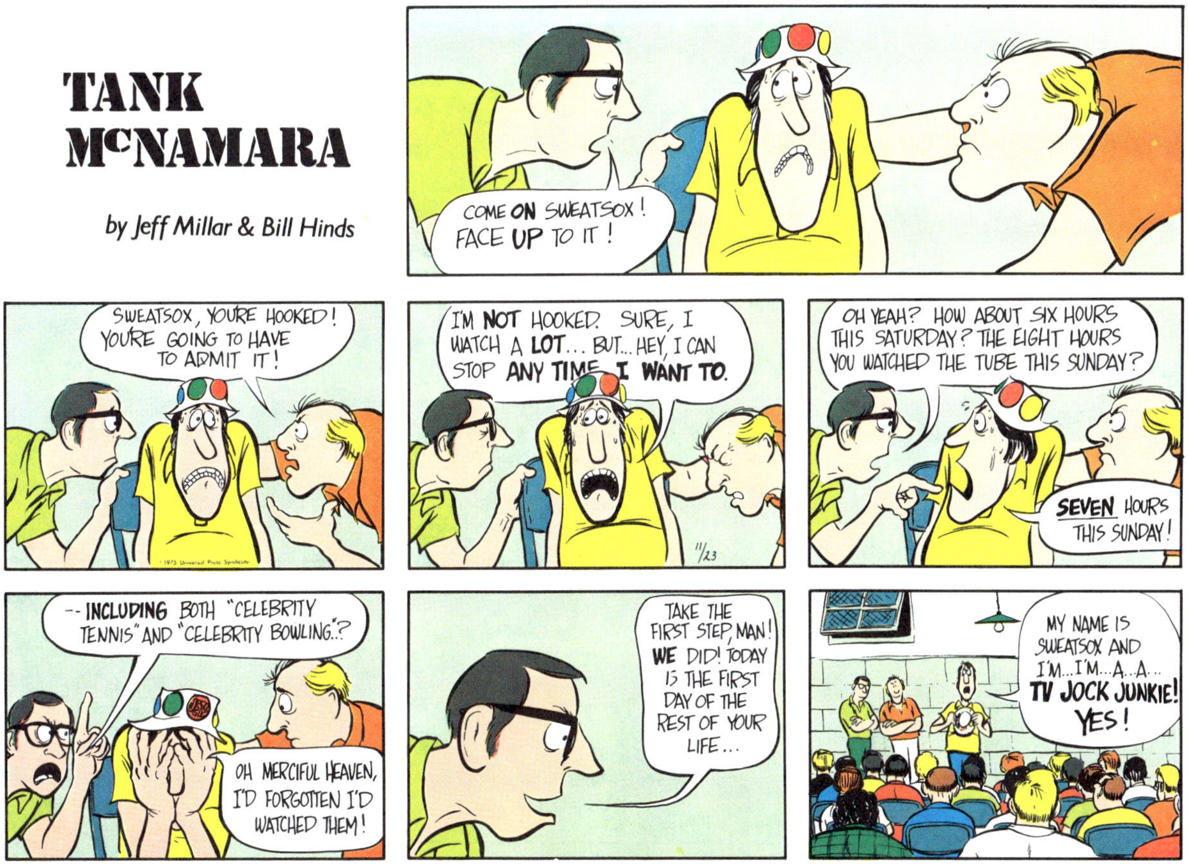

COME ON SWEATSOX! FACE UP TO IT!
SWEATSOX, YOU'RE HOOKED! YOU'RE GOING TO HAVE TO ADMIT IT!
I'M NOT HOOKED. SURE, I WATCH A LOT... BUT... HEY, I CAN STOP ANY TIME I WANT TO.
11/23
OH YEAH? HOW ABOUT SIX HOURS THIS SATURDAY? THE EIGHT HOURS YOU WATCHED THE TUBE THIS SUNDAY?
SEVEN HOURS THIS SUNDAY!
--INCLUDING BOTH "CELEBRITY TENNIS" AND "CELEBRITY BOWLING."?
OH MERCIFUL HEAVEN, I'D FORGOTTEN I'D WATCHED THEM!
TAKE THE FIRST STEP, MAN! WE DID! TODAY IS THE FIRST DAY OF THE REST OF YOUR LIFE...
MY NAME IS SWEATSOX AND I'M...I'M...A...A... TV JOCK JUNKIE! YES!

TANK McNAMARA

by Jeff Millar & Bill Hinds

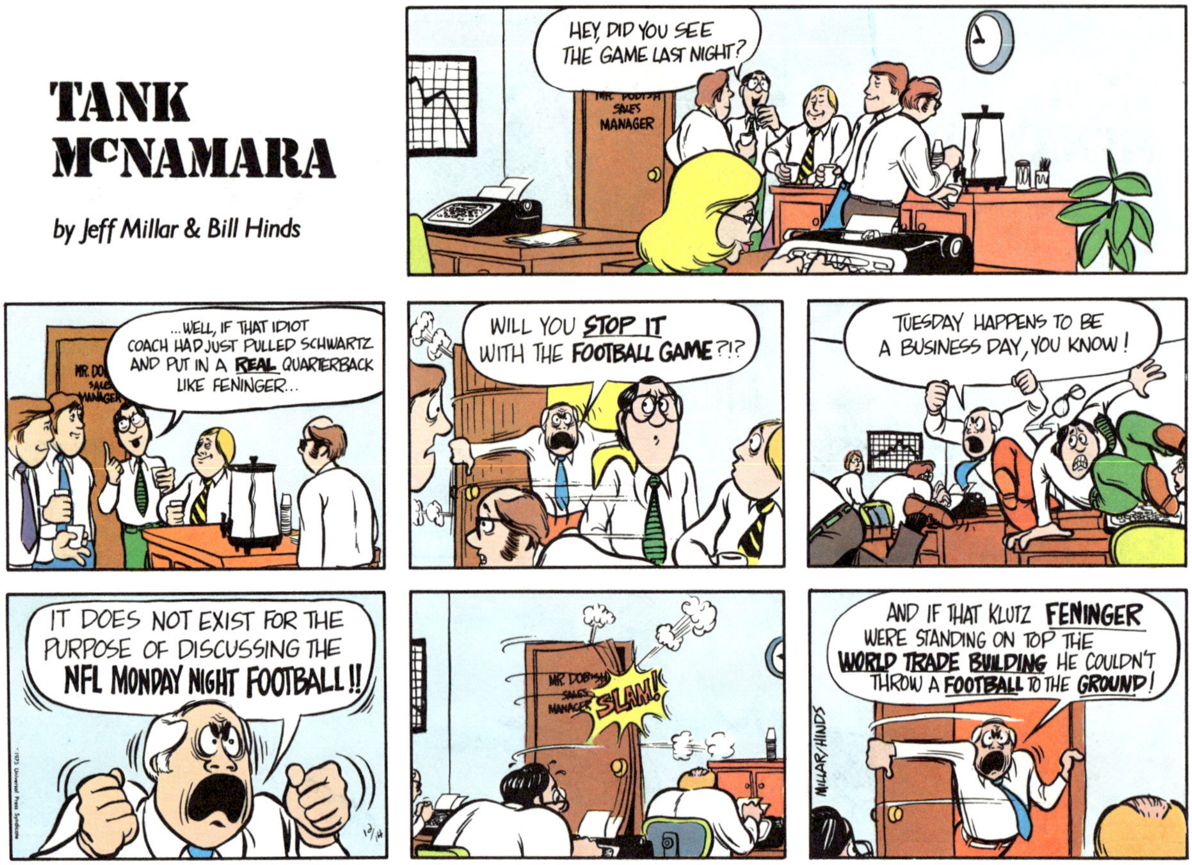
HEY, DID YOU SEE THE GAME LAST NIGHT?
MR. DOBISH SALES MANAGER
...WELL, IF THAT IDIOT COACH HAD JUST PULLED SCHWARTZ AND PUT IN A REAL QUARTERBACK LIKE FENINGER...
WILL YOU STOP IT WITH THE FOOTBALL GAME?!?
TUESDAY HAPPENS TO BE A BUSINESS DAY, YOU KNOW!
IT DOES NOT EXIST FOR THE PURPOSE OF DISCUSSING THE NFL MONDAY NIGHT FOOTBALL!!
SLAM!
AND IF THAT KLUTZ FENINGER WERE STANDING ON TOP THE WORLD TRADE BUILDING HE COULDN'T THROW A FOOTBALL TO THE GROUND!
MILLAR/HINDS

TANK McNAMARA

by Jeff Millar & Bill Hinds

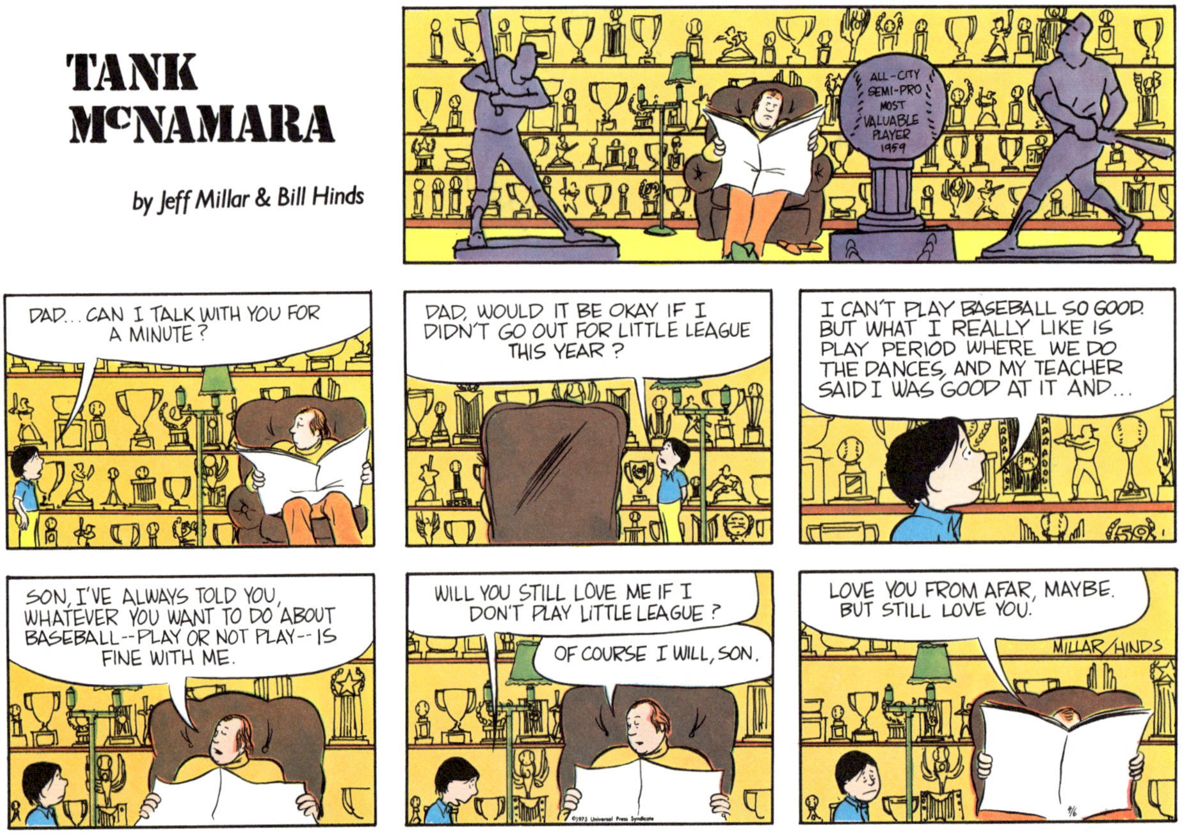
ALL-CITY SEMI-PRO MOST VALUABLE PLAYER 1959
DAD... CAN I TALK WITH YOU FOR A MINUTE?
DAD, WOULD IT BE OKAY IF I DIDN'T GO OUT FOR LITTLE LEAGUE THIS YEAR?
I CAN'T PLAY BASEBALL SO GOOD. BUT WHAT I REALLY LIKE IS PLAY PERIOD WHERE WE DO THE DANCES, AND MY TEACHER SAID I WAS GOOD AT IT AND...
SON, I'VE ALWAYS TOLD YOU, WHATEVER YOU WANT TO DO ABOUT BASEBALL--PLAY OR NOT PLAY--IS FINE WITH ME.
WILL YOU STILL LOVE ME IF I DON'T PLAY LITTLE LEAGUE?
OF COURSE I WILL, SON.
LOVE YOU FROM AFAR, MAYBE. BUT STILL LOVE YOU.
MILLAR/HINDS

So now Tank is starting to look a bit more like he does today. The changes in Tank's appearance, as best as I can tell, were gradual and unintentional. At least I don't recall sitting down with Bill and our deciding that Tank's eyes should move closer together, that his jaw should get bigger. I have grown to suspect that the metamorphosis in the way Tank wears his hair parallels what Hinds does with his.

A lot of things in *Tank* just happen without design. I don't even remember how I came upon his name. I was typing out a gag, came upon the point where I needed a character's name, and my fingers produced Tank.

Because of the nature of the collaboration, there's the principle of uncertainty involved; I like to think it enriches our work. Little accidents, small misunderstandings happen; the result is almost always better than what I had intended. I will discover that Bill has made a character black, or a female (I seldom specify gender of short-lived characters). "Hmmm," I'll think. "That's interesting." I'll keep the character in mind, see if the gender-job relationship can be used next time.

The mad-scientist character (Dr. Tszap — there, I just named him) was intended to be a one-shot appearance. I asked Bill for a "cliché mad-scientist type," and he came up with this image. I thought it was so funny that I started writing more mad-scientist gags just to make Bill draw him again.

What else would you like to know? *Have we ever met Charles Schulz?* No. *Mort Walker?* No. *Dik Browne?* No. Sorry. Cartoonists tend to live in the Northeast. *What's Garry Trudeau really like, and can you help me get an original from him?* I don't know, and no. *Has a pro athlete ever gotten mad at you and punched you (separately or at the same time) in the nose(s) for something you said about him?* Not yet. *Were either of you athletes yourselves?* I would now be a veteran linebacker for the Packers were it not for the fact that, after I had made the seventh grade football team, I became paralyzingly afraid of getting hurt. When the going got tough, I, unlike the tough, got going right out of the football program. It was the final sensible act of my life. Bill warmed benches at Little League parks across Southwest Houston. We play occasional lumbering tennis. *How do you stay topical?* The three-week lead time makes us guess a lot. Sometimes we hold our breath and pray, and sometimes the prayers are not heard (okay, we promise, no more Notre Dame jokes). Jimmy Connors and Chris Evert called off their engagement the weekend before we were to start a series of jokes about their wedding, the creeps. *How do we split the money?* Fifty-fifty with the Syndicate, those robbers, then fifty-fifty with each other. *Are you rich?* Don't make us laugh.

Sometimes I say that we do it for money and ego, and sometimes I say we do it for ego and money. It's too much hard work to do it just for the money, and it takes too much time to do it just for the ego. Face it, it's fun. We put our friends' names in the strip. Those with a sense of humor we draw into the strip.

Bill tells me it's a real ice-breaker with girls. And I have made amends . . . finally, finally . . . for all the Student Council elections I lost to jocks when I was in high school.

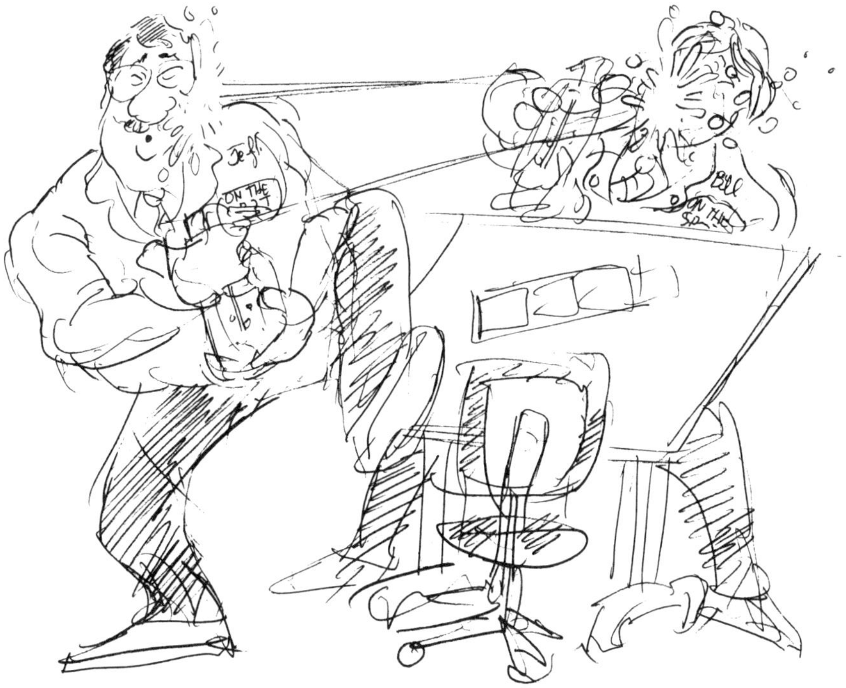
Jeff
ON THE
Bill

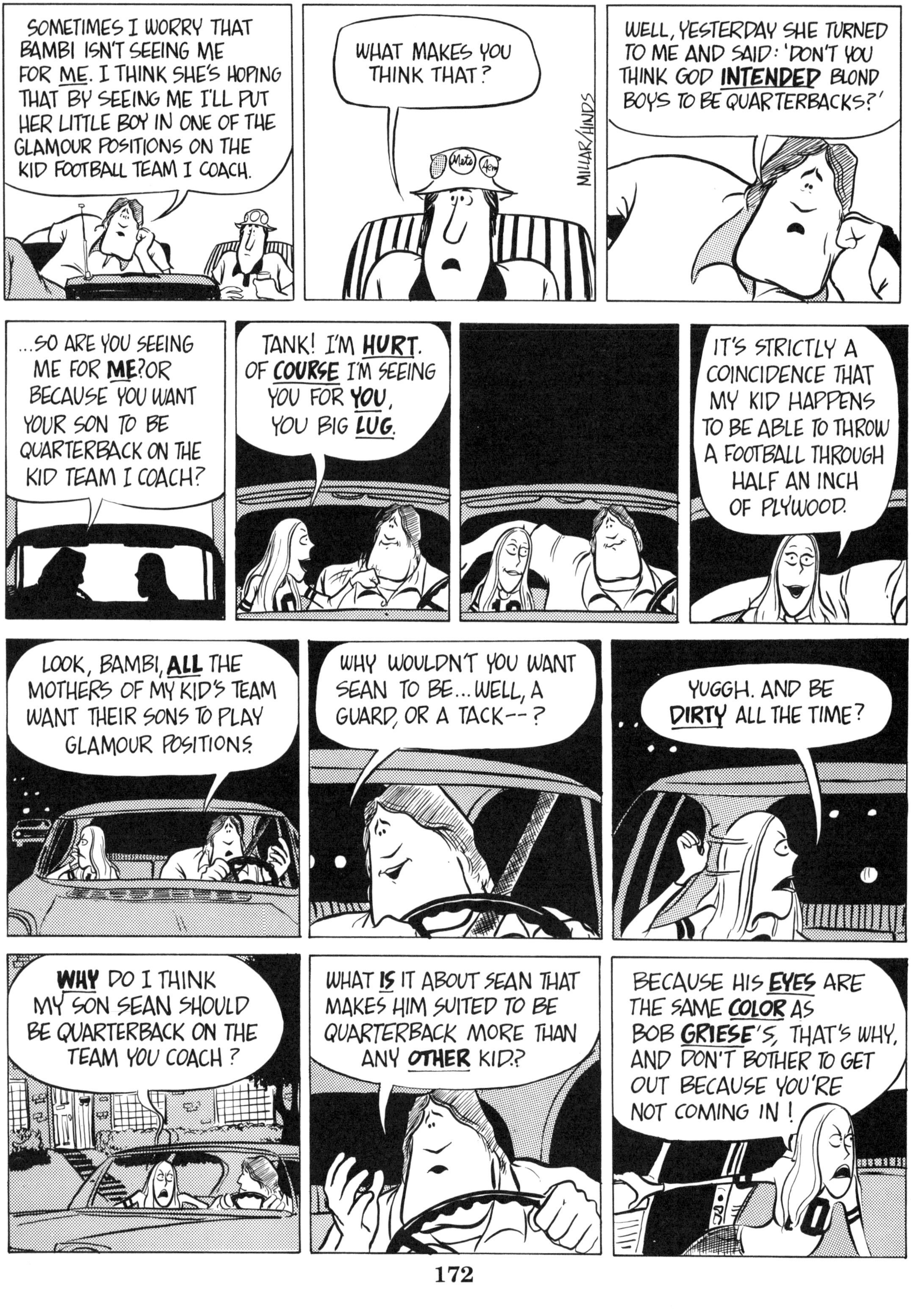
SOMETIMES I WORRY THAT BAMBI ISN'T SEEING ME FOR ME. I THINK SHE'S HOPING THAT BY SEEING ME I'LL PUT HER LITTLE BOY IN ONE OF THE GLAMOUR POSITIONS ON THE KID FOOTBALL TEAM I COACH.
WHAT MAKES YOU THINK THAT?
MILLAR/HINDS
WELL, YESTERDAY SHE TURNED TO ME AND SAID: 'DON'T YOU THINK GOD INTENDED BLOND BOYS TO BE QUARTERBACKS?'
...SO ARE YOU SEEING ME FOR ME? OR BECAUSE YOU WANT YOUR SON TO BE QUARTERBACK ON THE KID TEAM I COACH?
TANK! I'M HURT. OF COURSE I'M SEEING YOU FOR YOU, YOU BIG LUG.
IT'S STRICTLY A COINCIDENCE THAT MY KID HAPPENS TO BE ABLE TO THROW A FOOTBALL THROUGH HALF AN INCH OF PLYWOOD.
LOOK, BAMBI, ALL THE MOTHERS OF MY KID'S TEAM WANT THEIR SONS TO PLAY GLAMOUR POSITIONS.
WHY WOULDN'T YOU WANT SEAN TO BE... WELL, A GUARD, OR A TACK--?
YUGGH. AND BE DIRTY ALL THE TIME?
WHY DO I THINK MY SON SEAN SHOULD BE QUARTERBACK ON THE TEAM YOU COACH?
WHAT IS IT ABOUT SEAN THAT MAKES HIM SUITED TO BE QUARTERBACK MORE THAN ANY OTHER KID?
BECAUSE HIS EYES ARE THE SAME COLOR AS BOB GRIESE'S, THAT'S WHY, AND DON'T BOTHER TO GET OUT BECAUSE YOU'RE NOT COMING IN!

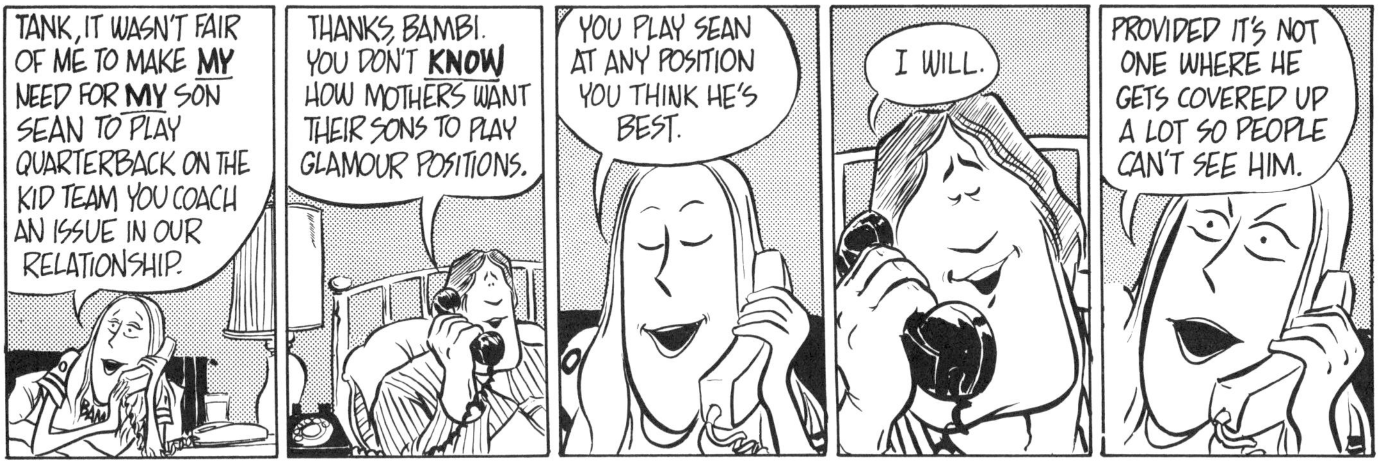
TANK, IT WASN'T FAIR OF ME TO MAKE MY NEED FOR MY SON SEAN TO PLAY QUARTERBACK ON THE KID TEAM YOU COACH AN ISSUE IN OUR RELATIONSHIP.
THANKS, BAMBI. YOU DON'T KNOW HOW MOTHERS WANT THEIR SONS TO PLAY GLAMOUR POSITIONS.
YOU PLAY SEAN AT ANY POSITION YOU THINK HE'S BEST.
I WILL.
PROVIDED IT'S NOT ONE WHERE HE GETS COVERED UP A LOT SO PEOPLE CAN'T SEE HIM.

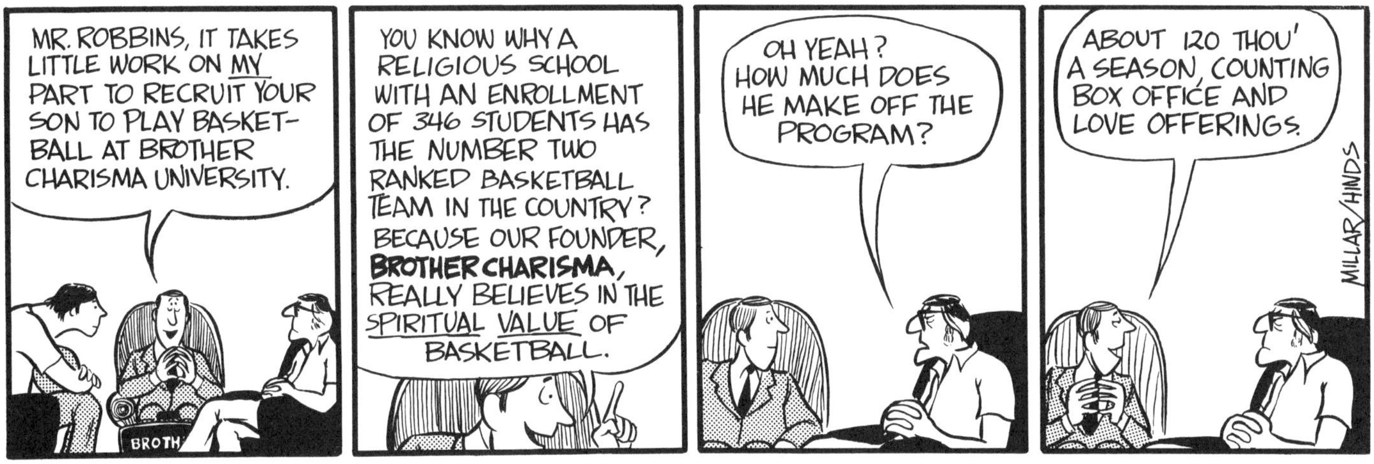
MR. ROBBINS, IT TAKES LITTLE WORK ON MY PART TO RECRUIT YOUR SON TO PLAY BASKETBALL AT BROTHER CHARISMA UNIVERSITY.
BROTH
YOU KNOW WHY A RELIGIOUS SCHOOL WITH AN ENROLLMENT OF 346 STUDENTS HAS THE NUMBER TWO RANKED BASKETBALL TEAM IN THE COUNTRY? BECAUSE OUR FOUNDER, BROTHER CHARISMA, REALLY BELIEVES IN THE SPIRITUAL VALUE OF BASKETBALL.
OH YEAH? HOW MUCH DOES HE MAKE OFF THE PROGRAM?
ABOUT 120 THOU' A SEASON, COUNTING BOX OFFICE AND LOVE OFFERINGS.
MILLAR/HINDS

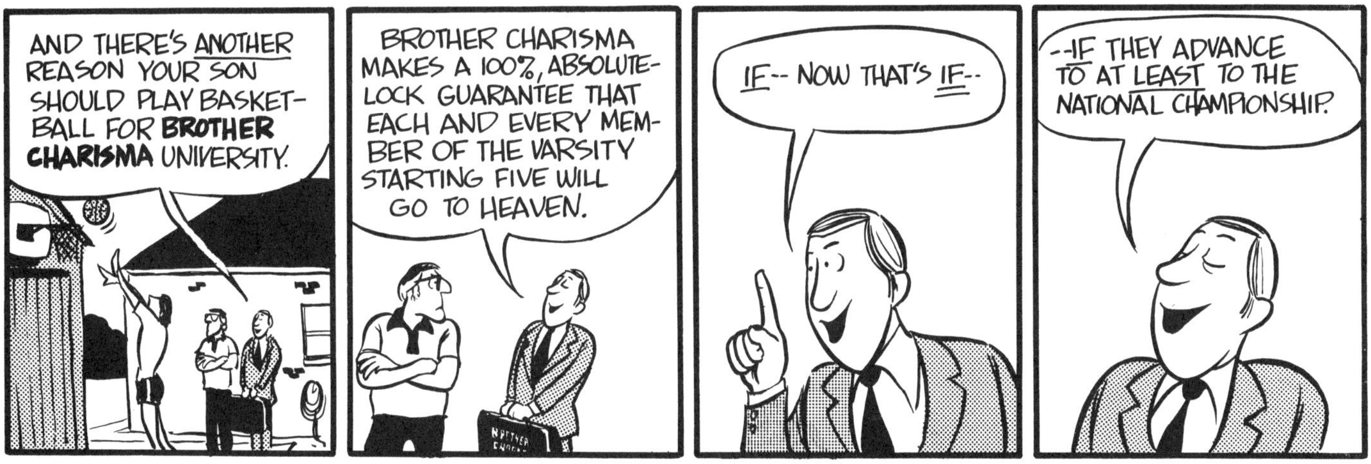
AND THERE'S ANOTHER REASON YOUR SON SHOULD PLAY BASKETBALL FOR BROTHER CHARISMA UNIVERSITY.
BROTHER CHARISMA MAKES A 100%, ABSOLUTE-LOCK GUARANTEE THAT EACH AND EVERY MEMBER OF THE VARSITY STARTING FIVE WILL GO TO HEAVEN.
IF -- NOW THAT'S IF --
--IF THEY ADVANCE TO AT LEAST TO THE NATIONAL CHAMPIONSHIP.

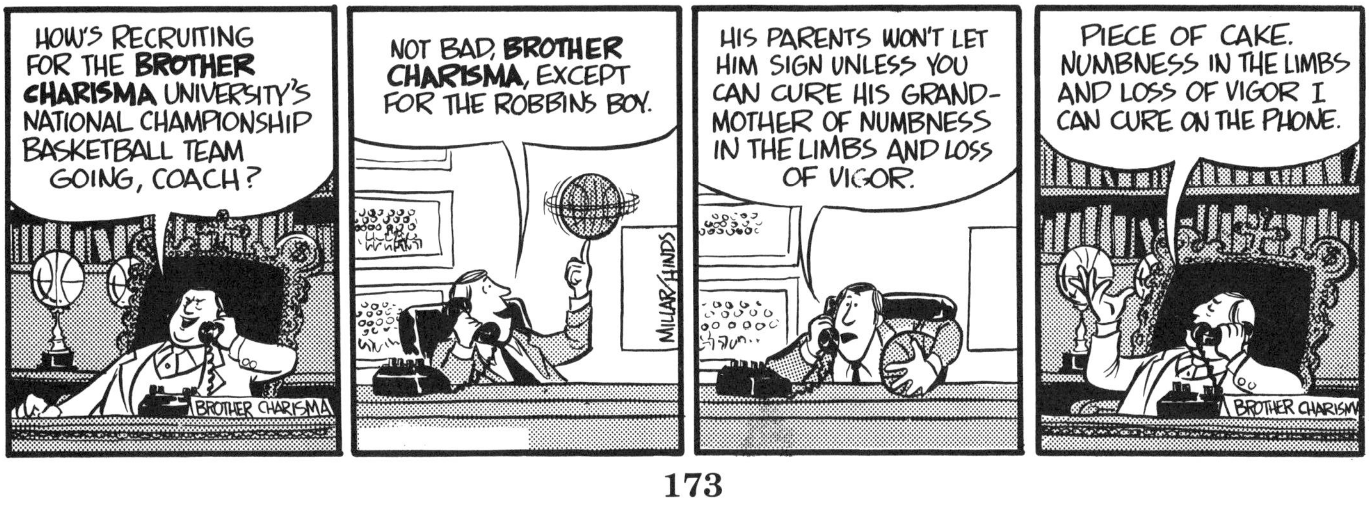
HOW'S RECRUITING FOR THE BROTHER CHARISMA UNIVERSITY'S NATIONAL CHAMPIONSHIP BASKETBALL TEAM GOING, COACH?
BROTHER CHARISMA
NOT BAD, BROTHER CHARISMA, EXCEPT FOR THE ROBBINS BOY.
MILLAR/HINDS
HIS PARENTS WON'T LET HIM SIGN UNLESS YOU CAN CURE HIS GRANDMOTHER OF NUMBNESS IN THE LIMBS AND LOSS OF VIGOR.
PIECE OF CAKE. NUMBNESS IN THE LIMBS AND LOSS OF VIGOR I CAN CURE ON THE PHONE.
BROTHER CHARISM

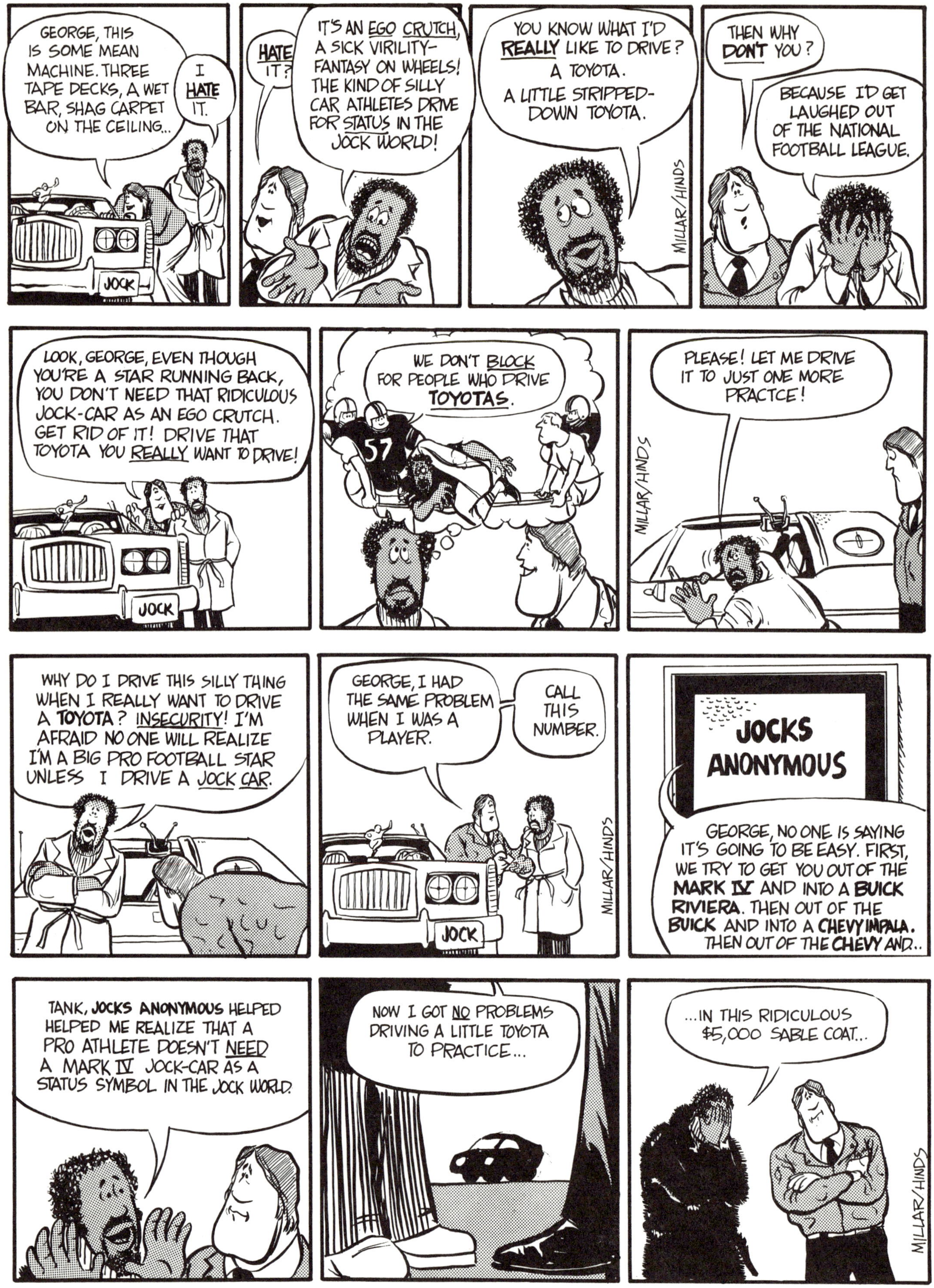
GEORGE, THIS IS SOME MEAN MACHINE. THREE TAPE DECKS, A WET BAR, SHAG CARPET ON THE CEILING...
I HATE IT.
JOCK
HATE IT?
IT'S AN EGO CRUTCH, A SICK VIRILITY-FANTASY ON WHEELS! THE KIND OF SILLY CAR ATHLETES DRIVE FOR STATUS IN THE JOCK WORLD!
YOU KNOW WHAT I'D REALLY LIKE TO DRIVE? A TOYOTA. A LITTLE STRIPPED-DOWN TOYOTA.
MILLAR/HINDS
THEN WHY DON'T YOU?
BECAUSE I'D GET LAUGHED OUT OF THE NATIONAL FOOTBALL LEAGUE.
LOOK, GEORGE, EVEN THOUGH YOU'RE A STAR RUNNING BACK, YOU DON'T NEED THAT RIDICULOUS JOCK-CAR AS AN EGO CRUTCH. GET RID OF IT! DRIVE THAT TOYOTA YOU REALLY WANT TO DRIVE!
JOCK
WE DON'T BLOCK FOR PEOPLE WHO DRIVE TOYOTAS.
57
MILLAR/HINDS
PLEASE! LET ME DRIVE IT TO JUST ONE MORE PRACTCE!
WHY DO I DRIVE THIS SILLY THING WHEN I REALLY WANT TO DRIVE A TOYOTA? INSECURITY! I'M AFRAID NO ONE WILL REALIZE I'M A BIG PRO FOOTBALL STAR UNLESS I DRIVE A JOCK CAR.
GEORGE, I HAD THE SAME PROBLEM WHEN I WAS A PLAYER.
CALL THIS NUMBER.
JOCK
MILLAR/HINDS
JOCKS ANONYMOUS
GEORGE, NO ONE IS SAYING IT'S GOING TO BE EASY. FIRST, WE TRY TO GET YOU OUT OF THE MARK IV AND INTO A BUICK RIVIERA. THEN OUT OF THE BUICK AND INTO A CHEVY IMPALA. THEN OUT OF THE CHEVY AND..
TANK, JOCKS ANONYMOUS HELPED HELPED ME REALIZE THAT A PRO ATHLETE DOESN'T NEED A MARK IV JOCK-CAR AS A STATUS SYMBOL IN THE JOCK WORLD.
NOW I GOT NO PROBLEMS DRIVING A LITTLE TOYOTA TO PRACTICE...
...IN THIS RIDICULOUS $5,000 SABLE COAT...
MILLAR/HINDS

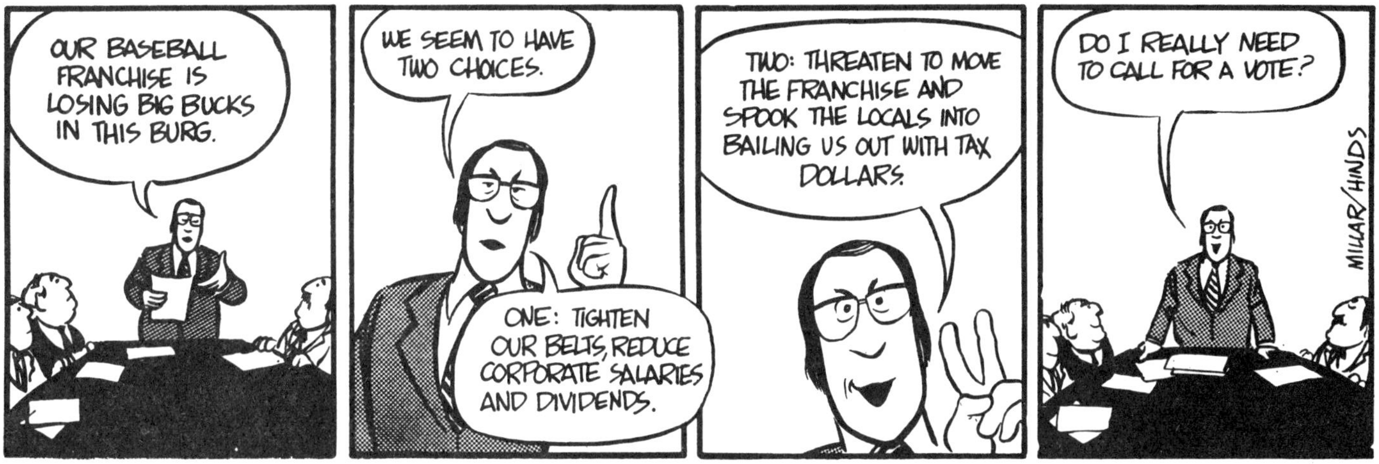
OUR BASEBALL FRANCHISE IS LOSING BIG BUCKS IN THIS BURG.
WE SEEM TO HAVE TWO CHOICES.
ONE: TIGHTEN OUR BELTS, REDUCE CORPORATE SALARIES AND DIVIDENDS.
TWO: THREATEN TO MOVE THE FRANCHISE AND SPOOK THE LOCALS INTO BAILING US OUT WITH TAX DOLLARS.
DO I REALLY NEED TO CALL FOR A VOTE?
MILLAR/HINDS

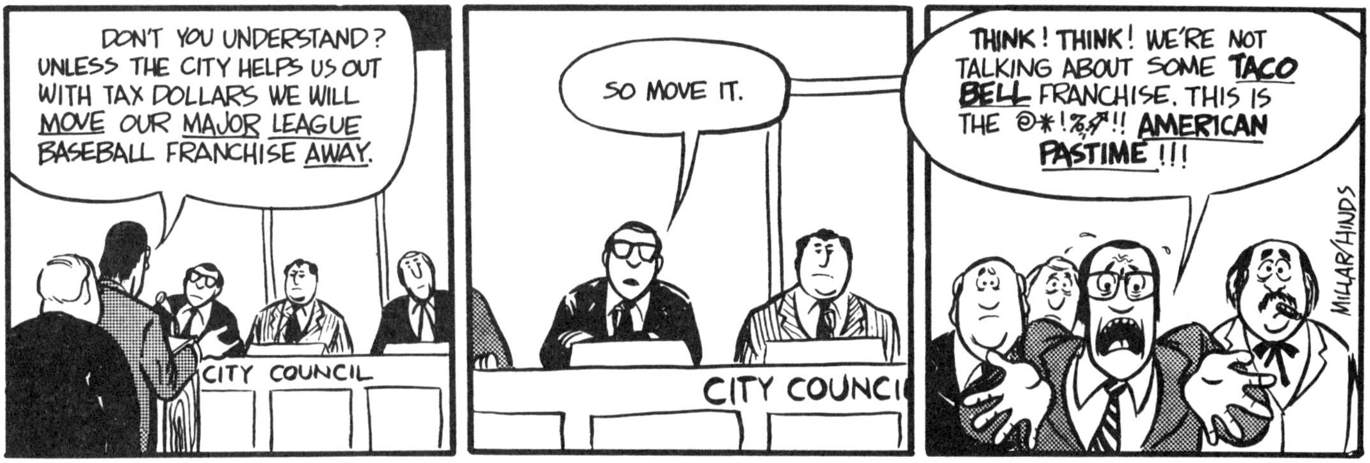
DON'T YOU UNDERSTAND? UNLESS THE CITY HELPS US OUT WITH TAX DOLLARS WE WILL MOVE OUR MAJOR LEAGUE BASEBALL FRANCHISE AWAY.
CITY COUNCIL
SO MOVE IT.
CITY COUNCI
THINK! THINK! WE'RE NOT TALKING ABOUT SOME TACO BELL FRANCHISE. THIS IS THE @*!%#!! AMERICAN PASTIME!!!
MILLAR/HINDS

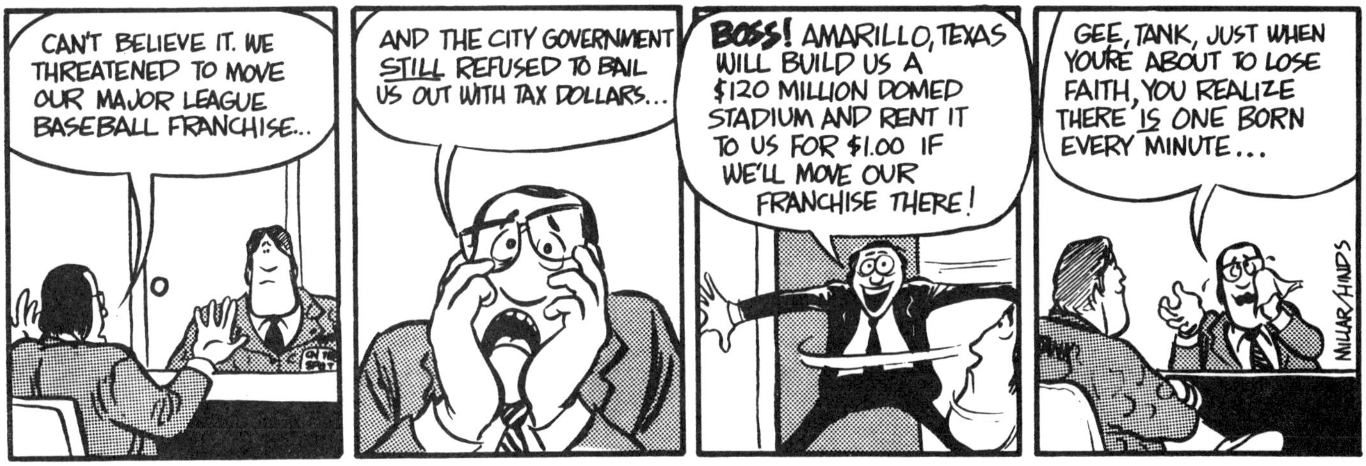
CAN'T BELIEVE IT. WE THREATENED TO MOVE OUR MAJOR LEAGUE BASEBALL FRANCHISE...
AND THE CITY GOVERNMENT STILL REFUSED TO BAIL US OUT WITH TAX DOLLARS...
BOSS! AMARILLO, TEXAS WILL BUILD US A $120 MILLION DOMED STADIUM AND RENT IT TO US FOR $1.00 IF WE'LL MOVE OUR FRANCHISE THERE!
GEE, TANK, JUST WHEN YOU'RE ABOUT TO LOSE FAITH, YOU REALIZE THERE IS ONE BORN EVERY MINUTE...
MILLAR/HINDS

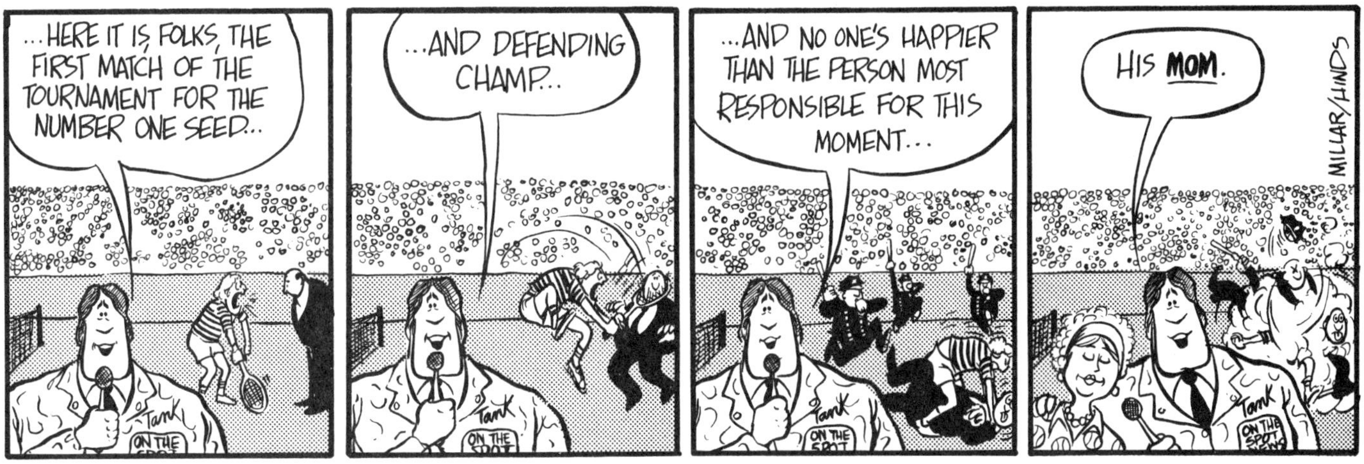
...HERE IT IS, FOLKS, THE FIRST MATCH OF THE TOURNAMENT FOR THE NUMBER ONE SEED...
...AND DEFENDING CHAMP...
...AND NO ONE'S HAPPIER THAN THE PERSON MOST RESPONSIBLE FOR THIS MOMENT...
HIS MOM.
MILLAR/HINDS

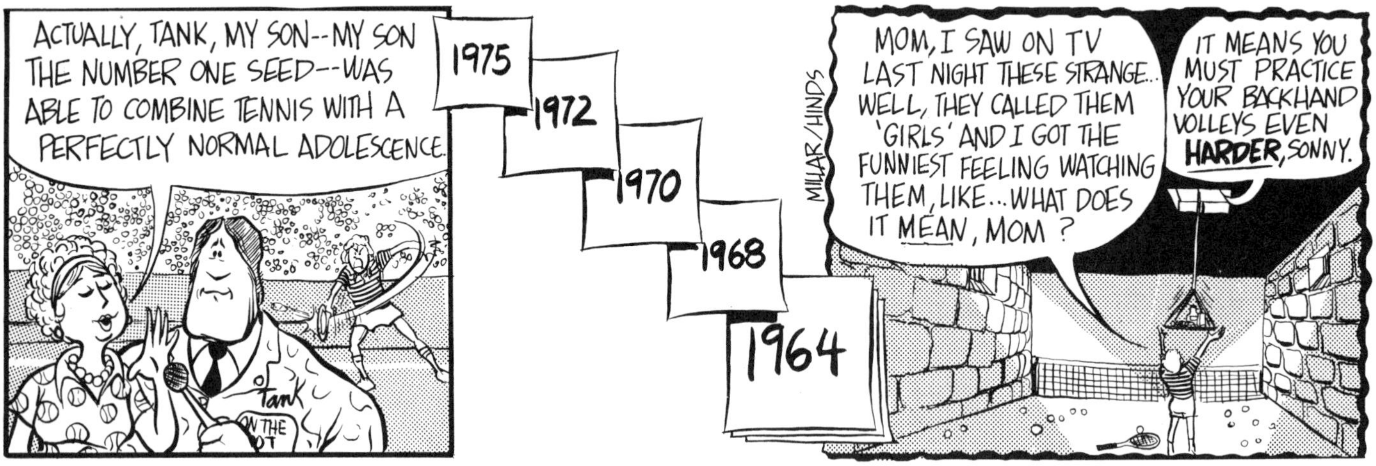
ACTUALLY, TANK, MY SON--MY SON THE NUMBER ONE SEED--WAS ABLE TO COMBINE TENNIS WITH A PERFECTLY NORMAL ADOLESCENCE.
1975
1972
1970
1968
1964
MILLAR/HINDS
MOM, I SAW ON TV LAST NIGHT THESE STRANGE... WELL, THEY CALLED THEM 'GIRLS' AND I GOT THE FUNNIEST FEELING WATCHING THEM, LIKE... WHAT DOES IT MEAN, MOM ?
IT MEANS YOU MUST PRACTICE YOUR BACKHAND VOLLEYS EVEN HARDER, SONNY.

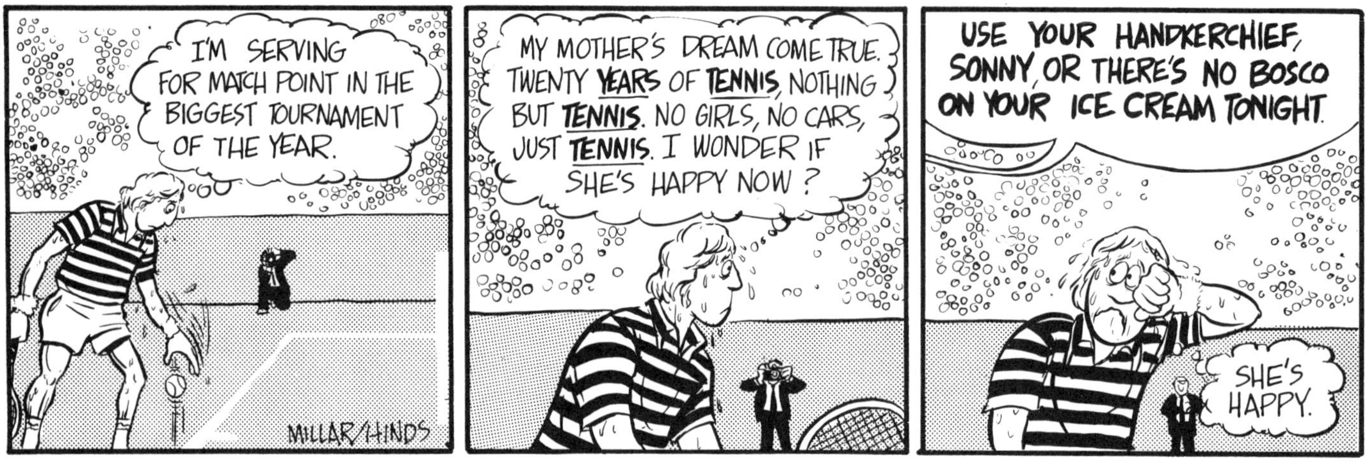
I'M SERVING FOR MATCH POINT IN THE BIGGEST TOURNAMENT OF THE YEAR.
MILLAR/HINDS
MY MOTHER'S DREAM COME TRUE. TWENTY YEARS OF TENNIS, NOTHING BUT TENNIS. NO GIRLS, NO CARS, JUST TENNIS. I WONDER IF SHE'S HAPPY NOW ?
USE YOUR HANDKERCHIEF, SONNY, OR THERE'S NO BOSCO ON YOUR ICE CREAM TONIGHT.
SHE'S HAPPY.

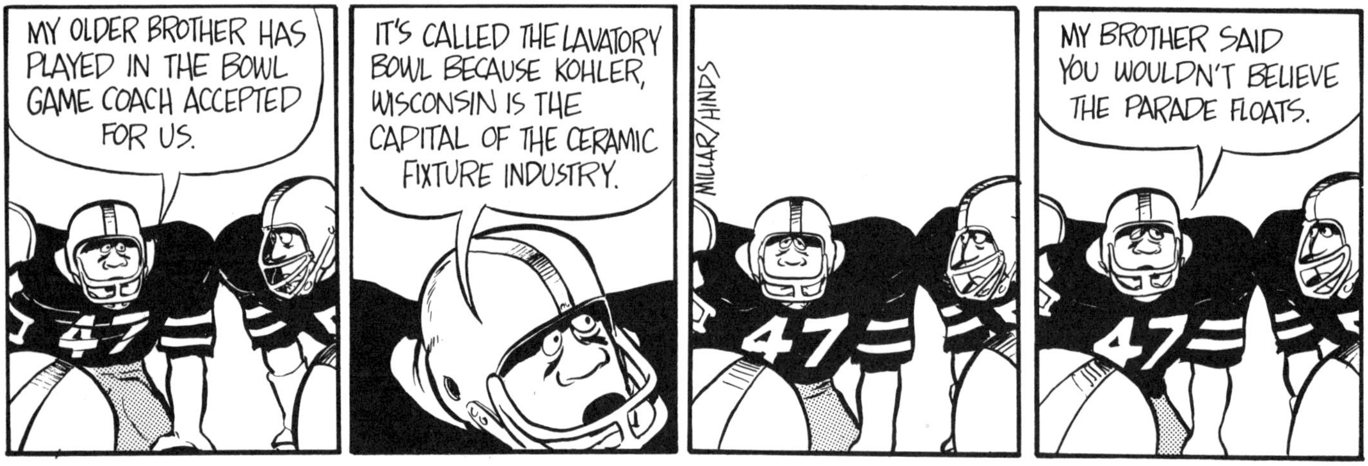
MY OLDER BROTHER HAS PLAYED IN THE BOWL GAME COACH ACCEPTED FOR US.
IT'S CALLED THE LAVATORY BOWL BECAUSE KOHLER, WISCONSIN IS THE CAPITAL OF THE CERAMIC FIXTURE INDUSTRY.
MILLAR/HINDS
MY BROTHER SAID YOU WOULDN'T BELIEVE THE PARADE FLOATS.

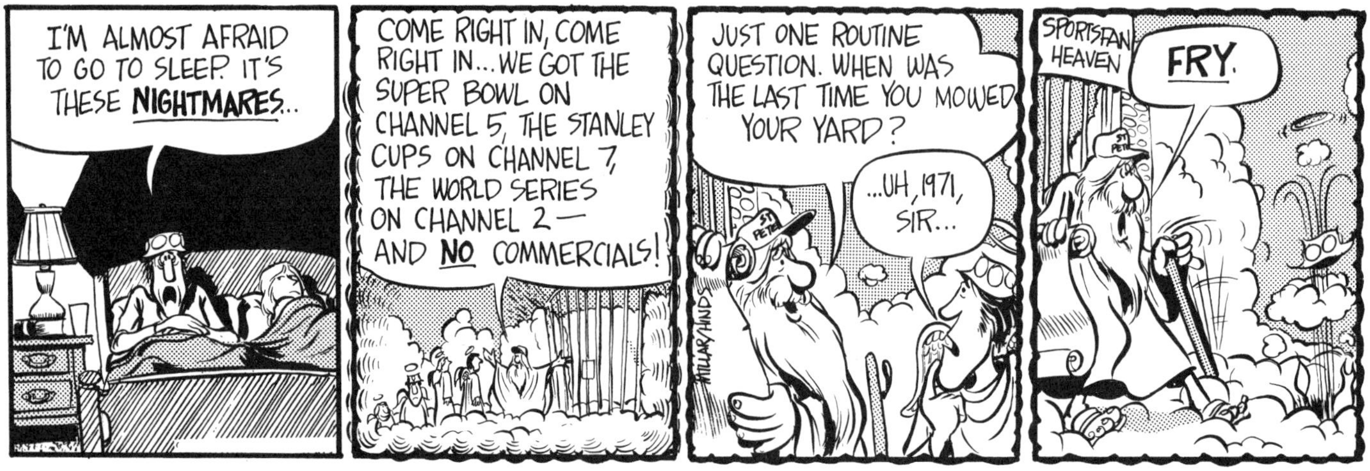
I'M ALMOST AFRAID TO GO TO SLEEP. IT'S THESE NIGHTMARES...
COME RIGHT IN, COME RIGHT IN... WE GOT THE SUPER BOWL ON CHANNEL 5, THE STANLEY CUPS ON CHANNEL 7, THE WORLD SERIES ON CHANNEL 2— AND NO COMMERCIALS!
JUST ONE ROUTINE QUESTION. WHEN WAS THE LAST TIME YOU MOWED YOUR YARD ?
...UH, 1971, SIR...
MILLAR/HINDS
SPORTSFAN HEAVEN
FRY.

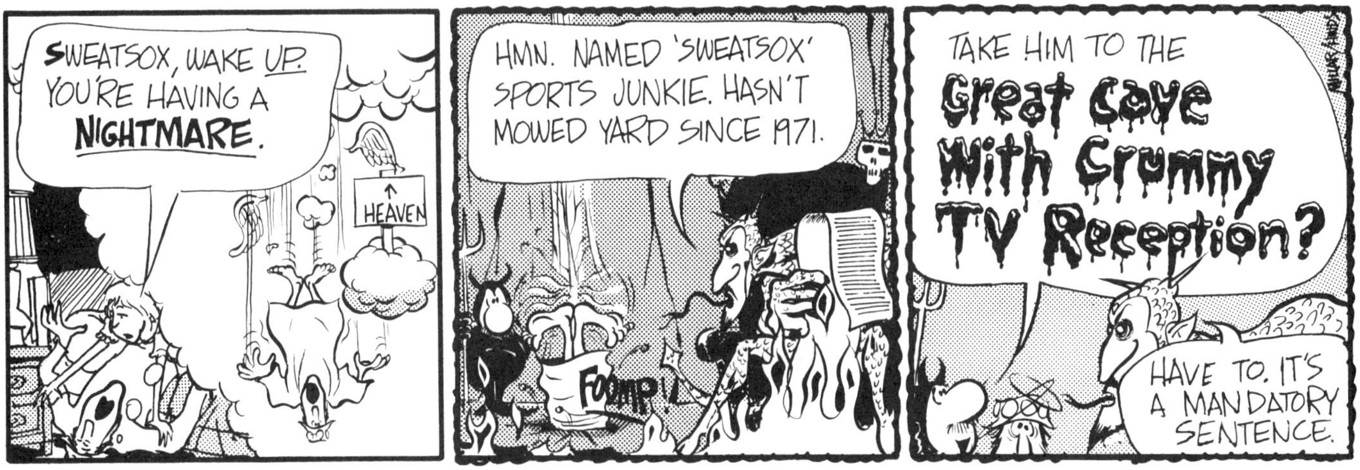
SWEATSOX, WAKE UP. YOU'RE HAVING A NIGHTMARE.
HEAVEN
HMN. NAMED 'SWEATSOX' SPORTS JUNKIE. HASN'T MOWED YARD SINCE 1971.
FOOMP!!
TAKE HIM TO THE Great Cave With Crummy TV Reception?
HAVE TO. IT'S A MANDATORY SENTENCE.

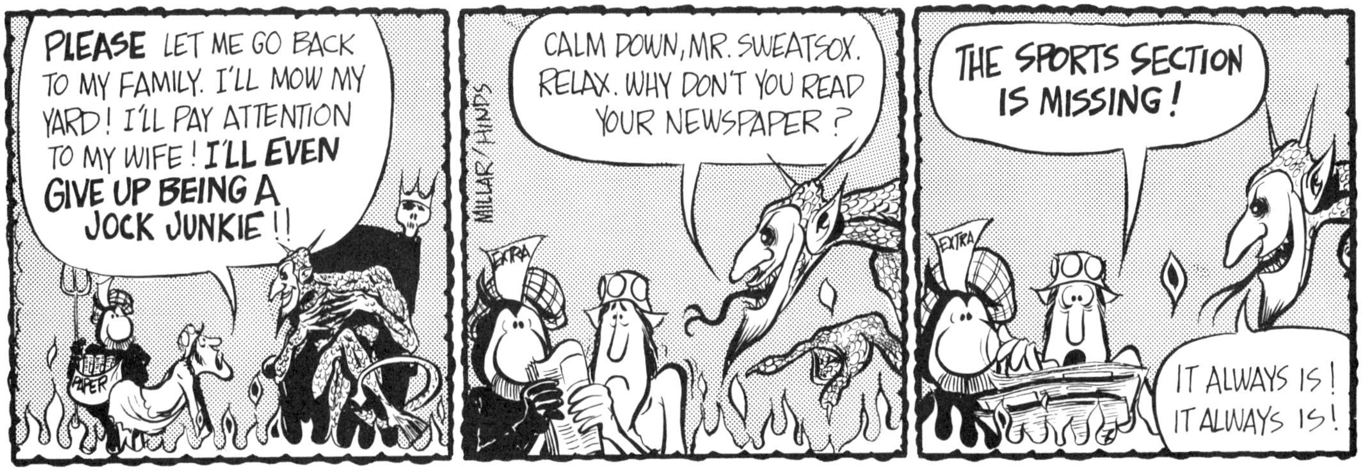
PLEASE LET ME GO BACK TO MY FAMILY. I'LL MOW MY YARD! I'LL PAY ATTENTION TO MY WIFE! I'LL EVEN GIVE UP BEING A JOCK JUNKIE!!
PAPER
MILLAR/HINDS
CALM DOWN, MR. SWEATSOX. RELAX. WHY DON'T YOU READ YOUR NEWSPAPER?
EXTRA
THE SPORTS SECTION IS MISSING!
EXTRA
IT ALWAYS IS! IT ALWAYS IS!

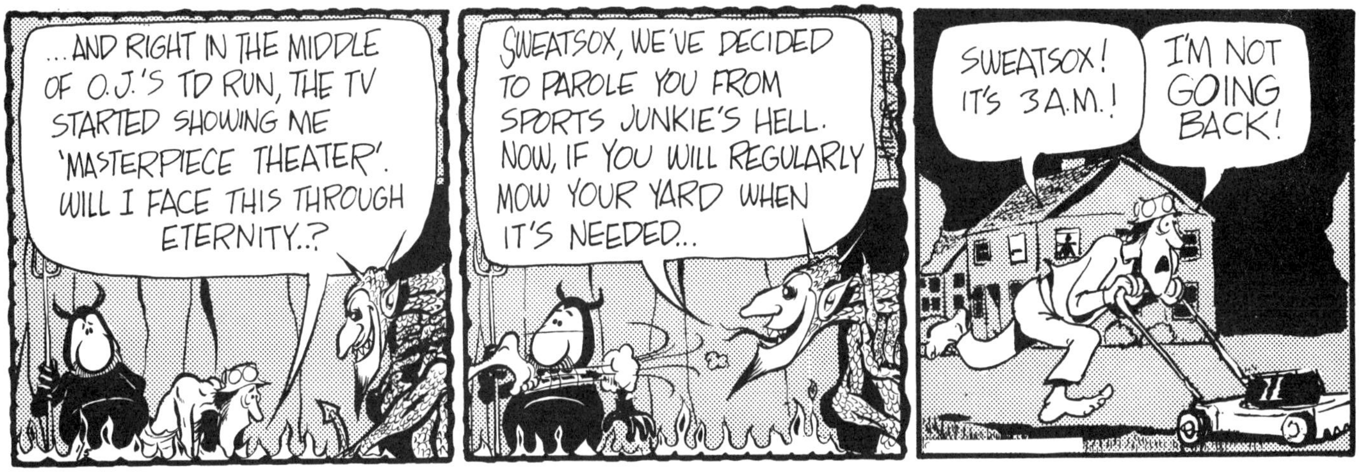
...AND RIGHT IN THE MIDDLE OF O.J.'S TD RUN, THE TV STARTED SHOWING ME 'MASTERPIECE THEATER'. WILL I FACE THIS THROUGH ETERNITY..?
SWEATSOX, WE'VE DECIDED TO PAROLE YOU FROM SPORTS JUNKIE'S HELL. NOW, IF YOU WILL REGULARLY MOW YOUR YARD WHEN IT'S NEEDED...
SWEATSOX! IT'S 3 A.M.!
I'M NOT GOING BACK!

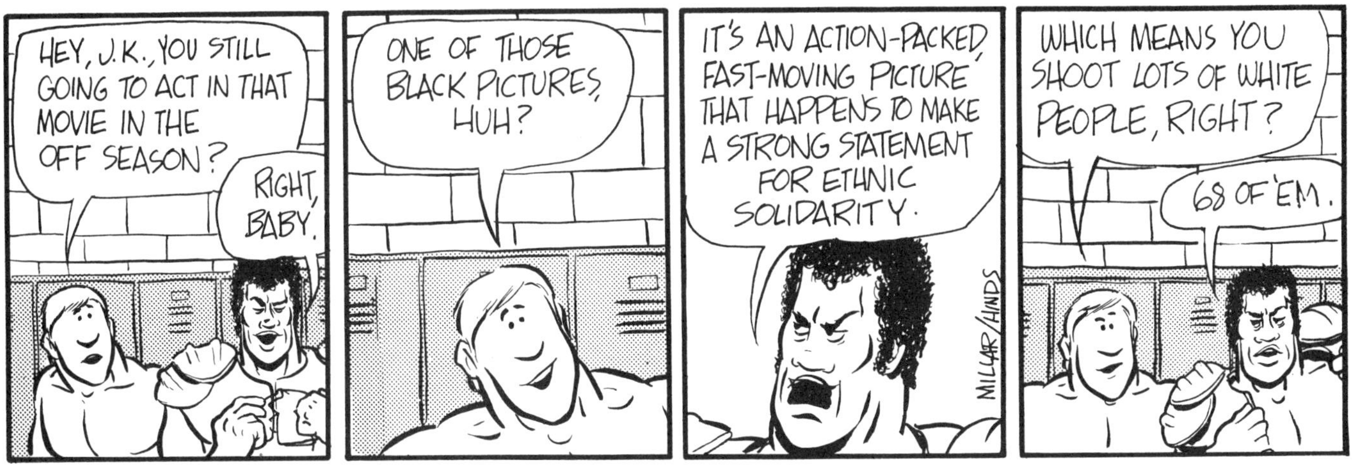
HEY, J.K., YOU STILL GOING TO ACT IN THAT MOVIE IN THE OFF SEASON?
RIGHT, BABY.
ONE OF THOSE BLACK PICTURES, HUH?
IT'S AN ACTION-PACKED, FAST-MOVING PICTURE THAT HAPPENS TO MAKE A STRONG STATEMENT FOR ETHNIC SOLIDARITY.
MILLAR/HINDS
WHICH MEANS YOU SHOOT LOTS OF WHITE PEOPLE, RIGHT?
68 OF 'EM.

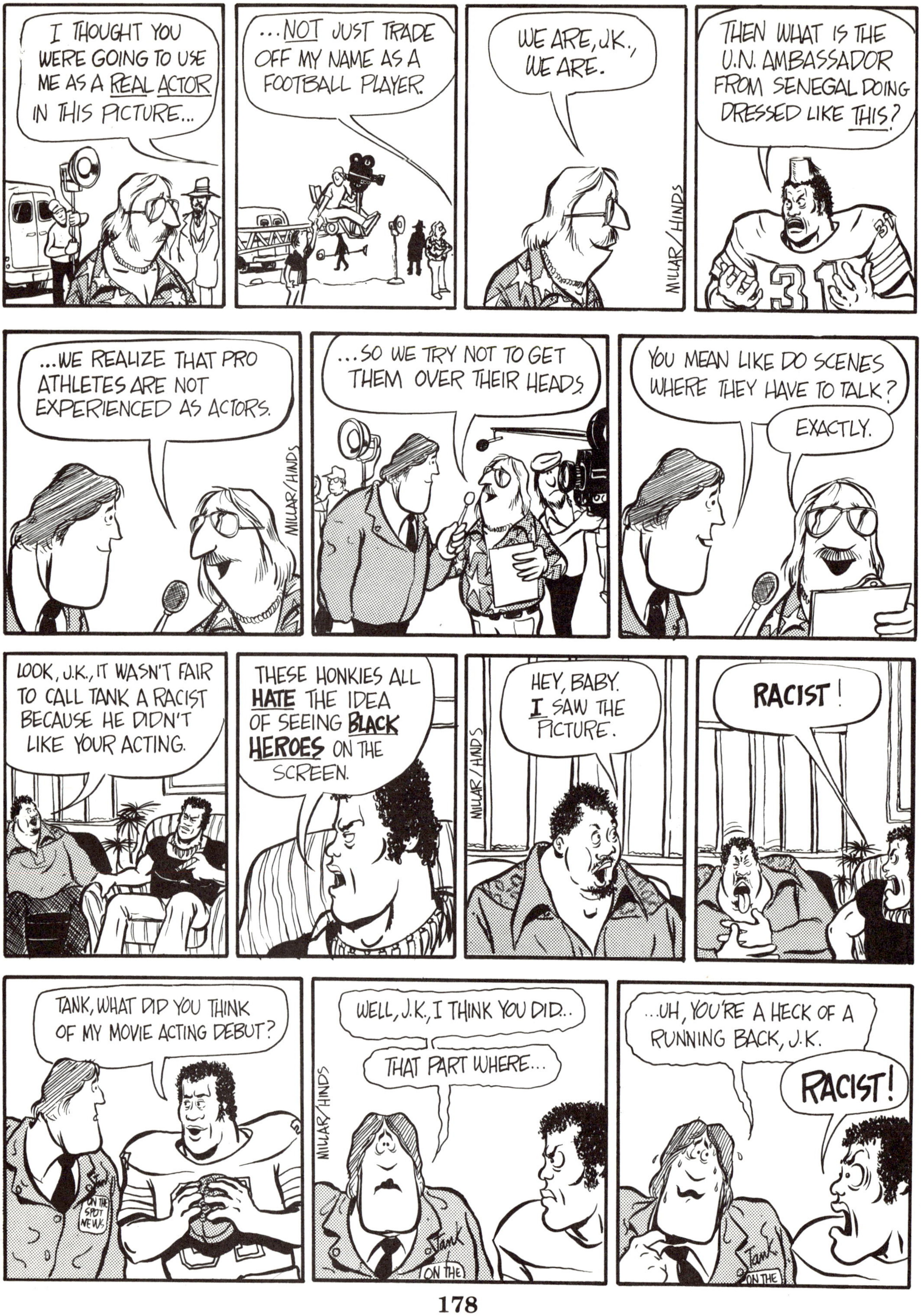

I THOUGHT YOU WERE GOING TO USE ME AS A REAL ACTOR IN THIS PICTURE...
...NOT JUST TRADE OFF MY NAME AS A FOOTBALL PLAYER.
WE ARE, J.K., WE ARE.
MILLAR/HINDS
THEN WHAT IS THE U.N. AMBASSADOR FROM SENEGAL DOING DRESSED LIKE THIS?
...WE REALIZE THAT PRO ATHLETES ARE NOT EXPERIENCED AS ACTORS.
MILLAR/HINDS
...SO WE TRY NOT TO GET THEM OVER THEIR HEADS.
YOU MEAN LIKE DO SCENES WHERE THEY HAVE TO TALK?
EXACTLY.
LOOK, J.K., IT WASN'T FAIR TO CALL TANK A RACIST BECAUSE HE DIDN'T LIKE YOUR ACTING.
THESE HONKIES ALL HATE THE IDEA OF SEEING BLACK HEROES ON THE SCREEN.
MILLAR/HINDS
HEY, BABY. I SAW THE PICTURE.
RACIST!
TANK, WHAT DID YOU THINK OF MY MOVIE ACTING DEBUT?
ON THE SPOT NEWS
MILLAR/HINDS
WELL, J.K., I THINK YOU DID..
THAT PART WHERE...
...UH, YOU'RE A HECK OF A RUNNING BACK, J.K.
RACIST!

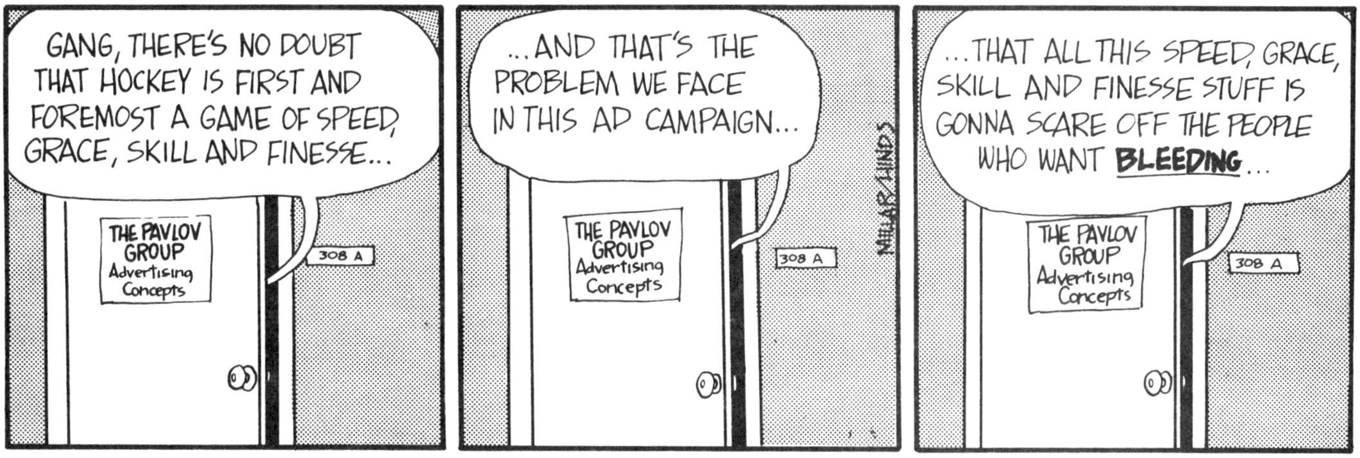
GANG, THERE'S NO DOUBT THAT HOCKEY IS FIRST AND FOREMOST A GAME OF SPEED, GRACE, SKILL AND FINESSE...
THE PAVLOV GROUP Advertising Concepts
308 A
...AND THAT'S THE PROBLEM WE FACE IN THIS AD CAMPAIGN...
MILLAR/HINDS
...THAT ALL THIS SPEED, GRACE, SKILL AND FINESSE STUFF IS GONNA SCARE OFF THE PEOPLE WHO WANT **BLEEDING**...

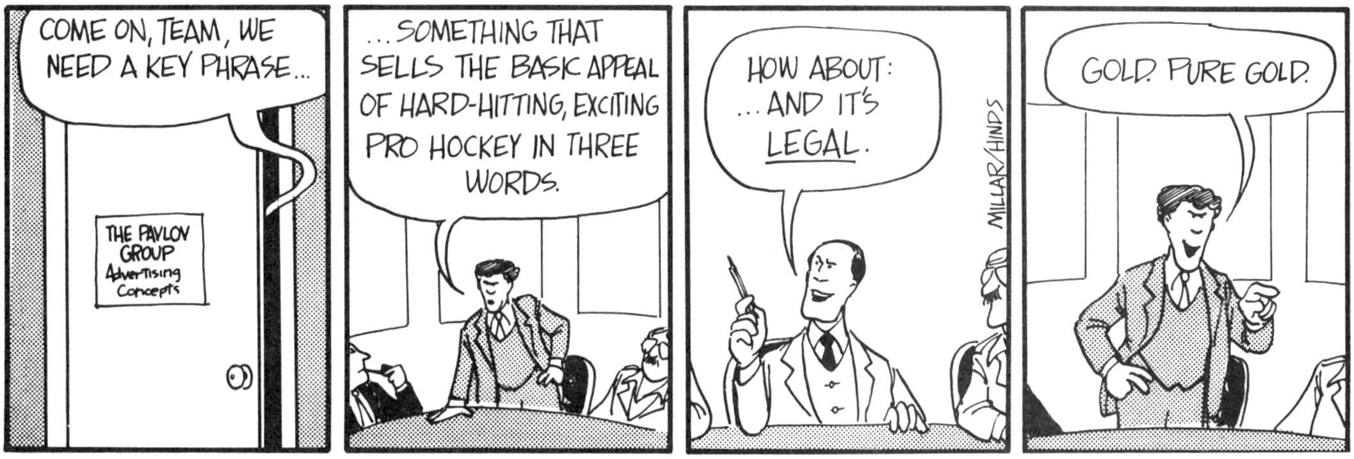
COME ON, TEAM, WE NEED A KEY PHRASE...
THE PAVLOV GROUP Advertising Concepts
...SOMETHING THAT SELLS THE BASIC APPEAL OF HARD-HITTING, EXCITING PRO HOCKEY IN THREE WORDS.
HOW ABOUT: ...AND IT'S LEGAL.
MILLAR/HINDS
GOLD. PURE GOLD.

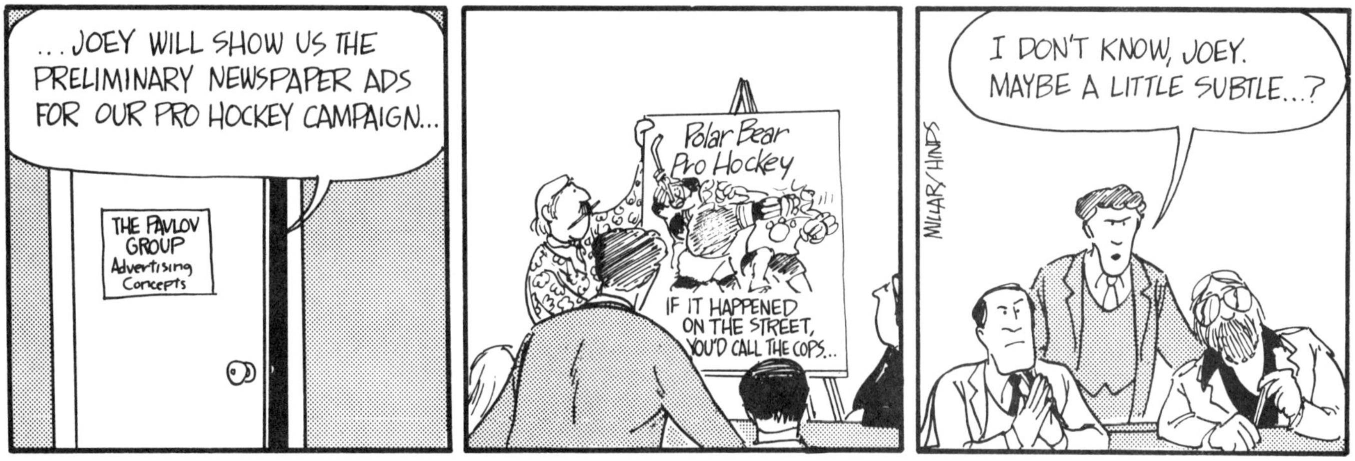
...JOEY WILL SHOW US THE PRELIMINARY NEWSPAPER ADS FOR OUR PRO HOCKEY CAMPAIGN...
THE PAVLOV GROUP Advertising Concepts
Polar Bear Pro Hockey
IF IT HAPPENED ON THE STREET, YOU'D CALL THE COPS...
MILLAR/HINDS
I DON'T KNOW, JOEY. MAYBE A LITTLE SUBTLE...?

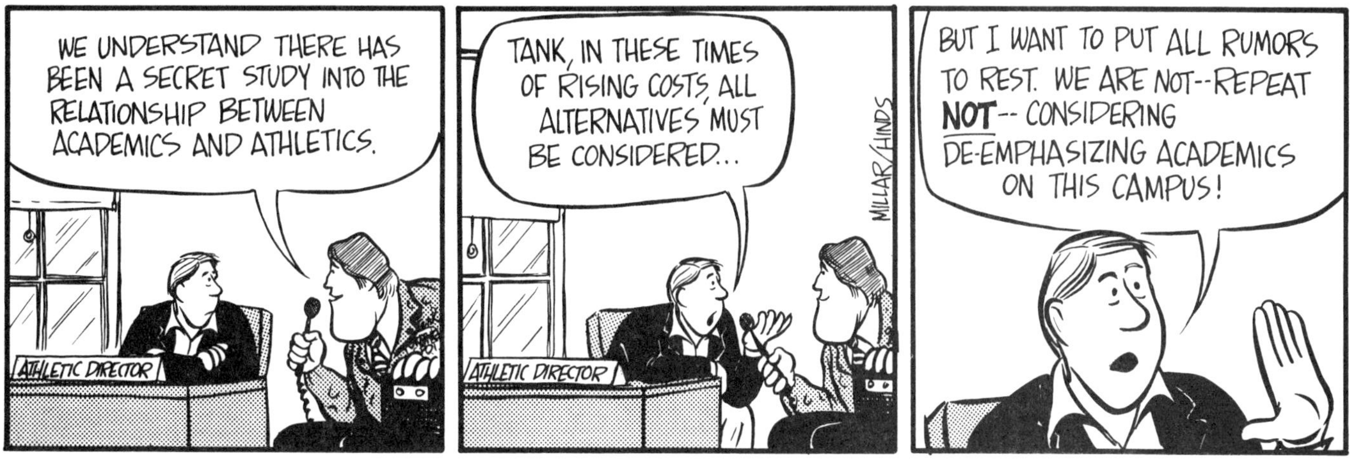
WE UNDERSTAND THERE HAS BEEN A SECRET STUDY INTO THE RELATIONSHIP BETWEEN ACADEMICS AND ATHLETICS.
ATHLETIC DIRECTOR
TANK, IN THESE TIMES OF RISING COSTS, ALL ALTERNATIVES MUST BE CONSIDERED...
ATHLETIC DIRECTOR
MILLAR/HINDS
BUT I WANT TO PUT ALL RUMORS TO REST. WE ARE NOT--REPEAT **NOT**-- CONSIDERING DE-EMPHASIZING ACADEMICS ON THIS CAMPUS!

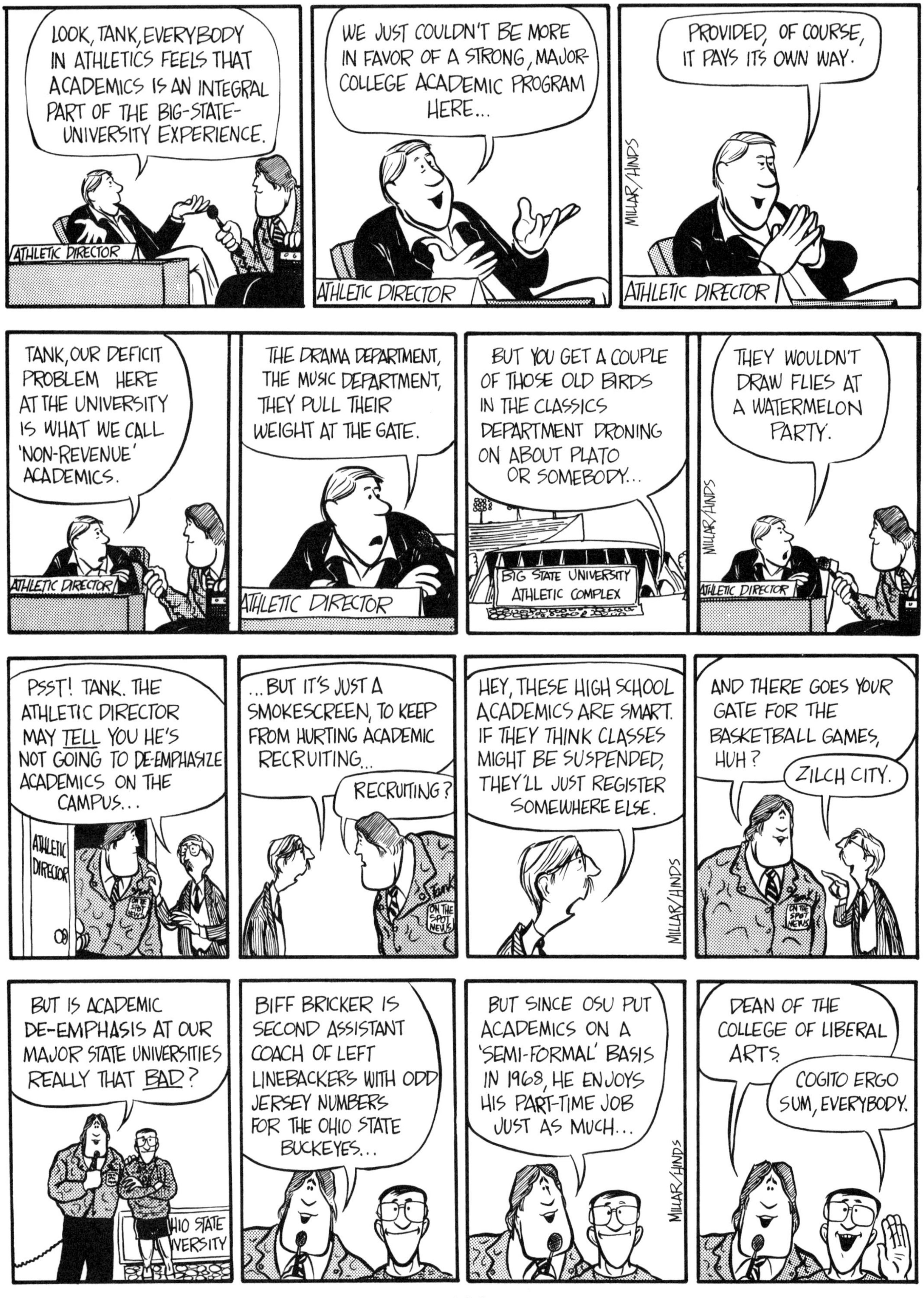
LOOK, TANK, EVERYBODY IN ATHLETICS FEELS THAT ACADEMICS IS AN INTEGRAL PART OF THE BIG-STATE-UNIVERSITY EXPERIENCE.
ATHLETIC DIRECTOR
WE JUST COULDN'T BE MORE IN FAVOR OF A STRONG, MAJOR-COLLEGE ACADEMIC PROGRAM HERE...
ATHLETIC DIRECTOR
MILLAR/HINDS
PROVIDED, OF COURSE, IT PAYS ITS OWN WAY.
ATHLETIC DIRECTOR
TANK, OUR DEFICIT PROBLEM HERE AT THE UNIVERSITY IS WHAT WE CALL 'NON-REVENUE' ACADEMICS.
ATHLETIC DIRECTOR
THE DRAMA DEPARTMENT, THE MUSIC DEPARTMENT, THEY PULL THEIR WEIGHT AT THE GATE.
ATHLETIC DIRECTOR
BUT YOU GET A COUPLE OF THOSE OLD BIRDS IN THE CLASSICS DEPARTMENT DRONING ON ABOUT PLATO OR SOMEBODY...
BIG STATE UNIVERSITY ATHLETIC COMPLEX
MILLAR/HINDS
THEY WOULDN'T DRAW FLIES AT A WATERMELON PARTY.
ATHLETIC DIRECTOR
PSST! TANK. THE ATHLETIC DIRECTOR MAY TELL YOU HE'S NOT GOING TO DE-EMPHASIZE ACADEMICS ON THE CAMPUS...
ATHLETIC DIRECTOR
...BUT IT'S JUST A SMOKESCREEN, TO KEEP FROM HURTING ACADEMIC RECRUITING...
RECRUITING?
HEY, THESE HIGH SCHOOL ACADEMICS ARE SMART. IF THEY THINK CLASSES MIGHT BE SUSPENDED, THEY'LL JUST REGISTER SOMEWHERE ELSE.
MILLAR/HINDS
AND THERE GOES YOUR GATE FOR THE BASKETBALL GAMES, HUH?
ZILCH CITY.
BUT IS ACADEMIC DE-EMPHASIS AT OUR MAJOR STATE UNIVERSITIES REALLY THAT BAD?
HIO STATE
VERSITY
BIFF BRICKER IS SECOND ASSISTANT COACH OF LEFT LINEBACKERS WITH ODD JERSEY NUMBERS FOR THE OHIO STATE BUCKEYES...
BUT SINCE OSU PUT ACADEMICS ON A 'SEMI-FORMAL' BASIS IN 1968, HE ENJOYS HIS PART-TIME JOB JUST AS MUCH...
MILLAR/HINDS
DEAN OF THE COLLEGE OF LIBERAL ARTS.
COGITO ERGO SUM, EVERYBODY.

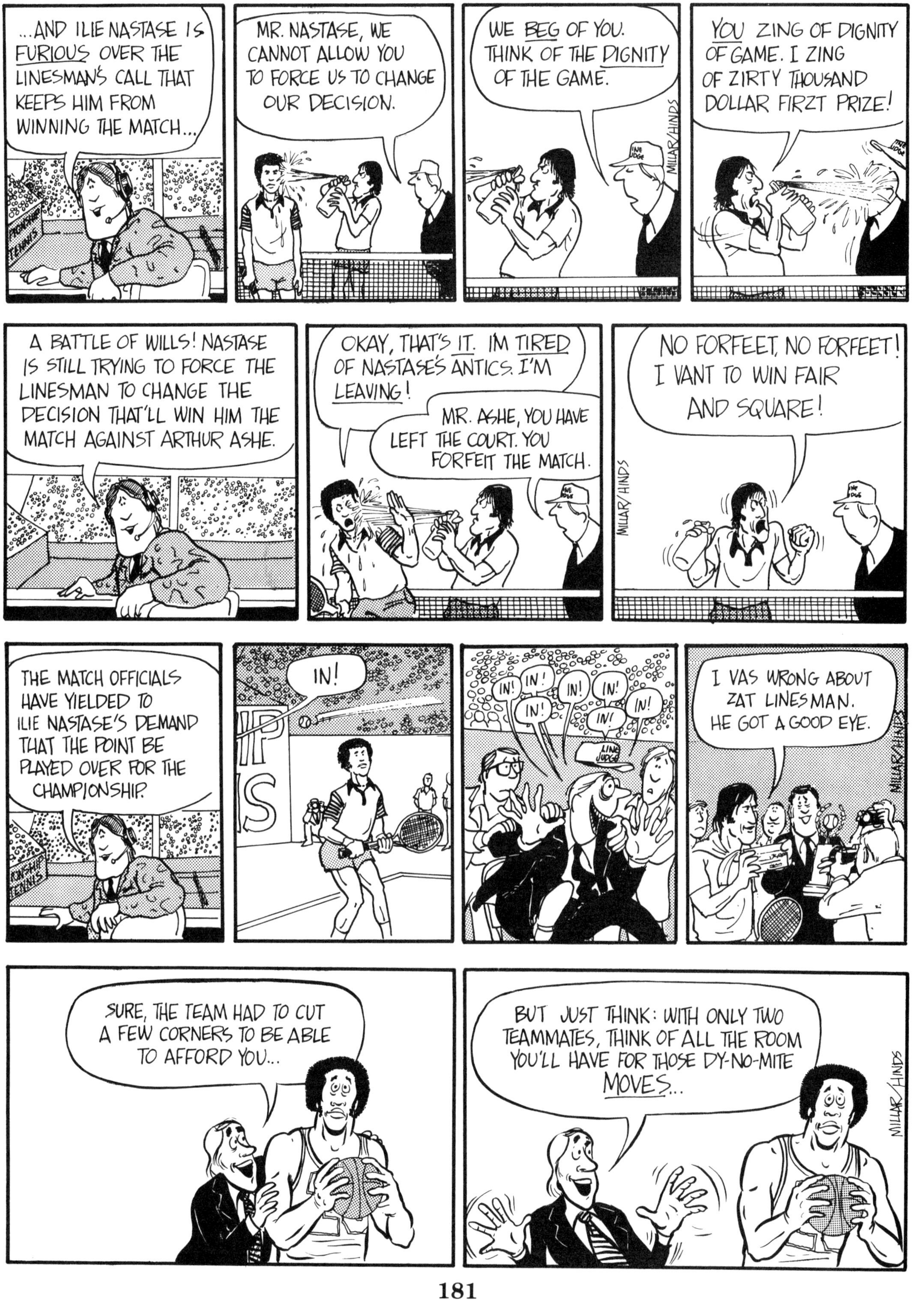
...AND ILIE NASTASE IS FURIOUS OVER THE LINESMAN'S CALL THAT KEEPS HIM FROM WINNING THE MATCH...
MR. NASTASE, WE CANNOT ALLOW YOU TO FORCE US TO CHANGE OUR DECISION.
WE BEG OF YOU. THINK OF THE DIGNITY OF THE GAME.
MILLAR/HINDS
YOU ZING OF DIGNITY OF GAME. I ZING OF ZIRTY THOUSAND DOLLAR FIRZT PRIZE!
A BATTLE OF WILLS! NASTASE IS STILL TRYING TO FORCE THE LINESMAN TO CHANGE THE DECISION THAT'LL WIN HIM THE MATCH AGAINST ARTHUR ASHE.
OKAY, THAT'S IT. I'M TIRED OF NASTASE'S ANTICS. I'M LEAVING!
MR. ASHE, YOU HAVE LEFT THE COURT. YOU FORFEIT THE MATCH.
MILLAR/HINDS
NO FORFEET, NO FORFEET! I VANT TO WIN FAIR AND SQUARE!
THE MATCH OFFICIALS HAVE YIELDED TO ILIE NASTASE'S DEMAND THAT THE POINT BE PLAYED OVER FOR THE CHAMPIONSHIP.
IN!
IN! IN! IN! IN! IN! IN! IN!
LINE JUDGE
I VAS WRONG ABOUT ZAT LINESMAN. HE GOT A GOOD EYE.
MILLAR/HINDS
SURE, THE TEAM HAD TO CUT A FEW CORNERS TO BE ABLE TO AFFORD YOU...
BUT JUST THINK: WITH ONLY TWO TEAMMATES, THINK OF ALL THE ROOM YOU'LL HAVE FOR THOSE DY-NO-MITE MOVES...
MILLAR/HINDS

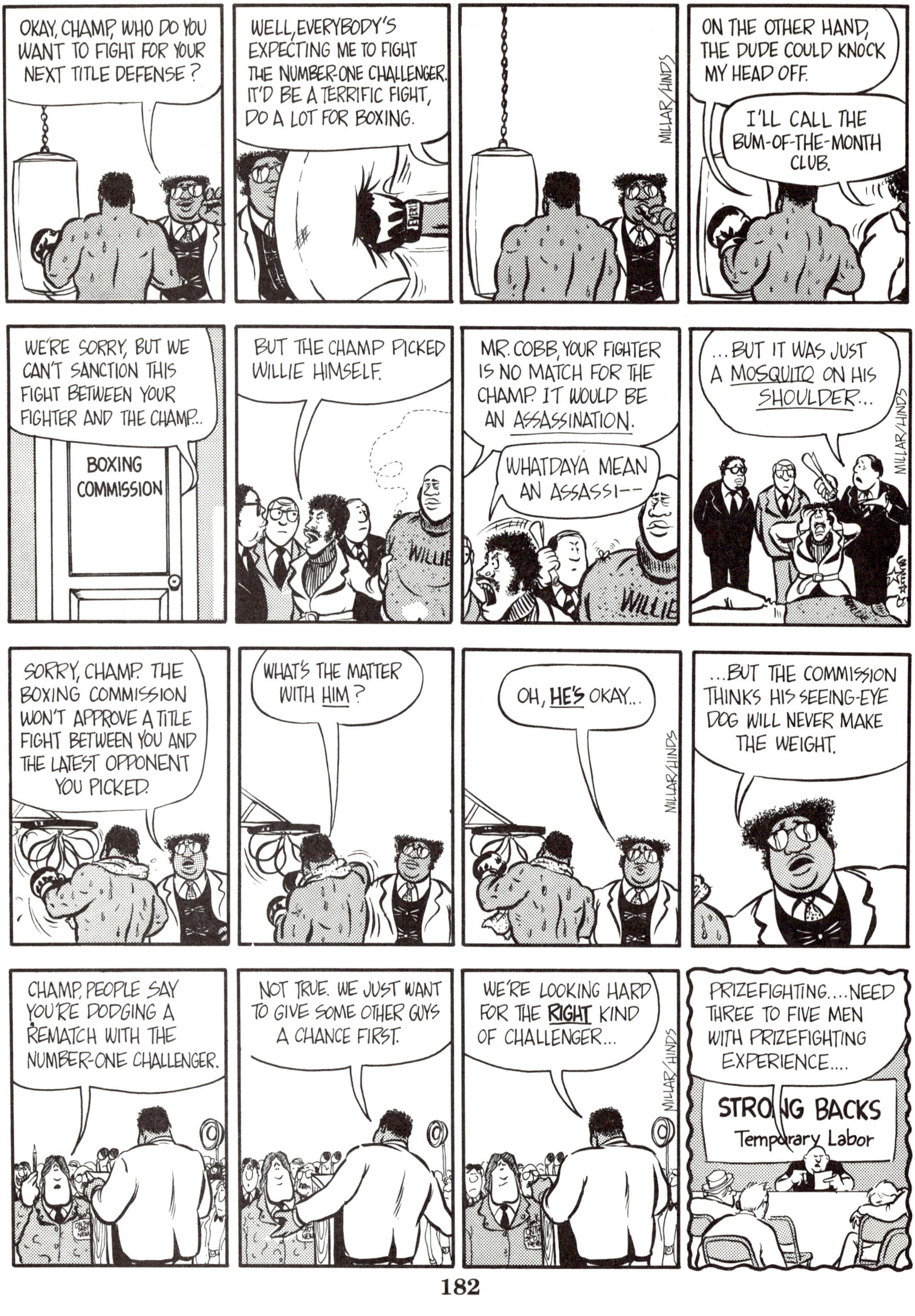
OKAY, CHAMP, WHO DO YOU WANT TO FIGHT FOR YOUR NEXT TITLE DEFENSE?
WELL, EVERYBODY'S EXPECTING ME TO FIGHT THE NUMBER-ONE CHALLENGER. IT'D BE A TERRIFIC FIGHT, DO A LOT FOR BOXING.
MILLAR/HINDS
ON THE OTHER HAND, THE DUDE COULD KNOCK MY HEAD OFF.
I'LL CALL THE BUM-OF-THE-MONTH CLUB.
WE'RE SORRY, BUT WE CAN'T SANCTION THIS FIGHT BETWEEN YOUR FIGHTER AND THE CHAMP...
BOXING COMMISSION
BUT THE CHAMP PICKED WILLIE HIMSELF.
WILLIE
MR. COBB, YOUR FIGHTER IS NO MATCH FOR THE CHAMP. IT WOULD BE AN ASSASSINATION.
WHATDAYA MEAN AN ASSASSI--
WILLIE
...BUT IT WAS JUST A MOSQUITO ON HIS SHOULDER...
MILLAR/HINDS
SORRY, CHAMP. THE BOXING COMMISSION WON'T APPROVE A TITLE FIGHT BETWEEN YOU AND THE LATEST OPPONENT YOU PICKED.
WHAT'S THE MATTER WITH HIM?
OH, HE'S OKAY...
MILLAR/HINDS
...BUT THE COMMISSION THINKS HIS SEEING-EYE DOG WILL NEVER MAKE THE WEIGHT.
CHAMP, PEOPLE SAY YOU'RE DODGING A REMATCH WITH THE NUMBER-ONE CHALLENGER.
NOT TRUE. WE JUST WANT TO GIVE SOME OTHER GUYS A CHANCE FIRST.
WE'RE LOOKING HARD FOR THE RIGHT KIND OF CHALLENGER...
MILLAR/HINDS
PRIZEFIGHTING....NEED THREE TO FIVE MEN WITH PRIZEFIGHTING EXPERIENCE....
STRONG BACKS
Temporary Labor

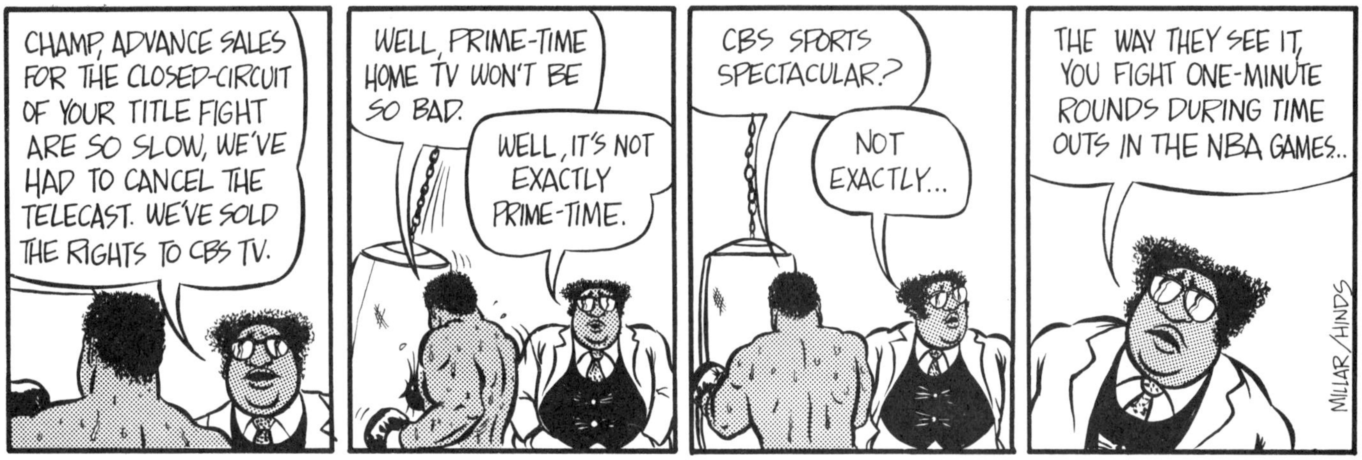
CHAMP, ADVANCE SALES FOR THE CLOSED-CIRCUIT OF YOUR TITLE FIGHT ARE SO SLOW, WE'VE HAD TO CANCEL THE TELECAST. WE'VE SOLD THE RIGHTS TO CBS TV.
WELL, PRIME-TIME HOME TV WON'T BE SO BAD.
WELL, IT'S NOT EXACTLY PRIME-TIME.
CBS SPORTS SPECTACULAR?
NOT EXACTLY...
THE WAY THEY SEE IT, YOU FIGHT ONE-MINUTE ROUNDS DURING TIME OUTS IN THE NBA GAMES..
MILLAR/HINDS

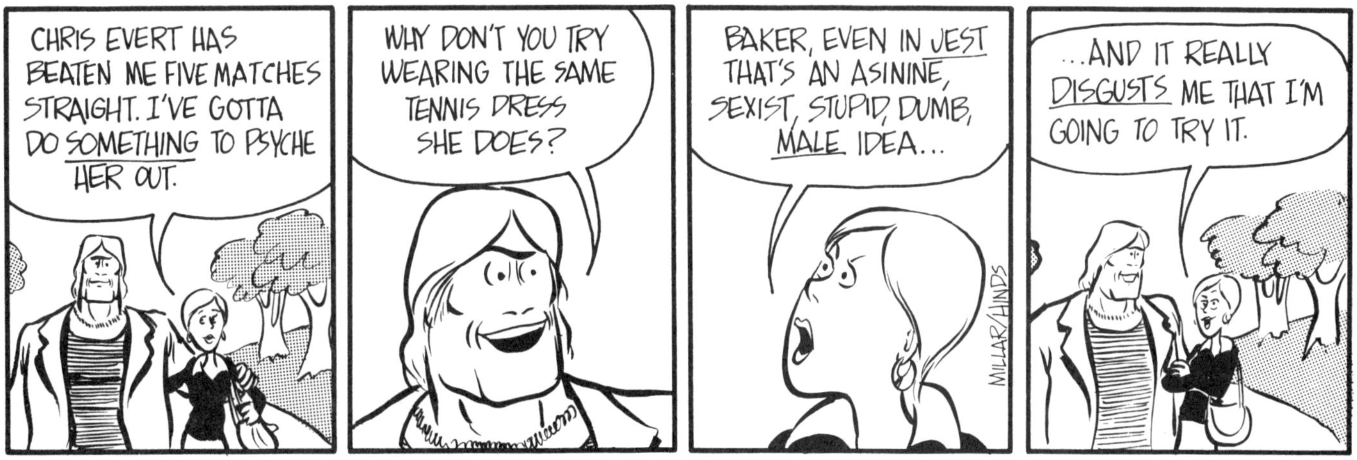
CHRIS EVERT HAS BEATEN ME FIVE MATCHES STRAIGHT. I'VE GOTTA DO SOMETHING TO PSYCHE HER OUT.
WHY DON'T YOU TRY WEARING THE SAME TENNIS DRESS SHE DOES?
BAKER, EVEN IN JEST THAT'S AN ASININE, SEXIST, STUPID, DUMB, MALE IDEA...
MILLAR/HINDS
...AND IT REALLY DISGUSTS ME THAT I'M GOING TO TRY IT.

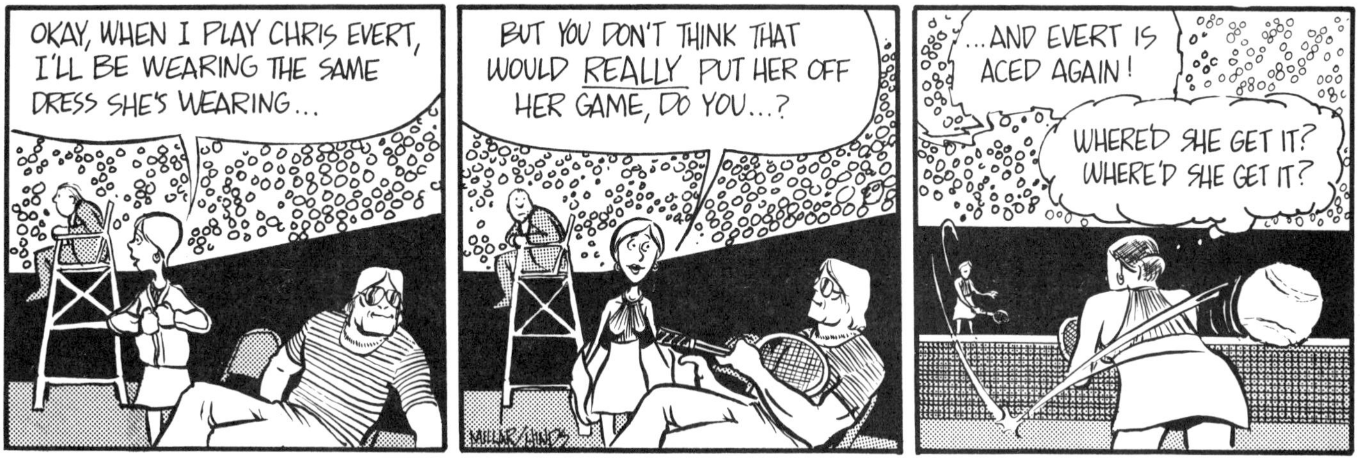
OKAY, WHEN I PLAY CHRIS EVERT, I'LL BE WEARING THE SAME DRESS SHE'S WEARING...
BUT YOU DON'T THINK THAT WOULD REALLY PUT HER OFF HER GAME, DO YOU...?
MILLAR/HINDS
...AND EVERT IS ACED AGAIN!
WHERE'D SHE GET IT? WHERE'D SHE GET IT?

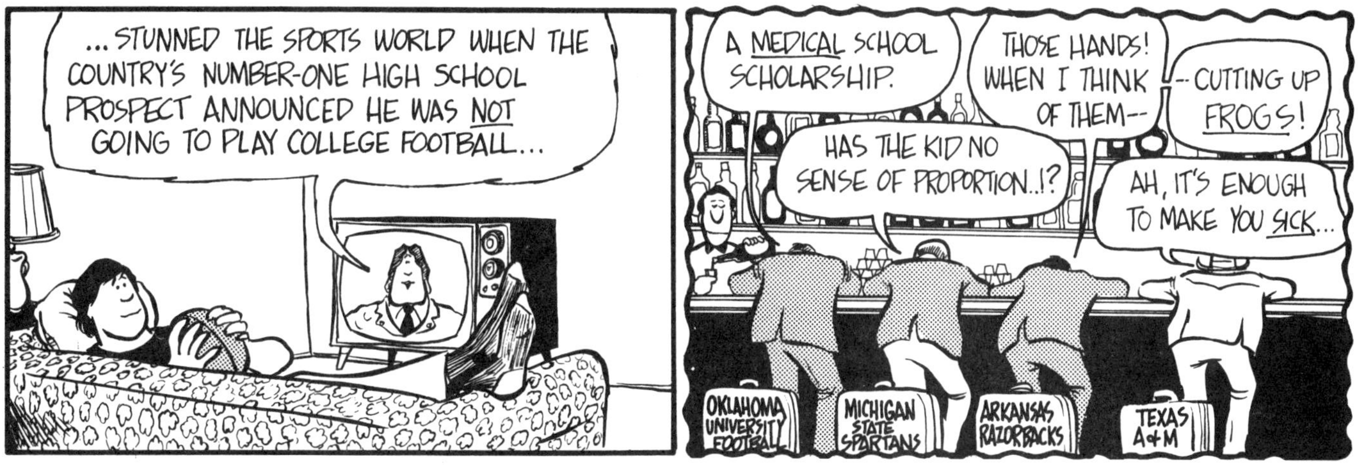
...STUNNED THE SPORTS WORLD WHEN THE COUNTRY'S NUMBER-ONE HIGH SCHOOL PROSPECT ANNOUNCED HE WAS NOT GOING TO PLAY COLLEGE FOOTBALL...
A MEDICAL SCHOOL SCHOLARSHIP.
THOSE HANDS! WHEN I THINK OF THEM--
--CUTTING UP FROGS!
HAS THE KID NO SENSE OF PROPORTION..!?
AH, IT'S ENOUGH TO MAKE YOU SICK...
OKLAHOMA UNIVERSITY FOOTBALL
MICHIGAN STATE SPARTANS
ARKANSAS RAZORBACKS
TEXAS A&M

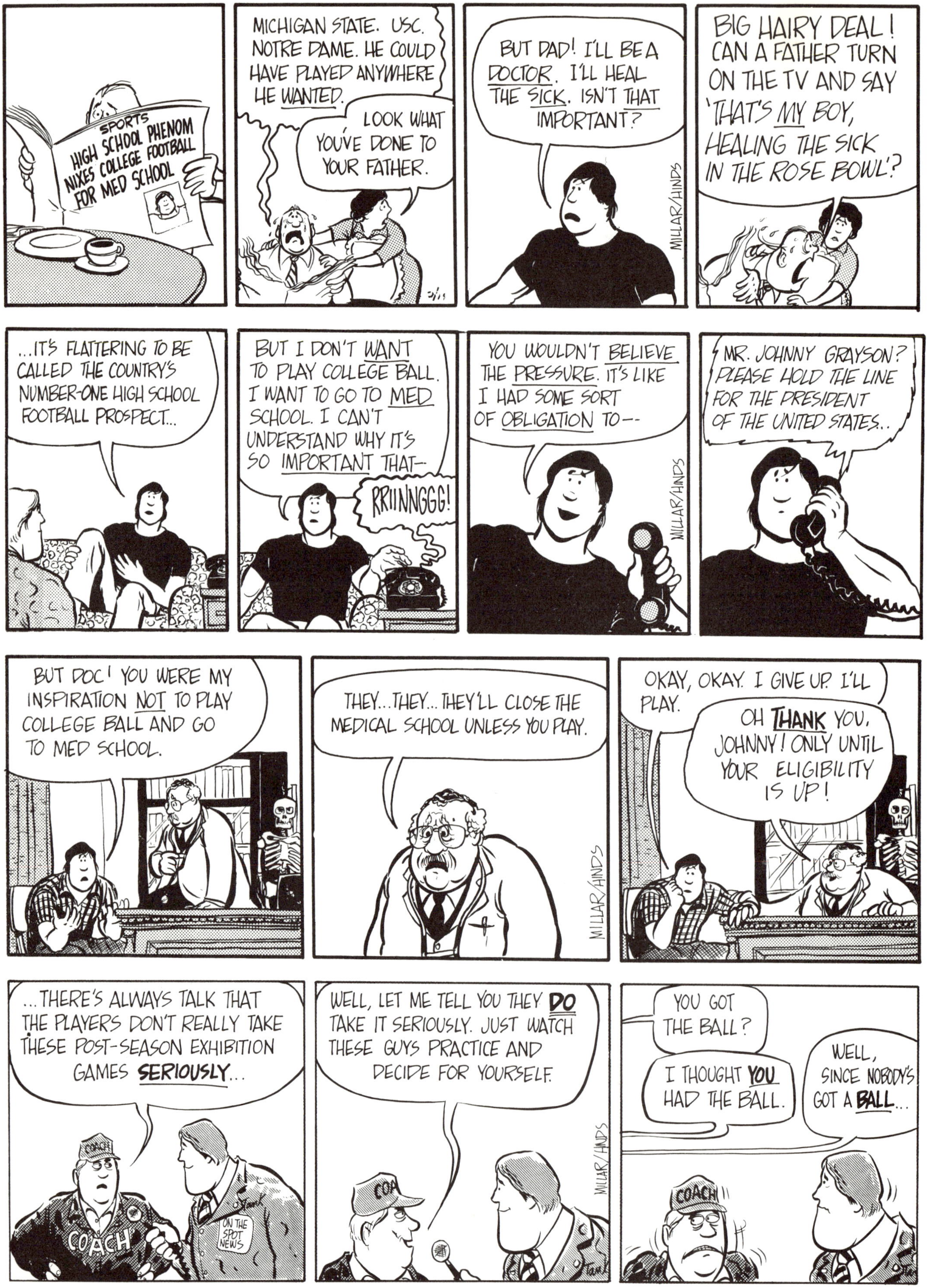
SPORTS
HIGH SCHOOL PHENOM NIXES COLLEGE FOOTBALL FOR MED SCHOOL
MICHIGAN STATE. USC. NOTRE DAME. HE COULD HAVE PLAYED ANYWHERE HE WANTED.
LOOK WHAT YOU'VE DONE TO YOUR FATHER.
BUT DAD! I'LL BE A DOCTOR. I'LL HEAL THE SICK. ISN'T THAT IMPORTANT?
MILLAR/HINDS
BIG HAIRY DEAL! CAN A FATHER TURN ON THE TV AND SAY 'THAT'S MY BOY, HEALING THE SICK IN THE ROSE BOWL'?
...IT'S FLATTERING TO BE CALLED THE COUNTRY'S NUMBER-ONE HIGH SCHOOL FOOTBALL PROSPECT...
BUT I DON'T WANT TO PLAY COLLEGE BALL. I WANT TO GO TO MED SCHOOL. I CAN'T UNDERSTAND WHY IT'S SO IMPORTANT THAT--
RRIINNGGG!
YOU WOULDN'T BELIEVE THE PRESSURE. IT'S LIKE I HAD SOME SORT OF OBLIGATION TO--
MILLAR/HINDS
MR. JOHNNY GRAYSON? PLEASE HOLD THE LINE FOR THE PRESIDENT OF THE UNITED STATES..
BUT DOC! YOU WERE MY INSPIRATION NOT TO PLAY COLLEGE BALL AND GO TO MED SCHOOL.
THEY...THEY...THEY'LL CLOSE THE MEDICAL SCHOOL UNLESS YOU PLAY.
MILLAR/HINDS
OKAY, OKAY. I GIVE UP. I'LL PLAY.
OH THANK YOU, JOHNNY! ONLY UNTIL YOUR ELIGIBILITY IS UP!
...THERE'S ALWAYS TALK THAT THE PLAYERS DON'T REALLY TAKE THESE POST-SEASON EXHIBITION GAMES SERIOUSLY...
COACH
COACH
ON THE SPOT NEWS
WELL, LET ME TELL YOU THEY DO TAKE IT SERIOUSLY. JUST WATCH THESE GUYS PRACTICE AND DECIDE FOR YOURSELF.
MILLAR/HINDS
YOU GOT THE BALL?
I THOUGHT YOU HAD THE BALL.
WELL, SINCE NOBODY'S GOT A BALL...
COACH

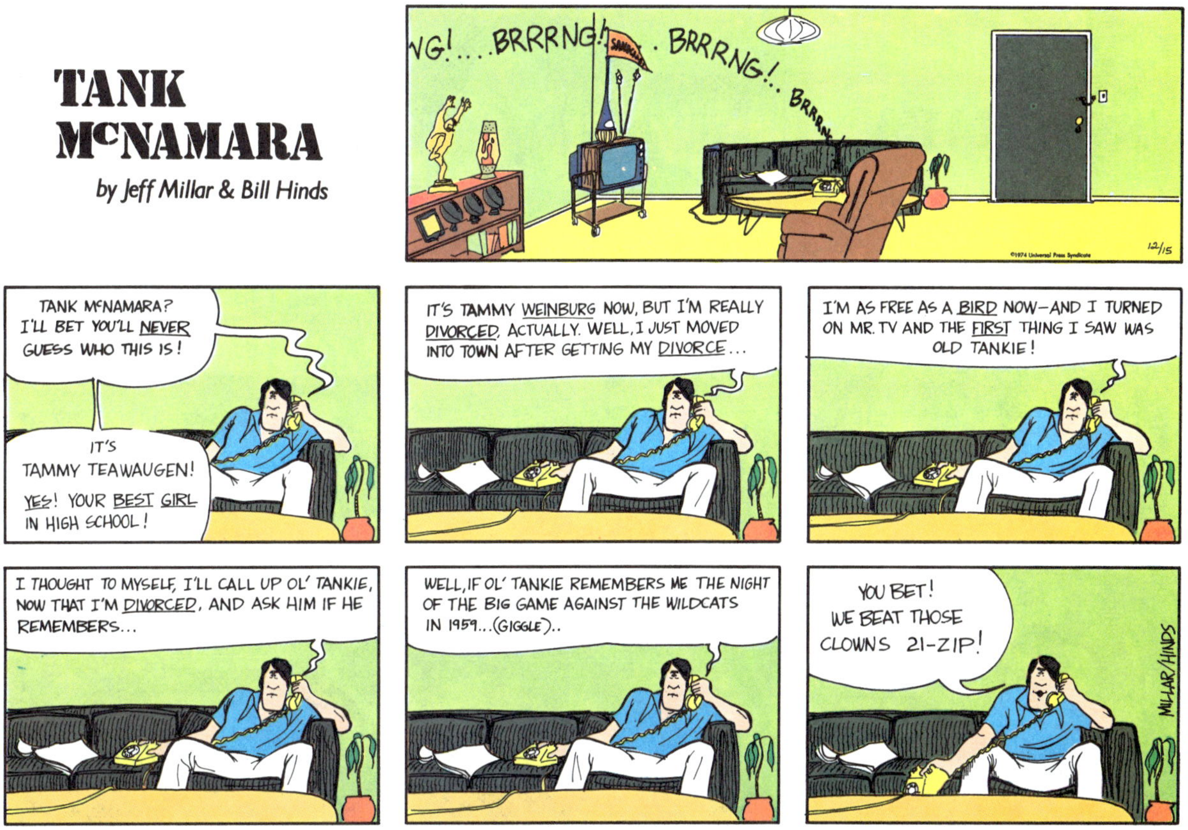

TANK McNAMARA
by Jeff Millar & Bill Hinds
NG!....BRRRNG!...BRRRNG!..BRRRNG
©1974 Universal Press Syndicate
12/15
TANK McNAMARA? I'LL BET YOU'LL NEVER GUESS WHO THIS IS!
IT'S TAMMY TEAWAUGEN! YES! YOUR BEST GIRL IN HIGH SCHOOL!
IT'S TAMMY WEINBURG NOW, BUT I'M REALLY DIVORCED, ACTUALLY. WELL, I JUST MOVED INTO TOWN AFTER GETTING MY DIVORCE...
I'M AS FREE AS A BIRD NOW—AND I TURNED ON MR. TV AND THE FIRST THING I SAW WAS OLD TANKIE!
I THOUGHT TO MYSELF, I'LL CALL UP OL' TANKIE, NOW THAT I'M DIVORCED, AND ASK HIM IF HE REMEMBERS...
WELL, IF OL' TANKIE REMEMBERS ME THE NIGHT OF THE BIG GAME AGAINST THE WILDCATS IN 1959...(GIGGLE)..
YOU BET! WE BEAT THOSE CLOWNS 21-ZIP!
MILLAR/HINDS

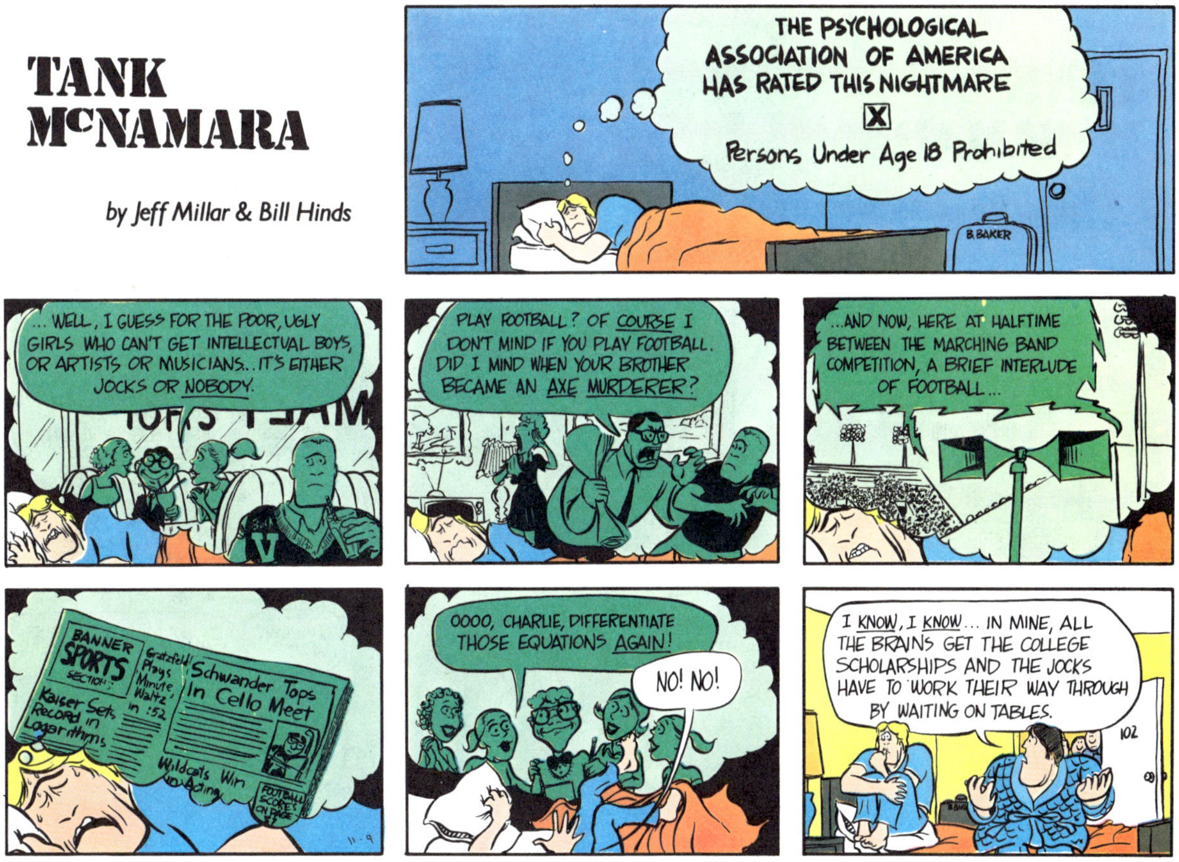

TANK McNAMARA
by Jeff Millar & Bill Hinds
THE PSYCHOLOGICAL ASSOCIATION OF AMERICA HAS RATED THIS NIGHTMARE
X
Persons Under Age 18 Prohibited
B. BAKER
... WELL, I GUESS FOR THE POOR, UGLY GIRLS WHO CAN'T GET INTELLECTUAL BOYS, OR ARTISTS OR MUSICIANS... IT'S EITHER JOCKS OR NOBODY.
PLAY FOOTBALL? OF COURSE I DON'T MIND IF YOU PLAY FOOTBALL. DID I MIND WHEN YOUR BROTHER BECAME AN AXE MURDERER?
...AND NOW, HERE AT HALFTIME BETWEEN THE MARCHING BAND COMPETITION, A BRIEF INTERLUDE OF FOOTBALL...
BANNER SPORTS SECTION
Gratzfeld Plays Minute Waltz in :52
Schwander Tops In Cello Meet
Kaiser Sets Record in Logarithms
Wildcats Win
FOOTBALL SCORES ON PAGE
11-9
OOOO, CHARLIE, DIFFERENTIATE THOSE EQUATIONS AGAIN!
NO! NO!
I KNOW, I KNOW... IN MINE, ALL THE BRAINS GET THE COLLEGE SCHOLARSHIPS AND THE JOCKS HAVE TO WORK THEIR WAY THROUGH BY WAITING ON TABLES.
102

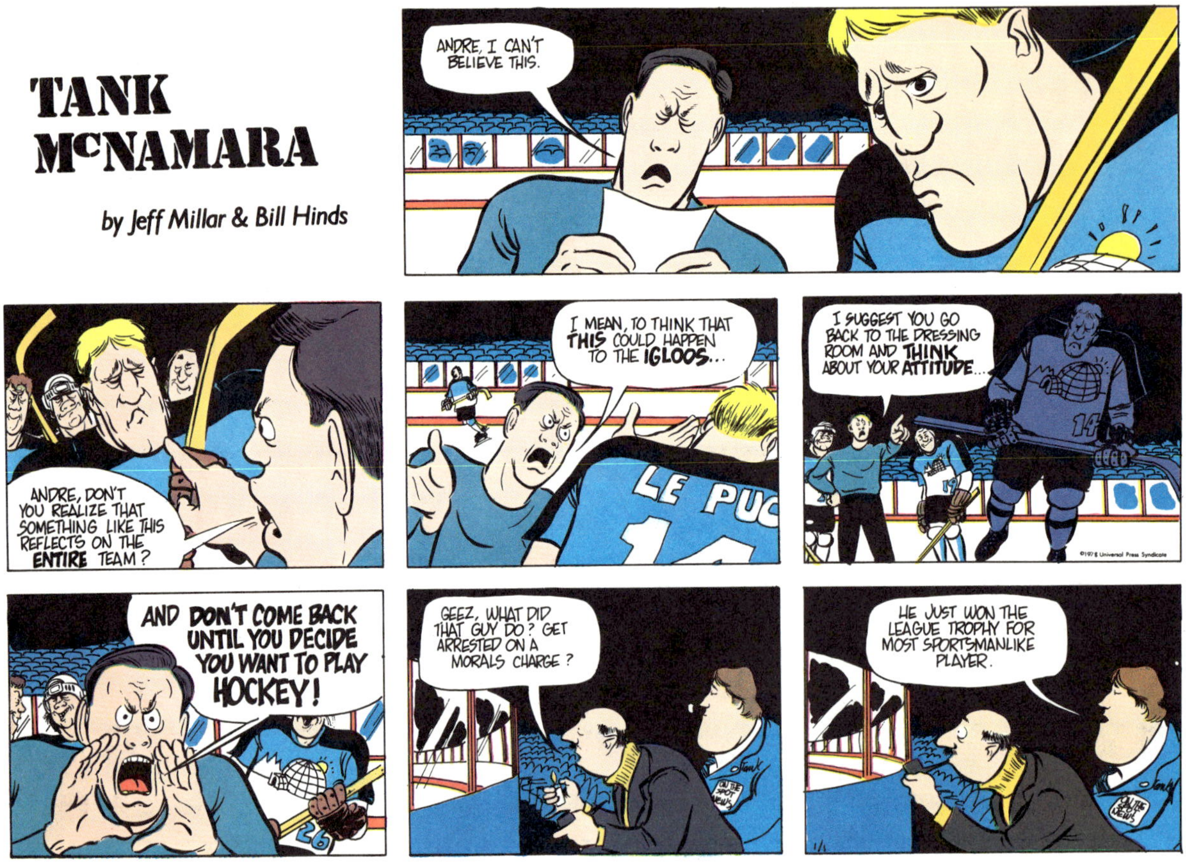
TANK McNAMARA
by Jeff Millar & Bill Hinds
ANDRE, I CAN'T BELIEVE THIS.
ANDRE, DON'T YOU REALIZE THAT SOMETHING LIKE THIS REFLECTS ON THE ENTIRE TEAM?
I MEAN, TO THINK THAT THIS COULD HAPPEN TO THE IGLOOS...
LE PUC
I SUGGEST YOU GO BACK TO THE DRESSING ROOM AND THINK ABOUT YOUR ATTITUDE...
AND DON'T COME BACK UNTIL YOU DECIDE YOU WANT TO PLAY HOCKEY!
GEEZ, WHAT DID THAT GUY DO? GET ARRESTED ON A MORALS CHARGE?
HE JUST WON THE LEAGUE TROPHY FOR MOST SPORTSMANLIKE PLAYER.

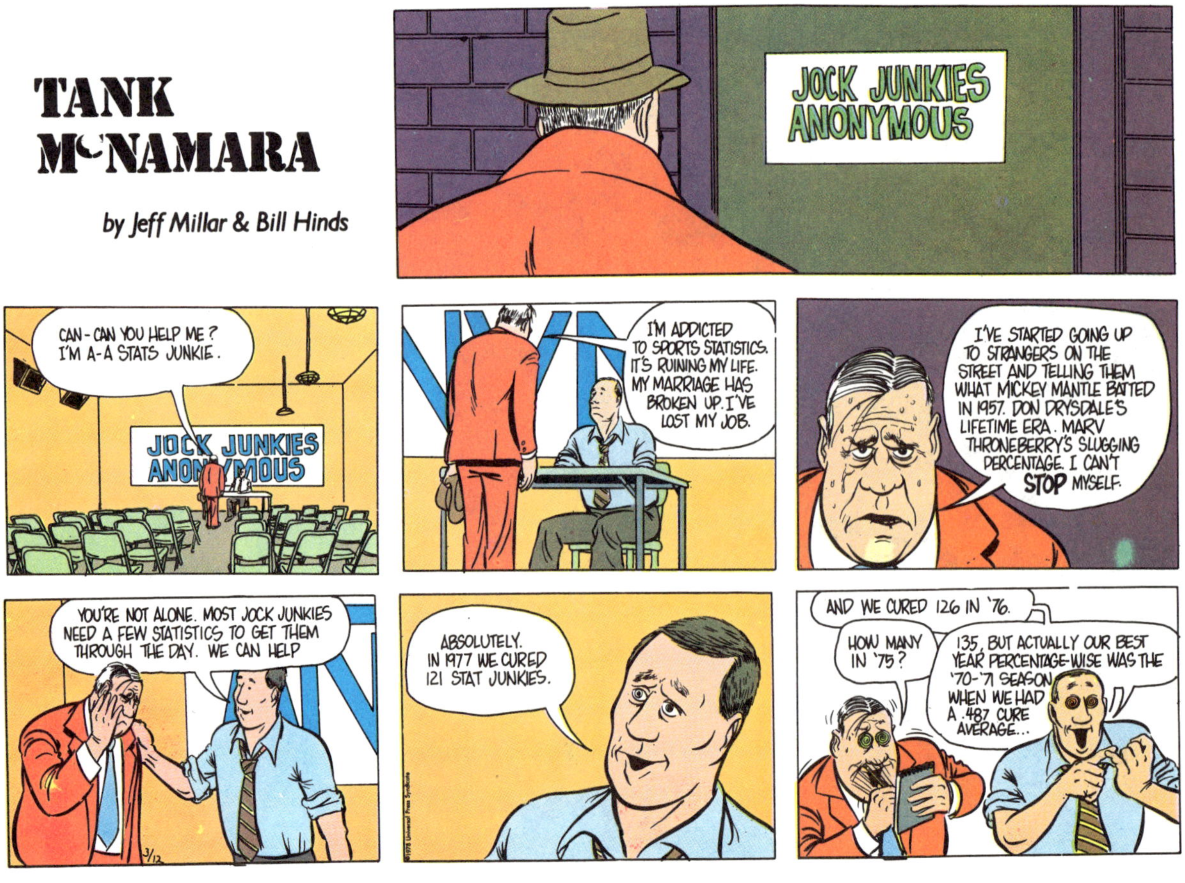
TANK McNAMARA
by Jeff Millar & Bill Hinds
JOCK JUNKIES ANONYMOUS
CAN-CAN YOU HELP ME? I'M A-A STATS JUNKIE.
I'M ADDICTED TO SPORTS STATISTICS. IT'S RUINING MY LIFE. MY MARRIAGE HAS BROKEN UP. I'VE LOST MY JOB.
I'VE STARTED GOING UP TO STRANGERS ON THE STREET AND TELLING THEM WHAT MICKEY MANTLE BATTED IN 1957. DON DRYSDALE'S LIFETIME ERA. MARV THRONEBERRY'S SLUGGING PERCENTAGE. I CAN'T STOP MYSELF.
YOU'RE NOT ALONE. MOST JOCK JUNKIES NEED A FEW STATISTICS TO GET THEM THROUGH THE DAY. WE CAN HELP
ABSOLUTELY. IN 1977 WE CURED 121 STAT JUNKIES.
AND WE CURED 126 IN '76.
HOW MANY IN '75?
135, BUT ACTUALLY OUR BEST YEAR PERCENTAGE-WISE WAS THE '70-'71 SEASON WHEN WE HAD A .487 CURE AVERAGE...

TANK McNAMARA

by Jeff Millar & Bill Hinds

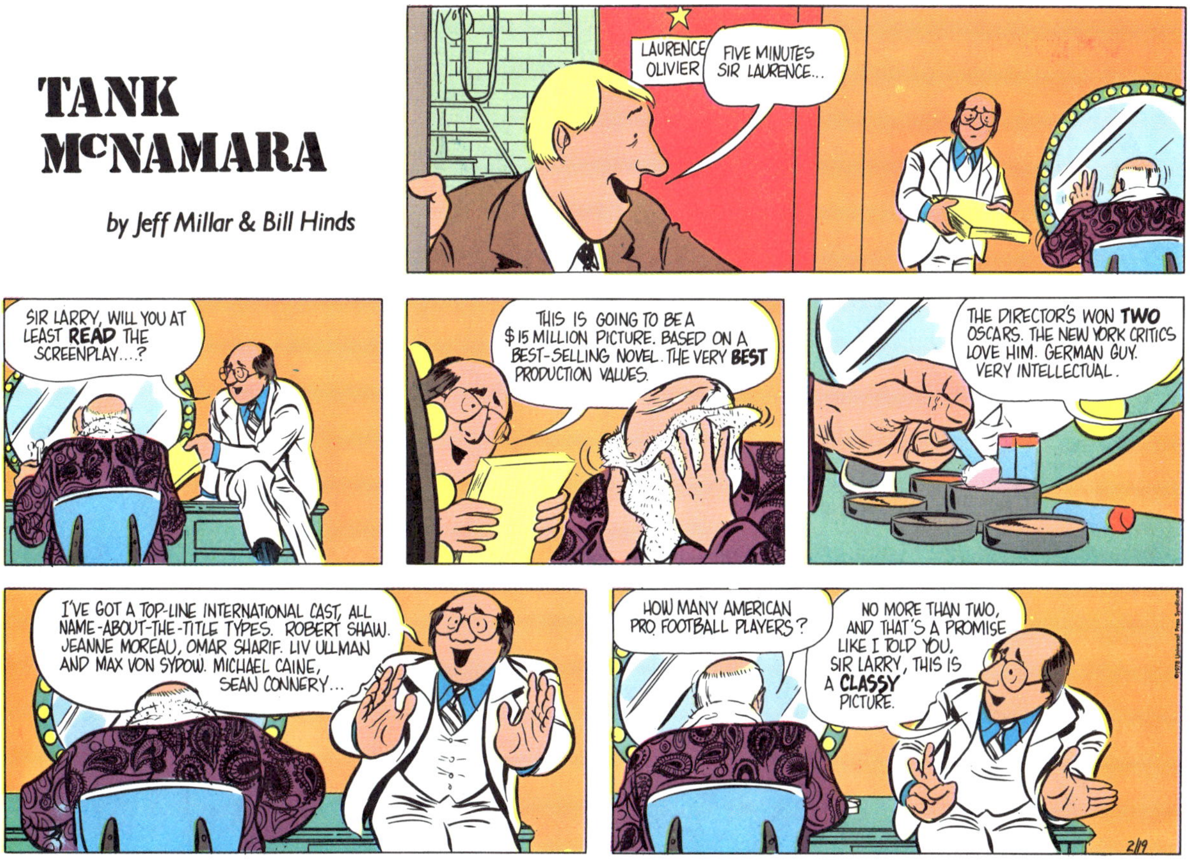
LAURENCE OLIVIER
FIVE MINUTES SIR LAURENCE...
SIR LARRY, WILL YOU AT LEAST **READ** THE SCREENPLAY...?
THIS IS GOING TO BE A $15 MILLION PICTURE. BASED ON A BEST-SELLING NOVEL. THE VERY **BEST** PRODUCTION VALUES.
THE DIRECTOR'S WON **TWO** OSCARS. THE NEW YORK CRITICS LOVE HIM. GERMAN GUY. VERY INTELLECTUAL.
I'VE GOT A TOP-LINE INTERNATIONAL CAST, ALL NAME-ABOUT-THE-TITLE TYPES. ROBERT SHAW. JEANNE MOREAU, OMAR SHARIF. LIV ULLMAN AND MAX VON SYDOW. MICHAEL CAINE, SEAN CONNERY...
HOW MANY AMERICAN PRO FOOTBALL PLAYERS?
NO MORE THAN TWO, AND THAT'S A PROMISE LIKE I TOLD YOU, SIR LARRY, THIS IS A **CLASSY** PICTURE.
2/19

TANK McNAMARA

by Jeff Millar & Bill Hinds

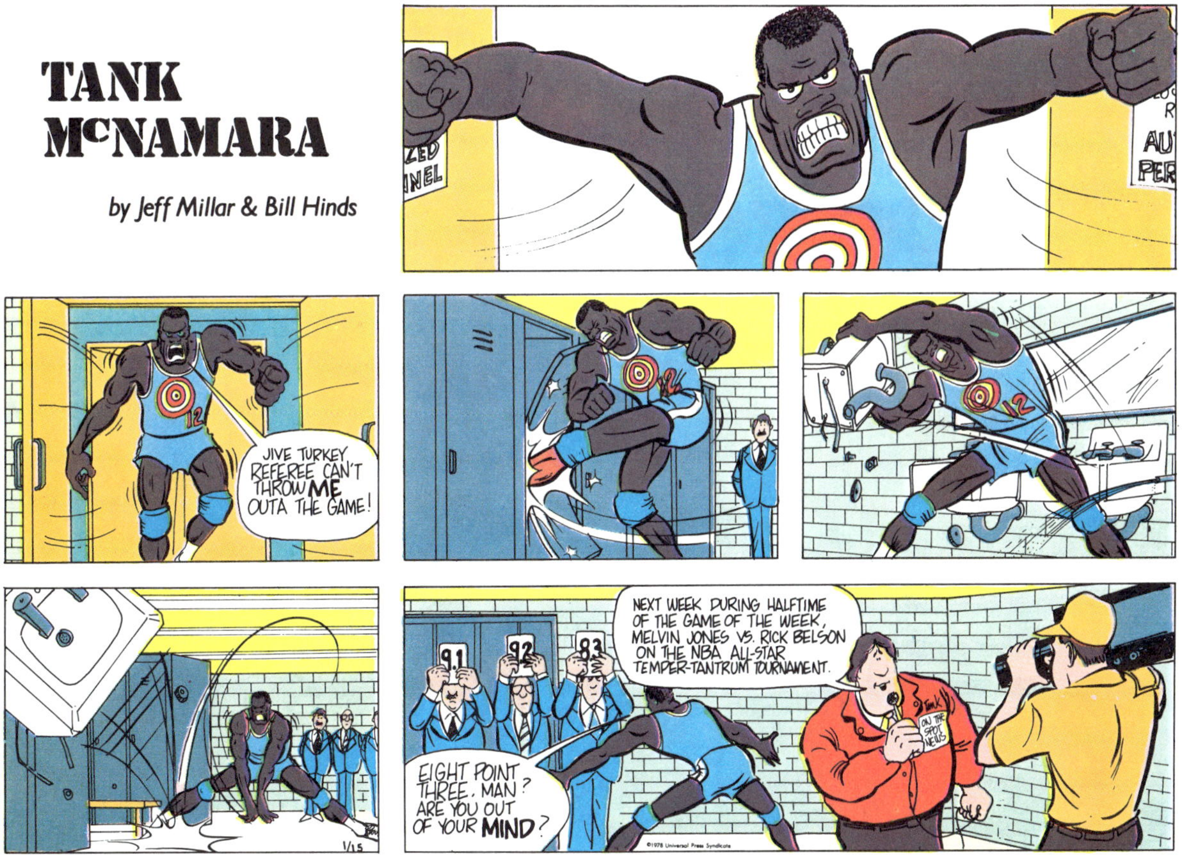
JIVE TURKEY REFEREE CAN'T THROW **ME** OUTA THE GAME!
1/15
9.1
9.2
8.3
NEXT WEEK DURING HALFTIME OF THE GAME OF THE WEEK, MELVIN JONES VS. RICK BELSON ON THE NBA ALL-STAR TEMPER-TANTRUM TOURNAMENT.
EIGHT POINT THREE, MAN? ARE YOU OUT OF YOUR **MIND**?
©1978 Universal Press Syndicate

TANK McNAMARA

by Jeff Millar & Bill Hinds

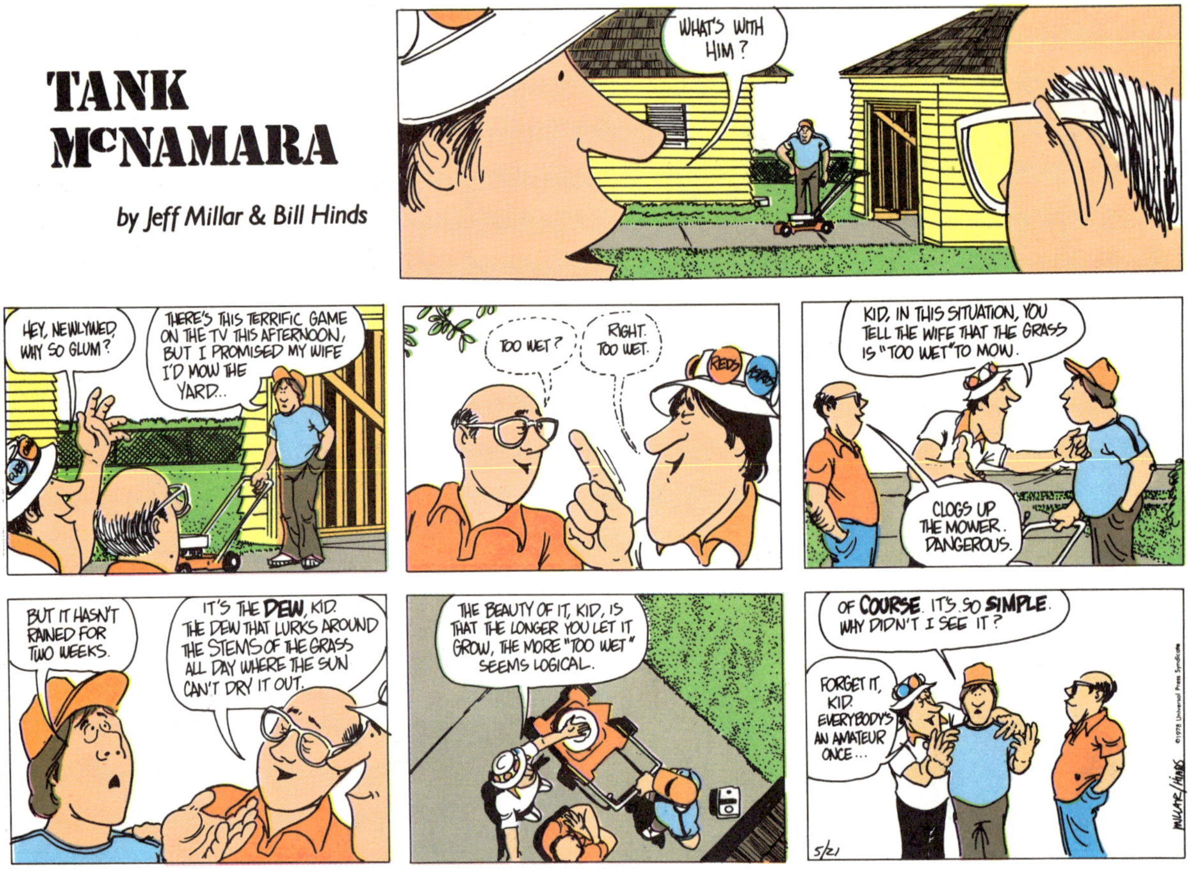
WHAT'S WITH HIM?
HEY, NEWLYWED, WHY SO GLUM?
THERE'S THIS TERRIFIC GAME ON THE TV THIS AFTERNOON, BUT I PROMISED MY WIFE I'D MOW THE YARD...
TOO WET?
RIGHT. TOO WET.
REDS
KID, IN THIS SITUATION, YOU TELL THE WIFE THAT THE GRASS IS "TOO WET" TO MOW.
CLOGS UP THE MOWER. DANGEROUS.
BUT IT HASN'T RAINED FOR TWO WEEKS.
IT'S THE DEW, KID. THE DEW THAT LURKS AROUND THE STEMS OF THE GRASS ALL DAY WHERE THE SUN CAN'T DRY IT OUT.
THE BEAUTY OF IT, KID, IS THAT THE LONGER YOU LET IT GROW, THE MORE "TOO WET" SEEMS LOGICAL.
OF COURSE. IT'S SO SIMPLE. WHY DIDN'T I SEE IT?
FORGET IT, KID. EVERYBODY'S AN AMATEUR ONCE...
5/21
MILLAR/HINDS

TANK McNAMARA

by Jeff Millar & Bill Hinds

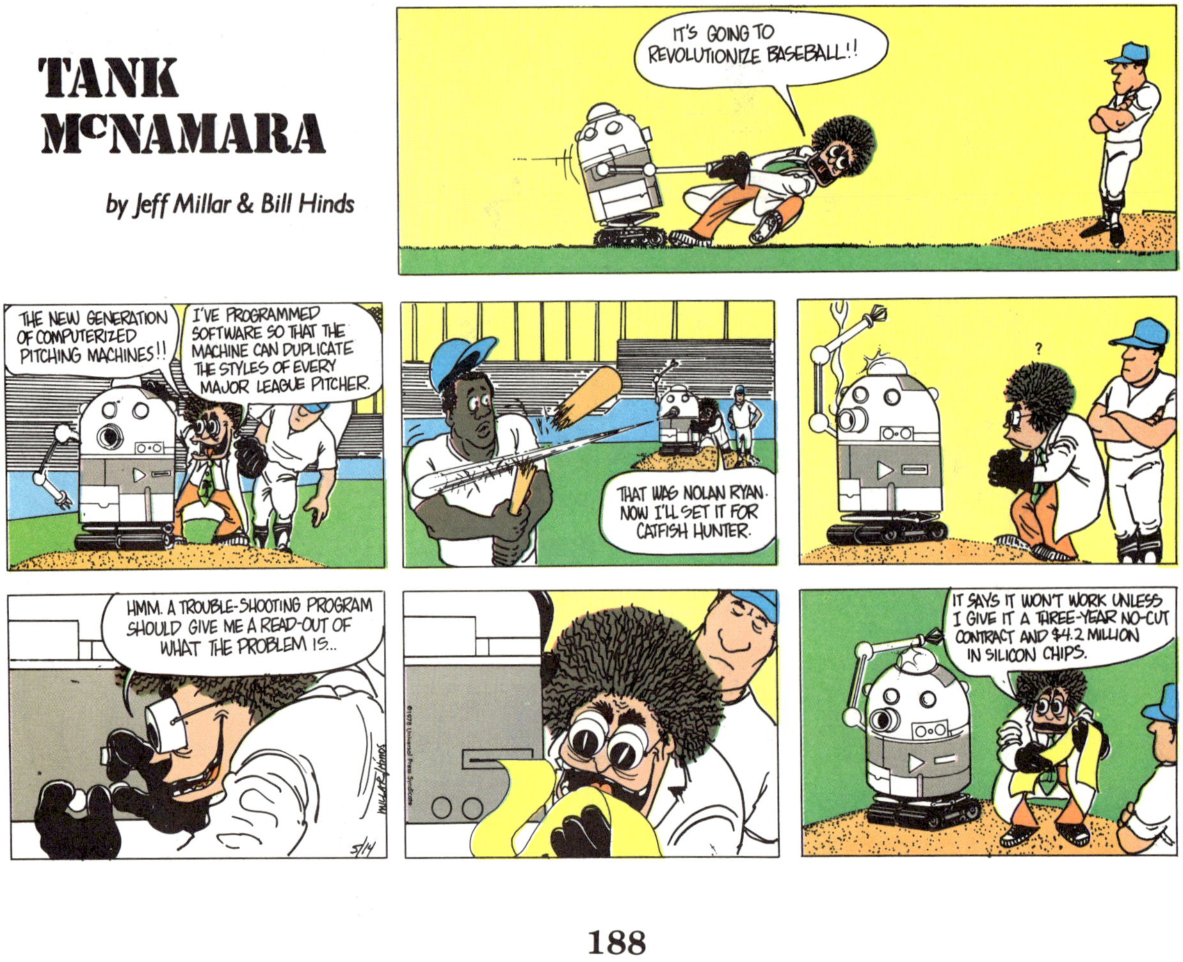
IT'S GOING TO REVOLUTIONIZE BASEBALL!!
THE NEW GENERATION OF COMPUTERIZED PITCHING MACHINES!!
I'VE PROGRAMMED SOFTWARE SO THAT THE MACHINE CAN DUPLICATE THE STYLES OF EVERY MAJOR LEAGUE PITCHER.
THAT WAS NOLAN RYAN. NOW I'LL SET IT FOR CATFISH HUNTER.
?
HMM. A TROUBLE-SHOOTING PROGRAM SHOULD GIVE ME A READ-OUT OF WHAT THE PROBLEM IS...
5/14
MILLAR/HINDS
IT SAYS IT WON'T WORK UNLESS I GIVE IT A THREE-YEAR NO-CUT CONTRACT AND $4.2 MILLION IN SILICON CHIPS.

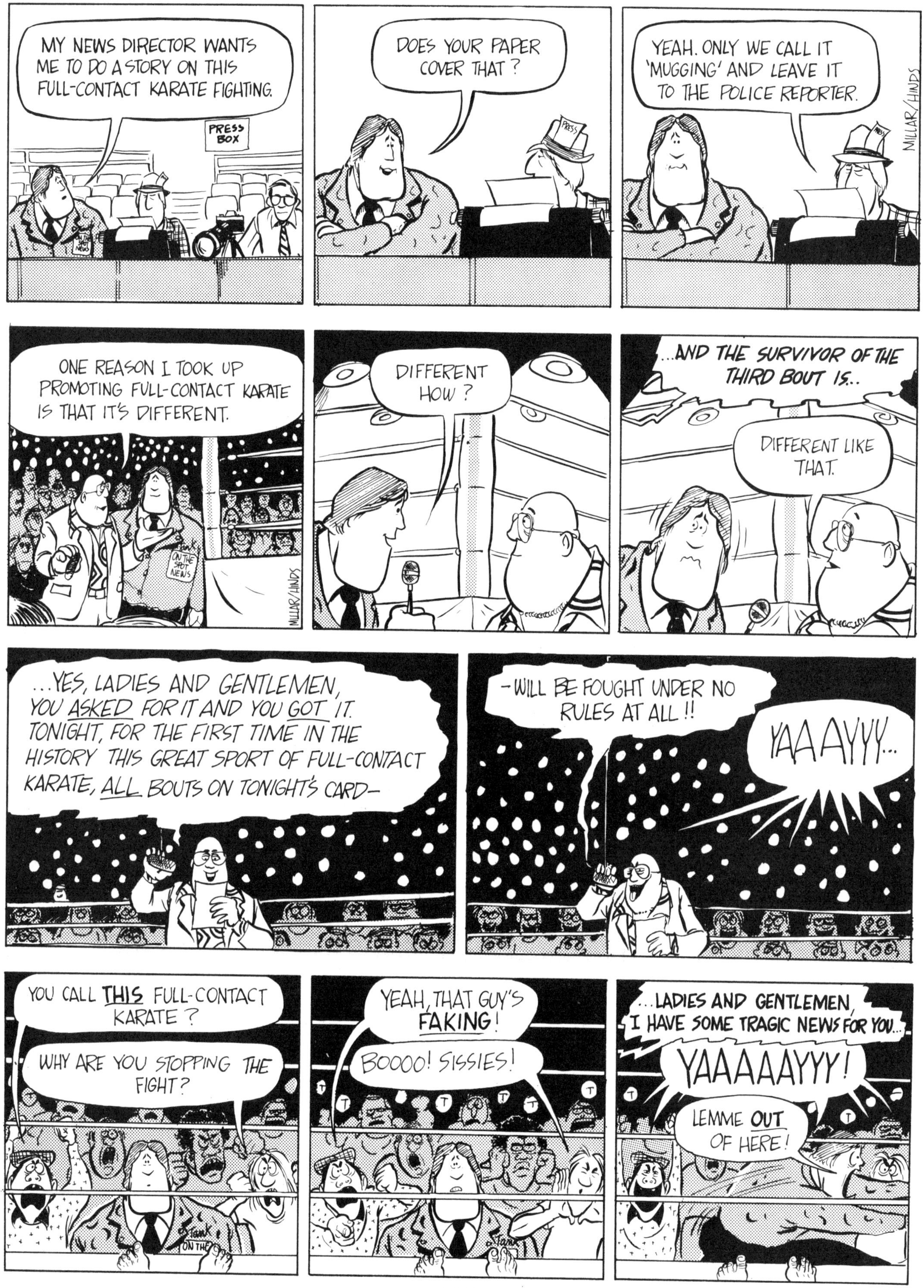
MY NEWS DIRECTOR WANTS ME TO DO A STORY ON THIS FULL-CONTACT KARATE FIGHTING.
PRESS BOX
DOES YOUR PAPER COVER THAT?
YEAH. ONLY WE CALL IT 'MUGGING' AND LEAVE IT TO THE POLICE REPORTER.
MILLAR/HINDS
ONE REASON I TOOK UP PROMOTING FULL-CONTACT KARATE IS THAT IT'S DIFFERENT.
ON THE SPOT NEWS
MILLAR/HINDS
DIFFERENT HOW?
...AND THE SURVIVOR OF THE THIRD BOUT IS...
DIFFERENT LIKE THAT.
...YES, LADIES AND GENTLEMEN, YOU ASKED FOR IT AND YOU GOT IT. TONIGHT, FOR THE FIRST TIME IN THE HISTORY THIS GREAT SPORT OF FULL-CONTACT KARATE, ALL BOUTS ON TONIGHT'S CARD—
—WILL BE FOUGHT UNDER NO RULES AT ALL!!
YAAAYYY...
YOU CALL THIS FULL-CONTACT KARATE?
WHY ARE YOU STOPPING THE FIGHT?
YEAH, THAT GUY'S FAKING!
BOOOO! SISSIES!
...LADIES AND GENTLEMEN, I HAVE SOME TRAGIC NEWS FOR YOU...
YAAAAAYYY!
LEMME OUT OF HERE!

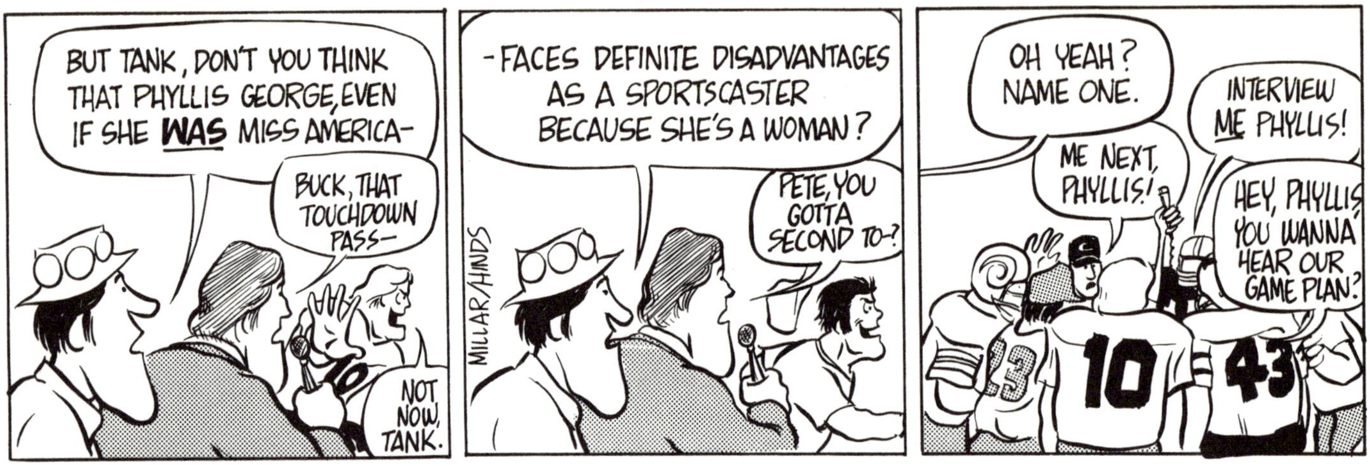
BUT TANK, DON'T YOU THINK THAT PHYLLIS GEORGE, EVEN IF SHE **WAS** MISS AMERICA-
BUCK, THAT TOUCHDOWN PASS—
NOT NOW, TANK.
10
-FACES DEFINITE DISADVANTAGES AS A SPORTSCASTER BECAUSE SHE'S A WOMAN?
PETE, YOU GOTTA SECOND TO-?
MILLAR/HINDS
OH YEAH? NAME ONE.
ME NEXT, PHYLLIS!
INTERVIEW ME PHYLLIS!
HEY, PHYLLIS YOU WANNA HEAR OUR GAME PLAN?
13
10
43

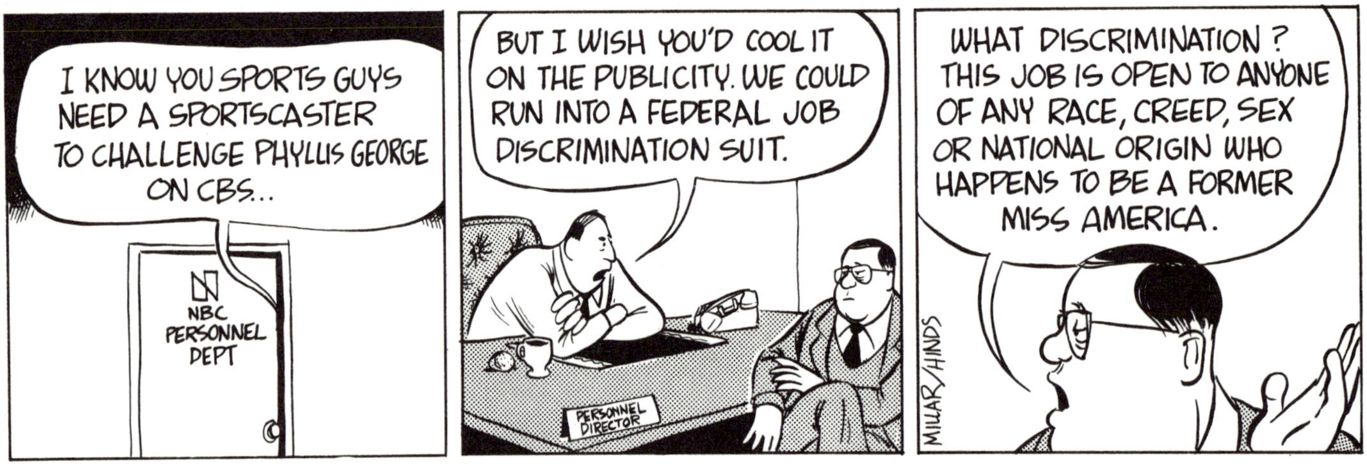
I KNOW YOU SPORTS GUYS NEED A SPORTSCASTER TO CHALLENGE PHYLLIS GEORGE ON CBS...
NBC PERSONNEL DEPT
BUT I WISH YOU'D COOL IT ON THE PUBLICITY. WE COULD RUN INTO A FEDERAL JOB DISCRIMINATION SUIT.
PERSONNEL DIRECTOR
WHAT DISCRIMINATION? THIS JOB IS OPEN TO ANYONE OF ANY RACE, CREED, SEX OR NATIONAL ORIGIN WHO HAPPENS TO BE A FORMER MISS AMERICA.
MILLAR/HINDS

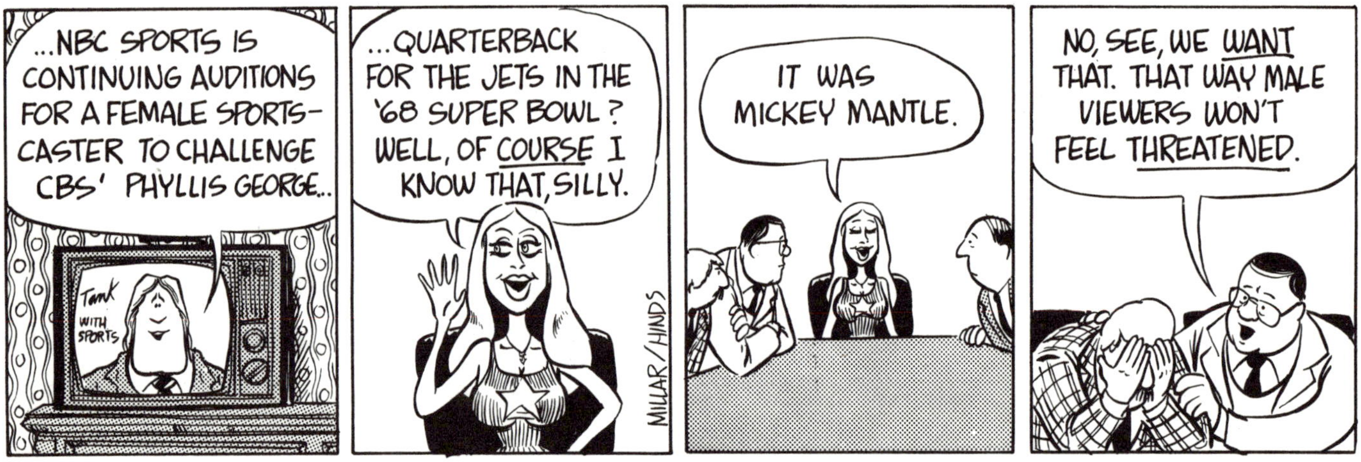
...NBC SPORTS IS CONTINUING AUDITIONS FOR A FEMALE SPORTS-CASTER TO CHALLENGE CBS' PHYLLIS GEORGE...
Tank WITH SPORTS
...QUARTERBACK FOR THE JETS IN THE '68 SUPER BOWL? WELL, OF COURSE I KNOW THAT, SILLY.
MILLAR/HINDS
IT WAS MICKEY MANTLE.
NO, SEE, WE WANT THAT. THAT WAY MALE VIEWERS WON'T FEEL THREATENED.

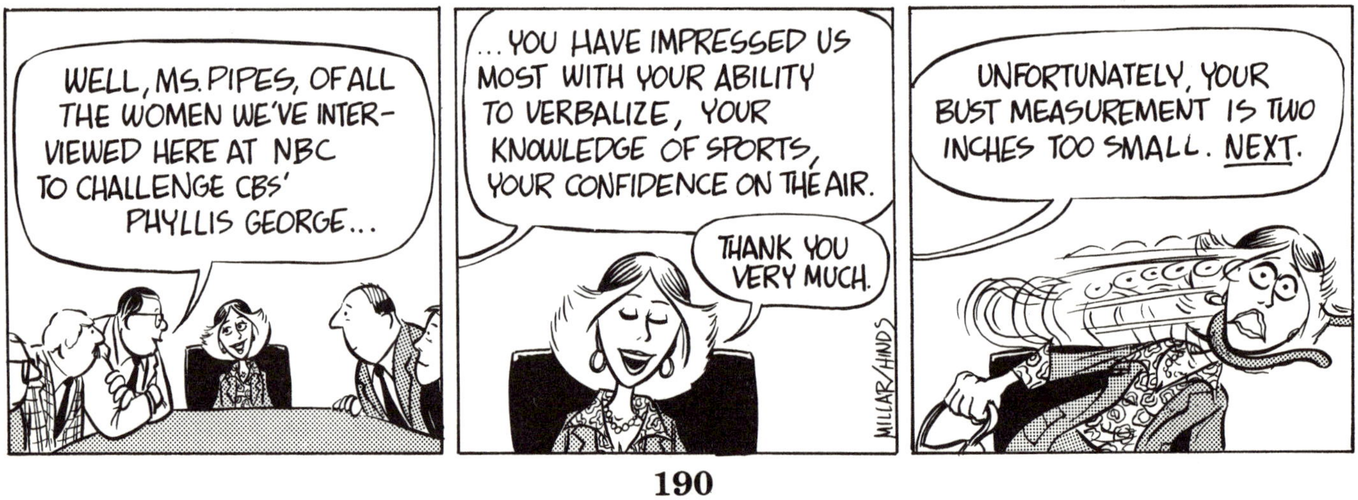
WELL, MS. PIPES, OF ALL THE WOMEN WE'VE INTER-VIEWED HERE AT NBC TO CHALLENGE CBS' PHYLLIS GEORGE...
...YOU HAVE IMPRESSED US MOST WITH YOUR ABILITY TO VERBALIZE, YOUR KNOWLEDGE OF SPORTS, YOUR CONFIDENCE ON THE AIR.
THANK YOU VERY MUCH.
MILLAR/HINDS
UNFORTUNATELY, YOUR BUST MEASUREMENT IS TWO INCHES TOO SMALL. NEXT.

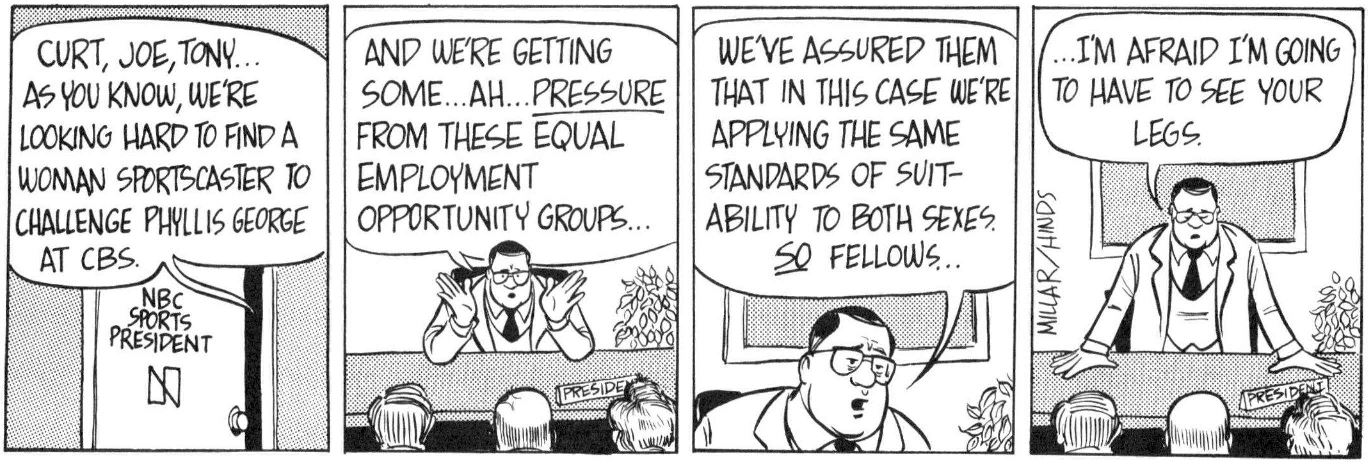
CURT, JOE, TONY... AS YOU KNOW, WE'RE LOOKING HARD TO FIND A WOMAN SPORTSCASTER TO CHALLENGE PHYLLIS GEORGE AT CBS.
NBC SPORTS PRESIDENT
AND WE'RE GETTING SOME...AH...PRESSURE FROM THESE EQUAL EMPLOYMENT OPPORTUNITY GROUPS...
WE'VE ASSURED THEM THAT IN THIS CASE WE'RE APPLYING THE SAME STANDARDS OF SUITABILITY TO BOTH SEXES. SO FELLOWS...
...I'M AFRAID I'M GOING TO HAVE TO SEE YOUR LEGS.
MILLAR/HINDS

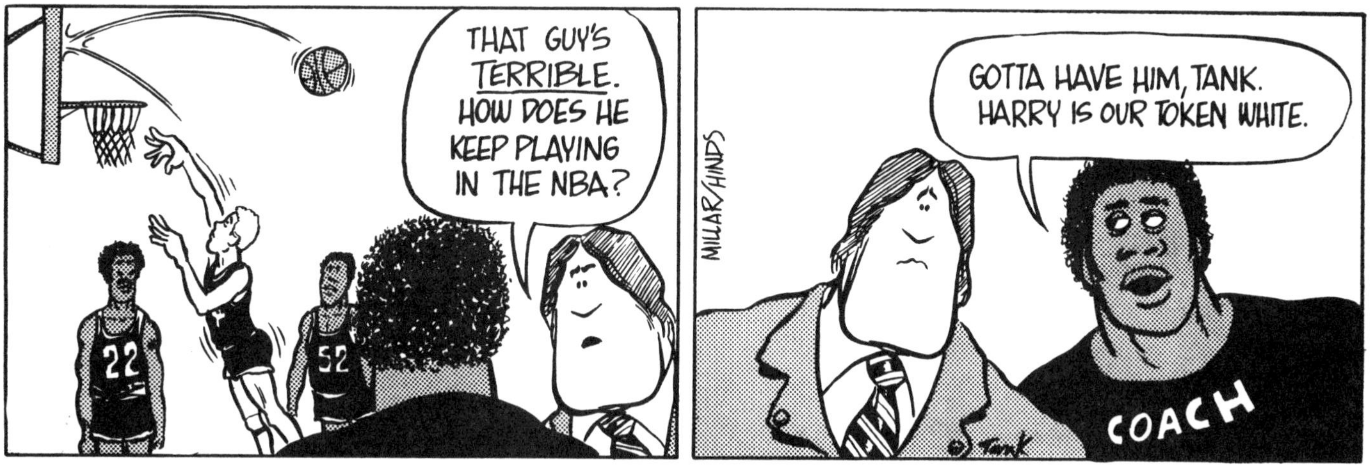
THAT GUY'S TERRIBLE. HOW DOES HE KEEP PLAYING IN THE NBA?
22
52
MILLAR/HINDS
GOTTA HAVE HIM, TANK. HARRY IS OUR TOKEN WHITE.
COACH

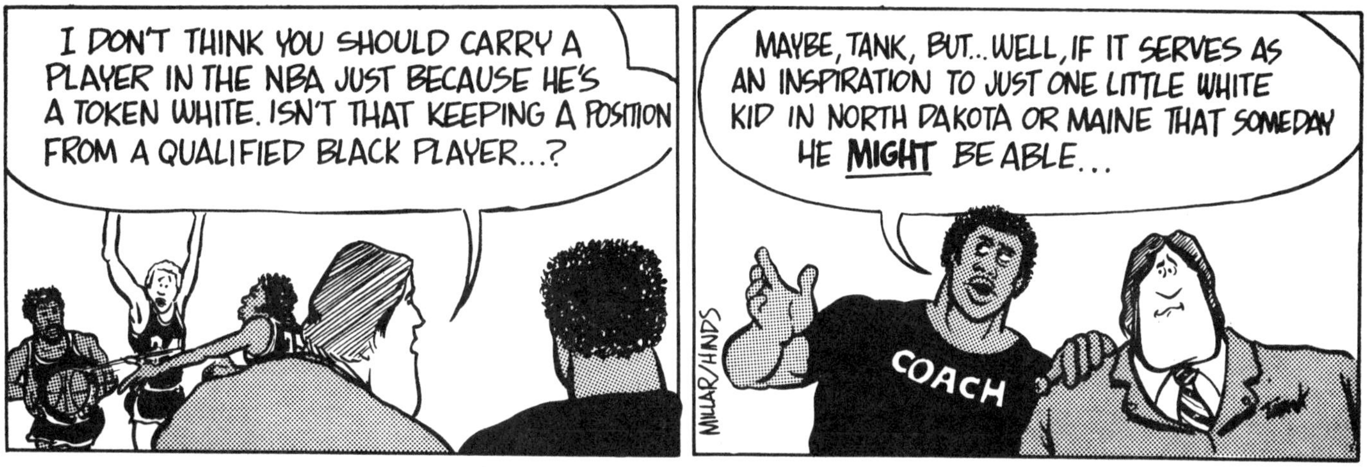
I DON'T THINK YOU SHOULD CARRY A PLAYER IN THE NBA JUST BECAUSE HE'S A TOKEN WHITE. ISN'T THAT KEEPING A POSITION FROM A QUALIFIED BLACK PLAYER...?
MILLAR/HINDS
MAYBE, TANK, BUT...WELL, IF IT SERVES AS AN INSPIRATION TO JUST ONE LITTLE WHITE KID IN NORTH DAKOTA OR MAINE THAT SOMEDAY HE MIGHT BE ABLE...
COACH

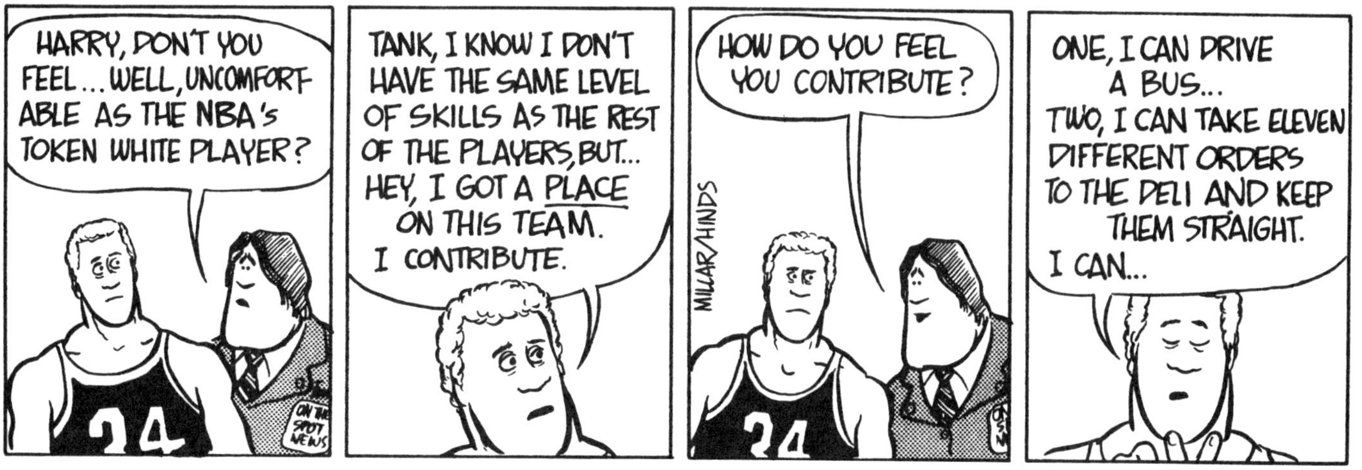
HARRY, DON'T YOU FEEL... WELL, UNCOMFORTABLE AS THE NBA's TOKEN WHITE PLAYER?
ON THE SPOT NEWS
TANK, I KNOW I DON'T HAVE THE SAME LEVEL OF SKILLS AS THE REST OF THE PLAYERS, BUT... HEY, I GOT A PLACE ON THIS TEAM. I CONTRIBUTE.
MILLAR/HINDS
HOW DO YOU FEEL YOU CONTRIBUTE?
ONE, I CAN DRIVE A BUS... TWO, I CAN TAKE ELEVEN DIFFERENT ORDERS TO THE DELI AND KEEP THEM STRAIGHT. I CAN...

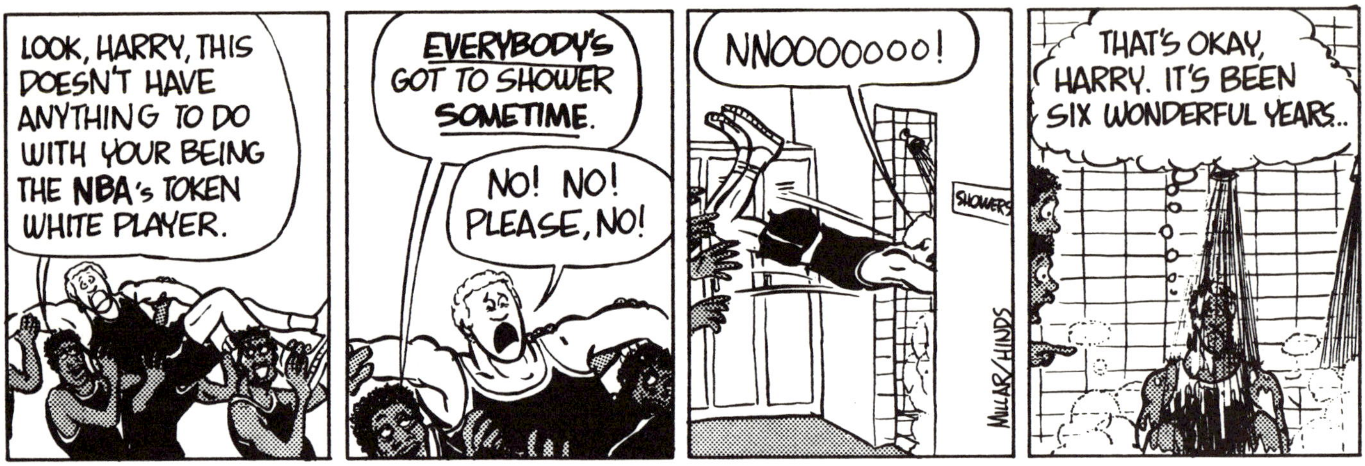
LOOK, HARRY, THIS DOESN'T HAVE ANYTHING TO DO WITH YOUR BEING THE NBA's TOKEN WHITE PLAYER.
EVERYBODY'S GOT TO SHOWER SOMETIME.
NO! NO! PLEASE, NO!
NNOOOOOOO!
SHOWERS
MILLAR/HINDS
THAT'S OKAY, HARRY. IT'S BEEN SIX WONDERFUL YEARS...

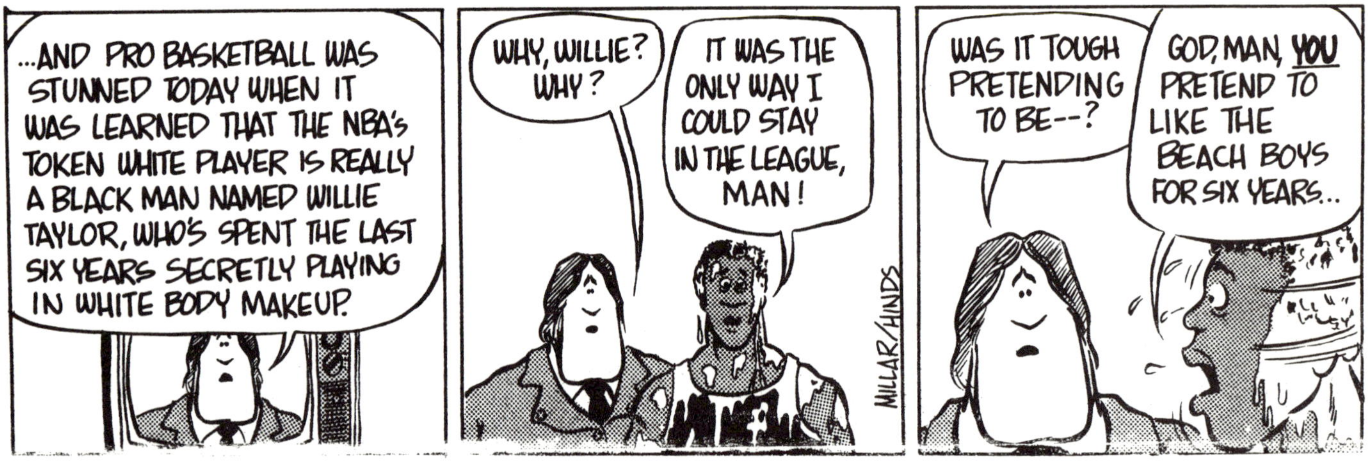
...AND PRO BASKETBALL WAS STUNNED TODAY WHEN IT WAS LEARNED THAT THE NBA's TOKEN WHITE PLAYER IS REALLY A BLACK MAN NAMED WILLIE TAYLOR, WHO'S SPENT THE LAST SIX YEARS SECRETLY PLAYING IN WHITE BODY MAKEUP.
WHY, WILLIE? WHY?
IT WAS THE ONLY WAY I COULD STAY IN THE LEAGUE, MAN!
MILLAR/HINDS
WAS IT TOUGH PRETENDING TO BE--?
GOD, MAN, YOU PRETEND TO LIKE THE BEACH BOYS FOR SIX YEARS...

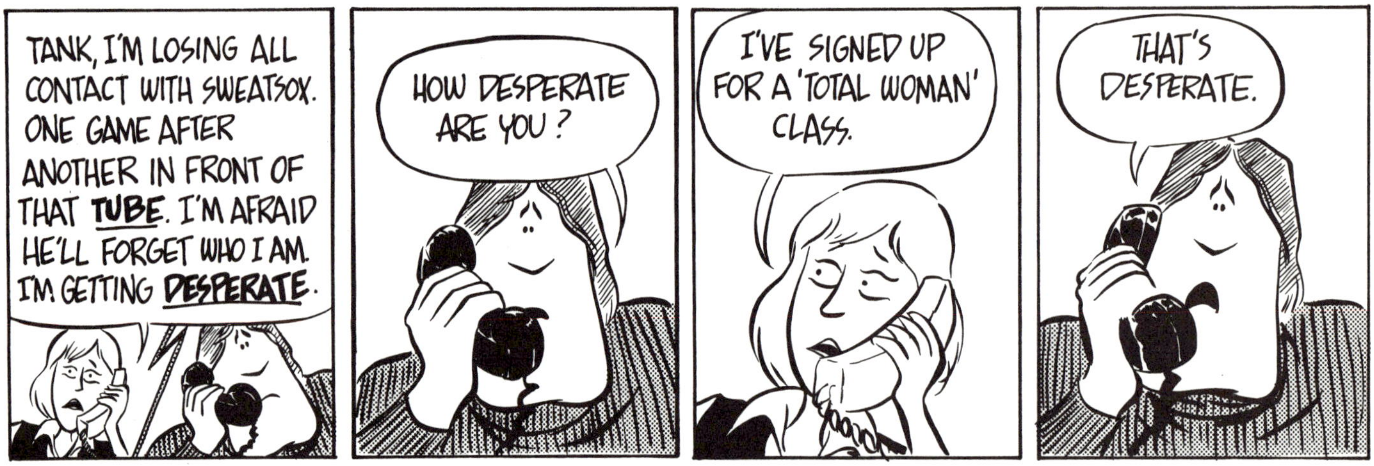
TANK, I'M LOSING ALL CONTACT WITH SWEATSOX. ONE GAME AFTER ANOTHER IN FRONT OF THAT TUBE. I'M AFRAID HE'LL FORGET WHO I AM. I'M GETTING DESPERATE.
HOW DESPERATE ARE YOU?
I'VE SIGNED UP FOR A 'TOTAL WOMAN' CLASS.
THAT'S DESPERATE.

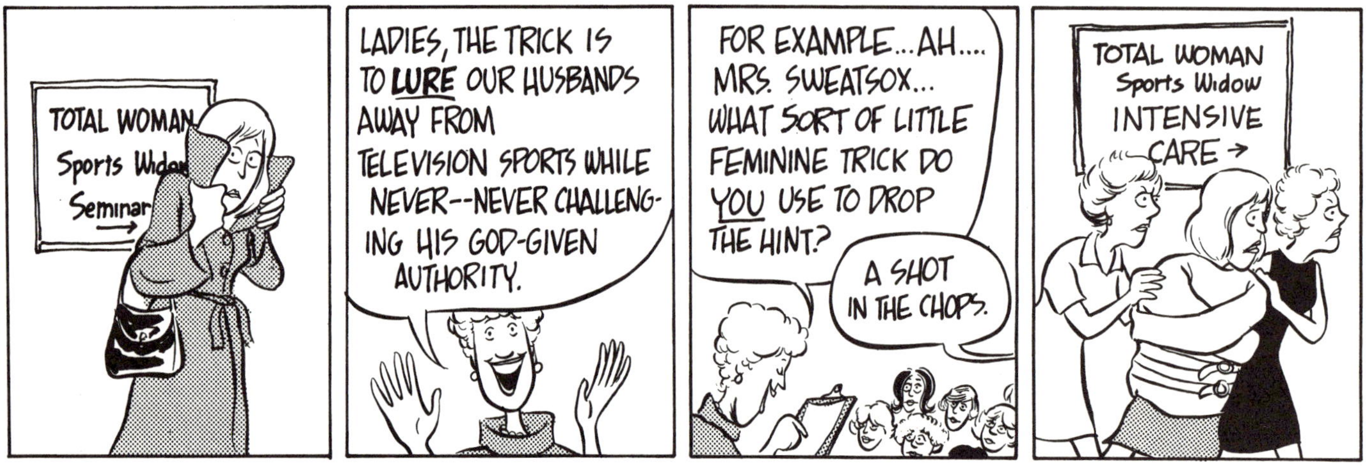
TOTAL WOMAN Sports Widow Seminar →
LADIES, THE TRICK IS TO LURE OUR HUSBANDS AWAY FROM TELEVISION SPORTS WHILE NEVER--NEVER CHALLENGING HIS GOD-GIVEN AUTHORITY.
FOR EXAMPLE...AH.... MRS. SWEATSOX... WHAT SORT OF LITTLE FEMININE TRICK DO YOU USE TO DROP THE HINT?
A SHOT IN THE CHOPS.
TOTAL WOMAN Sports Widow INTENSIVE CARE →

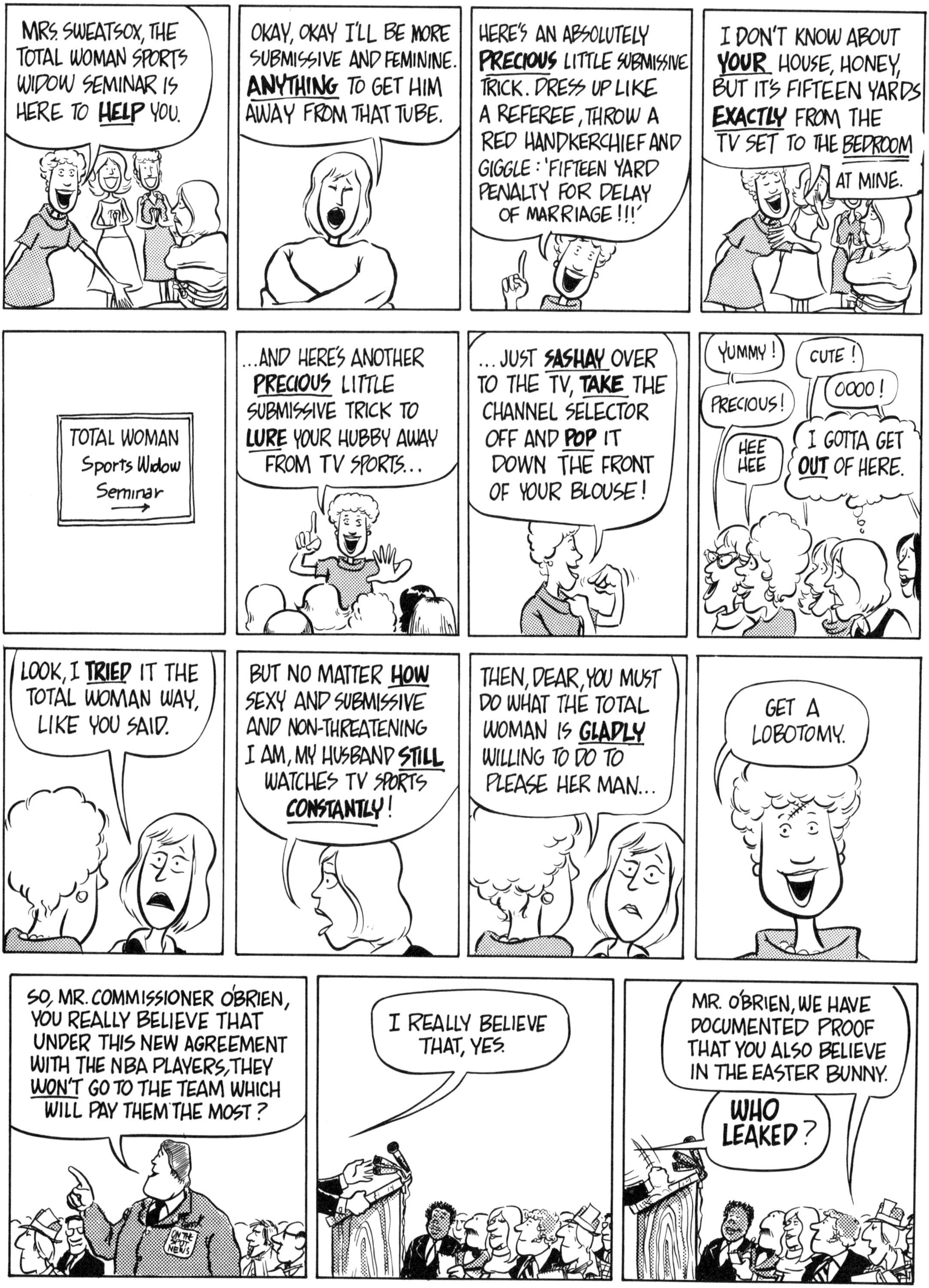
MRS. SWEATSOX, THE TOTAL WOMAN SPORTS WIDOW SEMINAR IS HERE TO HELP YOU.
OKAY, OKAY I'LL BE MORE SUBMISSIVE AND FEMININE. ANYTHING TO GET HIM AWAY FROM THAT TUBE.
HERE'S AN ABSOLUTELY PRECIOUS LITTLE SUBMISSIVE TRICK. DRESS UP LIKE A REFEREE, THROW A RED HANDKERCHIEF AND GIGGLE: 'FIFTEEN YARD PENALTY FOR DELAY OF MARRIAGE!!!'
I DON'T KNOW ABOUT YOUR HOUSE, HONEY, BUT IT'S FIFTEEN YARDS EXACTLY FROM THE TV SET TO THE BEDROOM
AT MINE.
TOTAL WOMAN Sports Widow Seminar →
...AND HERE'S ANOTHER PRECIOUS LITTLE SUBMISSIVE TRICK TO LURE YOUR HUBBY AWAY FROM TV SPORTS...
... JUST SASHAY OVER TO THE TV, TAKE THE CHANNEL SELECTOR OFF AND POP IT DOWN THE FRONT OF YOUR BLOUSE!
YUMMY!
CUTE!
OOOO!
PRECIOUS!
HEE HEE
I GOTTA GET OUT OF HERE.
LOOK, I TRIED IT THE TOTAL WOMAN WAY, LIKE YOU SAID.
BUT NO MATTER HOW SEXY AND SUBMISSIVE AND NON-THREATENING I AM, MY HUSBAND STILL WATCHES TV SPORTS CONSTANTLY!
THEN, DEAR, YOU MUST DO WHAT THE TOTAL WOMAN IS GLADLY WILLING TO DO TO PLEASE HER MAN...
GET A LOBOTOMY.
SO, MR. COMMISSIONER O'BRIEN, YOU REALLY BELIEVE THAT UNDER THIS NEW AGREEMENT WITH THE NBA PLAYERS, THEY WON'T GO TO THE TEAM WHICH WILL PAY THEM THE MOST?
ON THE SPOT NEWS
I REALLY BELIEVE THAT, YES.
MR. O'BRIEN, WE HAVE DOCUMENTED PROOF THAT YOU ALSO BELIEVE IN THE EASTER BUNNY.
WHO LEAKED?

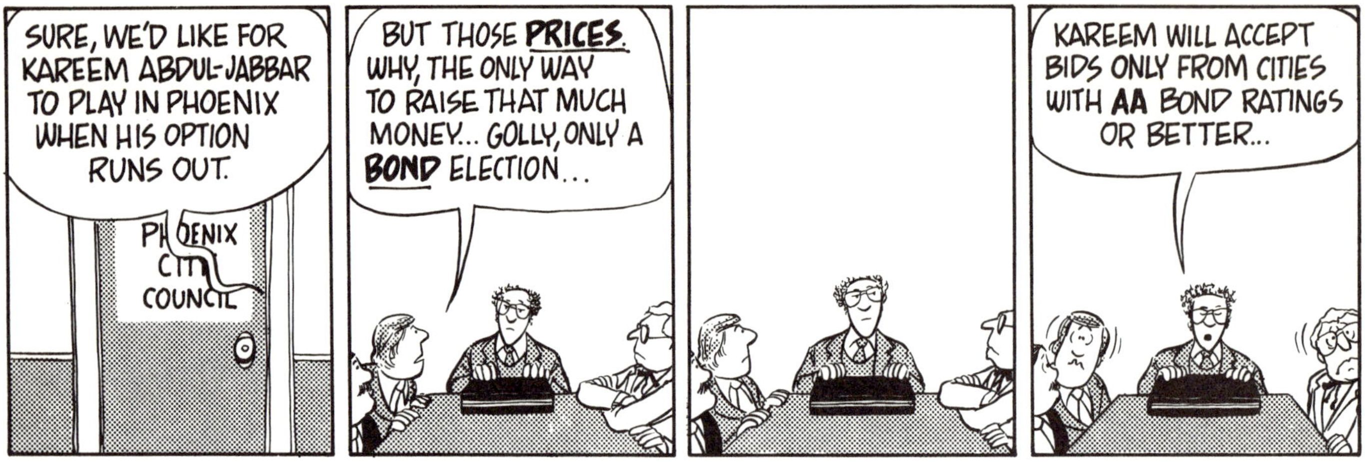

SURE, WE'D LIKE FOR KAREEM ABDUL-JABBAR TO PLAY IN PHOENIX WHEN HIS OPTION RUNS OUT.
BUT THOSE PRICES. WHY, THE ONLY WAY TO RAISE THAT MUCH MONEY... GOLLY, ONLY A BOND ELECTION...
KAREEM WILL ACCEPT BIDS ONLY FROM CITIES WITH AA BOND RATINGS OR BETTER...

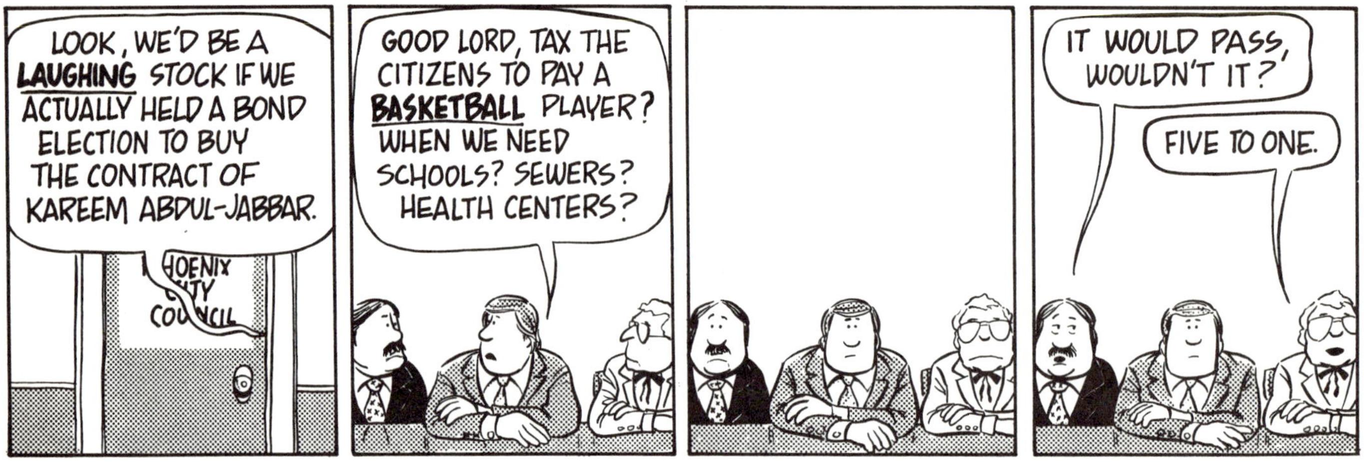

LOOK, WE'D BE A LAUGHING STOCK IF WE ACTUALLY HELD A BOND ELECTION TO BUY THE CONTRACT OF KAREEM ABDUL-JABBAR.
GOOD LORD, TAX THE CITIZENS TO PAY A BASKETBALL PLAYER? WHEN WE NEED SCHOOLS? SEWERS? HEALTH CENTERS?
IT WOULD PASS, WOULDN'T IT?
FIVE TO ONE.

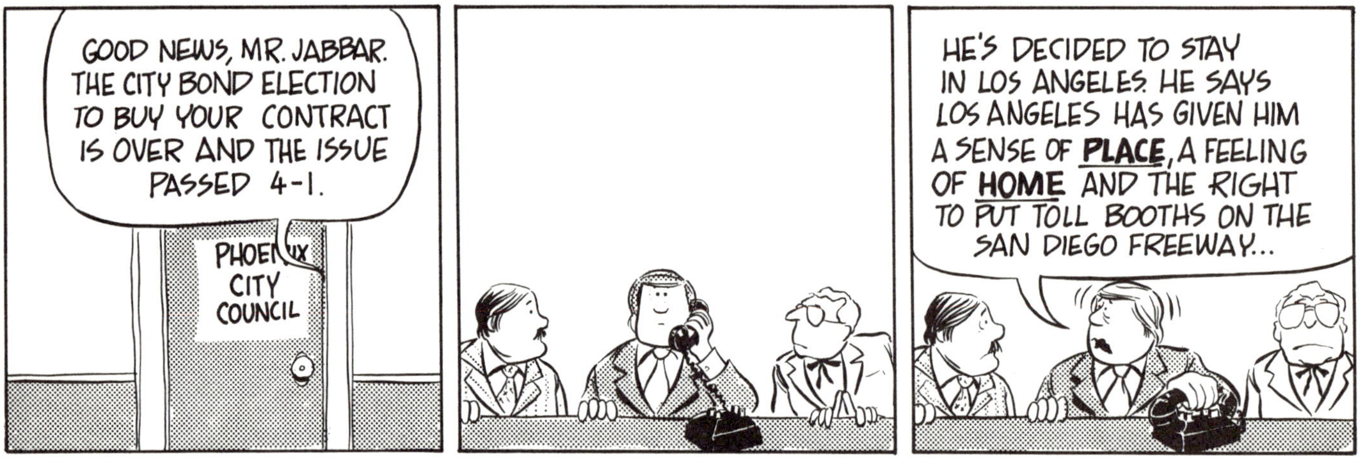

GOOD NEWS, MR. JABBAR. THE CITY BOND ELECTION TO BUY YOUR CONTRACT IS OVER AND THE ISSUE PASSED 4-1.
CITY COUNCIL
HE'S DECIDED TO STAY IN LOS ANGELES. HE SAYS LOS ANGELES HAS GIVEN HIM A SENSE OF PLACE, A FEELING OF HOME AND THE RIGHT TO PUT TOLL BOOTHS ON THE SAN DIEGO FREEWAY...

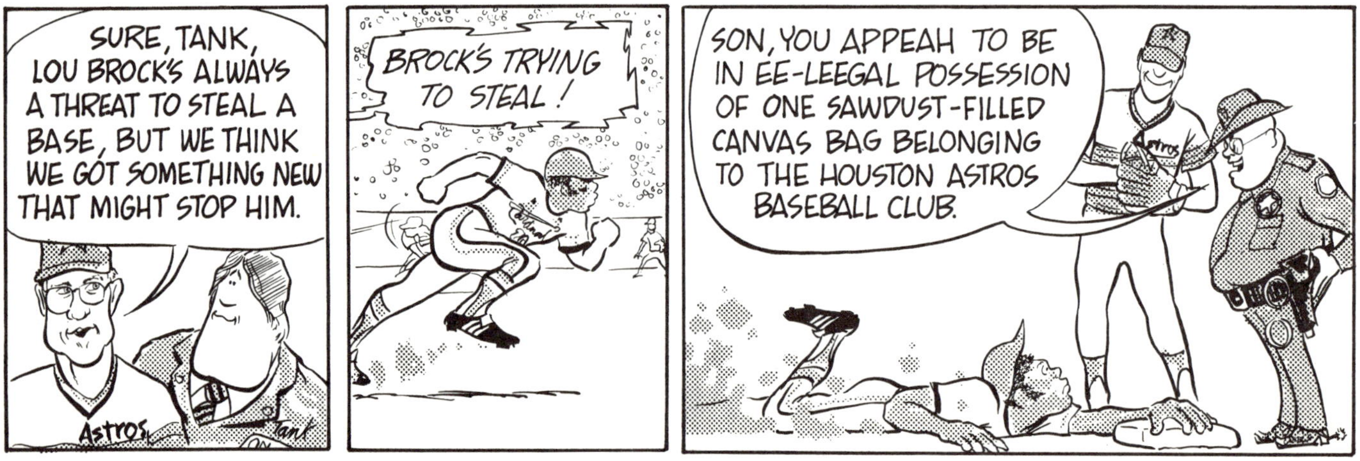

SURE, TANK, LOU BROCK'S ALWAYS A THREAT TO STEAL A BASE, BUT WE THINK WE GOT SOMETHING NEW THAT MIGHT STOP HIM.
Astros
BROCK'S TRYING TO STEAL!
SON, YOU APPEAH TO BE IN EE-LEEGAL POSSESSION OF ONE SAWDUST-FILLED CANVAS BAG BELONGING TO THE HOUSTON ASTROS BASEBALL CLUB.

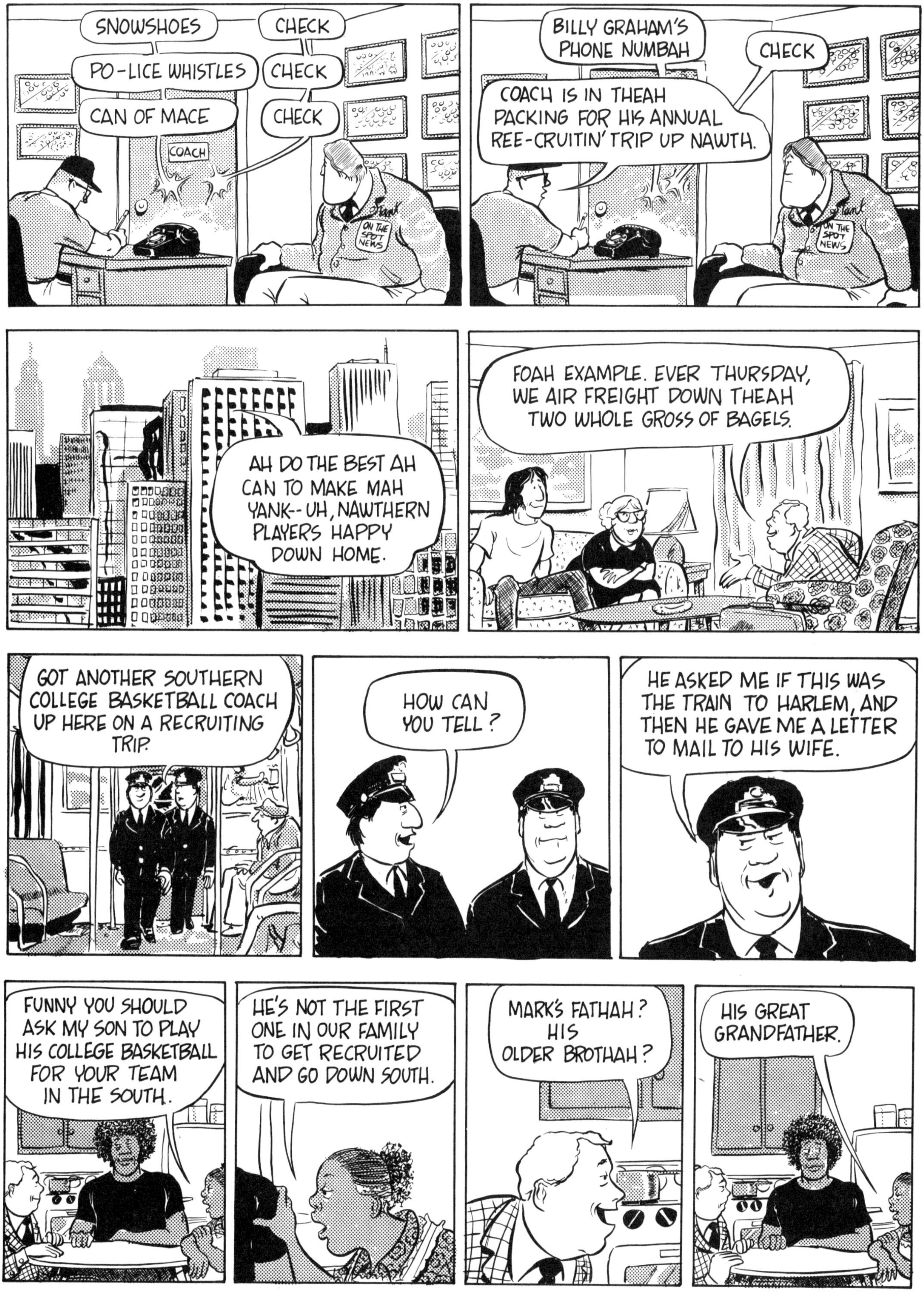
SNOWSHOES
CHECK
PO-LICE WHISTLES
CHECK
CAN OF MACE
CHECK
COACH
ON THE SPOT NEWS
BILLY GRAHAM'S PHONE NUMBAH
CHECK
COACH IS IN THEAH PACKING FOR HIS ANNUAL REE-CRUITIN' TRIP UP NAWTH.
AH DO THE BEST AH CAN TO MAKE MAH YANK-- UH, NAWTHERN PLAYERS HAPPY DOWN HOME.
FOAH EXAMPLE. EVER THURSDAY, WE AIR FREIGHT DOWN THEAH TWO WHOLE GROSS OF BAGELS.
GOT ANOTHER SOUTHERN COLLEGE BASKETBALL COACH UP HERE ON A RECRUITING TRIP.
HOW CAN YOU TELL?
HE ASKED ME IF THIS WAS THE TRAIN TO HARLEM, AND THEN HE GAVE ME A LETTER TO MAIL TO HIS WIFE.
FUNNY YOU SHOULD ASK MY SON TO PLAY HIS COLLEGE BASKETBALL FOR YOUR TEAM IN THE SOUTH.
HE'S NOT THE FIRST ONE IN OUR FAMILY TO GET RECRUITED AND GO DOWN SOUTH.
MARK'S FATHAH? HIS OLDER BROTHAH?
HIS GREAT GRANDFATHER.

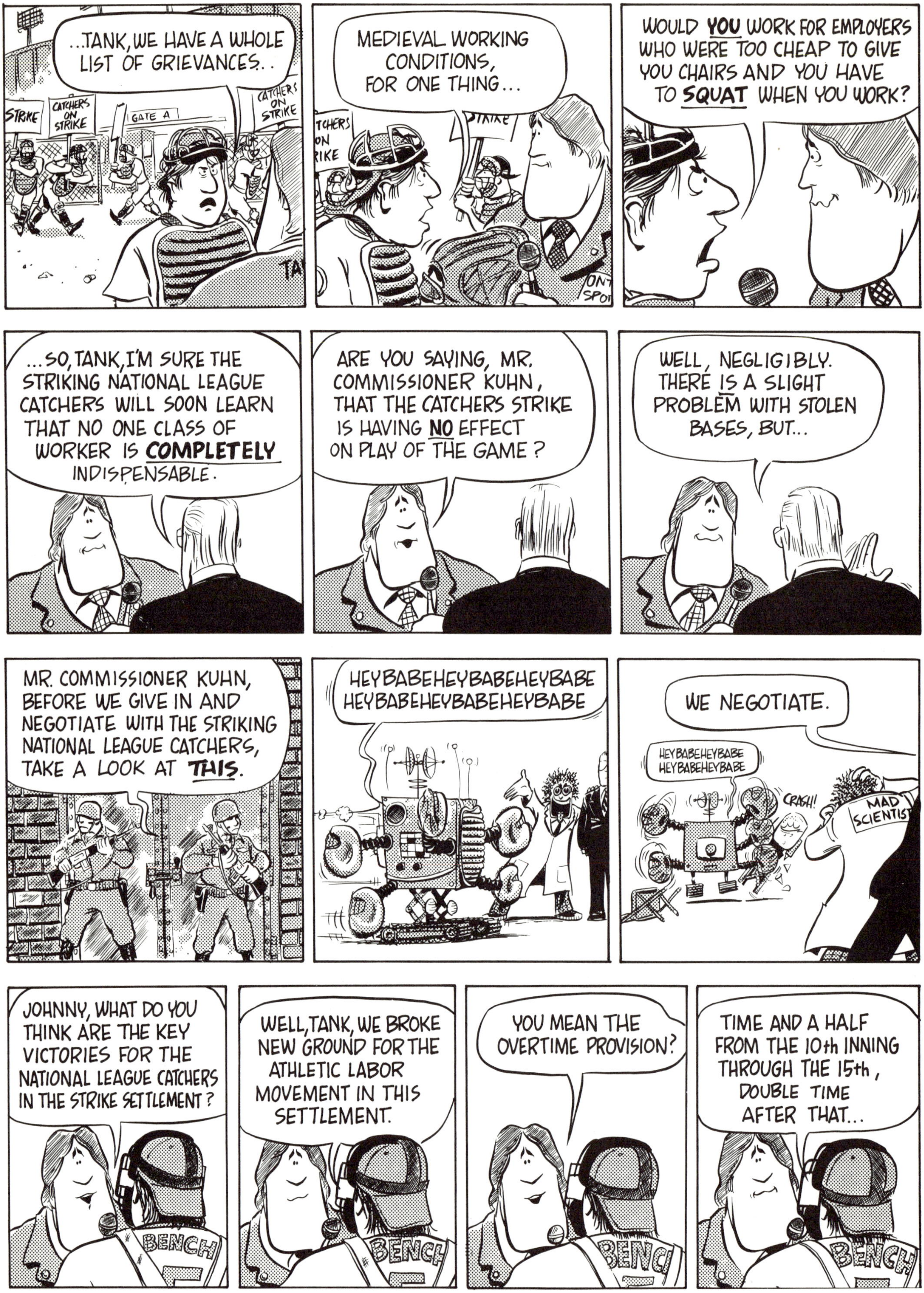
...TANK, WE HAVE A WHOLE LIST OF GRIEVANCES...
STRIKE
CATCHERS ON STRIKE
GATE A
CATCHERS ON STRIKE
MEDIEVAL WORKING CONDITIONS, FOR ONE THING...
WOULD YOU WORK FOR EMPLOYERS WHO WERE TOO CHEAP TO GIVE YOU CHAIRS AND YOU HAVE TO SQUAT WHEN YOU WORK?
...SO, TANK, I'M SURE THE STRIKING NATIONAL LEAGUE CATCHERS WILL SOON LEARN THAT NO ONE CLASS OF WORKER IS COMPLETELY INDISPENSABLE.
ARE YOU SAYING, MR. COMMISSIONER KUHN, THAT THE CATCHERS STRIKE IS HAVING NO EFFECT ON PLAY OF THE GAME?
WELL, NEGLIGIBLY. THERE IS A SLIGHT PROBLEM WITH STOLEN BASES, BUT...
MR. COMMISSIONER KUHN, BEFORE WE GIVE IN AND NEGOTIATE WITH THE STRIKING NATIONAL LEAGUE CATCHERS, TAKE A LOOK AT THIS.
HEYBABEHEYBABEHEYBABE HEYBABEHEYBABEHEYBABE
WE NEGOTIATE.
HEYBABEHEYBABE HEYBABEHEYBABE
CRASH!
MAD SCIENTIST
JOHNNY, WHAT DO YOU THINK ARE THE KEY VICTORIES FOR THE NATIONAL LEAGUE CATCHERS IN THE STRIKE SETTLEMENT?
BENCH
WELL, TANK, WE BROKE NEW GROUND FOR THE ATHLETIC LABOR MOVEMENT IN THIS SETTLEMENT.
YOU MEAN THE OVERTIME PROVISION?
TIME AND A HALF FROM THE 10th INNING THROUGH THE 15th, DOUBLE TIME AFTER THAT...

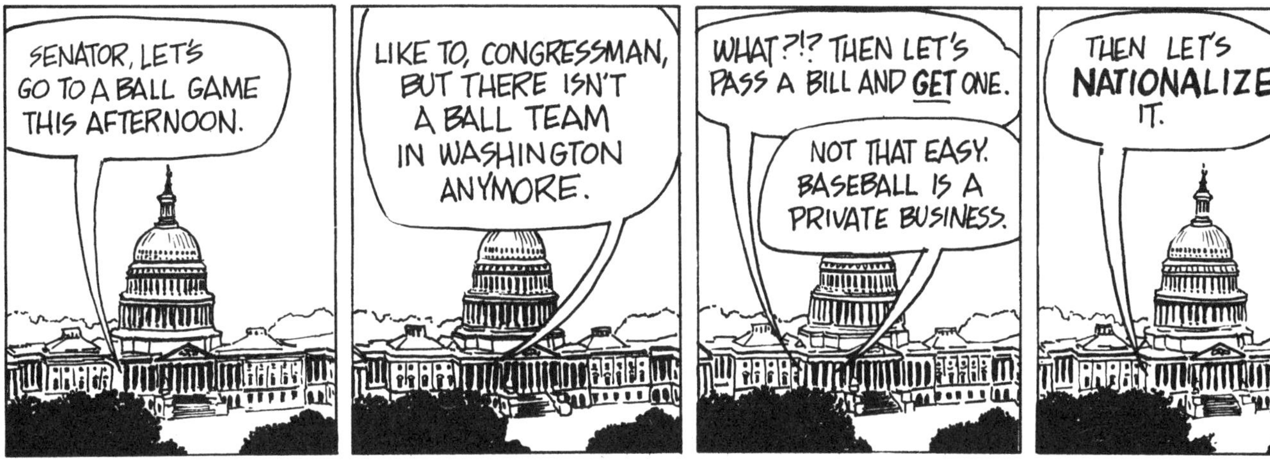
SENATOR, LET'S GO TO A BALL GAME THIS AFTERNOON.
LIKE TO, CONGRESSMAN, BUT THERE ISN'T A BALL TEAM IN WASHINGTON ANYMORE.
WHAT?!? THEN LET'S PASS A BILL AND GET ONE.
NOT THAT EASY. BASEBALL IS A PRIVATE BUSINESS.
THEN LET'S NATIONALIZE IT.
MILLAR/HINDS

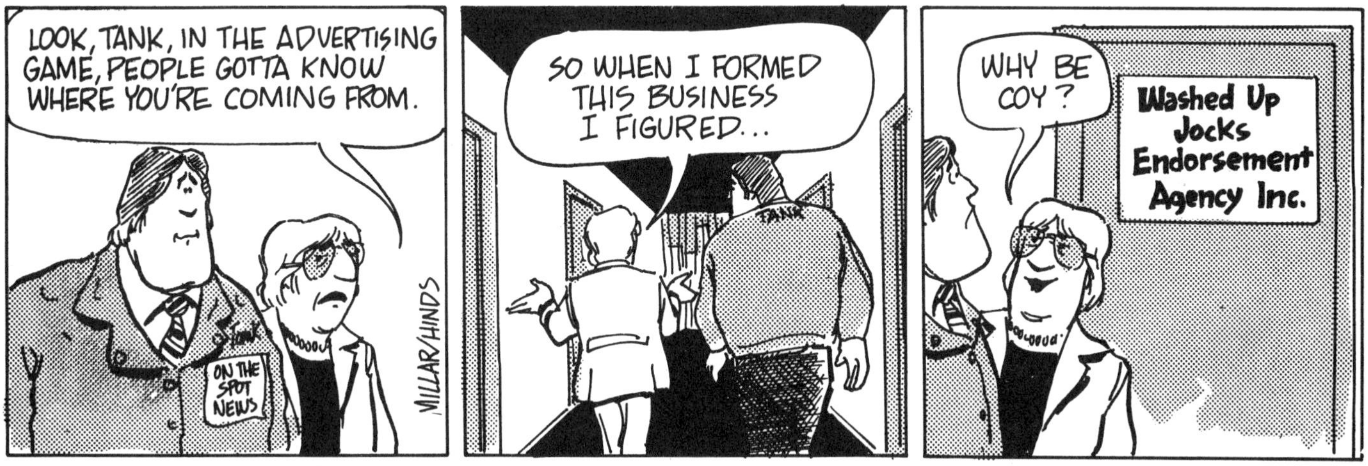
LOOK, TANK, IN THE ADVERTISING GAME, PEOPLE GOTTA KNOW WHERE YOU'RE COMING FROM.
ON THE SPOT NEWS
MILLAR/HINDS
SO WHEN I FORMED THIS BUSINESS I FIGURED...
TANK
WHY BE COY?
Washed Up Jocks Endorsement Agency Inc.

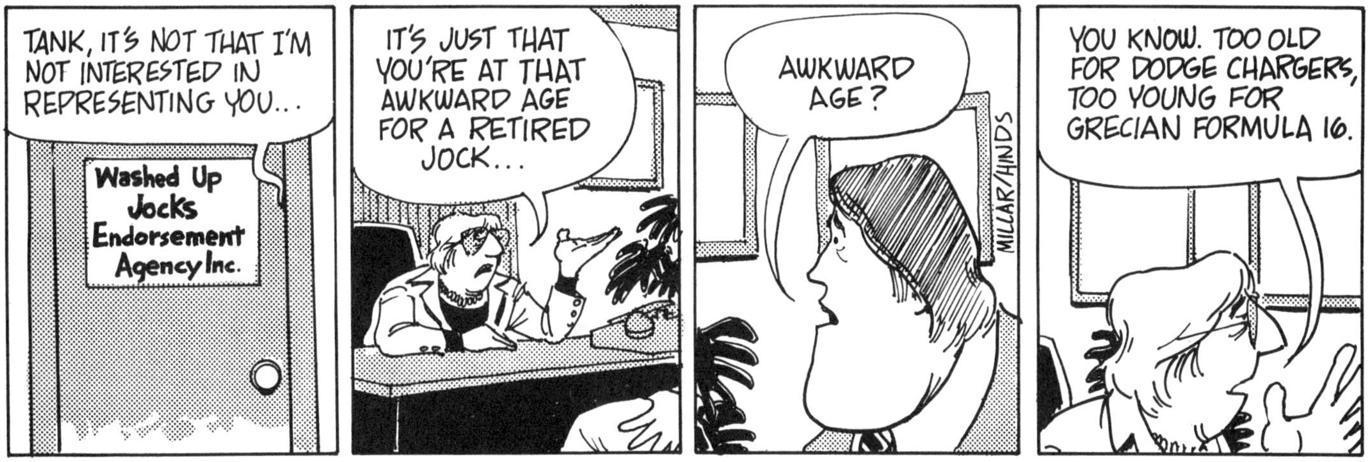
TANK, IT'S NOT THAT I'M NOT INTERESTED IN REPRESENTING YOU...
Washed Up Jocks Endorsement Agency Inc.
IT'S JUST THAT YOU'RE AT THAT AWKWARD AGE FOR A RETIRED JOCK...
AWKWARD AGE?
MILLAR/HINDS
YOU KNOW. TOO OLD FOR DODGE CHARGERS, TOO YOUNG FOR GRECIAN FORMULA 16.

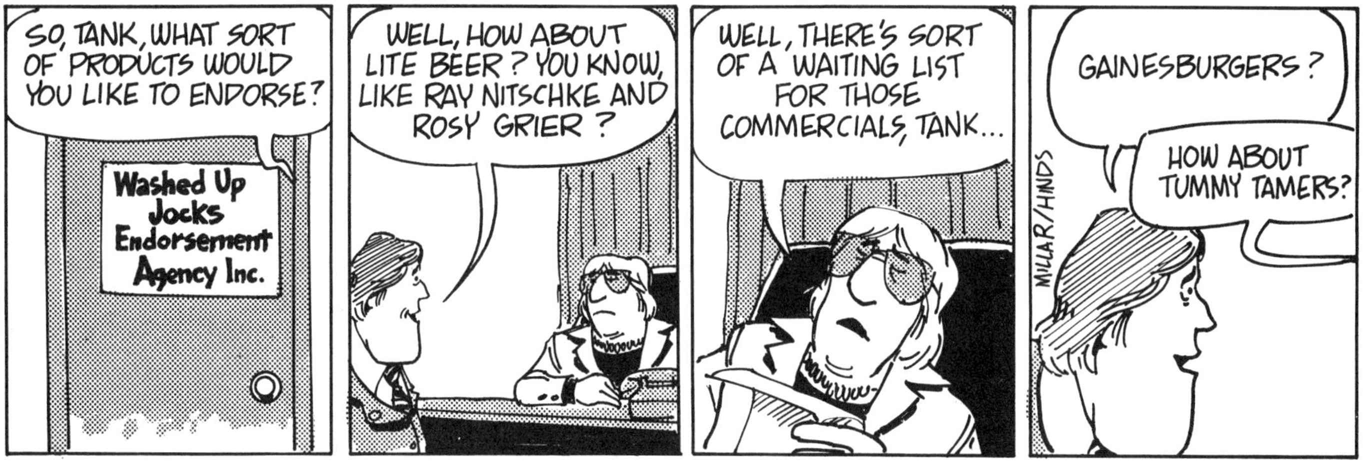
SO, TANK, WHAT SORT OF PRODUCTS WOULD YOU LIKE TO ENDORSE?
Washed Up Jocks Endorsement Agency Inc.
WELL, HOW ABOUT LITE BEER? YOU KNOW, LIKE RAY NITSCHKE AND ROSY GRIER?
WELL, THERE'S SORT OF A WAITING LIST FOR THOSE COMMERCIALS, TANK...
MILLAR/HINDS
GAINESBURGERS?
HOW ABOUT TUMMY TAMERS?

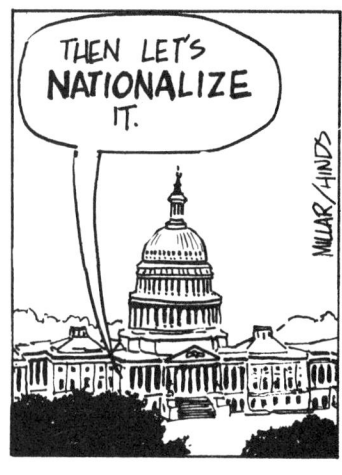

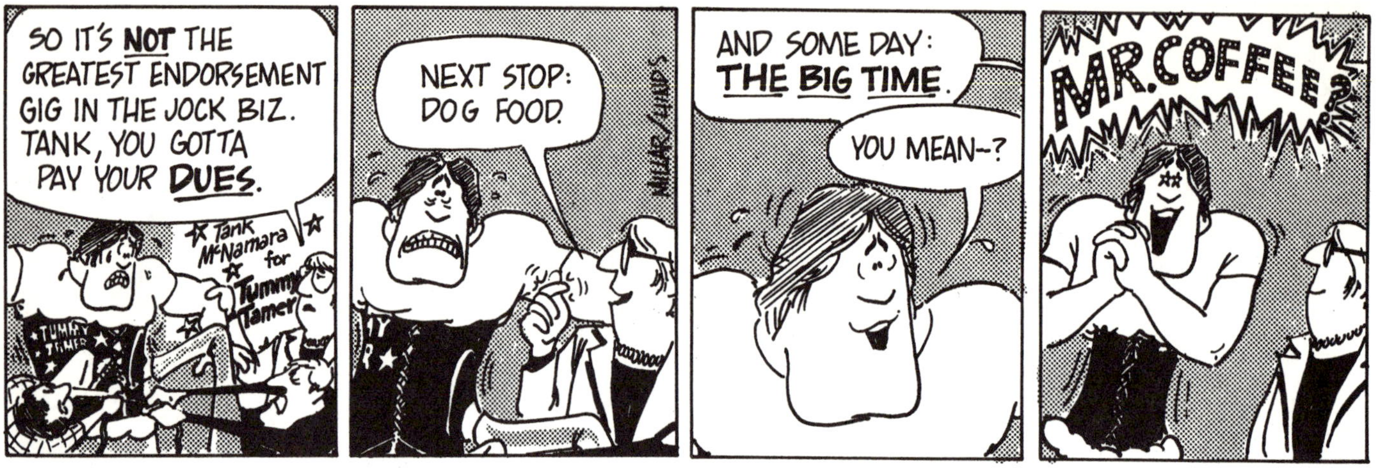
SO IT'S NOT THE GREATEST ENDORSEMENT GIG IN THE JOCK BIZ. TANK, YOU GOTTA PAY YOUR DUES.
Tank McNamara for Tummy Tamer
NEXT STOP: DOG FOOD.
MILLAR/HINDS
AND SOME DAY: THE BIG TIME.
YOU MEAN--?
MR. COFFEE?

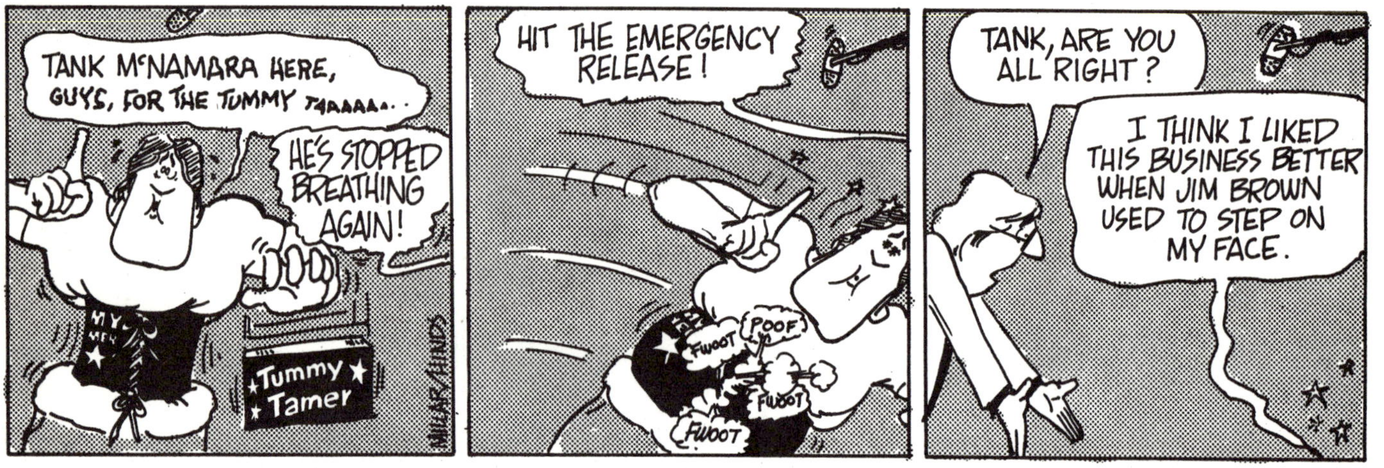
TANK McNAMARA HERE, GUYS, FOR THE TUMMY TAAAAA...
HE'S STOPPED BREATHING AGAIN!
Tummy Tamer
MILLAR/HINDS
HIT THE EMERGENCY RELEASE!
FWOOT
POOF
FWOOT
FWOOT
TANK, ARE YOU ALL RIGHT?
I THINK I LIKED THIS BUSINESS BETTER WHEN JIM BROWN USED TO STEP ON MY FACE.

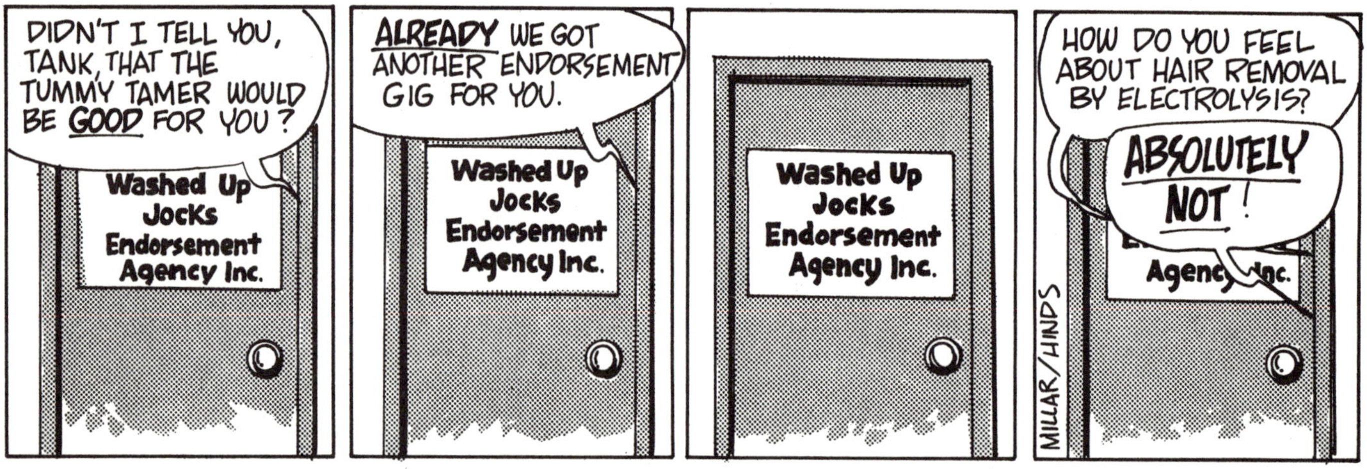
DIDN'T I TELL YOU, TANK, THAT THE TUMMY TAMER WOULD BE GOOD FOR YOU?
Washed Up Jocks Endorsement Agency Inc.
ALREADY WE GOT ANOTHER ENDORSEMENT GIG FOR YOU.
Washed Up Jocks Endorsement Agency Inc.
Washed Up Jocks Endorsement Agency Inc.
HOW DO YOU FEEL ABOUT HAIR REMOVAL BY ELECTROLYSIS?
ABSOLUTELY NOT!
MILLAR/HINDS

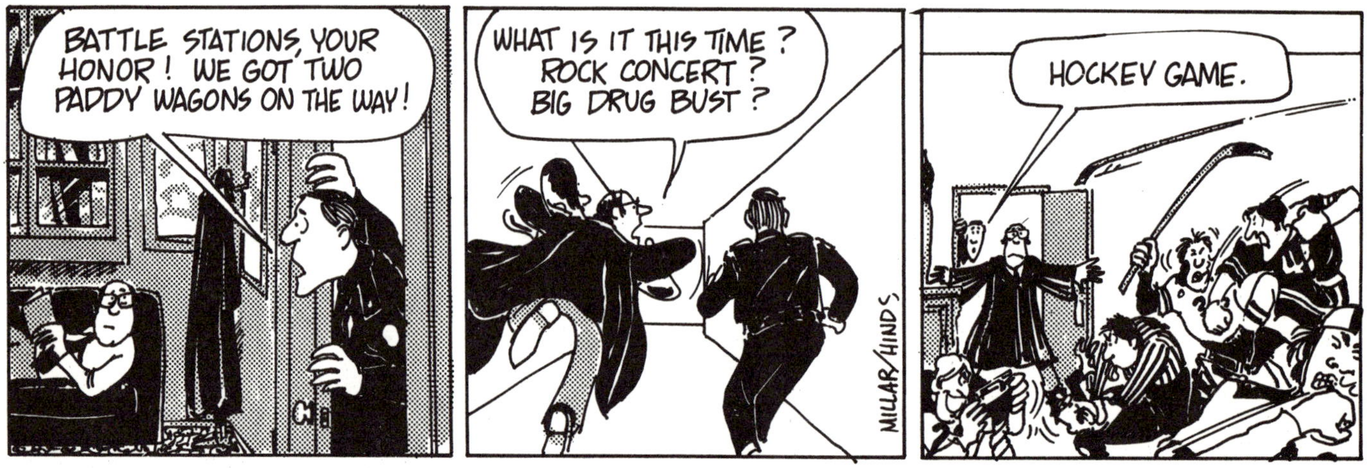
BATTLE STATIONS, YOUR HONOR! WE GOT TWO PADDY WAGONS ON THE WAY!
WHAT IS IT THIS TIME? ROCK CONCERT? BIG DRUG BUST?
MILLAR/HINDS
HOCKEY GAME.

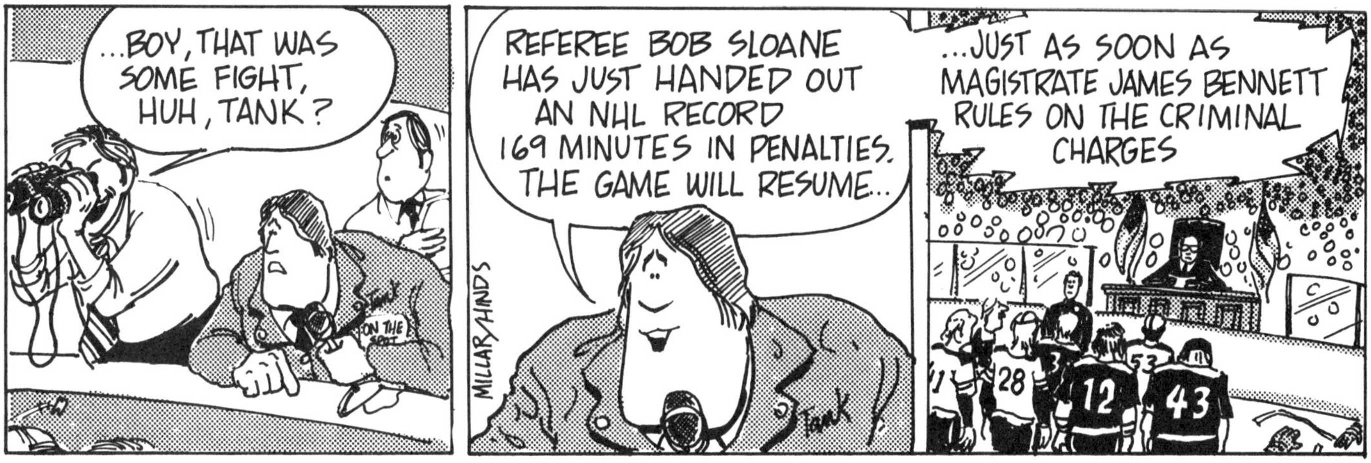
...BOY, THAT WAS SOME FIGHT, HUH, TANK?
MILLAR/HINDS
REFEREE BOB SLOANE HAS JUST HANDED OUT AN NHL RECORD 169 MINUTES IN PENALTIES. THE GAME WILL RESUME...
...JUST AS SOON AS MAGISTRATE JAMES BENNETT RULES ON THE CRIMINAL CHARGES

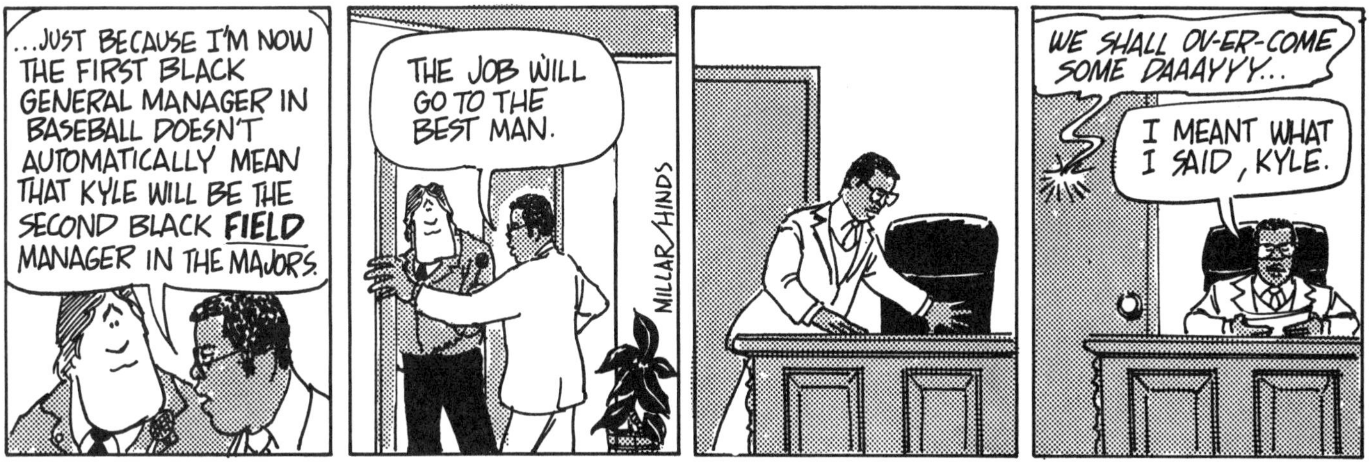
...JUST BECAUSE I'M NOW THE FIRST BLACK GENERAL MANAGER IN BASEBALL DOESN'T AUTOMATICALLY MEAN THAT KYLE WILL BE THE SECOND BLACK FIELD MANAGER IN THE MAJORS.
THE JOB WILL GO TO THE BEST MAN.
MILLAR/HINDS
WE SHALL OV-ER-COME SOME DAAAYYY...
I MEANT WHAT I SAID, KYLE.

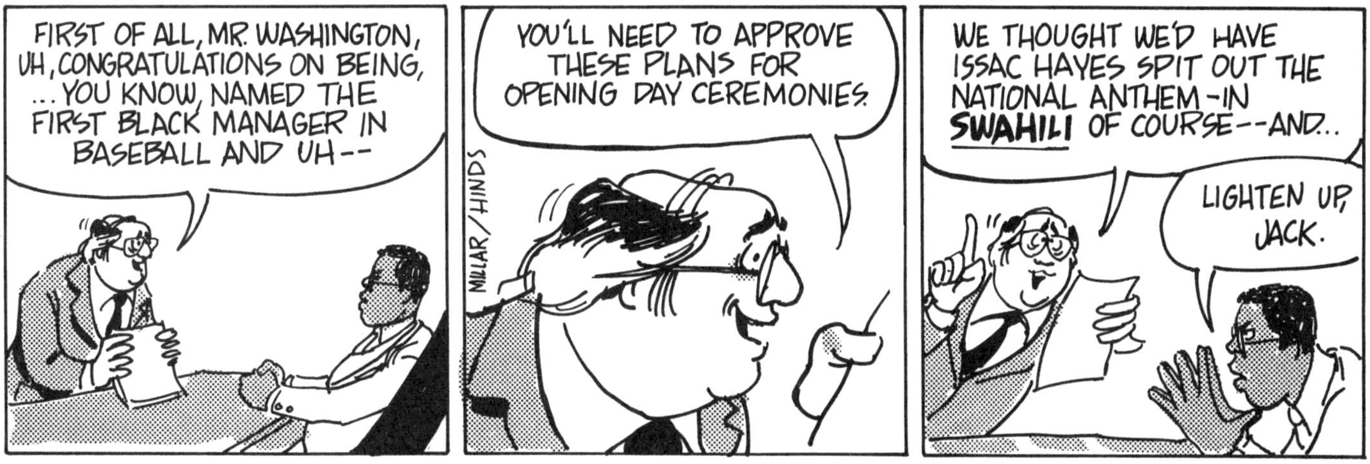
FIRST OF ALL, MR. WASHINGTON, UH, CONGRATULATIONS ON BEING, ...YOU KNOW, NAMED THE FIRST BLACK MANAGER IN BASEBALL AND UH--
MILLAR/HINDS
YOU'LL NEED TO APPROVE THESE PLANS FOR OPENING DAY CEREMONIES.
WE THOUGHT WE'D HAVE ISSAC HAYES SPIT OUT THE NATIONAL ANTHEM-IN SWAHILI OF COURSE--AND...
LIGHTEN UP, JACK.

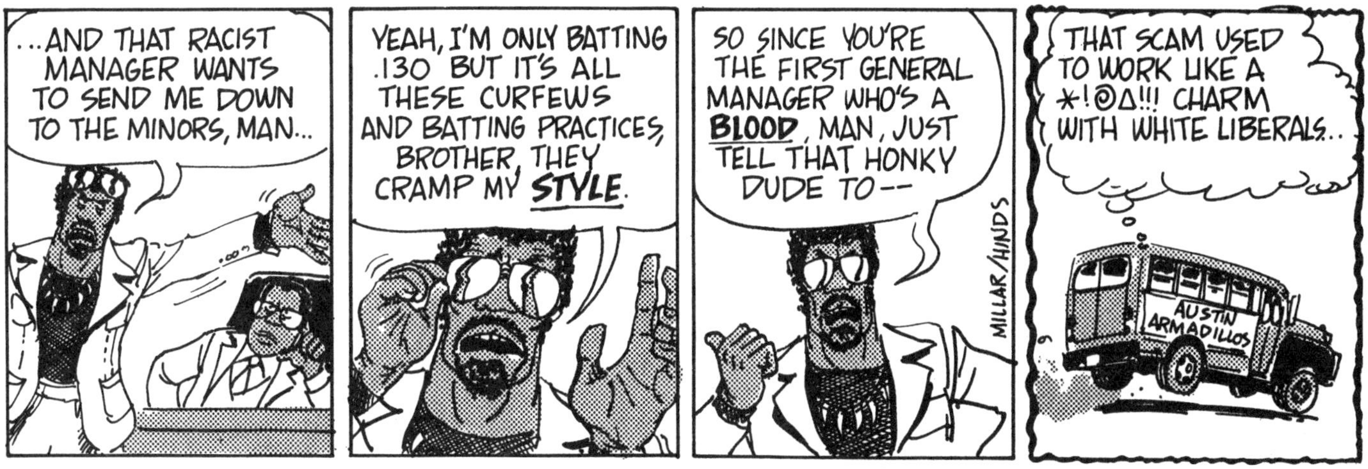
...AND THAT RACIST MANAGER WANTS TO SEND ME DOWN TO THE MINORS, MAN...
YEAH, I'M ONLY BATTING .130 BUT IT'S ALL THESE CURFEWS AND BATTING PRACTICES, BROTHER, THEY CRAMP MY STYLE.
SO SINCE YOU'RE THE FIRST GENERAL MANAGER WHO'S A BLOOD, MAN, JUST TELL THAT HONKY DUDE TO--
MILLAR/HINDS
THAT SCAM USED TO WORK LIKE A *!@Δ!!! CHARM WITH WHITE LIBERALS...
AUSTIN ARMADILLOS

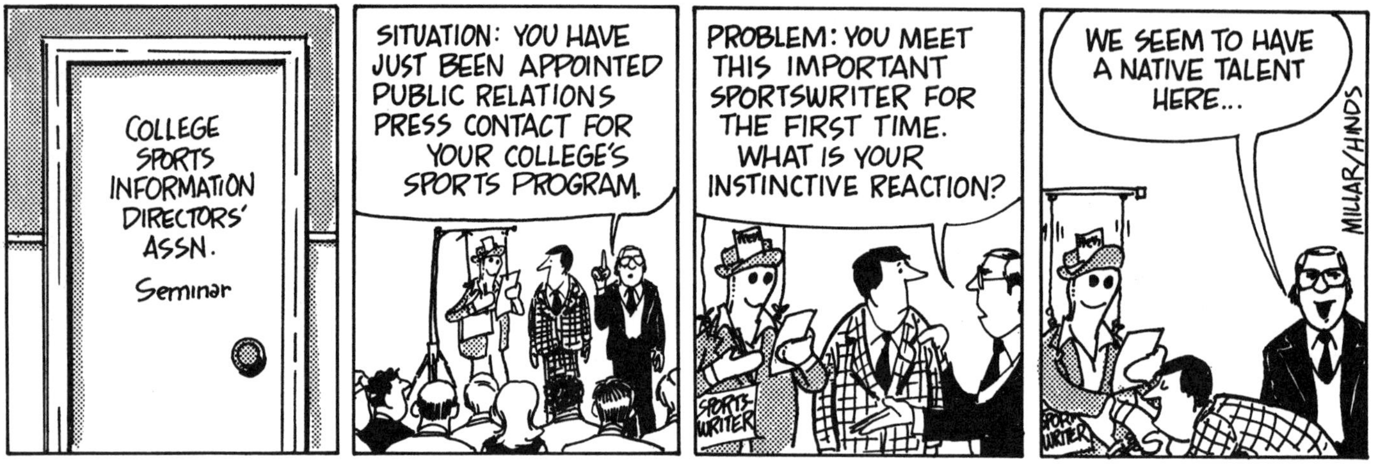
COLLEGE SPORTS INFORMATION DIRECTORS' ASSN. Seminar
SITUATION: YOU HAVE JUST BEEN APPOINTED PUBLIC RELATIONS PRESS CONTACT FOR YOUR COLLEGE'S SPORTS PROGRAM.
PROBLEM: YOU MEET THIS IMPORTANT SPORTSWRITER FOR THE FIRST TIME. WHAT IS YOUR INSTINCTIVE REACTION?
SPORTS WRITER
WE SEEM TO HAVE A NATIVE TALENT HERE...
MILLAR/HINDS

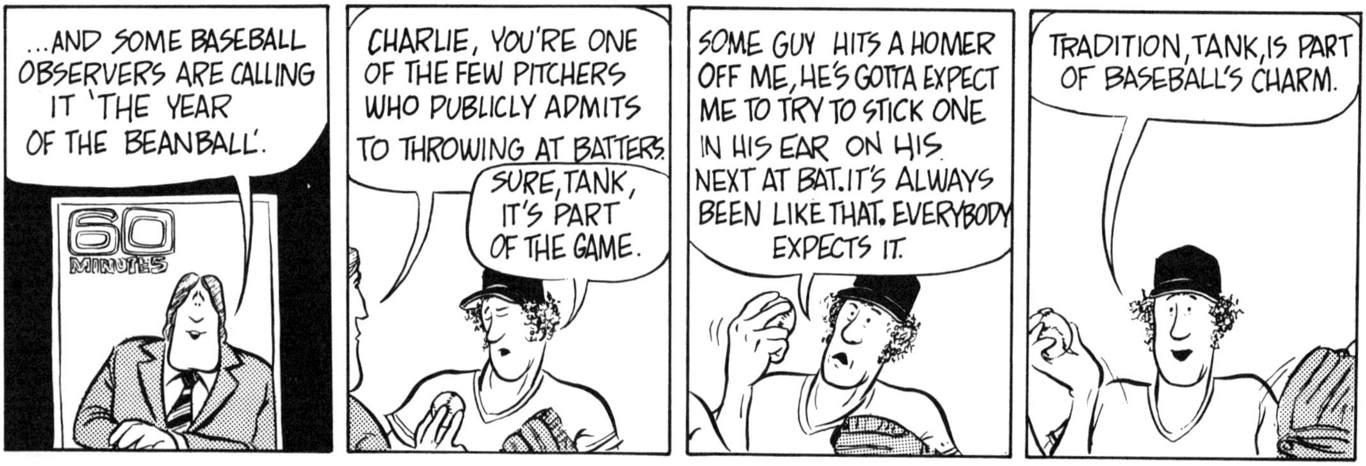
...AND SOME BASEBALL OBSERVERS ARE CALLING IT 'THE YEAR OF THE BEANBALL'.
60 MINUTES
CHARLIE, YOU'RE ONE OF THE FEW PITCHERS WHO PUBLICLY ADMITS TO THROWING AT BATTERS.
SURE, TANK, IT'S PART OF THE GAME.
SOME GUY HITS A HOMER OFF ME, HE'S GOTTA EXPECT ME TO TRY TO STICK ONE IN HIS EAR ON HIS NEXT AT BAT. IT'S ALWAYS BEEN LIKE THAT. EVERYBODY EXPECTS IT.
TRADITION, TANK, IS PART OF BASEBALL'S CHARM.

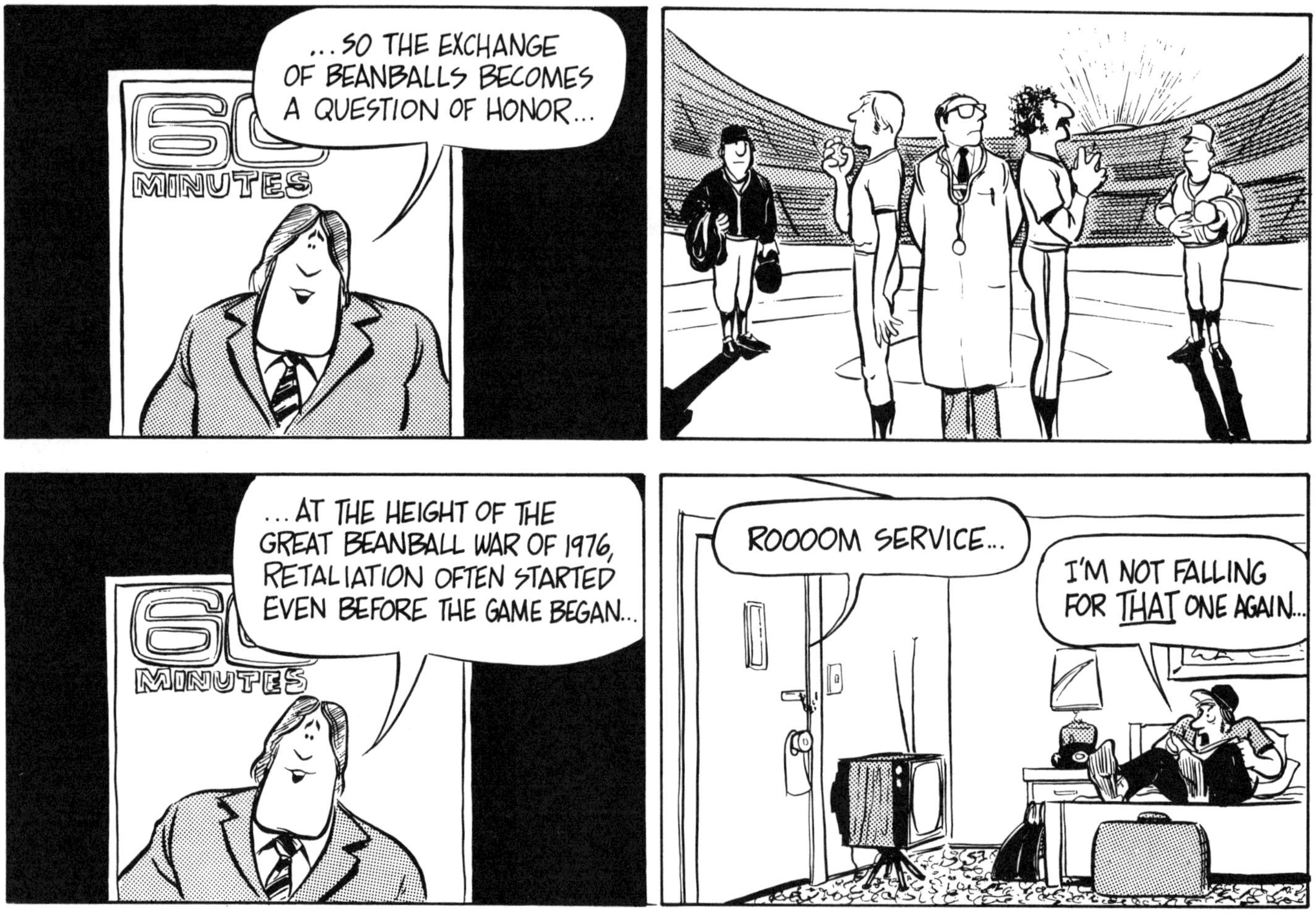
...SO THE EXCHANGE OF BEANBALLS BECOMES A QUESTION OF HONOR...
60 MINUTES
...AT THE HEIGHT OF THE GREAT BEANBALL WAR OF 1976, RETALIATION OFTEN STARTED EVEN BEFORE THE GAME BEGAN...
ROOOOM SERVICE...
I'M NOT FALLING FOR THAT ONE AGAIN...

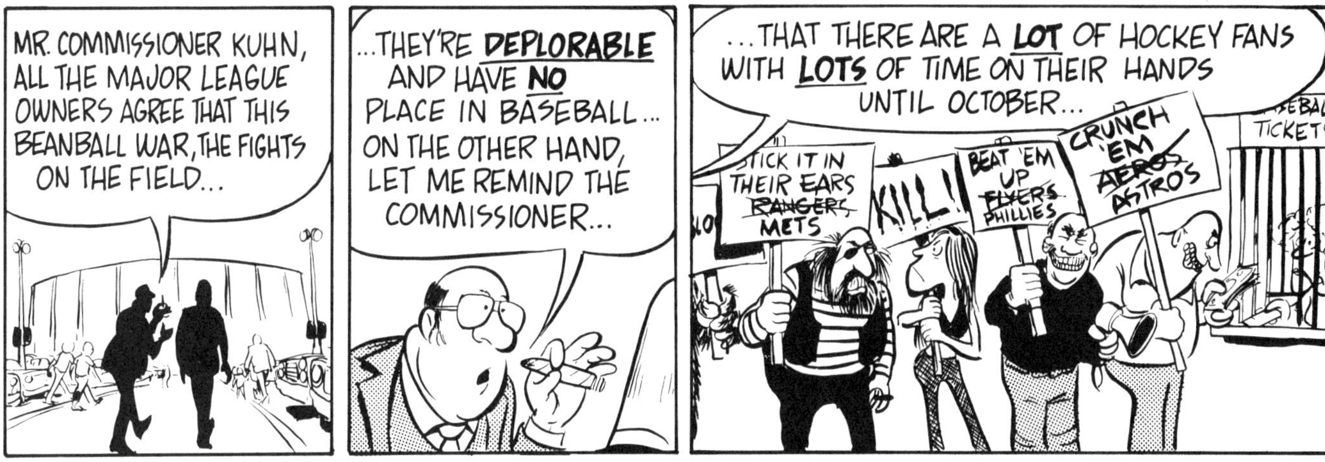
MR. COMMISSIONER KUHN, ALL THE MAJOR LEAGUE OWNERS AGREE THAT THIS BEANBALL WAR, THE FIGHTS ON THE FIELD...
...THEY'RE DEPLORABLE AND HAVE NO PLACE IN BASEBALL... ON THE OTHER HAND, LET ME REMIND THE COMMISSIONER...
...THAT THERE ARE A LOT OF HOCKEY FANS WITH LOTS OF TIME ON THEIR HANDS UNTIL OCTOBER...
STICK IT IN THEIR EARS RANGERS METS
KILL!
BEAT 'EM UP FLYERS PHILLIES
CRUNCH 'EM AEROS ASTROS
TICKETS

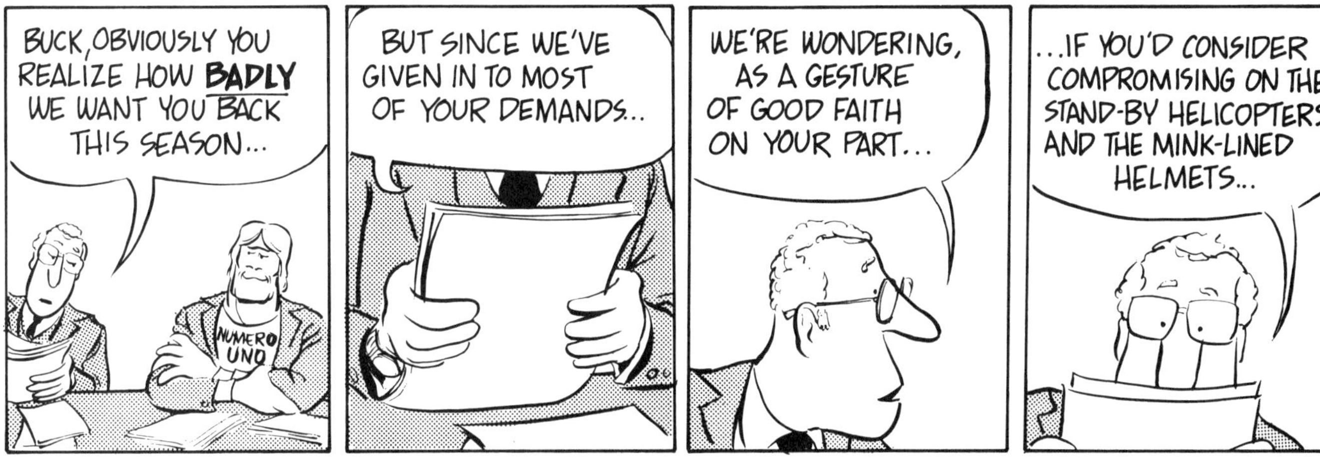
BUCK, OBVIOUSLY YOU REALIZE HOW BADLY WE WANT YOU BACK THIS SEASON...
NUMERO UNO
BUT SINCE WE'VE GIVEN IN TO MOST OF YOUR DEMANDS...
WE'RE WONDERING, AS A GESTURE OF GOOD FAITH ON YOUR PART...
...IF YOU'D CONSIDER COMPROMISING ON THE STAND-BY HELICOPTERS AND THE MINK-LINED HELMETS...

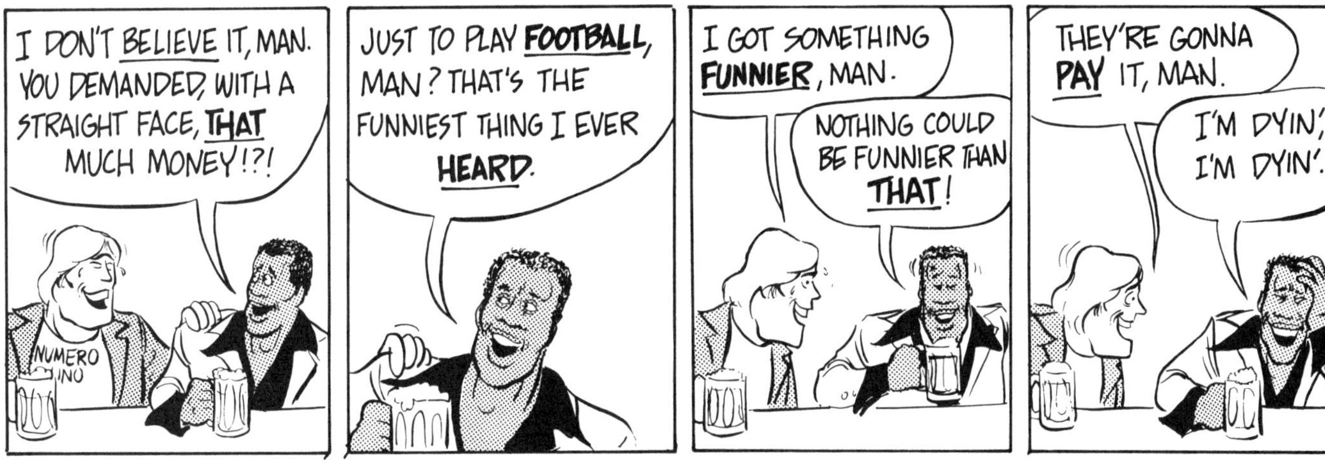
I DON'T BELIEVE IT, MAN. YOU DEMANDED, WITH A STRAIGHT FACE, THAT MUCH MONEY!?!
NUMERO UNO
JUST TO PLAY FOOTBALL, MAN? THAT'S THE FUNNIEST THING I EVER HEARD.
I GOT SOMETHING FUNNIER, MAN.
NOTHING COULD BE FUNNIER THAN THAT!
THEY'RE GONNA PAY IT, MAN.
I'M DYIN', I'M DYIN'.

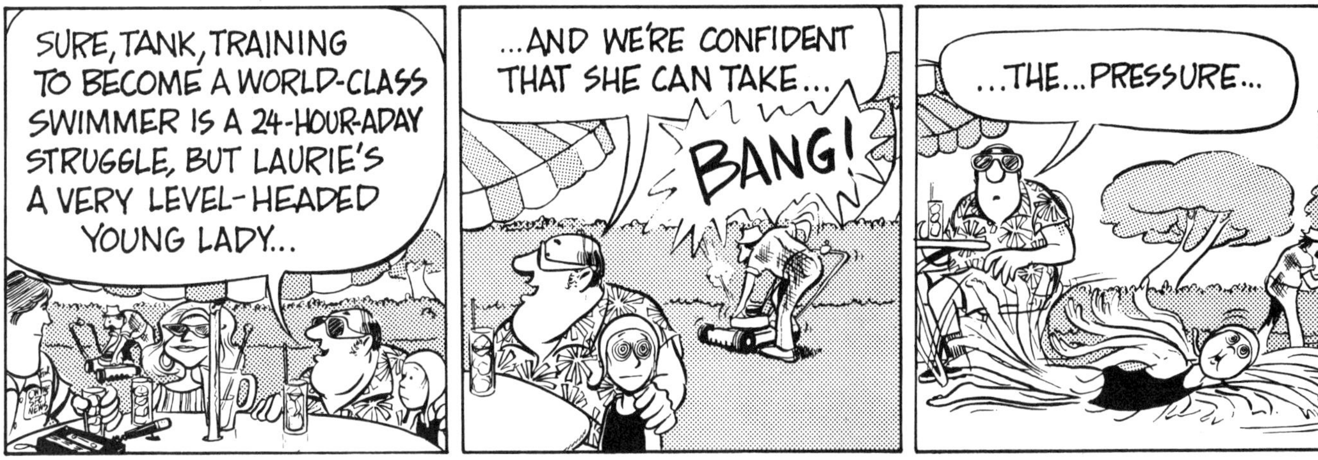
SURE, TANK, TRAINING TO BECOME A WORLD-CLASS SWIMMER IS A 24-HOUR-ADAY STRUGGLE, BUT LAURIE'S A VERY LEVEL-HEADED YOUNG LADY...
...AND WE'RE CONFIDENT THAT SHE CAN TAKE...
BANG!
...THE...PRESSURE...

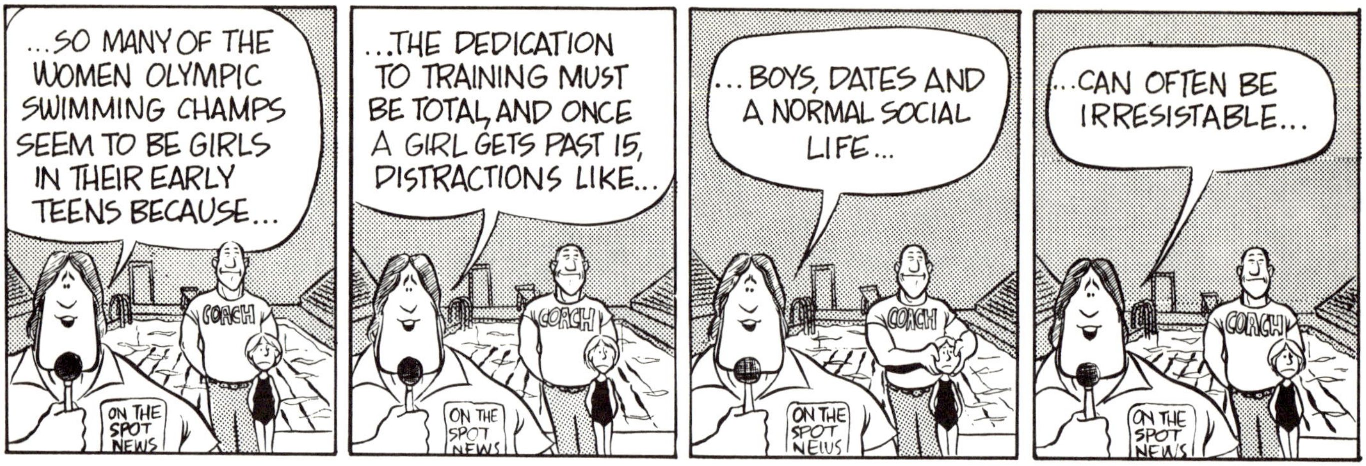
...SO MANY OF THE WOMEN OLYMPIC SWIMMING CHAMPS SEEM TO BE GIRLS IN THEIR EARLY TEENS BECAUSE...
COACH
ON THE SPOT NEWS
...THE DEDICATION TO TRAINING MUST BE TOTAL, AND ONCE A GIRL GETS PAST 15, DISTRACTIONS LIKE...
...BOYS, DATES AND A NORMAL SOCIAL LIFE...
...CAN OFTEN BE IRRESISTABLE...

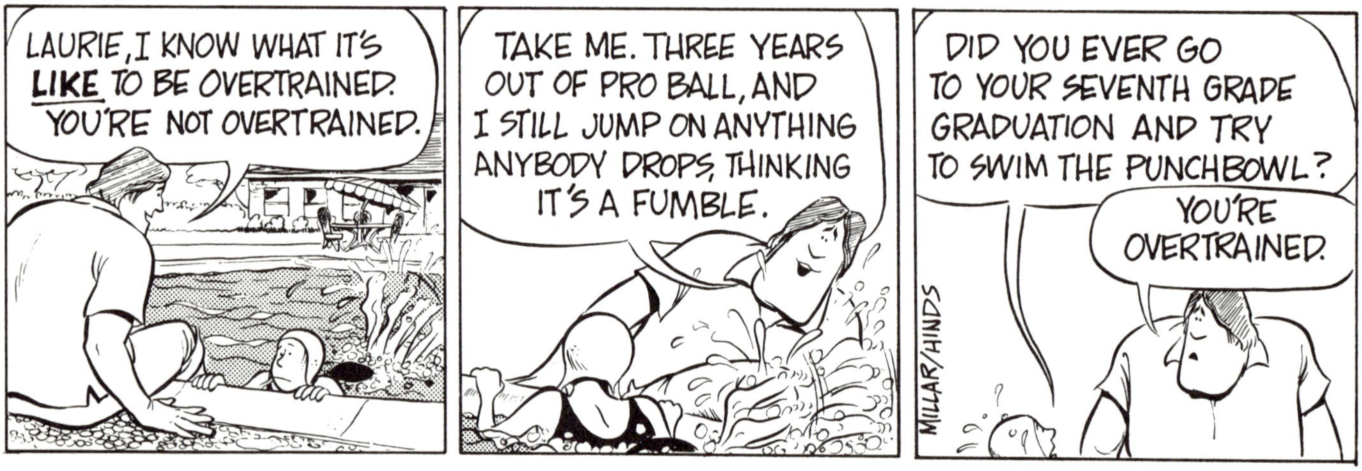
LAURIE, I KNOW WHAT IT'S **LIKE** TO BE OVERTRAINED. YOU'RE NOT OVERTRAINED.
TAKE ME. THREE YEARS OUT OF PRO BALL, AND I STILL JUMP ON ANYTHING ANYBODY DROPS, THINKING IT'S A FUMBLE.
DID YOU EVER GO TO YOUR SEVENTH GRADE GRADUATION AND TRY TO SWIM THE PUNCHBOWL?
YOU'RE OVERTRAINED.
MILLAR/HINDS

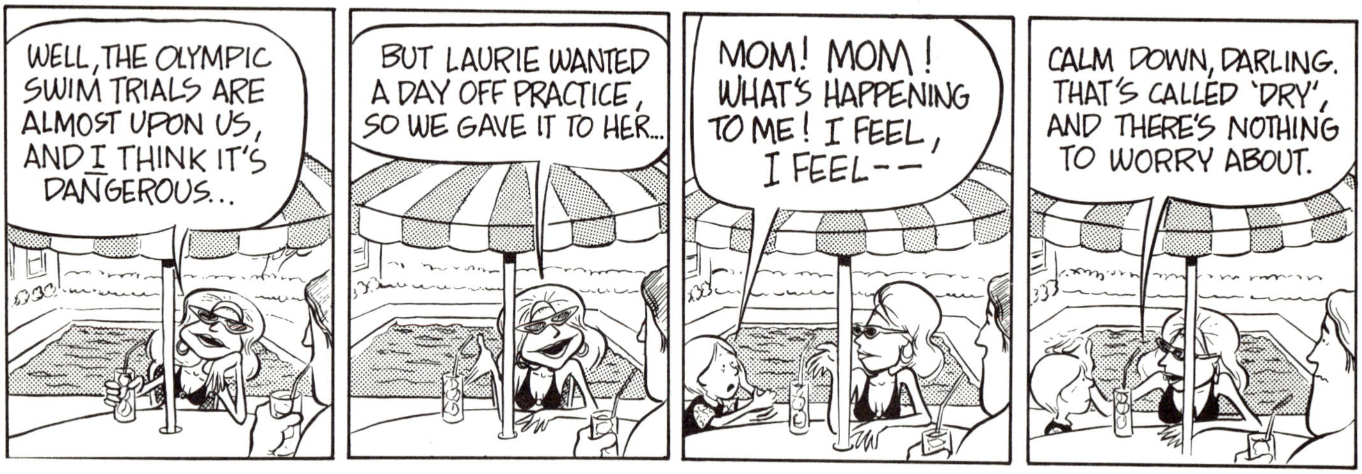
WELL, THE OLYMPIC SWIM TRIALS ARE ALMOST UPON US, AND I THINK IT'S DANGEROUS...
BUT LAURIE WANTED A DAY OFF PRACTICE, SO WE GAVE IT TO HER...
MOM! MOM! WHAT'S HAPPENING TO ME! I FEEL, I FEEL--
CALM DOWN, DARLING. THAT'S CALLED 'DRY', AND THERE'S NOTHING TO WORRY ABOUT.

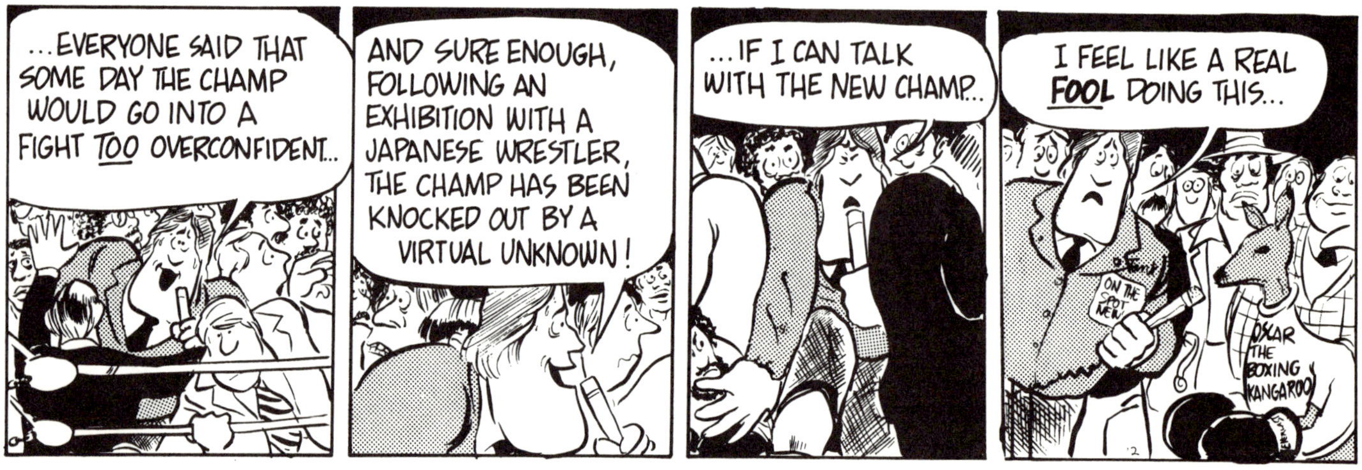
...EVERYONE SAID THAT SOME DAY THE CHAMP WOULD GO INTO A FIGHT TOO OVERCONFIDENT...
AND SURE ENOUGH, FOLLOWING AN EXHIBITION WITH A JAPANESE WRESTLER, THE CHAMP HAS BEEN KNOCKED OUT BY A VIRTUAL UNKNOWN!
...IF I CAN TALK WITH THE NEW CHAMP...
I FEEL LIKE A REAL **FOOL** DOING THIS...
ON THE SPOT NEWS
OSCAR THE BOXING KANGAROO

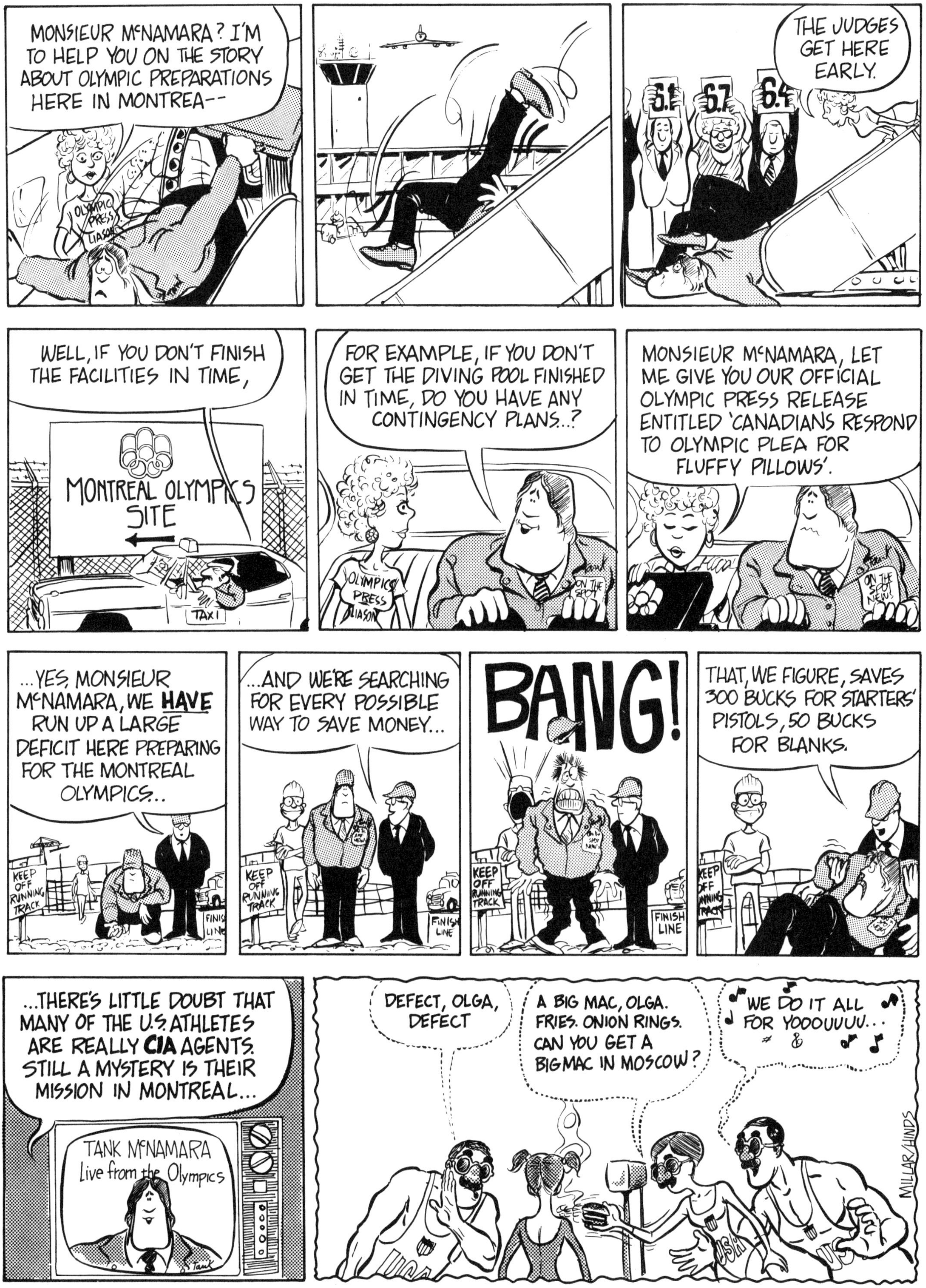
MONSIEUR McNAMARA? I'M TO HELP YOU ON THE STORY ABOUT OLYMPIC PREPARATIONS HERE IN MONTREA--
OLYMPIC PRESS LIASON
THE JUDGES GET HERE EARLY.
6.1
6.7
6.4
WELL, IF YOU DON'T FINISH THE FACILITIES IN TIME,
MONTREAL OLYMPICS SITE
TAXI
FOR EXAMPLE, IF YOU DON'T GET THE DIVING POOL FINISHED IN TIME, DO YOU HAVE ANY CONTINGENCY PLANS...?
OLYMPICS PRESS LIASON
ON THE SPOT
MONSIEUR McNAMARA, LET ME GIVE YOU OUR OFFICIAL OLYMPIC PRESS RELEASE ENTITLED 'CANADIANS RESPOND TO OLYMPIC PLEA FOR FLUFFY PILLOWS'.
ON THE SPOT NEWS
...YES, MONSIEUR McNAMARA, WE **HAVE** RUN UP A LARGE DEFICIT HERE PREPARING FOR THE MONTREAL OLYMPICS...
KEEP OFF RUNNING TRACK
FINISH LINE
...AND WE'RE SEARCHING FOR EVERY POSSIBLE WAY TO SAVE MONEY...
KEEP OFF RUNNING TRACK
FINISH LINE
BANG!
KEEP OFF RUNNING TRACK
FINISH LINE
THAT, WE FIGURE, SAVES 300 BUCKS FOR STARTERS' PISTOLS, 50 BUCKS FOR BLANKS.
KEEP OFF RUNNING TRACK
...THERE'S LITTLE DOUBT THAT MANY OF THE U.S. ATHLETES ARE REALLY **CIA** AGENTS. STILL A MYSTERY IS THEIR MISSION IN MONTREAL...
TANK McNAMARA Live from the Olympics
DEFECT, OLGA, DEFECT
A BIG MAC, OLGA. FRIES. ONION RINGS. CAN YOU GET A BIG MAC IN MOSCOW?
WE DO IT ALL FOR YOOOUUUU...
MILLAR/HINDS

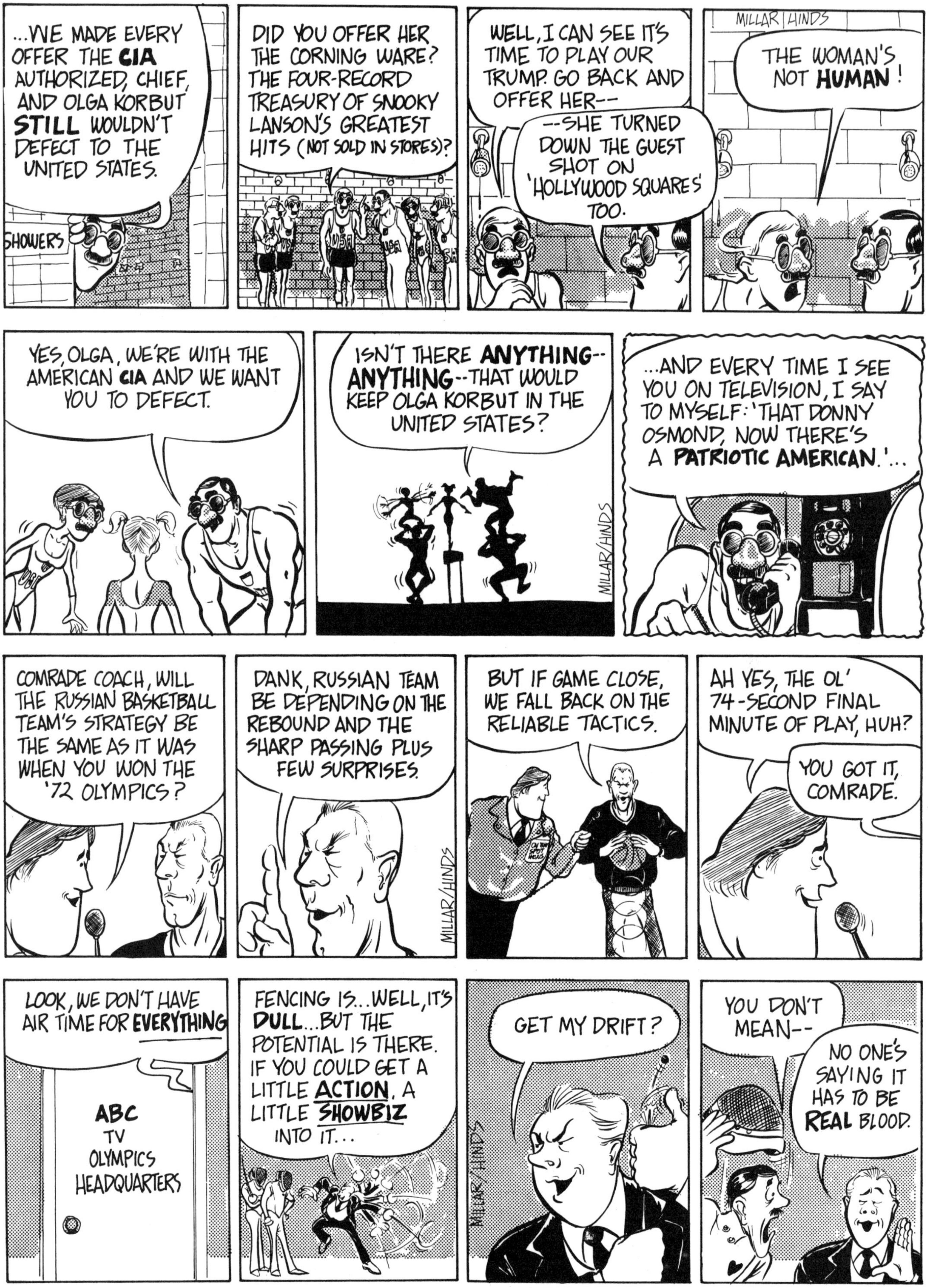
...WE MADE EVERY OFFER THE CIA AUTHORIZED, CHIEF, AND OLGA KORBUT STILL WOULDN'T DEFECT TO THE UNITED STATES.
SHOWERS
DID YOU OFFER HER THE CORNING WARE? THE FOUR-RECORD TREASURY OF SNOOKY LANSON'S GREATEST HITS (NOT SOLD IN STORES)?
WELL, I CAN SEE IT'S TIME TO PLAY OUR TRUMP. GO BACK AND OFFER HER--
--SHE TURNED DOWN THE GUEST SHOT ON 'HOLLYWOOD SQUARES' TOO.
MILLAR/HINDS
THE WOMAN'S NOT HUMAN!
YES, OLGA, WE'RE WITH THE AMERICAN CIA AND WE WANT YOU TO DEFECT.
ISN'T THERE ANYTHING--ANYTHING--THAT WOULD KEEP OLGA KORBUT IN THE UNITED STATES?
MILLAR/HINDS
...AND EVERY TIME I SEE YOU ON TELEVISION, I SAY TO MYSELF: 'THAT DONNY OSMOND, NOW THERE'S A PATRIOTIC AMERICAN.'...
COMRADE COACH, WILL THE RUSSIAN BASKETBALL TEAM'S STRATEGY BE THE SAME AS IT WAS WHEN YOU WON THE '72 OLYMPICS?
DANK, RUSSIAN TEAM BE DEPENDING ON THE REBOUND AND THE SHARP PASSING PLUS FEW SURPRISES.
MILLAR/HINDS
BUT IF GAME CLOSE, WE FALL BACK ON THE RELIABLE TACTICS.
AH YES, THE OL' 74-SECOND FINAL MINUTE OF PLAY, HUH?
YOU GOT IT, COMRADE.
LOOK, WE DON'T HAVE AIR TIME FOR EVERYTHING
ABC TV OLYMPICS HEADQUARTERS
FENCING IS...WELL, IT'S DULL...BUT THE POTENTIAL IS THERE. IF YOU COULD GET A LITTLE ACTION, A LITTLE SHOWBIZ INTO IT...
MILLAR/HINDS
GET MY DRIFT?
YOU DON'T MEAN--
NO ONE'S SAYING IT HAS TO BE REAL BLOOD.

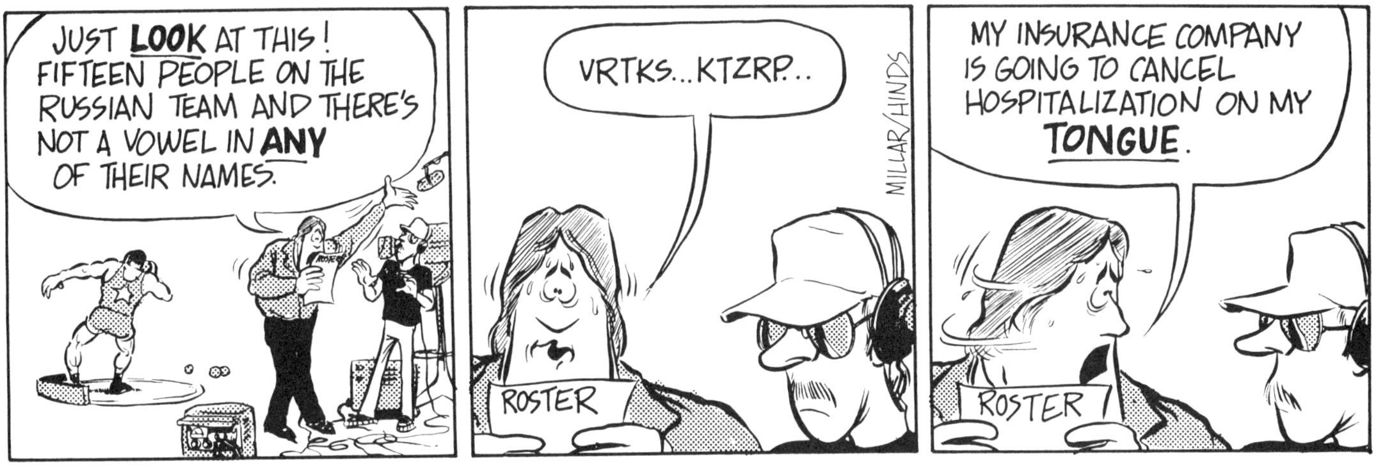
JUST **LOOK** AT THIS! FIFTEEN PEOPLE ON THE RUSSIAN TEAM AND THERE'S NOT A VOWEL IN **ANY** OF THEIR NAMES.
VRTKS...KTZRP...
ROSTER
MILLAR/HINDS
MY INSURANCE COMPANY IS GOING TO CANCEL HOSPITALIZATION ON MY **TONGUE**.
ROSTER

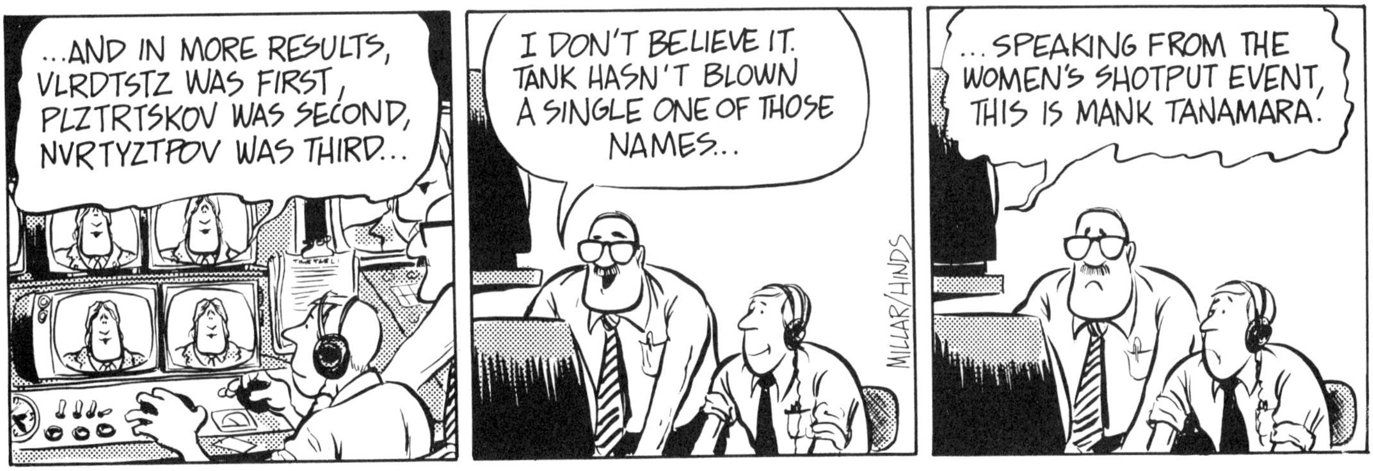
...AND IN MORE RESULTS, VLRDTSTZ WAS FIRST, PLZTRTSKOV WAS SECOND, NVRTYZTPOV WAS THIRD...
I DON'T BELIEVE IT. TANK HASN'T BLOWN A SINGLE ONE OF THOSE NAMES...
MILLAR/HINDS
...SPEAKING FROM THE WOMEN'S SHOTPUT EVENT, THIS IS MANK TANAMARA.

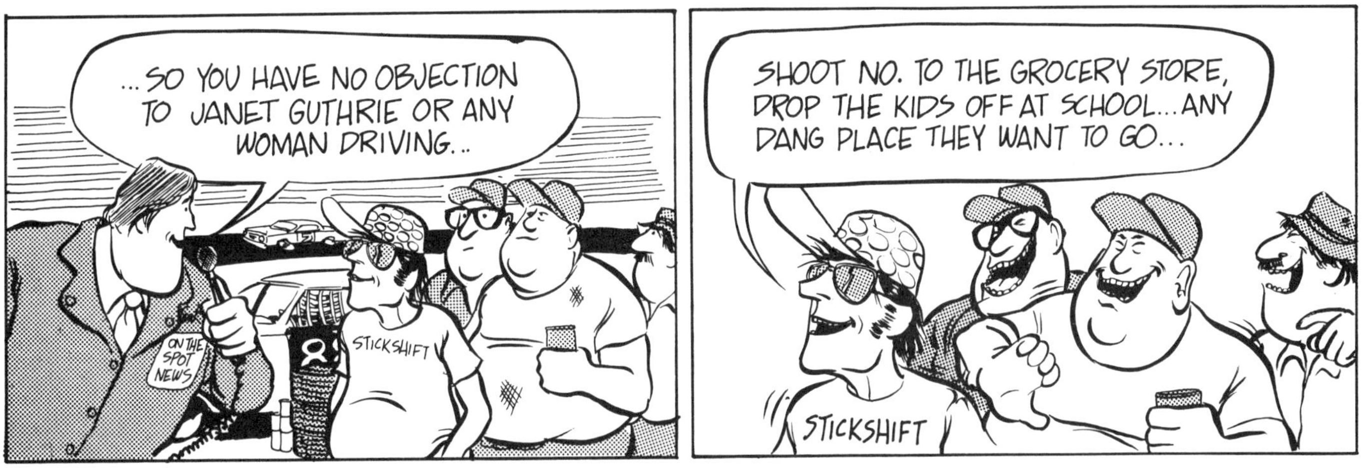
...SO YOU HAVE NO OBJECTION TO JANET GUTHRIE OR ANY WOMAN DRIVING...
ON THE SPOT NEWS
STICKSHIFT
SHOOT NO. TO THE GROCERY STORE, DROP THE KIDS OFF AT SCHOOL... ANY DANG PLACE THEY WANT TO GO...
STICKSHIFT

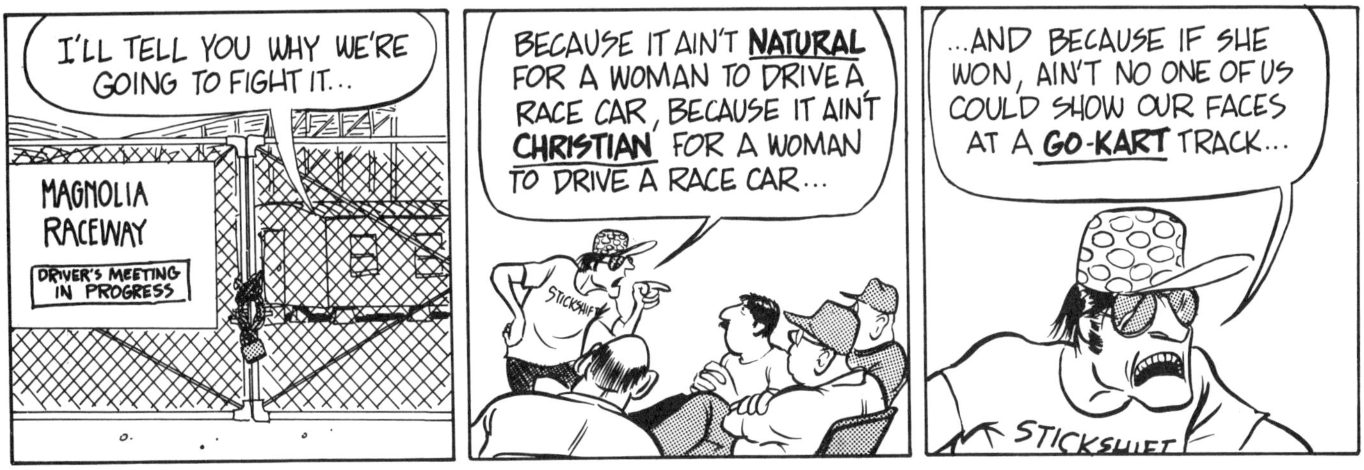
I'LL TELL YOU WHY WE'RE GOING TO FIGHT IT...
MAGNOLIA RACEWAY
DRIVER'S MEETING IN PROGRESS
BECAUSE IT AIN'T **NATURAL** FOR A WOMAN TO DRIVE A RACE CAR, BECAUSE IT AIN'T **CHRISTIAN** FOR A WOMAN TO DRIVE A RACE CAR...
STICKSHIFT
...AND BECAUSE IF SHE WON, AIN'T NO ONE OF US COULD SHOW OUR FACES AT A **GO-KART** TRACK...

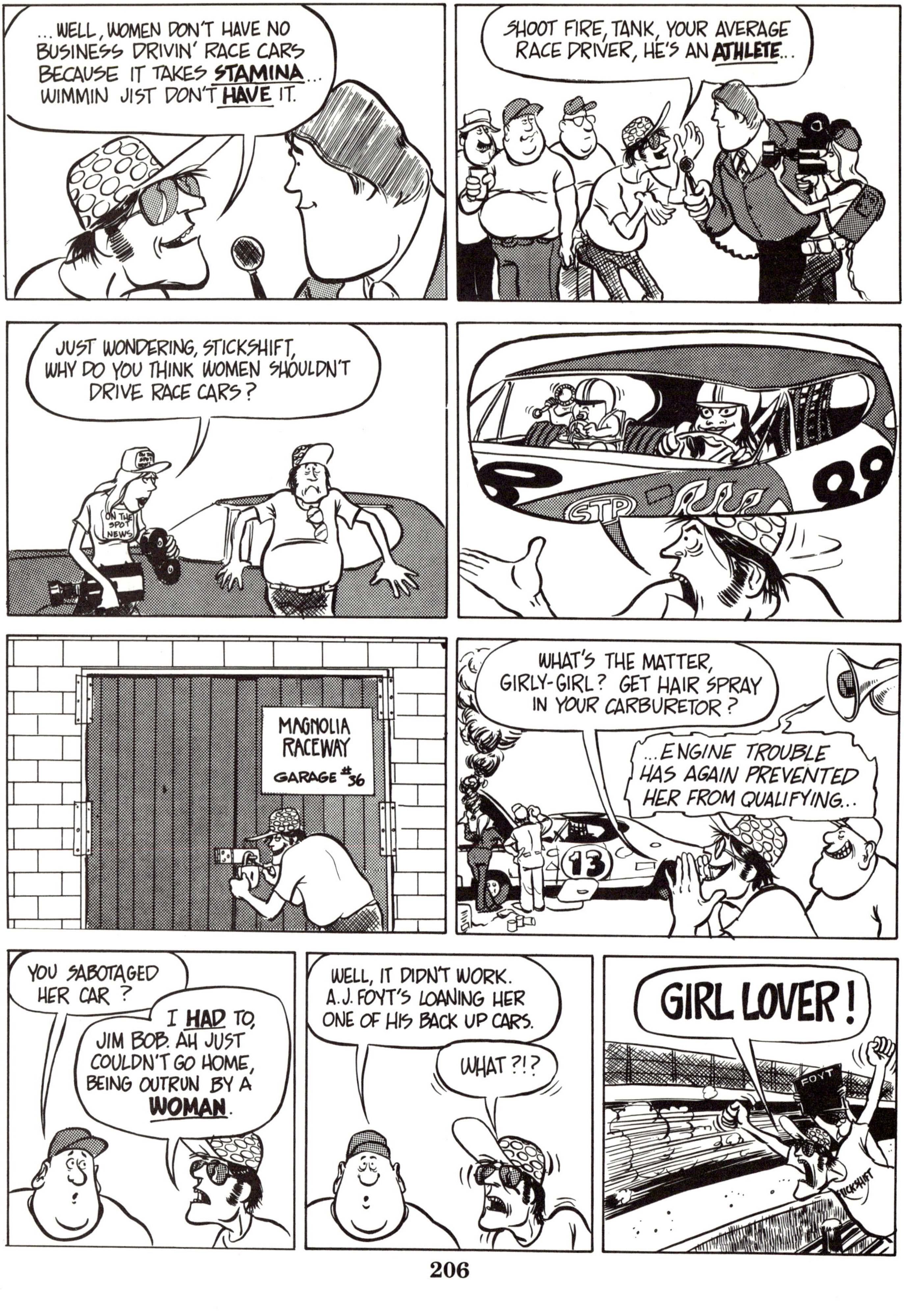
...WELL, WOMEN DON'T HAVE NO BUSINESS DRIVIN' RACE CARS BECAUSE IT TAKES STAMINA... WIMMIN JIST DON'T HAVE IT.
SHOOT FIRE, TANK, YOUR AVERAGE RACE DRIVER, HE'S AN ATHLETE...
JUST WONDERING, STICKSHIFT, WHY DO YOU THINK WOMEN SHOULDN'T DRIVE RACE CARS?
ON THE SPOT NEWS
STP
99
MAGNOLIA RACEWAY
GARAGE #36
WHAT'S THE MATTER, GIRLY-GIRL? GET HAIR SPRAY IN YOUR CARBURETOR?
...ENGINE TROUBLE HAS AGAIN PREVENTED HER FROM QUALIFYING...
13
YOU SABOTAGED HER CAR?
I HAD TO, JIM BOB. AH JUST COULDN'T GO HOME, BEING OUTRUN BY A WOMAN.
WELL, IT DIDN'T WORK. A.J. FOYT'S LOANING HER ONE OF HIS BACK UP CARS.
WHAT?!?
GIRL LOVER!
FOYT
STICKSHIFT

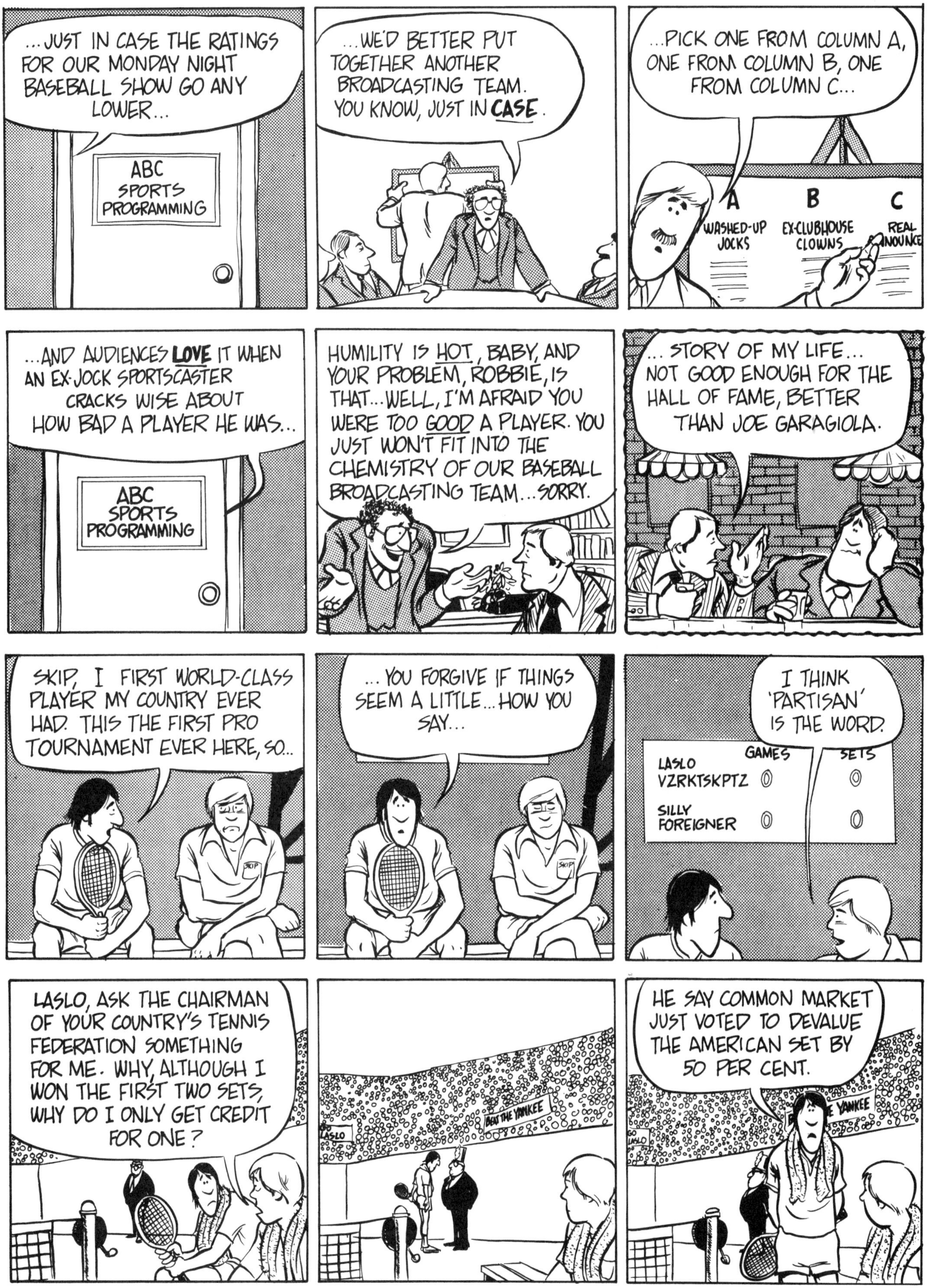
...JUST IN CASE THE RATINGS FOR OUR MONDAY NIGHT BASEBALL SHOW GO ANY LOWER...
ABC SPORTS PROGRAMMING
...WE'D BETTER PUT TOGETHER ANOTHER BROADCASTING TEAM. YOU KNOW, JUST IN CASE.
...PICK ONE FROM COLUMN A, ONE FROM COLUMN B, ONE FROM COLUMN C...
A WASHED-UP JOCKS
B EX-CLUBHOUSE CLOWNS
C REAL ANOUNCE
...AND AUDIENCES LOVE IT WHEN AN EX-JOCK SPORTSCASTER CRACKS WISE ABOUT HOW BAD A PLAYER HE WAS...
ABC SPORTS PROGRAMMING
HUMILITY IS HOT, BABY, AND YOUR PROBLEM, ROBBIE, IS THAT...WELL, I'M AFRAID YOU WERE TOO GOOD A PLAYER. YOU JUST WON'T FIT INTO THE CHEMISTRY OF OUR BASEBALL BROADCASTING TEAM...SORRY.
... STORY OF MY LIFE... NOT GOOD ENOUGH FOR THE HALL OF FAME, BETTER THAN JOE GARAGIOLA.
SKIP, I FIRST WORLD-CLASS PLAYER MY COUNTRY EVER HAD. THIS THE FIRST PRO TOURNAMENT EVER HERE, SO...
SKIP
... YOU FORGIVE IF THINGS SEEM A LITTLE...HOW YOU SAY...
SKIP
I THINK 'PARTISAN' IS THE WORD.
GAMES SETS
LASLO VZRKTSKPTZ 0 0
SILLY FOREIGNER 0 0
LASLO, ASK THE CHAIRMAN OF YOUR COUNTRY'S TENNIS FEDERATION SOMETHING FOR ME. WHY, ALTHOUGH I WON THE FIRST TWO SETS, WHY DO I ONLY GET CREDIT FOR ONE?
GO LASLO
BEAT THE YANKEE
HE SAY COMMON MARKET JUST VOTED TO DEVALUE THE AMERICAN SET BY 50 PER CENT.
GO LASLO
YANKEE

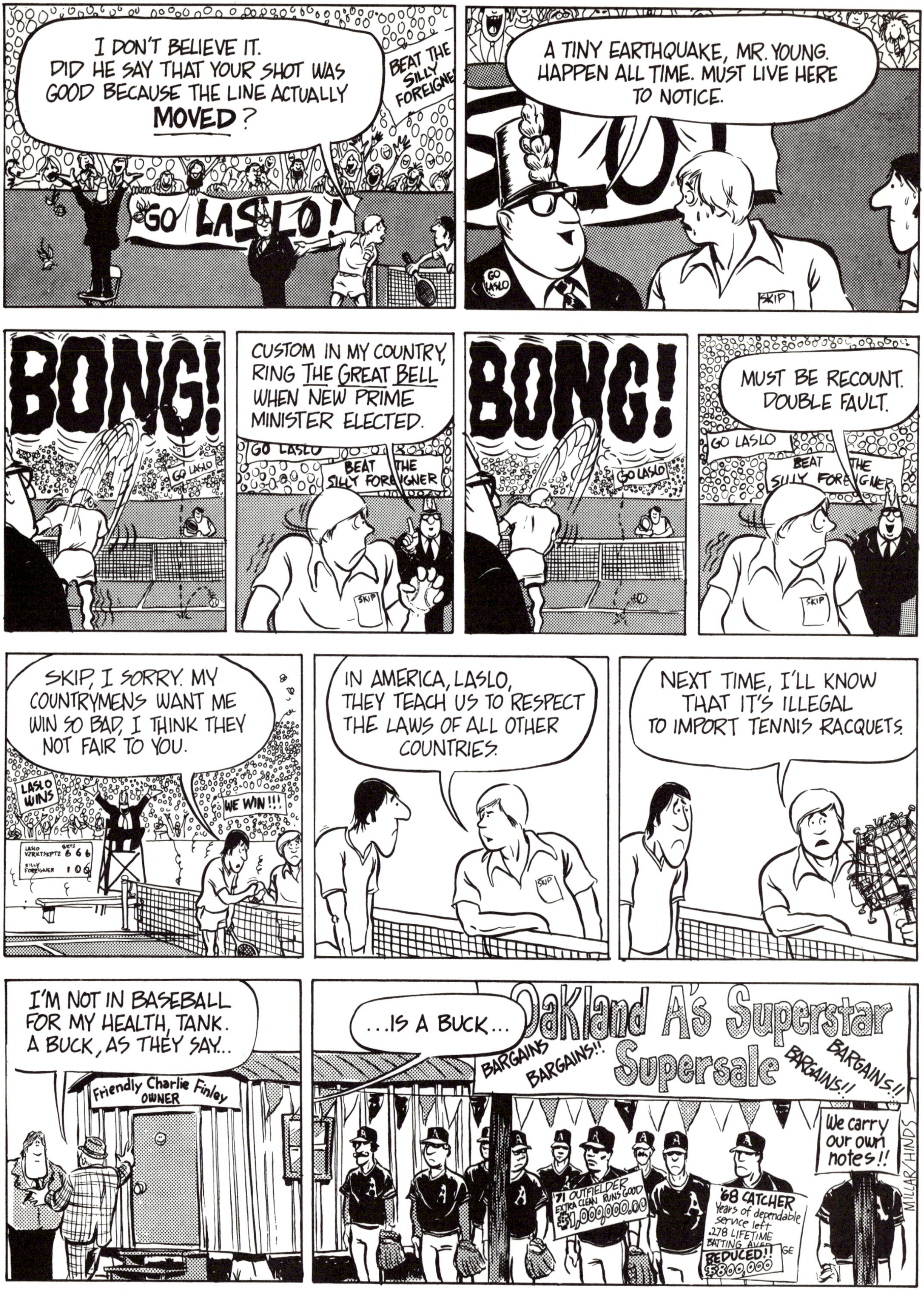
I DON'T BELIEVE IT. DID HE SAY THAT YOUR SHOT WAS GOOD BECAUSE THE LINE ACTUALLY MOVED?
BEAT THE SILLY FOREIGNE
GO LASLO!
A TINY EARTHQUAKE, MR. YOUNG. HAPPEN ALL TIME. MUST LIVE HERE TO NOTICE.
GO LASLO
SKIP
BONG!
GO LASLO
CUSTOM IN MY COUNTRY, RING THE GREAT BELL WHEN NEW PRIME MINISTER ELECTED.
GO LASLO
BEAT THE SILLY FOREIGNER
SKIP
BONG!
GO LASLO
MUST BE RECOUNT. DOUBLE FAULT.
GO LASLO
BEAT THE SILLY FOREIGNER
SKIP
SKIP, I SORRY. MY COUNTRYMENS WANT ME WIN SO BAD, I THINK THEY NOT FAIR TO YOU.
LASLO WINS
WE WIN!!!
IN AMERICA, LASLO, THEY TEACH US TO RESPECT THE LAWS OF ALL OTHER COUNTRIES.
SKIP
NEXT TIME, I'LL KNOW THAT IT'S ILLEGAL TO IMPORT TENNIS RACQUETS.
I'M NOT IN BASEBALL FOR MY HEALTH, TANK. A BUCK, AS THEY SAY...
Friendly Charlie Finley OWNER
...IS A BUCK...
Oakland A's Superstar Supersale
BARGAINS BARGAINS!! BARGAINS!! BARGAINS!!
We carry our own notes!!
'71 OUTFIELDER EXTRA CLEAN RUNS GOOD $1,000,000.00
'68 CATCHER Years of dependable service left .278 LIFETIME BATTING AVERAGE REDUCED!! $800,000
MILLAR/HINDS

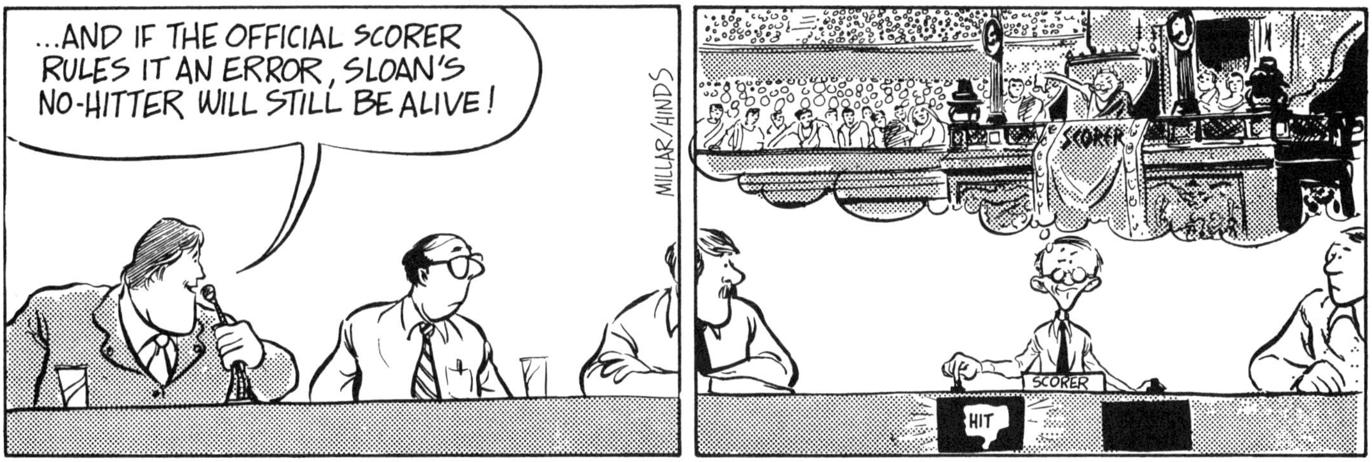
...AND IF THE OFFICIAL SCORER RULES IT AN ERROR, SLOAN'S NO-HITTER WILL STILL BE ALIVE!
MILLAR/HINDS
SCORER
SCORER
HIT

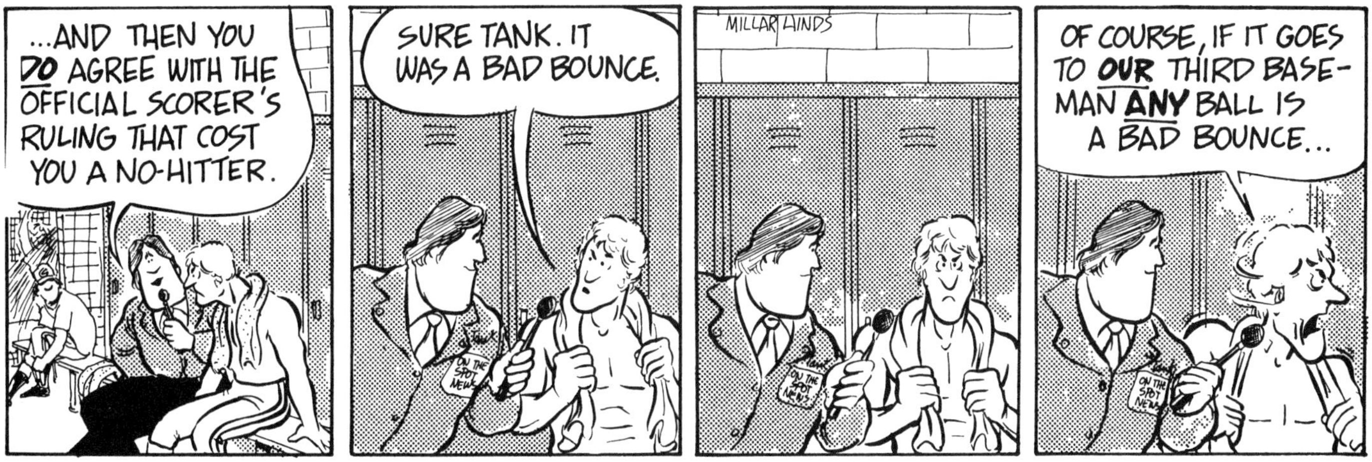
...AND THEN YOU DO AGREE WITH THE OFFICIAL SCORER'S RULING THAT COST YOU A NO-HITTER.
SURE TANK. IT WAS A BAD BOUNCE.
MILLAR/HINDS
OF COURSE, IF IT GOES TO OUR THIRD BASE-MAN ANY BALL IS A BAD BOUNCE...
ON THE SPOT NEWS

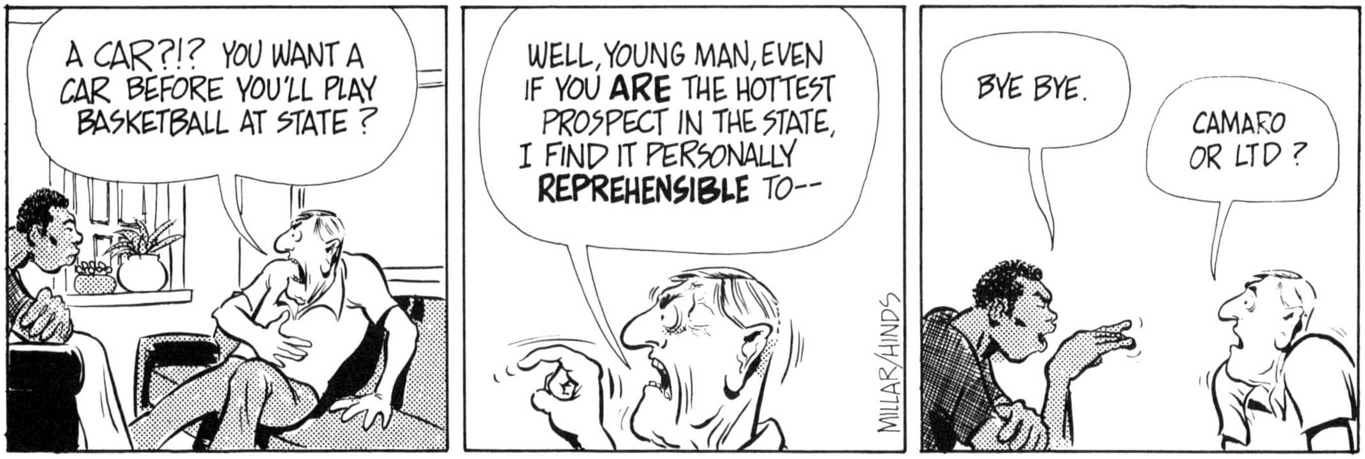
A CAR?!? YOU WANT A CAR BEFORE YOU'LL PLAY BASKETBALL AT STATE?
WELL, YOUNG MAN, EVEN IF YOU ARE THE HOTTEST PROSPECT IN THE STATE, I FIND IT PERSONALLY REPREHENSIBLE TO--
MILLAR/HINDS
BYE BYE.
CAMARO OR LTD?

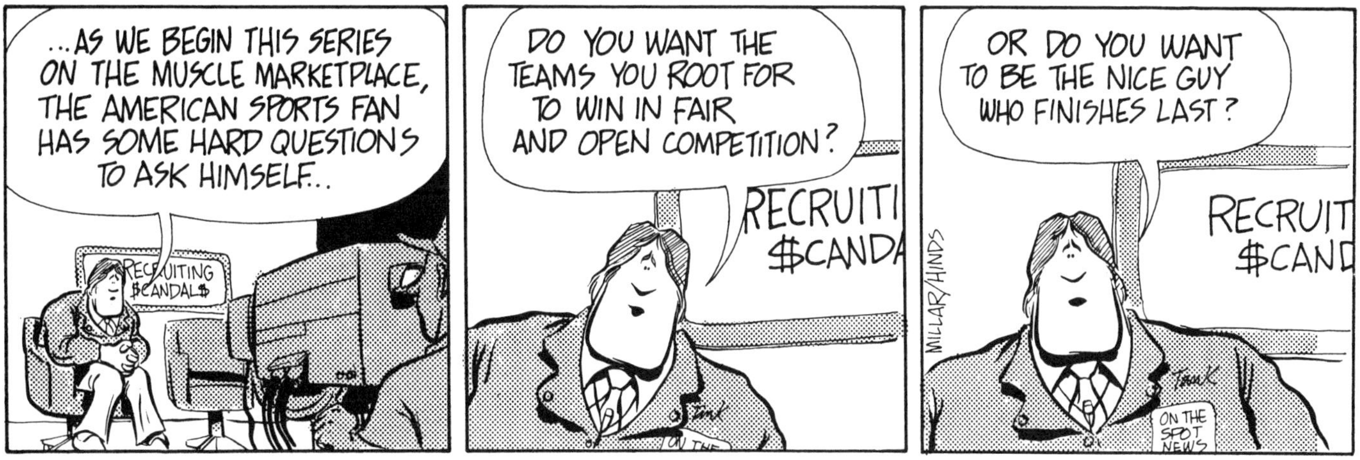
...AS WE BEGIN THIS SERIES ON THE MUSCLE MARKETPLACE, THE AMERICAN SPORTS FAN HAS SOME HARD QUESTIONS TO ASK HIMSELF...
RECRUITING $CANDAL$
DO YOU WANT THE TEAMS YOU ROOT FOR TO WIN IN FAIR AND OPEN COMPETITION?
RECRUITI $CANDA
MILLAR/HINDS
OR DO YOU WANT TO BE THE NICE GUY WHO FINISHES LAST?
RECRUIT $CAND
ON THE SPOT NEWS

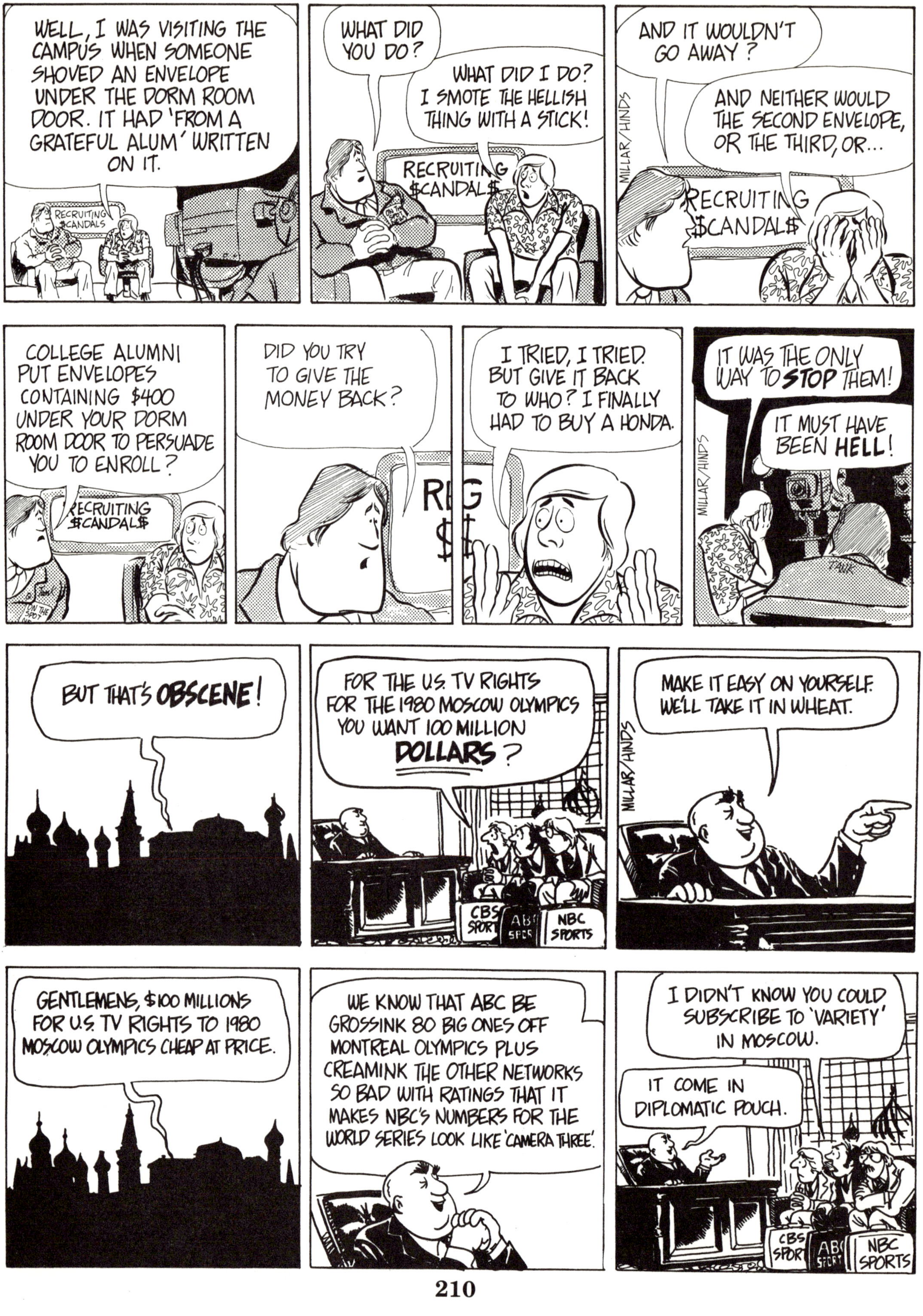
WELL, I WAS VISITING THE CAMPUS WHEN SOMEONE SHOVED AN ENVELOPE UNDER THE DORM ROOM DOOR. IT HAD 'FROM A GRATEFUL ALUM' WRITTEN ON IT.
RECRUITING $CANDALS
WHAT DID YOU DO?
WHAT DID I DO? I SMOTE THE HELLISH THING WITH A STICK!
RECRUITING $CANDAL$
AND IT WOULDN'T GO AWAY?
AND NEITHER WOULD THE SECOND ENVELOPE, OR THE THIRD, OR...
MILLAR/HINDS
RECRUITING $CANDAL$
COLLEGE ALUMNI PUT ENVELOPES CONTAINING $400 UNDER YOUR DORM ROOM DOOR TO PERSUADE YOU TO ENROLL?
RECRUITING $CANDAL$
DID YOU TRY TO GIVE THE MONEY BACK?
I TRIED, I TRIED. BUT GIVE IT BACK TO WHO? I FINALLY HAD TO BUY A HONDA.
IT WAS THE ONLY WAY TO **STOP** THEM!
IT MUST HAVE BEEN **HELL**!
MILLAR/HINDS
BUT THAT'S **OBSCENE**!
FOR THE U.S. TV RIGHTS FOR THE 1980 MOSCOW OLYMPICS YOU WANT 100 MILLION **DOLLARS**?
MILLAR/HINDS
CBS SPORT
NBC SPORTS
MAKE IT EASY ON YOURSELF. WE'LL TAKE IT IN WHEAT.
GENTLEMENS, $100 MILLIONS FOR U.S. TV RIGHTS TO 1980 MOSCOW OLYMPICS CHEAP AT PRICE.
WE KNOW THAT ABC BE GROSSINK 80 BIG ONES OFF MONTREAL OLYMPICS PLUS CREAMINK THE OTHER NETWORKS SO BAD WITH RATINGS THAT IT MAKES NBC'S NUMBERS FOR THE WORLD SERIES LOOK LIKE 'CAMERA THREE'.
I DIDN'T KNOW YOU COULD SUBSCRIBE TO 'VARIETY' IN MOSCOW.
IT COME IN DIPLOMATIC POUCH.
CBS SPORT
NBC SPORTS

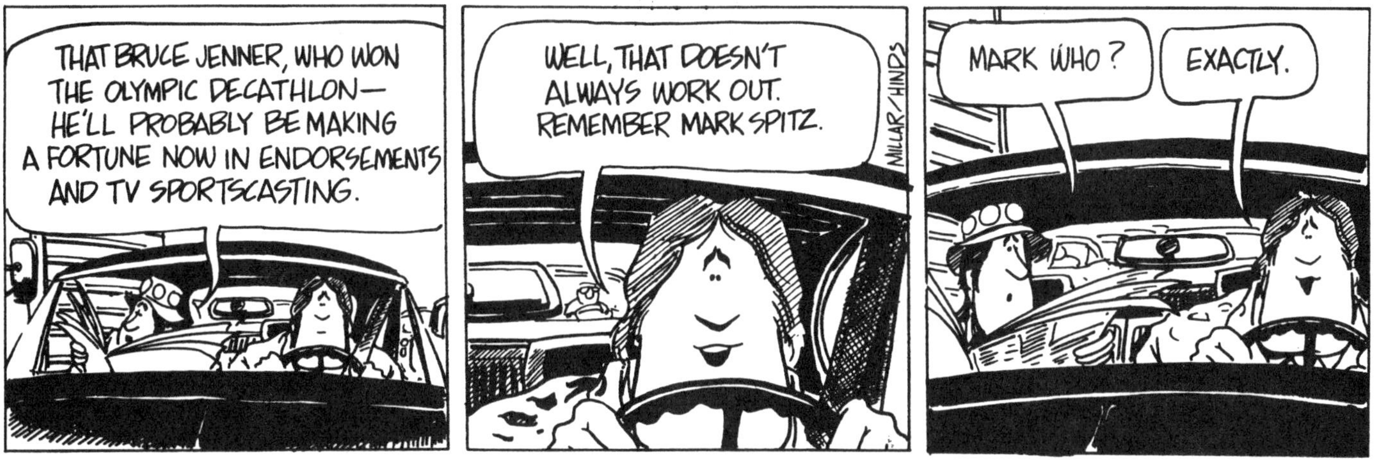
THAT BRUCE JENNER, WHO WON THE OLYMPIC DECATHLON— HE'LL PROBABLY BE MAKING A FORTUNE NOW IN ENDORSEMENTS AND TV SPORTSCASTING.
WELL, THAT DOESN'T ALWAYS WORK OUT. REMEMBER MARK SPITZ.
MILLAR/HINDS
MARK WHO?
EXACTLY.

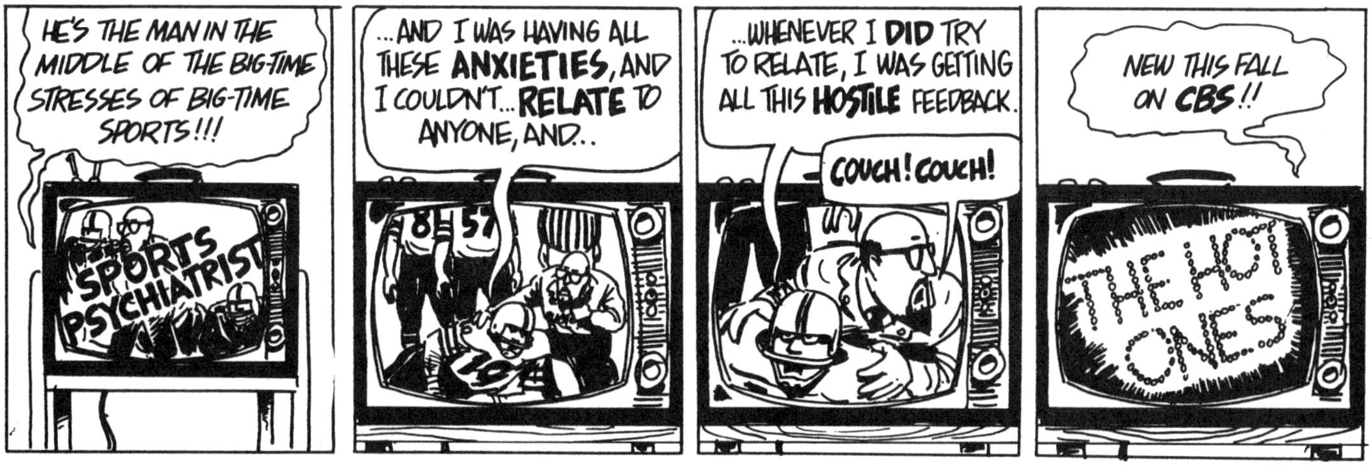
HE'S THE MAN IN THE MIDDLE OF THE BIG-TIME STRESSES OF BIG-TIME SPORTS!!!
SPORTS PSYCHIATRIST
...AND I WAS HAVING ALL THESE ANXIETIES, AND I COULDN'T...RELATE TO ANYONE, AND...
...WHENEVER I DID TRY TO RELATE, I WAS GETTING ALL THIS HOSTILE FEEDBACK.
COUCH! COUCH!
NEW THIS FALL ON CBS!!
THE HOT ONES

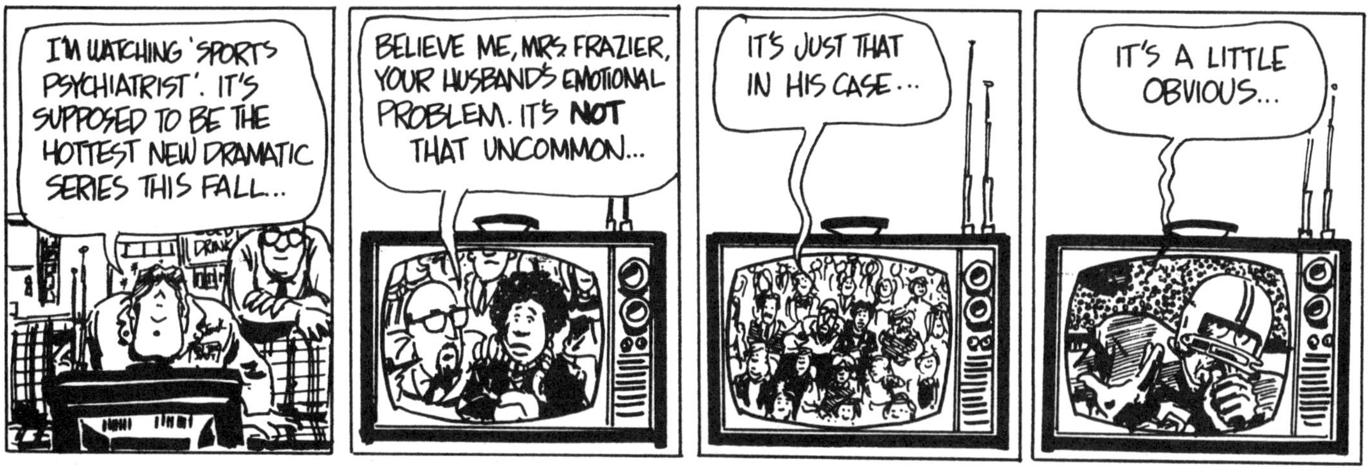
I'M WATCHING 'SPORTS PSYCHIATRIST'. IT'S SUPPOSED TO BE THE HOTTEST NEW DRAMATIC SERIES THIS FALL...
BELIEVE ME, MRS. FRAZIER, YOUR HUSBAND'S EMOTIONAL PROBLEM. IT'S NOT THAT UNCOMMON...
IT'S JUST THAT IN HIS CASE...
IT'S A LITTLE OBVIOUS...

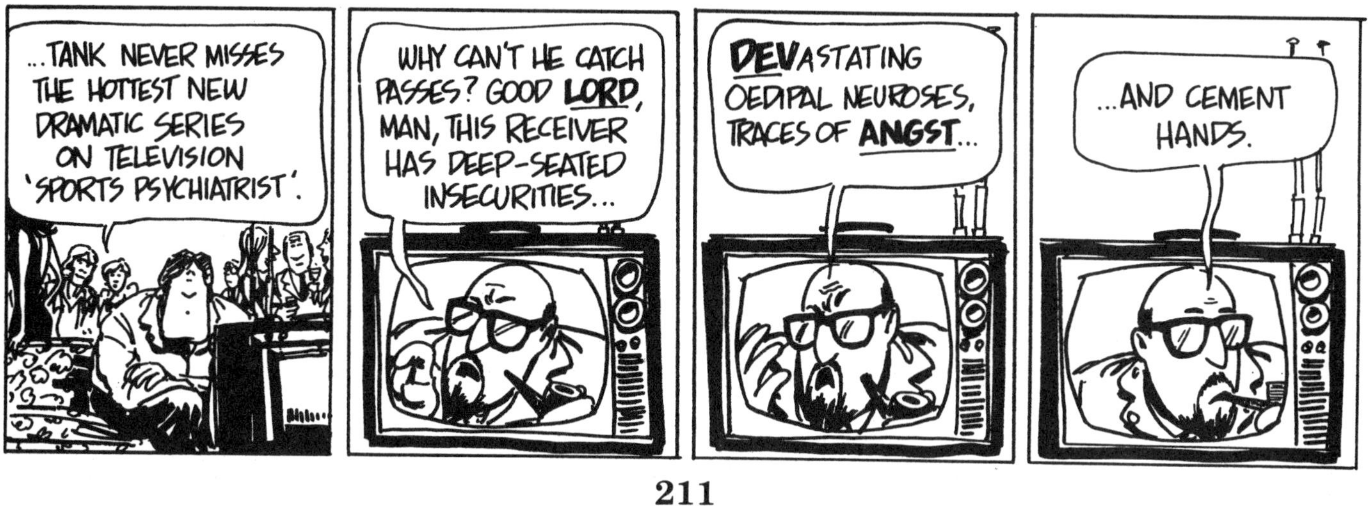
...TANK NEVER MISSES THE HOTTEST NEW DRAMATIC SERIES ON TELEVISION 'SPORTS PSYCHIATRIST'.
WHY CAN'T HE CATCH PASSES? GOOD LORD, MAN, THIS RECEIVER HAS DEEP-SEATED INSECURITIES...
DEVASTATING OEDIPAL NEUROSES, TRACES OF ANGST...
...AND CEMENT HANDS.

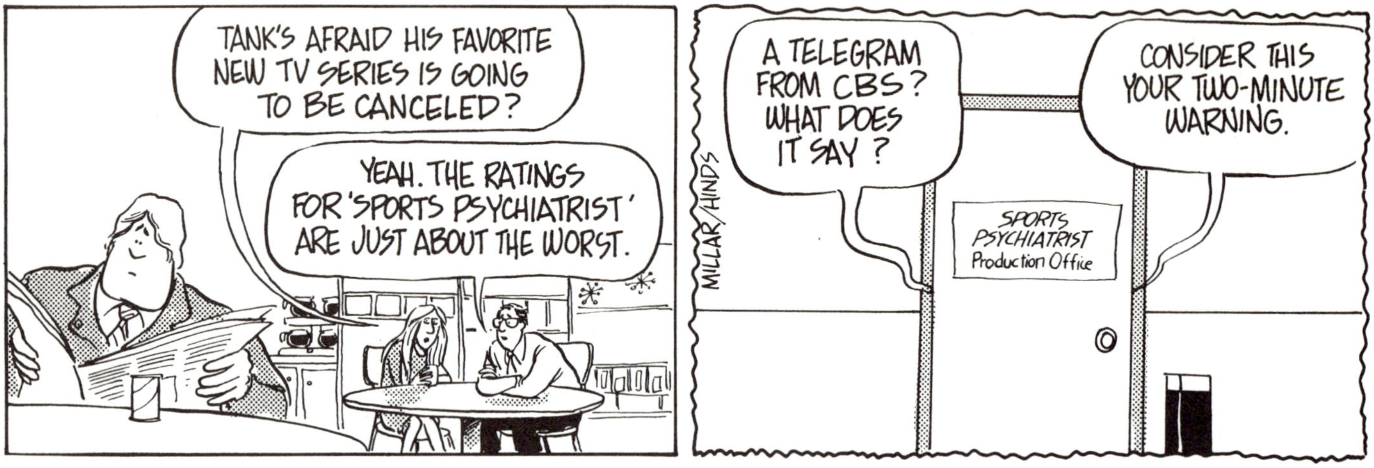
TANK'S AFRAID HIS FAVORITE NEW TV SERIES IS GOING TO BE CANCELED?
YEAH. THE RATINGS FOR 'SPORTS PSYCHIATRIST' ARE JUST ABOUT THE WORST.
MILLAR/HINDS
A TELEGRAM FROM CBS? WHAT DOES IT SAY?
CONSIDER THIS YOUR TWO-MINUTE WARNING.
SPORTS PSYCHIATRIST Production Office

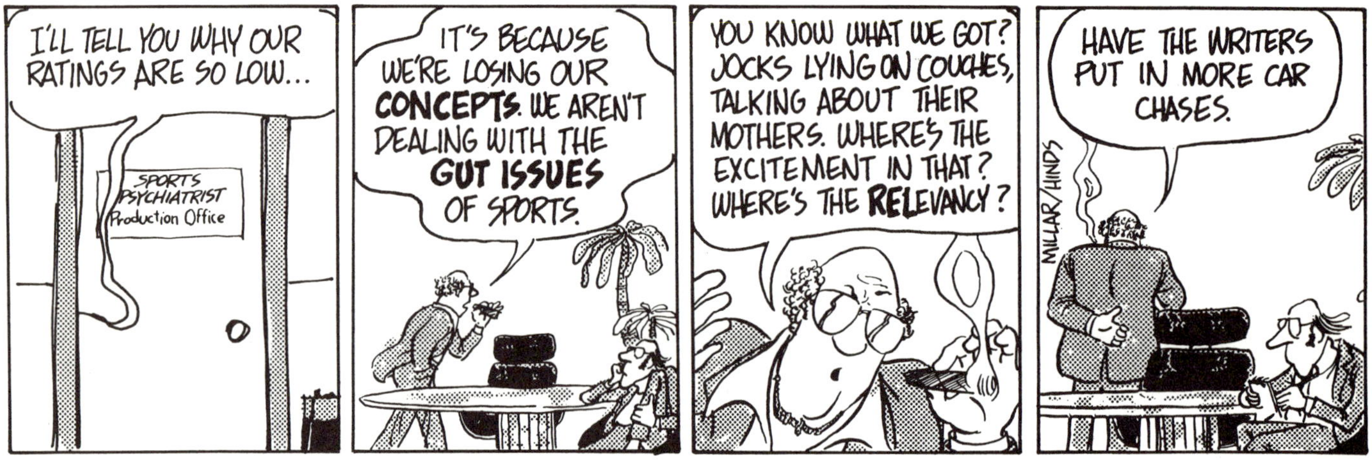
I'LL TELL YOU WHY OUR RATINGS ARE SO LOW...
SPORTS PSYCHIATRIST Production Office
IT'S BECAUSE WE'RE LOSING OUR CONCEPTS. WE AREN'T DEALING WITH THE GUT ISSUES OF SPORTS.
YOU KNOW WHAT WE GOT? JOCKS LYING ON COUCHES, TALKING ABOUT THEIR MOTHERS. WHERE'S THE EXCITEMENT IN THAT? WHERE'S THE RELEVANCY?
HAVE THE WRITERS PUT IN MORE CAR CHASES.
MILLAR/HINDS

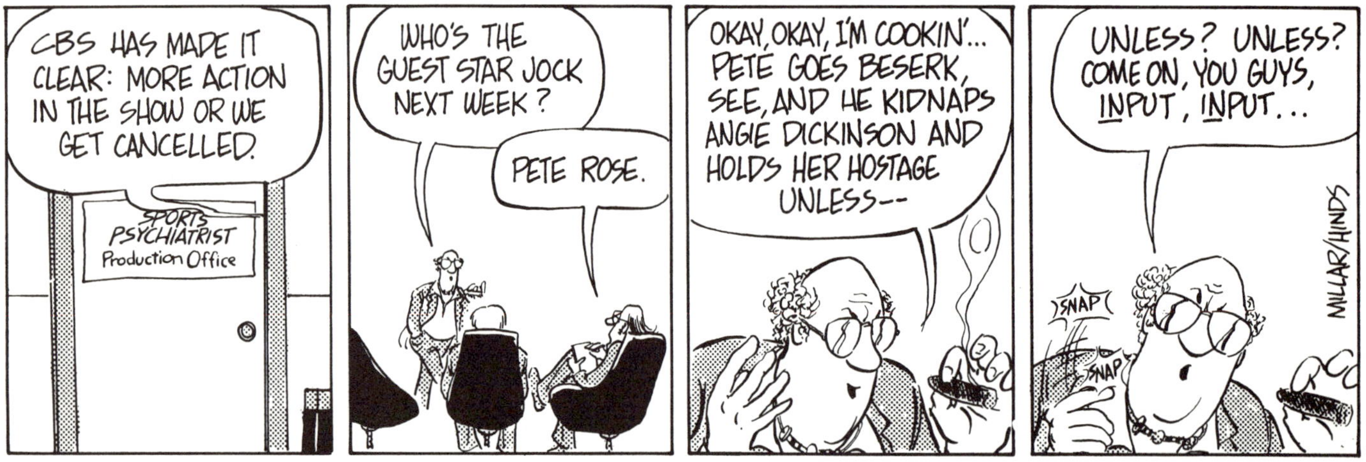
CBS HAS MADE IT CLEAR: MORE ACTION IN THE SHOW OR WE GET CANCELLED.
SPORTS PSYCHIATRIST Production Office
WHO'S THE GUEST STAR JOCK NEXT WEEK?
PETE ROSE.
OKAY, OKAY, I'M COOKIN'... PETE GOES BESERK, SEE, AND HE KIDNAPS ANGIE DICKINSON AND HOLDS HER HOSTAGE UNLESS--
UNLESS? UNLESS? COME ON, YOU GUYS, INPUT, INPUT...
SNAP
SNAP
MILLAR/HINDS

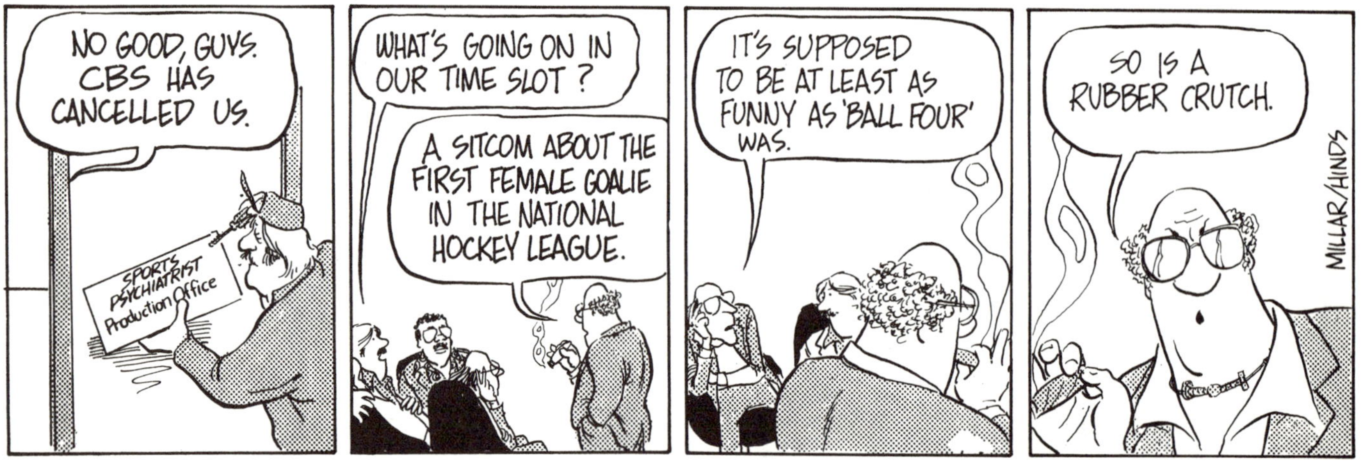
NO GOOD, GUYS. CBS HAS CANCELLED US.
SPORTS PSYCHIATRIST Production Office
WHAT'S GOING ON IN OUR TIME SLOT?
A SITCOM ABOUT THE FIRST FEMALE GOALIE IN THE NATIONAL HOCKEY LEAGUE.
IT'S SUPPOSED TO BE AT LEAST AS FUNNY AS 'BALL FOUR' WAS.
SO IS A RUBBER CRUTCH.
MILLAR/HINDS

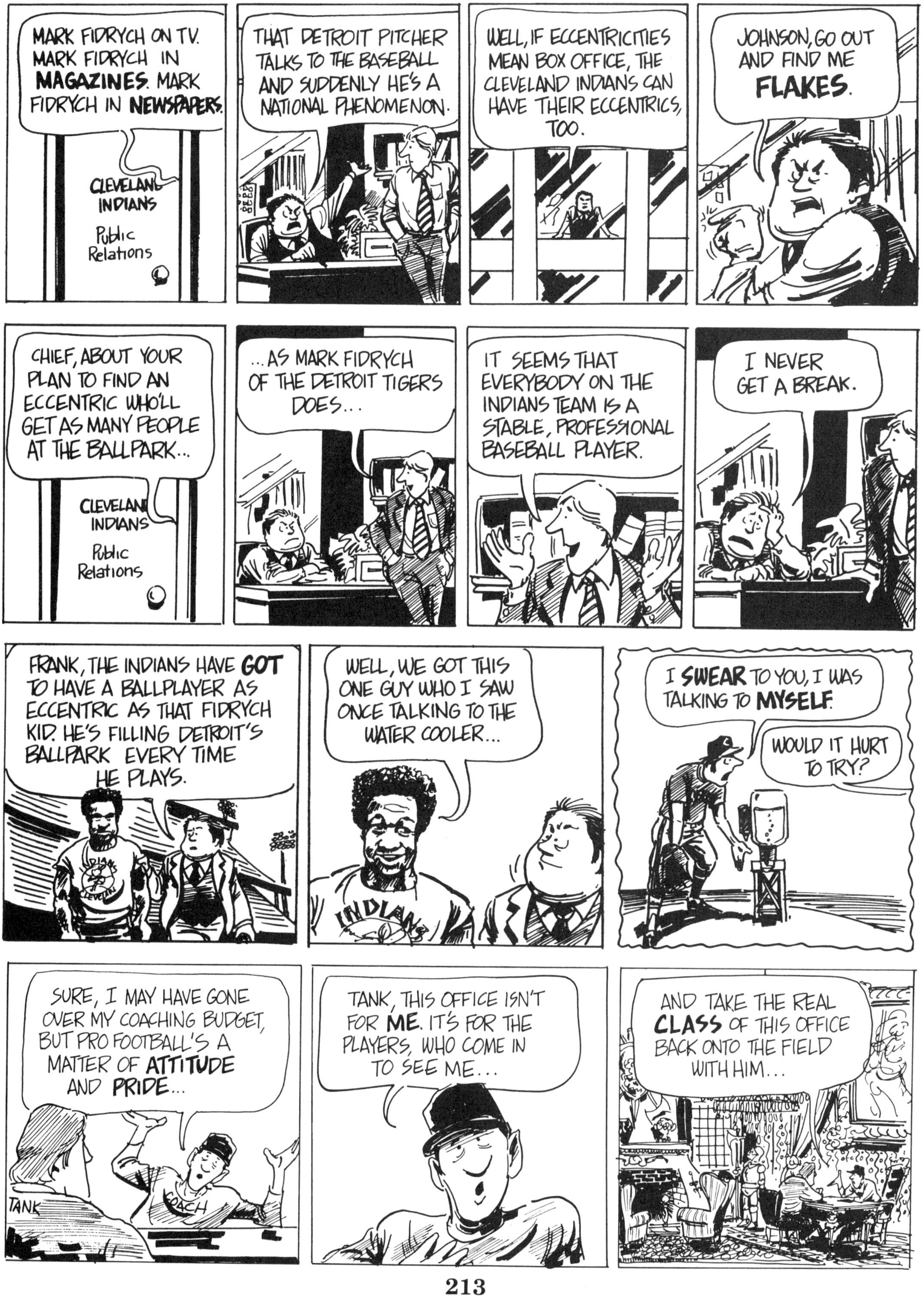
MARK FIDRYCH ON T.V. MARK FIDRYCH IN MAGAZINES. MARK FIDRYCH IN NEWSPAPERS.
CLEVELAND INDIANS
Public Relations
THAT DETROIT PITCHER TALKS TO THE BASEBALL AND SUDDENLY HE'S A NATIONAL PHENOMENON.
WELL, IF ECCENTRICITIES MEAN BOX OFFICE, THE CLEVELAND INDIANS CAN HAVE THEIR ECCENTRICS, TOO.
JOHNSON, GO OUT AND FIND ME FLAKES.
CHIEF, ABOUT YOUR PLAN TO FIND AN ECCENTRIC WHO'LL GET AS MANY PEOPLE AT THE BALLPARK...
CLEVELAND INDIANS
Public Relations
...AS MARK FIDRYCH OF THE DETROIT TIGERS DOES...
IT SEEMS THAT EVERYBODY ON THE INDIANS TEAM IS A STABLE, PROFESSIONAL BASEBALL PLAYER.
I NEVER GET A BREAK.
FRANK, THE INDIANS HAVE GOT TO HAVE A BALLPLAYER AS ECCENTRIC AS THAT FIDRYCH KID. HE'S FILLING DETROIT'S BALLPARK EVERY TIME HE PLAYS.
WELL, WE GOT THIS ONE GUY WHO I SAW ONCE TALKING TO THE WATER COOLER...
INDIANS
I SWEAR TO YOU, I WAS TALKING TO MYSELF.
WOULD IT HURT TO TRY?
SURE, I MAY HAVE GONE OVER MY COACHING BUDGET, BUT PRO FOOTBALL'S A MATTER OF ATTITUDE AND PRIDE...
TANK
COACH
TANK, THIS OFFICE ISN'T FOR ME. IT'S FOR THE PLAYERS, WHO COME IN TO SEE ME...
AND TAKE THE REAL CLASS OF THIS OFFICE BACK ONTO THE FIELD WITH HIM...

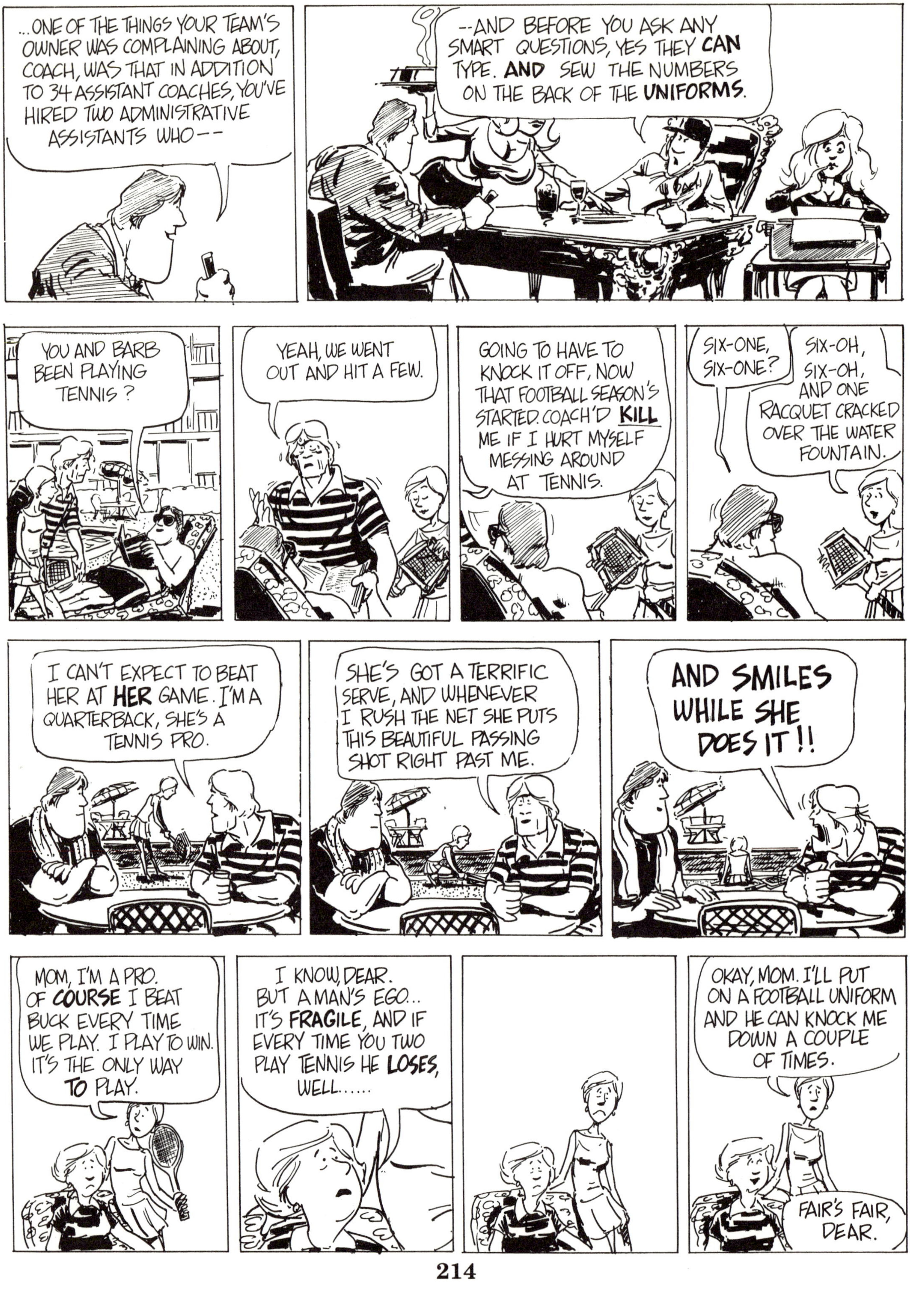
...ONE OF THE THINGS YOUR TEAM'S OWNER WAS COMPLAINING ABOUT, COACH, WAS THAT IN ADDITION TO 34 ASSISTANT COACHES, YOU'VE HIRED TWO ADMINISTRATIVE ASSISTANTS WHO--
--AND BEFORE YOU ASK ANY SMART QUESTIONS, YES THEY **CAN** TYPE. **AND** SEW THE NUMBERS ON THE BACK OF THE **UNIFORMS**.
YOU AND BARB BEEN PLAYING TENNIS ?
YEAH, WE WENT OUT AND HIT A FEW.
GOING TO HAVE TO KNOCK IT OFF, NOW THAT FOOTBALL SEASON'S STARTED. COACH'D **KILL** ME IF I HURT MYSELF MESSING AROUND AT TENNIS.
SIX-ONE, SIX-ONE?
SIX-OH, SIX-OH, AND ONE RACQUET CRACKED OVER THE WATER FOUNTAIN.
I CAN'T EXPECT TO BEAT HER AT **HER** GAME. I'M A QUARTERBACK, SHE'S A TENNIS PRO.
SHE'S GOT A TERRIFIC SERVE, AND WHENEVER I RUSH THE NET SHE PUTS THIS BEAUTIFUL PASSING SHOT RIGHT PAST ME.
AND SMILES WHILE SHE DOES IT !!
MOM, I'M A PRO. OF **COURSE** I BEAT BUCK EVERY TIME WE PLAY. I PLAY TO WIN. IT'S THE ONLY WAY **TO** PLAY.
I KNOW, DEAR. BUT A MAN'S EGO... IT'S **FRAGILE**, AND IF EVERY TIME YOU TWO PLAY TENNIS HE **LOSES**, WELL......
OKAY, MOM. I'LL PUT ON A FOOTBALL UNIFORM AND HE CAN KNOCK ME DOWN A COUPLE OF TIMES.
FAIR'S FAIR, DEAR.

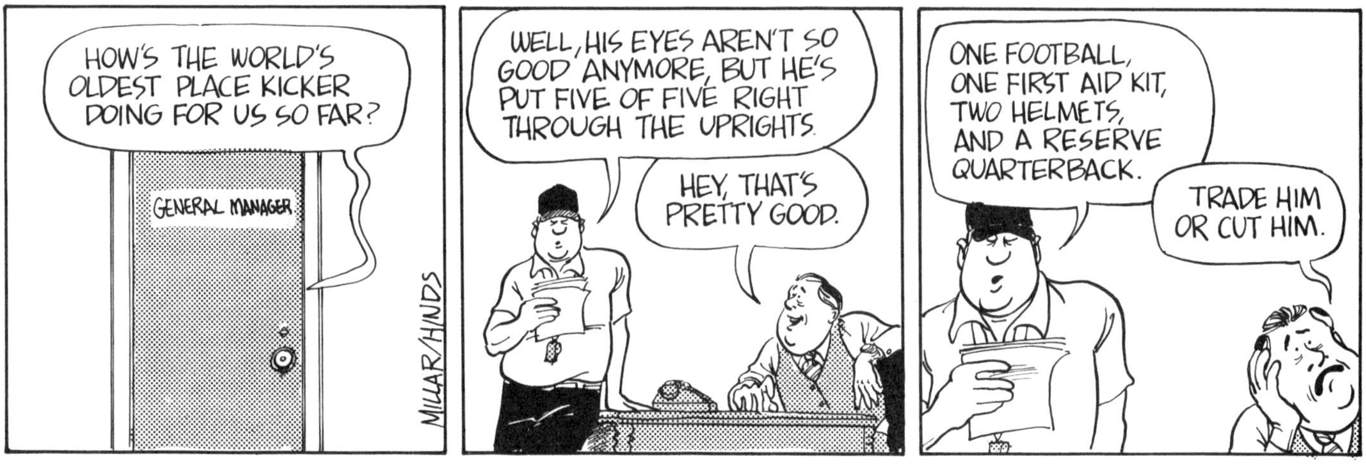
HOW'S THE WORLD'S OLDEST PLACE KICKER DOING FOR US SO FAR?
GENERAL MANAGER
MILLAR/HINDS
WELL, HIS EYES AREN'T SO GOOD ANYMORE, BUT HE'S PUT FIVE OF FIVE RIGHT THROUGH THE UPRIGHTS.
HEY, THAT'S PRETTY GOOD.
ONE FOOTBALL, ONE FIRST AID KIT, TWO HELMETS, AND A RESERVE QUARTERBACK.
TRADE HIM OR CUT HIM.

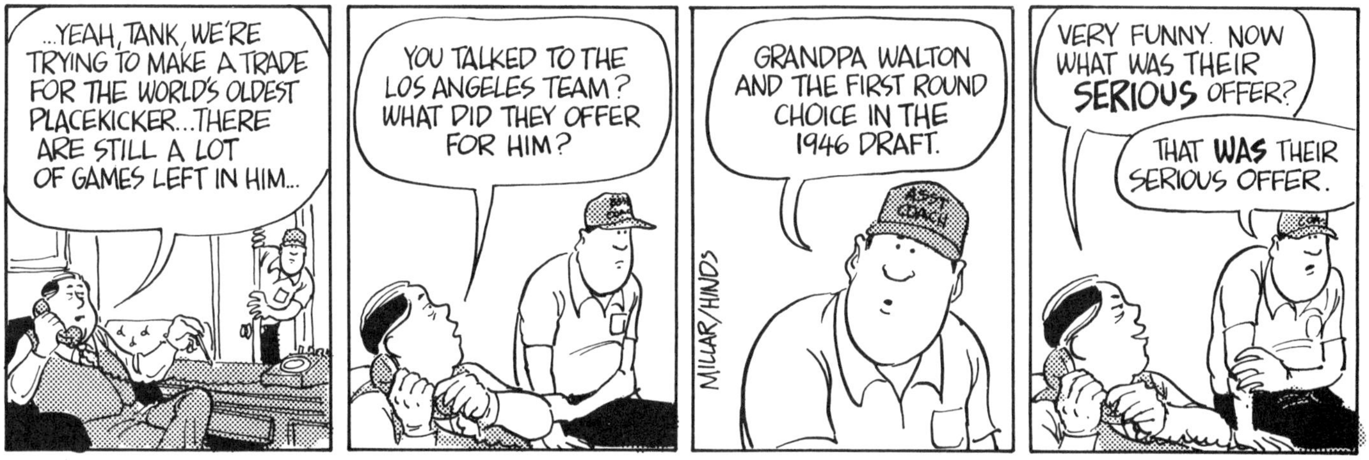
...YEAH, TANK, WE'RE TRYING TO MAKE A TRADE FOR THE WORLD'S OLDEST PLACEKICKER...THERE ARE STILL A LOT OF GAMES LEFT IN HIM...
YOU TALKED TO THE LOS ANGELES TEAM? WHAT DID THEY OFFER FOR HIM?
MILLAR/HINDS
GRANDPA WALTON AND THE FIRST ROUND CHOICE IN THE 1946 DRAFT.
ASST COACH
VERY FUNNY. NOW WHAT WAS THEIR **SERIOUS** OFFER?
THAT **WAS** THEIR SERIOUS OFFER.

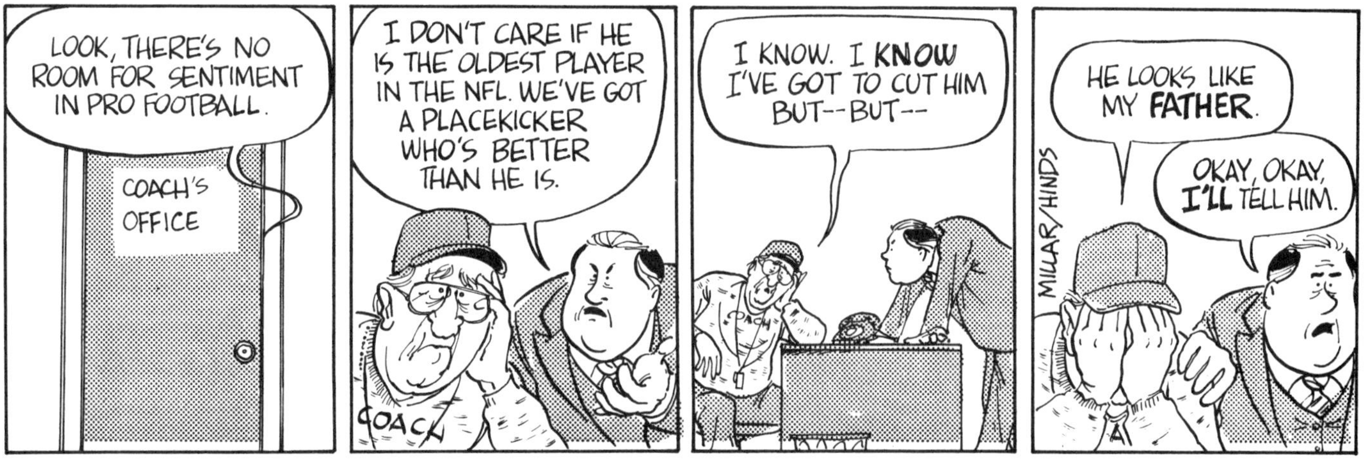
LOOK, THERE'S NO ROOM FOR SENTIMENT IN PRO FOOTBALL.
COACH'S OFFICE
I DON'T CARE IF HE IS THE OLDEST PLAYER IN THE NFL. WE'VE GOT A PLACEKICKER WHO'S BETTER THAN HE IS.
COACH
I KNOW. I **KNOW** I'VE GOT TO CUT HIM BUT--BUT--
MILLAR/HINDS
HE LOOKS LIKE MY **FATHER**.
OKAY, OKAY, **I'LL** TELL HIM.

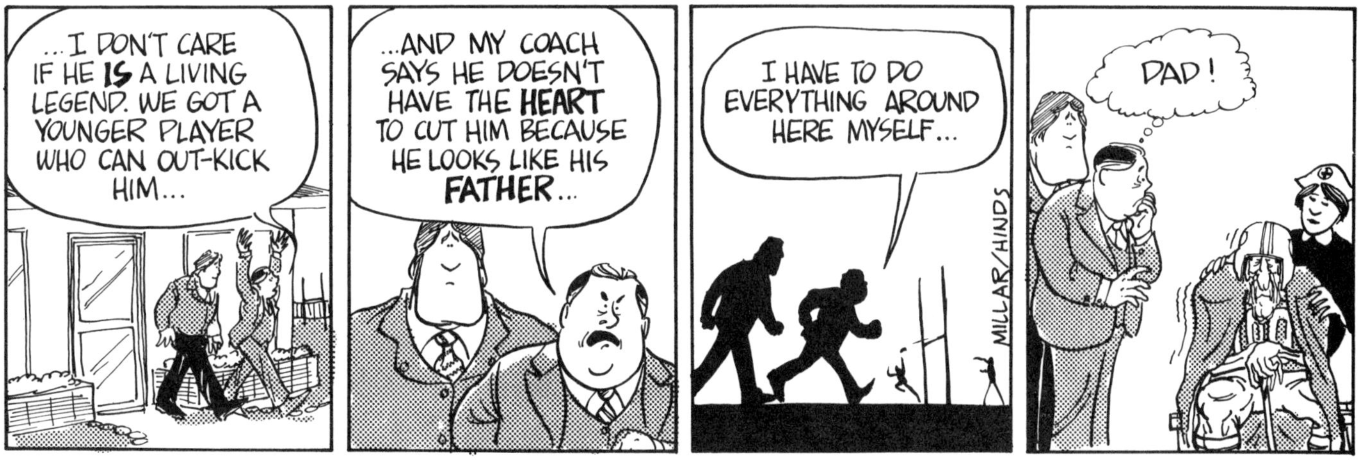
...I DON'T CARE IF HE **IS** A LIVING LEGEND. WE GOT A YOUNGER PLAYER WHO CAN OUT-KICK HIM...
...AND MY COACH SAYS HE DOESN'T HAVE THE **HEART** TO CUT HIM BECAUSE HE LOOKS LIKE HIS **FATHER**...
I HAVE TO DO EVERYTHING AROUND HERE MYSELF...
MILLAR/HINDS
DAD!

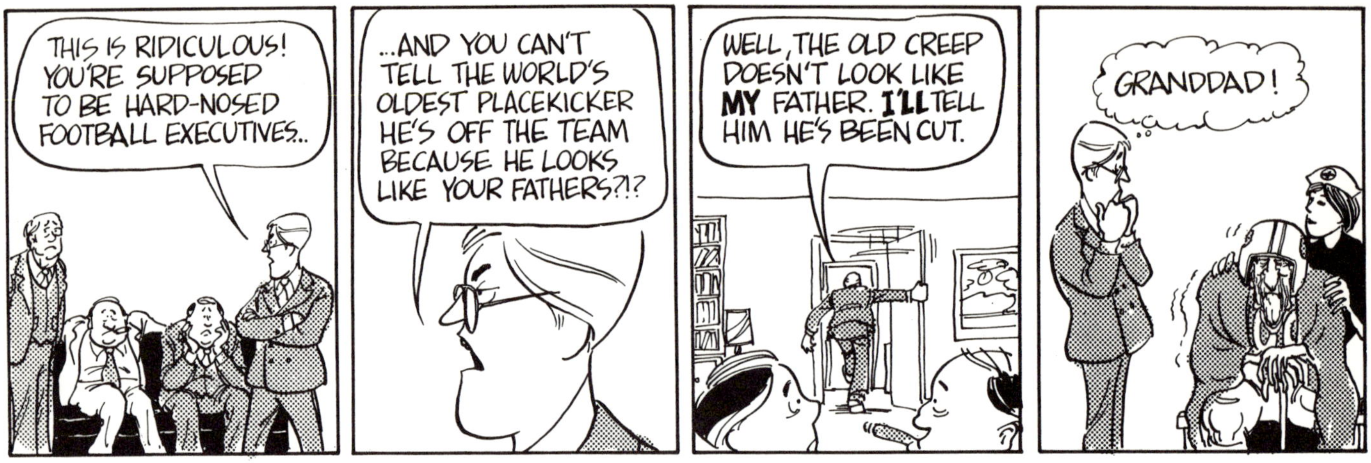
THIS IS RIDICULOUS! YOU'RE SUPPOSED TO BE HARD-NOSED FOOTBALL EXECUTIVES..
...AND YOU CAN'T TELL THE WORLD'S OLDEST PLACEKICKER HE'S OFF THE TEAM BECAUSE HE LOOKS LIKE YOUR FATHERS?!?
WELL, THE OLD CREEP DOESN'T LOOK LIKE **MY** FATHER. **I'LL** TELL HIM HE'S BEEN CUT.
GRANDDAD!

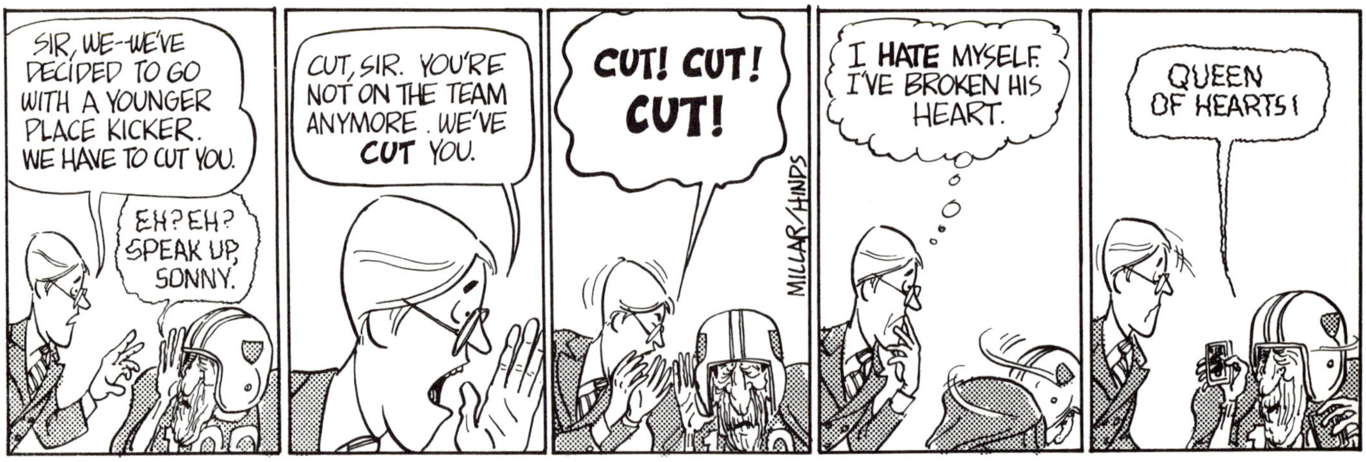
SIR, WE--WE'VE DECIDED TO GO WITH A YOUNGER PLACE KICKER. WE HAVE TO CUT YOU.
EH? EH? SPEAK UP, SONNY.
CUT, SIR. YOU'RE NOT ON THE TEAM ANYMORE. WE'VE **CUT** YOU.
CUT! CUT! CUT!
MILLAR/HINDS
I **HATE** MYSELF. I'VE BROKEN HIS HEART.
QUEEN OF HEARTS!

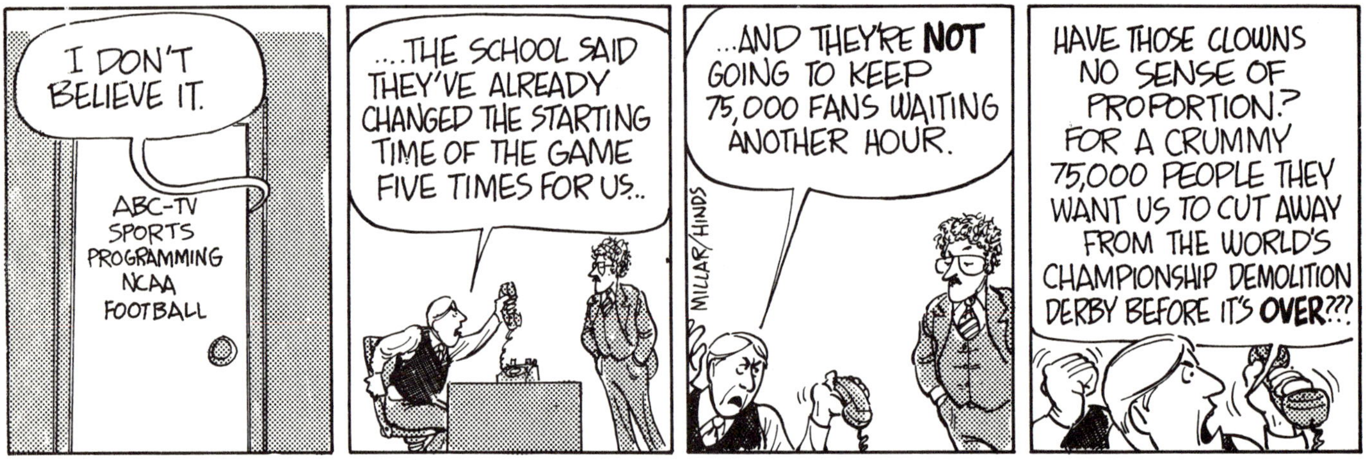
I DON'T BELIEVE IT.
ABC-TV SPORTS PROGRAMMING NCAA FOOTBALL
....THE SCHOOL SAID THEY'VE ALREADY CHANGED THE STARTING TIME OF THE GAME FIVE TIMES FOR US..
MILLAR/HINDS
...AND THEY'RE **NOT** GOING TO KEEP 75,000 FANS WAITING ANOTHER HOUR.
HAVE THOSE CLOWNS NO SENSE OF PROPORTION? FOR A CRUMMY 75,000 PEOPLE THEY WANT US TO CUT AWAY FROM THE WORLD'S CHAMPIONSHIP DEMOLITION DERBY BEFORE IT'S **OVER**???

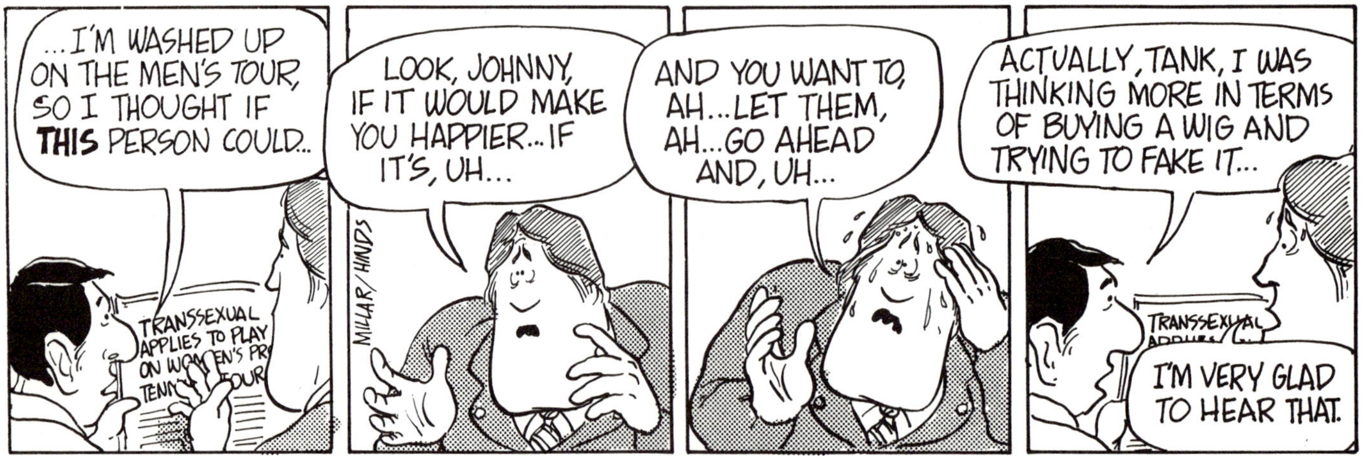
...I'M WASHED UP ON THE MEN'S TOUR, SO I THOUGHT IF **THIS** PERSON COULD...
TRANSSEXUAL APPLIES TO PLAY
LOOK, JOHNNY, IF IT WOULD MAKE YOU HAPPIER...IF IT'S, UH...
MILLAR/HINDS
AND YOU WANT TO, AH...LET THEM, AH...GO AHEAD AND, UH...
ACTUALLY, TANK, I WAS THINKING MORE IN TERMS OF BUYING A WIG AND TRYING TO FAKE IT...
TRANSSEXUAL
I'M VERY GLAD TO HEAR THAT.

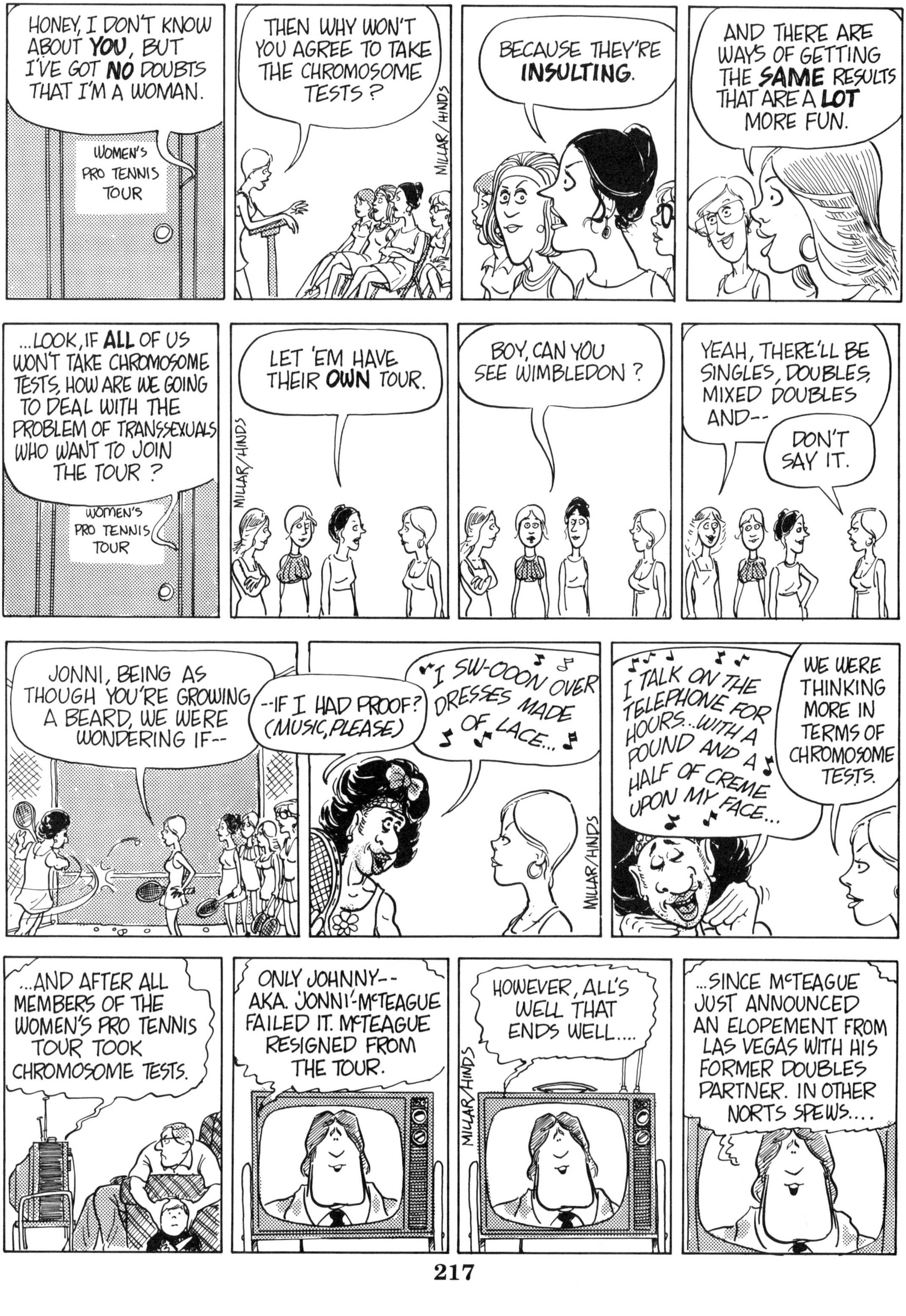
HONEY, I DON'T KNOW ABOUT **YOU**, BUT I'VE GOT **NO** DOUBTS THAT I'M A WOMAN.
WOMEN'S PRO TENNIS TOUR
THEN WHY WON'T YOU AGREE TO TAKE THE CHROMOSOME TESTS?
MILLAR/HINDS
BECAUSE THEY'RE **INSULTING**.
AND THERE ARE WAYS OF GETTING THE **SAME** RESULTS THAT ARE A **LOT** MORE FUN.
...LOOK, IF **ALL** OF US WON'T TAKE CHROMOSOME TESTS, HOW ARE WE GOING TO DEAL WITH THE PROBLEM OF TRANSSEXUALS WHO WANT TO JOIN THE TOUR?
WOMEN'S PRO TENNIS TOUR
MILLAR/HINDS
LET 'EM HAVE THEIR **OWN** TOUR.
BOY, CAN YOU SEE WIMBLEDON?
YEAH, THERE'LL BE SINGLES, DOUBLES, MIXED DOUBLES AND--
DON'T SAY IT.
JONNI, BEING AS THOUGH YOU'RE GROWING A BEARD, WE WERE WONDERING IF--
--IF I HAD PROOF? (MUSIC, PLEASE)
I SW-OOON OVER DRESSES MADE OF LACE...
MILLAR/HINDS
I TALK ON THE TELEPHONE FOR HOURS...WITH A POUND AND A HALF OF CREME UPON MY FACE...
WE WERE THINKING MORE IN TERMS OF CHROMOSOME TESTS.
...AND AFTER ALL MEMBERS OF THE WOMEN'S PRO TENNIS TOUR TOOK CHROMOSOME TESTS.
ONLY JOHNNY--AKA. 'JONNI'-McTEAGUE FAILED IT. McTEAGUE RESIGNED FROM THE TOUR.
MILLAR/HINDS
HOWEVER, ALL'S WELL THAT ENDS WELL....
...SINCE McTEAGUE JUST ANNOUNCED AN ELOPEMENT FROM LAS VEGAS WITH HIS FORMER DOUBLES PARTNER. IN OTHER NORTS SPEWS....

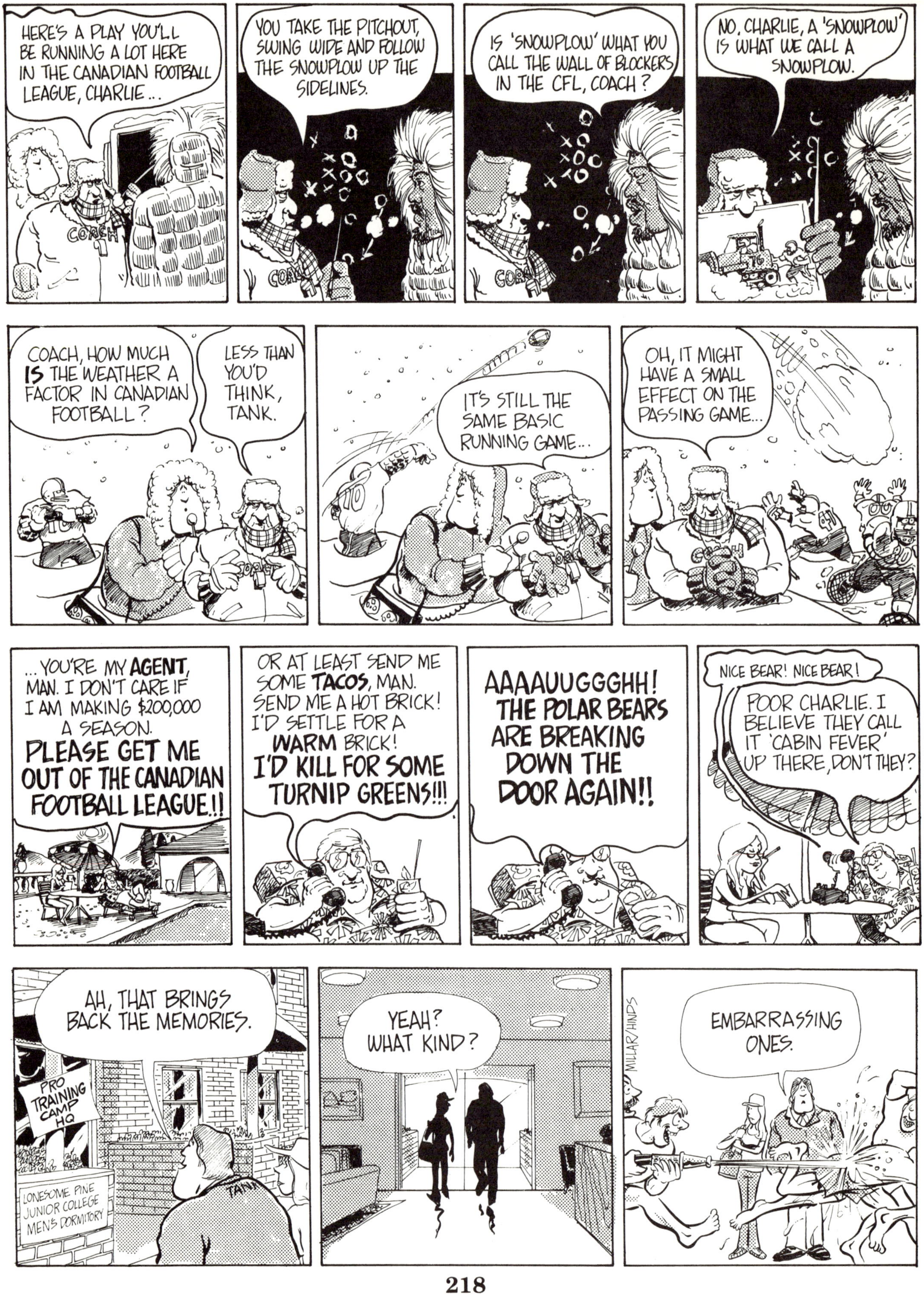
HERE'S A PLAY YOU'LL BE RUNNING A LOT HERE IN THE CANADIAN FOOTBALL LEAGUE, CHARLIE...
COACH
YOU TAKE THE PITCHOUT, SWING WIDE AND FOLLOW THE SNOWPLOW UP THE SIDELINES.
IS 'SNOWPLOW' WHAT YOU CALL THE WALL OF BLOCKERS IN THE CFL, COACH?
NO, CHARLIE, A 'SNOWPLOW' IS WHAT WE CALL A SNOWPLOW.
COACH, HOW MUCH **IS** THE WEATHER A FACTOR IN CANADIAN FOOTBALL?
LESS THAN YOU'D THINK, TANK.
IT'S STILL THE SAME BASIC RUNNING GAME...
OH, IT MIGHT HAVE A SMALL EFFECT ON THE PASSING GAME...
COACH
...YOU'RE MY **AGENT**, MAN. I DON'T CARE IF I AM MAKING $200,000 A SEASON.
PLEASE GET ME OUT OF THE CANADIAN FOOTBALL LEAGUE!!
OR AT LEAST SEND ME SOME **TACOS**, MAN. SEND ME A HOT BRICK! I'D SETTLE FOR A **WARM** BRICK!
I'D KILL FOR SOME TURNIP GREENS!!!
AAAAUUGGGHH! THE POLAR BEARS ARE BREAKING DOWN THE DOOR AGAIN!!
NICE BEAR! NICE BEAR!
POOR CHARLIE. I BELIEVE THEY CALL IT 'CABIN FEVER' UP THERE, DON'T THEY?
AH, THAT BRINGS BACK THE MEMORIES.
PRO TRAINING CAMP HQ
LONESOME PINE JUNIOR COLLEGE MEN'S DORMITORY
TANK
YEAH? WHAT KIND?
MILLAR/HINDS
EMBARRASSING ONES.

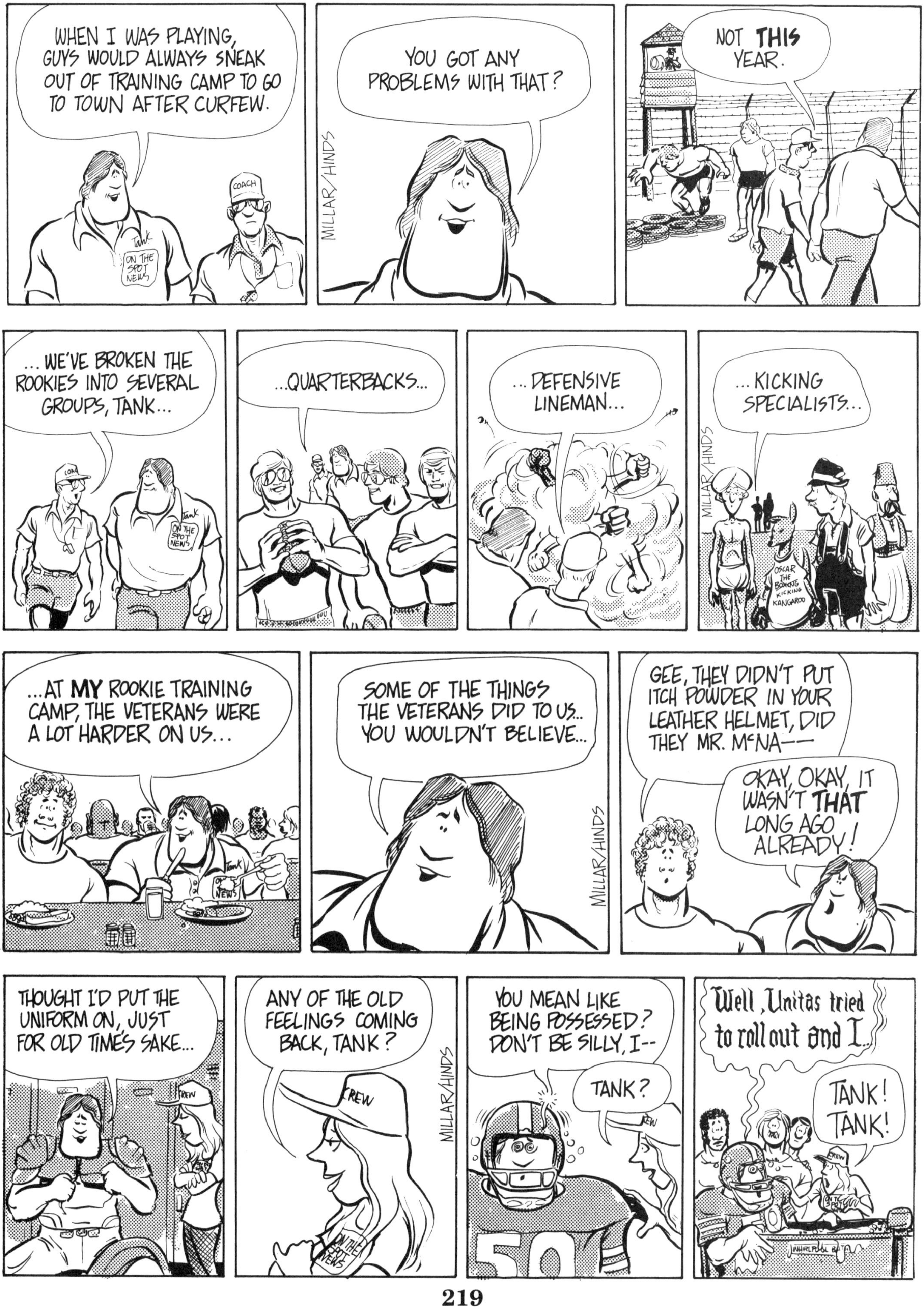
WHEN I WAS PLAYING, GUYS WOULD ALWAYS SNEAK OUT OF TRAINING CAMP TO GO TO TOWN AFTER CURFEW.
TANK
ON THE SPOT NEWS
COACH
MILLAR/HINDS
YOU GOT ANY PROBLEMS WITH THAT?
NOT THIS YEAR.
... WE'VE BROKEN THE ROOKIES INTO SEVERAL GROUPS, TANK...
...QUARTERBACKS...
... DEFENSIVE LINEMAN...
MILLAR/HINDS
... KICKING SPECIALISTS...
OSCAR THE BOXING KICKING KANGAROO
...AT MY ROOKIE TRAINING CAMP, THE VETERANS WERE A LOT HARDER ON US...
SOME OF THE THINGS THE VETERANS DID TO US.. YOU WOULDN'T BELIEVE...
MILLAR/HINDS
GEE, THEY DIDN'T PUT ITCH POWDER IN YOUR LEATHER HELMET, DID THEY MR. McNA--
OKAY, OKAY, IT WASN'T THAT LONG AGO ALREADY!
THOUGHT I'D PUT THE UNIFORM ON, JUST FOR OLD TIME'S SAKE...
CREW
ANY OF THE OLD FEELINGS COMING BACK, TANK?
MILLAR/HINDS
YOU MEAN LIKE BEING POSSESSED? DON'T BE SILLY, I--
TANK?
50
Well, Unitas tried to roll out and I...
TANK! TANK!
WHIRLPOOL BATH

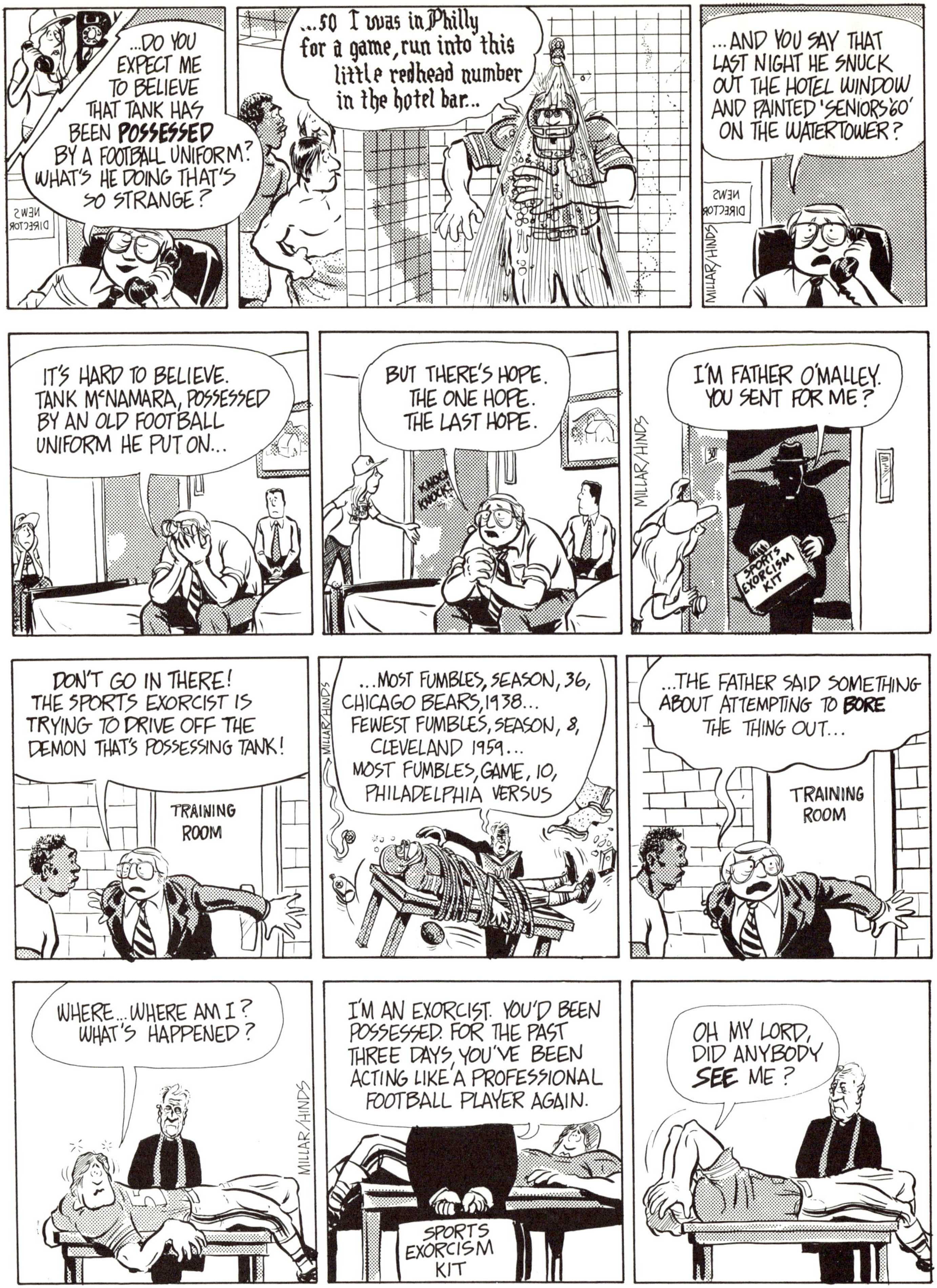
...DO YOU EXPECT ME TO BELIEVE THAT TANK HAS BEEN POSSESSED BY A FOOTBALL UNIFORM? WHAT'S HE DOING THAT'S SO STRANGE?
NEWS DIRECTOR
...SO I was in Philly for a game, run into this little redhead number in the hotel bar...
...AND YOU SAY THAT LAST NIGHT HE SNUCK OUT THE HOTEL WINDOW AND PAINTED 'SENIORS '60' ON THE WATERTOWER?
NEWS DIRECTOR
MILLAR/HINDS
IT'S HARD TO BELIEVE. TANK McNAMARA, POSSESSED BY AN OLD FOOTBALL UNIFORM HE PUT ON...
BUT THERE'S HOPE. THE ONE HOPE. THE LAST HOPE.
KNOCK KNOCK!
I'M FATHER O'MALLEY. YOU SENT FOR ME?
MILLAR/HINDS
SPORTS EXORCISM KIT
DON'T GO IN THERE! THE SPORTS EXORCIST IS TRYING TO DRIVE OFF THE DEMON THAT'S POSSESSING TANK!
TRAINING ROOM
MILLAR/HINDS
...MOST FUMBLES, SEASON, 36, CHICAGO BEARS, 1938... FEWEST FUMBLES, SEASON, 8, CLEVELAND 1959... MOST FUMBLES, GAME, 10, PHILADELPHIA VERSUS
...THE FATHER SAID SOMETHING ABOUT ATTEMPTING TO BORE THE THING OUT...
TRAINING ROOM
WHERE...WHERE AM I? WHAT'S HAPPENED?
MILLAR/HINDS
I'M AN EXORCIST. YOU'D BEEN POSSESSED. FOR THE PAST THREE DAYS, YOU'VE BEEN ACTING LIKE A PROFESSIONAL FOOTBALL PLAYER AGAIN.
SPORTS EXORCISM KIT
OH MY LORD, DID ANYBODY SEE ME?

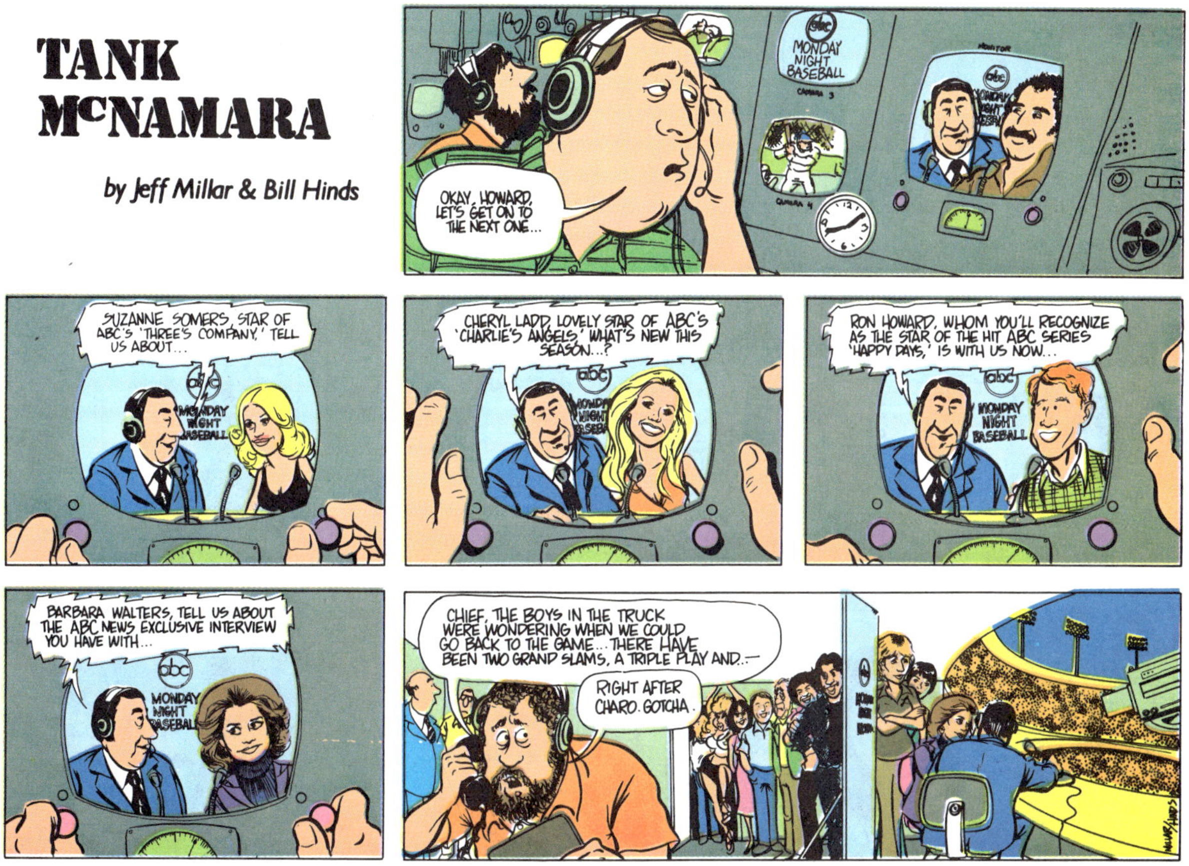
TANK McNAMARA
by Jeff Millar & Bill Hinds
MONDAY NIGHT BASEBALL
OKAY, HOWARD, LET'S GET ON TO THE NEXT ONE...
SUZANNE SOMERS, STAR OF ABC'S 'THREE'S COMPANY,' TELL US ABOUT...
CHERYL LADD, LOVELY STAR OF ABC'S 'CHARLIE'S ANGELS,' WHAT'S NEW THIS SEASON...?
RON HOWARD, WHOM YOU'LL RECOGNIZE AS THE STAR OF THE HIT ABC SERIES 'HAPPY DAYS,' IS WITH US NOW...
BARBARA WALTERS, TELL US ABOUT THE ABC NEWS EXCLUSIVE INTERVIEW YOU HAVE WITH...
CHIEF, THE BOYS IN THE TRUCK WERE WONDERING WHEN WE COULD GO BACK TO THE GAME... THERE HAVE BEEN TWO GRAND SLAMS, A TRIPLE PLAY AND...
RIGHT AFTER CHARO. GOTCHA.

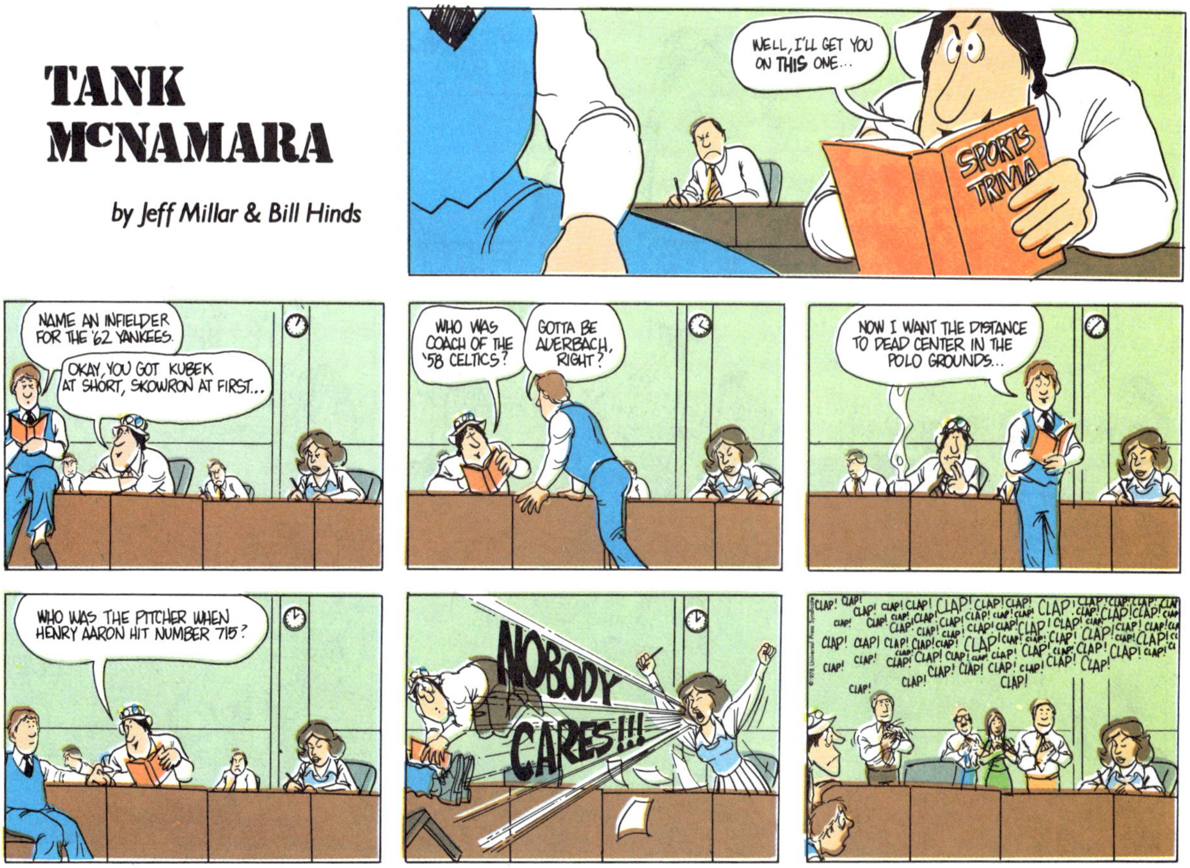
TANK McNAMARA
by Jeff Millar & Bill Hinds
WELL, I'LL GET YOU ON THIS ONE...
SPORTS TRIVIA
NAME AN INFIELDER FOR THE '62 YANKEES.
OKAY, YOU GOT KUBEK AT SHORT, SKOWRON AT FIRST...
WHO WAS COACH OF THE '58 CELTICS?
GOTTA BE AUERBACH, RIGHT?
NOW I WANT THE DISTANCE TO DEAD CENTER IN THE POLO GROUNDS...
WHO WAS THE PITCHER WHEN HENRY AARON HIT NUMBER 715?
NOBODY CARES!!!
CLAP! CLAP! CLAP! CLAP! CLAP! CLAP! CLAP! CLAP!

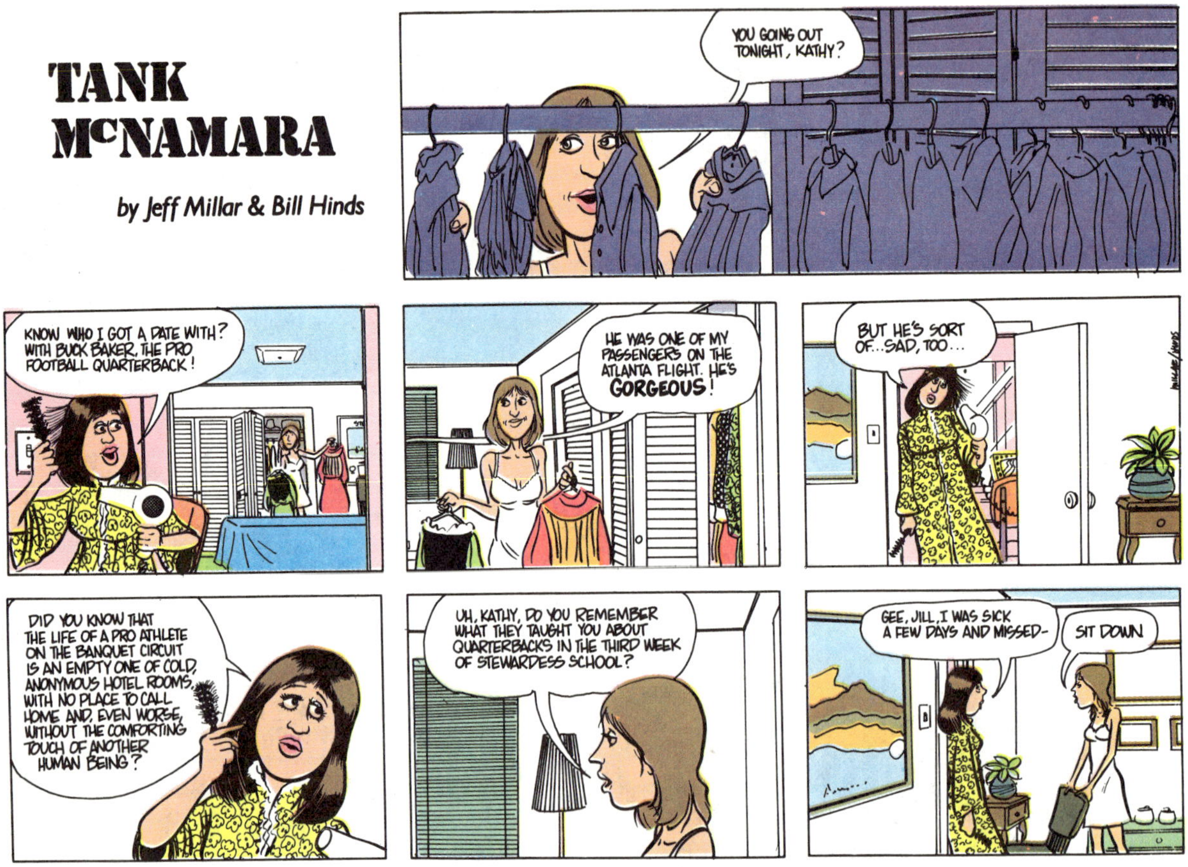
TANK McNAMARA
by Jeff Millar & Bill Hinds
YOU GOING OUT TONIGHT, KATHY?
KNOW WHO I GOT A DATE WITH? WITH BUCK BAKER, THE PRO FOOTBALL QUARTERBACK!
HE WAS ONE OF MY PASSENGERS ON THE ATLANTA FLIGHT. HE'S GORGEOUS!
BUT HE'S SORT OF... SAD, TOO...
DID YOU KNOW THAT THE LIFE OF A PRO ATHLETE ON THE BANQUET CIRCUIT IS AN EMPTY ONE OF COLD, ANONYMOUS HOTEL ROOMS, WITH NO PLACE TO CALL HOME AND, EVEN WORSE, WITHOUT THE COMFORTING TOUCH OF ANOTHER HUMAN BEING?
UH, KATHY, DO YOU REMEMBER WHAT THEY TAUGHT YOU ABOUT QUARTERBACKS IN THE THIRD WEEK OF STEWARDESS SCHOOL?
GEE, JILL, I WAS SICK A FEW DAYS AND MISSED–
SIT DOWN.

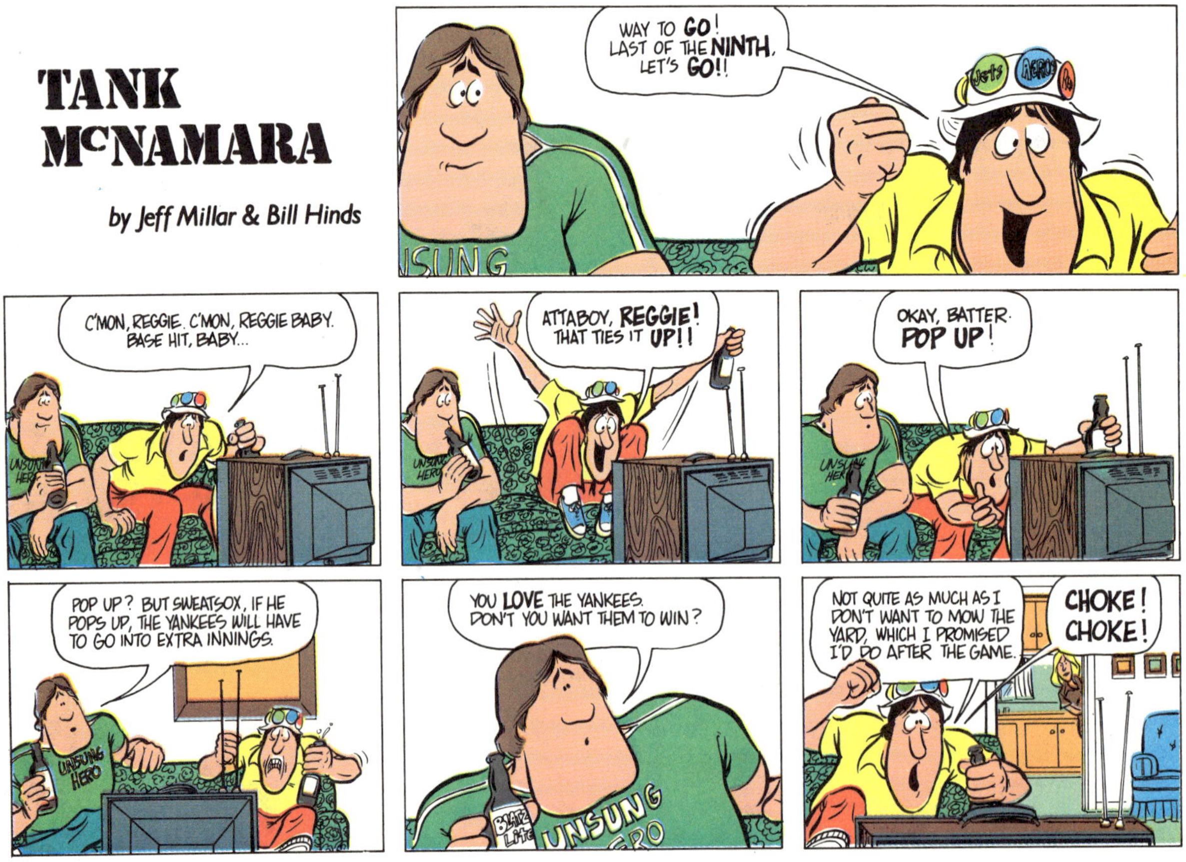
TANK McNAMARA
by Jeff Millar & Bill Hinds
WAY TO GO! LAST OF THE NINTH, LET'S GO!!
C'MON, REGGIE.. C'MON, REGGIE BABY. BASE HIT, BABY...
ATTABOY, REGGIE! THAT TIES IT UP!!
OKAY, BATTER. POP UP!
POP UP? BUT SWEATSOX, IF HE POPS UP, THE YANKEES WILL HAVE TO GO INTO EXTRA INNINGS.
YOU LOVE THE YANKEES. DON'T YOU WANT THEM TO WIN?
NOT QUITE AS MUCH AS I DON'T WANT TO MOW THE YARD, WHICH I PROMISED I'D DO AFTER THE GAME.
CHOKE! CHOKE!

TANK McNAMARA

by Jeff Millar & Bill Hinds

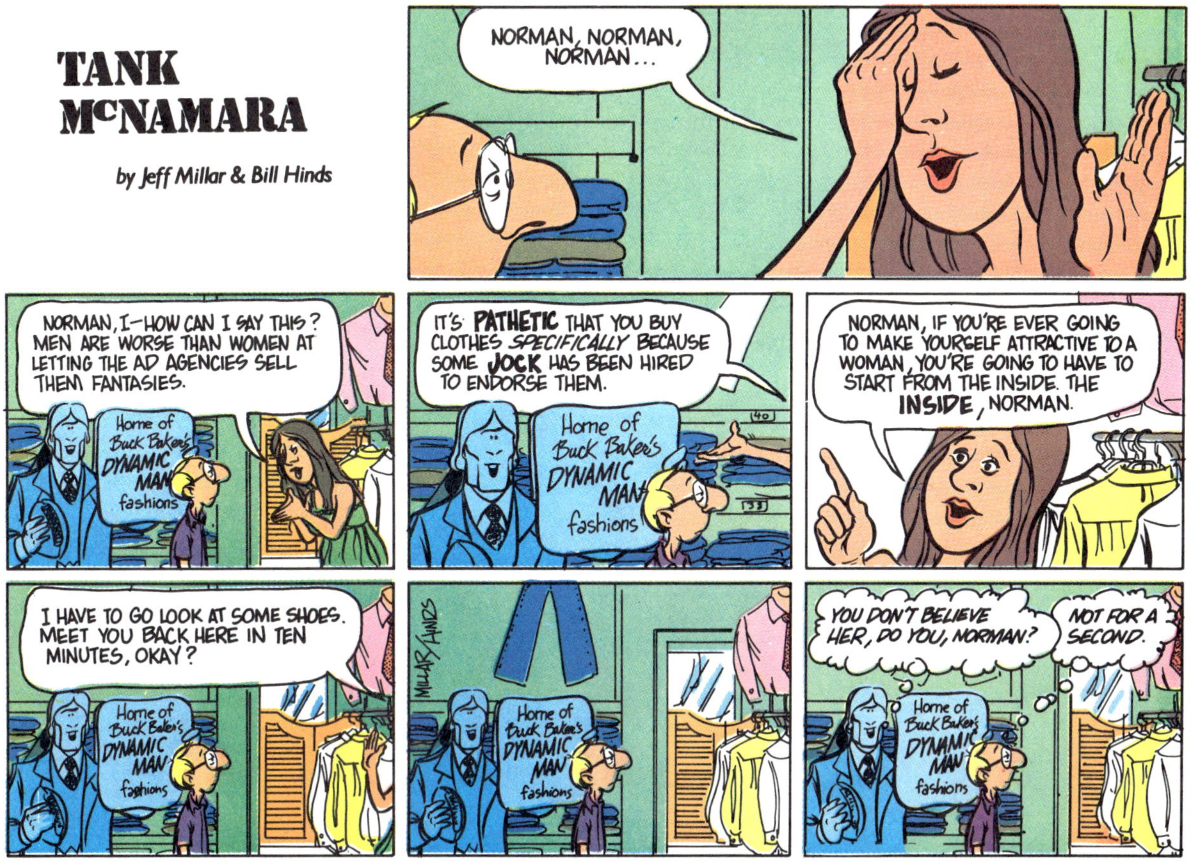
NORMAN, NORMAN, NORMAN...
NORMAN, I—HOW CAN I SAY THIS? MEN ARE WORSE THAN WOMEN AT LETTING THE AD AGENCIES SELL THEM FANTASIES.
Home of Buck Baker's DYNAMIC MAN fashions
IT'S PATHETIC THAT YOU BUY CLOTHES SPECIFICALLY BECAUSE SOME JOCK HAS BEEN HIRED TO ENDORSE THEM.
Home of Buck Baker's DYNAMIC MAN fashions
NORMAN, IF YOU'RE EVER GOING TO MAKE YOURSELF ATTRACTIVE TO A WOMAN, YOU'RE GOING TO HAVE TO START FROM THE INSIDE. THE INSIDE, NORMAN.
I HAVE TO GO LOOK AT SOME SHOES. MEET YOU BACK HERE IN TEN MINUTES, OKAY?
Home of Buck Baker's DYNAMIC MAN fashions
MILLAR / HINDS
Home of Buck Baker's DYNAMIC MAN fashions
YOU DON'T BELIEVE HER, DO YOU, NORMAN?
NOT FOR A SECOND.
Home of Buck Baker's DYNAMIC MAN fashions

TANK McNAMARA

by Jeff Millar & Bill Hinds

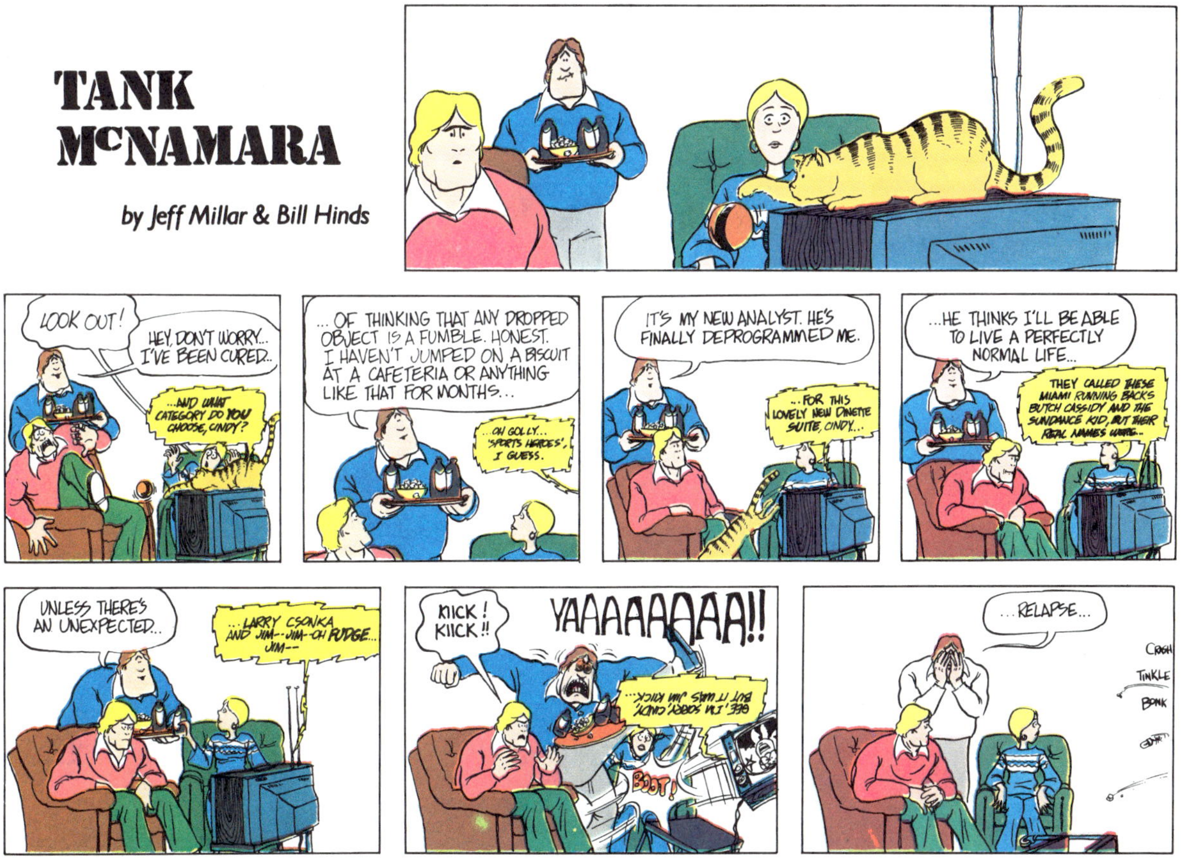
LOOK OUT!
HEY, DON'T WORRY... I'VE BEEN CURED...
...AND WHAT CATEGORY DO YOU CHOOSE, CINDY?
...OF THINKING THAT ANY DROPPED OBJECT IS A FUMBLE. HONEST. I HAVEN'T JUMPED ON A BISCUIT AT A CAFETERIA OR ANYTHING LIKE THAT FOR MONTHS...
...OH GOLLY... 'SPORTS HEROES', I GUESS.
IT'S MY NEW ANALYST. HE'S FINALLY DEPROGRAMMED ME.
...FOR THIS LOVELY NEW DINETTE SUITE, CINDY...
...HE THINKS I'LL BE ABLE TO LIVE A PERFECTLY NORMAL LIFE...
THEY CALLED THESE MIAMI RUNNING BACKS BUTCH CASSIDY AND THE SUNDANCE KID, BUT THEIR REAL NAMES WERE...
UNLESS THERE'S AN UNEXPECTED...
...LARRY CSONKA AND JIM--JIM--OH FUDGE... JIM--
KIICK! KIICK!!
YAAAAAAAA!!
GEE, I'M SORRY, CINDY, BUT IT WAS JIM KIICK...
BOOT!
...RELAPSE...
CRASH
TINKLE
BONK

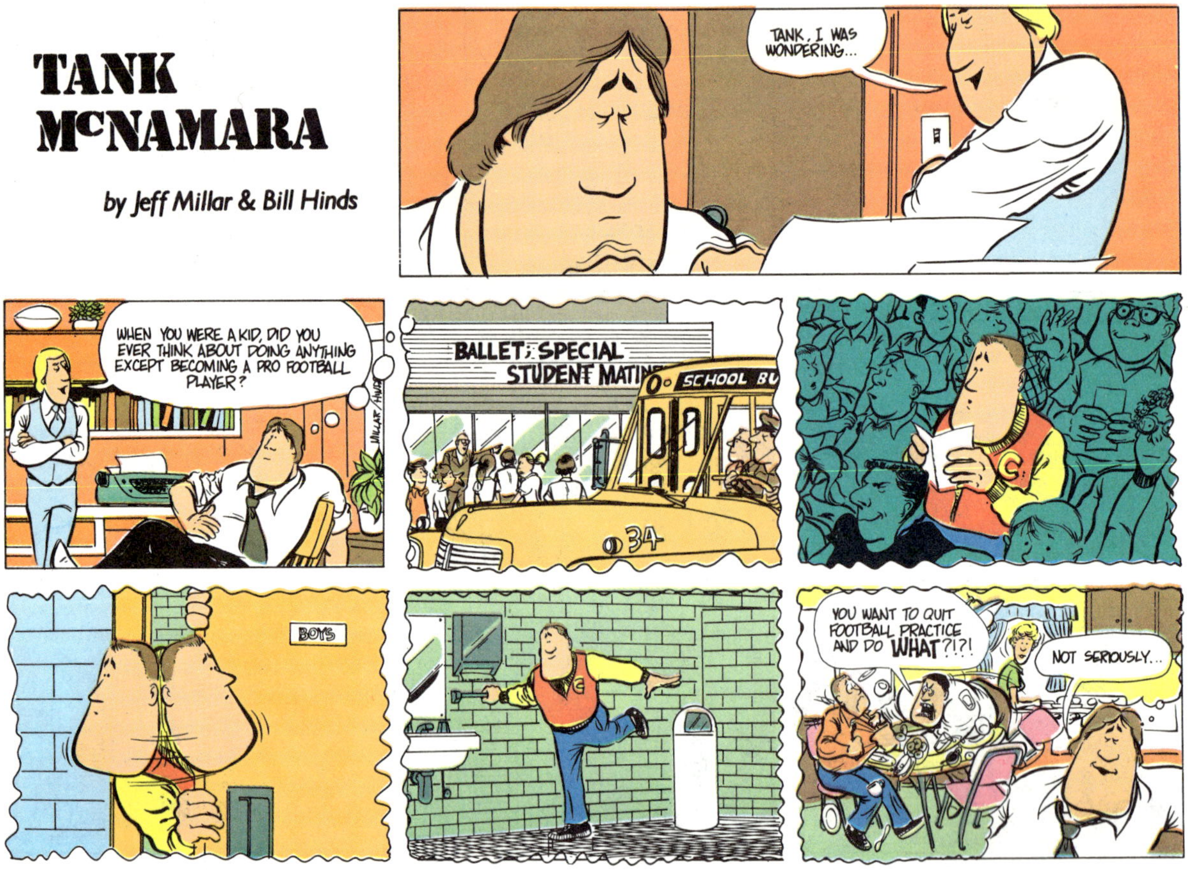
TANK McNAMARA
by Jeff Millar & Bill Hinds
TANK, I WAS WONDERING...
WHEN YOU WERE A KID, DID YOU EVER THINK ABOUT DOING ANYTHING EXCEPT BECOMING A PRO FOOTBALL PLAYER?
BALLET; SPECIAL STUDENT MATIN
SCHOOL BU
34
BOYS
YOU WANT TO QUIT FOOTBALL PRACTICE AND DO WHAT?!?!
NOT SERIOUSLY...

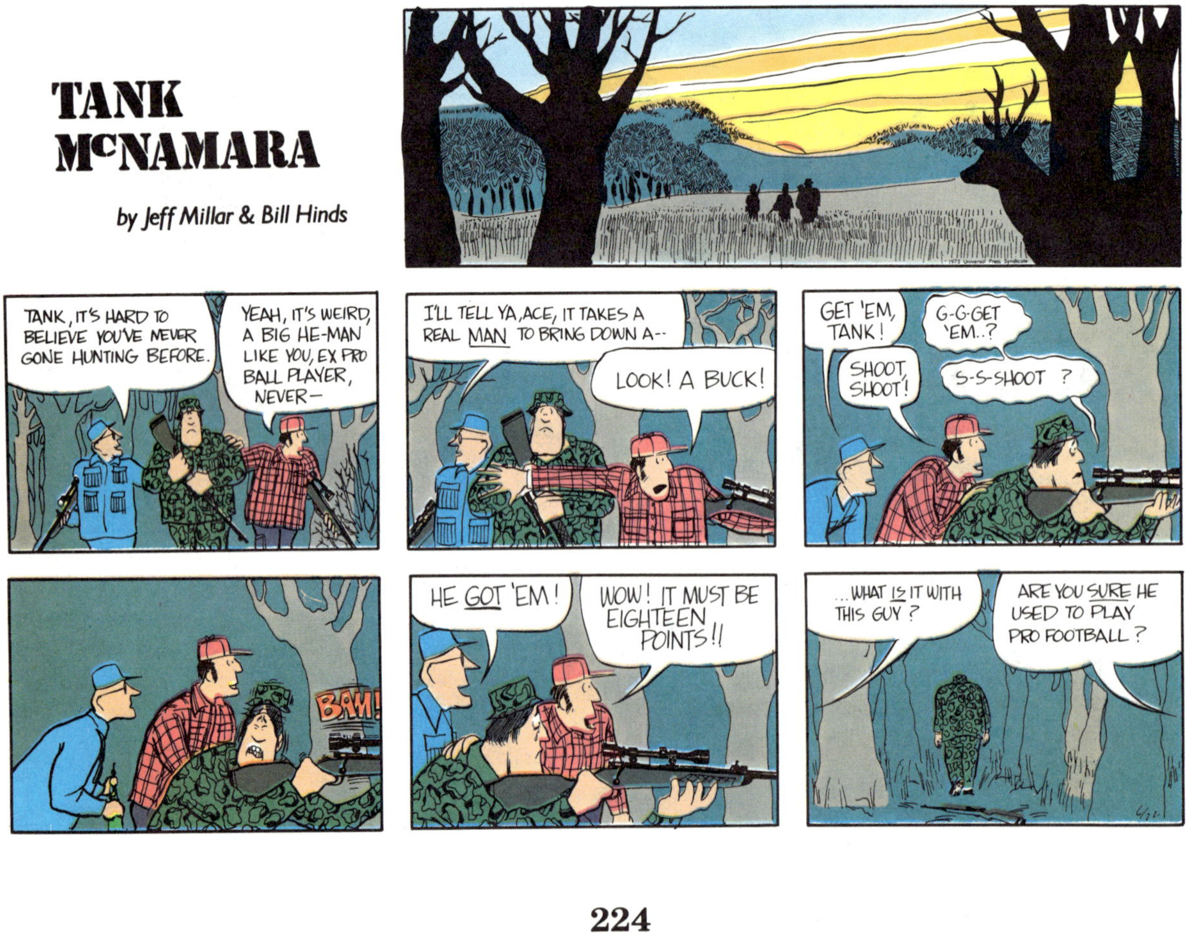
TANK McNAMARA
by Jeff Millar & Bill Hinds
TANK, IT'S HARD TO BELIEVE YOU'VE NEVER GONE HUNTING BEFORE.
YEAH, IT'S WEIRD, A BIG HE-MAN LIKE YOU, EX PRO BALL PLAYER, NEVER—
I'LL TELL YA, ACE, IT TAKES A REAL MAN TO BRING DOWN A--
LOOK! A BUCK!
GET 'EM, TANK!
G-G-GET 'EM..?
SHOOT, SHOOT!
S-S-SHOOT ?
BAM!
HE GOT 'EM!
WOW! IT MUST BE EIGHTEEN POINTS!!
...WHAT IS IT WITH THIS GUY?
ARE YOU SURE HE USED TO PLAY PRO FOOTBALL?